S0-AXJ-746

BEGINNING
WINDOWS® PHONE 7 APPLICATION DEVELOPMENT

BEGINNING

Windows® Phone 7 Application Development

BUILDING WINDOWS® PHONE APPLICATIONS USING SILVERLIGHT® AND XNA®

Nick Lecrenski
Karli Watson
Robert Fonseca-Ensor

Wiley Publishing, Inc.

Beginning Windows® Phone 7 Application Development: Building Windows® Phone Applications Using Silverlight® and XNA®

Published by
Wiley Publishing, Inc.
10475 Crosspoint Boulevard
Indianapolis, IN 46256
www.wiley.com

Copyright © 2011 Wiley Publishing, Inc., Indianapolis, Indiana

Published simultaneously in Canada

ISBN: 978-0-470-91233-1
ISBN: 978-1-118-09628-4 (ebk)
ISBN: 978-1-118-09629-1 (ebk)
ISBN: 978-1-118-09630-7 (ebk)

Manufactured in the United States of America

10 9 8 7 6 5 4 3 2 1

For general information on our other products and services please contact our Customer Care Department within the United States at (877) 762-2974, outside the United States at (317) 572-3993 or fax (317) 572-4002.

Wiley also publishes its books in a variety of electronic formats. Some content that appears in print may not be available in electronic books.

Library of Congress Control Number: 2011920899

*This book is dedicated to my beautiful wife, Kristie,
and my daughters, Tabetha and Cheyenne.*

—NICK LECRENSKI

For donna.

—KARLI WATSON

For the love of my life, Cara.

—ROBERT FONSECA-ENSOR

CREDITS

ACQUISITIONS EDITOR
Paul Reese

PROJECT EDITOR
Ginny Bess Munroe

TECHNICAL EDITOR
Jonathan Marbutt

PRODUCTION EDITOR
Kathleen Wisor

COPY EDITOR
Kitty Wilson

EDITORIAL DIRECTOR
Robyn B. Siesky

EDITORIAL MANAGER
Mary Beth Wakefield

FREELANCER EDITORIAL MANAGER
Rosemarie Graham

ASSOCIATE DIRECTOR OF MARKETING
David Mayhew

PRODUCTION MANAGER
Tim Tate

VICE PRESIDENT AND EXECUTIVE GROUP PUBLISHER
Richard Swadley

VICE PRESIDENT AND EXECUTIVE PUBLISHER
Barry Pruett

ASSOCIATE PUBLISHER
Jim Minatel

PROJECT COORDINATOR, COVER
Katie Crocker

PROOFREADER
Nancy Carrasco

INDEXER
Robert Swanson

COVER DESIGNER
Michael Trent

COVER IMAGE
© iStock/Oleksiy Mark

ABOUT THE AUTHORS

NICK LECRENSKI is a developer with 10 years of experience in a wide range of Microsoft technologies including Visual C++, C#, VB, VB.NET, SQL Server, .NET Framework, ASP.NET, AJAX, Silverlight, and more. He has a BS in Computer Science and has worked in various fields from biometrics to financial services. He is also the founder and lead developer of MyFitnessJournal.com, a fitness training website that currently utilizes Silverlight technology. He is also the author of *Silverlight 4: Problem - Design - Solution*, available from www.wrox.com.

KARLI WATSON is an IT contractor and author currently working in London in the financial sector. For the most part, he immerses himself in .NET (in particular, C#) and has written numerous books in the field for several publishers. He specializes in communicating complex ideas in a way that is accessible to anyone with a passion to learn, and he spends much of his time playing with technology to find new things to teach people. During those (seemingly few) times where he isn't doing the previous, Karli is probably wishing he was hurtling down a mountain on a snowboard or possibly trying to get his novel published. Either way, you'll know him by his brightly colored clothes.

ROBERT FONSECA-ENSOR is a software engineer consulting with Infusion (www.infusion.com). From New Zealand, he currently lives in London. He specializes in user interface development and has been working with Microsoft Surface, Silverlight, and WPF for the past four years. Rob has a strong passion for learning new things and then teaching them to others. He enjoys attending and presenting at .NET user groups so much that he started the Canary Wharf .NET User Group. He plans to become a university professor "as soon as he gets sick of coding in the real world," which isn't going to happen soon. Rob's wife is an IOS developer, and together they have built and released a couple of successful iPhone games. Now that his weekends are writing-free, he plans to churn out some awesome WP7 games, so watch your back. Rob keeps a blog at www.robfe.com, and has a twitter account at www.twitter.com/robfe.

ACKNOWLEDGMENTS

I WOULD LIKE TO THANK EVERYONE at Wrox who had a part in helping to get this book to print. First, I would like to thank my family for supporting me on another book writing endeavor. I would also like to take the time to thank Paul Reese for giving me the opportunity to work on another book project and Ginny Munroe, our primary editor, who fought to keep us all on track and on time, which was no easy task. I would also like to thank Jonathan Marbutt, our technical editor, for checking all of our code and offering valuable input during the writing process. Finally, I would also like to thank my co-authors, Karli and Robert, for their great work on this project and ensuring that all of the material will help our readers realize the goal of developing mobile applications on the new Windows Phone 7 platform.

—NICK

THANKS TO ALL AT WROX for their hard work in making my writing as good as it can be. In no particular order, thanks especially to Paul Reese for getting things off the ground, Ginny for infinite patience and good humour, and Kitty for her wordsmithing. Also, thanks to my fellow authors, including many congratulations to Rob for getting through that "difficult first book!"

—KARLI

I COULD NEVER HAVE GOTTEN this far if not for my darling wife, Cara. You're inspirational, patient, and wonderful. Thank you for all the support you give me. Thanks to the staff at Wrox for all their support and patience, especially Ginny and Paul. To all my mentors: Karli, Ben Gracewood, Dr. Rick Mugridge, Dr. Ewan Tempero, David Okey, Alan Goodison, and especially my parents — thank you for believing in me.

—ROBERT

CONTENTS

INTRODUCTION

TEN YEARS AGO, who would have thought that with the power of web and desktop applications, you would eventually be able to duplicate much of that power on something as small as a cellphone? There was a time not that long ago when the cellphone's primary purpose was to just make a phone call. In fact, just the capability to make a phone call anywhere was impressive. Things have changed. Now, with no less than three major smartphone platforms, cellphone users can do just about anything on a phone that previously required a PC. You can shop, do tax calculations, play games, browse the web, read the news, and so on. Of course, this means that as a developer, you officially have a new platform to consider when writing your own applications. Fortunately, the new Windows Phone 7 platform provides developers with one of the most robust, easy-to-use programming environments currently available for mobile application development.

When the first wave of smartphones hit the market, many required special development kits that were available only at a high cost through the specific phone manufacturers. The Windows Mobile platform, of course, was always different in that aspect. With the Windows Mobile platform, developers could write mobile applications using existing .NET technologies, and have a familiar development environment in Visual Studio. The previous incarnations of Windows Mobile development were not, however, without their shortcomings. In many cases, because the hardware was not standardized, applications written for one hardware device might not have functioned the same on another device. This dilemma and the high cost of specialized development toolkits were the problems that the latest wave of smartphone development platforms aimed to solve. In order for any mobile development market to explode and foster rich application development, hardware features needed to be standardized, and the cost to enter the mobile development space had to come down drastically.

The Windows Phone 7 development platform has done an impressive job solving these problems. The development environment is free, the hardware is finally standardized, and there is a rich abundance of developer information on the web and in this book. As an additional bonus, the choice to use Silverlight as the main development platform means that in many cases applications written for the Silverlight web-based platform can be easily ported to the phone device, and vice versa. It is no doubt an exciting time to be a developer and there is no better time than now to get familiar with the Windows Phone 7 development tools and platform. When you complete this book, you will be armed with the knowledge and skills to create your own rich mobile applications and games. You will find that developing applications for the platform is a rewarding and painless experience, and we all look forward to seeing the next generation of rich mobile applications starting with yours.

WHO THIS BOOK IS FOR

This book is specifically geared at readers who have an interest in learning mobile phone application development on the Windows Phone 7 platform. You should be familiar with basic programming constructs and methodologies. You do not, however, need any previous experience in mobile development, Silverlight, or Windows Phone 7. Familiarity with Microsoft development tools, such as Visual Studio and Expression Blend, is helpful but is not required. This book guides you through the required features of these tools in order to facilitate application development on the Windows Phone 7 platform.

WHAT THIS BOOK COVERS

This book covers everything you need to write rich mobile applications for Windows Phone 7. The following is a brief outline of each chapter:

➤ Chapter 1, "Introducing Windows Phone 7" — Introduce yourself to Windows Phone 7 development.

➤ Chapter 2, "Jaw-Dropping Apps with the Help of Silverlight" — Develop applications using Silverlight.

➤ Chapter 3, "Spice Up Your App with Shapes, Colors, Brushes, and Transforms" — Learn how to use Shapes, Colors, Brushes, and Transform objects.

➤ Chapter 4, "Advanced User Interface Techniques: Styles, Templates, and the Visual State Manager" — Learn interface techniques including styles, templates, and how to create animations using the Visual State Manager.

➤ Chapter 5, "Isolated Storage, Page Navigation, and the Application Life Cycle" — Understand data storage using the Silverlight Isolated Storage feature, and multipage applications.

➤ Chapter 6, "Interacting with the Hardware" — Use hardware interactions, FM Radio, and Accelerometer.

➤ Chapter 7, "Launchers, Choosers, and Advanced User Input" — Learn about launchers and choosers.

➤ Chapter 8, "Windows Phone 7 Services and Cloud Services" — Consume Windows Phone 7 Cloud Services.

➤ Chapter 9, "Creating and Consuming Web Services" — Consume external web services.

➤ Chapter 10, "Web Services Push Notifications" — Understand web services and how to use push notifications.

➤ Chapter 11, "XNA for Windows Phone 7" — Develop games with XNA.

➤ Chapter 12, "Microsoft Expression Blend" — Use Expression Blend.

➤ Chapter 13, "Using the Silverlight for Windows Phone Toolkit and Creating Panoramic User Interfaces" — Understand panoramic displays and the Silverlight Toolkit.

➤ Chapter 14, "Patterns, Frameworks, and Tests" — Use development patterns and test your applications.

➤ Chapter 15, "Publishing Your Application" — Publish your application to the Windows Phone 7 Marketplace.

➤ Appendix A, "Solutions to Exercises" — Get the solutions to the chapter exercises.

WHAT YOU NEED TO USE THIS BOOK

To follow this book and to compile and run the sample applications, you need the following:

➤   Windows 7, Windows Vista, Windows XP, Windows Server 2008, or Windows Server 2003.

➤   The latest release of the Windows Phone 7 developer tools. These are freely available from Microsoft at `http://create.msdn.com`. A free edition of Visual Studio 2010, XNA Game Studio, and Expression Blend designed for Windows Phone 7 development are included in these tools.

➤   Installation of the Silverlight for Windows Phone 7 Toolkit. A free toolkit is available at `http://silverlight.codeplex.com/`.

CONVENTIONS

To help you get the most from the text and keep track of what's happening, we've used several conventions throughout the book.

> **WARNING** *Boxes like this one hold important, not-to-be forgotten information that is directly relevant to the surrounding text.*

> **COMMON MISTAKES** *These areas hold important information about common mistakes that can be made while coding a particular feature.*

> **NOTE** *Tips, hints, tricks, and asides to the current discussion look like this.*

As for other conventions in the text:

➤   New terms and important words are *highlighted* in italics.

➤   Keyboard combinations are treated like this: Ctrl+R.

➤   Filenames, URLs, and code within the text are treated like this: `persistence.properties`.

This book uses monofont type with no highlighting for most code examples. This book also uses bold to emphasize code that is of particular importance in the present context.

SOURCE CODE

As you work through the examples in this book, either type the code manually or use the source-code files that accompany the book. All of the source code used in this book is available for download at www.wrox.com. On the site, simply locate the book's title (either by using the Search box or by using one of the title lists) and click the Download Code link on the book's detail page to obtain all the source code for the book.

 NOTE *Because many books have similar titles, you might find it easiest to search by ISBN; this book's ISBN is 978-0-470-91233-1.*

After you download the code, decompress it with your favorite compression tool. Alternately, you can go to the main Wrox code download page at www.wrox.com/dynamic/books/download.aspx to see the code available for this book and all other Wrox books.

ERRATA

We make every effort to ensure that there are no errors in the text or in the code. However, no one is perfect, and mistakes do occur. If you find an error in one of our books, like a spelling mistake or faulty piece of code, we would be very grateful for your feedback. By sending in errata, you might save another reader hours of frustration, and at the same time you will be helping us provide even higher quality information.

To find the errata page for this book, go to www.wrox.com and locate the title using the Search box or one of the title lists. Then, on the book details page, click the Errata link. On this page you can view all errata that have been submitted for this book and posted by Wrox editors.

 NOTE *A complete book list, including links to each book's errata, is also available at* www.wrox.com/misc-pages/booklist.shtml.

If you don't spot "your" error on the Errata page, go to www.wrox.com/contact/techsupport .shtml and complete the form there to send us the error you have found. We'll check the information and, if appropriate, post a message to the book's errata page and fix the problem in subsequent editions of the book.

P2P.WROX.COM

For author and peer discussion, join the P2P forums at p2p.wrox.com. The forums are a web-based system on which you can post messages relating to Wrox books and related technologies and interact with other readers and technology users. The forums offer a subscription feature to email you topics of interest of your choosing when new posts are made to the forums. Wrox authors, editors, other industry experts, and your fellow readers are present on these forums.

At p2p.wrox.com you will find a number of different forums that will help you not only as you read this book, but also as you develop your own applications. To join the forums, just follow these steps:

1. Go to p2p.wrox.com and click the Register link.

2. Read the terms of use and click Agree.

3. Complete the required information to join as well as any optional information you wish to provide, and click Submit.

4. You will receive an email with information describing how to verify your account and complete the joining process.

 NOTE *You can read messages in the forums without joining P2P, but in order to post your own messages, you must join.*

Once you join, you can post new messages and respond to messages other users post. You can read messages at any time on the web. If you would like to have new messages from a particular forum emailed to you, click the Subscribe to this Forum icon by the forum name in the forum listing.

For more information about how to use the Wrox P2P, be sure to read the P2P FAQs for answers to questions about how the forum software works, as well as many common questions specific to P2P and Wrox books. To read the FAQs, click the FAQ link on any P2P page.

1

Introducing Windows Phone 7

WHAT YOU WILL LEARN IN THIS CHAPTER:

➤ Learning the history of the Windows Mobile platform

➤ Understanding the new Windows Phone 7 platform

➤ Understanding the differences between Silverlight and XNA

➤ Using Windows Phone 7 development tools

➤ Creating your first Windows Phone 7 app

As you may have noticed lately, mobile application development is at the forefront of the industry. Not since the glory days of the mid- to late 1990s has it been quite this exciting to be a software developer. Why all this new excitement about a hardware platform that has existed for quite some time? You don't have to look much further than the introduction of cheaper smartphones to the masses. Even grandma and grandpa probably have a smartphone by now, and they may want to know when you are going to start writing your own mobile app. Of course, to do so, you need to pick a smartphone platform. Given that you have picked this book, it's safe to assume that you're going to write applications for the latest entry into the smartphone world: Windows Phone 7.

Even though we seem to be entering an era where Droid and iPhone are becoming the dominant platforms for mobile development, it is important to note that Microsoft actually did have a viable mobile development platform before most of the other companies even had any plans to enter this market. So although Microsoft is seemingly late to the party, it really isn't: It has quite a bit of history and experience in mobile development. In fact, in many ways, Windows Phone 7 provides developers with an even richer set of tools and programming opportunities than either the Droid or iPhone platforms.

THE WINDOWS MOBILE PLATFORM

Prior to the current generation of smartphone hardware, most users were relegated to using simple cellphones that could deal with calls, text messages, and possibly a handful of basic games or applications. More often than not, these applications weren't much more powerful than a glorified calculator. There was no app store, no programming interface was available to you, and unless you were an official partner with one of the major cell networks, you simply couldn't write custom applications for your phone, let alone share them with others. The original Pocket PC hardware teamed with the first version of Windows Mobile to change this.

The Windows Mobile platform came on the scene in 2000, on the Pocket PC hardware. It provided developers with some of the first legitimate opportunities to create applications for mobile devices. Although geared primarily toward power users and corporate accounts, this new mobile operating system offered versions of Word, Excel, Outlook, Internet Explorer, Windows Media Player, and more. Obviously, this was not going to be just your standard cellphone with limited capabilities. Along with the operating system, Microsoft released a set of developer tools that allowed those with a C++ background to develop native applications for the Pocket PC.

So if custom applications could be developed and the Pocket PC was available, why did it take the iPhone to make mobile computing catch on? For starters, although the Pocket PC and its successors continued to use various releases of Windows Mobile, the platform stayed geared toward power and corporate users. Data plans for such devices were costly, and the devices were often out of the price range of standard cellphone users. Besides, who wants to browse the Web at extremely slow speeds on a tiny little screen? In the early 2000s, home computers and broadband modems were better suited for browsing. Browsing the web on mobile devices was often slow and painful. It also didn't help that in order to use Windows Mobile devices, you had to use a stylus pen. Those devices weren't nearly as simple and powerful as today's multitouch mobile devices.

Another issue, in addition to cost, user experience, and data speed, was testing applications across a myriad of devices. Developers who were interested in creating Windows Mobile solutions also had to wrestle with the fact that with each new release of the Windows Mobile operating system, many new devices would also be released. Some of these new devices would have screen resolutions and features that were not supported in existing applications. Developers therefore had to worry about porting and testing their applications across a wide variety of devices. Applications written for one Windows Mobile device were not always guaranteed to work on another similar device. This further hurt any chance of building up a large user base for various applications and in turn hurt the overall mobile development market.

Here Comes the iPhone

In 2007, after a myriad of Windows Mobile releases, along with various versions of the popular BlackBerry devices, Apple jumped into the fray and released a phone completely designed from the ground up with the everyday consumer in mind. The first iPhone hit the market, forever changing mobile computing. There was no denying that this new phone was slick and easy for just about anybody to use. The iPhone brought better web browsing, better camera functionality, and a fluid touchscreen interface, including multitouch and even gestures such as "pinch" and "flick." It didn't take long for people who tried the phone to fall in love with its features.

In addition to all offering new hardware features, the iPhone was the first smartphone to allow anybody to develop custom applications for the phone and even distribute them with the intent of potentially making a profit. The concept of having only one standardized device along with a public marketplace to easily distribute and collect royalty payments sounded like the Holy Grail that developers had been waiting for with regard to mobile application development.

Of course if users hadn't bought iPhone devices in droves, there wouldn't have been much benefit to spending valuable resource time on iPhone development. However, because Apple partnered with AT&T, it was able to make the iPhone somewhat affordable and available to an extremely large audience. This is just what the doctor ordered for the then-stagnant mobile development landscape.

After just a few years and a couple of revisions of the proprietary operating system used by the iPhone, its popularity soared and essentially set the standard for what users were looking for from a smartphone. People who had never before considered using cellphones for anything other than making calls and sending text messages were suddenly checking sports scores, watching video clips, and even posting status updates to their Facebook accounts. As with any other new technology, competition was sure to arrive.

Android Arrives

There was simply no way that the success of the iPhone was going to go unnoticed by the other major players in the computing world. Sales of existing Windows Mobile devices began to plummet, as users began to demand iPhone functionality in all their mobile devices, regardless of the manufacturer.

Microsoft and a small company called Google began to take notice of the iPhone and the rapidly growing consumer market for smartphone devices. Google quickly set to work on its own mobile solution, but instead of focusing on hardware, Google actually went to work on its own mobile operating system that would include many of the innovations found in the iPhone's proprietary system. However, Google would offer the operating system for free, and it would also release its own software development platform that would not be as closed and proprietary as that of the iPhone. Google was hoping to attract even more developers to create rich mobile applications for devices running its Android operating system. In addition to the operating system and development tools, Google opened an app store similar to iTunes, where users of Android-based devices could be able to easily find rich mobile applications to load onto their devices. The Google-based marketplace soon offered thousands of applications, many of which were free or very low cost because there were no expensive licensing fees involved with Android application development.

Not long after the release of the Android operating system, cellphone manufacturers began releasing devices that made use of Google's technology. At that point, the mobile development marketplace was beginning to seem lucrative to cellphone carriers, and Google capitalized on the fact that iPhone development and devices were available only through AT&T's networks. All other carriers would be free to latch on to Android and offer their customers features similar to those of the iPhone with much lower costs. The largest cellphone provider, Verizon, released the Droid phone based on the Android operating system. Google's new entry into the mobile marketplace was pretty much guaranteed to explode just like the iPhone had. In fact, at the time of this writing, Android-based devices have actually started to do just that, even outselling new iPhone devices in some U.S. markets.

A Microsoft Reboot

With the success of the iPhone and the explosion of Android-based devices onto the scene, Windows Mobile device sales again took a hit. It became increasingly clear to Microsoft that its current Windows Mobile solution was not going to cut it. Rather than continue on the current path and release another version of the existing Windows Mobile operating system, Microsoft decided to go back to the drawing board and start over, with a clear plan of attack, to revive its struggling mobile division.

To ensure that the next generation of Windows Mobile satisfied the needs of the exploding consumer market for mobile devices, Microsoft revamped every aspect of its mobile operating system. To create a successful product, Microsoft needed to touch on all the areas of concern for consumers and developers in previous releases of Windows Mobile. At the Mobile World Congress in 2010, Microsoft officially took the covers off the first version of its mobile reboot: Windows Phone 7 Series.

It didn't take long to see that this was not the traditional Microsoft mobile platform. Everything about this operating system was different. From the new multitouch capabilities to the slick Metro user interface, designers at the conference instantly took to the new release. In the old days, Microsoft had offered a multitude of devices with varying screen resolutions and hardware features. Finally, Windows Phone 7 Series promised a standardized set of hardware. And, importantly, it offered an SDK and development platform that utilized .NET and Silverlight, two technologies that already had a massive developer base. To the excitement of many, developers already utilizing Silverlight in their solutions became Windows Phone 7 Series developers overnight.

Despite heavy competition from Google and Apple, there was more than enough promise even in this early stage that the new Microsoft entry into the mobile computing world would surely become a hit and continue to provide needed competition in the mobile development world.

At MIX 2010, Microsoft released the first edition of development tools so that developers everywhere could start working on Windows Phone 7 Series solutions. Unlike Android and iPhone development, Windows Phone 7 Series development made use of tools that were already very familiar to developers in Visual Studio. Harnessing Visual Studio, .NET, and Silverlight allowed Microsoft to drastically reduce the learning curve normally associated with mobile development. MIX 2010 provided attendees with exciting demos of Silverlight applications as well as powerful games that even had Xbox 360 integration by making use of the already available and familiar XNA development platform. Now even making mobile games would be something that any developer would be able to jump into.

Microsoft wasted no time in announcing the creation of its own app store and developer program that would allow Windows Phone 7 Series developers to create and distribute applications as well as potentially generate profits for their work. In September 2010, Microsoft offered the final release of its development tools, including an updated and even more powerful emulator for testing. Developers were encouraged to finalize applications and get ready for the impending release of Windows Phone hardware. At the same time, the official name of the new operating system was shortened to the easier-to-remember Windows Phone 7.

THE WINDOWS PHONE 7 PLATFORM

The Windows Phone 7 platform has been officially released, and the first wave of devices utilizing the operating system is hitting the market. It's time to start learning how to use the platform to create your own mobile applications and solutions and perhaps even make some money through the new Windows Phone 7 application marketplace.

In the next section, you'll get a brief overview of the Windows Phone 7 platform and a look at the developer tools that are available. Before you finish, you'll have built your first working Windows Phone 7 application. To get started, let's take a quick look at the major components of this new platform.

Windows Phone 7 Hardware Specifications

To avoid many of the problems that plagued application development in previous versions of the Windows mobile operating system, Microsoft decided to follow the lead of Google and Apple and come up with a hard list of requirements for hardware vendors. Rather than allow for an unlimited set of hardware configurations, Microsoft has been specific about the capabilities each Windows Phone 7 device must have. A user should be able to pick up any given Windows Phone 7 device and recognize how to use it without a major learning curve. No two devices should be so different from each other that they're difficult to use or program against. Ultimately, as a Windows Phone 7 developer, you're expected to develop applications against Microsoft's constrained list of potential hardware features. If you do, you won't have to worry about porting your application several times for it to run correctly across a myriad of Windows Phone 7 devices released by various cellphone manufacturers.

Table 1-1 lists the minimum hardware requirements for all Windows Phone 7 devices.

TABLE 1-1: Minimum Hardware Requirements for Windows Phone 7 Devices

FEATURE	REQUIREMENT
Capacitive multitouch screen	Must support four or more contact points, 800x400 resolution
Sensors	Must have GPS, accelerometer, compass, light, and proximity
Camera	Minimum of 5 megapixels, a flash, and a camera button
Multimedia	Codec acceleration
Memory	Minimum 256MB RAM, Minimum 8GB Flash
GPU	Support for DirectX 9
CPU	Minimum ARMv7 Cortex/Scorpion
Hardware buttons	Separate Start, Search, and Back buttons

As you can see from Table 1-1, Microsoft has not created a basic smartphone. Windows Phone 7 devices are on par with both Android-based devices and iPhones. They're powerful and enable rich application development.

Windows Phone 7 Architecture

In addition to the powerful list of standardized hardware features, the Windows Phone 7 platform provides developers with an architecture conducive to rapid and rich application development. The Windows Phone 7 architecture is divided among four main components:

➤ Runtime components

➤ Tools

➤ Cloud services

➤ Portal services

Runtime Components

A good place to start getting familiar with the Windows Phone 7 architecture is to take a look at the various runtime components. Figure 1-1 shows a complete list of the items that make up the runtime piece.

FIGURE 1-1: Windows Phone 7 runtime components.

The two main development paths for Windows Phone 7 consist of applications utilizing Silverlight technology and rich mobile games created using the XNA tools. Silverlight is the latest technology release by Microsoft to assist in the development of Rich Internet Applications (RIA). Now in its fourth revision, Silverlight has enabled .NET developers to create web-based applications that present users with rich user interfaces and quick response times not typically seen without delving into the realm of Windows Presentation Foundation (WPF) or thick client solutions. We're not saying that RIA apps couldn't be developed with existing Asynchronous JavaScript And XML (AJAX)-based solutions, but Silverlight presents developers with a way to create RIA apps in a familiar .NET language without having to worry about the discrepancies in how browsers behave with JavaScript.

Silverlight does require the end user to install a small lightweight plug-in similar to the popular Flash plug-in. The installation, however, is fast, not typically a painful experience for end users.

Offering the capability to create rich web-based applications without the distribution headaches that can sometimes accompany thick client development, Silverlight has exploded in popularity. Many large companies — such as Netflix, Continental Airlines, and Kelley Blue Book — use it.

As you will soon see, Silverlight development for the Windows Phone 7 platform is similar to Silverlight development for the web. Although Windows Phone 7 uses a custom version of Silverlight, most of the functionality available on the web is also available in the mobile version of the runtime. Silverlight also provides a powerful suite of controls that you can use in your applications to handle the display of data, user input, and more. In addition, most of these controls have already been customized to make use of the new Metro user interface style that is inherent to Windows Phone 7.

As great as Silverlight is for developing rich applications, the XNA platform equally excels at providing a powerful platform for developing games. The XNA toolkit was originally released to assist developers in writing DirectX-style games for the PC. Over time, the XNA toolkit was expanded to provide the libraries and tools needed to produce custom games for the Xbox 360. With the introduction of the XNA Creators Club, for the first time ever, developers had the ability to not only create console games but also distribute them to other gamers without expensive licensing fees and special versions of the console. The XNA platform streamlined many of the elements of DirectX and for an even faster development time for both PC and Xbox 360 games.

 NOTE *In Chapter 11 of this book, you'll see how to make use of the very same XNA platform to create rich and interactive games for the Windows Phone 7 platform.*

In addition to XNA and Silverlight, the runtime components include a media element. Media is rapidly becoming an important aspect to every smartphone, including Windows Phone 7 devices. In Windows Mobile, the multimedia functionality was most often based on the standard Windows Media Player software. In the case of Windows Phone 7, the multimedia story is being written using the same great components that are integrated in the popular Zune music device from Microsoft. As you will see, the interactions with multimedia elements in the Windows Phone 7 are similar to those in the Zune. In most cases, you can consider a Windows Phone 7 device a Zune that's used to play and manage media files such as music and video. The Windows Phone 7 development tools provide you with full access to all the Zune-like features for managing and playing music and video through your own custom application.

Of course, no Windows Phone 7 device is complete without the capability to make a phone call. Incredibly, in many smartphones, the ability to make a simple phone call can sometimes be overshadowed by the other features of the phone, leaving users with the impression that the smartphone can do everything well except actually make a phone call. Rest assured, this is not the case with Windows Phone 7. Not only are Windows Phone 7 devices capable of running rich mobile applications, but these devices can also make and handle phone calls. Later on, when we take a look at the developer tools, you'll see how you can make use of many of the phone features in your own applications and how Windows Phone 7 ensures that your applications behave correctly when phone events (such as calls and text messages) occur. Microsoft wants a flawless user experience with these devices, so Windows Phone 7 specifies rules that applications must follow to ensure that applications can never interfere with the most basic usage of the phone features, such as like calling and texting. In order to help facilitate following those rules, Windows Phone 7 provides you with several application life cycle event handlers that you can add custom code to if necessary. These event handlers allow you to easily save and restore application data to memory or a physical storage device so that when the interruption has completed, your application can be restored exactly the way it was left, and the user can easily pick up the app where they left off.

The runtime components include powerful sensors that your application can use. Windows Phone 7 includes the capabilities for your application to use the GPS, accelerometer, compass, light, and proximity features. In the case of the accelerometer, there is even built-in support in the emulator for testing and rearranging your user interface according to the orientation of the device.

Finally, no application is complete without data. In the first version of Windows Phone 7, there is not a compact version of SQL Server, as there was in some versions of Windows Mobile; however, you still have ways of storing and retrieving data. Windows Phone 7 uses the Silverlight concept *of Isolated Storage in order to facilitate the storing and retrieval of data on the device.* At the heart of Isolated Storage is a set of application programming interface (API) calls for storing and retrieving any kind of data. This really is a simplified way of doing things, but it is still very powerful and can take care of your data needs in many ways just as easily as the SQL Server CE edition used to do.

Cloud Services

With the release of Windows Phone 7, Microsoft has provided developers with a host of cloud-based services that developers can tap into for their own applications. Figure 1-2 highlights the cloud services available as of this writing.

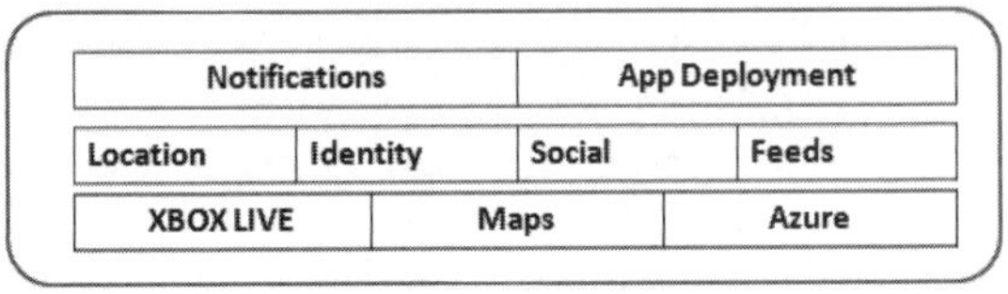

FIGURE 1-2: Windows Phone 7 cloud services

As you can see in Figure 1-2, there are many powerful services available to you for application development. One of the most interesting of them is the notification service. With this service, you have a unique way to "push" data and messages to a Windows Phone 7 device. This can provide you with the ability to create custom alerts for things such as sports scores, weather alerts, and more. Thanks to the notification service, your application doesn't necessarily have to poll in order to get data. The best part of the notification service is that you don't have to use a complex set of operations in order to use it.

The location service enables applications to access the user's physical location information. You can easily query for the location through a simple API call or listen for specific location events so that your application is notified when the user's location has changed. Although location information can be acquired from the GPS hardware, the cloud-based location service also makes use of cell tower information and even Wi-Fi to provide various levels of location accuracy.

Microsoft has produced an extensive web-based API for Xbox LIVE services and Windows Azure so that your mobile applications can tap into things like the Xbox LIVE achievements system, profile, and more. You can also easily use the new Windows Azure computing platform for additional web service functionality. Windows Phone 7 fully supports Azure web services, so you can take advantage of existing Azure web services or develop new custom web services. You can even leverage the new SQL Azure platform for relational database access in the cloud.

One final cloud service that can create some interesting application possibilities is the new Bing Maps control. This new control enables you to harness the full power of Bing Maps functionality right from your Windows Phone 7 application.

Portal Services

In addition to the various cloud services available, Microsoft also makes available several portal services for managing your applications. Figure 1-3 shows the various portal services available.

Registration	Marketplace
Validation	Billing
Certification	Application updates
Publishing	

FIGURE 1-3: Windows Phone 7 portal services.

Windows Mobile lacked top-notch support for application deployment and distribution. These two areas of concern have been completely revamped in Windows Phone 7. First, the deployment of applications has changed drastically. Instead of unrestricted deployment of apps, you now have an environment similar to that of the iPhone. Application developers for Windows Phone 7 need to register to distribute apps, and all application distribution is done through the new App Hub Site. The Marketplace is a one-stop shop for users to download and install new applications. It's similar to the iPhone and Android models of distribution.

The portal services don't stop here, however. Services for validating and certifying application code also exist to ensure that no malicious code makes it into a Windows Phone 7 device. When you're through testing your code in the emulator and on a development device, you essentially gain another pair of eyes to make sure nothing you did in your app interferes with the overall user experience on the phone. The validation and certification service teams look for anything that could potentially bring down the phone or any malicious code that violates the terms of service agreements. Although at first this might sound like a potential headache, you're likely to come to the conclusion that it's better to be safe than sorry. You don't want to go through all the work of developing an application and distributing it only for it to become known as the app that breaks the phone.

Another interesting portal service related to the App Hub is the billing service. Windows Phone 7 provides developers with additional API functionality that facilitates the creation of free, paid, and trial modes for applications. There's now an easy way to designate your app as freeware, pay to use, monthly billing, and more. Also, with just a few calls, you can restrict various features of your app, depending on whether the user is currently in a trial mode or has paid for the full version. Don't worry. Chapter 15 is devoted to covering the marketplace and all the various aspects of setting up your application for deployment and potentially generating revenue.

Finally, the App Hub also provides an easy place to manage and distribute application updates. There's now a simple way to manage updates to your application. You can even control whether updates are to be made available free of charge or for a cost. Users of your app have a designated place to go to see if new updates are available, and Windows Phone 7 ensures that the update process goes quickly and without incident.

Developer Tools

The final component of the Windows Phone 7 architecture is the developer tools. Unlike in Windows Mobile, Windows Phone 7 specializes in providing developers with perhaps the best overall mobile development experience. By utilizing its flagship Visual Studio product for the main development tool, Microsoft has given potential developers an industry-leading integrated development environment (IDE) to work with. It has also provided the new Expression Blend tool that enables designers to work fluidly with developers to create the best overall user experience possible for mobile applications. Perhaps the best part of this is that Microsoft has made available a completely free version of the Visual Studio and Expression Blend that can be used specifically for Windows Phone 7 application development. Figure 1-4 shows the full list of developer tools that are part of the Windows Phone 7 architecture.

Visual Studio	XNA Game Studio
Expression Blend	Documentation
Samples	Community
Packaging	Developer guidance

FIGURE 1-4: Windows 7 developer tools.

No discussion of the Windows Phone 7 architecture would be complete without an overview of the powerful developer tools that are made available. Microsoft has made sure that all Windows Phone 7 development can be performed with the familiar Visual Studio. Unlike with Windows Mobile development, you now even have the option of downloading and developing with Visual Studio Express Edition. This edition is the recommended version for this book and has the best price point you can ask for: It's free. This great tool also has a commercial license; so you can create great Windows Phone 7 applications with Visual Studio Express, and you can sell them!

Visual Studio Express offers the majority of developer features you would normally get from the professional version of the software, so this isn't just some "watered down" version of an IDE. You'll see throughout this book that you can develop the same high-quality rich applications with the Express Edition of the software as with Visual Studio Professional.

In addition to Visual Studio, Microsoft has also released a developer tool called Expression Blend. This tool offers designers a way to get into the game and still stay in sync with developers. All too often, designers are forced to create great user interfaces in a design tool, only to find that a developer can't fully translate that user interface into something that works in code. This is not the case anymore. With Expression Blend, designers actually work with the same project and files as developers, but they still have access to design tools that aren't found in Visual Studio and are typically found only in specialized designer software. You'll see how easy it is for a designer to create rich animated user interfaces and ensure that those user interfaces don't change or lose functionality as the developer integrates them into an application. You'll also see how Expression Blend works with Extensible Application Markup Language (XAML) for user interface elements. XAML is also used for Silverlight user interfaces, so there's no need to convert anything into Visual Studio. Designers can just create a user interface in Expression Blend, and developers can quickly grab the generated XAML code, add some event handlers, and run with it.

Last but certainly not least, Windows Phone 7 comes with a powerful developer community. By making Silverlight and XNA the primary development tools for creating Windows Phone 7 applications, Microsoft has ensured that you instantly have a large development community at your disposal as you develop applications. There are thousands of existing Silverlight and XNA developers and a large percentage of the articles and resources you'll find related to those two development technologies are relevant to Windows Phone 7 programming as well.

GETTING STARTED WITH WINDOWS PHONE 7 DEVELOPMENT

Now that you have some history of the Windows Mobile platform and a high-level understanding of the Windows Phone 7 architecture, it's time to get moving toward real application development. By now you're no doubt excited about the endless possibilities in store for your own app development and ready to get your hands on the development tools.

To get started, you need to first get a copy of Visual Studio. Although we cover Expression Blend in Chapter 12, the majority of this book and exercises utilize Visual Studio 2010 Express for Windows Phone. If you happen to have an existing copy of Visual Studio 2010 Professional or better, that works, too; you just need to download and install the Windows Phone 7 developer tools. The installation package can detect existing Visual Studio 2010 installations, so you don't have to worry about that.

After downloading the installation package, you start the program and follow the onscreen wizard steps. There isn't much to it other than accepting the licensing agreement. Once the process completes, you can start developing Windows Phone 7 solutions.

Navigating through Visual Studio 2010 Express Edition

The installation process takes care of installing Visual Studio 2010 Express Edition, the required Silverlight tools for Windows Phone 7, and the emulator that you use for testing applications right from your local machine. At this point, you need to get familiar with the Visual Studio environment, so run Visual Studio using the newly installed shortcut under the Start menu.

When the program starts, you see the welcome screen shown in Figure 1-5. This is essentially always your starting point for development. From this page, you can start a new Windows Phone 7 project or quickly access projects that you've recently worked with.

FIGURE 1-5: Visual Studio 2010 startup screen.

Visual Studio provides many features that are commonly found in development environments. A solution view allows you to see all your project source code and folders. You also have areas where you can view local variables and watch variables. You can move around all the windows in Visual Studio and dock them according to your preferences. In addition, you also have access to several toolbars that can assist in your development. The one you will likely use most often is the Build toolbar. This toolbar provides a "play"-style icon that starts the debugger; in the case of Windows Phone 7 development, it also starts the emulator software for testing.

Along with these toolbars and windows, Visual Studio also offers the features you've come to expect in a development environment, such as the ability to easily add breakpoints, refactor code, find and replace code, use syntax coloring, and of course use IntelliSense to help find classes, methods, and properties as you type.

Perhaps the best way to get familiar with the development environment is to dig right in. In the following Try It Out, you'll create your first Windows Phone 7 application. In continuing with the tradition set forth in many other development books, you'll create a "Hello, World" app.

TRY IT OUT "Hello, World" for Windows Phone 7

To see how easy it is to develop a Windows Phone 7 app, follow these steps to create a simple "Hello, World" app:

1. Start Visual Studio 2010 Express Edition and select File ➪ New Project.

2. At the top of the New Project window, choose the Windows Phone Application project template. In the Name field, enter **HelloWindowsPhone7** for the project name, as shown in Figure 1-6.

FIGURE 1-6: Creating a new project.

3. When the project finishes loading, you're presented with a split screen view, as shown in Figure 1-7. Part of the screen shows the Windows Phone emulator, and the other part shows the XAML source code required for the screen currently being displayed. We cover the XAML code in Chapter 2, so don't worry about modifying any of that code at this point. Just take a look around and get a feel for the project layout. Double-click some additional source files to look at more source code. The important thing to note here is that everything you need to produce a running Windows Phone application is already here in the Windows Phone Application project template.

FIGURE 1-7: Windows Phone 7 project layout.

4. Take a look at the Solution Explorer in Figure 1-7, and you see that the project consists of several source code files. Every Windows Phone 7 application contains an `App.xaml` file. This file basically represents the overall application. Although there's no user interface designed for this file, there are some entries in the XAML code. XAML code is not just restricted to user interface elements; it can, in fact, hold objects that other pages can use. In this case, the `App.xaml` file holds any resources that should be globally available to the application. In the following code, you can see that there is a `PhoneApplicationService` declared with a couple of event handlers for the various phone events, including launch, activate, deactivate, and close. Listing 1-1 shows the App .xaml file that is created with every new Windows Phone 7 project.

Available for download on Wrox.com

LISTING 1-1: Default App.xaml

```
<Application
    x:Class="HelloWindowsPhone_7.App"
    xmlns="http://schemas.microsoft.com/winfx/2006/xaml/presentation"
```

continues

LISTING 1-1 *(continued)*

```
    xmlns:x="http://schemas.microsoft.com/winfx/2006/xaml"
    xmlns:phone="clr-namespace:Microsoft.Phone.Controls;assembly=Microsoft.Phone"
    xmlns:shell="clr-namespace:Microsoft.Phone.Shell;assembly=Microsoft.Phone">

    <!--Application Resources-->
    <Application.Resources>
    </Application.Resources>

    <Application.ApplicationLifetimeObjects>
        <!--Required object that handles lifetime events for the application-->
        <shell:PhoneApplicationService
            Launching="Application_Launching" Closing="Application_Closing"
            Activated="Application_Activated"
            Deactivated="Application_Deactivated"/>
    </Application.ApplicationLifetimeObjects>
</Application>
```

Code Snippet HelloWindowsPhone7\App.xaml

5. You might be wondering where the actual event handlers are for the `PhoneApplicationService` events. They're located in the `App.xaml.cs` file, also known as the code-behind file. In Silverlight applications, you essentially have an `.xaml` component that holds all the declarative XAML code, and you have a corresponding `.xaml.cs` code-behind file to hold any source code related to the page. The default Windows Phone 7 project creates empty event handlers for the four main application life cycle events in the `App.xaml.cs` file. If you wanted to execute custom logic during any of these events, the following code is where you'd need to do it:

Available for
download on
Wrox.com

```
// Code to execute when the application is launching (eg, from Start)
// This code will not execute when the application is reactivated
private void Application_Launching(object sender, LaunchingEventArgs e)
{
}

// Code to execute when the application is activated (brought to foreground)
// This code will not execute when the application is first launched
private void Application_Activated(object sender, ActivatedEventArgs e)
{
}

// Code to execute when the application is deactivated (sent to background)
// This code will not execute when the application is closing
private void Application_Deactivated(object sender, DeactivatedEventArgs e)
{
}

// Code to execute when the application is closing (eg, user hit Back)
// This code will not execute when the application is deactivated
private void Application_Closing(object sender, ClosingEventArgs e)
{
}
```

Code Snippet HelloWindowsPhone7\App.xaml.cs

6. The next file that is required for Windows Phone 7 applications is the `MainPage.xaml` file shown in Listing 1-2. Although the name of this file is not a requirement, most of the content of the file is required. Open up the MainPage.xaml file and examine its contents. The main user interface that you see in the split screen is essentially designed using the XAML code in this file. At the top of the following code, you see the `PhoneApplicationPage` declaration. This is always the topmost parent object for your application. Any additional screens are considered children of this object. As you can see, the main layout of the user interface is created using a `Grid` control, which is another Silverlight control that handles the layout of additional controls.

LISTING 1-2: Default MainPage.xaml

```xml
<phone:PhoneApplicationPage
    x:Class="HelloWindowsPhone_7.MainPage"
    xmlns="http://schemas.microsoft.com/winfx/2006/xaml/presentation"
    xmlns:x="http://schemas.microsoft.com/winfx/2006/xaml"
    xmlns:phone="clr-namespace:Microsoft.Phone.Controls;assembly=Microsoft.Phone"
    xmlns:shell="clr-namespace:Microsoft.Phone.Shell;assembly=Microsoft.Phone"
    xmlns:d="http://schemas.microsoft.com/expression/blend/2008"
    xmlns:mc="http://schemas.openxmlformats.org/markup-compatibility/2006"
    mc:Ignorable="d" d:DesignWidth="480" d:DesignHeight="768"
    FontFamily="{StaticResource PhoneFontFamilyNormal}"
    FontSize="{StaticResource PhoneFontSizeNormal}"
    Foreground="{StaticResource PhoneForegroundBrush}"
    SupportedOrientations="Portrait" Orientation="Portrait"
    shell:SystemTray.IsVisible="True">

    <!--LayoutRoot is the root grid where all page content is placed-->
    <Grid x:Name="LayoutRoot" Background="Transparent">
        <Grid.RowDefinitions>
            <RowDefinition Height="Auto"/>
            <RowDefinition Height="*"/>
        </Grid.RowDefinitions>

        <!--TitlePanel contains the name of the application and page title-->
        <StackPanel x:Name="TitlePanel" Grid.Row="0" Margin="12,17,0,28">
            <TextBlock x:Name="ApplicationTitle" Text="MY APPLICATION"
Style="{StaticResource PhoneTextNormalStyle}"/>
            <TextBlock x:Name="PageTitle" Text="Hello Windows Phone 7"
Margin="9,-7,0,0" Style="{StaticResource PhoneTextTitle1Style}"/>
        </StackPanel>

        <!--ContentPanel - place additional content here-->
        <Grid x:Name="ContentPanel" Grid.Row="1" Margin="12,0,12,0"></Grid>
    </Grid>

    <!--Sample code showing usage of ApplicationBar-->
    <!--<phone:PhoneApplicationPage.ApplicationBar>
        <shell:ApplicationBar IsVisible="True" IsMenuEnabled="True">
```

continues

LISTING 1-2 *(continued)*

```
            <shell:ApplicationBarIconButton IconUri="/Images/appbar_button1.png"
    Text="Button 1"/>
            <shell:ApplicationBarIconButton IconUri="/Images/appbar_button2.png"
    Text="Button 2"/>
            <shell:ApplicationBar.MenuItems>
                <shell:ApplicationBarMenuItem Text="MenuItem 1"/>
                <shell:ApplicationBarMenuItem Text="MenuItem 2"/>
            </shell:ApplicationBar.MenuItems>
        </shell:ApplicationBar>
    </phone:PhoneApplicationPage.ApplicationBar>-->
</phone:PhoneApplicationPage>
```

Cod Snippet HelloWindowsPhone7\MainPage.xaml

 NOTE *Don't worry too much about understanding of the code at this point as the next chapter takes a much closer look at XAML and Silverlight in general. By the end of the next chapter, you should be able to understand every line of this code.*

7. Now you're ready to change the text being displayed in the phone. Click the box with the words "page name," and the box becomes highlighted. This control is called a `TextBlock` control, and it's a Silverlight-based control that allows you to display static text. After you make this control active, you should see a new set of properties displayed in the lower-right corner, in the Properties window. By default, the `Text` property should be in focus, and here you can change the text being displayed to `Hello, Windows Phone 7`. Finally, press Enter, and you should see the text displayed in the emulator change to reflect what you just typed.

8. Build and run this program in the Windows Phone emulator by clicking the green triangle in the top toolbar (see Figure 1-8). Clicking the green triangle is the fastest way to build a Windows Phone project. If there are no compiler errors, Visual Studio starts the emulator and runs your new application in a mock Windows Phone 7 device, as shown in Figure 1-9.

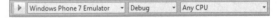

FIGURE 1-8: Starting the emulator.

FIGURE 1-9: The Windows Phone 7 emulator

9. Notice that the phone screen is not wide enough to actually display all of the text. The Windows Phone 7 device relies on scrolling and panoramic displays of user interfaces. You'll see later on how to take advantage of this feature. With the application now running, you have a great test environment that does an excellent job of simulating a real Windows Phone 7 device.

10. To change the orientation of the device, click the orientation tool in the toolbar. After you click this tool, you see your phone flipped sideways, as shown in Figure 1-10. This has obvious implications for applications, but don't worry. The Windows Phone 7 API makes sure to give you event handlers when orientation changes take place. In those event handlers, you can add code to redisplay your user interface using the appropriate screen orientation. The emulator does, however, provide a great way to test and ensure that your app behaves properly when this actually happens.

11. Stop the emulator and finish running your program by clicking the square Stop icon on the toolbar shown in Figure 1-11.

FIGURE 1-10: Alternate orientation.

FIGURE 1-11: Stop the emulator.

How It Works

In this example, you created a simple "Hello, World" Windows Phone 7 application. You had a chance to take a look around Visual Studio 2010 Express to see that your source code files fall under the Solution Explorer. You were also introduced to your first Silverlight control, TextBlock, which enables you to easily add static text to a Windows Phone app.

In this example, you changed the default text displayed by clicking on the control and altering the Text property in the Properties window. In fact, all Silverlight control properties are available right from this window, so as you move forward in this book, you'll be doing plenty of work here. You always have the option of changing property values in code through the XAML, and you'll see how to do that later on. The Properties window offers an easy way to scan all the available properties of a given control and make changes, if necessary.

Finally, you ran your new application in the Windows Phone 7 emulator software. This powerful program emulates an actual Windows Phone 7 device and allows you to test a program before deploying it to actual hardware.

COMMON MISTAKES *When you stop debugging an application, Visual Studio takes you back to the normal split view showing the user interface and source code. It doesn't actually shut down the emulator software. This is by design. Keeping the emulator running dramatically speeds up the build process and ensures that the emulator is ready to go when you want to start debugging your application again. Don't worry that something didn't shut down right; this is Visual Studio's way of making sure no development time is wasted by going through the emulator startup process more than necessary.*

SUMMARY

This chapter provides a brief history of Windows Phone 7. You learned how this platform has evolved over time and how fierce competition from Google and Apple led to Microsoft redesigning its entire mobile operating system from the ground up.

You also learned how Windows Phone 7 differs from Windows Mobile in fundamental ways, starting with the hardware specification. Instead of allowing for just about any hardware configuration cellphone providers could come up with, Microsoft has created a strict set of minimum requirements that must be met in every Windows Phone 7 device. Thanks to these requirements, you don't need to develop applications and port them over to a myriad of devices.

You learned about the various pieces that make up the architecture of the Windows Phone 7 platform: the runtime components, cloud services, portal services, and tools.

In this chapter, you also got an overview of how the new Windows Phone Marketplace allows users to easily find and install your apps.

You walked through the installation of the free developer tools. After taking a quick tour of Visual Studio 2010, you created your first Windows Phone 7 application. Finally, after compiling and building your new "Hello, World" app, you ran and tested the program by using the emulator software, which allows you to see how your finished application will look when it's deployed to actual device hardware.

EXERCISES

1. True or False: Windows Phone development requires the use of Visual Studio 2010 Professional Version or better.

2. The Windows Phone architecture consists of which of the following components? (Choose All That Apply)

a)   Runtime components

b)   Cloud services

c)   WCF RIA services

d)   WPF

e)   Portal services

f)   Tools

3. True or False: You can distribute applications developed for Windows Phone 7 to any device by simply making the executable available on your own website for others to download.

4. What purpose does the `TextBlock` control serve in an application?

5. What is the function of the `PhoneApplicationPage` control that is found in all Windows Phone 7 apps?

Answers to Exercises can be found in Appendix A.

▶ **WHAT YOU LEARNED IN THIS CHAPTER**

TOPIC	KEY CONCEPTS
Windows Mobile platform	Windows Mobile has evolved to its current incarnation, Windows Phone 7, through years of market research and intense competition and, more recently, a much larger consumer marketplace for smartphones in general. Some of the drawbacks of Windows Mobile were the need to use a stylus for user input and the need to support countless screen resolutions and devices. Windows Phone 7 has addressed such issues through the use of a strict minimum hardware specification that includes a requirement for a capacitive multitouch screen.
Windows Phone 7 architecture	The Windows Phone 7 architecture includes four major components: runtime components, cloud services, portal services, and developer tools. Included in the runtime components are the .NET runtime, Silverlight, XNA, sensors, data, and media management. The cloud services include support for Xbox LIVE integration, social networking, Bing Maps, location, identity, and notifications. The portal services assist you in certification, deployment, and distribution of applications through the validation, certification, publishing, and registration services. You may be able to profit from your applications and ensure that they're made available to all Windows Phone 7 users by distributing them through the new and improved Windows Phone Marketplace. Finally, the powerful developer tools in Windows Phone 7 include the familiar Visual Studio 2010, the new Expression Blend for designers, plenty of sample applications, and an extensive community of .NET and Silverlight developers.
Visual Studio 2010 Express Edition	Visual Studio 2010 is your primary development tool for creating Windows Phone 7 applications. Visual Studio allows you to edit both XAML and code-behind files. You can also easily compile and build applications by using the Build toolbar. You can use the Windows Phone 7 emulator software to easily test your apps without actual hardware.
App.xaml	All Windows Phone 7 applications require an `App.xaml` file that holds important resources that need to be made globally available to other pages in a project.

TOPIC	KEY CONCEPTS
MainPage.xaml	Although it doesn't have to be named `MainPage.xaml`, there will always be a page like this that contains the top-level `PhoneApplicationPage` control. This control is responsible for acting like the top-level window of your application. All other controls and user interface elements must reside in the context of this control.
Windows Phone emulator	When you're ready to being testing an application, you can run the Windows Phone emulator software to get a feel for how your app will look in a Windows Phone environment without actually having to take the time to deploy it to a physical piece of hardware. The emulator supports many of the same features as a real Windows Phone device, including the accelerometer. This allows you to test your application in both vertical and horizontal configurations, depending on the current orientation of the phone.

2

Jaw-Dropping Apps with the Help of Silverlight

WHAT YOU WILL LEARN IN THIS CHAPTER:

➤ Understanding the Requirements for Windows Phone 7 Development

➤ Developing User Interfaces with XAML

➤ Understanding the Anatomy of a Windows Phone 7 App

➤ Using Silverlight controls

➤ Creating your first Silverlight application for Windows Phone 7

In the previous chapter, you learned about the history of the Windows Mobile platform and got a basic overview of the new Windows Phone 7 platform. In this chapter, you'll see how to fully make use of Silverlight and the supplied user interface controls to make rich Windows Phone 7 apps. The Silverlight controls enable you to collect user input, display images, lay out data entry forms, and more.

It's important to note that this chapter assumes some basic programming knowledge. You need to know basics such as variables, loop constructs, and so on. Additionally, you should have some basic knowledge of C# and .NET development in general. If you're looking for additional information or help programming in C#, you should refer to one of the many available beginning or professional-level C# books currently on the market today. *Beginning Visual C#* by Karli Watson (Wrox Press, 2010) is a great place to start! You don't, however, need to worry about being an expert in using Visual Studio. This chapter covers everything you need to know about the latest Integrated Development Environment (IDE) and how it relates to programming for Windows Phone 7.

REQUIREMENTS FOR WINDOWS PHONE 7 DEVELOPMENT

Back at the MIX 2010 conference, when the new Windows Phone 7 platform was originally introduced to the masses, there were many comments to the effect that if you're currently a Silverlight developer, then you're already a Windows Phone 7 developer. For the most part, this is pretty much the case. If you've spent a decent amount of time developing web solutions using Silverlight technology, then much of the information covered in this chapter will be familiar to you. If you've never heard of Silverlight or if you've never had the time to take an extensive look at it, don't worry. This chapter goes into detail about all the controls available in the Windows Phone 7 SDK. If you're already a Silverlight developer, you'll still want to work your way through this chapter as the Silverlight runtime that exists on the phone is a subset of the full-blown version available on the web. You should become familiar with the controls available for the phone and which controls are currently not supported.

The following is a complete list of requirements for Windows Phone 7 development:

➤   Visual Studio 2010 Express for Windows Phone 7

➤   Windows Phone 7 Developer Tools

➤   Knowledge of the C# programming language and the .NET framework

➤   Silverlight and/or XNA libraries and tools

WHAT IS SILVERLIGHT?

What is this Silverlight thing, and what is Extensible Application Markup Language (XAML)? Silverlight, which is now in its fourth iteration, was originally developed to provide developers with a way to create rich Internet applications, using standard .NET tools and languages. Rich Internet applications (RIA) became the de facto standard for Web 2.0–style applications. These applications typically would forgo the traditional post-back model where users click a link and the entire page is refreshed with new data. Instead, RIA web applications make use of a new programming standard called Asynchronous JavaScript and XML (AJAX) in order to update only the parts of the web page that actually need to be updated instead of refreshing the entire page.

Taking advantage of RIA's updating method enhances the end user experience; users don't have to sit and wait for an entire page to be reloaded when only one small area is actually being changed. It also reduces the actual bandwidth used on the web server because a much smaller amount of data is transmitted over the wire.

AJAX-based solutions were typically written using raw HTML and JavaScript. As you may know, trying to write an application using raw HTML and JavaScript presents several challenges. When working in an AJAX environment, you need to test against many different web browsers, and each one has its own slightly different take on how JavaScript calls are supposed to perform. In addition, not all browsers support CSS in the same way, so a site that looks great in Firefox doesn't usually look exactly the same in Internet Explorer without some tweaking of CSS and JavaScript. This problem is one of the main things that Silverlight for the web tries to address.

Silverlight provides web developers with another way to create RIA-style web applications. The runtime itself works as a plug-in for the browser that's similar to Flash. Because it's a plug-in, all the user interface code you write occurs on the client PC, so you don't have to worry about page refreshes. In addition, the user interface can be written using XAML and the .NET runtime. Therefore, if you've been developing Windows-based solutions using .NET, you can easily transfer your skills without having to learn JavaScript and all the various ways different web browsers handle it. Silverlight also takes care of cross-browser compatibility issues. If you write code to run in Silverlight, it'll work the same in every browser. You should still do your own application testing in a variety of browsers, but for the most part, Microsoft has done the heavy lifting to ensure that your web applications run the same, regardless of the browser.

Another nice benefit of Silverlight is that traditionally, if you were doing .NET development, you had no way to target a non-Windows platform. This is no longer the case as Silverlight is supported on multiple platforms and in many popular web browsers. Table 2-1 lists the operating systems and browsers that Silverlight 4 supports.

TABLE 2-1: Platforms and Browsers Supported in Silverlight 4

OPERATING SYSTEM	BROWSERS
Windows 7	Internet Explorer (6, 7, 8), Firefox 3, Safari (3, 4), Chrome 4
Windows Vista	Internet Explorer (6, 7, 8), Firefox 3, Safari (3, 4), Chrome 4
Windows Server 2008	Internet Explorer (7, 8), Firefox 3, Chrome 4
Windows Server 2008 R2	Internet Explorer 8, Firefox 3, Chrome 4
Windows XP SP2, SP3	Internet Explorer (6, 7, 8), Firefox 3, Chrome 4
Windows 2000 SP4	Internet Explorer 6
Mac OS 10.4.11 +	Firefox 3, Safari (3, 4)

As you can see, Silverlight is supported across a wide variety of operating systems and browsers. Perhaps more importantly, Silverlight is also the preferred development platform for the Windows Phone. Therefore, porting applications written using Silverlight for the web to Windows Phone doesn't take much effort. In fact, most of the code carries over just fine. The only real work usually comes from working with the smaller screen that the phone provides.

 NOTE *If you want some more information on Silverlight for the web, take a look at www.silverlight.net. At this site, you can visit the Get Started section for much more detail on all the features available in the full version of Silverlight 4. You can also see Silverlight in action by checking out some major sites like those of Netflix, NASA, and NBC Sports.*

What Is XAML?

Now that you have some background information on what Silverlight actually is, it's time to take a look at how it's involved in the development of Windows Phone 7 applications. Remember that all Windows Phone applications are written using either Silverlight or XNA. We'll get to XNA in Chapter 11, but for now the rule-of-thumb is that if you're developing a consumer application that deals with data, text, and so on, you'll most likely use Silverlight. If you want to create games, you'll focus mostly on XNA as it provides libraries and project templates specific for writing games on the Windows Phone.

All Silverlight development begins and ends with XAML. If you've ever worked with XML or HTML, then XAML won't be difficult to understand.

When working with HTML, you typically declare controls on a page where you need some kind of user interactivity — for example, `<input>` for buttons or `<img>` for displaying images. When using XAML, you do something similar to create a user interface. For example, if you wanted to put a button on a page along with some text, you can do so in XAML with something like the following:

```
<Button Content="Click this button" />
```

To display an image on the page, you could add something like this:

```
<Image Source="MyImage.png" />
```

It's pretty simple so far. As you can see, XAML syntax is similar to that of HTML, so when you have a feel for how to declare all of the various controls, it won't take you long to get your user interface up-and-running.

One important benefit of using XAML to create a user interface is that you can completely separate your code from your design. When you use a declarative language such as XAML, you can also use tools such as Expression Blend to create rich user interfaces without worrying about them looking different after they're delivered to the developer. If you've worked with web development before, you might know that some designers prefer to create a rich user interface using software such as Photoshop. However, you can't just put Photoshop files into Visual Studio and start writing code against them. With XAML, you can literally take the XAML code generated by a design tool, place it into Visual Studio, and start coding the application

The Anatomy of a Windows Phone Application

Before delving into some of the individual controls available in Silverlight, you should probably become more familiar with what goes into the Windows Phone 7 application template you used in Chapter 1. Some of these topics will be covered in greater detail later on, but before working with the controls and creating more projects, it'll help to get a better understanding of some of the files that appear with each new project being created in Visual Studio Express.

Development Starts with MainPage.xaml

You typically start your application development with the `MainPage.xaml` file. In this chapter, all the code you write will be either in this page or in the code-behind file `MainPage.xaml.cs`. There's no requirement that this page be called `MainPage`, but when you're learning your way through Windows Phone 7 development, you probably want to just stick with the default. When you first create a Windows Phone 7 application using the Visual Studio template, you see the following code in `MainPage.xaml`:

```
<phone:PhoneApplicationPage
    x:Class="WindowPhoneApp.MainPage"
    xmlns="http://schemas.microsoft.com/winfx/2006/xaml/presentation"
    xmlns:x="http://schemas.microsoft.com/winfx/2006/xaml"
    xmlns:phone="clr-namespace:Microsoft.Phone.Controls;assembly=Microsoft.Phone"
    xmlns:shell="clr-namespace:Microsoft.Phone.Shell;assembly=Microsoft.Phone"
    xmlns:d="http://schemas.microsoft.com/expression/blend/2008"
    xmlns:mc="http://schemas.openxmlformats.org/markup-compatibility/2006"
    mc:Ignorable="d" d:DesignWidth="480" d:DesignHeight="768"
    FontFamily="{StaticResource PhoneFontFamilyNormal}"
    FontSize="{StaticResource PhoneFontSizeNormal}"
    Foreground="{StaticResource PhoneForegroundBrush}"
    SupportedOrientations="Portrait" Orientation="Portrait"
    shell:SystemTray.IsVisible="True">

    <!--LayoutRoot is the root grid where all page content is placed-->
    <Grid x:Name="LayoutRoot" Background="Transparent">
        <Grid.RowDefinitions>
            <RowDefinition Height="Auto"/>
            <RowDefinition Height="*"/>
        </Grid.RowDefinitions>

        <!--TitlePanel contains the name of the application and page title-->
        <StackPanel x:Name="TitlePanel" Grid.Row="0" Margin="12,17,0,28">
            <TextBlock x:Name="ApplicationTitle" Text="MY APPLICATION"
Style="{StaticResource PhoneTextNormalStyle}"/>
            <TextBlock x:Name="PageTitle" Text="page name" Margin="9,-7,0,0"
Style="{StaticResource PhoneTextTitle1Style}"/>
        </StackPanel>

        <!--ContentPanel - place additional content here-->
        <Grid x:Name="ContentPanel" Grid.Row="1" Margin="12,0,12,0"></Grid>
    </Grid>

<!--Sample code showing usage of ApplicationBar-->
<!--<phone:PhoneApplicationPage.ApplicationBar>
<shell:ApplicationBar IsVisible="True" IsMenuEnabled="True">
<shell:ApplicationBarIconButton IconUri="/Images/appbar_button1.png"
Text="Button 1"/>
<shell:ApplicationBarIconButton IconUri="/Images/appbar_button2.png"
Text="Button 2"/>
<shell:ApplicationBar.MenuItems>
<shell:ApplicationBarMenuItem Text="MenuItem 1"/>
<shell:ApplicationBarMenuItem Text="MenuItem 2"/>
```

```
</shell:ApplicationBar.MenuItems>
</shell:ApplicationBar>
</phone:PhoneApplicationPage.ApplicationBar>-->

</phone:PhoneApplicationPage>
```

We dissect some of the features of this file in upcoming chapters. For now, there are a couple of important things to note about the preceding code. First, every Windows Phone application requires an instance of the `PhoneApplicationPage` control. There must always be at least one of these controls declared. Although you can have additional pages in your app, each page should have the following control declared:

```
<phone:PhoneApplicationPage x:Class="WindowPhoneApp.MainPage"
```

In this page, a couple of default `TextBlock` controls display the application name and the title of the currently displayed page. The application name can be found in the `ApplicationTitle` text block:

```
<TextBlock x:Name="ApplicationTitle" Text="MY APPLICATION" Style="{StaticResource
PhoneTextNormalStyle}"/>
```

Don't worry about `StaticResource` yet; it will be covered later. For now, note that you can change the app title that's displayed by simply changing the `Text` property from MY APPLICATION to something more relevant for your app.

The current page title is also declared in the following `TextBlock` declaration:

```
<TextBlock x:Name="PageTitle" Text="page name" Margin="9,-7,0,0"
Style="{StaticResource PhoneTextTitle1Style}"/>
```

Once again, you can easily modify this by changing the `Text` property from page name to something more appropriate.

The next area that's important to note is the `ContentPanel` grid control. All the Silverlight controls that you use on the page will reside inside this control. The following code shows a `Button` control sitting inside `ContentPanel`:

```
<!--ContentPanel - place additional content here-->
<Grid x:Name="ContentPanel" Grid.Row="1" Margin="12,0,12,0"></Grid>
    <Button x:Name="MainButton" Content="Click Me" />
</Grid>
```

The MainPage.xaml.cs Code-Behind File

The `MainPage.xaml.cs` file is the code-behind page for the `MainPage.xaml` file. All your control interactions and code will reside in this file, including any event handlers. Code-behind and events are covered in greater depth later in this chapter. For now, notice in the following code that is generated by default that the file doesn't contain much aside from a constructor for the page:

```
using System;
using System.Collections.Generic;
using System.Linq;
```

```
using System.Net;
using System.Windows;
using System.Windows.Controls;
using System.Windows.Documents;
using System.Windows.Input;
using System.Windows.Media;
using System.Windows.Media.Animation;
using System.Windows.Shapes;
using Microsoft.Phone.Controls;

namespace test
{
    public partial class MainPage : PhoneApplicationPage
    {
        // Constructor
        public MainPage()
        {
            InitializeComponent();
        }
    }
}
```

The App.xaml Page

The App.xaml page, which is not displayed on the phone, contains resources and settings that are global to your entire application. When you first create a new project, you're presented with the following code in the App.xaml file:

```
<Application
    x:Class="test.App"
    xmlns="http://schemas.microsoft.com/winfx/2006/xaml/presentation"
    xmlns:x="http://schemas.microsoft.com/winfx/2006/xaml"
    xmlns:phone="clr-namespace:Microsoft.Phone.Controls;assembly=Microsoft.Phone"
    xmlns:shell="clr-namespace:Microsoft.Phone.Shell;assembly=Microsoft.Phone">

    <!--Application Resources-->
    <Application.Resources>
    </Application.Resources>

    <Application.ApplicationLifetimeObjects>
    <!--Required object that handles lifetime events for the application-->
    <shell:PhoneApplicationService
        Launching="Application_Launching" Closing="Application_Closing"
        Activated="Application_Activated" Deactivated="Application_Deactivated"/>
    </Application.ApplicationLifetimeObjects>

</Application>
```

As you can probably guess from the comments, you put shared resources in the Application .Resources section. There's also a section that declares PhoneApplicationService, which is a globally available service you can use to detect important phone events, such as Launching, Closing, Activated, and Deactivated. Default implementations of these event handlers are created for you in the App.xaml.cs file. In later chapters, you'll learn more about these events and how to use them in your app.

The App.xaml.cs Code-Behind File

The App.xaml.cs file, shown in Listing 2-1, is the code-behind for the App.xaml file. In this file's code, you'll find default handlers for several of the PhoneApplicationService events and additional application initialization code. Listing 2-1 shows the default contents of the App.xaml.cs file.

LISTING 2-1 App.xaml.cs

```csharp
using System;
using System.Collections.Generic;
using System.Linq;
using System.Net;
using System.Windows;
using System.Windows.Controls;
using System.Windows.Documents;
using System.Windows.Input;
using System.Windows.Media;
using System.Windows.Media.Animation;
using System.Windows.Navigation;
using System.Windows.Shapes;
using Microsoft.Phone.Controls;
using Microsoft.Phone.Shell;

namespace BeginningWindowsPhone7
{
    public partial class App : Application
    {
        /// <summary>
        /// Provides easy access to the root frame of the Phone Application.
        /// </summary>
        /// <returns>The root frame of the Phone Application.</returns>
        public PhoneApplicationFrame RootFrame { get; private set; }

        /// <summary>
        /// Constructor for the Application object.
        /// </summary>
        public App()
        {
            // Global handler for uncaught exceptions.
            UnhandledException += Application_UnhandledException;

            // Show graphics profiling information while debugging.
            if (System.Diagnostics.Debugger.IsAttached)
            {
                // Display the current frame rate counters.
                Application.Current.Host.Settings.EnableFrameRateCounter =
true;

                // Show the areas of the app that are being redrawn in each
                // frame.
                //Application.Current.Host.Settings.EnableRedrawRegions = true;

                // Enable non-production analysis visualization mode,
```

```
                // which shows areas of a page that are being GPU accelerated
                // with a colored overlay.
                //Application.Current.Host.Settings.EnableCacheVisualization =
true;
            }

            // Standard Silverlight initialization
            InitializeComponent();

            // Phone-specific initialization
            InitializePhoneApplication();
        }

        // Code to execute when the application is launching (eg, from Start)
        // This code will not execute when the application is reactivated
        private void Application_Launching(object sender, LaunchingEventArgs e)
        {
        }

        // Code to execute when the application is activated (brought to
        // foreground)
        // This code will not execute when the application is first launched
        private void Application_Activated(object sender, ActivatedEventArgs e)
        {
        }

        // Code to execute when the application is deactivated (sent to
        // background)
        // This code will not execute when the application is closing
        private void Application_Deactivated(object sender,
DeactivatedEventArgs e)
        {
        }

        // Code to execute when the application is closing (eg, user hit Back)
        // This code will not execute when the application is deactivated
        private void Application_Closing(object sender, ClosingEventArgs e)
        {
        }

        // Code to execute if a navigation fails
        private void RootFrame_NavigationFailed(object sender,
NavigationFailedEventArgs e)
        {
            if (System.Diagnostics.Debugger.IsAttached)
            {
                // A navigation has failed; break into the debugger
                System.Diagnostics.Debugger.Break();
            }
        }

        // Code to execute on Unhandled Exceptions
        private void Application_UnhandledException(object sender,
```

continues

LISTING 2-1 *(continued)*

```
ApplicationUnhandledExceptionEventArgs e)
        {
            if (System.Diagnostics.Debugger.IsAttached)
            {
                // An unhandled exception has occurred; break into the debugger
                System.Diagnostics.Debugger.Break();
            }
        }

#region Phone application initialization

        // Avoid double-initialization
        private bool phoneApplicationInitialized = false;

        // Do not add any additional code to this method
        private void InitializePhoneApplication()
        {
            if (phoneApplicationInitialized)
                return;

            // Create the frame but don't set it as RootVisual yet; this
            // allows the splash
            // screen to remain active until the application is ready to render.
            RootFrame = new PhoneApplicationFrame();
            RootFrame.Navigated += CompleteInitializePhoneApplication;

            // Handle navigation failures
            RootFrame.NavigationFailed += RootFrame_NavigationFailed;

            // Ensure we don't initialize again
            phoneApplicationInitialized = true;
        }

        // Do not add any additional code to this method
        private void CompleteInitializePhoneApplication(object sender,
NavigationEventArgs e)
        {
            // Set the root visual to allow the application to render
            if (RootVisual != RootFrame)
                RootVisual = RootFrame;

            // Remove this handler since it is no longer needed
            RootFrame.Navigated -= CompleteInitializePhoneApplication;
        }

#endregion
    }
}
```

The WMAppManifest.xaml Page

The WMAppManifest.xaml file holds many application-specific settings, including what page should be loaded upon startup. The following is the default version of WMAppManifest.xaml that's created when a new project first loads:

```xml
<?xml version="1.0" encoding="utf-8"?>

<Deployment xmlns="http://schemas.microsoft.com/windowsphone/2009/deployment"
    AppPlatformVersion="7.0">
<App xmlns="" ProductID="{477fbe79-ad5e-412f-bd70-6685237ad47a}" Title="test"
    RuntimeType="Silverlight" Version="1.0.0.0" Genre="apps.normal"
    Author="Author"
    Description="Sample description" Publisher="Wrox">
    <IconPath IsRelative="true" IsResource="false">ApplicationIcon.png</IconPath>
    <Capabilities>
        <Capability Name="ID_CAP_GAMERSERVICES"/>
        <Capability Name="ID_CAP_IDENTITY_DEVICE"/>
        <Capability Name="ID_CAP_IDENTITY_USER"/>
        <Capability Name="ID_CAP_LOCATION"/>
        <Capability Name="ID_CAP_MEDIALIB"/>
        <Capability Name="ID_CAP_MICROPHONE"/>
        <Capability Name="ID_CAP_NETWORKING"/>
        <Capability Name="ID_CAP_PHONEDIALER"/>
        <Capability Name="ID_CAP_PUSH_NOTIFICATION"/>
        <Capability Name="ID_CAP_SENSORS"/>
        <Capability Name="ID_CAP_WEBBROWSERCOMPONENT"/>
    </Capabilities>
    <Tasks>
        <DefaultTask  Name ="_default" NavigationPage="MainPage.xaml"/>
    </Tasks>
    <Tokens>
        <PrimaryToken TokenID="testToken" TaskName="_default">
            <TemplateType5>
                <BackgroundImageURI IsRelative="true"
    IsResource="false">Background.png</BackgroundImageURI>
                <Count>0</Count>
                <Title>Beginning Windows Phone 7 Development</Title>
            </TemplateType5>
        </PrimaryToken>
    </Tokens>
</App>
</Deployment>
```

Note that the line starting with <DefaultTask is responsible for determining which page loads on application startup. If you want to change the name of MainPage.xaml or use an alternate startup page, you need to change this value to reflect that change.

The Application Splash Screen

The splash screen image is displayed as your application is being loaded in the background. By default, every project has an image called SplashScreenImage.jpg that shows a clock. You're allowed to change this image to anything you like. Just be sure to name your splash screen image **SplashScreenImage.jpg** because this is what the runtime will be looking for when your application starts up.

The Application Icon

By default, the project template provides your app with an application icon (`ApplicationIcon.png`) that looks similar to the sun. As with the splash screen, you can customize this icon by replacing this file with your own image, as long as you use the same filename. The application icon will be displayed in the list of installed applications on a phone.

Developing with Silverlight Controls

Perhaps the best way to become familiar with both Silverlight and XAML is to take a look at some actual examples of each. As stated earlier, Silverlight for Windows Phone consists of a subset of the Silverlight for the web platform. The majority of controls that are available for the web are also available on the phone, but there are a few exceptions. Table 2-2 shows the full list of controls that you can use in your Windows Phone applications, along with a brief description of what they're used for.

TABLE 2-2: Silverlight Controls

CONTROL	DESCRIPTION
Border	Creates a border around another user interface object.
Button	Enables user interaction using a mouse click.
Canvas container	Enables you to absolutely position elements on the screen.
Control class	Acts as a generic base class for most controls; contains several properties and methods used by controls.
Grid control	Enables you to arrange additional controls in a table-like format.
HyperlinkButton button	Provides you with the ability to create HTML hyperlinks to external content, while providing characteristics of a standard Button control.
Image	Displays an image file in one of the supported formats (JPEG or PNG).
ListBox data container	Presents items in a list format.
MediaElement	Displays media such as music or video.
PasswordBox text box	Enables password input. Users can type a password and text will be converted on-the-fly to ***** (asterisk) characters.
ProgressBar bar controls	Shows the end user the current progress of a long-running operation.
RadioButton	Enables the user to select from a list of options.

CONTROL	DESCRIPTION
ScrollViewer	Enables you to host scrollable content. If your page will take up more than the available screen space, ScrollViewer enables the end user to easily scroll to view additional page information.
Slider	Enables the user to change a value using a sliding scale control.
StackPanel	Enables you to lay out (stack) other controls either vertically or horizontally.
TextBlock	Enables you to display plain text.
TextBox	Provides users with a way to enter data.

Common Control Properties

Because almost all Silverlight controls inherit from the Control base class, all controls have several properties available. The first and perhaps most important is the x:Name property. This property allows you to assign a name to a control so that you can easily access it, along with all of its properties from other places in XAML code or from your page logic code. In the following code, for example, a Button control is assigned a name so that it can be accessed later on in code:

```
<Button x:Name="MyWindowsPhoneButton" />
```

Almost all controls allow you to specify a size using the Height and Width properties. Using the following code, you can easily create small, medium, and large buttons by making use of these two properties:

```
<Button x:Name="SmallButton" Height="10" Width="10" />
<Button x:Name="MediumButton" Height="50" Width="50" />
<Button x:Name="LargeButton" Height="100" Width="100" />
```

Another important property in Silverlight is the Visibility property. As you can probably guess, the Visibility property enables you to show and hide a particular control. Setting this property requires the use of an enumeration value. An enumeration value is basically a variable that has multiple options — not just true and false. In this case, the Visibility enumerator offers two choices: Visible and Collapsed. The following code shows this in action:

```
<Button x:Name="VisibleButton" Visibility="Visible" />
<Button x:Name="HiddenButton" Visibility="Collapsed" />
```

Now you can set the height and width of a control and even toggle whether the control should show up on the page.

What if you want to change the font or text style of the Button control? The Silverlight controls make it easy to do just that. You can use a couple of different properties when changing the font or text style of a control. Table 2-3 shows the various properties available, along with some of the options.

TABLE 2-3: Font and Text Styles for Silverlight Controls

PROPERTY	EXAMPLES OF VALUES	XAML CODE
FontFamily	Arial, Times New Roman	`<Button Content="Button1" FontFamily="Arial" />`
FontSize	8, 10, 11, 12	`<Button Content="Button1" FontSize="12" />`
FontStretch	Condensed, Normal, Expanded	`<Button Content="Button1" FontStretch="Expanded" />`
FontStyle	Normal, Italic	`<Button Content="ItalicButton" FontStyle="Italic" />`
FontWeight	Thin, ExtraLight, Light, Normal, Medium, SemiBold, Bold, ExtraBold, Black, ExtraBlack	`<Button Content="BoldButton" FontWeight="Bold" />`

Silverlight provides several additional properties that are common to all controls. The `IsEnabled` property allows you to toggle the user's ability to interact with a given control while still making sure the control is visible. The `Background` and `Foreground` properties enable you to customize the control's background and foreground text with solid colors, gradients, and even images. The `Margin` and `Padding` properties that are available work similarly to the HTML equivalent margin and padding CSS properties. These two properties enable you to create some space around controls. Table 2-4 shows these additional properties, along with the possible values and even some XAML code to get you started using them.

TABLE 2-4: Additional Common Control Properties

PROPERTY	VALUES	XAML CODE
IsEnabled	True, False	`<Button Content="Disabled Button" IsEnabled="False" />`
Margin	1 or 1, 1, 1, 1 (representing left, top, right, and bottom, respectively)	`<Button Content="Button With Set Margin" Margin="5" />`
Padding	1 or 1, 1, 1, 1 (representing left, top, right, and bottom, respectively)	`<Button Content="Padded Button" Padding="5" />`
Background	Any valid color, such as Red, Blue, Green, or Yellow	`<Button Content="Red Background" Background="Red" />`
Foreground	Any valid color, such as Red, Blue, Green, or Yellow	`<Button Content="Blue Text" Foreground="Blue" />`

Layout Controls

The first group of controls we need to cover is the layout controls. Layout controls enable you to position other controls on the page in an orderly fashion.

The Canvas Control

The most basic of the layout controls is perhaps the `Canvas` control. This control works similarly to a raw HTML page. You can add any other controls to a `Canvas` control, and you can influence their position by setting X and Y coordinates for the controls. The following code shows a `Canvas` object with two `Button` controls set to display at different locations in the `Canvas` control:

```
<Canvas x:Name="MainCanvas">
    <Button Canvas.Top="20" Canvas.Left="20" Content="Top Button" />
    <Button Canvas.Top="200" Canvas.Left="50" Content="Lower Button" />
</Canvas>
```

As you can see, you set the coordinates of the two `Button` controls by using the `Top` and `Left` properties of the parent `Canvas` object. This mechanism, called *attached properties*, is a feature specific to XAML. Attached properties allow a control to access properties that may belong to its parent. In this case, you want the `Button` controls to be positioned relative to the `Canvas` control, so for the first button, setting the `Top` and `Left` values to `20` will position the control 20 pixels from the top of the `Canvas` and 20 pixels from the left. If you were to run the previous code using the Windows Phone emulator, you would see the buttons in the appropriate location on the screen, as shown in Figure 2-1.

You may have noticed the additional `x:Name="MainCanvas"` line in the code. If you think you'll need to access a control in your code or somewhere else in XAML, you should name it in this way as that is the standard naming convention for Silverlight controls.

FIGURE 2-1: The `Canvas` control.

The Grid Control

All the layout controls are essentially hosts for other controls, but the `Grid` control is perhaps one of the most flexible in that it allows you to arrange controls in a table-like format; it's similar to the HTML `<table>` tag. With a `Grid` control, you set up rows and columns and use attached properties to assign controls to those rows and columns. To start, you simply declare a new `Grid` control like this:

```
<Grid x:Name="MainGrid"></Grid>
```

Just in case you need to access the `Grid` later on, you give it the name `MainGrid`. You need to tell the `Grid` control how many rows and columns will be required. In this case, assume that you want a three-by-three table-like structure, so tell the `Grid` control that you need three rows and three columns. You do this by using the `Grid.RowDefinitions` and `Grid.ColumnDefinitions` properties. The following code demonstrates how to use these properties to create the three-by-three table structure:

```
<Grid x:Name="MainGrid">
    <Grid.RowDefinitions>
```

```
            <RowDefinition />
            <RowDefinition />
            <RowDefinition />
        </Grid.RowDefinitions>
        <Grid.ColumnDefinitions>
            <ColumnDefinition />
            <ColumnDefinition />
            <ColumnDefinition />
        </Grid.ColumnDefinitions>
    </Grid>
```

This isn't too difficult. You just add a `RowDefinition` and `ColumnDefinition` declaration for each row and column you want in the `Grid` control. Then you can add some controls to the various rows and columns. The following code adds `Button` controls to the `Grid` control, in various rows and columns:

```
<Grid x:Name="MainGrid">
    <Grid.RowDefinitions>
        <RowDefinition />
        <RowDefinition />
        <RowDefinition />
    </Grid.RowDefinitions>
    <Grid.ColumnDefinitions>
        <ColumnDefinition />
        <ColumnDefinition />
        <ColumnDefinition />
    </Grid.ColumnDefinitions>
    <Button Grid.Row="0" Grid.Column="0" Content="Button 1" />
    <Button Grid.Row="1" Grid.Column="1" Content="Button 2" />
    <Button Grid.Row="2" Grid.Column="2" Content="Button 3" />
</Grid>
```

Note that just as in the case of the `Canvas` control, an attached property from the parent `Grid` control is used to assign where the button should actually reside. This differs from the traditional HTML table design, where you have actual markup for each row and column. With the `Grid` control, you just need to make sure the controls being included are declared between the `<Grid>` and `</Grid>` tags.

Running the previous code in the emulator produces the table structure shown in Figure 2-2.

The `Grid` control is also flexible in how the various rows and columns can be sized. With regard to row sizing, the `Grid` control automatically tries to size rows according to the object with the largest height that's been placed in the row. This is similar to how standard HTML tables size themselves. For the most part, the same rules apply to column widths by default. You do, however, have control over the row and column size, thanks to the `Height` property of the `RowDefinition` object and the `Width` property of the `ColumnDefinition` object. The following code shows the standard way to set these values when customizing a `Grid` control:

FIGURE 2-2: Grid control layout.

```
<Grid x:Name="MainGrid">
    <Grid.RowDefinitions>
```

```
        <RowDefinition Height="100" />
        <RowDefinition Height="50" />
    </Grid.RowDefinitions>
    <Grid.ColumnDefinitions>
        <ColumnDefinition Width="100" />
        <ColumnDefinition Width="50" />
    </Grid.ColumnDefinitions>
</Grid>
```

In addition to setting the height and width, you can also use "star sizing". This great feature of the Grid control allows you to create an even more dynamic layout with your Grid control. If you set the Height property or Width property to *, the Grid control will automatically stretch that Row or Column to make use of all the remaining available space. For example, if you want to create a table layout with three columns, where the first column stretches to take up all the space that's not being used by the last two columns, you set a fixed-width value for the last two columns and use the * value for the first column. The following code shows this in action by creating a three-column Grid control with a fixed width assigned to the last two columns:

```
<Grid x:Name="MainGrid" ShowGridLines="True">
    <Grid.RowDefinitions>
        <RowDefinition />
    </Grid.RowDefinitions>
    <Grid.ColumnDefinitions>
        <ColumnDefinition Width="*" />
        <ColumnDefinition Width="100" />
        <ColumnDefinition Width="55"/>
    </Grid.ColumnDefinitions>
        <TextBlock Grid.Row="0" Grid.Column="0" TextWrapping="Wrap"
            Text="This column takes up all remaining available space" />
        <TextBlock Grid.Row="0" Grid.Column="1" TextWrapping="Wrap"
Text="100 Pixel Column" />
        <TextBlock Grid.Row="0" Grid.Column="2" TextWrapping="Wrap"
Text="55 Pixel Column" />
</Grid>
```

When this code is run in the emulator, you see that the first TextBlock control stretches to take up all the remaining space not being used by the last two columns (see Figure 2-3).

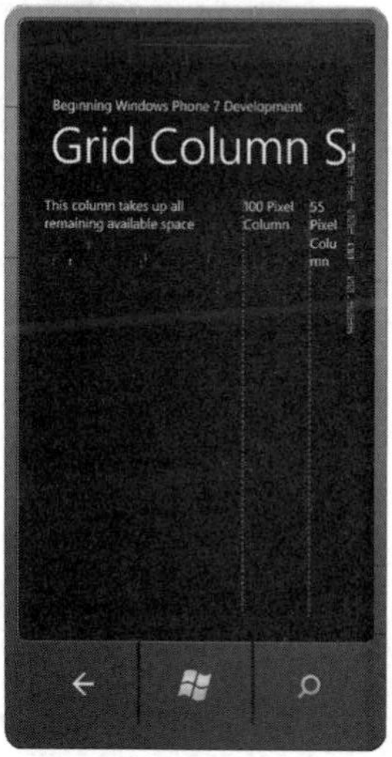

The StackPanel Control

The StackPanel control doesn't really mimic an existing HTML control, but it can be extremely useful for Silverlight control layouts, especially under Windows Phone. The main job of the StackPanel control is to "stack" other controls either vertically or horizontally. This might not seem like a big deal, but it provides a very simple way to lay out controls in either direction.

Many times when you don't really need the complexity of a Grid control or a table-like structure, you can use the StackPanel control instead. For example, to create a data entry form on a phone, you would want to make

FIGURE 2-3: Grid column sizing.

sure all the controls are vertically stacked so that they all fit on the smaller phone screen. Without StackPanel, you'd have to resort to tricky Margin and Padding configurations, and you might have difficulty getting the items to look exactly the way you want them.

In the following code, TextBlock, TextBox, and Button controls are placed inside a StackPanel control in a way that keeps the controls aligned vertically. Some margin settings have been modified in order to make some room between the controls:

```
<StackPanel Orientation="Vertical">
    <TextBlock Text="First Name" Margin="10" />
    <TextBox x:Name="FirstName" />
    <Button x:Name="Submit" Content="Submit" />
</StackPanel>
```

Note that the Orientation property of the StackPanel control is set to Vertical. This is the default behavior of the control, so ordinarily if you want to stack items vertically, you can leave out this property declaration. However, if you want to flip the items horizontally, you need to add this property. Figures 2-4 and 2-5 show both vertical and horizontal versions of the same data entry form.

FIGURE 2-4: A vertical StackPanel control.

FIGURE 2-5: A horizontal StackPanel control.

As you can see, using the StackPanel is a quick and easy way to put together a vertical layout of controls on the phone. In case the user decides to change the orientation of the phone, you can write code that switches the orientation of the StackPanel control to match.

The Border Control

Another great layout control is the Border control. This control gives you an incredibly easy way to add borders to any existing control on the screen. Border essentially works as a host to other controls sitting inside it. So, using the previous example, if you wanted to have a blue border around the data entry form created in the `StackPanel` control, you'd need to simply place the `StackPanel` control inside a `Border` control, like this:

```
<Border>
    <StackPanel>
        <TextBlock Text="First Name" Margin="10" />
        <TextBox x:Name="FirstName" />
        <Button x:Name="Submit" Content="Submit" />
    </StackPanel>
</Border>
```

Once you place the `StackPanel` control in the `Border` control, you can change the style of the border, using properties such as `BorderBrush` and `BorderThickness`. In this example, you want a blue border, and you want it to be visible, so you should probably add a little thickness to the line being drawn. The following code should do the trick:

```
<Border BorderBrush="Red" BorderThickness="5">
```

The nice thing about the `BorderBrush` property is that you can set it to any valid color or even an image. The `BorderThickness` property follows the same pattern as the `Margin` and `Padding` properties of other controls: You can set the entire thickness with a numeric value such as 5, or you can individually set the left, top, right, and bottom values with a comma-delimited value such as `0,0,5,5`.

The ScrollViewer Control

You can probably guess what the `ScrollViewer` control is responsible for. Because you're no longer operating in the context of a web browser when developing for Windows Phone, you don't have the benefit of a scroll bar automatically appearing when your content goes off the screen vertically. So if you have a lengthy data entry form or some other content that won't quite fit vertically on the screen, you can simply wrap all the content and controls inside a `ScrollViewer` control.

The following code shows a data entry form with a number of fields that don't all fit on the phone's screen at the same time. In order to remedy the issue and allow the user to scroll through the content, the form is wrapped inside a `ScrollViewer` control:

```
<ScrollViewer>
    <StackPanel>
        <TextBlock Text="First Name" Margin="10" />
        <TextBox x:Name="FirstName" />
        <TextBlock Text="Last Name" Margin="10" />
        <TextBox x:Name="LastName" />
        <TextBlock Text="Address" Margin="10" />
        <TextBox x:Name="Address" />
        <TextBlock Text="Phone" Margin="10" />
        <TextBox x:Name="Phone" />
        <TextBlock Text="Email Address" Margin="10" />
        <TextBox x:Name="Email" />
        <Button x:Name="SubmitForm" Content="Submit" />
    </StackPanel>
</ScrollViewer>
```

When you run the code in the emulator, at first you see only a partial display of the form (see Figure 2-6).

However, if you hold down the left mouse button and drag upward, you see the rest of the form, as shown in Figure 2-7.

FIGURE 2-6: A partial view of a data entry form.

FIGURE 2-7: A data entry form's additional fields.

As you can see, `ScrollViewer` is a great control to use when you have content that doesn't fit in the confines of the phone screen.

Now it's time to put some of these layout controls to use. In the following Try It Out section, you'll create a quick sample application that makes use of the `Grid`, `StackPanel`, `ScrollViewer`, and some additional controls, including `TextBlock`, `TextBox`, and `Button`, to create a fluid data entry layout.

TRY IT OUT   Creating a Scrollable Data Entry Form

In the following exercise, you create a scrollable data entry form.

1. Start Visual Studio 2010 Express Edition and select File ➪ New Project.

2. From the New Project list, choose the new Windows Phone application template and in the Name field, enter **DataEntry** for the project name. Wait for the project to finish loading in Visual Studio.

3. When the project is loaded, change the title of the app from the default My Application title. To do so, find the following code segment in `MainPage.xaml`:

```
<StackPanel x:Name="TitlePanel" Grid.Row="0" Margin="12,17,0,28">
    <TextBlock x:Name="ApplicationTitle" Text="MY APPLICATION"
Style="{StaticResource PhoneTextNormalStyle}"/>
        <TextBlock x:Name="PageTitle" Text="page name" Margin="9,-7,0,0"
```

```
            Style="{StaticResource PhoneTextTitle1Style}"/>
        </StackPanel>
        Code Snippet DataEntry\MainPage.xaml
```

Change it to the following:

```
<StackPanel x:Name="TitlePanel" Grid.Row="0" Margin="12,17,0,28">
    <TextBlock x:Name="ApplicationTitle" Text="Data Entry App Using Scrollviewer"
Style="{StaticResource PhoneTextNormalStyle}"/>
    <TextBlock x:Name="PageTitle" Text="Main Form" Margin="9,-7,0,0"
Style="{StaticResource PhoneTextTitle1Style}"/>
</StackPanel>
```

Code Snippet DataEntry\MainPage.xaml

When creating a new Windows Phone 7 application, you can find the `TextBlock` control named `ApplicationTitle` and modify it to the desired app name. In this case, you're calling the app `Data Entry App Using ScrollViewer`. You'll no doubt come up with better names for your applications, but this will do for now.

4. Locate the main `Grid` control that contains all other controls on the page (in this case, `ContentPanel`) and add the `ScrollViewer` control. Although you could remove this control and replace it with something else, you should just leave it in place for this example and treat it as the topmost parent for your app. Then simply add the `ScrollViewer` control, as in the following code:

```
<Grid x:Name="ContentPanel" Grid.Row="1" Margin="12,0,12,0">
    <ScrollViewer>
    </ScrollViewer>
</Grid>
```

Code Snippet DataEntry\MainPage.xaml

5. Add the data entry controls by adding the following code inside the `ScrollViewer` control:

```
<StackPanel>
    <TextBlock Text="First Name" Margin="10" />
    <TextBox x:Name="FirstName" />
    <TextBlock Text="Last Name" Margin="10" />
    <TextBox x:Name="LastName" />
    <TextBlock Text="Address" Margin="10" />
    <TextBox x:Name="Address" />
    <TextBlock Text="Address 2" Margin="10" />
    <TextBox x:Name="Address2" />
    <TextBlock Text="Primary Phone" Margin="10" />
    <TextBox x:Name="Phone" />
    <TextBlock Text="Cell Phone" Margin="10" />
    <TextBox x:Name="CellPhone" />
    <TextBlock Text="Email Address" Margin="10" />
    <TextBox x:Name="Email" />
    <Button Content="Submit" />
</StackPanel>
```

Code Snippet DataEntry\MainPage.xaml

You should now have everything in place for your simple data entry screen.

 NOTE *As you can see in Figure 2-8, the fields don't all quite fit on the phone screen in the Visual Studio designer window, so you can see that using a* `ScrollViewer` *control is the way to go here.*

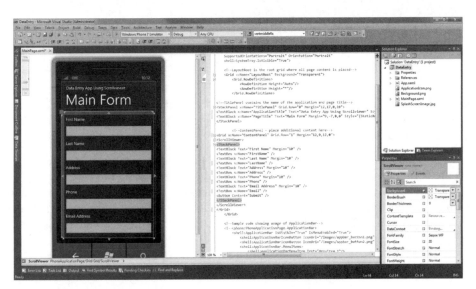

FIGURE 2-8: The Visual Studio Designer window hiding controls.

6. Build and run the application in the emulator by pressing F5 or clicking the Debug icon in the toolbar. Once the app is running, you should be able to use your mouse to scroll the phone display in order to see the last few data entry fields and the Submit button.

How It Works

In this example, you created a simple data entry screen with several fields. Because the screen display of the Windows Phone device was not large enough to contain all the available fields, you needed to provide the user with a means to scroll through all the fields. By containing all your data entry controls in a `ScrollViewer` control, you were able to easily provide this functionality with just two lines of code.

Programming with Silverlight

Now that you've seen some of the basic layout controls Silverlight for Windows Phone 7 has to offer, it's time to take an in-depth look at some of the remaining controls you can use and how to program with them. Being able to lay out controls is nice, but interactivity with the various controls is the crux of a Windows Phone application.

The Code-Behind

Before getting into the additional controls, let's take a look at the other side of XAML. As you've seen, you can visually put together a user interface by using XAML and the Visual Studio designer. However, you also need a way to make use of these various controls in order for users to interact with your app. By default, every XAML file in a Windows Phone 7 project has a corresponding xaml.cs file. This file is where you typically add the source code to handle loading data into controls, user input, and more. All the examples so far have involved adding XAML control declarations to the MainPage.xaml file. If you expand that file in the Solution Explorer of Visual Studio, you also see a file called MainPage.xaml.cs. The following code shows the contents of MainPage.xaml.cs when you first create a new Windows Phone 7 project:

```
using System;
using System.Collections.Generic;
using System.Linq;
using System.Net;
using System.Windows;
using System.Windows.Controls;
using System.Windows.Documents;
using System.Windows.Input;
using System.Windows.Media;
using System.Windows.Media.Animation;
using System.Windows.Shapes;
using Microsoft.Phone.Controls;

namespace DataEntry
{
    public partial class MainPage : PhoneApplicationPage
    {
        // Constructor
        public MainPage()
        {
            InitializeComponent();
        }
    }
}
```

There's not much to this code, but there are some interesting points. First, notice how the MainPage class inherits from the PhoneApplicationPage class. All your screens/XAML pages should also inherit from either PhoneApplicationPage or another base page that in turn inherits from PhoneApplicationPage. Aside from this, there's not much to see here other than some standard using statements, the default namespace, and the constructor for the MainPage class. So far it looks like any old C# class. The most important thing to note is that this file is considered a code-behind file. This means that all the programming code you intend to write that makes use of the controls added to the .xaml page should be added in this file.

To get a better feel for how this works, let's look at a simple example. Remember early in the chapter when we talked about the x:Name property that all controls have? Well, in this code-behind file, you can access any control on the XAML page by simply typing its name in the editor. Visual Studio then shows a pop-up box that lists all the available methods and properties you can use. This great feature is called IntelliSense and you'll no doubt find it to be one of the best features of the

Visual Studio environment. Figure 2-9 shows the IntelliSense feature in action after you type FirstName from the Try It Out data entry example.

FIGURE 2-9: Visual Studio IntelliSense.

Notice in Figure 2-9 that IntelliSense shows all the properties and methods that match what you're typing, and it also shows the documentation for the selected property or method. This can come in very handy and can also save you the time of having to look up the method in online or offline documentation.

Handling Control Events

Most applications written for Windows Phone 7 require the use of Silverlight controls and interactivity with those controls. For example, there wouldn't be much use for a Button control if there were no way for application code to detect when the Button control is clicked by the user. Silverlight enables interactivity between controls and an application through the use of events. An event is essentially a message that's sent from a control to any application listening for that particular message.

The way this typically works is that in your code-behind, you register or subscribe for particular events from a given control. When such an event takes place, a designated area in your code is used to handle that event. One of the most common events is a Click event, which is usually triggered when a user clicks on a Button control with the mouse; however, this control can also apply to mouse clicks that are performed on other controls displayed on the screen.

A program can subscribe to events in one of two ways. The first is to declare an event handler right in the XAML code for the control. Let's say you want to make something happen in your program when a user clicks a given Button control. You can declare the Button control in XAML along with a method name assigned to the Click event, as in the following code:

```
<Button x:Name="ButtonControl" Content="Click Me" Click="ButtonControl_Click" />
```

In this case, you've assigned the Click event to a method called ButtonControl_Click. Somewhere in your code-behind page, you need to add this method. In the following code, the ButtonControl_Click method is declared in the code-behind, along with the standard method signature that the Click event is looking for:

```
private void ButtonControl_Click(object sender, RoutedEventArgs e)
{
    //Handle button click here
}
```

You might wonder what the sender and e parameters are for and why they're required. Remember that every event in Silverlight is essentially a message being sent back to your program. Assigning the Click event to the ButtonControl_Click method tells the Button control where to send the message. The Button control also needs to actually send the message itself. The Click event expects a certain method signature that includes the sender parameter, which will always be the control itself, as well as the RoutedEventArgs parameter e, which includes any message data.

A control event always passes a copy of itself as the sender parameter. There's always some type of EventArgs-style parameter being passed in. These parameters can change, depending on the control that fires the event. In some cases, such as a mouse click, you may see that the EventArgs parameter contains X and Y coordinates that tell exactly where on the screen the mouse was clicked. In this particular case, for the Button Click event, there isn't any important message data, so you won't find anything in the e parameter. Besides, all the information you need from the Click event is that the Click event occurred.

Once you have this event handler set up, you can run any code you like. For example, you could show a message that lets the user know that you've detected the user clicking the Button control, as in the following code:

```
private void ButtonControl_Click(object sender, RoutedEventArgs e)
{
    MessageBox.Show("You have clicked the Button");
}
```

In addition to setting up the control event handler right in the XAML code, you also have the option of setting up event handlers in the code-behind. You can do this right in the constructor of the page, or you can wait until the page has completely finished loading. As you might have guessed, the page has several messages you can subscribe to, including a Loaded event, so you know for certain that all the controls have been drawn on the screen and are available for use. The following code sets up an event handler for the page Loaded event and in that handler creates the event handler for the Click event of the Button control:

```
public MainPage()
{
    InitializeComponent();
    this.Loaded += new RoutedEventHandler(MainPage_Loaded);
}

private void MainPage_Loaded(object sender, RoutedEventArgs e)
{
    ButtonControl.Click += new RoutedEventHandler(ButtonControl_Click);
}

private void ButtonControl_Click(object sender, RoutedEventArgs e)
{
    MessageBox.Show("You have clicked the Button");
}
```

As you can imagine, it can be tough to memorize all the different events that you can make use of for each of the Silverlight controls. Don't worry, though: You can easily make use of the IntelliSense feature in Visual Studio to display all of a given control's events, just as you did with the method and property list in this section.

Interactive Controls

Now that you know where to put your code, it's time to take an in-depth look at some of the controls you're likely to use in your own applications.

The TextBlock Control

When you need to display static text in an application, TextBlock is your control of choice. All the properties you'd expect for a control like this are available, including the ability to select font type, size, color, and so on. To use a TextBlock control, you can either type in the XAML declaration or drag and drop the TextBlock control from the list of available Silverlight controls in the Visual Studio control toolbox. The following code declares a new TextBlock in XAML code with the Text property set. It also selects a font type, size, color, weight, and style, via the FontFamily, FontSize, Foreground, FontWeight, and FontStyle properties:

```
<TextBlock x:Name="StaticText" Text="This is some static text"
    FontFamily="Arial" FontSize="12" FontStyle="Italic"
    FontWeight="Bold" Foreground="Blue" />
```

This seems simple enough. Now what if you want to make some changes to the static text programmatically? In this case, you can jump right back to the code-behind and use IntelliSense to find the property you want to change. In this case, assume that you want to change the text when the program starts to "This program has started". To do this right in the constructor, you can simply add the following code and run the debugger/emulator to see your changes:

```
public MainPage()
{
    InitializeComponent();

    StaticText.Text = "This program has started";
}
```

The TextBox Control

Just as the TextBlock control is useful for displaying text on the screen, the TextBox control is equally useful for collecting data input from the user. The TextBox control is very similar in features to the standard HTML <input> tag. When using the TextBox control, you'll often simply add the control to your XAML and set the Width and possibly Foreground or Background properties of the control. The following code adds a simple 100-by-200-pixel TextBox control to the screen and sets the Background color to yellow:

```
<TextBox x:Name="UserInputBox" Width="200" Height="100" Background="Yellow" />
```

Once the control is displayed, you wait for the user to input data into the TextBox control, and from the code-behind file, you can easily retrieve the data entered and store it in a variable by using the Text property, as shown here:

```
string userInput = UserInputBox.Text;
```

At this point, whatever the user typed into the TextBox control is stored in the userInput variable and can be used in your program.

The Button Control

When users complete a data entry operation, they look for a way to notify the program that they're done. They usually do this by using some kind of button on the screen. Naturally, Silverlight for Windows Phone 7 provides a `Button` control for just this purpose.

You have many options when declaring a `Button` control in your XAML code. By default, you can simply add a standard-looking button with text by using the following code:

```
<Button x:Name="StandardButton" Content="This is a standard button" />
```

This declaration of a `Button` control produces a standard-looking button on the screen, as shown in Figure 2-10.

This is a standard button

FIGURE 2-10: A standard `Button` control.

You might be wondering why the `Button` control uses a `Content` property instead of a `Text` for setting the text of the control. Well, a `Button` control is capable of using just about any other control as its content. This incredibly slick feature of Silverlight allows for all sorts of interesting possibilities for `Button` controls. By default, the `Content` property can be set to a text string, and that works fine. The previous code runs and displays a standardized Windows Phone 7 button. However, you could also easily use another control, such as an `Image` control, as the `Content` property of the `Button` control. This would effectively make the `Image` control itself a `Button` control. The following code shows how it works.

> **NOTE** *Instead of terminating the control declaration with* `/>`*, you declare the* `Button` *control and the* `Button.Content` *property in a separate section of the XAML. You can do this with any of the control properties:*
>
> ```
> <Button x:Name="ImageButton">
>     <Button.Content>
>         <Image Source="Background.png" />
>     </Button.Content>
> </Button>
> ```

As you can see in Figure 2-11, instead of the standard Windows Phone `Button` control, you now see an image that can be clicked just like the standard button.

You'll often use the `Button` control in order to submit a form or change the currently displayed screen on the phone in some way. In order to detect whether the user has clicked the `Button` control, you need to subscribe to the `Click` event. Previously in this chapter, you saw multiple ways of subscribing to control events, and you should be familiar with how to subscribe and handle the `Click` event for the `Button` control. The following code gives you a quick refresher,

FIGURE 2-11: An `ImageButton` control.

subscribing to the `Click` event in XAML and adding its corresponding event handler in the code-behind file:

```
<Button x:Name="ButtonControl" Content="Click Me" Click="ButtonControl_Click" />
private void ButtonControl_Click(object sender, RoutedEventArgs e)
{
    MessageBox.Show("You have clicked the Button");
}
```

The HyperlinkButton Control

The `HyperlinkButton` control behaves similarly to a standard `Button` control. It has many of the same events that you can subscribe to, including the `Click` event. However, unlike the `Button` control, the `HyperlinkButton` control renders itself on the screen as a standard hyperlink. This can be a useful control when you want to present a link to additional application content or content on the web.

When adding a `HyperlinkButton` control to your XAML, you first need to determine how you'll use it. For example, if you were simply looking to add a link to an external website, such as www.wrox.com, you'd add the following XAML code:

```
<HyperlinkButton x:Name="WroxLink" Content="Wrox.com"
    NavigateUri="http://www.wrox.com" TargetName="_blank"/>
```

There are a couple of important things to notice about this control declaration. First, you should always set the `Content` property of the control to something that makes sense to the user. In this case, you're just trying to display a standard hyperlink to an external site, so adding text works just fine. You could also use the trick you learned with the `Button` control: Use an `Image` control for the `Content` property. That would create a hyperlink out of the image being displayed. You should also note that the `NavigateUri` property is used to direct the user to www.wrox.com. You can go ahead and set this property to any valid web address. Finally, `TargetName` is required and should be set to `_blank`. When you set this property to `_blank`, the Windows Phone launches a copy of the internal web browser and navigates directly to the web pages assigned in the `NavigateUri` property.

 COMMON MISTAKES You might expect the `HyperlinkButton` control to have a property called `NavigateUrl` instead of `NavigateUri`. Uri, in this case, is actually more flexible. Uri stands for *uniform resource identifier*. It allows your application to use a `HyperlinkButton` control to link to any valid resource, whether it's an external HTML page on the web or an embedded resource. So, for example, if you wanted to change the currently displayed screen to a page called `SecondScreen.xaml`, you could easily do this by simply assigning the `NavigateUri` property to a string such as `/SecondScreen.xaml`. The Uri object is smart enough to take a look at your internal Windows Phone 7 project and find that XAML page to perform the navigation. Internally, the phone uses `NavigationService` to actually switch the currently displayed screen.

The ProgressBar Control

Any time you have a potentially lengthy operation taking place on a phone, it's important to let the user know that the operation is running. One of the most standard ways of letting the user know that something is happening in the background is to use some kind of progress bar. The ProgressBar control is simple to use; it requires only that you set the Minimum and Maximum properties to get started. The Minimum and Maximum properties will set the range of the ProgressBar and the Value property is used to determine how much of the ProgressBar if filled. The percentage of filled space will be calculated based on the Minimum and Maximum property values.

TRY IT OUT   Manipulating a Progress Bar

In the following exercise, you manipulate a progress bar.

1. Create a new project, using the Windows Phone 7 application template, and name the project **ProgressBarSample**.

2. Add a ProgressBar control and a Button control to the ContentPanel control, as shown in Listing 2-2:

LISTING 2-2 MainPage.xaml

```xaml
<phone:PhoneApplicationPage
    x:Class="ProgressBarSample.MainPage"
    xmlns="http://schemas.microsoft.com/winfx/2006/xaml/presentation"
    xmlns:x="http://schemas.microsoft.com/winfx/2006/xaml"
    xmlns:phone="clr-namespace:Microsoft.Phone.Controls;assembly=Microsoft.Phone"
    xmlns:shell="clr-namespace:Microsoft.Phone.Shell;assembly=Microsoft.Phone"
    xmlns:d="http://schemas.microsoft.com/expression/blend/2008"
    xmlns:mc="http://schemas.openxmlformats.org/markup-compatibility/2006"
    mc:Ignorable="d" d:DesignWidth="480" d:DesignHeight="768"
    FontFamily="{StaticResource PhoneFontFamilyNormal}"
    FontSize="{StaticResource PhoneFontSizeNormal}"
    Foreground="{StaticResource PhoneForegroundBrush}"
    SupportedOrientations="Portrait" Orientation="Portrait"
    shell:SystemTray.IsVisible="True">

    <!--LayoutRoot is the root grid where all page content is placed-->
    <Grid x:Name="LayoutRoot" Background="Transparent">
        <Grid.RowDefinitions>
            <RowDefinition Height="Auto"/>
            <RowDefinition Height="*"/>
        </Grid.RowDefinitions>

        <!--TitlePanel contains the name of the application and page title-->
        <StackPanel x:Name="TitlePanel" Grid.Row="0" Margin="12,17,0,28">
            <TextBlock x:Name="ApplicationTitle" Text="Progress Bar Sample App"
    Style="{StaticResource PhoneTextNormalStyle}"/>
```

continues

LISTING 2-2 *(continued)*

```
        </StackPanel>

        <!--ContentPanel - place additional content here-->
        <Grid x:Name="ContentPanel" Grid.Row="1" Margin="12,0,12,0">
            <StackPanel>
                <ProgressBar x:Name="MainProgress" Value="0" Minimum="0"
Maximum="100" />
                <Button x:Name="MoveProgress" Content="Step Progress" />
            </StackPanel>
        </Grid>
    </Grid>

</phone:PhoneApplicationPage>
```

Code Listing ProgressBarSample\MainPage.xaml

3. In the `MainPage.xaml.cs` file, edit the constructor to subscribe to the `Loaded` event for the page so that it looks as follows:

```
public MainPage()
{
    InitializeComponent();
    this.Loaded += new RoutedEventHandler(MainPage_Loaded);
}
```

Code Snippet ProgressBarSample\MainPage.xaml.cs

4. Subscribe to the `Click` event in the `Loaded` event handler and create a new handler for the event:

```
private void MainPage_Loaded(object sender, RoutedEventArgs e)
{
    MoveProgress.Click += new RoutedEventHandler(MoveProgress_Click);
}
```

Code Snippet ProgressBarSample\MainPage.xaml.cs

5. In the `Click` event handler, manipulate the current value of `ProgressBar` by adding 10 to the current `Value` property:

```
private void MoveProgress_Click(object sender, RoutedEventArgs e)
{
    MainProgress.Value += 10;
}
```

Code Snippet ProgressBarSample\MainPage.xaml.cs

6. Run the application in the emulator by pressing F5 or clicking the debugger icon in Visual Studio.

7. Click the `Button` control several times and watch the `ProgressBar` display increase. Figure 2-12 shows the `ProgressBar` control after several `Button` control clicks.

How It Works

In this example, you added a `ProgressBar` control to the screen. You can see how easy it is to manipulate the current progress value in order to advance the progress being displayed. In this case, you simply added 10 to the `Value` property of the `ProgressBar` control every time the `Button` control was clicked. Because the `Maximum` property of the control was set to 100, it will take 10 clicks in order for the `ProgressBar` control to be filled.

FIGURE 2-12: The `ProgressBar` control in action.

The Image Control

The `Image` control enables you to display an image on a phone screen. The control supports both `.png` and `.jpg` formats for images. There's currently no support for formats such as `.gif`, `.tiff`, and some of the other image formats out there. When using the `Image` control, you'll want to set the `Source` property to the path where your image can be found. For example, say you want to display an image called `wrox.jpg`, which is in the `Images` directory of your project. The following XAML would create an `Image` control and display `wrox.jpg`:

```
<Image Source="Images\wrox.jpg" />
```

Easy enough, right? In addition to just setting the `Source` property to the image that you want displayed, you can also modify additional attributes of the image, such as whether the image should stretch to fill all available space or whether the image should be somewhat translucent.

By default, the `Image` control is set to display an image and fill all available space, scaling the image as necessary. The XAML declaration used previously would result in the image being stretched to fill up the entire `StackPanel` space by default. In this case, you'd end up with something like what's shown in Figure 2-13.

Now suppose you don't want the `Image` control to stretch and take up all the available space in the `StackPanel` control. In this case, you could make use of the `Stretch` property. There are four valid choices for this

FIGURE 2-13: A stretched image control.

property: `Fill`, `None`, `Uniform`, and `UniformToFill`. By default, the
`Image` control uses a `Stretch` value of `UniformToFill`. In this example,
you could force the image to be displayed in its normal size by setting the
`Stretch` property to `None`, as in the following code. This would result in
a much smaller version of the image being displayed (see Figure 2-14).

```
<Image Source="Images\wrox.jpg" Stretch="None" />
```

The default value of `UniformToFill` is basically a variation on the
`Fill` value. `Fill` results in the `Image` control being stretched to fill all
available space, but the original aspect ratio of the image isn't preserved.
`UniformToFill` does the same stretching operation but keeps the aspect
ratio of the image intact. `UniformToFill` does, however, clip the image
if the dimensions don't match the destination of the image. This means
that if the original image used was larger than the size of the `StackPanel`
control, the image would be stretched and preserve its aspect ratio, but
the image would also be clipped in order to remain contained in the
`StackPanel` control.

FIGURE 2-14: An
unstretched image.

The PasswordBox Control

The `PasswordBox` control is basically a specialized version of the `TextBox` control. As you might
guess, the `PasswordBox` control comes in handy if you need to create a data entry form and want to
hide the actual text being entered in the `TextBox` control. All the same properties that are part of
the standard `TextBox` control exist in `PasswordBox`. The only major difference is that in the code-
behind, instead of accessing the `Text` property to collect the data that's input, you use the `Password`
property. In addition, you can control what character is displayed in the `PasswordBox` control as the
user is typing the sensitive information (for example, *). You can set the character to be displayed by
using the `PasswordChar` property.

TRY IT OUT   **Entering a Username and Password**

In this exercise, you enter a username and password.

1. Create a new project, using the Windows Phone 7 application template, and name the project
PasswordSample.

2. Add to `MainPage.xaml` a simple user login form with `TextBlock`, `TextBox`, `PasswordBox`, and
`Button` controls. This is shown here in Listing 2-3:

LISTING 2-3 MainPage.xaml

```
<phone:PhoneApplicationPage
        x:Class="PasswordSample.MainPage"
        xmlns="http://schemas.microsoft.com/winfx/2006/xaml/presentation"
        xmlns:x="http://schemas.microsoft.com/winfx/2006/xaml"
```

```
        xmlns:phone="clr-namespace:Microsoft.Phone.Controls;assembly=Microsoft.Phone"
        xmlns:shell="clr-namespace:Microsoft.Phone.Shell;assembly=Microsoft.Phone"
        xmlns:d="http://schemas.microsoft.com/expression/blend/2008"
        xmlns:mc="http://schemas.openxmlformats.org/markup-compatibility/2006"
        mc:Ignorable="d" d:DesignWidth="480" d:DesignHeight="768"
        FontFamily="{StaticResource PhoneFontFamilyNormal}"
        FontSize="{StaticResource PhoneFontSizeNormal}"
        Foreground="{StaticResource PhoneForegroundBrush}"
        SupportedOrientations="Portrait" Orientation="Portrait"
        shell:SystemTray.IsVisible="True">

        <!--LayoutRoot is the root grid where all page content is placed-->
        <Grid x:Name="LayoutRoot" Background="Transparent">
            <Grid.RowDefinitions>
                <RowDefinition Height="Auto"/>
                <RowDefinition Height="*"/>
            </Grid.RowDefinitions>

            <!--TitlePanel contains the name of the application and page title-->
            <StackPanel x:Name="TitlePanel" Grid.Row="0" Margin="12,17,0,28">
                <TextBlock x:Name="ApplicationTitle" Text="Password Sample App"
        Style="{StaticResource PhoneTextNormalStyle}"/>
                <TextBlock x:Name="PageTitle" Text="Login Page" Margin="9,-7,0,0"
        Style="{StaticResource PhoneTextTitle1Style}"/>
            </StackPanel>

            <!--ContentPanel - place additional content here-->
            <Grid x:Name="ContentPanel" Grid.Row="1" Margin="12,0,12,0">
                <StackPanel>
                    <TextBlock Text="Username:" Margin="10" />
                    <TextBox x:Name="UserName" />
                    <TextBlock Text="Password:" Margin="10" />
                    <PasswordBox x:Name="PasswordControl" PasswordChar="*" />
                    <Button x:Name="LoginButton" Content="Login"
        Click="LoginButton_Click" />
                </StackPanel>
            </Grid>
        </Grid>
</phone:PhoneApplicationPage>
```

Code Snippet PasswordSample\MainPage.xaml

3.   Edit the `MainPage.xaml.cs` code-behind file so that it looks like the code in Listing 2-4.

LISTING 2-4 MainPage.xaml.cs

```
using System;
using System.Collections.Generic;
using System.Linq;
using System.Net;
using System.Windows;
```

continues

LISTING 2-4 *(continued)*

```
using System.Windows.Controls;
using System.Windows.Documents;
using System.Windows.Input;
using System.Windows.Media;
using System.Windows.Media.Animation;
using System.Windows.Shapes;
using Microsoft.Phone.Controls;

namespace PasswordSample
{
    public partial class MainPage : PhoneApplicationPage
    {
        // Constructor
        public MainPage()
        {
            InitializeComponent();
        }

        private void LoginButton_Click(object sender, RoutedEventArgs e)
        {
            if (UserName.Text == "user" && PasswordControl.Password ==
"winphone7")
                MessageBox.Show("Successful Login");
            else
                MessageBox.Show("Login Failed");
        }
    }
}
```

Code Snippet PasswordSample\MainPage.xaml.cs

4. Build and run the application by pressing the F5 key or clicking the debugger icon on the toolbar.

5. Test the application by entering the username **user** and the password **winphone7**. Figure 2-15 shows the app in action.

6. Try using incorrect login information to make sure the "Login Failed" message appears.

How It Works

In this example, you created a simple login page for an application, using a combination of Silverlight controls you've seen in this chapter. You captured the username with a standard `TextBox` control and made use of the `PasswordBox` control to give the user a way to enter password information without displaying the plain text on the screen.

In the code-behind, you compared the values of the `Text` property of the `TextBox` control and the `Password` property of the `PasswordBox` control

FIGURE 2-15: The password app.

against hard-coded values and showed the user a pass or fail login message, based on the results of the comparison.

For a simple example like this, hardcoding the username and password to compare against is acceptable, but in your own applications, you'll almost always want to compare against values stored in a database somewhere. To accomplish this, you need to connect to a web service, using the web service connectivity tools available for Windows Phone.

The RadioButton Control

The RadioButton control gives you a way to add a list of possible choices to display to the user. Often, these types of controls can be used to select from among various program options, and sometimes they're used to poll users in surveys. To make use of a RadioButton control in your app, you can add the following XAML:

```
<RadioButton IsChecked="false" Content="Option 1" />
```

The IsChecked property determines whether the radio button is selected, and the Content property is used to display the text alongside the option. Most of the time, you'll make use of this control with a set of additional options. The behavior you would be looking for in this case is to have a set of RadioButton controls from which only one selection is considered valid. The RadioButton control provides this functionality by making available the GroupName property. If you have multiple RadioButton controls on a page and they're all assigned to the same GroupName property, the user will be allowed to select only one of the options at a time. In the following code, three RadioButton controls are added to the screen, and the GroupName property is used to ensure that only one selection is valid at a time:

```
<RadioButton x:Name="Option1"  GroupName="Test"
    IsChecked="true" Content="Other" />
<RadioButton x:Name="Option2" GroupName="Test"
    IsChecked="False" Content="Android" />
<RadioButton x:Name="Option3" GroupName="Test"
    IsChecked="False" Content="iPhone" />
<RadioButton x:Name="Option4" GroupName="Test"
    IsChecked="False" Content="Windows Phone 7" />
```

In this example, the Other option is checked by default, and selecting one of the other options automatically unchecks the Option1 control. For example, in Figure 2-16, the user has selected Windows Phone 7 as the preferred smartphone platform.

The ListBox Control

The ListBox control allows you to easily display a vertical list of items on the screen. The easiest way to use it is to simply add a ListBox declaration on your page, along with some items in the ListBox.Items property, as in the following code:

FIGURE 2-16: A group of RadioButton controls.

```
<ListBox x:Name="MainList">
    <ListBox.Items>
    <ListBoxItem Content="Item 1" IsSelected="True" />
    <ListBoxItem Content="Item 2" />
    <ListBoxItem Content="Item 3" />
    <ListBoxItem Content="Item 4" />
    <ListBoxItem Content="Item 5" />
    </ListBox.Items>
</ListBox>
```

The `ListBox` control also has an `ItemsSource` property that you can use in the code-behind page. You can assign the `ItemsSource` property to just about any type of collection. Because most of the time you won't know ahead of time what content should be placed in the list, you'll most likely need to set the `ItemsSource` property with code such as the following:

```
List<string> items = new List<string>();

items.Add("Dynamic Item 1");
items.Add("Dynamic Item 2");
items.Add("Dynamic Item 3");
items.Add("Dynamic Item 4");
items.Add("Dynamic Item 5");

MainList.ItemsSource = items;
```

In this code, you create a generic list of `string` objects and add several items to the collection. Then you set the `ItemsSource` property to the collection.

> **NOTE** *If you're not familiar with the concept of C# collections or generics in general, refer to* Beginning Visual C# 2010 *by Karli Watson (Wrox Press, 2010) for an excellent tutorial on both subjects. For now, just be aware that you can create collections by using* `List<object type>` *and set those collections to the* `ItemsSource` *property.*

`ListBox` is very flexible about what types of objects it supports. You can use the `ListBox` control to display strings, images, other controls, and so on. You can even customize many of the visual elements of the `ListBox` control, along with the items being displayed, by using control templates.

The Slider Control

The `Slider` control is most often used in conjunction with another control, such as a `TextBox` control, but you can also use it in many other ways. The standard usage is to enable the user to increase or decrease a value by sliding a finger over the control. The `Slider` control supports both horizontal and vertical display.

When using the `Slider` control, you normally set some properties that are similar to those of the `ProgressBar` control, such as the `Minimum` and `Maximum` values, as well as the current value. In order to tie this in with a `TextBox` control, you then listen for the changed event on the `Slider` control and update the `Text` property in the `TextBox` control accordingly.

TRY IT OUT **Using the Slider Control**

In this exercise, you learn how to use the `Slider` control.

1. Create a new Windows Phone 7 project by using Visual Studio Express and name it **SliderSample**.

2. Modify `MainPage.xaml` to look like the code in Listing 2-5:

LISTING 2-5 MainPage.xaml

```xml
<phone:PhoneApplicationPage
    x:Class="SliderSample.MainPage"
    xmlns="http://schemas.microsoft.com/winfx/2006/xaml/presentation"
    xmlns:x="http://schemas.microsoft.com/winfx/2006/xaml"
    xmlns:phone="clr-namespace:Microsoft.Phone.Controls;assembly=Microsoft.Phone"
    xmlns:shell="clr-namespace:Microsoft.Phone.Shell;assembly=Microsoft.Phone"
    xmlns:d="http://schemas.microsoft.com/expression/blend/2008"
    xmlns:mc="http://schemas.openxmlformats.org/markup-compatibility/2006"
    mc:Ignorable="d" d:DesignWidth="480" d:DesignHeight="768"
    FontFamily="{StaticResource PhoneFontFamilyNormal}"
    FontSize="{StaticResource PhoneFontSizeNormal}"
    Foreground="{StaticResource PhoneForegroundBrush}"
    SupportedOrientations="Portrait" Orientation="Portrait"
    shell:SystemTray.IsVisible="True">

    <!--LayoutRoot is the root grid where all page content is placed-->
    <Grid x:Name="LayoutRoot" Background="Transparent">
        <Grid.RowDefinitions>
            <RowDefinition Height="Auto"/>
            <RowDefinition Height="*"/>
        </Grid.RowDefinitions>

        <!--TitlePanel contains the name of the application and page title-->
        <StackPanel x:Name="TitlePanel" Grid.Row="0" Margin="12,17,0,28">
            <TextBlock x:Name="ApplicationTitle" Text="Slider Sample App"
Style="{StaticResource PhoneTextNormalStyle}"/>
        </StackPanel>

        <!--ContentPanel - place additional content here-->
        <Grid x:Name="ContentPanel" Grid.Row="1" Margin="12,0,12,0">
            <StackPanel Orientation="Horizontal">
                <TextBox x:Name="CurrentValue" Height="75"
Width="150" VerticalAlignment="Top" TextAlignment="Center" />
                <Slider x:Name="MainSlider" Minimum="0" Maximum="100"
Value="0" Orientation="Horizontal" Width="300" VerticalAlignment="Top"
ValueChanged="MainSlider_ValueChanged"/>
            </StackPanel>
        </Grid>
```

continues

LISTING 2-5 *(continued)*

```
            </Grid>

</phone:PhoneApplicationPage>
```

Code Snippet SliderSample\MainPage.xaml

 NOTE *Observe in this code how the* ValueChanged *event of the* Slider *control is being subscribed to.*

3. Add the MainSlider_ValueChanged method in the MainPage.xaml.cs file and set the Text property of the TextBox control to the current Value property of the Slider control, as shown here in Listing 2-6:

LISTING 2-6 MainPage.xaml.cs

```
using System;
using System.Collections.Generic;
using System.Linq;
using System.Net;
using System.Windows;
using System.Windows.Controls;
using System.Windows.Documents;
using System.Windows.Input;
using System.Windows.Media;
using System.Windows.Media.Animation;
using System.Windows.Shapes;
using Microsoft.Phone.Controls;

namespace SliderSample
{
    public partial class MainPage : PhoneApplicationPage
    {
        // Constructor
        public MainPage()
        {
            InitializeComponent();
        }

        private void MainSlider_ValueChanged(object sender,
RoutedPropertyChangedEventArgs<double> e)
        {
            CurrentValue.Text = Math.Round(MainSlider.Value,0).ToString();
        }
    }
}
```

Code Snippet SliderSample\MainPage.xaml.cs

Note how the `Round` method of the `Math` class is used to ensure that the number being set in the `Text` property of the `TextBox` control doesn't include any decimal values. Also, the `ToString` method is used on the result in order to convert the number to a text-based representation that works with the `TextBox` control.

4. Build and run the application in the emulator by pressing F5 or clicking the debugger icon in the toolbar. Now try to use the slider, noting how the current value appears in the `TextBox` control as soon as you let go of the mouse. Figure 2-17 shows this in action.

How It Works

In this example, you used a `Slider` control to manipulate the text being displayed in a `TextBox` control. In order to do this, you needed to subscribe to the `ValueChanged` event of the `Slider` control. In that event, you simply grabbed the current `Value` property of the `Slider` control, which is set when the user stops the sliding motion or when the mouse button is released in the emulator. You then rounded that value to get rid of any decimal values and converted it to a `String` value that could be used by the `Text` property of the `TextBox` control.

FIGURE 2-17: Using a `Slider` control.

 NOTE *In the next chapter, you'll see how to use a technique called element binding to perform exactly the same operation as the* `Slider` *control, with no code in the code-behind at all. This is a very powerful feature, and with data binding, it can dramatically reduce the amount of code you need to write.*

The MediaElement Control

The powerful `MediaElement` control allows you to easily embed and play a multitude of media files, including music and video files. Using the control is simple. You just add the following XAML to your page:

```
<MediaElement AutoPlay="True" Source="http://ecn.channel9.msdn.com/o9/te/
NorthAmerica/2010/wmv/Key01_300k.wmv" />
```

In this example, you're embedding a video from the Microsoft channel9 site, which is a valuable resource for developers using Microsoft technologies. Believe it or not, this is all that's required to use the `MediaElement` control and get video playing from an external site.

Users expect to be able to change the orientation of a device in order to maximize the screen space available for a video. In order to enable this functionality, you need to support the `Landscape` orientation in the app. Doing this is simple and requires only one change in the `MainPage` `.xaml` file. In the `PhoneApplicationPage` XAML declaration, there are attributes called

`SupportedOrientation` and `Orientation`. Because users viewing media will most likely want to view the video in landscape mode, you can set `SupportedOrientation` to `Landscape` and the default `Orientation` property to `Landscape`. Then, when you run the application, the video plays in landscape mode automatically. Figure 2-18 shows the video being played on startup in this mode. Figure 2-19 shows what happens when you click the change orientation button on the emulator in order to run the app in landscape mode.

Most users also want some type of control over the video, such as the ability to stop, pause, rewind, fast forward, and play. By default, the `MediaElement` control doesn't provide buttons for these actions, but you can add them relatively easily by making use of the Windows Phone application bar. In the next chapter, you'll see how to use of this feature in your applications to provide a consistent user interface for users across all Windows Phone 7 applications.

FIGURE 2-18:
`MediaElement` in portrait orientation.

FIGURE 2-19: `MediaElement` in landscape orientation.

SUMMARY

This chapter covers a lot of material. You were introduced to the Silverlight runtime. You were also introduced to the XAML programming language, which is used to design user interfaces in Silverlight, both for the web and the phone. Next, the chapter provided a thorough introduction to various Silverlight controls you'll be using as you create Windows Phone 7 apps. You should have a good understanding of concepts such as control event handling, adding code to the code-behind file, and setting and retrieving values from the various Silverlight controls.

In the next chapter, you'll learn about some complex controls that are available for Windows Phone 7 development. You'll also explore some more advanced Silverlight programming concepts, such as element binding, data binding, transforms, themes, and more.

EXERCISES

1. True or False: Windows Phone 7 applications support only vertical display orientations.

2. Which of the following properties should you set when you want to have multiple RadioButton controls on a page but with only one valid choice?

    a)   ButtonGroup

    b)   MatchingGroup

    c)   GroupName

    d)   RadioElements

3. What Silverlight layout control should you use if you want to host several controls in a vertical or horizontal layout?

4. When using the HyperlinkButton control, which property must be set if you want the phone to automatically launch its internal web browser and navigate to the destination page?

5. What are the two ways you can subscribe to Silverlight control events?

Answers to the Exercises can be found in the Appendix.

▶ **WHAT YOU LEARNED IN THIS CHAPTER**

TOPIC	KEY CONCEPTS
Using XAML	XAML is the default programming language you use when designing a user interface for Windows Phone 7 with the Silverlight runtime. It has an XML-like syntax and can be edited by hand or by using design-time tools.
Working with the default application files	All Windows Phone 7 applications generated using the standard app template consists of several common files, including `App.xaml`, `App.xaml.cs`, `MainPage.xaml`, `MainPage.xaml.cs`, `WMAppManifest.xml`, `SplashScreenImage.jpg`, and `ApplicationIcon.png`.
	In this chapter, you worked with `MainPage.xaml` and `MainPage.xaml.cs`, but you can also add additional pages to your application. You should also be familiar with the purpose of `App.xaml`, `App.xaml.cs`, and `WMAppManifest.xml`, which contain application-wide settings and resources. `App.xaml.cs` also includes handlers for several important phone events that you'll see later on in the book.
Taking advantage of Silverlight controls	You should now be familiar with many of the Silverlight controls available for Windows Phone 7 development. These include several layout controls, such as `Canvas`, `Grid`, `StackPanel`, and `Border`. In addition, there are many interactive controls, such as `Button`, `HyperlinkButton`, `MediaElement`, `ListBox`, `Slider`, `Image`, `RadioButton`, `ProgressBar`, `TextBlock`, `TextBox`, and `PasswordBox`. You have seen how to set and read properties of these controls both in XAML and in the code-behind file.
Using code-behind	Every XAML page in an application normally has a corresponding `xaml.cs` file that should contain all the application code. This file should contain application logic and event handlers for control events you're interested in capturing.
Handling events	Silverlight controls all have various user interface events that can be subscribed to. You can take advantage of this functionality to add dynamic functionality and user interactivity to an application. You can also access important properties and status information related to the control events you have subscribed to.

3

Spice Up Your App with Shapes, Colors, Brushes, and Transforms

WHAT YOU WILL LEARN IN THIS CHAPTER:

➤ Using Brushes to paint objects

➤ Drawing shapes using Silverlight shape controls

➤ Adding and working with Silverlight Color objects

➤ Modifying controls with transforms

In this chapter, you'll learn about Silverlight features and techniques that will help you create rich and unique applications for the Windows Phone platform. You'll use different shape objects, including the `Ellipse`, `Rectangle`, `Line`, `Polygon`, `Polyline`, and `Path`, and you'll learn to use `Brush` and `Color` objects. In this chapter you'll also learn how to apply transform effects, such as rotate, skew, and other effects, to Silverlight controls.

WORKING WITH SHAPES

The majority of the time, the standard set of Silverlight controls is all you need to create rich Windows Phone 7 applications. However, depending on the app, you may need additional capabilities, such as drawing. For example, if you write a basic paint program or perhaps a photo editing solution on the phone, you need the ability to draw basic shapes on the screen. In addition to the standard controls, Silverlight provides a set of basic shapes. Using these shapes is simple and straightforward. In no time, you can get a basic paint program up-and-running. With the multitouch capabilities of the Windows Phone 7 hardware, you can create some intriguing solutions.

The Ellipse Control

The Ellipse control provides a simple way to create circle-type objects on the screen. A handful of properties make up the definition of the ellipse. At a minimum, you should count on setting the Height and Width properties, which determine the overall size and shape of the ellipse. In addition, you should set the Stroke property, which determines the outline color of the ellipse. You also have several options related to Stroke, such as StrokeThickness, that allow for further customization.

You add an Ellipse control with code like the following:

```
<Ellipse x:Name="MainEllipse" Width="200" Stroke="White" StrokeThickness="5"
Height="100" Fill="Blue" />
```

In this case, you'd create a blue ellipse with a relatively thick white outline, as shown in Figure 3-1.

This shape closely resembles an oval. You can also use the Ellipse control to easily create a perfect circle. Just make sure the Height and Width properties are the same, with code like the following:

```
<Ellipse x:Name="MainEllipse" Width="200" Stroke="White" StrokeThickness="5"
Height="200" Fill="Blue" />
```

Figure 3-2 shows the result.

FIGURE 3-1: An Ellipse control.

FIGURE 3-2: Drawing a circle using an Ellipse control.

What if you want to create an application where you don't want to add the Ellipse control directly in the XAML code? You can instead create an instance of the Ellipse control from the code-behind. The following code creates exactly the same ellipse as before, inside a method called DrawEllipse:

```
private void DrawEllipse()
{
    Ellipse oval = new Ellipse();

    oval.Stroke = new SolidColorBrush(Colors.White);
    oval.StrokeThickness = 5;
    oval.Height = 100;
    oval.Width = 200;
    oval.Fill = new SolidColorBrush(Colors.Blue);

    ContentPanel.Children.Add(oval);
}
```

The same properties that you would have used directly in the XAML code are available in the code-behind. As you can see, you still set the Stroke, StrokeThickness, Height, Width, and Fill properties. There are a couple differences, though, in how you actually set these properties. First, when setting the Stroke property in the code-behind, you don't use a string representation of the color, such as "White". The Silverlight runtime converts the XAML string into an appropriate Brush object, but it can't do that from the code-behind file. Instead, you need to create a new SolidColorBrush object and use the System.Colors enumerator to pick the color of the brush. The SolidColorBrush and other Brush objects are covered later in this chapter in much more detail, but for now just understand that using SolidColorBrush is a way to paint an object with just one color, in this case white.

The System.Colors enumerator contains many of the default system colors that are available on a Windows Phone 7 device. There are additional ways of setting the color that are more flexible, and they're covered later in this chapter as well.

As is the case with the Stroke property, the Fill property must make use of a SolidColorBrush object instead of just a text string. Finally, you need to add the new Ellipse object to the screen. In this case, the example assumes that the control will be added to an existing StackPanel control. The StackPanel control, like many of the layout controls, has a property called Children. This property has a method called Add that enables you to add new controls as children of the StackPanel control. This gives you a simple way to dynamically create and add new controls to the screen. In addition to the Add method, the Children property also has Insert and Remove methods that enable you to insert new controls in a specific order and remove existing controls from the panel.

The Rectangle Control

The Rectangle control has many of the same properties as the Ellipse control. You can declare a Rectangle control with the following code:

```
<Rectangle x:Name="MainRectangle" Height="100" Width="200" Stroke="Green"
StrokeThickness="5" Fill="Red" />
```

This code draws a rectangle shape on the screen similar to the one shown in Figure 3-3.

You can also use the `Rectangle` control to create a perfect square shape by setting the `Width` and `Height` properties to the same value. As with the `Ellipse` control, you can easily control the `Stroke`, `StrokeThickness`, and `Fill` properties. You can also easily create an instance of a `Rectangle` control in the code-behind by using code similar to the following:

```
private void DrawRectangle()
{
    Rectangle rect = new Rectangle();

    rect.Stroke = new SolidColorBrush(Colors.Green);
    rect.StrokeThickness = 5;
    rect.Height = 100;
    rect.Width = 200;
    rect.Fill = new SolidColorBrush(Colors.Red);

    ContentPanel.Children.Add(rect);
}
```

FIGURE 3-3: A `Rectangle` control.

A couple of additional properties of the `Rectangle` control are interesting: `RadiusX` and `RadiusY`. You can use these properties when you need to draw a `Rectangle` shape with rounded corners. For example, the following XAML sets these properties to a value of `10`, which results in the rounded rectangle shape shown in Figure 3-4:

```
<Rectangle x:Name="MainRectangle" Height="100" Width="200" Stroke="Blue"
StrokeThickness="5" Fill="White" RadiusX="20" RadiusY="20" />
```

FIGURE 3-4: A rounded `Rectangle` control.

The RadiusX and RadiusY properties create an ellipse shape in the background that rounds off each of the four corners of the rectangle.

The Line Control

The Line control draws a line on the screen between two points. You can use XAML code similar to the following to add a Line control to the screen:

```
<Line x:Name="MainLine" Stroke="Red" StrokeThickness="5" X1="20" Y1="10" X2="150"
Y2="200" />
```

Only a couple of properties are required to draw the Line control on the screen. The Stroke and StrokeThickness properties work the same way they did for the Ellipse and Rectangle controls. In this case, you'll set the Line control to Red and about 5 pixels in thickness. Next, you need to set the points to which the Line control connects. You can set the starting point of the line by using the X1 and Y1 properties. You declare the ending point of the line by using the X2 and Y2 properties. Running the preceding XAML code in the emulator results in a red Line control being drawn diagonally across the screen, as shown in Figure 3-5.

Creating a Line control dynamically in the code-behind should look familiar, based on what you've seen from the previous shapes. The following code re-creates the same red Line control on the screen previously created using XAML code.

FIGURE 3-5: A Line control.

```
private void DrawLine()
{
    Line line = new Line();

    line.Stroke = new SolidColorBrush(Colors.Red);
    line.StrokeThickness = 5;
    line.X1 = 20;
    line.X2 = 150;
    line.Y1 = 10;
    line.Y2 = 200;

    ContentPanel.Children.Add(line);
}
```

Now that you understand how to use the Line control, let's look at how to use it in a simple paint program that shows off some of the multitouch features of a Windows Phone 7 device, along with the drawing and capabilities of Silverlight.

TRY IT OUT Drawing Lines with the Touchscreen

In this exercise, you will see how to create an application that draws Line objects on the screen as the user moves their finger, or if using the emulator software, as the mouse is dragged across the emulator screen.

1. Create a new Windows Phone application using the Windows Phone 7 application template and name this application **PhonePaint.**

2. When the project finishes loading, modify the MainPage.xaml file to look like Listing 3-1:

LISTING 3-1: MainPage.xaml

```xml
<phone:PhoneApplicationPage
    x:Class="PhonePaint.MainPage"
    xmlns="http://schemas.microsoft.com/winfx/2006/xaml/presentation"
    xmlns:x="http://schemas.microsoft.com/winfx/2006/xaml"
    xmlns:phone="clr-namespace:Microsoft.Phone.Controls;assembly=Microsoft.Phone"
    xmlns:shell="clr-namespace:Microsoft.Phone.Shell;assembly=Microsoft.Phone"
    xmlns:d="http://schemas.microsoft.com/expression/blend/2008"
    xmlns:mc="http://schemas.openxmlformats.org/markup-compatibility/2006"
    mc:Ignorable="d" d:DesignWidth="480" d:DesignHeight="768"
    FontFamily="{StaticResource PhoneFontFamilyNormal}"
    FontSize="{StaticResource PhoneFontSizeNormal}"
    Foreground="{StaticResource PhoneForegroundBrush}"
    SupportedOrientations="Portrait" Orientation="Portrait"
    shell:SystemTray.IsVisible="True">

    <!--LayoutRoot is the root grid where all page content is placed-->
    <Grid x:Name="LayoutRoot" Background="Transparent">
        <Grid.RowDefinitions>
            <RowDefinition Height="Auto"/>
            <RowDefinition Height="*"/>
        </Grid.RowDefinitions>

        <!--TitlePanel contains the name of the application and page title-->
        <StackPanel x:Name="TitlePanel" Grid.Row="0" Margin="12,17,0,28">
            <TextBlock x:Name="ApplicationTitle" Text="PhonePaint App"
Style="{StaticResource PhoneTextNormalStyle}"/>
        </StackPanel>

        <!--ContentPanel - place additional content here-->
        <Grid x:Name="ContentPanel" Grid.Row="1" Margin="12,0,12,0">
            <Canvas x:Name="MainCanvas" HorizontalAlignment="Stretch"
VerticalAlignment="Stretch" Background="Black" />
        </Grid>
    </Grid>
</phone:PhoneApplicationPage>
```

Code Snippet PhonePaint\MainPage.xaml

3. Add functionality in the code-behind to detect where the user touches the screen to draw a line. Modify `MainPage.xaml.cs` to match the code shown here in Listing 3-2:

LISTING 3-2: MainPage.xaml.cs

```csharp
using System;
using System.Collections.Generic;
using System.Linq;
using System.Net;
using System.Windows;
using System.Windows.Controls;
using System.Windows.Documents;
using System.Windows.Input;
using System.Windows.Media;
using System.Windows.Media.Animation;
using System.Windows.Shapes;
using Microsoft.Phone.Controls;

namespace PhonePaint
{
    public partial class MainPage : PhoneApplicationPage
    {
        private Point startingPoint;
        private Point endingPoint;

        // Constructor
        public MainPage()
        {
            InitializeComponent();
            this.Loaded += new RoutedEventHandler(MainPage_Loaded);
        }

        private void MainPage_Loaded(object sender, RoutedEventArgs e)
        {
            MainCanvas.MouseLeftButtonDown += new
MouseButtonEventHandler(MainCanvas_MouseLeftButtonDown);
            MainCanvas.MouseLeftButtonUp += new
MouseButtonEventHandler(MainCanvas_MouseLeftButtonUp);
        }

        private void MainCanvas_MouseLeftButtonDown(object sender,
MouseButtonEventArgs e)
        {
            startingPoint = e.GetPosition(MainCanvas);
        }

        private void MainCanvas_MouseLeftButtonUp(object sender,
MouseButtonEventArgs e)
        {
```

continues

LISTING 3-2 *(continued)*

```
            endingPoint = e.GetPosition(MainCanvas);

            Line line = new Line();

            line.Stroke = new SolidColorBrush(Colors.White);
            line.StrokeThickness = 5;
            line.X1 = startingPoint.X;
            line.Y1 = startingPoint.Y;
            line.X2 = endingPoint.X;
            line.Y2 = endingPoint.Y;

            MainCanvas.Children.Add(line);
        }
    }
}
```

Code Snippet PhonePaint\MainPage.xaml.cs

4. Build and run the application by pressing the F5 key or clicking the debugger symbol in the toolbar.

5. When the app runs in the emulator, try to press down with the mouse on the screen and then release. A white line is drawn in the area where you dragged the mouse. Figure 3-6 shows several lines drawn in the Canvas area.

How It Works

In this Try It Out, you created a simple Windows Phone 7 painting program. To start, you added a Canvas control to the screen and set the HorizontalAlignment and VerticalAlignment properties to Stretch. These properties control where the Canvas lines up in relationship to the parent Grid control. These two properties exist on all Silverlight controls, and you can also use values such as Center, Top, Left, and Right. However, using the value Stretch ensures that the Canvas control takes up all the available screen space.

You also set a background color for the Canvas control as it defaults to transparent. If the Canvas control is transparent, the lines being drawn won't appear on the screen.

FIGURE 3-6: Drawing lines on a Canvas control.

With the Canvas control ready to go, you added a couple of event handlers in the code-behind file to handle both the MouseLeftButtonDown and MouseLeftButtonUp events. The reason you need to handle these events is that the Line control requires both a starting point and an ending point. The MouseLeftButtonDown event provides access to a GetPosition method that can be used to get the X and Y coordinates of the current mouse location when the button is pressed. The X and Y coordinates represent the starting point for the Line control to be drawn. Because you also need the ending point of the Line control, you need to save the current value of GetPosition in a class member variable so it can be used when the MouseLeftButtonUp event is fired.

When you finally capture the MouseLeftButtonUp event, you can use the same GetPosition method to capture the ending point of the Line control. Now, using the same code you saw previously, you can dynamically create a Line control and add it to the Children property of the Canvas control.

Although this example works for drawing Line controls on-the-fly, depending on the mouse or touch motions, it would be nice to draw the line as you're dragging the mouse or as the user drags a finger across the screen. Making this improvement simply requires subscribing to additional mouse events. (Hint: Try to look at the MouseMove event and see if you can come up with a way to draw the line on the Canvas control every time this event is fired.)

The Polygon Control

The Polygon control draws a closed series of connected lines. This control works similarly to the Line control in that it relies on you giving it a set of points from which to draw the object. Instead of using multiple X and Y values for properties, however, the Polygon control uses a property called Points. This property is set with a list of comma-delimited X and Y coordinate pairs. The following code shows the declaration of a basic Polygon control resembling a triangle:

```
<Polygon x:Name="MainPolygon" Fill="White"
    Stroke="Red" StrokeThickness="5" Points="10,10,100,200,300,10" />
```

A basic three-point triangle shape is drawn using the XAML declaration of the Polygon control (see Figure 3-7). Just as was the case with the previous shape controls, you can also set the Fill and Stroke colors and the StrokeThickness property to customize the outline of the shape.

When creating this control from the code-behind, you need to do more work than with the straight XAML declaration. For example, in the following code, you create a DrawPolygon method to take care of drawing the triangle:

```
private void DrawPolygon()
{
    Polygon poly = new Polygon();

    poly.Stroke = new SolidColorBrush(Colors.Red);
    poly.StrokeThickness = 5;
    poly.Fill = new SolidColorBrush(Colors.White);

    // Add polygon points

    poly.Points.Add(new Point(10, 10));
```

FIGURE 3-7: A Polygon control.

```
        poly.Points.Add(new Point(100, 200));
        poly.Points.Add(new Point(300, 10));

        ContentPanel.Children.Add(poly);
    }
```

Note that you need to add each individual point to the `Points` collection of the `Polygon` control. This isn't difficult, as you can easily create a new instance of the `Point` object by using the necessary `x` and `y` coordinates.

In addition to adding `Point` objects to the `Points` collection, you can also create your own `PointCollection` object and then assign it to the `Points` property. The `PointCollection` is a .NET collection object that is available in Silverlight. It gives you a little more control in the way you add points dynamically in the code-behind and assign them to the `Points` property of the `Polygon` control.

The Polyline Control

The `Polyline` control gives you a way to create a multiple-point line that doesn't end up as a closed shape, like the `Polygon` control. You declare an instance of a `Polyline` control in XAML the same way you do for the `Polygon` control. Figure 3-8 shows the multipoint line generated with the following XAML code:

```
<Polyline x:Name="MainPolyline" Stroke="White"
    StrokeThickness="5" Points="10,10,100,200,300,10,300,250" />
```

The main difference between the `Polyline` control and the `Polygon` control is that the ending point and starting point of the line are not automatically connected by the runtime. With the `Polygon` control, just adding three points to the `Points` property is enough to create the triangle shape. When using the `Polyline` control, you don't draw the last line segment without adding another reference to the starting point.

Creating an instance of the `Polyline` control shape in the code-behind follows the same pattern you've seen with the other shape controls. As you can see in the following example, it's almost identical to the `Polygon` control, except in this code snippet, the `PointCollection` object discussed earlier is used, and then an instance of that object is assigned to the `Points` property of the `Polyline` control:

```
private void DrawPolyline()
{
    Polyline poly = new Polyline();
```

FIGURE 3-8: A `Polyline` control.

```
        PointCollection collection = new PointCollection();

        poly.Stroke = new SolidColorBrush(Colors.White);
        poly.StrokeThickness = 5;

        collection.Add(new Point(10, 10));
        collection.Add(new Point(100, 200));
        collection.Add(new Point(300, 10));
        collection.Add(new Point(300, 250));

        poly.Points = collection;
        ContentPanel.Children.Add(poly);
    }
```

One thing you might have noticed is that the `Fill` property is not set in this example. The `Fill` property is still available when you use the `Polyline` control, and in fact the area immediately surrounding the lines being drawn will be filled with the specified color. Figure 3-9 shows the same `Polyline` control shown in Figure 3-8, but with the `Fill` property set.

FIGURE 3-9: A `Polyline` control with the `Fill` property set.

WORKING WITH COLORS

Now that you're familiar with the basic shape controls available in Windows Phone 7, it's time to take a look at some of the color-management features. Although this isn't a terribly complex subject, you need to know the various ways you can construct colors for things like the `SolidColorBrush` object and basic `Fill` and `Background` properties of various controls.

As you've already seen, when working with XAML, you can easily type a color name into the `Background`, `Foreground`, and `Fill` properties of controls, and the Silverlight runtime will convert the string value into a valid color resource. When setting colors for various objects in XAML, you can choose from any valid HTML color code or you can use one of the string representations of the available colors. You can find a complete list of available colors in the online MSDN (www.msdn .microsoft.com) documentation by searching for the System.Colors enumeration.

Sometimes you need even more control of the color or need to set the color in the code-behind page. For example, if you have a new `SolidColorBrush` object and want to use one of the available colors, you'd probably expect to be able to use code similar to the following:

```
ContentPanel.Background = new SolidColorBrush("SeaGreen");
```

Unfortunately, this won't work. You can only use the color strings when setting the color in XAML. So how do you set the color in the code-behind? The first choice you have is to use one of the values available in the `Colors` enumeration, as you've seen previously, using code similar to the following:

```
ContentPanel.Background = new SolidColorBrush(Colors.White);
```

The downside to this is that the `Colors` enumerator does not contain many colors. In fact, it holds only the basic colors and a handful of system colors. This doesn't appear to give you the flexibility that you need. To still be able to set the color from the code-behind, you need to use the static `FromArgb` method available on the `Color` class. This method enables you to set the color by specifying the alpha, red, green, and blue components of the color you want to choose. The following code sets the background to white by using red, green, and blue values of 255, which are the maximum values of each, as well as setting the alpha component to 255, meaning fully visible:

```
ContentPanel.Background = new SolidColorBrush(Color.FromArgb(255, 255, 255, 255));
```

This doesn't seem as easy as using a string-based representation of a color or the simple HTML color codes you're already familiar with. There is, however, a relatively straightforward way to at least make use of the HTML color codes, and all it takes is some basic string parsing.

Assume that you want to set the color to something like #FF0033 because the `FromArgb` method requires an alpha component that effectively works as a transparency flag. The following Try It Out has you add that component to the beginning of the HTML color code.

TRY IT OUT   Using HTML Color Codes in the Code-Behind

In this exercise, you'll add a component to the beginning of the HTML color code. For the alpha, you can use a value from 00 all the way to FF for fully visible. For this example, the HTML color code becomes #FFFF0033. Follow these steps:

1. Create a new Windows Phone 7 project and name it **ColorConversion**.

2. When the project finishes loading, open `MainPage.xaml.cs` and update the code to look like the code here in Listing 3-3:

LISTING 3-3: MainPage.xaml.cs

```
using System;
using System.Collections.Generic;
using System.Linq;
using System.Net;
using System.Windows;
using System.Windows.Controls;
using System.Windows.Documents;
```

```
using System.Windows.Input;
using System.Windows.Media;
using System.Windows.Media.Animation;
using System.Windows.Shapes;
using Microsoft.Phone.Controls;

namespace ColorConversion
{
    public partial class MainPage : PhoneApplicationPage
    {
        // Constructor
        public MainPage()
        {
            InitializeComponent();
            ContentPanel.Background = GetSolidColorBrush("#FFFF0033");
        }

        private SolidColorBrush GetSolidColorBrush(string htmlColor)
        {
            byte alpha = 0;
            byte red = 0;
            byte green = 0;
            byte blue = 0;

            alpha = (byte)Convert.ToInt32(htmlColor.Substring(1, 2),16);
            red = (byte)Convert.ToInt32(htmlColor.Substring(3, 2),16);
            green = (byte)Convert.ToInt32(htmlColor.Substring(5, 2),16);
            blue = (byte)Convert.ToInt32(htmlColor.Substring(7, 2),16);

            if (String.IsNullOrEmpty(htmlColor) || htmlColor.Length < 9)
                throw new Exception("Invalid html color code supplied,
use #FFFFFFFF format");

            return new SolidColorBrush(Color.FromArgb(alpha, red, green, blue));
        }
    }
}
```

Code Snippet ColorConversion\MainPage.xaml.cs

3. Build and run the application in the emulator. Notice how the background color of the application has changed to the HTML color code specified in the constructor of the MainPage class.

How It Works

The goal of this example is to get a method that enables you to use standard HTML color codes to set a color for a Brush object. In XAML, you can use the color codes, but in the code-behind, that procedure is not supported. In the previous code, you created the GetSolidColorBrush method to return a SolidColorBrush control that can be used as the background for the app. Of course, you could modify this routine to just return a `Color` object as well, which might be more useful in your own applications. In this case, though, the goal was to set the `Background` property of the main content panel in the application and to do it from the code-behind file.

The `GetSolidColorBrush` method works by taking a standard HTML color code with the added alpha value discussed earlier. It then converts that color code to a set of red, green, and blue values that the `FromArgb` method can use. In this example, you parsed the HTML color code string by using the `Substring` function that's available on all `String` objects in .NET. You used the alpha to represent the first two characters after the # sign. In addition, you knew that the red, green, and blue components of an HTML color code are 2 bytes each and make up the rest of the string.

You couldn't just use the parsed string values, so you needed to convert them to integer values. By using `Convert.ToInt32` with the additional parameter of `16`, you essentially told the runtime that the two characters converted represent a base 16 number between 0 and 255. So after the conversion took place, you had an integer value representing your string.

Finally, because the `FromArgb` method requires byte objects as opposed to integer values, you simply cast the result of the conversion by using the (byte) syntax.

In this example, you got a reusable method that uses the standard HTML color codes instead of trying to figure out red, green, and blue numeric components for each of the colors.

USING BRUSHES

Now that you have an understanding of how to manipulate and use colors in Silverlight, it's time to take a more in-depth look at the `Brush` object, along with all the available types of brushes that can be used to fill Silverlight controls.

The SolidColorBrush Object

As you've seen in the previous code samples, the `SolidColorBrush` object is used primarily to fill a shape or control with a single solid color. You can use any of the available runtime colors in XAML or in the code-behind that you've seen before. In the following code, you set the `Fill` property of a `Rectangle` shape to a blue `SolidColorBrush` object, resulting in the rectangle being filled as shown in Figure 3-10:

```
MainRect.Fill = new SolidColorBrush(Colors.Blue);
```

The LinearGradientBrush Object

The `LinearGradientBrush` is a `Brush` object that enables you to create horizontal, vertical, and diagonal gradients to use for filling objects via the `Background` or `Fill` property. Like the `SolidColorBrush`, it is easy

FIGURE 3-10:
A `SolidColorBrush`
object.

to use in XAML or in the code-behind. To fill the same `Rectangle` object used in the preceding section with a horizontal gradient, you can use XAML code such as the following:

```
<Rectangle x:Name="MainRect" Height="300" Width="300">
    <Rectangle.Fill>
        <LinearGradientBrush StartPoint="0,0.5" EndPoint="1,0.5">
            <GradientStop Color="Black" Offset="0.0" />
            <GradientStop Color="White" Offset="0.5" />
        </LinearGradientBrush>
    </Rectangle.Fill>
</Rectangle>
```

Unlike with `SolidColorBrush`, with `LinearGradientBrush` you need to be concerned with a few different attributes. First, it's important that you tell the `Brush` where to start the gradient and where to finish it. To do this, you set the `StartPoint` and `EndPoint` properties. By default, the runtime maps coordinate 0, 0 to the top left of the object being filled and 1, 1 as the bottom right. This means you can start and end the gradient anywhere in between those coordinates. To produce a horizontal gradient like the one shown in Figure 3-11, you start the gradient at 0, 5, which is halfway down the left side of the object. Then you end the gradient at 1, 0.5, with 1 being the right border of the object and 0.5 being halfway down the side.

You can set any number of `GradientStop` objects, and each one represents a color associated with the gradient. In this case, only two stops were used to get a black-and-white gradient to appear. The `Offset` property determines where on the object to start the color. In this case, you want a 50/50 split of black and white, so you tell the black `GradientStop` object to start at 0 and the white `GradientStop` object to start halfway down the object, at 0.5.

FIGURE 3-11: A `LinearGradientBrush` object.

Creating a vertical gradient is just as easy as creating a horizontal one. All you need to do is set the appropriate starting and ending points. The following XAML changes the previous example from a horizontal gradient to a vertical one that also starts off black, is white in the middle, and is black again at the end of the gradient:

```
<Rectangle x:Name="MainRect" Height="300" Width="300">
    <Rectangle.Fill>
        <LinearGradientBrush StartPoint="0.5,0.0" EndPoint="0.5,1">
            <GradientStop Color="Black" Offset="0.0" />
            <GradientStop Color="White" Offset="0.5" />
            <GradientStop Color="Black" Offset="1.0" />
        </LinearGradientBrush>
    </Rectangle.Fill>
</Rectangle>
```

As you can see, you need to declare only one additional `GradientStop` object. Figure 3-12 shows the new version of the gradient.

FIGURE 3-12: A horizontal
`LinearGradientBrush`
object.

It's not difficult to create rich horizontal, vertical, and diagonal gradients for object and shape fills or backgrounds. You can also create an instance of the `LinearGradientBrush` object in the code-behind by using code similar to the following:

```
LinearGradientBrush brush = new LinearGradientBrush();

brush.StartPoint = new Point(0, 0);
brush.EndPoint = new Point(1, 1);
brush.GradientStops.Add(new GradientStop { Color=Colors.Black, Offset=0.0 });
brush.GradientStops.Add(new GradientStop { Color=Colors.White, Offset=0.5 });

MainRect.Fill = brush;
```

This code creates a diagonal gradient, using black and white. Notice how the `LinearGradientBrush` object has a `GradientStops` collection that you can use in the code-behind to add new `GradientStop` declarations for each color. You may also have noticed that instead of setting the `Color` and `Offset` properties of the `GradientStop` object in the constructor, the .NET object initialization syntax is used. This method is used because the `GradientStop` object doesn't provide a constructor with parameters for `Color` and `Offset`. This syntax has been available since .NET version 3.5 enables you to circumvent this limitation and assign the property values in one line of code. This is a time saver for initializing objects.

The RadialGradientBrush Object

`RadialGradientBrush` works similarly to `LinearGradientBrush`. The major difference is that instead of the gradient being drawn from left to right or top to bottom, with `RadialGradientBrush` the gradient is drawn in a circle from a center point that you specify. Using the `Rectangle` shape again, the following code assigns the black-and-white gradient fill but uses `RadialGradientBrush` instead:

```
<Rectangle.Fill>
    <RadialGradientBrush Center="0.5,0.5" GradientOrigin="0.5,0.5">
        <GradientStop Color="Black" Offset="0.0" />
        <GradientStop Color="White" Offset="1.0" />
    </RadialGradientBrush>
</Rectangle.Fill>
```

This XAML code produces the gradient fill shown in Figure 3-13:

You need to know a few things about creating and using the `RadialGradientBrush` object. First, there are no starting and ending point properties that need to be set. By default, the gradient is drawn from the center of the object being filled. You can control this, however, by setting the `Center` property. In the previous code, the `Center` property was set to 0.5, 0.5, which is the same as the default value. Once again, this `Brush` object uses the same coordinate system as `LinearGradientBrush`, where the top-left point of the object is 0, 0 and the bottom-right point of the object is 1, 1.

You can use two additional properties to manipulate the overall size of the circular gradient being drawn. By using the `RadiusX` and `RadiusY` properties, you can easily increase or decrease the overall radius of the gradient object.

Creating an instance of this `Brush` object in the code-behind is similar to creating a `LinearGradientBrush` object in that you need to add `GradientStop` objects to the `GradientStops` collection. The following code creates the same `RadialGradientBrush` object and fills the `Rectangle` object with it:

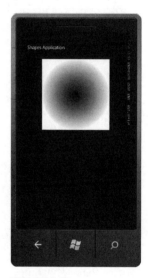

FIGURE 3-13:
A `RadialGradientBrush` object.

```
RadialGradientBrush brush = new RadialGradientBrush();

brush.GradientStops.Add(new GradientStop { Color = Colors.Black, Offset = 0.0 });
brush.GradientStops.Add(new GradientStop { Color = Colors.White, Offset = 1.0 });

MainRect.Fill = brush;
```

The ImageBrush Object

Solid fill colors and gradients are interesting and can be useful in most cases. However, when you're using Silverlight for Windows Phone 7, you can also use a couple more unique `Brush` objects, such as `ImageBrush`. With the `ImageBrush` object, you can easily paint the `Fill` property of the `Rectangle` object or the `Background` property of another Silverlight control with an image.

The following XAML code uses the same `Rectangle` object from the previous examples but this time paints the `Fill` property with an image of a Wrox Press book cover (see Figure 3-14):

```
<Rectangle.Fill>
    <ImageBrush ImageSource="wrox.png" Stretch="Fill" />
</Rectangle.Fill>
```

As you can see, you need only one line of code to make the `Background` or `Fill` property of a Silverlight control an image. The `ImageBrush` object uses many of the same properties that you saw with the `Image` control. `ImageBrush` uses an `ImageSource` property to set the image being used for the brush, and the `Stretch` property determines whether the image should be stretched to the dimensions of the object being painted.

Creating and using `ImageBrush` from the code-behind is just as simple:

```
ImageBrush brush = new ImageBrush();

brush.ImageSource = new BitmapImage(new Uri("wrox.png", UriKind.Relative));
brush.Stretch = Stretch.Fill;

MainRect.Fill = brush;
```

FIGURE 3-14:
An `ImageBrush` object.

Notice in the code-behind version of creating the `ImageBrush` that you can't simply use a string-based path to the image file you want displayed for the `ImageSource` property. Instead, you need to create an instance of a `BitmapImage` object that contains the path to the actual image file. When declaring the `ImageBrush` object in XAML, the runtime takes care of creating a new `BitmapImage` object to be displayed in the background by simply using the path to the file you entered in the declaration. You don't get that same behavior, however, when you set this property from the code-behind page. For the most part, though, it doesn't really add much additional code. As with the creation of a `SolidColorBrush` object using an HTML color code, this difference in behavior from the XAML-based declaration can cause problems if you don't watch for it and make the necessary code changes.

APPLYING TRANSFORMS

At this point, you should have a good understanding of the various shapes, colors, and brushes you can use in Windows Phone 7 applications. Next you will see how to make use of various transform effects like rotation, scaling, skewing, and translation.

The RotateTransform Object

You can rotate just about any Silverlight object without having to create complicated rotation algorithms. Instead, Silverlight provides the `RotateTransform` object, which you can easily apply to various controls and shapes to rotate them a specified number of degrees.

You use the `RotateTransform` object in XAML as follows:

```
<TextBlock x:Name="RotatedText" Margin="50" Text="This text has been rotated">
    <TextBlock.RenderTransform>
        <RotateTransform Angle="45" />
    </TextBlock.RenderTransform>
</TextBlock>
```

This seems simple enough. Basically, in this example, you rotate a `TextBlock` object 45 degrees by adding a `RotateTransform` object with the `Angle` property set to the `RenderTransform` property of the `TextBlock` control. To better understand how this works, first take a look at the `RenderTransform` property of the `TextBlock` object. All Silverlight controls contain an attached property called `RenderTransform` that enables you to specify a type of transform to apply during the rendering of the object. In this case, you add a simple rotation to the text. You can't ask for an easier way to rotate an object than this. Figure 3-15 shows the rotation in action.

Adding the rotation effect to the same `TextBlock` control from the code-behind is just as easy. You simply create a new `RotateTransform` object, set the `Angle` property, and assign it to the `RenderTransform` property of the `TextBlock` object, as in the following code:

FIGURE 3-15:
A `RotateTransform` object.

```
RotatedText.RenderTransform = new RotateTransform { Angle = 45 };
```

You can use this effect for any Silverlight control in Windows Phone 7, which means you can create a `RotateTransform` object and assign it to the `RenderTransform` property of an `Image` object, a `Button` object, a `RadioButton` object, and so on.

The `Angle` property can accept values from 0 to 360, as expected, but you should also be aware of a couple of additional properties of `RotateTransform`. By default, `RotateTransform` applies the angle rotation to the object, starting at coordinates 0, 0 or the top-left area of the object. You can control this by setting both the `CenterX` and `CenterY` properties of the `RotateTransform` object. By modifying these two additional properties, you can force the area of rotation to start somewhere other than 0, 0. To see how this works, look at the following XAML code, which centers a `Button` control inside a `Border` container:

```
<Border Margin="0,10,0,0" BorderThickness="5" BorderBrush="White" Width="300"
Height="300">
    <Button Content="Rotated Button" HorizontalAlignment="Center"
VerticalAlignment="Center">
    </Button>
</Border>
```

This XAML code produces the screen shown in Figure 3-16.

FIGURE 3-16: A centered
`Button` control.

You can use the following XAML code to apply a basic `RotateTransform` object to the `Button`
control and rotate it 90 degrees:

```
<Border Margin="0,10,0,0" BorderThickness="5" BorderBrush="White" Width="300"
Height="300">
    <Button Content="Rotated Button" HorizontalAlignment="Center"
VerticalAlignment="Center">
        <Button.RenderTransform>
            <RotateTransform Angle="90" />
        </Button.RenderTransform>
    </Button>
</Border>
```

This XAML code produces the screen shown in Figure 3-17.

As you can see in Figure 3-17, although the `RotateTransform` object rotates the `Button` control 90
degrees, it does so by rotating from the top left of the control, which doesn't really have the desired
effect of both rotating the `Button` control and keeping it inside the `Border` object. You can solve
this problem rather easily by modifying the `CenterX` property. The following XAML code makes
the necessary adjustments to these properties, rotating the `Button` control while keeping it inside the
`Border` control (see Figure 3-18):

```
<Border Margin="0,10,0,0" BorderThickness="5" BorderBrush="White" Width="300"
Height="300">
    <Button Content="Rotated Button" HorizontalAlignment="Center"
VerticalAlignment="Center">
        <Button.RenderTransform>
            <RotateTransform Angle="90" CenterX="50" />
        </Button.RenderTransform>
    </Button>
</Border>
```

FIGURE 3-17: A rotated `Button` control.

FIGURE 3-18: A rotated `Button` control in a border.

The ScaleTransform Object

When applied to the `RenderTransform` property of a Silverlight control, `ScaleTransform` scales the item larger or smaller, depending on the desired effect. In the following XAML code, you declare a standard `TextBlock` control along with an additional version of the `TextBlock` control that uses the `ScaleTransform` control in order to triple its overall size:

```
<TextBlock Margin="10" Text="Rotated Text" />
<TextBlock Margin="10" Text="Rotated Text">
    <TextBlock.RenderTransform>
        <ScaleTransform ScaleX="3" ScaleY="3" />
    </TextBlock.RenderTransform>
</TextBlock>
```

To make this work, you need to set two properties: `ScaleX` and `ScaleY`. You can easily enlarge or shrink the control by setting these values to anything from `0` on up. If you use a value less than 1, you'll see the `TextBlock` object shrink accordingly. In this case, you want to triple the overall size of the `TextBlock` control, so you use a value of 3 for both properties. Figure 3-19 shows both the original `TextBlock` control and the scaled `TextBlock` control.

FIGURE 3-19: A `ScaleTransform` object on a `TextBlock` control.

You can apply the `ScaleTransform` effect in the code-behind much the same way you use `RotateTransform`. The following code applies the same tripling of size for the additional `TextBlock` control:

```
ScaleTransform transform = new ScaleTransform { ScaleX = 3, ScaleY = 3 };
ScaledTextBlock.RenderTransform = transform;
```

 Once again, you can easily apply this scaling effect to any Silverlight control or shape by applying it to the `RenderTransform` *property of the specified control.*

The SkewTransform Control

You can easily skew objects by using the `SkewTransform` control. This control works basically the same as the `ScaleTransform`: You add it to the `RenderTransform` property of the object being skewed. In the following XAML code, you apply the `SkewTransform` object to the `TextBlock` control, with the goal of creating a 45-degree slanted version of the text:

```
<TextBlock x:Name="SkewedTextBlock" FontSize="50" Margin="10" Text="Skewed Text">
    <TextBlock.RenderTransform>
        <SkewTransform AngleX="45" AngleY="0" />
    </TextBlock.RenderTransform>
</TextBlock>
```

For this effect, you need to use the `AngleX` and `AngleY` properties to control the skew effect. To slant the text 45 degrees horizontally, you need only the `AngleX` property. Figure 3-20 shows the effect in action.

FIGURE 3-20:
A `SkewTransform` object.

By now, you can probably guess how to apply this effect in the code-behind page. As with the other transform effects, you once again create an instance of `SkewTransform`, set the angle properties, and assign the `SkewTransform` object to the `RenderTransform` property of the object:

```
SkewTransform transform = new SkewTransform { AngleX = 45, AngleY = 0 };
SkewedTextBlock.RenderTransform = transform;
```

As with the other transform objects, you also have the option of manipulating the origin of the skew effect by setting the `CenterX` and `CenterY` properties.

The TranslateTransform Object

The `TranslateTransform` effect provides a simple way to alter the location of an object on the screen. The following XAML code shows a basic example of this effect used on a `Button` control:

```
<Button x:Name="MainButton" Width="200" Content="Click Me">
    <Button.RenderTransform>
        <TranslateTransform X="5" Y="5" />
    </Button.RenderTransform>
</Button>
```

For the `TranslateTransform` object, the only properties that need to be set are the `X` and `Y` coordinates of the destination location for the object. Although these can be set in XAML, as in this example, this really isn't practical because the move would happen before the end user even saw the original location.

TRY IT OUT   Moving a Rectangle Control

In the following steps, you'll make the effect a little more interesting by using it in the code-behind.

1. Create a new Windows Phone 7 project and name it **MovingRectangleDemo**.

2. When the project finishes loading, replace the contents of `MainPage.xaml` with the code shown here in Listing 3-4:

Available for
download on
Wrox.com

LISTING 3-4: MainPage.xaml

```
<phone:PhoneApplicationPage
    x:Class="MovingRectangleDemo.MainPage"
    xmlns="http://schemas.microsoft.com/winfx/2006/xaml/presentation"
    xmlns:x="http://schemas.microsoft.com/winfx/2006/xaml"
    xmlns:phone="clr-namespace:Microsoft.Phone.Controls;assembly=Microsoft.Phone"
    xmlns:shell="clr-namespace:Microsoft.Phone.Shell;assembly=Microsoft.Phone"
    xmlns:d="http://schemas.microsoft.com/expression/blend/2008"
    xmlns:mc="http://schemas.openxmlformats.org/markup-compatibility/2006"
    mc:Ignorable="d" d:DesignWidth="480" d:DesignHeight="768"
    FontFamily="{StaticResource PhoneFontFamilyNormal}"
    FontSize="{StaticResource PhoneFontSizeNormal}"
```

continues

LISTING 3-4 *(continued)*

```
          Foreground="{StaticResource PhoneForegroundBrush}"
          SupportedOrientations="Portrait" Orientation="Portrait"
          shell:SystemTray.IsVisible="True">

    <!--LayoutRoot is the root grid where all page content is placed-->
    <Grid x:Name="LayoutRoot" Background="Transparent">
        <Grid.RowDefinitions>
            <RowDefinition Height="Auto"/>
            <RowDefinition Height="*"/>
        </Grid.RowDefinitions>

        <!--TitlePanel contains the name of the application and page title-->
        <StackPanel x:Name="TitlePanel" Grid.Row="0" Margin="12,17,0,28">
            <TextBlock x:Name="ApplicationTitle" Text="Moving Rectangle Demo"
Style="{StaticResource PhoneTextNormalStyle}"/>
        </StackPanel>

        <!--ContentPanel - place additional content here-->
        <Grid x:Name="ContentPanel" Grid.Row="1" Margin="12,0,12,0">
            <StackPanel>
                <Rectangle x:Name="MainRect" Width="200"
Height="200" Fill="White" HorizontalAlignment="Left" VerticalAlignment="Top" />
                <Button Margin="0,300,0,0" Width="300"
Content="Move Rectangle" />
            </StackPanel>
        </Grid>
    </Grid>
</phone:PhoneApplicationPage>
```

Code Snippet MovingRectangleDemo\MainPage.xaml

3. Open `MainPage.xaml.cs` and replace the existing code with the code shown here in Listing 3-5:

LISTING 3-5: MainPage.xaml.cs

```
using System;
using System.Collections.Generic;
using System.Linq;
using System.Net;
using System.Windows;
using System.Windows.Controls;
using System.Windows.Documents;
using System.Windows.Input;
using System.Windows.Media;
using System.Windows.Media.Animation;
using System.Windows.Shapes;
using Microsoft.Phone.Controls;

namespace MovingRectangleDemo
{
    public partial class MainPage : PhoneApplicationPage
```

```
                {
                    private TranslateTransform transform = null;

                    // Constructor
                    public MainPage()
                    {
                        InitializeComponent();
                        this.Loaded += new RoutedEventHandler(MainPage_Loaded);

                        transform = new TranslateTransform();
                    }

                    private void MainPage_Loaded(object sender, RoutedEventArgs e)
                    {
                        MoveRect.Click += new RoutedEventHandler(MoveRect_Click);
                    }

                    private void MoveRect_Click(object sender, RoutedEventArgs e)
                    {
                        transform.X += 1;
                        transform.Y += 1;

                        MainRect.RenderTransform = transform;
                    }
                }
            }
```

Code Snippet MovingRectangleDemo\MainPage.xaml.cs

4. Build and run the application in the emulator and click the move rectangle button to force the Rectangle control to be moved. Notice how the Rectangle control moves diagonally across the screen with each click.

5. Modify the MoveRect_Click method as follows to increase the X and Y coordinates of the translation effect by 5 pixels for each click:

Available for
download on
Wrox.com

```
private void MoveRect_Click(object sender, RoutedEventArgs e)
{
    transform.X += 5;
    transform.Y += 5;

    MainRect.RenderTransform = transform;
}
```

Code Snippet MovingRectangleDemo\MainPage.xaml.cs

How It Works

In this example, your goal was to move the Rectangle control a certain number of pixels each time the Button control was clicked. In order to make this happen, you declared a class-level variable for the TranslateTransform object so that with each click, you only needed to increase the current value of the X and Y coordinates, and then you could reapply the transform to the Rectangle object.

The TransformGroup Object

All the transform effects we've examined so far seem pretty great. They're easy to use and take care of the complex math formulas required to generate the effects. However, there's one major drawback to all of them: You must use the `RenderTransform` property of the control, and you can assign only one transform effect to that property. So if you wanted to perform more advanced scenarios in an application, such as mixing multiple effects, the `RenderTransform` property would not give you that ability, at least using the methods you've seen so far.

To get around what seems like a big limitation of the `RenderTransform` property, you can use the `TransformGroup` object. The `RenderTransform` property of a Silverlight control also accepts this object in place of a single transform effect. `TransformGroup` has one purpose: to hold an ordered collection of transform effects. Let's look at a simple example. In the following XAML code, an `Image` control is both rotated and scaled using `TransformGroup`:

```
<Image Source="wrox.png" Stretch="None" HorizontalAlignment="Center"
VerticalAlignment="Center">
    <Image.RenderTransform>
        <TransformGroup>
            <RotateTransform Angle="45" />
            <ScaleTransform ScaleX="2" ScaleY="2" />
        </TransformGroup>
    </Image.RenderTransform>
</Image>
```

Because `RotateTransform` is listed first, this effect actually takes place before `ScaleTransform`. Figure 3-21 shows `TransformGroup` taking effect.

FIGURE 3-21: Multiple transform effects using `TransformGroup`.

Of course, as in all the other examples, you can also use `TransformGroup` from the code-behind page. Here's the code to do so:

```
TransformGroup group = new TransformGroup();

group.Children.Add(new RotateTransform { Angle = 45 });
group.Children.Add(new ScaleTransform { ScaleX = 2, ScaleY = 2 });

MainImage.RenderTransform = group;
```

This code generates the same output as the XAML. The only real difference here is that you're adding transform objects to the `Children` property of `TransformGroup`.

TRY IT OUT Experimenting with Transforms

In the following steps, you'll put together all this new knowledge of transforms in a cool little application.

1. Create a new Windows Phone 7 project and name it **TransformDemo**.

2. Replace the contents of `MainPage.xaml` with the code shown in Listing 3-6:

Available for download on Wrox.com

LISTING 3-6: MainPage.xaml

```
<phone:PhoneApplicationPage
    x:Class="TransformDemo.MainPage"
    xmlns="http://schemas.microsoft.com/winfx/2006/xaml/presentation"
    xmlns:x="http://schemas.microsoft.com/winfx/2006/xaml"
    xmlns:phone="clr-namespace:Microsoft.Phone.Controls;assembly=Microsoft.Phone"
    xmlns:shell="clr-namespace:Microsoft.Phone.Shell;assembly=Microsoft.Phone"
    xmlns:d="http://schemas.microsoft.com/expression/blend/2008"
    xmlns:mc="http://schemas.openxmlformats.org/markup-compatibility/2006"
    mc:Ignorable="d" d:DesignWidth="480" d:DesignHeight="768"
    FontFamily="{StaticResource PhoneFontFamilyNormal}"
    FontSize="{StaticResource PhoneFontSizeNormal}"
    Foreground="{StaticResource PhoneForegroundBrush}"
    SupportedOrientations="Portrait" Orientation="Portrait"
    shell:SystemTray.IsVisible="True">

    <!--LayoutRoot is the root grid where all page content is placed-->
    <Grid x:Name="LayoutRoot" Background="Transparent">
        <Grid.RowDefinitions>
            <RowDefinition Height="Auto"/>
            <RowDefinition Height="*"/>
        </Grid.RowDefinitions>

        <!--TitlePanel contains the name of the application and page title-->
        <StackPanel x:Name="TitlePanel" Grid.Row="0" Margin="12,17,0,28">
            <TextBlock x:Name="ApplicationTitle" Text="Transform Demo App"
    Style="{StaticResource PhoneTextNormalStyle}"/>
        </StackPanel>

        <!--ContentPanel - place additional content here-->
```

continues

LISTING 3-6 *(continued)*

```xml
                <Grid x:Name="ContentPanel" Grid.Row="1" Margin="12,0,12,0">
                    <StackPanel>
                        <Image x:Name="MainImage" HorizontalAlignment="Center"
VerticalAlignment="Top" Source="wrox.png"
Stretch="None" Margin="0,10,0,0" />
                        <StackPanel Orientation="Horizontal" Margin="0,100,0,0">
                            <TextBlock Text="Enter Angle for RotateTransform"
TextWrapping="Wrap" Width="175" />
                            <TextBox x:Name="RotateAngle" Text="0" Width="75" />
                            <Button x:Name="ApplyRotation" Content="Apply" />
                        </StackPanel>
                        <StackPanel Orientation="Horizontal" Margin="0,10,0,0">
                            <TextBlock Text="Enter X and Y for ScaleTransform"
TextWrapping="Wrap" Width="175" />
                            <TextBox x:Name="ScaleX" Text="1" Width="75" />
                            <TextBox x:Name="ScaleY" Text="1" Width="75" />
                            <Button x:Name="ApplyScale" Content="Apply" />
                        </StackPanel>
                        <StackPanel Orientation="Horizontal" Margin="0,10,0,0">
                            <TextBlock Text="Enter X and Y for SkewTransform"
TextWrapping="Wrap" Width="175" />
                            <TextBox x:Name="SkewX" Text="0" Width="75" />
                            <TextBox x:Name="SkewY" Text="0" Width="75" />
                            <Button x:Name="ApplySkew" Content="Apply" />
                        </StackPanel>
                        <StackPanel Orientation="Horizontal" Margin="0,10,0,0">
                            <TextBlock Text="Enter X and Y for TranslateTransform"
TextWrapping="Wrap" Width="175" />
                            <TextBox x:Name="TranslateX" Text="0" Width="75" />
                            <TextBox x:Name="TranslateY" Text="0" Width="75" />
                            <Button x:Name="ApplyTranslate" Content="Apply" />
                        </StackPanel>
                        <Button Margin="0,10,0,0" Content="Apply All"
x:Name="ApplyAll" />
                    </StackPanel>
                </Grid>
        </Grid>
</phone:PhoneApplicationPage>
```

Code Snippet TransformDemo\MainPage.xaml

3. Enter the following code from Listing 3-7 in the `MainPage.xaml.cs` file:

LISTING 3-7: MainPage.xaml.cs

```csharp
using System;
using System.Collections.Generic;
using System.Linq;
using System.Net;
using System.Windows;
```

```csharp
using System.Windows.Controls;
using System.Windows.Documents;
using System.Windows.Input;
using System.Windows.Media;
using System.Windows.Media.Animation;
using System.Windows.Shapes;
using Microsoft.Phone.Controls;

namespace TransformDemo
{
    public partial class MainPage : PhoneApplicationPage
    {
        // Constructor
        public MainPage()
        {
            InitializeComponent();
            this.Loaded += new RoutedEventHandler(MainPage_Loaded);
        }

        private void MainPage_Loaded(object sender, RoutedEventArgs e)
        {
            ApplyRotation.Click += new RoutedEventHandler(ApplyRotation_Click);
            ApplyScale.Click += new RoutedEventHandler(ApplyScale_Click);
            ApplySkew.Click += new RoutedEventHandler(ApplySkew_Click);
            ApplyTranslate.Click += new
RoutedEventHandler(ApplyTranslate_Click);
            ApplyAll.Click += new RoutedEventHandler(ApplyAll_Click);
        }

        private void ApplyAll_Click(object sender, RoutedEventArgs e)
        {
            TransformGroup group = new TransformGroup();

            group.Children.Add(new TranslateTransform { X =
Convert.ToDouble(TranslateX.Text), Y = Convert.ToDouble(TranslateY.Text) });
            group.Children.Add(new SkewTransform { AngleX =
Convert.ToDouble(SkewX.Text), AngleY = Convert.ToDouble(SkewY.Text) });
            group.Children.Add(new ScaleTransform { ScaleX =
Convert.ToDouble(ScaleX.Text), ScaleY = Convert.ToDouble(ScaleY.Text) });
            group.Children.Add(new RotateTransform { Angle =
Convert.ToDouble(RotateAngle.Text) });

            MainImage.RenderTransform = group;
        }

        private void ApplyTranslate_Click(object sender, RoutedEventArgs e)
        {
            MainImage.RenderTransform = new TranslateTransform { X =
Convert.ToDouble(TranslateX.Text), Y = Convert.ToDouble(TranslateY.Text) };
        }

        private void ApplySkew_Click(object sender, RoutedEventArgs e)
```

continues

LISTING 3-7 *(continued)*

```
        {
            MainImage.RenderTransform = new SkewTransform { AngleX =
Convert.ToDouble(SkewX.Text), AngleY = Convert.ToDouble(SkewY.Text) };
        }

        private void ApplyScale_Click(object sender, RoutedEventArgs e)
        {
            MainImage.RenderTransform = new ScaleTransform { ScaleX =
Convert.ToDouble(ScaleX.Text), ScaleY = Convert.ToDouble(ScaleY.Text) };
        }

        private void ApplyRotation_Click(object sender, RoutedEventArgs e)
        {
            MainImage.RenderTransform = new RotateTransform { Angle =
Convert.ToDouble(RotateAngle.Text) };
        }
    }
}
```

Code Snippet TransformDemo\MainPage.xaml.cs

4. Build and run the application in the emulator. At this point, you should see the screen shown in Figure 3-22.

FIGURE 3-22: A transform demo app.

5. Play around with some of the transform effects by entering an angle for RotateTransform and clicking the Apply button. Each individual Apply button should render the associated transform effect.

6. Enter data for all the transforms, and then click the Apply All button to see the cumulative effect of all the transforms being applied.

7. Add a new button called Spin to the XAML, underneath the Apply All button:

```
<Button Margin="0,10,0,0" Content="Apply All" x:Name="ApplyAll" />
<Button Margin="0,10,0,0" Content="Spin" x:Name="Spin" />
```

8. Add a new event handler for the Click event for this button in the code-behind file. To do so, add the following line in the MainPage_Loaded method:

```
Spin.Click += new RoutedEventHandler(Spin_Click);
```

9. Add the following Spin_Click method somewhere in the code-behind file:

```
private void Spin_Click(object sender, RoutedEventArgs e)
{
    DispatcherTimer timer = new DispatcherTimer();
    timer.Interval = new TimeSpan(1000);
    timer.Tick += (se, ev) =>
    {
        angle += 5;
        MainImage.RenderTransform = new RotateTransform { Angle = angle };
    };
    timer.Start();
}
```

10. Add a class-level variable called angle at the top of the class declaration:

```
public partial class MainPage : PhoneApplicationPage
    {
        private int angle = 0;
```

11. Build and run the application again in the emulator and click the Spin button. Notice that the Image control is now automatically rotated continuously around the top-left corner of the image.

How It Works

In this example, you created a relatively simple data entry form that allows the user to experience all the various transform effects available in Windows Phone 7. You added an Image control that will be manipulated by the various transform objects. After you created the form in XAML, most of the real work took place in the code-behind. First, you created event handlers for all of the Button object Click events. In each of these events, you simply created an instance of the appropriate transform object and set the current RenderTransform property of the Image control. Because the user enters the values in a TextBox control, the code will retrieve the contents of the TextBox controls as string values, which don't do much good as Angle and X, Y coordinates. In this case you wanted to allow the user to enter decimal values, so you used the Convert.ToDouble method on the Text property of the TextBox controls.

To show off the ability to mix and match transforms, you added an event handler for the Apply All Button control. In this event handler, you created a new TransformGroup object and collected all the values entered by the user for the various transform effects. Then, in the following code, you added instances of these effects to the `Children` property of `TransformGroup`:

```
private void ApplyAll_Click(object sender, RoutedEventArgs e)
{
    TransformGroup group = new TransformGroup();

    group.Children.Add(new TranslateTransform {
X = Convert.ToDouble(TranslateX.Text), Y = Convert.ToDouble(TranslateY.Text) });
    group.Children.Add(new SkewTransform { AngleX = Convert.ToDouble(SkewX.Text),
AngleY = Convert.ToDouble(SkewY.Text) });
    group.Children.Add(new ScaleTransform { ScaleX = Convert.ToDouble(ScaleX.Text),
ScaleY = Convert.ToDouble(ScaleY.Text) });
    group.Children.Add(new RotateTransform { Angle =
Convert.ToDouble(RotateAngle.Text) });

    MainImage.RenderTransform = group;
}
```

Code Snippet TransformDemo\MainPage.xaml.cs

Finally, you added a button called Spin. In the `Click` event handler for this `Button` control, you added some interesting code that effectively rotates the image over and over again, around the top-left corner of the control. In that code, first, you created a new object called `DispatcherTimer`. In Silverlight for Windows Phone 7, this is the preferred way to create a `timer` object. `DispatcherTimer` offers a very simple way to have a task repeated on a timed basis. The first property you set is the `Interval` property:

```
timer.Interval = new TimeSpan(1000);
```

In this case, you created a new `TimeSpan` object of 1,000 milliseconds, or 1 second. You were therefore setting the `timer` object to fire every second so you could run custom code. You did this by utilizing the `Tick` event, like so:

```
timer.Tick += (se, ev) =>
{
    angle += 5;
    MainImage.RenderTransform = new RotateTransform { Angle = angle };
};
```

Here you used a relatively new feature of .NET that allows you to add event-handling code inline, without creating a new separate method. Sometimes it can be nice for debugging purposes to keep the event-handling code close to the actual event declaration; if you don't have a large amount of code required for the event handler, this shortcut can be useful. In this `Tick` event, you basically added 5 degrees to the current value of the class-level `angle` variable. Then you created a new `RotateTransform` object, using that angle, and applied it to the `Image` control.

Finally, you started the `timer` object by using the following line of code:

```
timer.Start();
```

The `Start` method then begins running the timer, and it continues every second forever. A good addition to this program would be to offer the user some way of stopping the rotation. You could do this by calling the `Stop` method of the `timer` variable. You could add a new `Button` control that handles this, or you could customize the `Spin Button` code to handle it based on whether the timer is currently running.

SUMMARY

You should now have a good understanding of most of the Silverlight techniques you can use when writing apps for Windows Phone 7. This chapter touched on some important concepts, such as shapes, colors, brushes, and transforms. You should be able to draw all sorts of shapes and fill them with solid-color and gradient backgrounds. You now know how easy it is to apply transform effects such as rotation, scaling, skewing, and even moving objects.

EXERCISES

1. True or False: Silverlight supports using HTML color codes to create a `SolidColorBrush` object in the code-behind file.

2. Which of the following are not valid `Shape` controls in Silverlight for Windows Phone 7? (Choose all that apply.)

    a)   `Triangle`

    b)   `Circle`

    c)   `Polyline`

    d)   `Polygon`

    e)   `Rectangle`

3. When you use the `TransformGroup` object, does the order in which transform effects are added matter?

4. What is the preferred method of repeating a task on a timed basis in Silverlight?

5. Which of the following are not valid transform effects in Silverlight? (Choose all that apply.)

    a)   `RotateTransform`

    b)   `TranslateTransform`

    c)   `SpinTransform`

    d)   `SkewTransform`

    e)   `SlideTransform`

    f)   `FadeTransform`

Answers to the Exercises can be found in the Appendix.

▶ WHAT YOU LEARNED IN THIS CHAPTER

TOPIC	KEY CONCEPTS
Shapes	Silverlight for Windows Phone 7 enables you to use several shape objects to draw various items on the screen. These include the `Line`, `Ellipse`, `Rectangle`, `Polyline`, `Polygon`, and `Path` controls.
Colors	When using colors in Silverlight, you have several options. You can easily set the color by using a text value, such as `Red`, `Blue`, `Green`, and so on in the XAML code, or you can use HTML color codes in XAML. However, things get a little more complicated in the code-behind file. You can't simply use the same text-based assignments in the code-behind file; instead, you need to use one of the basic `Color` objects in the `Colors` enumeration. Alternatively, you can use the `Color.FromARGB` method and supply separate alpha, red, green, and blue values. If you want to make use of HTML color codes, you need to generate your own custom conversion method to parse the color code string into separate red, green, and blue values.
Brushes	When creating backgrounds or fills for various controls and shapes, you have many options at your disposal. You can use one solid color with `SolidColorBrush`, or you can create complex backgrounds using gradients, with the `LinearGradientBrush` and the `RadialGradientBrush` objects. You aren't even limited to just colors in Silverlight when you develop Windows Phone 7 apps; you can even use images as backgrounds and fills by using `ImageBrush`.
Transforms	Silverlight provides several transform effects that you can use with very little code and no complicated algorithms. You can rotate, scale, skew, and move objects by using the `RotateTransform`, `SkewTransform`, `ScaleTransform`, and `TranslateTransform` objects. You can use more than one effect at a time by using the `TransformGroup` object.
Timers	When you need to create a repeatable task on a timed basis, you can use the `DispatcherTimer` object, which enables you to run custom code every time its `Tick` event is fired.

Advanced User Interface Techniques: Styles, Templates, and the Visual State Manager

WHAT YOU WILL LEARN IN THIS CHAPTER:

➤ Customizing controls with styles

➤ Understanding how Silverlight controls work by modifying control templates

➤ Creating rich control animations with the Visual State Manager

➤ Creating your own powerful custom controls for your Windows Phone 7 applications

It's time to take a more in-depth look at some powerful features of Silverlight that you can use to get even more control over how controls look and behave. By the end of this chapter, you should have a solid understanding of how the controls work behind the scenes, and you should be armed with enough information to customize the standard Silverlight controls.

You've seen that all Silverlight controls have some basic attributes and properties that control things such as background and foreground colors. Now you'll see how to set up control styles that you can apply to multiple instances of controls to drastically reduce the amount of XAML code required. Then you'll see how to use the control templates to make changes to the behavior of some of the standard controls. In many cases, this is an easier process than writing a custom control from scratch.

Next up is coverage of the Visual State Manager. This feature of Silverlight makes it simple to perform complex animations and change the way different control states act. For example, if you want to change the color of a Button control when the user presses it, you can modify the default states of the Button control to achieve the desired effect.

UNDERSTANDING CONTROL STYLES

If you've done any considerable amount of web development, especially using HTML, you've probably figured out the tremendous advantages of using CSS to control the look of various HTML elements in your website. CSS allows you to easily configure the various styles of controls, and its powerful cascading rules allow you to apply styles to multiple controls with minimal amounts of code. An additional benefit of CSS is that it allows you to separate the styles of the HTML elements from the HTML elements themselves. Although you can declare CSS style information inline next to the element to be affected, more often you put all the necessary style information in a separate file and include it at the top of the web page.

So far in this book, you've seen how to manipulate various Silverlight control styles by setting values for properties such as Background, BorderBrush, Margin, and Padding. All the work you've been doing has been inline and right next to the control being affected. In the following code, you can see how this would be a time-consuming task, especially with a set of Button controls that have similar style information:

```
<Button Margin="10,10,5,5" Padding="5" Background="Beige"
    Foreground="Black" Content="Click Me" />
<Button Margin="10,10,5,5" Padding="5" Background="Beige"
    Foreground="Black" Content="Click Me" />
<Button Margin="10,10,5,5" Padding="5" Background="Beige"
    Foreground="Black" Content="Click Me" />
<Button Margin="10,10,5,5" Padding="5" Background="Beige"
    Foreground="Black" Content="Click Me" />
<Button Margin="10,10,5,5" Padding="5" Background="Beige"
    Foreground="Black" Content="Click Me" />
<Button Margin="10,10,5,5" Padding="5" Background="Beige"
    Foreground="Black" Content="Click Me" />
```

Looking at the amount of similar code in each control's XAML declaration might make you wish that Silverlight would provide something similar to CSS to reduce the amount of work involved. In this example, there are six Button controls drawn on the screen. The only difference between them is in the Content property. You essentially have duplicate values for Margin, Padding, Background, and Foreground. This is just a simple example; imagine how this technique can quickly spiral out of control when applied throughout an entire application. And then consider what would happen if the client decided he wanted a blue button instead of a beige one. In this case, you would have to traverse every Button control in the entire application and make the change to the Background property. Not only would this be time-consuming (although you can make the argument that Find and Replace would help out), it is also error prone because even with Find and Replace, you need to make sure you're using the entire application as the scope of the search. Quite simply, it is easy to make a mistake if you try to globally change the color of all the Button controls. It also adds a tremendous amount of duplicate XAML code, and you want to avoid duplicate code if possible.

When you face a problem such as this, you can turn to control styles. By making use of controls styles, you can reduce the previous XAML code to the following:

```
<Button Style="{StaticResource ButtonStyle}" />
<Button Style="{StaticResource ButtonStyle}" />
<Button Style="{StaticResource ButtonStyle}" />
<Button Style="{StaticResource ButtonStyle}" />
<Button Style="{StaticResource ButtonStyle}" />
```

As you can see, this is a dramatically smaller amount of code. Let's take a look at how the control styling works in Silverlight. First, you need to pick out which properties are common to the controls you want to style. In the previous example, this includes the Margin, Padding, Background, Foreground, and Content properties. It is highly unlikely that in a real-world application you'd have the same Content properties for several Button controls, but in this simple case, that's what you have. Now the goal is to set up a style resource that can be shared across all of the Button controls. Style declarations in XAML are considered resources, and most controls have a Resource property that's capable of holding styles. Once styles are added to the resource property, they're available for any of the child controls. In this case, let's assume that you have a StackPanel control holding all these Button controls. To declare the style for the Button controls, you simply use the StackPanel.Resources attached property, as shown in the following example:

```
<StackPanel.Resources>
    <Style x:Key="ButtonStyle" TargetType="Button">
        <Setter Property="Margin" Value="10,10,5,5" />
        <Setter Property="Padding" Value="5" />
        <Setter Property="Background" Value="Beige" />
        <Setter Property="Foreground" Value="Black" />
        <Setter Property="Content" Value="Click Me" />
    </Style>
</StackPanel.Resources>
```

Going further into the code, you can see how a new Style object is declared with two attributes, x:Key and TargetType. The x:Key attribute is used to differentiate between several styles. TargetType tells the runtime for which type of control this style is valid. In this case, you're applying the style to Button controls — hence the Button TargetType. This is important because the properties set in the style must exist in the target control, or errors will occur. Setting TargetType to the right kind of control ensures that only valid properties are used in the style declaration. Moving forward after the Style object is declared, you see several Setter statements, like this one:

```
<Setter Property="Margin" Value="10,10,5,5" />
```

The syntax here is pretty straightforward. You simply set the Property attribute to the property on the control you wish to set, and you set the Value attribute to the value of that property. In this case, Margin, Padding, Background, Foreground, and Content all have Setter declarations. Finally, you tell the Button control itself which style to use, using the following syntax:

```
<Button Style="{StaticResource ButtonStyle}" />
```

Here you're telling the Silverlight runtime to look for a `Style` resource with the `x:Key` name `ButtonStyle`. Because the declaration of `ButtonStyle` exists in the immediate `StackPanel` parent, it is found, and the style is applied. In fact, as long as a style exists with the specified `x:Key` property in one of the parent objects of the control, the style will be applied successfully.

Application Styles

When you need to create styles that should be made available to controls throughout an application, you can use application-level style resources. This is not much different from what you just saw when placing the style object inside the `StackPanel.Resources` area. In fact, the declaration of the style object doesn't need to change at all — only its location does. In the previous example, you could make `ButtonStyle` visible to all `Button` controls in your application by simply placing that style in the `App.xaml` file, under the `Application.Resources` section:

```
<Application.Resources>
    <Style x:Key="ButtonStyle" TargetType="Button">
        <Setter Property="Margin" Value="10,10,5,5" />
        <Setter Property="Padding" Value="5" />
        <Setter Property="Background" Value="Beige" />
        <Setter Property="Foreground" Value="Black" />
        <Setter Property="Content" Value="Click Me" />
    </Style>
</Application.Resources>
```

The `Application.Resources` section is a great place to put style objects that you want to make available to controls throughout an application. When you do this, any `Button` object on any XAML page can easily access `ButtonStyle`, and any changes that are necessary can be made in one central location, under the `Application.Resources` section in the `App.xaml` file.

TRY IT OUT **Using Application Resources**

In this example, you will create control styles in the `App.xaml` file so that they can be shared between controls on multiple pages.

1. Create a new Windows Phone application, using the Windows Phone 7 application template, and name it **ApplicationStyles**.

2. After the project finishes loading, modify the `MainPage.xaml` file so that it looks like the code in Listing 4-1:

LISTING 4-1: MainPage.xaml

```
<phone:PhoneApplicationPage
    x:Class="ApplicationStyles.MainPage"
    xmlns="http://schemas.microsoft.com/winfx/2006/xaml/presentation"
```

```
    xmlns:x="http://schemas.microsoft.com/winfx/2006/xaml"
    xmlns:phone="clr-namespace:Microsoft.Phone.Controls;assembly=Microsoft.Phone"
    xmlns:shell="clr-namespace:Microsoft.Phone.Shell;assembly=Microsoft.Phone"
    xmlns:d="http://schemas.microsoft.com/expression/blend/2008"
    xmlns:mc="http://schemas.openxmlformats.org/markup-compatibility/2006"
    mc:Ignorable="d" d:DesignWidth="480" d:DesignHeight="768"
    FontFamily="{StaticResource PhoneFontFamilyNormal}"
    FontSize="{StaticResource PhoneFontSizeNormal}"
    Foreground="{StaticResource PhoneForegroundBrush}"
    SupportedOrientations="Portrait" Orientation="Portrait"
    shell:SystemTray.IsVisible="True">

    <!--LayoutRoot is the root grid where all page content is placed-->
    <Grid x:Name="LayoutRoot" Background="Transparent">
        <Grid.RowDefinitions>
            <RowDefinition Height="Auto"/>
            <RowDefinition Height="*"/>
        </Grid.RowDefinitions>

        <!--TitlePanel contains the name of the application and page title-->
        <StackPanel x:Name="TitlePanel" Grid.Row="0" Margin="12,17,0,28">
            <TextBlock x:Name="ApplicationTitle"
Text="Application Style Demo" Style="{StaticResource
PhoneTextNormalStyle}"/>
        </StackPanel>

        <!--ContentPanel - place additional content here-->
        <Grid x:Name="ContentPanel" Grid.Row="1" Margin="12,0,12,0">
            <StackPanel>
                <TextBlock Text="Email" />
                <TextBox x:Name="Email" />
                <TextBlock Text="Message" />
                <TextBox x:Name="Message" />
                <Button Content="Send Message" />
            </StackPanel>
        </Grid>
    </Grid>
</phone:PhoneApplicationPage>
```

Code Snippet ApplicationStyles\MainPage.xaml

3. You now have a standard looking data entry form, without style information or properties set on any of the controls. Right-click the top of the project and select Add New Item from the context menu. Choose Windows Phone Portrait Page and call it `AdditionalPage.xaml`, as shown in Figure 4-1.

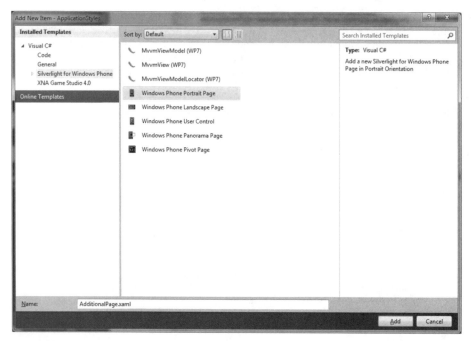

FIGURE 4-1: Adding a new page to a project.

4. Replace the code in the newly added page with the code shown here in Listing 4-2:

LISTING 4-2: AdditionalPage.xaml

```xml
<phone:PhoneApplicationPage
    x:Class="ApplicationStyles.AdditionalPage"
    xmlns="http://schemas.microsoft.com/winfx/2006/xaml/presentation"
    xmlns:x="http://schemas.microsoft.com/winfx/2006/xaml"
    xmlns:phone="clr-namespace:Microsoft.Phone.Controls;assembly=Microsoft.Phone"
    xmlns:shell="clr-namespace:Microsoft.Phone.Shell;assembly=Microsoft.Phone"
    xmlns:d="http://schemas.microsoft.com/expression/blend/2008"
    xmlns:mc="http://schemas.openxmlformats.org/markup-compatibility/2006"
    FontFamily="{StaticResource PhoneFontFamilyNormal}"
    FontSize="{StaticResource PhoneFontSizeNormal}"
    Foreground="{StaticResource PhoneForegroundBrush}"
    SupportedOrientations="Portrait" Orientation="Portrait"
    mc:Ignorable="d" d:DesignHeight="768" d:DesignWidth="480"
    shell:SystemTray.IsVisible="True">

    <!--LayoutRoot is the root grid where all page content is placed-->
    <Grid x:Name="LayoutRoot" Background="Transparent">
        <Grid.RowDefinitions>
            <RowDefinition Height="Auto"/>
```

```
                <RowDefinition Height="*"/>
        </Grid.RowDefinitions>

        <!--TitlePanel contains the name of the application and page title-->
        <StackPanel x:Name="TitlePanel" Grid.Row="0" Margin="12,17,0,28">
                <TextBlock x:Name="ApplicationTitle" Text="Application Style Demo"
    Style="{StaticResource PhoneTextNormalStyle}"/>
        </StackPanel>

        <!--ContentPanel - place additional content here-->
        <Grid x:Name="ContentPanel" Grid.Row="1" Margin="12,0,12,0">
            <StackPanel>
                <TextBlock Text="First Name" />
                <TextBox x:Name="FirstName" />
                <TextBlock Text="Last Name" />
                <TextBox x:Name="LastName" />
                <TextBlock Text="Address" />
                <TextBox x:Name="Address" />
                <TextBlock Text="Phone" />
                <TextBox x:Name="Phone" />
                <TextBlock Text="Email" />
                <TextBox x:Name="Email" />
                <Button Content="Add New Contact" />
            </StackPanel>
        </Grid>
    </Grid>
</phone:PhoneApplicationPage>
```

Code Snippet ApplicationStyles\AdditionalPage.xaml

Now you have multiple data entry screens for a potential contact management application. Because your client has changed his mind about various aspects of the user interface on several occasions, you decide not to place any style information directly in the XAML pages. This turns out to be a great decision because the client has just requested a slight margin around every control on the forms and that the company color of blue be used for all text rendered on the screen. In addition, the client prefers that any `TextBox` controls have a yellow background so that users know they are required fields. If you use application-level styles, this should not be a problem.

5. Open the `App.xaml` file and add the style declarations to handle the margin area for all of the controls. To do this, modify `App.xaml` to contain the code shown in Listing 4-3:

LISTING 4-3: App.xaml

```
<Application
    x:Class="ApplicationStyles.App"
    xmlns="http://schemas.microsoft.com/winfx/2006/xaml/presentation"
    xmlns:x="http://schemas.microsoft.com/winfx/2006/xaml"
    xmlns:phone="clr-namespace:Microsoft.Phone.Controls;assembly=Microsoft.Phone"
```

continues

LISTING 4-3 *(continued)*

```
        xmlns:shell="clr-namespace:Microsoft.Phone.Shell;assembly=Microsoft.Phone">

        <!--Application Resources-->
        <Application.Resources>
            <Style x:Key="TextBlockStyle" TargetType="TextBlock">
                <Setter Property="Foreground" Value="Blue" />
                <Setter Property="Margin" Value="5" />
            </Style>
            <Style x:Key="TextBoxStyle" TargetType="TextBox">
                <Setter Property="Margin" Value="5" />
                <Setter Property="Background" Value="Yellow" />
            </Style>
            <Style x:Key="ButtonStyle" TargetType="Button">
                <Setter Property="Margin" Value="5" />
            </Style>
        </Application.Resources>

        <Application.ApplicationLifetimeObjects>
            <!--Required object that handles lifetime events for the application-->
            <shell:PhoneApplicationService
Launching="Application_Launching" Closing="Application_Closing"
Activated="Application_Activated" Deactivated="Application_Deactivated"/>
        </Application.ApplicationLifetimeObjects>

</Application>
```

Code Snippet ApplicationStyles\App.xaml

6. To assign the styles to the individual controls, open `MainPage.xaml` and modify the code to look as follows:

Available for download on Wrox.com

```
<StackPanel>
    <TextBlock Text="Email" Style="{StaticResource TextBlockStyle}" />
    <TextBox x:Name="Email" Style="{StaticResource TextBoxStyle}" />
    <TextBlock Text="Message" Style="{StaticResource TextBlockStyle}" />
    <TextBox x:Name="Message" Style="{StaticResource TextBoxStyle}" />
    <Button Content="Send Message" Style="{StaticResource ButtonStyle}" />
</StackPanel>
```

Code Snippet ApplicationStyles\MainPage.xaml

7. Open `AdditionalPage.xaml` and make the same changes to the controls on that data entry form:

Available for download on Wrox.com

```
<StackPanel>
    <TextBlock Text="First Name" Style="{StaticResource TextBlockStyle}" />
    <TextBox x:Name="FirstName" Style="{StaticResource TextBoxStyle}" />
    <TextBlock Text="Last Name" Style="{StaticResource TextBlockStyle}" />
    <TextBox x:Name="LastName" Style="{StaticResource TextBoxStyle}" />
```

```
    <TextBlock Text="Address" Style="{StaticResource TextBlockStyle}" />
    <TextBox x:Name="Address" Style="{StaticResource TextBoxStyle}" />
    <TextBlock Text="Phone" Style="{StaticResource TextBlockStyle}" />
    <TextBox x:Name="Phone" Style="{StaticResource TextBoxStyle}" />
    <TextBlock Text="Email" Style="{StaticResource TextBlockStyle}" />
    <TextBox x:Name="Email" Style="{StaticResource TextBoxStyle}" />
    <Button Content="Add New Contact" Style="{StaticResource ButtonStyle}" />
</StackPanel>
```

Code Snippet ApplicationStyles\AdditionalPage.xaml

Now if you take a look in the Visual Studio 2010 Designer, you can see that all the controls correctly share their respective styles. You can now easily change the overall style of the TextBox, TextBlock, or Button controls if the client requests additional changes.

How It Works

Although this is a simple example, it should give you a good feel for how powerful application-level control styling can be. In this example, you had two data entry screens in the application, and the client wanted the TextBox, TextBlock, and Button controls to share a similar look and feel. You could have set the Margin, Background, and Foreground properties right in the individual control declarations, but with only two data entry pages, doing so would have required a lot of XAML code. This would become extremely complex with 10 or more data entry screens. Also, this particular client has a tendency to request changes often. Now, however, you can make any style changes by just making modifications to the following code in the App.xaml file:

```
<Application.Resources>
    <Style x:Key="TextBlockStyle" TargetType="TextBlock">
        <Setter Property="Foreground" Value="Blue" />
        <Setter Property="Margin" Value="5" />
    </Style>
    <Style x:Key="TextBoxStyle" TargetType="TextBox">
        <Setter Property="Margin" Value="5" />
        <Setter Property="Background" Value="Yellow" />
    </Style>
    <Style x:Key="ButtonStyle" TargetType="Button">
        <Setter Property="Margin" Value="5" />
    </Style>
</Application.Resources>
```

BasedOn Styles

In the previous Try It Out, you might have noticed that the Margin property being set for each of the controls had the same value. Even though the same value was used, you still needed to explicitly add a Setter object for the Margin property on all the control styles declared. Now in this simple example, it isn't too painful to do so, but it would be nice to have a slightly better way of doing this — a way more like using CSS. Well, the answer is to use `BasedOn` styling. The concept of `BasedOn` styles in Silverlight involves creating a generic style with some common property assignments and then creating an additional style that has some different properties. Finally, you tell the new style to be based on the original style. Let's apply this to the previous example to see how this works.

Say that you want the `Margin`, `Padding`, and `Width` properties of all `TextBox` controls on your data entry form to be identical. The `Background` and `Height` properties of the controls will differ. Typically, if you want to use styles, you create a new style declaration, like this:

```
<Style x:Key="TextBoxStyle" TargetType="TextBox">
    <Setter Property="Margin" Value="5" />
    <Setter Property="Padding" Value="2" />
    <Setter Property="Width" Value="200" />
</Style>
```

Then you have some `TextBox` control declarations such as the following that use the `TextBoxStyle`, and you set their individual `Background` and `Height` properties because they differ between controls:

```
<TextBox Background="Blue" Height="50" Style="{StaticResource TextBoxStyle}" />
<TextBox Background="White" Height="100" Style="{StaticResource TextBoxStyle}" />
<TextBox Background="Yellow" Height="200" Style="{StaticResource TextBoxStyle}" />
```

The limitation of using only one style is evident in this example. Although you can separate the common properties, you still have style information in the main XAML declarations of the individual controls. By using `BasedOn` styling, you can eliminate this even further. With `BasedOn` styles, you create your original `TextBoxStyle` like so:

```
<Style x:Key="TextBoxStyle" TargetType="TextBox">
    <Setter Property="Margin" Value="5" />
    <Setter Property="Padding" Value="2" />
    <Setter Property="Width" Value="200" />
</Style>
```

Then you create an additional style containing the `Background` and `Height` properties, but you tell Silverlight to base it on the original style so that the new style automatically inherits the styles being set in the original `TextBoxStyle` declaration. Here's the new `BasedOn` version:

```
<Style x:Key="BlueStyle" TargetType="TextBox" BasedOn="{StaticResource
TextBoxStyle}">
    <Setter Property="Background" Value="Blue" />
    <Setter Property="Height" Value="50" />
</Style>

<Style x:Key="WhiteStyle" TargetType="TextBox" BasedOn="{StaticResource
TextBoxStyle}">
    <Setter Property="Background" Value="White" />
    <Setter Property="Height" Value="100" />
```

```
    </Style>

    <Style x:Key="YellowStyle" TargetType="TextBox" BasedOn="{StaticResource
    TextBoxStyle}">
        <Setter Property="Background" Value="Yellow" />
        <Setter Property="Height" Value="200" />
    </Style>
```

You now have three additional `Style` declarations that will automatically share the same values for `Margin`, `Padding`, and `Width`. The only thing left to do is to update the `TextBox` controls:

```
    <TextBox Style="{StaticResource BlueStyle}" />
    <TextBox Style="{StaticResource WhiteStyle}" />
    <TextBox Style="{StaticResource YellowStyle}" />
```

Each of the `TextBox` controls will not only use the appropriate style for `Background` and `Height`, but it will also have the same `Margin`, `Padding`, and `Width` values. Any time you find yourself creating `Style` declarations for similar controls that share many of the same properties, you can probably create a base style to derive from and make use of the `BasedOn` styling feature in Silverlight to further reduce the amount of XAML code needed.

Control Templates

Now that you have a solid grasp of how to customize the look of the various Silverlight controls by modifying style information, it's time to see how to further customize the appearance of controls — and, in many cases, the behavior of those controls — by using control templates. In Chapter 2, you saw how easy it can be to customize the default look and feel of a `Button` control by overriding the `Content` property. In most circumstances, the `Content` property is set to a text string and displayed as is. However, in Chapter 2 you saw how to change that so the `Content` property actually contains an `Image` as opposed to just a text-based string. That is the easiest way to customize controls, but it's not the only way. In fact, by using control templates, you can create much more advanced scenarios.

The first key to understanding custom control templates is to realize that at its core, a control template is just another version of a style. For instance, in the simple image button example, you start by creating a new style for the `Button` control:

```
    <Style x:Key="ImageButton" TargetType="Button">
    </Style>
```

Next, you override the default control template for the `Button` control. You do so by adding a `Setter` object for the `Template` property, like this:

```
    <Style x:Key="ImageButton" TargetType="Button">
        <Setter Property="Template">
            <Setter.Value>

            </Setter.Value>
        </Setter>
    </Style>
```

Notice that `Value` is not being set on the same line as `Property`, as in previous examples. That is just another way to set the property of a `Style` object. When you have a case like this one, where `Value` will actually take up more than one line of code, you just close the `Setter` tag and add a `Setter.Value` tag below, where you can finish the property assignment. At this point, you can add any valid Silverlight object you want. That's right. You can put anything here, and it will automatically act and behave like a standard `Button` control. So for the `ImageButton` example, you add the following:

```
<Style x:Key="ImageButton" TargetType="Button">
    <Setter Property="Template">
        <Setter.Value>
            <ControlTemplate>
                <Image Source="/SilverlightControls;component/Images/wrox.jpg"
 />
            </ControlTemplate>
        </Setter.Value>
    </Setter>
</Style>
```

If you now add to the page a `Button` control that uses this style, the image will display and act like a `Button` control, with all the standard `Button` events. Figure 4-2 shows this feature in action.

What if you want to set the width and height of the underlying `Image` control? Obviously, the `Button` control exposes the `Width` and `Height` properties. But they apply only to the `Button` control itself. Now that you have complete control over the template and the underlying controls that make up the `Button` control, how can you make use of the various properties available to `Button` controls? To achieve this, you need to use a concept called *template binding*.

FIGURE 4-2: Using a custom button template.

Template binding gives you a way to access the current values of various properties of the control being customized. For example, if you want the `Image` control in the previous example to make use of the `Height` and `Width` properties of the `Button` control, you simply set the `Image` control's `Height` and `Width` properties the same as in the XAML for the `Button` control. You do this with the following code:

```
<Style x:Key="ImageButton" TargetType="Button">
    <Setter Property="Template">
        <Setter.Value>
            <ControlTemplate>
                <Image Width="{TemplateBinding Width}" Height="{TemplateBinding
Height}" Source="/SilverlightControls;component/Images/wrox.jpg" />
            </ControlTemplate>
        </Setter.Value>
    </Setter>
</Style>
```

Note how the TemplateBinding is used here to set both the Width and Height of the Image control. Now when you run the application, you'll see that the Image control takes up only the space specified in the Button declaration. Figure 4-3 shows this in action.

FIGURE 4-3: Template binding for height and width.

You can use the TemplateBinding syntax for any of the existing Button properties. For example, to create a Button control that includes both the Image and TextBlock controls that used the existing Content property of the Button control, you could use XAML code like the following:

```
<Style x:Key="ImageButton" TargetType="Button">
    <Setter Property="Template">
        <Setter.Value>
            <ControlTemplate>
                    <StackPanel Height="{TemplateBinding Height}"
Width="{TemplateBinding Width}">
                        <Image Height="100" Width="100"
Source="/SilverlightControls;component/Images/wrox.jpg" />
                        <TextBlock Text="{TemplateBinding Content}" />
                    </StackPanel>
            </ControlTemplate>
        </Setter.Value>
    </Setter>
</Style>
```

Now you just add a `Button` control and set the `Content` property along with the `Height` and `Width` properties:

```
<Button Width="200" Height="200" Content="This is an image button"
Style="{StaticResource ImageButton}" />
```

When you run this example, it displays both the `Image` control and the `TextBlock` control, using the text set in the `Content` property of the `Button` control. Notice in Figure 4-4 that the entire area including both the `Image` and `TextBlock` controls is now clickable and works just like a standard `Button` control.

FIGURE 4-4: Template binding with a text block.

As you can imagine, using template binding along with the control templates opens up new possibilities for changing the default behavior of various Silverlight controls. Next, you'll try a slightly more complex example.

TRY IT OUT   Using Control Templates

In this example, you will use control templates to create a custom `Button` style.

1. Create a new Windows Phone 7 project in Visual Studio 2010 and call it **ControlTemplate**.

2. Open the `MainPage.xaml` file and replace the existing code with Listing 4-4:

LISTING 4-4: MainPage.xaml

```
<phone:PhoneApplicationPage
    x:Class="ControlTemplate.MainPage"
    xmlns="http://schemas.microsoft.com/winfx/2006/xaml/presentation"
    xmlns:x="http://schemas.microsoft.com/winfx/2006/xaml"
```

```
xmlns:phone="clr-namespace:Microsoft.Phone.Controls;assembly=Microsoft.Phone"
xmlns:shell="clr-namespace:Microsoft.Phone.Shell;assembly=Microsoft.Phone"
xmlns:d="http://schemas.microsoft.com/expression/blend/2008"
xmlns:mc="http://schemas.openxmlformats.org/markup-compatibility/2006"
mc:Ignorable="d" d:DesignWidth="480" d:DesignHeight="768"
FontFamily="{StaticResource PhoneFontFamilyNormal}"
FontSize="{StaticResource PhoneFontSizeNormal}"
Foreground="{StaticResource PhoneForegroundBrush}"
SupportedOrientations="Portrait" Orientation="Portrait"
shell:SystemTray.IsVisible="True">

    <!--LayoutRoot is the root grid where all page content is placed-->
    <Grid x:Name="LayoutRoot" Background="Transparent">
        <Grid.RowDefinitions>
            <RowDefinition Height="Auto"/>
            <RowDefinition Height="*"/>
        </Grid.RowDefinitions>

        <!--TitlePanel contains the name of the application and page title-->
        <StackPanel x:Name="TitlePanel" Grid.Row="0" Margin="12,17,0,28">
            <TextBlock x:Name="ApplicationTitle" Text="Control Template App"
Style="{StaticResource PhoneTextNormalStyle}"/>
        </StackPanel>

        <!--ContentPanel - place additional content here-->
        <Grid x:Name="ContentPanel" Grid.Row="1" Margin="12,0,12,0">
            <StackPanel>
                <Button x:Name="CustomButton" Content="Custom Styled Button"
Margin="10" Width="350" Height="350" BorderBrush="White"
BorderThickness="5"
Style="{StaticResource CustomButtonStyle}" />
                <Button x:Name="StandardButton"
Content="Standard Button" Margin="10" />
            </StackPanel>
        </Grid>
    </Grid>
</phone:PhoneApplicationPage>
```

Code Snippet ControlTemplate\MainPage.xaml

At this point, you have a couple of Button controls on the page. The first control uses a custom Button template, and the second just uses the standard Windows Phone 7 Button template.

3. Open the App.xaml file and replace its contents with the code shown in Listing 4-5, which contains the custom Button template.

LISTING 4-5: App.xaml

```
<Application
    x:Class="ControlTemplate.App"
    xmlns="http://schemas.microsoft.com/winfx/2006/xaml/presentation"
```

continues

LISTING 4-5 *(continued)*

```
    xmlns:x="http://schemas.microsoft.com/winfx/2006/xaml"
    xmlns:phone="clr-namespace:Microsoft.Phone.Controls;assembly=Microsoft.Phone"
    xmlns:shell="clr-namespace:Microsoft.Phone.Shell;assembly=Microsoft.Phone">

    <!--Application Resources-->
    <Application.Resources>
        <Style x:Key="CustomButtonStyle" TargetType="Button">
            <Setter Property="Template">
                <Setter.Value>
                    <ControlTemplate>
                        <Border Width="{TemplateBinding Width}"
Height="{TemplateBinding Height}" BorderBrush="{TemplateBinding
BorderBrush}" BorderThickness="{TemplateBinding BorderThickness}">
                            <StackPanel>
                                <Image Source="Images/wrox.png" Width="200"
Height="300" />
                                <TextBlock Text="{TemplateBinding Content}"
TextAlignment="Center" />
                            </StackPanel>
                        </Border>
                    </ControlTemplate>
                </Setter.Value>
            </Setter>
        </Style>
    </Application.Resources>

    <Application.ApplicationLifetimeObjects>
    <!--Required object that handles lifetime events for the application-->
        <shell:PhoneApplicationService
Launching="Application_Launching" Closing="Application_Closing"
Activated="Application_Activated" Deactivated="Application_Deactivated"/>
    </Application.ApplicationLifetimeObjects>

</Application>
```

Code Snippet ControlTemplate\App.xaml

4. Now with the template and Button controls declared, add some code-behind to prove that no matter what controls are included in the template, you still get all of the basic functionality of a standard Button control. To do this, open the MainPage.xaml.cs file and add the code shown in Listing 4-6 that contains Click event handlers for both the custom and standard Button controls:

LISTING 4-6: MainPage.xaml.cs

```
using System;
using System.Collections.Generic;
using System.Linq;
```

```
using System.Net;
using System.Windows;
using System.Windows.Controls;
using System.Windows.Documents;
using System.Windows.Input;
using System.Windows.Media;
using System.Windows.Media.Animation;
using System.Windows.Shapes;
using Microsoft.Phone.Controls;

namespace ControlTemplate
{
    public partial class MainPage : PhoneApplicationPage
    {
        // Constructor
        public MainPage()
        {
            InitializeComponent();
            this.Loaded += (s,e) =>
            {
                CustomButton.Click +=
new RoutedEventHandler(CustomButton_Click);
                StandardButton.Click +=
new RoutedEventHandler(StandardButton_Click);
};

        }

            private void StandardButton_Click(object sender, RoutedEventArgs e)
            {
                MessageBox.Show("Standard Button Clicked");
            }

            private void CustomButton_Click(object sender, RoutedEventArgs e)
            {
                MessageBox.Show("Custom Button Clicked");
            }
        }
    }
}
```

Code Snippet ControlTemplate\MainPage.xaml.cs

5. Build and run the application at this point. You should see the screen shown in Figure 4-5.

6. Click each of the Button controls. You should see the MessageBox control shown in Figure 4-6. Notice that both the standard and custom Button controls fire the Click event, even though your custom control template was created from scratch with StackPanel, Image, and TextBlock controls.

FIGURE 4-5: Custom and standard button controls.

FIGURE 4-6: A custom button being clicked.

How It Works

In this example, you created an application with two `Button` controls. One `Button` control uses a custom control template, and the other uses the standard Windows Phone 7 `Button` template. To create the template, you added a new `Style` object to the `App.xaml` file and added a `Setter` for the `Template` property. You also defined a custom control template from scratch. In this case, you created a `Button` control that was actually a combination of an image and text sitting below the image. So the user knows where to touch, you wrapped everything up in a `Border` control.

To prove that the custom control template still contains all the behaviors of a standard `Button` template, you added a `Click` event handler for both `Button` controls and just displayed a simple `MessageBox` control on the screen. As you can see, even though your new `Button` template doesn't look like the standard version, you can still touch or click the area associated with your custom control template and generate a `Click` event.

You should see the value of creating custom control templates. It basically enables you to completely change the way standard controls look and feel without losing the default methods and events associated with a control. In this case, you added simple `Image` and `TextBlock` controls, but you could just as easily have added a `Shape` control such as a `Polygon`, a `RadioButton`, `ComboBox`, or any of the other Silverlight controls. The control template mechanism is completely flexible and allows you to easily use existing `Button` property values by using the `TemplateBinding` syntax. In this example, you used `TemplateBinding` to set the `Text` property of the `TextBlock` control. This way, the text that is added to the `Content` property of the `Button` declaration will be displayed in the `TextBlock` control.

COMMON MISTAKES *Be warned that the* Text *property of the* TextBlock *control expects a string object. Using* TemplateBinding *doesn't give you automatic type checking, and the* Content *property of the* Button *control will accept just about any Silverlight control, including a string. If a user puts, for example, an* Image *control in the* Content *property, the application would crash because this is not a valid string for the* Text *property of the* TextBlock *control.* TemplateBinding *is flexible, but you need to use caution when property types might not completely match up.*

The Visual State Manager

Along with the capability to control the look and feel of controls with custom control templates, Silverlight also gives you the capability to manipulate the various states of the controls. The Visual State Manager is a feature in Silverlight that helps you customize the different styles that are applied to controls when they are pressed, have focus, are disabled, and are in other control states. For example, with the Button control, you can modify the control template for when the Button control is sitting idle on the page and when it is being pressed by the user, and you can even change the template that is used when the control is disabled, has focus, or loses focus.

NOTE *In addition to providing you with a mechanism to alter the control template for the various control states, the Visual State Manager also gives you a great way to create animations in your application.*

To get started, it helps to see some XAML code that shows off some control states and then break down the various pieces that are related to the Visual State Manager. The following is the default control template for a Button control in Silverlight for Windows Phone 7:

```
<ControlTemplate TargetType="Button">
    <Grid Background="Transparent">
        <VisualStateManager.VisualStateGroups>
            <VisualStateGroup x:Name="CommonStates">
                <VisualState x:Name="Normal"/>
                <VisualState x:Name="MouseOver"/>
                <VisualState x:Name="Pressed">
                    <Storyboard>
                        <ObjectAnimationUsingKeyFrames
Storyboard.TargetProperty="Foreground"
Storyboard.TargetName="ContentContainer">
                            <DiscreteObjectKeyFrame KeyTime="0"
```

```xml
                                      Value="{StaticResource PhoneBackgroundBrush}"/>
                                          </ObjectAnimationUsingKeyFrames>
                                          <ObjectAnimationUsingKeyFrames
Storyboard.TargetProperty="Background"
Storyboard.TargetName="ButtonBackground">
                                              <DiscreteObjectKeyFrame KeyTime="0"
Value="{StaticResource PhoneForegroundBrush}"/>
                                          </ObjectAnimationUsingKeyFrames>
                                          <ObjectAnimationUsingKeyFrames
Storyboard.TargetProperty="BorderBrush"
Storyboard.TargetName="ButtonBackground">
                                              <DiscreteObjectKeyFrame KeyTime="0"
Value="{StaticResource PhoneForegroundBrush}"/>
                                          </ObjectAnimationUsingKeyFrames>
                                  </Storyboard>
                          </VisualState>
                          <VisualState x:Name="Disabled">
                                  <Storyboard>
                                          <ObjectAnimationUsingKeyFrames
Storyboard.TargetProperty="Foreground"
Storyboard.TargetName="ContentContainer">
                                              <DiscreteObjectKeyFrame KeyTime="0"
Value="{StaticResource PhoneDisabledBrush}"/>
                                          </ObjectAnimationUsingKeyFrames>
                                          <ObjectAnimationUsingKeyFrames
Storyboard.TargetProperty="BorderBrush"
Storyboard.TargetName="ButtonBackground">
                                              <DiscreteObjectKeyFrame KeyTime="0"
Value="{StaticResource PhoneDisabledBrush}"/>
                                          </ObjectAnimationUsingKeyFrames>
                                          <ObjectAnimationUsingKeyFrames
Storyboard.TargetProperty="Background"
Storyboard.TargetName="ButtonBackground">
                                              <DiscreteObjectKeyFrame KeyTime="0"
Value="Transparent"/>
                                          </ObjectAnimationUsingKeyFrames>
                                  </Storyboard>
                          </VisualState>
                      </VisualStateGroup>
                  </VisualStateManager.VisualStateGroups>
                  <Border x:Name="ButtonBackground" BorderBrush="{TemplateBinding
BorderBrush}" BorderThickness="{TemplateBinding BorderThickness}"
Background="{TemplateBinding Background}" CornerRadius="0" Margin="{StaticResource
PhoneTouchTargetOverhang}">
                      <ContentControl x:Name="ContentContainer"
ContentTemplate="{TemplateBinding ContentTemplate}"
Content="{TemplateBinding Content}"
Foreground="{TemplateBinding Foreground}"
HorizontalContentAlignment="{TemplateBinding
HorizontalContentAlignment}" Padding="{TemplateBinding Padding}"
VerticalContentAlignment="{TemplateBinding VerticalContentAlignment}"/>
                  </Border>
          </Grid>
</ControlTemplate>
```

Notice the immediate reference to the Visual State Manager and the declaration of `VisualStateGroup` objects. When you're creating a custom control template or modifying an existing template, you have the ability to group `VisualState` objects. This allows you to place several related control states into a group. In this case, the `Normal`, `MouseOver`, `Pressed`, and `Disabled` states are included in a group called `CommonStates`:

```
<VisualStateGroup x:Name="CommonStates">
    <VisualState x:Name="Normal"/>
    <VisualState x:Name="MouseOver"/>
    <VisualState x:Name="Pressed">
    <VisualState x:Name="Disabled">
</VisualStateGroup>
```

The main reason for creating `VisualStateGroup` objects and placing individual states in a group is that the runtime is capable of handling more than one control state at a time. However, only one state from each group can be active at any given time. This means that for a `Button` control, the runtime will allow the `Button` to be in the `Pressed` state and display any styles or animations related to that state. It also allows another group, such as a `focused` state, because a `Button` control could be in the `Pressed` and `Focused` states at the same time. It is important to group any `VisualState` objects in a way that makes sense.

The `VisualState` object gives you a way to change the current style of a control dynamically, based on the state of that control. In the previous example, you created a `Button` control using a custom template that displayed an `Image` control and a `TextBlock` control. There were no `VisualState` objects declared for that control, so by default that custom `Button` control is always in the `Normal` state. You can, however, create a visual state for the `Pressed` state, and when the `Button` is pressed, you can change the opacity of the image, rotate it, or perform some other effect or animation.

All `VisualState` objects must be named using the `x:Name` syntax and you can create your own `VisualState` names. You're not limited to only `Normal`, `MouseOver`, `Pressed`, and `Disabled`. You therefore have flexibility, especially when you're creating your own custom controls, which you'll do later in this chapter.

Each `VisualState` object includes a `StoryBoard` object that will hold any animations or changes to the current control template. The first state that has a `StoryBoard` object is the `Pressed` state, which is triggered when the user touches the `Button` control on the screen. Here's the code for the `Pressed` state:

```
<VisualState x:Name="Pressed">
    <Storyboard>
        <ObjectAnimationUsingKeyFrames Storyboard.TargetProperty="Foreground"
Storyboard.TargetName="ContentContainer">
            <DiscreteObjectKeyFrame KeyTime="0" Value="{StaticResource
PhoneBackgroundBrush}"/>
        </ObjectAnimationUsingKeyFrames>
        <ObjectAnimationUsingKeyFrames Storyboard.TargetProperty="Background"
Storyboard.TargetName="ButtonBackground">
            <DiscreteObjectKeyFrame KeyTime="0" Value="{StaticResource
```

```
PhoneForegroundBrush}"/>
        </ObjectAnimationUsingKeyFrames>
        <ObjectAnimationUsingKeyFrames Storyboard.TargetProperty="BorderBrush"
Storyboard.TargetName="ButtonBackground">
            <DiscreteObjectKeyFrame KeyTime="0" Value="{StaticResource
PhoneForegroundBrush}"/>
        </ObjectAnimationUsingKeyFrames>
    </Storyboard>
</VisualState>
```

Let's break down each piece of this control state. First, there is a declaration of the required `Storyboard` object that holds any animations and effects that need to be applied to the `Button` control. Next is an `ObjectAnimationUsingKeyFrames` object. The goal of this object is to perform animation on a target object over a set of keyframes. This sounds much more complicated than it actually is. Basically, any animation will be performed over a set of keyframes and a total duration. The duration can be set to zero, which essentially makes the animation happen instantaneously. In this example, the animation targets the `Foreground` property of a control called `ContentContainer`. `ObjectAnimationUsingKeyFrames` declarations in XAML should always set the attached `Storyboard.TargetProperty` and `Storyboard.TargetName` properties. In this case, the goal of animation is to modify the `Foreground` property of the underlying `ContentControl` for the `Button` control. This is done using a `DiscreteObjectKeyFrame` object.

The `DiscreteKeyFrame` object has a `KeyTime` property that can be used to control at what point in the overall duration the change should take place, as well as a `Value` property that is the actual value to set. In this instance, `PhoneBackgroundBrush` is set against `ContentControl` at a `KeyTime` of zero or as soon as the user actually touches the `Button` control.

Next, another `ObjectAnimationUsingKeyFrames` is declared, and it causes another instant change to the `Button` style when pressed. This declaration again uses `DiscreteObjectKeyFrame` to change the `Background` property of the `Button` control to the `PhoneForegroundBrush` resource. Finally, one last `ObjectAnimationUsingKeyFrames` is used to change the `BorderBrush` property of the underlying `Border` control to `PhoneForegroundBrush`.

This is a lot of material to take in, but it gives you a quick look into what a full-blown control state might look like for one of the standard Silverlight for Windows Phone 7 controls. Here's a summary of what goes into the `Pressed` state:

➤ `Storyboard` is created to hold any animations.

➤ `ObjectAnimationUsingKeyFrames` objects are declared to hold potential keyframes and changes to make to the underlying style of the control.

➤ `DiscreteObjectKeyFrame` objects are used to control exactly when the change will occur and what the value of the target property should be upon completion of the animation.

A quick look through some of the other `Button` control states shows that this same basic technique is repeated to provide smooth animations for the various `Button` control states, such as `Disabled`. Perhaps the best part of all of this is that ultimately, for your own controls and customizations, you can simply create or modify existing control states, and the Visual State Manager will take care of all the hard work of transitioning between the various states and applying the necessary effects. Let's see if you can use the Visual State Manager to apply some transition effects in the existing custom control that you created in the earlier example. This can give you a better feel for how the feature works.

TRY IT OUT Using the Visual State Manager

In this example, you will see how to use the Visual State Manager feature of Silverlight in order to create custom state transitions.

1. Create a new Windows Phone 7 application in Visual Studio 2010 using the standard project template. Call this project **VisualStates**.

2. Open the App.xaml page and add the code shown in Listing 4-7 to form the basis of the custom control template created earlier:

Available for download on Wrox.com

LISTING 4-7: App.xaml

```
<Application
    x:Class="VisualStates.App"
    xmlns="http://schemas.microsoft.com/winfx/2006/xaml/presentation"
    xmlns:x="http://schemas.microsoft.com/winfx/2006/xaml"
    xmlns:phone="clr-namespace:Microsoft.Phone.Controls;assembly=Microsoft.Phone"
    xmlns:shell="clr-namespace:Microsoft.Phone.Shell;assembly=Microsoft.Phone">

    <!--Application Resources-->
    <Application.Resources>
        <Style x:Key="CustomButtonStyle" TargetType="Button">
            <Setter Property="Template">
                <Setter.Value>
                    <ControlTemplate>
                        <Border Width="{TemplateBinding Width}"
Height="{TemplateBinding Height}" BorderBrush="{TemplateBinding BorderBrush}"
BorderThickness="{TemplateBinding BorderThickness}">
                            <StackPanel>
                                <Image Source="Images/wrox.png" Width="200"
Height="300" />
                                <TextBlock Text="{TemplateBinding Content}"
TextAlignment="Center" />
                            </StackPanel>
                        </Border>
                    </ControlTemplate>
                </Setter.Value>
            </Setter>
        </Style>
    </Application.Resources>

    <Application.ApplicationLifetimeObjects>
        <!--Required object that handles lifetime events for the application-->
```

continues

```
            <shell:PhoneApplicationService
Launching="Application_Launching" Closing="Application_Closing"
Activated="Application_Activated" Deactivated="Application_Deactivated"/>
        </Application.ApplicationLifetimeObjects>
</Application>
```

Code Snippet VisualStates\App.xaml

3.   Now open `MainPage.xaml` and add the code shown in Listing 4-8, which includes a `Button` control that will use this style:

LISTING 4-8: MainPage.xaml

```
<phone:PhoneApplicationPage
    x:Class="VisualStates.MainPage"
    xmlns="http://schemas.microsoft.com/winfx/2006/xaml/presentation"
    xmlns:x="http://schemas.microsoft.com/winfx/2006/xaml"
    xmlns:phone="clr-namespace:Microsoft.Phone.Controls;assembly=Microsoft.Phone"
    xmlns:shell="clr-namespace:Microsoft.Phone.Shell;assembly=Microsoft.Phone"
    xmlns:d="http://schemas.microsoft.com/expression/blend/2008"
    xmlns:mc="http://schemas.openxmlformats.org/markup-compatibility/2006"
    mc:Ignorable="d" d:DesignWidth="480" d:DesignHeight="768"
    FontFamily="{StaticResource PhoneFontFamilyNormal}"
    FontSize="{StaticResource PhoneFontSizeNormal}"
    Foreground="{StaticResource PhoneForegroundBrush}"
    SupportedOrientations="Portrait" Orientation="Portrait"
    shell:SystemTray.IsVisible="True">

    <!--LayoutRoot is the root grid where all page content is placed-->
    <Grid x:Name="LayoutRoot" Background="Transparent">
        <Grid.RowDefinitions>
            <RowDefinition Height="Auto"/>
            <RowDefinition Height="*"/>
        </Grid.RowDefinitions>

        <!--TitlePanel contains the name of the application and page title-->
        <StackPanel x:Name="TitlePanel" Grid.Row="0" Margin="12,17,0,28">
            <TextBlock x:Name="ApplicationTitle" Text="Visual States App"
Style="{StaticResource PhoneTextNormalStyle}"/>
        </StackPanel>

        <!--ContentPanel - place additional content here-->
        <Grid x:Name="ContentPanel" Grid.Row="1" Margin="12,0,12,0">
            <Button x:Name="CustomButton" Width="250" Height="350"
Content="Custom Button" Style="{StaticResource CustomButtonStyle}" />
        </Grid>
    </Grid>
</phone:PhoneApplicationPage>
```

Code Snippet VisualStates\MainPage.xaml

4. Build and run the application. While the app is running, click the new custom `Button` control and see how there is no visual reference to the fact that a click/touch took place.

5. Decide what type of states this particular control should have. Obviously, because you want this control to behave as much like a standard `Button` control as possible, you should copy the main states that you saw in the standard `Button` template: `Normal`, `Pressed`, and `Disabled`. If you can create styles for these three major `Button` states, you should be able to give the user decent visual feedback that something has happened.

6. Add a `VisualStateGroup` object and declare these states by adding the following code to the existing `Button` style in `App.xaml`:

Available for download on Wrox.com

```
<ControlTemplate>
    <Grid>
        <VisualStateManager.VisualStateGroups>
            <VisualStateGroup x:Name="CommonButtonStates">
                <VisualState x:Name="Normal" />
                <VisualState x:Name="Pressed" />
                <VisualState x:Name="Disabled" />
            </VisualStateGroup>
        </VisualStateManager.VisualStateGroups>
        <Border x:Name="MainBorder" Width="{TemplateBinding Width}"
Height="{TemplateBinding Height}"
BorderBrush="{TemplateBinding BorderBrush}"
            <StackPanel>
                <Image x:Name="MainImage" Source="Images/wrox.png" Width="200"
Height="300" />
                <TextBlock x:Name="MainText" Text="{TemplateBinding Content}"
TextAlignment="Center" />
            </StackPanel>
        </Border>
    </Grid>
</ControlTemplate>
```

Code Snippet VisualStates\App.xaml

> **COMMON MISTAKES** *An important thing to note about this code is that you cannot simply add the* `VisualStateManager.VisualStateGroup` *declaration directly under the* `ControlTemplate` *tag.* `VisualStateManager` *is an attached property that's available to Silverlight controls only. The* `ControlTemplate` *tag defines the area where the custom style is going to be declared, but it doesn't interact at all with* `VisualStateManager`*. To create the control state groups, you need to attach* `VisualStateManager` *to a container. In this case, you added a simple* `Grid` *control as a wrapper around the main controls in the template. The* `Grid` *control won't affect the overall look and feel of the template, and it will automatically size itself according to the child controls, so* `Grid` *makes a perfect candidate to house the state groups.*

7. Decide what kind of effect you want to apply for the various states. The Normal state will look like the Button control when the control is just sitting there on a page and not being interacted with. This is the default state and in this case should just be left alone. The Pressed state is where you want to start your customization. Change the color of the Border control and make the Image and TextBlock controls slightly transparent when the user touches or clicks the Button control.

8. Change the color of the Border control by adding the following code to the Pressed state:

```xml
<VisualState x:Name="Pressed">
    <Storyboard>
        <ObjectAnimationUsingKeyFrames Duration="0"
Storyboard.TargetName="MainBorder"
Storyboard.TargetProperty="BorderBrush">
            <DiscreteObjectKeyFrame KeyTime="0" Value="Red" />
        </ObjectAnimationUsingKeyFrames>
    </Storyboard>
</VisualState>
```

Code Snippet VisualStates\App.xaml

9. Build and run the application and click the Button control in the emulator. You should see the color of the border change when the Button control is clicked. The change in border color is nice, but it seems like the Visual State Manager could do better. What if the change from white to red happened a little more smoothly, under an animation? In this case, you need to use another animation object available in Silverlight: a ColorAnimation object. Replace the existing VisualState code with the following:

```xml
<VisualState x:Name="Pressed">
    <Storyboard>
        <ColorAnimation Storyboard.TargetName="MainBorder"
Storyboard.TargetProperty="Border.BorderBrush.SolidColorBrush.Color" To="Red"
Duration="0:0:1" />
    </Storyboard>
  </VisualState>
```

Code Snippet VisualStates\App.xaml

Using the DoubleAnimation object is an easy way to animate a property represented by a double type. Opacity is always a double value type, so it makes a perfect candidate for the DoubleAnimation object.

10. Add the following code to the current VisualState object:

```xml
<VisualState x:Name="Pressed">
    <Storyboard>
        <ColorAnimation Storyboard.TargetName="MainBorder"
Storyboard.TargetProperty="Border.BorderBrush.SolidColorBrush.Color" To="Red"
Duration="0:0:1" />
        <DoubleAnimation Storyboard.TargetName="MainImage"
```

```
Storyboard.TargetProperty="Opacity" To=".5" Duration="0:0:1" />
        <DoubleAnimation Storyboard.TargetName="MainText"
Storyboard.TargetProperty="Opacity" To=".5" Duration="0:0:1" />
    </Storyboard>
</VisualState>
```

Code Snippet VisualStates\App.xaml

As you can see, the `DoubleAnimation` object is similar to `ColorAnimation` in that it takes the `TargetName` and `TargetProperty`, as well as the final value of what the object should be set to. Because you don't want to completely hide the controls but just fade them away a little bit, you set the `To` property to `0.5`. A fully visible `Opacity` value is always `1.0`.

11. Build and run the application now and see for yourself the smooth transition to a red `Border` control as well as the gradual fading of the `Image` and `TextBlock` controls.

12. Hide the `Image` and `TextBlock` controls and change the underlying `Background` so it looks like a typical disabled control. Once again, this should be no problem for the Visual State Manager. Simply add a new `Storyboard` to the `Disabled` state and enter the following code:

Available for
download on
Wrox.com

```
<VisualState x:Name="Disabled">
    <Storyboard>
        <DoubleAnimation Storyboard.TargetName="MainImage"
Storyboard.TargetProperty="Opacity" To=".1"
Duration="0" />
        <DoubleAnimation Storyboard.TargetName="MainText"
Storyboard.TargetProperty="Opacity" To=".1"
Duration="0" />
        <ColorAnimation Storyboard.TargetName="MainPanel"
Storyboard.TargetProperty=
"StackPanel.Background.SolidColorBrush.Color"
To="DarkGray" Duration="0" />
    </Storyboard>
</VisualState>
```

Code Snippet VisualStates\App.xaml

Because the `Button` control should be disabled, you want the `Image` and `TextBlock` controls to be barely visible. Therefore, you have to soothe the `Opacity` of these `DoubleAnimation` objects to `.1`. You also need to change the current `Background` of the `StackPanel` control to something that will make it obvious that this control cannot be used; `DarkGray` should get the point across.

13. To test this new state, modify the current `Button` declaration so that it looks like the following:

Available for
download on
Wrox.com

```
<Button x:Name="CustomButton" IsEnabled="False" Width="250" Height="350"
Content="Custom Button"
Style="{StaticResource CustomButtonStyle}" />
```

Code Snippet VisualStates\App.xaml

14. Build and run the app and notice the difference in the look of the control now that is in the `Disabled` state. Your control should now look similar to the one shown in Figure 4-7.

How It Works

In this example, the goal was to produce a custom `Button` control style that has various animation effects applied. You first created a new `VisualStateGroup` object to hold the various states of the control. Because you were building on a control you created previously, you wanted the custom button to give some visual feedback to the user when it was touched. This required adding states for `Pressed` and `Disabled`.

Although there are many different ways to perform the animations in the `Pressed` state, the easiest way to accomplish the desired effect in this example was to make use of the `ColorAnimation` and `DoubleAnimation` objects. Using the `ColorAnimation` object is an easy way to animate the color of the `Border` control that houses both the `Image` and `TextBlock` controls. You saw how to use the `Duration` property to create a smooth transition from a `White BorderBrush` setting to `Red`. In addition, it is easy to fade the `Image` and `TextBlock` controls by lowering the `Opacity` level with the `DoubleAnimation` object.

FIGURE 4-7: The disabled state for a custom button template.

Using the `DoubleAnimation` object is an easy way to change a property that uses a `double` type and does it under a smooth animation. In this case, you wanted both of the controls to fade a little bit and do so over the course of about a second. In a real-world version of this example, you probably shouldn't drag the `Pressed` state out that long, but setting `Duration` to one second allows you to easily see the transition in this example.

Next, you added code to handle the `Disabled` state. Most `Button` controls that are in the `Disabled` state provide some visual feedback to the user making it obvious that the `Button` control can't be clicked. Once again, you used `ColorAnimation` and `DoubleAnimation` objects to fade the control as well as make the traditional disabled control background color stand out. The only difference is that the animation in this case isn't done gradually over the course of one second because you don't want to give the impression that there is a window of time in which the `Button` control can be pressed. Instead, the animation is set to go off instantaneously when the control appears on the screen.

Finally, you might wonder how the Visual State Manager knows that the `Disabled` state should be triggered based on the `IsEnabled` property of the `Button` control. This is done behind the scenes when the `IsEnabled` property changes. An event handler is created to handle when the property changes, and the underlying source code determines which visual state to switch to based on the current value. The switching of states is done by a static helper method in the `VisualStates` class called `GoToState`. You will see more about this helper method soon, when you start creating your own custom Silverlight control.

Expression Blend

Before moving on to the discussion about how to create a custom control from scratch, you should first note that although you can make use of the VisualStateManager and the various animations and VisualState objects using Visual Studio 2010 Express, more often you'll find the job much easier using the new Expression Blend product. Expression Blend was built from the ground up to handle things like the Visual State Manager and associated animations much more easily than Visual Studio. Although it can sometimes be misconstrued as a designer-only piece of software, you as a developer should become familiar with it because you can use it to streamline some jobs that would take hundreds of manual lines of XAML code in Visual Studio. Later on in the book, you'll see some of the power of Expression Blend and how much easier it is to produce rich animations and control templates and states by using it.

User Controls

Now it's time to take a look at some additional control options in Silverlight. So far you've placed all your XAML code in one file, usually MainPage.xaml. This is great for simple examples, but as you can imagine, it doesn't promote code reuse or other best practices. You'll often find that the XAML code you're using on one page might also be beneficial on another page. In this case, you can use a custom user control. A user control consists of both a .xaml file and a .xaml.cs file.

When creating a custom user control, you can place any XAML you like in the .xaml file, and you can even add custom properties in the .xaml.cs file to set those properties in the XAML declaration of the user control. Let's take a look at a simple example of this. Assume that you have the following XAML code on the MainPage.xaml file:

```
<StackPanel>
    <TextBlock Margin="10" Text="This is a reusable section of code" />
    <Button Content="Click" />
</StackPanel>
```

Assume that this is an important piece of code that will potentially be duplicated on several pages in your Windows Phone 7 application. You can copy and paste this all over the place in your app, but you've probably been down that road before, only to find that when it comes time to make a change to something like the text being displayed in the TextBlock control, you'll be in for a real headache. Instead, the better thing to do is create a new custom user control. To do this, you right-click the project in the Solution Explorer, and then select Add ➪ New Item. In the screen that displays, you choose a new Windows Phone user control from the template selection, as shown in Figure 4-8.

FIGURE 4-8: A Windows Phone user control template.

At this point, you have a new file called `SampleControl.xaml` in your project. When you look at the generated code, you can see that there isn't much besides a `Grid` control that will be your root parent control. Turning the previous code into a custom user control is as simple as cutting and pasting the code into the `SampleControl.xaml` file, which leaves you with the following:

```
<UserControl x:Class="CustomUserControl.SampleControl"
    xmlns="http://schemas.microsoft.com/winfx/2006/xaml/presentation"
    xmlns:x="http://schemas.microsoft.com/winfx/2006/xaml"
    xmlns:d="http://schemas.microsoft.com/expression/blend/2008"
    xmlns:mc="http://schemas.openxmlformats.org/markup-compatibility/2006"
    mc:Ignorable="d"
    FontFamily="{StaticResource PhoneFontFamilyNormal}"
    FontSize="{StaticResource PhoneFontSizeNormal}"
    Foreground="{StaticResource PhoneForegroundBrush}"
    d:DesignHeight="480" d:DesignWidth="480">

    <Grid x:Name="LayoutRoot" Background="{StaticResource PhoneChromeBrush}">
        <StackPanel>
            <TextBlock Margin="10" Text="This is a reusable section of code" />
            <Button Content="Click" />
        </StackPanel>
    </Grid>
</UserControl>
```

If you look at the designer page for this custom user control, you can see that you no longer have all the traditional Windows Phone 7 page elements, such as the header and title. Instead, you see only the area representing the custom user control. Figure 4-9 shows the updated designer view.

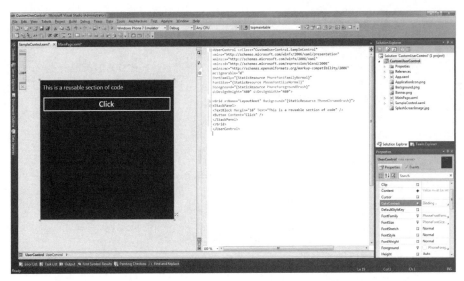

FIGURE 4-9: The designer view of a custom user control.

After the code is copied over, you have a new reusable custom user control that you can place on multiple pages of a Windows Phone 7 application. You might be wondering how to actually use the new user control. Well, you can't simply add a `SampleControl` tag to the `MainPage.xaml` file. Instead, you need to tell Visual Studio and the Silverlight runtime what namespace is used to reference the custom user control. If you open a `MainPage.xaml` file, you'd see several namespace declarations at the top of the file:

```
<phone:PhoneApplicationPage
    x:Class="CustomUserControl.MainPage"
    xmlns="http://schemas.microsoft.com/winfx/2006/xaml/presentation"
    xmlns:x="http://schemas.microsoft.com/winfx/2006/xaml"
    xmlns:phone="clr-namespace:Microsoft.Phone.Controls;assembly=Microsoft.Phone"
    xmlns:shell="clr-namespace:Microsoft.Phone.Shell;assembly=Microsoft.Phone"
    xmlns:d="http://schemas.microsoft.com/expression/blend/2008"
```

The namespace declarations that begin with `xmlns:` give you a way to reference controls that are outside the main Silverlight control scope. To reference this new `SampleControl` file, you can simply add a line like the following to that list of namespaces:

```
xmlsn:local="clr-namespace:CustomUserControl"
```

You're not restricted to calling this namespace local, but for controls that are part of your project, it is an easy naming convention to remember. Now you can easily reference a custom user control by adding a `local:SampleControl` tag to the XAML. Updating this example's `MainPage.xaml` file to use this control would give you the following code:

```
<phone:PhoneApplicationPage
    x:Class="CustomUserControl.MainPage"
    xmlns="http://schemas.microsoft.com/winfx/2006/xaml/presentation"
    xmlns:x="http://schemas.microsoft.com/winfx/2006/xaml"
    xmlns:phone="clr-namespace:Microsoft.Phone.Controls;assembly=Microsoft.Phone"
    xmlns:shell="clr-namespace:Microsoft.Phone.Shell;assembly=Microsoft.Phone"
    xmlns:d="http://schemas.microsoft.com/expression/blend/2008"
    xmlns:local="clr-namespace:CustomUserControl"
    xmlns:mc="http://schemas.openxmlformats.org/markup-compatibility/2006"
    mc:Ignorable="d" d:DesignWidth="480" d:DesignHeight="768"
    FontFamily="{StaticResource PhoneFontFamilyNormal}"
    FontSize="{StaticResource PhoneFontSizeNormal}"
    Foreground="{StaticResource PhoneForegroundBrush}"
    SupportedOrientations="Portrait" Orientation="Portrait"
    shell:SystemTray.IsVisible="True">

    <!--LayoutRoot is the root grid where all page content is placed-->
    <Grid x:Name="LayoutRoot" Background="Transparent">
        <Grid.RowDefinitions>
            <RowDefinition Height="Auto"/>
            <RowDefinition Height="*"/>
        </Grid.RowDefinitions>

        <!--TitlePanel contains the name of the application and page title-->
        <StackPanel x:Name="TitlePanel" Grid.Row="0" Margin="12,17,0,28">
            <TextBlock x:Name="ApplicationTitle" Text="Custom User Control"
Style="{StaticResource PhoneTextNormalStyle}"/>
        </StackPanel>

        <!--ContentPanel - place additional content here-->
        <Grid x:Name="ContentPanel" Grid.Row="1" Margin="12,0,12,0">
            <local:SampleControl x:Name="MainSampleControl" />
        </Grid>
    </Grid>
</phone:PhoneApplicationPage>
```

Now you only have one line of code on this page to present the user with controls located in `SampleControl`. You could now add this control to any other page in your application and easily make changes to the text being displayed across all pages by just making the change in the custom user control.

Another benefit of custom user controls is that you can add additional properties in the code-behind file that will allow you to set them in XAML code. In the previous example, the text displayed was hardcoded in the XAML file for `SampleControl`. You can add a new property called `DisplayText` in the code-behind, and that property will be available right in the `MainPage.xaml` declaration of `SampleControl`. This makes it simple for the text to be changed, depending on the page that hosts the control.

Custom Controls

Using custom user controls is a great way to separate common pieces of XAML code into reusable controls. You can even add some properties and methods to add functionality to a user control. Any time you find yourself copying and pasting large chunks of XAML code, you probably have a good candidate for a user control to be developed. However, custom user controls won't let you extend the behavior of an existing Silverlight control. If you need to add additional functionality to a `Button` control or an `Image` control, for example, a custom user control will not help you much. This is where custom control development comes into play.

Silverlight for Windows Phone 7 supports the development of custom controls that extend any of the existing standard control classes. You can simply create a class called `ImageButton` and extend the `Button` class to automatically inherit all the functionality of a `Button` control. You can then create a style template and add additional properties and functionality in the code-behind. At that point, you would have a brand-new control to reuse throughout your application whenever you need an `ImageButton` control. You can even extend things like the `Slider`, `ProgressBar`, `StackPanel`, and other controls. There are no limitations, and building the controls isn't terribly difficult. There are just a couple of rules you need to follow for property declarations and default control templates.

To get started with a custom control, simply pick a standard control whose functionality you want to extend, such as a `Slider` control. Then add a new class file to your project and extend the `Slider` class. Listing 4-9 shows the code for a custom `Slider` control:

Available for download on Wrox.com

LISTING 4-9: CustomSlider.cs

```csharp
using System;
using System.Net;
using System.Windows;
using System.Windows.Controls;
using System.Windows.Documents;
using System.Windows.Ink;
using System.Windows.Input;
using System.Windows.Media;
using System.Windows.Media.Animation;
using System.Windows.Shapes;

namespace CustomControl
{
    public class CustomSlider : Slider
    {

    }
}
```

Code Snippet CustomSliderControl\CustomSlider.cs

As you can see, all you need to do is inherit from the control you want to extend. This small bit of code is enough to build your project and create the control. You can then add the following line of XAML to one of your pages to begin using your new control:

```
<local:CustomSlider x:Name="CustomSliderControl" Value="50" Maximum="100"
Minimum="0" />
```

Code Snippet CustomSliderControl\MainPage.xaml

The `CustomSlider` control still contains all the properties you expect from the standard `Slider` control. It doesn't do anything to the way the `Slider` looks or behaves, however. As of now, this custom control doesn't do much of anything. Let's assume that for this example you want to add a `TextBlock` control underneath the `Slider` control that automatically displays the current `Value` property. This requires a couple of changes, including a change to the existing control template. By default, the custom control uses the standard `Slider` template. To change this, you need to modify the constructor so that it has this additional line:

```
public CustomSlider()
    : base()
{
    DefaultStyleKey = typeof(CustomSlider);
}
```

Code Snippet CustomSliderControl\CustomSlider.cs

This line of code tells Silverlight that instead of a `TargetType` of `Slider`, your control will use a `TargetType` of `CustomSlider`. The standard `Slider` template is overridden, and you no longer have any user interface for the control. When you change the `DefaultStyleKey` property, Silverlight expects to find your custom control template in a file called `Generic.xaml`, under a new folder called `Themes`. This may seem like a strange convention, but it's easy to follow. You just add to your project a new folder called `Themes` and add a new `.xaml` file called `Generic.xaml`. This special file is called an application resource file. Because all you want to do in this case is add a `TextBlock` control beneath the existing `Slider`, you probably shouldn't start with an entirely new control template. Instead, copy the existing default `Slider` template into the `Generic.xaml` file, and you're left with the code shown in Listing 4-10:

LISTING 4-10: Generic.xaml

```
<ResourceDictionary
    xmlns="http://schemas.microsoft.com/winfx/2006/xaml/presentation"
    xmlns:x="http://schemas.microsoft.com/winfx/2006/xaml"
    xmlns:local="clr-namespace:CustomControl"
    xmlns:vsm="clr-namespace:System.Windows;assembly=System.Windows"
    xmlns:System="clr-namespace:System;assembly=mscorlib"
    xmlns:d="http://schemas.microsoft.com/expression/blend/2008"
    xmlns:mc="http://schemas.openxmlformats.org/markup-compatibility/2006"
    mc:Ignorable="d">

    <ControlTemplate x:Key="PhoneScrollbarThumb" TargetType="Thumb">
        <Rectangle Fill="{TemplateBinding Background}" Height="{TemplateBinding
```

```
Height}" IsHitTestVisible="False" Width="{TemplateBinding Width}"/>
    </ControlTemplate>
    <ControlTemplate x:Key="PhoneSimpleRepeatButton" TargetType="RepeatButton">
        <Rectangle Fill="Transparent"/>
    </ControlTemplate>
    <ControlTemplate x:Key="PhoneSimpleThumb" TargetType="Thumb">
        <Rectangle Fill="Transparent"/>
    </ControlTemplate>
    <Style x:Key="SliderStyle1" TargetType="Slider">
        <Setter Property="BorderThickness" Value="0"/>
        <Setter Property="BorderBrush" Value="Transparent"/>
        <Setter Property="Maximum" Value="10"/>
        <Setter Property="Minimum" Value="0"/>
        <Setter Property="Value" Value="0"/>
        <Setter Property="Background" Value="{StaticResource
        PhoneContrastBackgroundBrush}"/>
        <Setter Property="Foreground" Value="{StaticResource PhoneAccentBrush}"/>
        <Setter Property="Template">
            <Setter.Value>
                <ControlTemplate TargetType="Slider">
                    <Grid Background="Transparent">
                        <VisualStateManager.VisualStateGroups>
                            <VisualStateGroup x:Name="CommonStates">
                                <VisualState x:Name="Normal"/>
                                <VisualState x:Name="MouseOver"/>
                                <VisualState x:Name="Disabled">
                                    <Storyboard>
                                        <DoubleAnimation Duration="0"
To="0.1" Storyboard.TargetProperty="Opacity"
Storyboard.TargetName="HorizontalTrack"/>
                                        <DoubleAnimation Duration="0"
To="0.1" Storyboard.TargetProperty="Opacity"
Storyboard.TargetName="VerticalTrack"/>
                                        <ObjectAnimationUsingKeyFrames
Storyboard.TargetProperty="Fill" Storyboard.TargetName="HorizontalFill">
                                            <DiscreteObjectKeyFrame
KeyTime="0" Value="{StaticResource PhoneDisabledBrush}"/>
                                        </ObjectAnimationUsingKeyFrames>
                                        <ObjectAnimationUsingKeyFrames
Storyboard.TargetProperty="Fill" Storyboard.TargetName="VerticalFill">
                                            <DiscreteObjectKeyFrame
KeyTime="0" Value="{StaticResource PhoneDisabledBrush}"/>
                                        </ObjectAnimationUsingKeyFrames>
                                    </Storyboard>
                                </VisualState>
                            </VisualStateGroup>
                        </VisualStateManager.VisualStateGroups>
                        <Grid x:Name="HorizontalTemplate"
Margin="{StaticResource PhoneHorizontalMargin}">
                            <Grid.ColumnDefinitions>
                                <ColumnDefinition Width="Auto"/>
                                    <ColumnDefinition Width="0"/>
                                    <ColumnDefinition Width="*"/>
                            </Grid.ColumnDefinitions>
                            <Rectangle x:Name="HorizontalTrack"
```

continues

LISTING 4-10 *(continued)*

```xml
Grid.ColumnSpan="3" Fill="{TemplateBinding Background}" Height="12"
IsHitTestVisible="False" Margin="0,22,0,50" Opacity="0.2"/>
                                <Rectangle x:Name="HorizontalFill"
Grid.Column="0" Fill="{TemplateBinding Foreground}" Height="12"
IsHitTestVisible="False" Margin="0,22,0,50"/>
                                <RepeatButton
x:Name="HorizontalTrackLargeChangeDecreaseRepeatButton"
Grid.Column="0"
IsTabStop="False" Template="{StaticResource PhoneSimpleRepeatButton}"/>
                                <RepeatButton
x:Name="HorizontalTrackLargeChangeIncreaseRepeatButton"
Grid.Column="2"
IsTabStop="False" Template="{StaticResource PhoneSimpleRepeatButton}"/>
                                <Thumb x:Name="HorizontalThumb"
Grid.Column="1" Margin="-1,0,0,0" RenderTransformOrigin="0.5,0.5"
Template="{StaticResource
PhoneSimpleThumb}" Width="1">
                                        <Thumb.RenderTransform>
                                            <ScaleTransform ScaleY="1"
ScaleX="32"/>
                                        </Thumb.RenderTransform>
                                    </Thumb>
                                </Grid>
                                <Grid x:Name="VerticalTemplate"
Margin="{StaticResource PhoneVerticalMargin}">
                                    <Grid.RowDefinitions>
                                        <RowDefinition Height="*"/>
                                        <RowDefinition Height="0"/>
                                        <RowDefinition Height="Auto"/>
                                    </Grid.RowDefinitions>
                                    <Rectangle x:Name="VerticalTrack"
Fill="{TemplateBinding Background}" IsHitTestVisible="False"
Margin="12,0"
Opacity="0.2" Grid.RowSpan="3" Width="12"/>
                                    <Rectangle x:Name="VerticalFill"
Fill="{TemplateBinding Foreground}" IsHitTestVisible="False"
Margin="12,0"
Grid.Row="2" Width="12"/>
                                    <RepeatButton
x:Name="VerticalTrackLargeChangeDecreaseRepeatButton"
IsTabStop="False"
Grid.Row="0" Template="{StaticResource PhoneSimpleRepeatButton}"/>
                                    <RepeatButton
x:Name="VerticalTrackLargeChangeIncreaseRepeatButton"
IsTabStop="False"
Grid.Row="2" Template="{StaticResource PhoneSimpleRepeatButton}"/>
                                    <Thumb x:Name="VerticalThumb" Height="1"
Margin="0,-1,0,0" Grid.Row="1" RenderTransformOrigin="0.5,0.5"
Template="{StaticResource PhoneSimpleThumb}">
                                        <Thumb.RenderTransform>
                                            <ScaleTransform ScaleY="32"
ScaleX="1"/>
```

```
                                        </Thumb.RenderTransform>
                                    </Thumb>
                                </Grid>
                            </Grid>
                        </ControlTemplate>
                    </Setter.Value>
                </Setter>
            </Style>
        </ResourceDictionary>
```

Code Lnippet CustomSliderControl\Themes\Generic.xaml

This seems like a lot of XAML code, and it should verify that you don't want to create a `Slider` control from scratch if you can use something that's already available. You might be wondering how you get at the current default style in the first place. The short answer is that you can't — at least not easily through Visual Studio 2010. You can do this in Expression Blend, however, which is another reason to look into that product if you plan on doing any heavy work with custom controls.

The `Slider` control has a couple of `Grid` controls available. The first supports horizontal display, and the second one enables a vertical slider. It's a safe bet that the `Slider` control functionality behind the scenes takes care of which one is actually displayed. For this example, assume that only the horizontal `Slider` controls can be used. To display the required `TextBlock` control, you simply add it to the existing `Grid` control. Before you do so, however, the current `Grid` control has only one row defined, and because you want the `TextBlock` control underneath the Slider, you need to add an additional row to the `Grid` control before adding the `TextBlock` control:

Available for download on Wrox.com

```
<Grid x:Name="HorizontalTemplate" Margin="{StaticResource PhoneHorizontalMargin}">
    <Grid.ColumnDefinitions>
        <ColumnDefinition Width="Auto"/>
        <ColumnDefinition Width="0"/>
        <ColumnDefinition Width="*"/>
    </Grid.ColumnDefinitions>
    <Grid.RowDefinitions>
        <RowDefinition />
        <RowDefinition />
    </Grid.RowDefinitions>
    <Rectangle x:Name="HorizontalTrack" Grid.ColumnSpan="3"
Fill="{TemplateBinding Background}" Height="12" IsHitTestVisible="False"
Margin="0,22,0,50"
Opacity="0.2"/>
    <Rectangle x:Name="HorizontalFill" Grid.Column="0"
Fill="{TemplateBinding Foreground}" Height="12"
IsHitTestVisible="False"
Margin="0,22,0,50"/>
    <RepeatButton x:Name="HorizontalTrackLargeChangeDecreaseRepeatButton"
Grid.Column="0" IsTabStop="False"
Template="{StaticResource PhoneSimpleRepeatButton}"/>
    <RepeatButton x:Name="HorizontalTrackLargeChangeIncreaseRepeatButton"
Grid.Column="2" IsTabStop="False"
Template="{StaticResource PhoneSimpleRepeatButton}"/>
```

```
        <Thumb x:Name="HorizontalThumb" Grid.Column="1" Margin="-1,0,0,0"
RenderTransformOrigin="0.5,0.5"
Template="{StaticResource PhoneSimpleThumb}" Width="1">
            <Thumb.RenderTransform>
                <ScaleTransform ScaleY="1" ScaleX="32"/>
            </Thumb.RenderTransform>
        </Thumb>
        <TextBlock x:Name="MainText" Grid.Row="1" Grid.Column="0" Grid.ColumnSpan="3"
Text="0" />
    </Grid>
```

Code Snippet CustomSliderControl\Themes\Generic.xaml

Now, if you build and run the application, you will see a `Slider` control and a `TextBlock` control below it, like the one shown in Figure 4-10.

The `TextBlock` control just displays the text 0, which isn't accurate. To fix this, you need to access the `TextBlock` control in the code-behind file. Because this control is declared in a template, you can't just use `MainText` syntax. Instead, as you do anytime you need access to a control from the template, you override the `OnApplyTemplate` method of the custom control. In this method, you can use a helper method called `GetTemplateChild`, passing in the name of the `TextBlock` control. The following code shows this method override:

FIGURE 4-10: A custom slider control.

```
private TextBlock mainText;

public override void OnApplyTemplate()
{
    base.OnApplyTemplate();

    mainText = GetTemplateChild("MainText") as TextBlock;
    mainText.Text = this.Value.ToString();
}
```

Code Snippet CustomSliderControl\CustomSlider.cs

Now at any point in the code, you can access the `TextBlock` control by using the private variable. Because the idea in this example is to change the text based on the `Value` property, you can simply hook into the `ValueChanged` event and update the text on the `TextBlock` control accordingly:

```
private void CustomSlider_Loaded(object sender, RoutedEventArgs e)
{
    this.ValueChanged += (s, ev) =>
    {
        if (mainText != null)
        mainText.Text = this.Value.ToString();
    };
}
```

Code Snippet CustomSliderControl\CustomSlider.cs

In this case, a simple lambda expression takes care of setting the value when the `ValueChanged` event is fired for the control. If you run the application at this point, you'll see the `TextBlock` control update when the `Slider` control is moved. Figure 4-11 shows this in action.

At this point, you know how to create the control, how to style it, and how to access controls declared in that style. The only other major point to developing custom controls that you need to be familiar with is `DependencyProperty`. Earlier you saw the limitations of custom properties on a user control. If you want to add custom properties to a custom control and enable things like data binding for it, you need to make use of `DependencyProperty`.

The basic concept is that you create a normal property. For this example, you might want the custom `Slider` control to allow the `TextBlock` control to be customized with custom text in a XAML declaration. This would allow a developer to modify the `Value` property being displayed to something with additional text, like `Current Value is: 750`. You need to add the property as you did for a custom user control, like this:

FIGURE 4-11: A custom slider control updating.

Available for download on Wrox.com

```
public string CustomText { get; set; }
```

Code Snippet CustomSliderControl\CustomSlider.cs

Then you need to add a corresponding `DependencyProperty` for it, using the following code:

Available for download on Wrox.com

```
public static readonly DependencyProperty CustomTextProperty =
    DependencyProperty.Register(
     "CustomText",
     typeof(string),
     typeof(CustomSlider), new PropertyMetadata(""));
```

Code Ssnippet CustomSliderControl\CustomSlider.cs

 COMMON MISTAKES *Note that the standard naming convention for* `DependencyProperty` *is to add the word* `Property` *to the currently declared property variable. In this case, you have a property called* `CustomText`, *so its corresponding* `DependencyProperty` *would be* `CustomTextProperty`. *Next, you set the value of that property by using a helper method called* `Register`. *This tells the Silverlight runtime a couple of things. The first parameter tells the runtime which custom property you're trying to register, and the second parameter tells the runtime what type of variable it is. Next, you need to tell the runtime what type of control this* `DependencyProperty` *is being declared for, which in this case is a* `CustomSlider` *type, and finally you add a* `PropertyMetadata` *object that essentially allows you to give a default value to the property.*

All `DependencyProperty` objects need to be declared `static` and `readonly`. Before using the new property, however, you need to update the event handler to make use of it. This way, the custom text will be displayed alongside the current `Value` property:

```
private void CustomSlider_Loaded(object sender, RoutedEventArgs e)
{
    this.ValueChanged += (s, ev) =>
    {
        if (mainText != null)
        mainText.Text = String.Format("{0} {1}", CustomText,
this.Value.ToString());
    };
}
```

Code Snippet CustomSliderControl\CustomSlider.cs

Now you can set the `CustomText` by using XAML code like the following:

```
<local:CustomSlider x:Name="CustomSliderControl" Value="750"
    Maximum="1000" Minimum="0" Width="300"
    VerticalAlignment="Top"
    CustomText="Here is some custom text"/>
```

Code Snippet CustomSliderControl\MainPage.xaml

Figure 4-12 shows the application running with the new code. Notice both the custom text and the current `Value` property of the `Slider`.

Although at first it might seem complicated, adding a `DependencyProperty` isn't that difficult. The concept is simple once you see an example, and you'll appreciate the benefits of doing so when you start using techniques like data binding in the next chapter.

With the knowledge of how to create a custom control in hand, it's time to try a slightly more complicated example so that you leave this chapter confident that you understand how to build custom controls for your own applications. For this example, you'll write an application that can display a list of books from a warehouse. In this list, you need to display an image, the title of the book, and a description. When users of the application click anywhere in this general area, they should be presented with pricing information for the book. When you go through the design process, you determine that the best way to approach this is to create a custom control. This way, when you're ready for data binding, the custom control will be able to handle different images, descriptions, titles, and pricing without requiring hardcoding of any values.

FIGURE 4-12: A custom control with additional text.

TRY IT OUT Creating a Custom Control

In this example, you will create a new custom control from scratch. You will see how to create custom properties that can be set in XAML code by using the `DependencyProperty` feature of Silverlight.

1. Create a new Windows Phone 7 project in Visual Studio 2010 and call it **CustomControl**.

2. Right-click the project and select Add ⇨ New Folder. Call this folder **Themes**.

3. Right-click the newly created folder and select Add ⇨ New Item ⇨ Windows Phone User Control. Call this control **Generic.xaml**. It will house the custom control template.

4. Open the `Generic.xaml` file and replace its contents with the code shown in Listing 4-11:

LISTING 4-11: Generic.xaml

```xml
<ResourceDictionary
    xmlns="http://schemas.microsoft.com/winfx/2006/xaml/presentation"
    xmlns:x="http://schemas.microsoft.com/winfx/2006/xaml"
    xmlns:local="clr-namespace:CustomControl"
    xmlns:vsm="clr-namespace:System.Windows;assembly=System.Windows"
    xmlns:System="clr-namespace:System;assembly=mscorlib"
    xmlns:d="http://schemas.microsoft.com/expression/blend/2008"
    xmlns:mc="http://schemas.openxmlformats.org/markup-compatibility/2006"
    mc:Ignorable="d">

    <Style TargetType="local:BookDetails">
        <Setter Property="Template">
            <Setter.Value>
                <ControlTemplate TargetType="local:BookDetails">
                    <Border BorderBrush="White" BorderThickness="2"
Margin="10">
                        <StackPanel Orientation="Horizontal">
                            <Image Source="{TemplateBinding CoverImage}"
Margin="10" />
                            <StackPanel>
                                <TextBlock Text="{TemplateBinding Title}"
Margin="10" />
                                <TextBlock
Text="{TemplateBinding Description}" Margin="10" />
                            </StackPanel>
                        </StackPanel>
                    </Border>
                </ControlTemplate>
            </Setter.Value>
        </Setter>
    </Style>
</ResourceDictionary>
```

Code Snippet CustomControl\Themes\Generic.xaml

This code will create the control template to be used. Notice how `TemplateBinding` is used to set the `Source` property of the `Image` control as well as the `Text` properties for the `TextBlock` controls.

5. Right-click the project and select Add ➪ New ➪ Class. Call this new class file `BookDetails.cs`.

6. Replace the contents of the generated class file with the code shown in Listing 4-12:

LISTING 4-12: BookDetails.cs

```csharp
using System;
using System.Net;
using System.Windows;
using System.Windows.Controls;
using System.Windows.Documents;
using System.Windows.Ink;
using System.Windows.Input;
using System.Windows.Media;
using System.Windows.Media.Animation;
using System.Windows.Shapes;
using System.Windows.Media.Imaging;

namespace CustomControl
{
    public class BookDetails : Button
    {
        public BookDetails()
            : base()
        {
            DefaultStyleKey = typeof(BookDetails);
            this.Loaded += new RoutedEventHandler(WroxDetails_Loaded);
        }

        private void WroxDetails_Loaded(object sender, RoutedEventArgs e)
        {
            this.Click += (s, ev) => { MessageBox.Show(String.Format("The
current price is {0}", Price)); };
        }

        public string Description
        {
            get { return (string)GetValue(DescriptionProperty); }
            set { SetValue(DescriptionProperty, value); }
        }

        public static readonly DependencyProperty DescriptionProperty =
DependencyProperty.Register("Description", typeof(string), typeof(BookDetails), new
PropertyMetadata("Description"));

        public string Title
```

```
        {
            get { return (string)GetValue(TitleProperty); }
            set { SetValue(TitleProperty, value); }
        }

        public static readonly DependencyProperty TitleProperty =
DependencyProperty.Register("Title", typeof(string), typeof(BookDetails), new
PropertyMetadata("Title"));

        public string Price
        {
            get { return (string)GetValue(PriceProperty); }
            set { SetValue(PriceProperty, value); }
        }

        public static readonly DependencyProperty PriceProperty =
DependencyProperty.Register("Price", typeof(string), typeof(BookDetails), new
PropertyMetadata("Price"));

        public BitmapImage CoverImage
        {
            get { return (BitmapImage)GetValue(CoverImageProperty); }
            set { SetValue(CoverImageProperty, value); }
        }

        public static readonly DependencyProperty CoverImageProperty =
DependencyProperty.Register("CoverImage", typeof(BitmapImage), typeof(BookDetails),
new PropertyMetadata(null));
    }
}
```

Code Snippet CustomControl\BookDetails.cs

7. To use the control, open `MainPage.xaml` and modify its contents to look like the code in Listing 4-13:

Available for download on Wrox.com

LISTING 4-13: MainPage.xaml

```
<phone:PhoneApplicationPage
    x:Class="CustomControl.MainPage"
    xmlns="http://schemas.microsoft.com/winfx/2006/xaml/presentation"
    xmlns:x="http://schemas.microsoft.com/winfx/2006/xaml"
    xmlns:phone="clr-namespace:Microsoft.Phone.Controls;assembly=Microsoft.Phone"
    xmlns:shell="clr-namespace:Microsoft.Phone.Shell;assembly=Microsoft.Phone"
    xmlns:d="http://schemas.microsoft.com/expression/blend/2008"
    xmlns:mc="http://schemas.openxmlformats.org/markup-compatibility/2006"
    xmlns:local="clr-namespace:CustomControl"
    mc:Ignorable="d" d:DesignWidth="480" d:DesignHeight="768"
```

continues

LISTING 4-13 *(continued)*

```
        FontFamily="{StaticResource PhoneFontFamilyNormal}"
        FontSize="{StaticResource PhoneFontSizeNormal}"
        Foreground="{StaticResource PhoneForegroundBrush}"
        SupportedOrientations="PortraitOrLandscape" Orientation="Portrait"
        shell:SystemTray.IsVisible="True">

    <!--LayoutRoot is the root grid where all page content is placed-->
    <Grid x:Name="LayoutRoot" Background="Transparent">
        <Grid.RowDefinitions>
            <RowDefinition Height="Auto"/>
            <RowDefinition Height="*"/>
        </Grid.RowDefinitions>

    <!--TitlePanel contains the name of the application and page title-->
    <StackPanel x:Name="TitlePanel" Grid.Row="0" Margin="12,17,0,28">
        <TextBlock x:Name="ApplicationTitle" Text="Custom Control App"
Style="{StaticResource PhoneTextNormalStyle}"/>
    </StackPanel>

    <!--ContentPanel - place additional content here-->
    <Grid x:Name="ContentPanel" Grid.Row="1" Margin="12,0,12,0">
        <ListBox x:Name="MainList">
            <local:BookDetails CoverImage="/Images/book1.png"
Title="Professional Windows Phone 7 Game Development: Creating Games using
XNA Game Studio 4"
Price="$44.99"
Description="Apps built for previous versions of Windows phones will
not run on the new Windows Phone 7, forcing developers to quickly get
up to speed on this new platform..." />
            <local:BookDetails CoverImage="/Images/book2.png"
Title="Windows Phone 7 Application Development: 24 Hour Trainer"
Price="$39.99"
Description="While numerous books cover both Silverlight and XNA,
there lacks a resource that covers the specifics of Windows Phone 7
development... "/>
            <local:BookDetails CoverImage="/Images/book3.png"
Title="Professional Windows Phone 7 Application Development: Building
Applications and Games Using Visual Studio, Silverlight, and XNA"
Price="$44.99"
Description="While numerous books cover both Silverlight and XNA,
there lacks a resource that covers the specifics of
Windows Phone 7 development..."/>
        </ListBox>
    </Grid>
</Grid>
</phone:PhoneApplicationPage>
```

Code Snippet CustomControl\MainPage.xaml

8. Build and run the application. You should see the screen shown in Figure 4-13.

How It Works

In this example, you developed a control capable of displaying the image of a book, its title, and a description. When the user clicks anywhere in the area of the control, the user should be notified of the current pricing information. To make this work, you created a new custom control and set up a custom control template in the `Generic.xaml` file. To ensure that no hardcoding of values takes place, you used `TemplateBinding` in the control template. Next, you set up several new properties in the custom control code-behind and made sure they were available for `TemplateBinding` and assignment in XAML by adding corresponding `DependencyProperty` objects.

FIGURE 4-13: A custom control sample application.

You saw earlier in this chapter how all these different techniques work, and by now, you should have a solid grasp of custom control concepts. The only other area of the code you should note is the `TemplateBinding` of the `Source` property for the `Image` control. Note that `DependencyProperty` is actually of the type `BitmapImage`. Even though in the control template declaration of the `Image` control you can get away with setting `Source` to a text-based string path to the actual image file, it won't work to simply bind to a `string` property in the custom control. Template binding of this particular property requires a `BitmapImage` object with a defined `URI` path to the actual image file.

SUMMARY

In this chapter, you learned more about the Silverlight runtime and customization of controls. First, you learned how to alter the look and feel of most of the standard Silverlight controls by modifying the various styles of controls. Control styling encourages code reuse by allowing you to set up styles that can be shared across similar controls. With `BasedOn` styling techniques, you can even create a base style for when controls need to share a basic set of styled properties such as `Margin`, `Padding`, `Background`, and `Foreground`. Next, you saw how to further alter the default look of controls by making use of custom control templates.

Also in this chapter, you learned how to use the Visual State Manager in order to provide smooth animations and a variety of control states for custom controls. The Visual State Manager provides an easy way to perform timed animations across several controls. It also makes it easy to change the style of various control states, such as the `Button` control's `Pressed` and `Disabled` states. You even saw how to create your own custom states, when necessary, for your own controls.

Finally, for times when the default Silverlight controls don't provide all the functionality you're looking for, you saw how to make use of custom user controls and custom controls. The custom user controls provide a nice way to reuse existing XAML across multiple pages in a Windows Phone 7 application. Custom controls take everything a step further and allow for ultimate flexibility and customization, right down to providing custom dependency properties that give you support for advanced scenarios such as data binding.

EXERCISES

1. You need to create several new styles for a custom `Button` control. However, each `Button` control will use the same value for `Margin`, `Padding`, and `Background`. What is the Silverlight styling technique that will best help you?

a) Application styling

b) Custom control templates

c) Implicit styling

d) `BasedOn` styles

2. Which of the following are valid animation objects that can be used with the Visual State Manager? (Choose all that apply.)

a) `ColorAnimation`

b) `DoubleAnimation`

c) `TranslateAnimation`

d) `SkewAnimation`

3. True or False: A control can be placed in multiple visual states at the same time.

4. When you're building custom controls, what technique should you use when you need programmatic access to a control declared in the XAML of your default control style?

a) Control templates

b) Application resources

c) Control programming

d) Override of `OnApplyTemplate`

5. True or False: When building custom controls, you must make use of dependency properties in order to allow for data binding and other advanced scenarios.

Answers to the Exercises can be found in the Appendix.

▶ **WHAT YOU LEARNED IN THIS CHAPTER**

TOPIC	KEY CONCEPTS
Styles	It is not required to declare property values in line with the Silverlight control declaration. You always have the option to pull those values out into a `Style` object so that those property values can be shared among similar controls.
BasedOn styling	`BasedOn` styling allows you to create a base style to apply to similar controls. This can come in handy when you have several property values that will be the same for all the controls of a similar type, but you also have some properties that will differ. The differing style objects can use `BasedOn` styling to inherit any of the styles that should be similar across controls.
Application resource styles	Although style declarations can be declared at the page level, it is often a better choice to pull these out into the `Application.Resources` section of the `App.xaml` file. Doing so ensures that the style objects are accessible to any page in a Windows Phone 7 application.
Control templates	You can easily modify the look and feel of the standard Silverlight controls by making use of custom control templates. By creating new control templates, you get to keep the various behaviors of a control but can replace the user interface of the control with anything you like.
The Visual State Manager	When you need to add smooth animations or simply set up several different control states, you can use the Visual State Manager. The Visual State Manager provides several different animation objects that make it easy to perform time-based animations on control properties.
Custom user controls	You can use custom `UserControl` objects when you find the need to reuse sections of your user interface XAML code.
Custom controls	For the ultimate in flexibility, you can create new custom controls from scratch. Creating custom controls gives you complete control of not only the look and feel of the controls but also their behaviors, states, and properties. You can gain programmatic access to any of the Silverlight objects declared in the custom control default template by overriding the `OnApplyTemplate` method in the custom control. You can also make use of `DependencyProperty` objects in order to support data binding and tools such as Expression Blend.

5

Isolated Storage, Page Navigation, and the Application Life Cycle

WHAT YOU WILL LEARN IN THIS CHAPTER:

➤ Storing data on a phone

➤ Including multiple pages in an application

➤ Understanding the life cycle of a Windows Phone 7 application

➤ Responding to phone events in an application

What good is an application without data? All Windows Phone 7 devices come with built-in memory for data storage, and your application can easily make use of that memory. This chapter begins with an overview of data storage techniques on the phone. You'll learn about the concept of Silverlight's Isolated Storage feature and how you can easily write and read data to and from Isolated Storage in your own applications.

This chapter also discusses the Silverlight Navigation Framework. So far, every example you've worked with has consisted of a simple one-page user interface. In some cases, this is all you need for a particular application. Many times, however, you'll find the need to display multiple pages, and you'll need to learn about the Silverlight navigation system that is in use on the Windows Phone 7 platform. You should be familiar with the concept of a page by now. In this chapter, you'll see how to easily navigate between multiple pages so that you can create more complex applications.

Finally, your application doesn't only need to be aware of the various phone events that can occur; it also needs to know how best to handle them. In this chapter, you'll learn what your application needs to do when incoming phone calls, text messages, and other interruptions occur. You'll also see how your application can run custom code during application startup and how to handle app shutdown properly.

ISOLATED STORAGE

Behind every good application, you'll find data. Without data, an application can't do much. Every application on some level needs to present, manipulate, retrieve, and store application-specific data. As you probably know, data can come from a wide variety of sources, ranging from local file systems and databases to third-party web services. When developing for the Windows Phone 7 platform, you have a built-in ability to access both local storage and web services for retrieval of data. In this chapter, you'll see how to use the local storage system called Isolated Storage.

How Windows Phone 7 Data Storage Works

All Windows Phone 7 devices are required to support data storage using the Isolated Storage file system mechanism. Because all Windows Phone 7 devices also are required to have on-board memory, you can be assured that the Isolated Storage system will be available for your application regardless of what physical hardware the user is working with.

Isolated Storage works by giving each application a physical data store to work with that is accessible only by that particular application. No application will be allowed access to either the underlying file system of the phone or any another application's Isolated Storage space As shown in Figure 5-1, Isolated Storage offers two different use cases for storing and retrieving data.

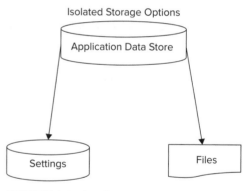

One method depicted in Figure 5-1 involves using an application-specific settings collection to quickly store and retrieve objects in code. This works similarly to a hash table concept or the `Session` object in ASP.NET programming. It is simple to use and provides a great way to quickly store application-specific user settings.

FIGURE 5-1: Isolated storage options.

In addition to the application settings collection, you can also use the Isolated Storage components to create physical folders and files with which to manipulate data. You can write data to files in text-based form or even serialize it, using some of the .NET serialization helper methods.

Getting Started Using Isolated Storage

The Isolated Storage concept in Windows Phone 7 is taken from the same concept that exists in the current version of Silverlight for the PC. Isolated Storage works similarly to a PC-based file system, with the important distinction that the actual underlying file system of the phone device is never accessible from the application. You can think of Isolated Storage as a sandbox of data storage for your application. Unlike a PC-based file system, which has set limitations on how much space your application can take up, Isolated Storage for Windows Phone has no such limitation; however, it would not be a good application practice to go out and utilize all the space available.

Isolated Storage uses any on-board memory of the phone and installed microSD card memory. The total amount of memory available for data storage depends on the number of applications installed, video clips, music, and photos that have already been stored on the device.

Just like a PC-based file system, Isolated Storage allows you to create both files and folders and store any kind of binary data your application might need, using just a few simple API calls. It also provides an easy-to-use name/value pair collection with which to store application settings. To get started, you need to import the namespaces related to both IO and Isolated Storage, using the following code:

```
using Sytem.IO;
using System.IO.IsolatedStorage
```

The IsolatedStorageSettings Object

After you import the namespaces, you need to get an instance of the Isolated Storage space for your specific application. It's important to note that each Windows Phone 7 application has its own instance of Isolated Storage to work with so that no application can read or write to anything other than its own space. This is a great security measure and ensures that a rogue application can never delete or corrupt any of the data required for your application. You have a couple of options at this point. The first is to simply add objects to the IsolatedStorageSettings object; this automatically takes care of storing objects in a name/value pair format.

For example, after declaring the appropriate using statements, you get an instance of the IsolatedStorageSettings object for your application, using the following code:

```
IsolatedStorageSettings settings = IsolatedStorageSettings.ApplicationSettings;
```

With an instance of the object, you can now add items to the settings collection, using code like the following:

```
settings.Add("FirstName", "Test");
settings.Add("LastName", "User");
```

When you have finished adding items to the collection, you persist these settings to Isolated Storage by using the Save method:

```
settings.Save();
```

This is all you have to do to store objects in Isolated Storage using the IsolatedStorageSettings object. Retrieving data is just as simple, as you can access any of the data by using the Key supplied earlier. For example, to get the FirstName object out of Isolated Storage, you can simply use the following code:

```
string firstName = settings["FirstName"].ToString();
```

Because `FirstName` is a string variable, this will work just fine. Keep in mind that you are not limited to just string variables in this collection. The second parameter of the `Add` method takes any object, so to retrieve any other type of object, you simply need to cast the result. For example, if you had stored a `Person` class instance in the `IsolatedStorageSettings` object, you could retrieve it by using the following:

```
Person testPerson = settings["TestPerson"] as Person;
```

The IsolatedStorageFile Object

The `IsolatedStorageSettings` object is simple and effective at storing objects to Isolated Storage when you don't necessarily need a full-blown directory structure with files in your application. If, however, your app needs more functionality and control over the data being stored in Isolated Storage, you can still work with traditional methods and write files and directories.

To work with files and directories in Isolated Storage, you need to get an instance of the Isolated Storage object for your application. This time, instead of the `IsolatedStorageSettings` object, you'll want to use the `IsolatedStorageFile` object, using code like the following:

```
IsolatedStorageFile fileSystem = IsolatedStorageFile.GetUserStoreForApplication();
```

The `IsolatedStorageFile` object has several properties that are useful when writing data to Isolated Storage. You can get the current amount of free space by making use of the `AvailableFreeSpace` property. This will return the total number of bytes available for storage on the device. In addition, you can use familiar IO methods in .NET for dealing with files and directories. The only difference is that the files and directories are created in your own assigned application space.

Assume that you want to read and write a file using the `IsolatedStorageFile` object. At this point, you have an instance of the object in the `fileSystem` variable. You can easily create a directory to hold your data file by using the `CreateDirectory` method:

```
fileSystem.CreateDirectory("ApplicationData");
```

Next, you can create a new `StreamWriter` object, using `IsolatedStorageFileStream` as the parameter to create the data file:

```
StreamWriter writer = new StreamWriter(new
IsolatedStorageFileStream("ApplicationData\\testfile.dat",
FileMode.CreateNew, fileSystem));
```

The file should now reside in `ApplicationData\testfile.dat`. You can now write data to the file by using any of the standard stream methods, such as `WriteLine`:

```
writer.WriteLine("This is some test data for the application");
```

Finally, you call the `Close` method on the `StreamWriter` object, and you're done. Reading the data back from Isolated Storage is just as simple, using the `StreamReader` .NET class. Again, you use the `IsolatedStorageFileStream` object to tell the `StreamReader` object which file to open:

```
StreamReader reader = new StreamReader(new
IsolatedStorageFileStream("ApplicationData\\testfile.dat",
FileMode.Open, fileSystem));
```

Next, you can simply call `ReadLine` to read back the data that was written to the file. You also call `Close` on the `StreamReader` object when you're done.

> **ISOLATED STORAGE ON THE EMULATOR**
>
> One thing to note about the use of Isolated Storage when using the emulator software is that as long as the emulator is running, the data residing in Isolated Storage is valid. This means that even if you have stopped debugging your application, if the emulator window is still being displayed, then data you wrote to Isolated Storage will still be available. If you want to clear all your application data from Isolated Storage, you can do so by simply closing down and restarting the emulator software.

TRY IT OUT Using Isolated Storage

In this example, you'll save and load data from a typical data entry form to Isolated Storage. By keeping the emulator software running and open, you can easily write data to Isolated Storage and retrieve it by stopping and restarting the debugger. Follow these steps:

1. Create a new Windows Phone 7 application in Visual Studio 2010, using the default application template. Call this project **IsolatedStorageSample**.

2. When the project has finished loading, open the `MainPage.xaml` file and replace its contents with the code in Listing 5-1:

Available for download on Wrox.com

LISTING 5-1: MainPage.xaml

```
<phone:PhoneApplicationPage
    x:Class="IsolatedStorageSample.MainPage"
    xmlns="http://schemas.microsoft.com/winfx/2006/xaml/presentation"
    xmlns:x="http://schemas.microsoft.com/winfx/2006/xaml"
    xmlns:phone="clr-namespace:Microsoft.Phone.Controls;assembly=Microsoft.Phone"
    xmlns:shell="clr-namespace:Microsoft.Phone.Shell;assembly=Microsoft.Phone"
    xmlns:d="http://schemas.microsoft.com/expression/blend/2008"
    xmlns:mc="http://schemas.openxmlformats.org/markup-compatibility/2006"
    mc:Ignorable="d" d:DesignWidth="480" d:DesignHeight="768"
    FontFamily="{StaticResource PhoneFontFamilyNormal}"
    FontSize="{StaticResource PhoneFontSizeNormal}"
```

continues

LISTING 5-1 *(continued)*

```
            Foreground="{StaticResource PhoneForegroundBrush}"
            SupportedOrientations="Portrait" Orientation="Portrait"
            shell:SystemTray.IsVisible="True">

    <!--LayoutRoot is the root grid where all page content is placed-->
        <Grid x:Name="LayoutRoot" Background="Transparent">
            <Grid.RowDefinitions>
                <RowDefinition Height="Auto"/>
                <RowDefinition Height="*"/>
            </Grid.RowDefinitions>

            <!--TitlePanel contains the name of the application and page title-->
            <StackPanel x:Name="TitlePanel" Grid.Row="0" Margin="12,17,0,28">
                <TextBlock x:Name="ApplicationTitle"
    Text="Isolated Storage Sample"
    Style="{StaticResource PhoneTextNormalStyle}"/>
            </StackPanel>

            <!--ContentPanel - place additional content here-->
            <StackPanel x:Name="ContentPanel" Grid.Row="1">
                <TextBlock Text="Name" Margin="10" />
                <TextBox x:Name="Name" />
                <TextBlock Text="Email" Margin="10" />
                <TextBox x:Name="Email" />
                <TextBlock Text="Phone" Margin="10" />
                <TextBox x:Name="Phone" />
                <Button HorizontalAlignment="Right" x:Name="Save" Content="Save" />
            </StackPanel>
        </Grid>
</phone:PhoneApplicationPage>
```

Code Snippet IsolatedStorageSample\MainPage.xaml

This simple data entry form will collect a name, an email address, and a phone number and save the data to Isolated Storage. In the code-behind file, you want to accomplish two objectives. First, you need to check whether data for this form already exists in Isolated Storage and, if so, load it and use it. Next, you need to handle writing changes to the data in a `Click` event handler for the `Save` button.

3. Open `MainPage.xaml.cs` and add the code shown in Listing 5-2:

Available for download on Wrox.com

LISTING 5-2: MainPage.xaml.cs

```
public MainPage()
{
    InitializeComponent();
    this.Loaded += new RoutedEventHandler(MainPage_Loaded);
```

```
    }

    private void MainPage_Loaded(object sender, RoutedEventArgs e)
    {
        Save.Click += new RoutedEventHandler(Save_Click);
        LoadDataFromIsolatedStorage();
    }

    private void LoadDataFromIsolatedStorage()
    {

    }

    private void Save_Click(object sender, RoutedEventArgs e)
    {

    }
```

Code Snippet IsolatedStorageSample\MainPage.xaml.cs

This code basically sets up the Click event handler for the Save Button control and also ensures that if any data exists in Isolated Storage already, it will populate the form with that data. Because you'll be using XML serialization, you need a class to hold the data entered on the data entry form.

4. Add the following class to MainPage.xaml.cs as an inner class of MainPage:

Available for
download on
Wrox.com

```
public class DataForm
{
    public string Name { get; set; }
    public string Email { get; set; }
    public string Phone { get; set; }
}
```

Code Snippet IsolatedStorageSample\MainPage.xaml.cs

At this point, both the Save_Click and LoadDataFromIsolatedStorage methods are empty. To load any existing data, you need an instance of the IsolatedStorageFile object for your application. Assume that the data will be stored in a file called user.dat. Also assume that the data is serialized into XML format.

5. Modify the LoadDataFromIsolatedStorage method to look like the following:

Available for
download on
Wrox.com

```
private void LoadDataFromIsolatedStorage()
{
    IsolatedStorageFile fileSystem =
IsolatedStorageFile.GetUserStoreForApplication();

    if (fileSystem.DirectoryExists("UserData"))
    {
```

```
        StreamReader reader = new StreamReader(new
IsolatedStorageFileStream("UserData\\user.dat", FileMode.Open, fileSystem));
        XmlSerializer serializer = new XmlSerializer(typeof(DataForm));

        DataForm data = serializer.Deserialize(reader) as DataForm;

        Name.Text = data.Name;
        Email.Text = data.Email;
        Phone.Text = data.Phone;

        reader.Close();
    }
}
```

Code Snippet IsolatedStorageSample\MainPage.xaml.cs

6. Save any changes to the data that has been loaded on the form in the Save_Click method. Update this method to look like the following:

```
private void Save_Click(object sender, RoutedEventArgs e)
{
    IsolatedStorageFile fileSystem =
IsolatedStorageFile.GetUserStoreForApplication();

    DataForm data = new DataForm { Name = Name.Text, Email = Email.Text,
Phone = Phone.Text };
    XmlSerializer serializer = new XmlSerializer(typeof(DataForm));

    fileSystem.CreateDirectory("UserData");
    StreamWriter writer = new StreamWriter(new
IsolatedStorageFileStream("UserData\\user.dat",
FileMode.CreateNew, fileSystem));

    serializer.Serialize(writer, data);
    writer.Close();
}
```

Code Snippet IsolatedStorageSample\MainPage.xaml.cs

7. Build and run the application in the emulator. The first time the app runs, you should see an empty data entry form similar to the one shown in Figure 5-2.

8. Enter some sample data and click the Save button.

9. Run the application in the emulator again. You should now see the previously saved changes loaded into the data entry form, which should look similar to Figure 5-3.

FIGURE 5-2: No data in Isolated Storage.

FIGURE 5-3: Data loaded from Isolated Storage.

How It Works

In this example, you created a simple data entry form and saved the data entered to an Isolated Storage file called `user.dat`. In addition to saving the data to the file, you also serialized the data to XML format, using the `XmlSerializer` helper class. When you first run the application, nothing is stored in the `user.dat` file. In fact, it doesn't even exist. The code first checks for the existence of the custom directory, and if it is there, the data is loaded into an `XmlSerializer` object and then a new `DataForm` object is created. From there, each of the data entry controls is populated with the respective value.

To ensure that any changes to the data entered are saved, you first create a custom directory and then create a new `StreamWriter` instance, using the required `IsolatedStorageFileStream` class. Because you need to persist the `DataForm` object values in XML form instead of using the `Write` or `WriteLine` methods of the `StreamWriter` class, you use the `Serialize` method of the `XmlSerializer` helper class, passing in both the instance of the `StreamWriter` object and the `DataForm` object itself.

Finally, you call the `Close` method of the `StreamWriter` object to persist the data to the actual `IsolatedStorageFileStream` object. Once the `Close` method has been called, the data is available in Isolated Storage for the application to load the next time it is run in the emulator. Remember that if you want to reset all this and clear the Isolated Storage values, you need to fully close the emulator software, not just stop the debugging session in Visual Studio.

USING THE NAVIGATION FRAMEWORK

So far in this book, you've been working with sample applications that contain one main page. In almost every real-world phone application, however, you need support for more pages. The Windows Phone 7 platform provides the simple-to-use Navigation Framework for navigating between pages in your application. You need to become familiar with just two objects — `NavigationContext` and `NavigationService` — to support multiple pages in your applications.

Getting to Know the Navigation Framework

When you create a new Windows Phone 7 project, you are given a `MainPage.xaml` file to work with. When you open this file, at the top of the page you see a declaration for a `PhoneApplicationPage` object. Each page in your app is an instance of this class type. But behind the scenes, there's also an object called `PhoneApplicationFrame`. This frame object is responsible for holding and displaying pages in your app. As you make use of multiple pages in your application, the pages will be loaded and displayed in this underlying frame object. Figure 5-4 shows an example of the object hierarchy between the frame and page.

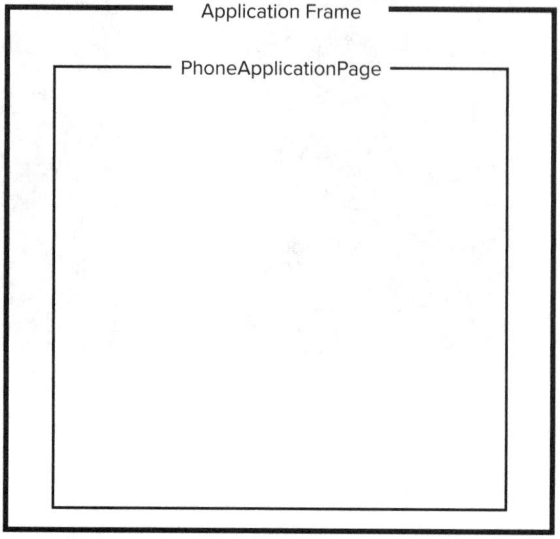

FIGURE 5-4: A navigation frame and page.

The NavigationService Class

The first class you should become familiar with when adding support for multiple pages in your app is `NavigationService`. This class provides several methods that enable you to switch the currently displayed page to a different page. You do this by using the `Navigate` method of the class. The `Navigate` method takes a parameter type of `URI` that typically points to a `.xaml` file to be displayed. Let's look at a simple example of this in action.

First, assume that a new project has been created, and in addition to `MainPage.xaml`, there's a page called `Page2.xaml`. You can easily display this new page by setting up a `Button` `Click` event handler that makes use of `NavigationService`. In the following code, the `Click` handler calls the `Navigate` method of `NavigationService` to tell the main frame object to display `Page2.xaml`. Take note that when declaring `URI`, you use `UriKind.Relative` to tell the system to look for `Page2` `.xaml` in the project, and not an external Internet type source:

```
NavigationService.Navigate(new Uri("/Page2.xaml", UriKind.Relative));
```

If you wanted to get back to the `MainPage.xaml` being displayed, you could have another `Button` control in `Page2.xaml` that uses the same `Navigate` method to tell the main frame control to redisplay `MainPage.xaml`. The following code redirects the user back to the first page:

```
NavigationService.Navigate(new Uri("/MainPage.xaml", UriKind.Relative));
```

In addition to the `Navigate` method, `NavigationService` also provides a few other methods for page switching, including `GoBack` and `GoForward`. As in a typical web browser, `NavigationService` contains a complete history of pages that have been displayed. Both the GoBack and GoForward methods work just like their browser button counterparts. The GoBack method navigates to the last displayed page, and the GoForward method navigates to move forward in the page history. Both of these methods, however, throw exceptions if there are no pages in the history to be navigated to. Therefore, it is best to check the CanGoBack and CanGoForward properties of NavigationService before using these methods to avoid having exceptions thrown.

Query Strings

In addition to basic navigation between pages, the Navigation Framework also provides support for query strings. You may be familiar with query strings if you've done any work with ASP or ASP.NET pages. Using a query string is an easy way to pass data back and forth between pages. For example, say that you want to redirect the user to a page that has specific details about a customer, such as CustomerDetails.xaml. Now assume that you need to load the information about the customer into this page, using an external web service. Presumably, you would need some kind of CustomerID field in order to do that. By using a query string, you can easily navigate to the CustomerDetails.xaml page, passing along the CustomerID of the customer information that should be loaded. You can do this with the Navigate method, using code like the following:

```
NavigationService.Navigate(new Uri("/CustomerDetails.xaml?CustomerID=111",
UriKind.Relative));
```

Now in the CustomerDetails page, you can make use of another object from the Navigation Framework called NavigationContext. This object gives you easy access to query string variables such as CustomerID. Using this class is simple, and you can extract the CustomerID with code such as the following:

```
string customerID = NavigationContext.QueryString["CustomerID"];
```

NavigationContext provides a QueryString property that can be checked for any passed-in query string variables.

Navigation Events

In addition to the NavigationService and NavigationContext classes, the Silverlight Navigation Framework also provides several important events for pages that can be used to determine when a user has navigated to a certain page and when a user leaves the page. When a user navigates to a page, you can run custom code by overriding the OnNavigatedTo method. Alternatively, you can run custom code when a user leaves a given page by overriding the OnNavigatedFrom method of the page. Using the previous example, you would most likely add code like the following in the CustomerDetails page to begin loading the customer data, using the CustomerID in the QueryString object:

```
protected override void OnNavigatedTo(System.Windows.Navigation.NavigationEventArgs
 e)
{
    base.OnNavigatedTo(e);
```

```
        string customerID = NavigationContext.QueryString["CustomerID"];
        LoadCustomerData(customerID);
    }
```

For example, you might use the OnNavigatedFrom event to confirm whether a user wants to leave a page before saving data. For example, assume that the user is looking at a data entry form and clicks the back button on the phone device. The NavigatedFrom event fires, and you could ask if the user wants to save data first. To do this, you use the following code:

```
protected override void OnNavigatedFrom(
System.Windows.Navigation.NavigationEventArgs
 e)
{
    base.OnNavigatedFrom(e);

    MessageBoxResult result =  MessageBox.Show("Do you wish to save your data?",
"Save Data", MessageBoxButton.OKCancel);

    if (result == MessageBoxResult.OK)
        SaveData();
}
```

After the data is saved or if the user clicks Cancel, the user is redirected back to the page most recently displayed.

Page State

When navigating between pages, it's important to keep track of any data that has been entered on data entry forms in your apps. An app is not user friendly if it forces a user to enter the same data more than once. Each PhoneApplicationPage object has its own State property that works just like the PhoneApplicationService.State object. The idea is that any form data or custom page data can be quickly stored in the State property of the page when a deactivating or activating event takes place. The easiest way to work with this State object is to save any page data to the State property in the OnNavigatedFrom event handler because it will automatically be called when an application is about to be deactivated or suspended. The following code shows an example of saving existing form data to the State property of the page when the user leaves the page:

```
protected override void OnNavigatedFrom(
System.Windows.Navigation.NavigationEventArgs
 e)
{
    base.OnNavigatedFrom(e);

    if (State.ContainsKey("CustomData"))
        State["CustomData"] = CustomDataClass;
    else
        State.Add("CustomData", CustomDataClass);
}
```

You can then easily restore the data from the `State` property in the `OnNavigatedTo` method override if any data has been saved. Again, the `OnNavigatedTo` method will be called when the `Activated` event is fired. Here is an example of data being loaded from the `State` property when the page is being navigated to. Note how the code first checks whether any data exists before attempting to access it as this may be the first time the user has navigated to this page:

```
protected override void OnNavigatedTo(System.Windows.Navigation.NavigationEventArgs
  e)
{
    base.OnNavigatedTo(e);

    if( State.ContainsKey("CustomData") )
        CustomDataClass = State["CustomData"] as CustomDataClass
}
```

As you can see, as with the `IsolatedStorageSettings` and `PhoneApplicationService.State` objects, you're dealing with a collection of name/value pairs. This may seem way too easy — and it really is easy. The Navigation Framework makes it simple to switch pages in your application and maintain the state of the controls on those pages, whether because the user is navigating between pages or the application is being deactivated or suspended.

TRY IT OUT Navigating between Pages

In this example, you'll create a simple multi-page Windows Phone 7 application. You'll see how to make use of both the `NavigationService` and `NavigationContext` classes. In addition, you'll see how to use the `State` property for pages to save and restore the information displayed on the page when the user navigates to and from that page. Follow these steps:

1. Create a new Windows Phone 7 project, using the default application template, and call it **NavigationSampleApp.**

2. When the project has finished loading, right-click the project node in the Solution Explorer and add to the project a new class called **Customer.cs**. This file holds the code representing a `Customer` object. Enter the code shown in Listing 5-3:

Available for download on Wrox.com

LISTING 5-3: Customer.cs

```
using System;
using System.Net;
using System.Windows;
using System.Windows.Controls;
using System.Windows.Documents;
using System.Windows.Ink;
using System.Windows.Input;
using System.Windows.Media;
using System.Windows.Media.Animation;
using System.Windows.Shapes;

namespace NavigationSample
```

continues

LISTING 5-3 *(continued)*

```
{
    public class Customer
    {
        public string ID { get; set; }
        public string FirstName { get; set; }
        public string LastName { get; set; }
        public string Email { get; set; }
        public string Address { get; set; }
        public string Phone { get; set; }
        public string TotalOrders { get; set; }
        public string FullName { get { return String.Format("{0} {1}",
FirstName, LastName); } }
    }
}
```

Code Snippet NavigationSampleApp\Customer.cs

3. Now you need a page to display the detailed customer information. The plan for this example is to display a `ListBox` control on the `MainPage.xaml` file that will show a list of customers but only display the `FullName` and `TotalOrders` properties for each customer in the list. Then the user will be able to select a customer from the `ListBox` control, and the `CustomerDetails.xaml` page will display the remaining properties. Right-click the project node in Solution Explorer and add a new phone portrait page from the list of templates. Call this file **CustomerDetails.xaml** and replace its contents with the code shown in Listing 5-4:

LISTING 5-4: CustomerDetails.xaml

```
<phone:PhoneApplicationPage
    x:Class="NavigationSample.CustomerDetails"
    xmlns="http://schemas.microsoft.com/winfx/2006/xaml/presentation"
    xmlns:x="http://schemas.microsoft.com/winfx/2006/xaml"
    xmlns:phone="clr-namespace:Microsoft.Phone.Controls;assembly=Microsoft.Phone"
    xmlns:shell="clr-namespace:Microsoft.Phone.Shell;assembly=Microsoft.Phone"
    xmlns:d="http://schemas.microsoft.com/expression/blend/2008"
    xmlns:mc="http://schemas.openxmlformats.org/markup-compatibility/2006"
    FontFamily="{StaticResource PhoneFontFamilyNormal}"
    FontSize="{StaticResource PhoneFontSizeNormal}"
    Foreground="{StaticResource PhoneForegroundBrush}"
    SupportedOrientations="Portrait" Orientation="Portrait"
    mc:Ignorable="d" d:DesignHeight="768" d:DesignWidth="480"
    shell:SystemTray.IsVisible="True">

    <!--LayoutRoot is the root grid where all page content is placed-->
    <Grid x:Name="LayoutRoot" Background="Transparent">
        <Grid.RowDefinitions>
            <RowDefinition Height="Auto"/>
            <RowDefinition Height="*"/>
        </Grid.RowDefinitions>

        <!--TitlePanel contains the name of the application and page title-->
```

```
            <StackPanel x:Name="TitlePanel" Grid.Row="0" Margin="12,17,0,28">
                <TextBlock x:Name="ApplicationTitle" Text="Navigation Sample App"
    Style="{StaticResource PhoneTextNormalStyle}"/>
                <TextBlock x:Name="PageTitle" Text="Customer Details"
    Margin="9,-7,0,0" Style="{StaticResource PhoneTextTitle1Style}"/>
            </StackPanel>

            <!--ContentPanel - place additional content here-->
            <Grid x:Name="ContentPanel" Grid.Row="1" Margin="12,0,12,0">
                <StackPanel>
                    <TextBlock x:Name="FirstName" />
                    <TextBlock x:Name="LastName" />
                    <TextBlock x:Name="Email" />
                    <TextBlock x:Name="Address" />
                    <TextBlock x:Name="Phone" />
                    <TextBlock x:Name="TotalOrders" />
                    <Button x:Name="Back" Content="Back To Customer List" />
                </StackPanel>
            </Grid>
        </Grid>
    </phone:PhoneApplicationPage>
```

Code Snippet NavigationSampleApp\CustomerDetails.xaml

4. To display both the `FullName` and `TotalOrders` properties, create a custom `ItemTemplate` for the `ListBox` control. To do so, open the `MainPage.xaml` file and replace its contents with the code shown in Listing 5-5:

LISTING 5-5: MainPage.xaml

```
<phone:PhoneApplicationPage
    x:Class="NavigationSample.MainPage"
    xmlns="http://schemas.microsoft.com/winfx/2006/xaml/presentation"
    xmlns:x="http://schemas.microsoft.com/winfx/2006/xaml"
    xmlns:phone="clr-namespace:Microsoft.Phone.Controls;assembly=Microsoft.Phone"
    xmlns:shell="clr-namespace:Microsoft.Phone.Shell;assembly=Microsoft.Phone"
    xmlns:d="http://schemas.microsoft.com/expression/blend/2008"
    xmlns:mc="http://schemas.openxmlformats.org/markup-compatibility/2006"
    mc:Ignorable="d" d:DesignWidth="480" d:DesignHeight="768"
    FontFamily="{StaticResource PhoneFontFamilyNormal}"
    FontSize="{StaticResource PhoneFontSizeNormal}"
    Foreground="{StaticResource PhoneForegroundBrush}"
    SupportedOrientations="Portrait" Orientation="Portrait"
    shell:SystemTray.IsVisible="True">

    <!--LayoutRoot is the root grid where all page content is placed-->
    <Grid x:Name="LayoutRoot" Background="Transparent">
        <Grid.RowDefinitions>
            <RowDefinition Height="Auto"/>
            <RowDefinition Height="*"/>
        </Grid.RowDefinitions>

        <!--TitlePanel contains the name of the application and page title-->
```

continues

LISTING 5-5 *(continued)*

```
        <StackPanel x:Name="TitlePanel" Grid.Row="0" Margin="12,17,0,28">
            <TextBlock x:Name="ApplicationTitle" Text="Navigation Sample App"
Style="{StaticResource PhoneTextNormalStyle}"/>
            <TextBlock x:Name="PageTitle" Text="Customer List" Margin="9,-7,0,0"
Style="{StaticResource PhoneTextTitle1Style}"/>
        </StackPanel>

        <!--ContentPanel - place additional content here-->
        <Grid x:Name="ContentPanel" Grid.Row="1" Margin="12,0,12,0">
            <ListBox x:Name="CustomerList" HorizontalContentAlignment="Stretch">
                <ListBox.ItemTemplate>
                    <DataTemplate>
                        <Border BorderBrush="Blue" BorderThickness="2">
                            <StackPanel>
                                <TextBlock Text="{Binding FullName}"
Margin="5" />
                                <TextBlock Text="{Binding TotalOrders}"
Margin="5" />
                            </StackPanel>
                        </Border>
                    </DataTemplate>
                </ListBox.ItemTemplate>
            </ListBox>
        </Grid>
    </Grid>
</phone:PhoneApplicationPage>
```

Code Snippet NavigationSampleApp\MainPage.xaml

 WARNING *Note the* ListBox *declaration and how the* ItemTemplate *is overridden to show a* StackPanel *with* TextBlock *controls for both of the desired properties.*

5. To create an application-level variable to hold the list of customers, open the App.xaml.cs file and add the following property declaration at the top of the file:

Available for download on Wrox.com

```
public List<Customer> customers { get; set; }
```

Code Snippet NavigationSampleApp\App.xaml.cs

6. You make the property public so all pages will have access to it. Before leaving this file, initialize the variable. To do this, in the App() constructor method, add the following line before the end of the method:

Available for download on Wrox.com

```
customers = new List<Customer>();
```

Code Snippet NavigationSampleApp\App.xaml.cs

7. Add some code to populate the collection of customers and tell the `ListBox` control to display the collection. To do this, open the `MainPage.xaml.cs` file and replace its contents with the code shown in 5-6:

LISTING 5-6: MainPage.xaml.cs

```csharp
using System;
using System.Collections.Generic;
using System.Linq;
using System.Net;
using System.Windows;
using System.Windows.Controls;
using System.Windows.Documents;
using System.Windows.Input;
using System.Windows.Media;
using System.Windows.Media.Animation;
using System.Windows.Shapes;
using Microsoft.Phone.Controls;

namespace NavigationSample
{
    public partial class MainPage : PhoneApplicationPage
    {
        // Constructor
        public MainPage()
        {
            InitializeComponent();

            this.Loaded += (se, ev) =>
            {
                LoadCustomers();
                CustomerList.SelectionChanged += new
SelectionChangedEventHandler(CustomerList_SelectionChanged);
            };
        }

        private void CustomerList_SelectionChanged(object sender,
SelectionChangedEventArgs e)
        {
            Customer selected = e.AddedItems[0] as Customer;
            NavigationService.Navigate(new
Uri(String.Format("/CustomerDetails.xaml?CustomerID={0}", selected.ID),
UriKind.Relative));
        }

        private void LoadCustomers()
        {
            List<Customer> customers = (App.Current as
NavigationSample.App).customers;

            if (customers.Count == 0)
            {
                customers.Add(new Customer { ID = "1", FirstName = "Test",
```

continues

LISTING 5-6 *(continued)*

```
                 LastName = "User1", Email = "testuser1@wiley.com", Phone = "555-555-9999",
                 Address = "1 Test St", TotalOrders = "12" });
                                 customers.Add(new Customer { ID = "2", FirstName = "Test",
                 LastName = "User2", Email = "testuser2@wiley.com", Phone = "555-555-8888",
                 Address = "2 Test St", TotalOrders = "24" });
                                 customers.Add(new Customer { ID = "3", FirstName = "Test",
                 LastName = "User3", Email = "testuser3@wiley.com", Phone = "555-555-7777",
                 Address = "3 Test St", TotalOrders = "36" });
                                 customers.Add(new Customer { ID = "4", FirstName = "Test",
                 LastName = "User4", Email = "testuser4@wiley.com", Phone = "555-555-6666",
                 Address = "4 Test St", TotalOrders = "48" });
                                 customers.Add(new Customer { ID = "5", FirstName = "Test",
                 LastName = "User5", Email = "testuser5@wiley.com", Phone = "555-555-5555",
                 Address = "5 Test St", TotalOrders = "60" });
                         }

                    CustomerList.ItemsSource = customers;
                 }
            }
        }
```

Code Snippet NavigationSampleApp\MainPage.xaml.cs

 NOTE *Note the* `SelectionChanged` *event handler and how the* `Navigate` *method of* `NavigationService` *is used with a query string parameter holding the* `ID` *of the selected customer. This lets the* `CustomerDetails` *page know which customer to load from the global customer list.*

8. The final step is to override the `OnNavigateTo` method of the `CustomerDetails.xaml.cs` file. In this method, you need to use the `NavigationContext` object to pull the selected `ID` from the query string. Then, you load the additional customer properties into the `TextBlock` controls. Finally, you provide the user with a way to navigate back to the customer list by once again calling the `Navigate` method of `NavigationService`, this time passing in the `MainPage.xaml` file destination. Open the `CustomerDetails.xaml.cs` file and replace its contents with the code shown in Listing 5-7:

LISTING 5-7: CustomerDetails.xaml.cs

Available for download on Wrox.com

```
using System;
using System.Collections.Generic;
using System.Linq;
using System.Net;
using System.Windows;
using System.Windows.Controls;
```

```csharp
using System.Windows.Documents;
using System.Windows.Input;
using System.Windows.Media;
using System.Windows.Media.Animation;
using System.Windows.Shapes;
using Microsoft.Phone.Controls;

namespace NavigationSample
{
    public partial class CustomerDetails : PhoneApplicationPage
    {
        public CustomerDetails()
        {
            InitializeComponent();
            this.Loaded += new RoutedEventHandler(CustomerDetails_Loaded);
        }

        protected void CustomerDetails_Loaded(object sender, RoutedEventArgs e)
        {
            Back.Click += new RoutedEventHandler(Back_Click);
        }

        protected void Back_Click(object sender, RoutedEventArgs e)
        {
            NavigationService.Navigate(new Uri("/MainPage.xaml",
UriKind.Relative));
        }

        protected override void
OnNavigatedTo(System.Windows.Navigation.NavigationEventArgs e)
        {
            base.OnNavigatedTo(e);
            string customerID = NavigationContext.QueryString["CustomerID"];

            List<Customer> customers = (App.Current as
NavigationSample.App).customers;
            Customer customer = customers.Where(c => c.ID ==
customerID).SingleOrDefault();

            if (customer != null)
            {
                FirstName.Text = String.Format("First Name: {0}",
customer.FirstName);
                LastName.Text = String.Format("Last Name: {0}",
customer.LastName);
                Address.Text = String.Format("Address: {0}", customer.Address);
                Phone.Text = String.Format("Phone: {0}", customer.Phone);
                Email.Text = String.Format("Email: {0}", customer.Email);
                TotalOrders.Text = String.Format("Total Orders: {0}",
customer.TotalOrders);
            }
        }
    }
}
```

Code Snippet NavigationSampleApp\CustomerDetails.xaml.cs

9. Build and run the app in the emulator. When the application starts, you should be presented with a customer list like the one shown in Figure 5-5.

10. Click one of the customers in the list, and you see the `CustomerDetails.xaml` screen shown in Figure 5-6. This screen displays the remaining properties of the selected `Customer` object.

FIGURE 5-5: Customer list.

FIGURE 5-6: Selected customer details.

How It Works

In this example, you created a multi-page phone application. To have more control over the properties displayed in the `ListBox` control, you used a custom `ItemTemplate` so that both the `FullName` and `TotalOrders` for each customer could be displayed. If you hadn't overridden the `ItemTemplate` property, you would have had to use the `DisplayMemberPath` property. However, this property would allow you to bind to only one of the customer properties, such as `FullName`. Next, you created an additional page to host the remaining customer properties. On this page, you overrode the `OnNavigatedTo` method and extracted the selected `CustomerID` property from the query string. The `NavigationContext` object provided easy access to that variable, and the `Navigate` method of the `NavigationService` provided the `MainPage.xaml.cs` file with the ability to pass the selected `ID` in the query string easily.

Finally, although the user can always get back to the main customer list by using the hardware back button on the phone, it's a good practice for an application to provide the user with a way to get back to the previous screen as well. You did this here by creating a `Click` event handler for a `Button` control and once again used the `Navigate` method of `NavigationService`, passing in a destination of `MainPage.xaml`. Alternatively, you could have used the `GoBack` method because in this particular case, that would have had the same effect. Just remember that to avoid a possible exception being thrown, you should check the `CanGoBack` property before actually calling `GoBack`.

THE APPLICATION LIFE CYCLE

Up to this point, you've created several small sample applications without worrying about what might happen if a phone call or text message were to arrive while your app is running. The goal of the Windows Phone 7 platform is to provide a smooth interface for users, so your application must handle these events gracefully. Luckily, the standard Windows Phone 7 project template creates default handlers for these events and gives you a boilerplate code to use when these events are fired. Before diving into the specifics, however, it's important to take a look at the overall application life cycle so that you are familiar with all the application states that will take place.

The Windows Phone 7 platform has a primary goal of providing a fast user experience, and one of the ways this is accomplished is by ensuring that the current application in the foreground is always treated with the highest priority. In most cases, the background application that was running is actually suspended. When users start your application, they're free at any time to hit one of the main buttons on the phone, including Back, Home, and Search. When this happens, you can expect that your application will no longer be in view of the user, and in most cases it will actually be suspended until the user decides to return to your app. As you'll see, the back button is somewhat of a special case in that if your application utilizes multiple pages, users will continue to navigate back until they hit the beginning landing page of your app, but one more press will send them back to the Windows Phone tile screen, and your application will be history.

The primary way that Windows Phone handles this termination of applications is not to simply kill the process, as it may do on a PC; instead, it relies on putting the application into active and inactive states. This gives the illusion that your application is still running in the background, consuming resources, when in fact this is not the case.

The Launching State

The first state of an application is the launching state. This state is triggered when a user selects your application icon from either a tile pinned to the Windows Phone 7 start page or from the list of installed applications. When a user selects your application, a Launched event is fired, and custom code can be executed in the event handler. Because all the previous sample exercises were created using the default Windows Phone 7 application template, the event handler declarations are already taken care of and built into your application. In fact, if you were to take a look at any newly created project that uses one of the Windows Phone 7 project templates, you would find empty event handlers for all the various application state events. For example, if you were to create a new project and open the App.xaml.cs file, you'd see the following:

```
private void Application_Launching(object sender, LaunchingEventArgs e)
{
}
```

As you can see, there is an event handler for everything except the running state. The reason for this is that once the Launched event has been handled, the application is considered to be running. Any code you put in page constructors or Loaded events is then executed as normal.

There are a couple of things to watch out for when handling the Launched event. First, you need to make sure that no long-running operations take place here. At this point, the user doesn't see your application running and is effectively waiting for it to launch. You don't want to go out and call an external web service or something as that will further delay the startup of your application. Users should be able to click your application icon and instantly be running and interacting with the app. In fact, the Windows Phone Marketplace certification process requires that an application start within 5 seconds. You should therefore avoid loading data from anything other than Isolated Storage, including loading data from external web services.

You also need to make sure that any time the Launched event is handled, it is treated as a brand-new instance of your application. If you receive the Launched event, it means that the user has started your application, with the intent of it being an application instance. This is not the same as reactivating your application after receiving a phone call or making use of launchers and choosers. You therefore don't want to restore any settings that may have been saved during the handling of a Deactivate event.

You might be wondering what kind of code should be put into the Application_Launching event handler. Well, loading data from Isolated Storage is typically an acceptable operation here. The only catch is that in order for your application to be accepted and certified in the Windows Phone Marketplace, the application needs to be in the running state within 5 seconds.

The Running State

After your application has been launched, it is considered to be in the running state. In this state, your application should perform its main functionality. Data can now safely be loaded from an external web service. There are no special event handlers for this state.

The Closing State

Your application reaches the closing state when a user presses the back button on the device enough times to get past your starting page and on to the main tile view or Windows Phone 7 home page. As with the launching state, a default event handler is added to the App.xaml.cs file, and in it you can put custom code to handle things like saving existing screen data to Isolated Storage or an external web service. If you open App.xaml.cs in any project, you'll see the following method declaration:

```
private void Application_Closing(object sender, ClosingEventArgs e)
{
}
```

Unlike with the deactivating state, you don't need to save any session style data here as the only way your application will appear in the foreground again is if the user starts a brand-new instance of the app.

The Deactivating State

The deactivating state is slightly different from the closing state **in that** your application is not fully terminated; rather, it is sent into a suspended mode. Your application can enter this state anytime an external phone event occurs, such as an incoming phone call or text message. Your application can also enter this state if the user presses the Start button on the device. Once again, a default empty event handler is generated for you in the App.xaml.cs file, and it looks like the following:

```
private void Application_Deactivated(object sender, DeactivatedEventArgs e)
{
}
```

The Windows Phone 7 platform provides a state object you can use to save any application-wide state information before the application is suspended. This class is called `PhoneApplicationService`, and it has a `State` property that allows for name/value pairs to be added. It is recommended that any application-level variables be stored here rather than in Isolated Storage because you have only a 10-second window to complete this event handler before the system suspends your app. Because the `PhoneApplicationService` class resides in memory, any operations performed against the `State` property are much faster than those in Isolated Storage. The following is a quick example of how you might use this.

Say that you have an application-level variable, called `CurrentUser`, that's shared between various pages of your app. The `CurrentUser` class has some basic properties, including `Name`, `Email`, and so on. It probably holds a reference to the information entered on a typical data entry form or even the currently logged-in user of the application if the app has a login system. Now when the application is suspended, you need to save the current value of the `CurrentUser` variable so that if the application is reactivated again, the user will be able to pick up where he or she left off. This is where the `PhoneApplicationService` class comes in handy.

In the following code, the `State` property is used to save the `CurrentUser` variable, ensuring that it will be restorable when the application is activated again later:

```
// Application Level Variable

public CurrentUser currentUser;

private void Application_Deactivated(object sender, DeactivatedEventArgs e)
{
    if (!PhoneApplicationService.Current.State.ContainsKey("CurrentUser"))
        PhoneApplicationService.Current.State.Add("CurrentUser", currentUser);
    else
        PhoneApplicationService.Current.State["CurrentUser"] = currentUser;
}
```

Notice the use of the `ContainsKey` method before you add the variable to the `State` property. This is required because each key must be unique, and your application could be deactivated multiple times while running.

The Activating State

The final state handler is the activating state. As you just saw, you use `PhoneApplicationService` to save any application-wide data to memory before your app is suspended. Then, when the activating event is triggered, you can safely use the `PhoneApplicationService` object once again to restore any data. As with the deactivating state, you shouldn't perform any Isolated Storage operations because you need to display the user interface as quickly as possible. Using the previous example, here is a potential event handler for an `Application_Activated` method:

```
private void Application_Activated(object sender, ActivatedEventArgs e)
{
    if( PhoneApplicationService.Current.State.ContainsKey("CurrentUser") )
        currentUser = PhoneApplicationService.Current.State["CurrentUser"]
```

```
    as CurrentUser;
    }
```

Once again, you use the `ContainsKey` method to check for the existence of any data before assigning it to the application-level variable.

TRY IT OUT   Handling Application States

In this example, you'll create a sample application that saves and restores both data global to the overall application and data important to each application page. You'll also see how to debug each of the application state event handlers by using the emulator. Follow these steps:

1. Create a new Windows Phone 7 application in Visual Studio 2010, using the default Windows Phone 7 project template. Call this project **ApplicationStateSample**.

2. When the project finishes loading, add a new page to the project. To do so, right-click the project node in the Solution Explorer and choose Add ➪ New Item ➪ Windows Phone Portrait Page. Call this page **AddUser.xaml**.

3. Now open the `MainPage.xaml` file and replace its contents with the code shown in Listing 5-8:

LISTING 5-8: MainPage.xaml

```xml
<phone:PhoneApplicationPage
    x:Class="ApplicationStateSample.MainPage"
    xmlns="http://schemas.microsoft.com/winfx/2006/xaml/presentation"
    xmlns:x="http://schemas.microsoft.com/winfx/2006/xaml"
    xmlns:phone="clr-namespace:Microsoft.Phone.Controls;assembly=Microsoft.Phone"
    xmlns:shell="clr-namespace:Microsoft.Phone.Shell;assembly=Microsoft.Phone"
    xmlns:d="http://schemas.microsoft.com/expression/blend/2008"
    xmlns:mc="http://schemas.openxmlformats.org/markup-compatibility/2006"
    mc:Ignorable="d" d:DesignWidth="480" d:DesignHeight="768"
    FontFamily="{StaticResource PhoneFontFamilyNormal}"
    FontSize="{StaticResource PhoneFontSizeNormal}"
    Foreground="{StaticResource PhoneForegroundBrush}"
    SupportedOrientations="Portrait" Orientation="Portrait"
    shell:SystemTray.IsVisible="True">

    <!--LayoutRoot is the root grid where all page content is placed-->
    <Grid x:Name="LayoutRoot" Background="Transparent">
        <Grid.RowDefinitions>
            <RowDefinition Height="Auto"/>
            <RowDefinition Height="*"/>
        </Grid.RowDefinitions>

        <!--TitlePanel contains the name of the application and page title-->
        <StackPanel x:Name="TitlePanel" Grid.Row="0" Margin="12,17,0,28">
            <TextBlock x:Name="ApplicationTitle"
    Text="Application State Sample" Style="{StaticResource PhoneTextNormalStyle}"/>
            <TextBlock x:Name="PageTitle" Text="User List"
    Margin="9,-7,0,0" Style="{StaticResource PhoneTextTitle1Style}"/>
```

```
                </StackPanel>

                <!--ContentPanel - place additional content here-->
                <Grid x:Name="ContentPanel" Grid.Row="1" Margin="12,0,12,0">
                    <StackPanel>
                        <ListBox x:Name="AllUsers" DisplayMemberPath="FullName"
    Margin="10" />
                        <Button x:Name="AddUser" Content="Add User" />
                    </StackPanel>
                </Grid>
            </Grid>
    </phone:PhoneApplicationPage>
```

Code Snippet ApplicationStateSample\MainPage.xaml

4. To display on the `MainPage.xaml` screen a `ListBox` control with a list of users that have been added to the system, right-click the project node in the Solution Explorer and select Add ➪ New Class. Call this class **AppUser.cs**. When the class is created, replace its contents with the code shown in Listing 5-9:

LISTING 5-9: AppUser.cs

```
using System;
using System.Net;
using System.Windows;
using System.Windows.Controls;
using System.Windows.Documents;
using System.Windows.Ink;
using System.Windows.Input;
using System.Windows.Media;
using System.Windows.Media.Animation;
using System.Windows.Shapes;

namespace ApplicationStateSample
{
    public class AppUser
    {
        public string FirstName { get; set; }
        public string LastName { get; set; }
        public string Email { get; set; }
        public string Phone { get; set; }
        public string FullName { get { return String.Format("{0} {1}",
    FirstName, LastName); } }
    }
}
```

Code Snippet ApplicationStateSample\AppUser.cs

Now you have a class that will represent each user, and the `ListBox` will ultimately display the `FullName` property for each user added to the system.

5. Add a global-level variable to hold all the users who have been added to the system. To do so, open `App.xaml.cs` and replace its contents with the code shown in Listing 5-10. As you do so, take note of the implementations created for each of the application state events:

LISTING 5-10: App.xaml.cs

```csharp
using System;
using System.Collections.Generic;
using System.Linq;
using System.Net;
using System.Windows;
using System.Windows.Controls;
using System.Windows.Documents;
using System.Windows.Input;
using System.Windows.Media;
using System.Windows.Media.Animation;
using System.Windows.Navigation;
using System.Windows.Shapes;
using Microsoft.Phone.Controls;
using Microsoft.Phone.Shell;
using System.IO.IsolatedStorage;

namespace ApplicationStateSample
{
    public partial class App : Application
    {
        /// <summary>
        /// Provides easy access to the root frame of the Phone Application.
        /// </summary>
        /// <returns>The root frame of the Phone Application.</returns>
        public PhoneApplicationFrame RootFrame { get; private set; }
        public List<AppUser> GlobalUserList { get; set; }

        /// <summary>
        /// Constructor for the Application object.
        /// </summary>
        public App()
        {
            // Global handler for uncaught exceptions.
            UnhandledException += Application_UnhandledException;

            // Show graphics profiling information while debugging.
            if (System.Diagnostics.Debugger.IsAttached)
            {
                // Display the current frame rate counters.
                Application.Current.Host.Settings.EnableFrameRateCounter =
true;

                // Show the areas of the app that are being redrawn in
                // each frame.
                //Application.Current.Host.Settings.EnableRedrawRegions = true;

                // Enable non-production analysis visualization mode,
                // which shows areas of a page that are being GPU
```

```
                    // accelerated with a colored overlay.
                    // Application.Current.Host.Settings.EnableCacheVisualization =
                    // true;

                    // Be sure to initialize the global list of users

                    GlobalUserList = new List<AppUser>();
                }

                // Standard Silverlight initialization
                InitializeComponent();

                // Phone-specific initialization
                InitializePhoneApplication();
            }

            // Code to execute when the application is launching (eg, from Start)
            // This code will not execute when the application is reactivated
            private void Application_Launching(object sender, LaunchingEventArgs e)
            {
                IsolatedStorageSettings settings =
IsolatedStorageSettings.ApplicationSettings;

                if (settings.Contains("UserList"))
                    GlobalUserList = settings["UserList"] as List<AppUser>;
            }

            // Code to execute when the application is activated
            // (brought to foreground)
            // This code will not execute when the application is first launched
            private void Application_Activated(object sender, ActivatedEventArgs e)
            {
                if (PhoneApplicationService.Current.State.ContainsKey("UserList"))
                    GlobalUserList =
PhoneApplicationService.Current.State["UserList"] as List<AppUser>;
            }

            // Code to execute when the application is deactivated
            // (sent to background)
            // This code will not execute when the application is closing
            private void Application_Deactivated(object sender,
DeactivatedEventArgs e)
            {
                if (!PhoneApplicationService.Current.State.ContainsKey("UserList"))
                    PhoneApplicationService.Current.State.Add("UserList",
GlobalUserList);
                else
                    PhoneApplicationService.Current.State["UserList"] =
GlobalUserList;
            }

            // Code to execute when the application is closing (eg, user hit Back)
            // This code will not execute when the application is deactivated
```

continues

LISTING 5-10 *(continued)*

```
        private void Application_Closing(object sender, ClosingEventArgs e)
        {
            IsolatedStorageSettings settings =
IsolatedStorageSettings.ApplicationSettings;

            if (!settings.Contains("UserList"))
                settings.Add("UserList", GlobalUserList);
            else
                settings["UserList"] = GlobalUserList;
        }

        // Code to execute if a navigation fails
        private void RootFrame_NavigationFailed(object sender,
NavigationFailedEventArgs e)
        {
            if (System.Diagnostics.Debugger.IsAttached)
            {
                // A navigation has failed; break into the debugger
                System.Diagnostics.Debugger.Break();
            }
        }

        // Code to execute on Unhandled Exceptions
        private void Application_UnhandledException(object sender,
ApplicationUnhandledExceptionEventArgs e)
        {
            if (System.Diagnostics.Debugger.IsAttached)
            {
                // An unhandled exception has occurred; break into the debugger
                System.Diagnostics.Debugger.Break();
            }
        }

#region Phone application initialization

        // Avoid double-initialization
        private bool phoneApplicationInitialized = false;

        // Do not add any additional code to this method
        private void InitializePhoneApplication()
        {
            if (phoneApplicationInitialized)
                return;

            // Create the frame but don't set it as RootVisual yet; this
            // allows the splash
            // screen to remain active until the application is ready to render.
            RootFrame = new PhoneApplicationFrame();
            RootFrame.Navigated += CompleteInitializePhoneApplication;

            // Handle navigation failures
```

```
            RootFrame.NavigationFailed += RootFrame_NavigationFailed;

            // Ensure we don't initialize again
            phoneApplicationInitialized = true;
        }

        // Do not add any additional code to this method
        private void CompleteInitializePhoneApplication(object sender,
NavigationEventArgs e)
        {
            // Set the root visual to allow the application to render
            if (RootVisual != RootFrame)
                RootVisual = RootFrame;

            // Remove this handler since it is no longer needed
            RootFrame.Navigated -= CompleteInitializePhoneApplication;
        }

    #endregion
        }
    }
```

Code Snippet ApplicationStateSample\App.xaml.cs

6. Create the data entry form for adding users by opening AddUser.xaml and replacing its contents
with the code shown in Listing 5-11:

LISTING 5-11: AddUser.xaml

```xml
<phone:PhoneApplicationPage
    x:Class="ApplicationStateSample.AddUser"
    xmlns="http://schemas.microsoft.com/winfx/2006/xaml/presentation"
    xmlns:x="http://schemas.microsoft.com/winfx/2006/xaml"
    xmlns:phone="clr-namespace:Microsoft.Phone.Controls;assembly=Microsoft.Phone"
    xmlns:shell="clr-namespace:Microsoft.Phone.Shell;assembly=Microsoft.Phone"
    xmlns:d="http://schemas.microsoft.com/expression/blend/2008"
    xmlns:mc="http://schemas.openxmlformats.org/markup-compatibility/2006"
    FontFamily="{StaticResource PhoneFontFamilyNormal}"
    FontSize="{StaticResource PhoneFontSizeNormal}"
    Foreground="{StaticResource PhoneForegroundBrush}"
    SupportedOrientations="Portrait" Orientation="Portrait"
    mc:Ignorable="d" d:DesignHeight="768" d:DesignWidth="480"
    shell:SystemTray.IsVisible="True">

    <!--LayoutRoot is the root grid where all page content is placed-->
    <Grid x:Name="LayoutRoot" Background="Transparent">
        <Grid.RowDefinitions>
            <RowDefinition Height="Auto"/>
            <RowDefinition Height="*"/>
        </Grid.RowDefinitions>

        <!--TitlePanel contains the name of the application and page title-->
```

continues

LISTING 5-11 *(continued)*

```xml
            <StackPanel x:Name="TitlePanel" Grid.Row="0" Margin="12,17,0,28">
                <TextBlock x:Name="ApplicationTitle"
Text="Application State Sample" Style="{StaticResource PhoneTextNormalStyle}"/>
                <TextBlock x:Name="PageTitle" Text="Add New User"
Margin="9,-7,0,0" Style="{StaticResource PhoneTextTitle1Style}"/>
            </StackPanel>

            <!--ContentPanel - place additional content here-->
            <Grid x:Name="ContentPanel" Grid.Row="1" Margin="12,0,12,0">
                <StackPanel>
                    <TextBlock Text="First Name" Margin="10" />
                    <TextBox x:Name="FirstName" />
                    <TextBlock Text="Last Name" Margin="10" />
                    <TextBox x:Name="LastName" />
                    <TextBlock Text="Email" Margin="10" />
                    <TextBox x:Name="Email" />
                    <TextBlock Text="Phone" Margin="10" />
                    <TextBox x:Name="Phone" />
                    <Button x:Name="Save" Content="Save User" />
                </StackPanel>
            </Grid>
        </Grid>
</phone:PhoneApplicationPage>
```

Code Snippet ApplicationStateSample\AddUser.xaml

Now with the user interface ready to go, you need to handle navigating to the data entry form, saving the data to the global list of users, and navigating back to the main screen. You should start with the main screen logic. This page will need to navigate to the add user page and load any list of users that may exist in the global variable. In addition, you'll want to reload the ListBox control after each user is added with the data entry form. You do this by checking the query string of NavigationContext for a reload parameter. That parameter should exist only when the user saves a new entry using the data entry form.

7. Open MainPage.xaml.cs and replace its contents with the code shown in Listing 5-12:

LISTING 5-12: MainPage.xaml.cs

```csharp
using System;
using System.Collections.Generic;
using System.Linq;
using System.Net;
using System.Windows;
using System.Windows.Controls;
using System.Windows.Documents;
using System.Windows.Input;
using System.Windows.Media;
using System.Windows.Media.Animation;
using System.Windows.Shapes;
```

```
using Microsoft.Phone.Controls;

namespace ApplicationStateSample
{
    public partial class MainPage : PhoneApplicationPage
    {
        // Constructor
        public MainPage()
        {
            InitializeComponent();
            this.Loaded += (se, ev) =>
            {
                AddUser.Click += new RoutedEventHandler(AddUser_Click);
                AllUsers.ItemsSource = (App.Current as
ApplicationStateSample.App).GlobalUserList;
            };
        }

        protected void AddUser_Click(object sender, RoutedEventArgs e)
        {
            NavigationService.Navigate(new Uri("/AddUser.xaml",
UriKind.Relative));
        }

        protected override void
OnNavigatedTo(System.Windows.Navigation.NavigationEventArgs e)
        {
            base.OnNavigatedTo(e);

            if (NavigationContext.QueryString.ContainsKey("reload"))
            {
                AllUsers.ItemsSource = (App.Current as
ApplicationStateSample.App).GlobalUserList;
            }
        }
    }
}
```

Code Snippet ApplicationStateSample\MainPage.xaml.cs

8. To save new user data to the global list of users and navigate back to the main screen, open the AddUser.xaml.cs file and replace its contents with the code shown in Listing 5-13:

LISTING 5-13: AddUser.xaml.cs

```
using System;
using System.Collections.Generic;
using System.Linq;
using System.Net;
using System.Windows;
using System.Windows.Controls;
using System.Windows.Documents;
```

continues

LISTING 5-13 *(continued)*

```
using System.Windows.Input;
using System.Windows.Media;
using System.Windows.Media.Animation;
using System.Windows.Shapes;
using Microsoft.Phone.Controls;

namespace ApplicationStateSample
{
    public partial class AddUser : PhoneApplicationPage
    {
        public AddUser()
        {
            InitializeComponent();
            this.Loaded += new RoutedEventHandler(AddUser_Loaded);
        }

        private void AddUser_Loaded(object sender, RoutedEventArgs e)
        {
            Save.Click += new RoutedEventHandler(Save_Click);
        }

        private void Save_Click(object sender, RoutedEventArgs e)
        {
            AppUser newUser = new AppUser { FirstName = FirstName.Text,
LastName = LastName.Text, Email = Email.Text, Phone = Phone.Text };
            App app = App.Current as ApplicationStateSample.App;

            app.GlobalUserList.Add(newUser);
            this.NavigationService.Navigate(new Uri("/MainPage.xaml?reload",
UriKind.Relative));
        }
    }
}
```

Code Snippet ApplicationStateSample\AddUser.xaml.cs

Now all of the code is set up and ready to run. Because you want to see the application state event handlers using the emulator software, you can try to see if they can be triggered one at a time. Before doing so, though, you should add some data to the application.

9. Build and run the application and click the Add User button. You should see the data entry screen shown in Figure 5-7.

10. Add a few test users to the system by filling out the fields on the data entry screen. Don't forget that you can press the Pause/Break key on the keyboard to use your PC keyboard for the data entry instead of using the virtual onscreen keyboard of the emulator. When you've finished adding users, you should be back at the main screen of the application, with a list of users displayed that's similar to the one shown in Figure 5-8.

FIGURE 5-7: Adding a new user.

FIGURE 5-8: A list of users.

11. Now that you have some data to work, try all the various application states in the emulator. To do so, set a breakpoint in the `Application_Deactivated` event handler. In order to trigger this event, simply click on the Windows Start key on the emulator screen. Notice how you now hit the breakpoint and can debug your `PhoneApplicationService` saving code.

12. Activate your application again. To do so, set another breakpoint on the `Application_Activated` event handler in the `App.xaml.cs` file. Click the back button on the emulator and notice how you hit your breakpoint and can now debug any code related to restoration of data from the `PhoneApplicationService` object.

13. To close your app, set a breakpoint on the `Application_Closing` event handler and then press the back button on the emulator until the main Windows Phone 7 tile screen appears. Notice how you now hit your breakpoint and can debug your Isolated Storage code.

14. Start a new instance of the application. Set a breakpoint on the `Application_Launching` event handler in the `App.xaml.cs` file and fully stop the debugging session while keeping the emulator software open. Press the F5 key to start up a new debugging session and notice how you now hit the breakpoint set. From here you can debug any loading of data from Isolated Storage that may be taking place.

How It Works

In this example, you handled application state events and used Isolated Storage, `PhoneApplicationService`, and the Navigation Framework.

The first thing to take a look at is the application-level variable that will hold all the users. At any time, you can create a public variable in the `App.xaml.cs` file, and all of your application pages will have access to it. In this case, you created a generic `List<AppUser>` object and initialized it in the constructor for the app. Next, you made sure that the data was never lost by saving/restoring from either Isolated Storage or the `PhoneApplicationService.State` object.

In the `Application_Closing` and `Application_Launching` event handlers, you used Isolated Storage to save/restore the list of users. Doing this ensures that the data will be available for future application sessions and not just the current running instance. However, if your application is interrupted by a phone call or text message or the user navigating with the Windows Start key, you save the current list of users quickly to memory by using the `PhoneApplicationService.State` object. You do this in both the `Application_Deactivated` and `Application_Activated` event handlers.

Another interesting aspect of the application is that when you've added a new user to the global list of users, you need to navigate back to the main application screen. The following code for the `Save_Click` method uses `NavigationService`, which is available to all pages in your application, to navigate to the `MainPage.xaml` file, but with a query string variable that tells the `ListBox` control to reload its contents with the latest version of the global user list:

Available for
download on
Wrox.com

```
private void Save_Click(object sender, RoutedEventArgs e)
{
        AppUser newUser = new AppUser { FirstName = FirstName.Text,
LastName = LastName.Text, Email = Email.Text, Phone = Phone.Text };
        App app = App.Current as ApplicationStateSample.App;

        app.GlobalUserList.Add(newUser);
        this.NavigationService.Navigate(new Uri("/MainPage.xaml?reload",
UriKind.Relative));
}
```

Code Snippet ApplicationStateSample\AddUser.xaml.cs

Also notice that the `App.Current` variable, which gives you an instance of the application object, needs to be cast to the `ApplicationStateSample.App` type. Otherwise, it won't know about the `GlobalUserList` variable.

Finally, you set breakpoints in each of the application state event handlers and made use of the emulator buttons and the Visual Studio debugger in a way that allows you to debug any code you have in these event handlers.

SUMMARY

In this chapter, you learned about several core Silverlight for Windows Phone 7 concepts, including Isolated Storage, page navigation, and application life cycle events. You saw several different ways to store data in your application, including using Isolated Storage as a file system as well as making use of the `IsolatedStorageSettings` object. Then you learned to create multi-page applications and navigate between pages, using the powerful Navigation Framework.

Finally, you saw that your application needs to be aware of the various phone events that can take place. Some of these events can put your application into a suspended state. To ensure a great user experience, you learned how to save your application state and page state so that it can quickly be restored when your application once again is brought to the foreground. You also learned how to debug code in the various event handlers, using the emulator software.

EXERCISES

1. Which of the following are valid options to use when saving data to Isolated Storage? (Choose all that apply.)

a)   `IsolatedStorageFile`

b)   `IsolatedMemoryFile`

c)   `IsolatedStorageSettings`

d)   `PhoneApplicationService`

2. True or False: When an application is in the running state, you can add custom code to the `Application_Running` event handler.

3. What is the maximum amount of space your application can use from Isolated Storage?

4. Which two method overrides can you use to run custom code when a user navigates both to and from a page?

5. Which of the following is not a valid application life cycle event handler?

a)   `Application_Activated`

b)   `Application_Closing`

c)   `Application_Suspended`

d)   `Application_Launching`

Answers to the Exercises can be found in the Appendix.

▶ **WHAT YOU LEARNED IN THIS CHAPTER**

TOPIC	KEY CONCEPTS
Isolated storage	You can quickly store data in Isolated Storage by using either the `Isolated StorageSettings` or `IsolatedStorageFile` objects. `IsolatedStorage Settings` allows you to easily save and restore data, using a name/value pair format. The `IsolatedStorageFile` object provides a full-blown file system that allows you to create directory structures and files. You can also serialize data to the files by using standard .NET serialization techniques.
Page navigation	An application can have more than one page, and you can easily control navigating between those pages by using the `Navigate`, `GoBack`, and `GoForward` methods of `NavigationService`. You can also pass data between pages by using a familiar query string format. You access the query string data by using the `NavigationContext` object.
Page state	When you need to maintain the state of controls on various pages, you can use the `State` property of the page to hold the values of controls. The `State` property provides a simple name/value pair collection from which to save and restore object data. To provide an excellent user experience, you should ensure that data form is saved in the `State` object when the user navigates away from the page and that it is reloaded when the user navigates back to the page. This way, the user won't need to reenter the form data.
Application events	During the application life cycle, several events need to be handled in an application. When an application is first started, the `Launched` event is fired, and you can write custom code in the `Application_Launching` event handler. When your application is to be shut down or terminated, the `Closing` event is fired, and you can save any application data in the `Application_Closing` event handler. When a phone interruption occurs, such as an incoming phone call or text message, your application will be suspended, and the `Deactivated` event will be fired. You can place custom code in the `Application_Deactivated` event handler. When your application is once again brought to the foreground, the `Activated` event is fired, and custom code and page state can be restored in the `Application_Activated` event handler. All the application life cycle event handlers can be found in the `App.xaml.cs` file.

Interacting with the Hardware

WHAT YOU WILL LEARN IN THIS CHAPTER:

➤ What's different about mobile development

➤ Responding to changes in device orientation

➤ Using the built-in Back button

➤ Communicating with users through vibration

➤ Using the FM radio

➤ Using the accelerometer sensor

One of the most exciting things about writing applications for mobile devices is that their capabilities can be vastly different from more "traditional" platforms. Mobile devices fit in the palm of your hand, and you can move them around, shake them, and interact with them in other unusual ways. If you tried to do that with a desktop PC, you'd probably only succeed in breaking something or injuring yourself.

In this chapter, you'll learn about the differences in capabilities between mobile devices and desktop PCs and how to write code that takes these differences into account. You also learn about the difficulties inherent in developing with an emulator that doesn't always give you access to these capabilities.

Specifically, after you've learned about the differences in capabilities, you'll look at how to determine the orientation of a device and ensure that your applications respond to orientation changes. This helps you ensure that your applications look good and function well, regardless of how users hold their devices — and it even allows you to introduce additional functionality.

Next, you look at the Back button. This button, along with the Search button, must be present on all devices that run Windows Phone 7, and its functionality must correspond with users' expectations. Although you can write code to respond to this button, you must be careful to ensure that the button still functions as users expect it to function.

One unique way to interact with users of mobile devices is vibration. You'll look at how to initiate vibration in a device and when you might want to do this. You'll also use your imagination a bit for this section, as clearly you cannot detect a vibrating emulator.

Next, you'll look at how to interact with the FM radio that is an optional extra for Windows Phone 7 devices.

Finally, you'll look at the built-in accelerometer sensor that all Windows Phone 7 devices contain. This sensor allows you to detect movement, either gentle or abrupt, and respond to that information. For example, you might use this information to detect whether a user has dropped the phone or simply shaken it to make something happen in a game you've written.

When you've mastered the techniques demonstrated in this chapter, you'll be well on your way to writing applications that get the best out of Windows Phone 7 devices.

WHAT'S DIFFERENT ABOUT MOBILE DEVICE APPLICATION DEVELOPMENT?

These days, you'll probably hear a lot of developers talk about writing applications for different *form factors*. This is a way to refer to the physical dimensions — and often the capabilities — of a device. The form factor of a computing device mostly concerns how big it is and, importantly, its screen resolution.

Developing for devices with smaller form factors is challenging. Compared with developing for PCs, you have a lot less screen area (often referred to as screen *real estate*) to play with. Recent developments such as multitouch zoom functionality in mobile web browsers and the Windows Phone 7 Pivot and Panorama controls have to a certain extent eased this restriction for users; however, you still have to consider form factor as you develop Windows Phone 7 applications.

The screen size and the lack of a mouse or human hand-sized keyboard are the major challenges in writing applications for mobile devices. Therefore, we address these issues right at the start of this section. In addition to these challenges, however, mobile devices have a number of benefits. These include:

➤ Mobility and location awareness though Global Positioning System (GPS) and/or other technologies

➤ Flexibility of use and detection of orientation and movement

➤ Haptic feedback, such as vibration

➤ Other built-in hardware features of devices, such as the Back button

All these features are either unique to mobile devices or are much more important in mobile devices than in desktop PCs. You can use some PC monitors in multiple orientations, but you don't tend to change the orientations of monitors often once they're set up, and it is unlikely that applications would need to be aware of any change; the operating system deals with that for you, and you simply change the dimensions that are available.

The applications that you write for mobile devices, on the other hand, not only respond to these novel features, but can also use them as core sources of user input. This means you can create completely unique types of applications, from games that users interact with through shaking and tilting, to applications whose functions depend on how a device is held.

The key thing for you as a developer to remember is to approach the difference in capabilities between desktop PCs and mobile devices as an opportunity, not a set of restrictions. It's fair to say that the hardware in a palm-sized device won't be as powerful as that in a desktop PC, but this doesn't mean you can't do great things with it, and you'll find that there are plenty of things that mobile devices can do that are simply not possible in bulky, immovable desktop PCs.

THE WINDOWS PHONE 7 HARDWARE SPECIFICATION

Along with the Windows Phone 7 operating system, Microsoft has also released a minimum hardware specification that devices must meet. This hardware specification makes it a lot easier for you as a developer because you know in advance what capabilities are available to you, regardless of the device manufacturer. It also means that you can write code that uses the application programming interfaces (APIs) that the operating system supplies rather than having to hook into device-specific hardware drivers. This means that the techniques you learn in this chapter apply to all Windows Phone 7 devices.

Among other features, all Windows Phone 7 devices must support the following:

➤ A multitouch screen

➤ A GPS for location services

➤ An accelerometer

➤ A compass

➤ A light sensor

➤ A proximity sensor

➤ A camera

➤ Start, Search, and Back hardware buttons

In this and the following chapters, you'll look at several of these features and learn some ways to use them. Several of the hardware features, including the accelerometer, fall under the general description of "sensor." This doesn't necessarily mean that they have a lot in common other than the most general of features, but hopefully Microsoft will provide some kind of generic framework. At the time of writing, not all sensors are available in the Windows Phone 7 SDK — the compass, light, and proximity sensors being notable omissions.

ALTERING DEVICE ORIENTATION

One of the simplest ways you can interact with a Windows Phone 7 device is to detect both its current orientation and when orientation changes occur. *Orientation*, in a mobile device sense, simply means whether you're holding it vertically upright or in another position, such as on its side. Vertical orientation is referred to as *portrait* orientation, and horizontal orientation is called *landscape* orientation.

You might wonder why orientation is important. Indeed, in many applications it isn't important. However, sometimes it's useful to know how the device is being held so that you can change the display accordingly. This enables you to enhance the usability of your applications. For example, you might display list data in a different way or change the layout of onscreen elements, depending on the orientation. Alternatively, you might want to force a particular orientation so that your application looks the same however the device is oriented.

The `PhoneApplicationPage` class exposes a property called, unsurprisingly, `Orientation`. This property is of the enumeration type `Microsoft.Phone.Controls.PageOrientation`, which has the members shown in Table 6-1.

TABLE 6-1 PageOrientation Enumeration Members

MEMBER	VALUE	DESCRIPTION
None	0	Indicates that no orientation information is available or specified. In practice, you probably won't see this value unless there are hardware problems.
Portrait	1	Indicates a portrait-type orientation, which includes both right-way-up and upside-down positions.
Landscape	2	Indicates a landscape-type orientation, with the device rotated 90 degrees to either the right or left.
PortraitUp	5	Indicates the right-way-up portrait-type orientation.
PortraitDown	9	Indicates the upside-down portrait-type orientation.
LandscapeLeft	18	Indicates a landscape-type orientation with the device rotated 90 degrees to the left.
LandscapeRight	34	Indicates a landscape-type orientation with the device rotated 90 degrees to the right.

The values defined for the `PageOrientation` enumeration members make it easier to detect whether a given orientation is portrait or landscape by using bitwise AND operations. You can write code as follows to determine whether the page orientation is portrait or landscape:

```
if (Orientation == PageOrientation.Landscape
    || Orientation == PageOrientation.LandscapeLeft
    || Orientation == PageOrientation.LandscapeRight)
{
    // Orientation is landscape-type.
}
```

With the values defined, though, you can instead write the following more readable code:

```
if ((Orientation & PageOrientation.Landscape) == PageOrientation.Landscape)
{
    // Orientation is landscape-type.
}
```

Configuring Supported Orientations

You've probably noticed by now that every Silverlight Windows Phone application that you create using Visual Studio 2010 Express for Windows Phone includes the following code in its main page XAML:

```
<phone:PhoneApplicationPage ... SupportedOrientations="Portrait" ... >
```

The `SupportedOrientations` property, which is of type `SupportedPageOrientation`, enables you to declare what orientations an application supports: portrait, orientation, or both. You can use the `PortraitOrLandscape` value to declare that a page supports both orientation types.

The value of this property determines the allowed values of the `Orientation` property. If you set it to `Portrait`, you'll only see the `Orientation` values `PortraitUp` and `PortraitDown`, never `LandscapeLeft` or `LandscapeRight`. In addition, no orientation change events (detailed in the next section) will be raised for the unsupported orientations.

Responding to Orientation Changes

The `PhoneApplicationPage` class exposes an event that relates to orientation changes: `OrientationChanged`. This event is raised when an orientation change is detected. It passes event arguments of type `OrientationChangedEventArgs`, which has an `Orientation` property that specifies the new orientation. However, it is worth noting that when this event is raised, there is no information available about the previous orientation.

Now that you've seen how orientation is specified and detected, it's time to look at an example.

TRY IT OUT   Orientation Detection

The following steps show the effects of orientation changes and how to respond to these changes with or without changing the supported orientations.

1.   Create a new application using the Windows Phone Application template called `OrientationDetection`.

2.   Modify the code in `MainPage.xaml.cs` so that it looks like Listing 6-1.

LISTING 6-1: Modifying the code in MainPage.xaml.cs

```
public partial class MainPage : PhoneApplicationPage
{
    private PageOrientation preChangeOrientation;

    public MainPage()
    {
        InitializeComponent();

        preChangeOrientation = Orientation;
        OrientationChanged +=
            new EventHandler<OrientationChangedEventArgs>(
                MainPage_OrientationChanged);
    }

    public static DependencyProperty PreviousOrientationProperty =
        DependencyProperty.Register(
            "PreviousOrientation",
            typeof(PageOrientation),
            typeof(MainPage),
            new PropertyMetadata(PageOrientation.None));

    public PageOrientation PreviousOrientation
    {
        get
        {
            return (PageOrientation)GetValue(PreviousOrientationProperty);
        }
        set
        {
            SetValue(PreviousOrientationProperty, value);
        }
    }

    private void MainPage_OrientationChanged(
        object sender, OrientationChangedEventArgs e)
    {
        PreviousOrientation = preChangeOrientation;

        if ((PreviousOrientation == PageOrientation.LandscapeLeft
            && e.Orientation == PageOrientation.PortraitUp)
            || (PreviousOrientation == PageOrientation.PortraitUp
            && e.Orientation == PageOrientation.LandscapeRight)
            || (PreviousOrientation == PageOrientation.LandscapeRight
            && e.Orientation == PageOrientation.PortraitDown)
            || (PreviousOrientation == PageOrientation.PortraitDown
            && e.Orientation == PageOrientation.LandscapeLeft))
        {
```

```
      // Counterclockwise rotation.
      RotateArrowLeft.Begin();
   }
   else
   {
      // Clockwise rotation.
      RotateArrowRight.Begin();
   }

   preChangeOrientation = Orientation;
   }
}
```

Code Snippet OrientationDetection\MainPage.xaml.cs

3. Modify the code in `MainPage.xaml` so that it looks like Listing 6-2.

LISTING 6-2: Modifying the code in MainPage.xaml

```xml
<phone:PhoneApplicationPage ... SupportedOrientations="PortraitOrLandscape"
  Name="Root">
  <phone:PhoneApplicationPage.Resources>
    <Storyboard x:Name="RotateArrowRight">
      <DoubleAnimationUsingKeyFrames Duration="00:00:01"
        Storyboard.TargetName="ArrowGrid"
        Storyboard.TargetProperty=
          "(UIElement.RenderTransform).(RotateTransform.Angle)">
        <DiscreteDoubleKeyFrame KeyTime="00:00:00" Value="-90" />
        <EasingDoubleKeyFrame KeyTime="00:00:01" Value="0">
          <EasingDoubleKeyFrame.EasingFunction>
            <BounceEase />
          </EasingDoubleKeyFrame.EasingFunction>
        </EasingDoubleKeyFrame>
      </DoubleAnimationUsingKeyFrames>
    </Storyboard>
    <Storyboard x:Name="RotateArrowLeft">
      <DoubleAnimationUsingKeyFrames Duration="00:00:01"
        Storyboard.TargetName="ArrowGrid"
        Storyboard.TargetProperty=
          "(UIElement.RenderTransform).(RotateTransform.Angle)">
        <DiscreteDoubleKeyFrame KeyTime="00:00:00" Value="90" />
        <EasingDoubleKeyFrame KeyTime="00:00:01" Value="0">
          <EasingDoubleKeyFrame.EasingFunction>
            <BounceEase />
          </EasingDoubleKeyFrame.EasingFunction>
        </EasingDoubleKeyFrame>
      </DoubleAnimationUsingKeyFrames>
    </Storyboard>
  </phone:PhoneApplicationPage.Resources>
```

continues

LISTING 6-2 *(continued)*

```xml
<Grid x:Name="LayoutRoot" Background="Transparent">
  <Grid.RowDefinitions>
    <RowDefinition Height="Auto" />
    <RowDefinition Height="Auto" />
    <RowDefinition Height="*" />
  </Grid.RowDefinitions>
  <Grid.ColumnDefinitions>
    <ColumnDefinition />
    <ColumnDefinition />
  </Grid.ColumnDefinitions>

  <TextBlock Grid.Row="0" HorizontalAlignment="Right"
    Text="Current Orientation: " />
  <TextBlock Grid.Row="1" HorizontalAlignment="Right"
    Text="Previous Orientation: " />
  <TextBlock Grid.Row="0" Grid.Column="1"
    Text="{Binding ElementName=Root, Path=Orientation}" />
  <TextBlock Grid.Row="1" Grid.Column="1"
    Text="{Binding ElementName=Root, Path=PreviousOrientation}" />

  <Grid x:Name="ArrowGrid" Grid.Row="2" Grid.ColumnSpan="2"
    HorizontalAlignment="Center" VerticalAlignment="Center">
    <Grid.RenderTransform>
      <RotateTransform Angle="0" CenterX="100" CenterY="100" />
    </Grid.RenderTransform>
    <Grid.RowDefinitions>
      <RowDefinition Height="200" />
      <RowDefinition Height="Auto" />
    </Grid.RowDefinitions>
    <Grid.ColumnDefinitions>
      <ColumnDefinition Width="200" />
    </Grid.ColumnDefinitions>

    <Path Stroke="{StaticResource PhoneBorderBrush}" Stretch="Fill"
      StrokeThickness="8" Fill="{StaticResource PhoneSubtleBrush}"
      Data="M 3 10 7 10 7 5 10 5 5 0 0 5 3 5 Z" />
    <TextBlock Style="{StaticResource PhoneTextExtraLargeStyle}" Grid.Row="1"
      Text="THIS WAY IS UP" TextWrapping="Wrap" TextAlignment="Center" />
  </Grid>
</Grid>
</phone:PhoneApplicationPage>
```

Code Snippet OrientationDetection\MainPage.xaml

4.   Run the application. Figure 6-1 shows the result.

FIGURE 6-1: PortraitUp
orientation.

FIGURE 6-2: LandscapeLeft orientation.

5. Tap the Rotate Left button in the emulator controls. Figure 6-2 shows the result you get when the animation finishes.

6. Tap the Rotate Right button in the emulator controls.

7. Stop the application, and then modify the code in MainPage.xaml as follows:

```
<phone:PhoneApplicationPage ... SupportedOrientations="Portrait" Name="Root">
```

8. Run the application and then tap the Rotate Left button in the emulator controls. Figure 6-3 shows the result.

FIGURE 6-3: The result of disabling support for landscape orientation.

How It Works

In this example, you created a simple application that shows which way is up, according to the device orientation. As you've seen, you don't have to do a lot for that to happen as changes in orientation automatically result in changes to layout. If you don't write code to act on orientation changes, the layout of your application will be reformatted automatically — assuming that you leave the default "all orientations supported" code in place.

To display previous orientations when changes occur, you add a dependency property, `PreviousOrientation`, and bind that property and the `Orientation` property to text boxes:

```
<TextBlock Grid.Row="0" Grid.Column="1"
  Text="{Binding ElementName=Root, Path=Orientation}" />
<TextBlock Grid.Row="1" Grid.Column="1"
  Text="{Binding ElementName=Root, Path=PreviousOrientation}" />
```

You also keep a reference to the current orientation in a private field called `preChangeOrientation`, so that in the `MainPage_OrientationChanged()` event handler you have access to both the current and new orientations. You provide an initial value to this field in the page constructor:

```
public MainPage()
{
    InitializeComponent();

    preChangeOrientation = Orientation;
    OrientationChanged +=
        new EventHandler<OrientationChangedEventArgs>(
            MainPage_OrientationChanged);
}
```

During the processing of the `MainPage_OrientationChanged()` event handler, you update `PreviousOrientation` as follows:

```
private void MainPage_OrientationChanging(
        object sender, OrientationChangedEventArgs e)
{
    PreviousOrientation = preChangeOrientation;
```

Also in this event handler, you use the current and new orientations to determine whether a clockwise or counterclockwise rotation has occurred, and you fire off one of two animations (`RotateArrowLeft` or `RotateArrowRight`) accordingly:

```
if ((PreviousOrientation == PageOrientation.LandscapeLeft
    && e.Orientation == PageOrientation.PortraitUp)
    || (PreviousOrientation == PageOrientation.PortraitUp
    && e.Orientation == PageOrientation.LandscapeRight)
    || (PreviousOrientation == PageOrientation.LandscapeRight
    && e.Orientation == PageOrientation.PortraitDown)
    || (PreviousOrientation == PageOrientation.PortraitDown
    && e.Orientation == PageOrientation.LandscapeLeft))
```

```
    {
       // Counterclockwise rotation.
       RotateArrowLeft.Begin();
    }
    else
    {
       // Clockwise rotation.
       RotateArrowRight.Begin();
    }
```

Finally, the event handler stores a reference to the new orientation, ready for use in the next change event:

```
       preChangeOrientation = Orientation;
    }
```

After testing this code, you experimented with changing the supported orientations. By disabling support for landscape orientation, you managed to force the arrow to point left instead of up since no change in orientation occurred.

 COMMON MISTAKES *It is worth noting that if you remove support for a given orientation, the* Orientation *property will never get updated to that orientation. Also, no changes or changing events occur. You can see this in Figure 6-3, which shows that the* Orientation *and* PreviousOrientation *properties did not change when the emulator orientation was changed.*

Device Orientation Best Practices

A Windows Phone 7 device, by default, reformats your layout when the orientation changes; therefore, you must design for this from the start. Otherwise, you might find out much later that your application looks bad or, worse, fails to work properly simply due to an orientation change.

Wherever possible, you should ensure that your application interface updates intuitively with orientation changes, with rearrangement of layout as required. It is also best to avoid large changes in functionality in most cases, as such changes can overcomplicate the interface. Don't be afraid to support only certain orientations when necessary; this is far better than an accidental switch into an unusable layout.

The downloadable code for this chapter includes an additional sample called ListOrientation that provides an example of changing the layout of a list when the page orientation changes. The code is not listed here as it is fairly trivial, but it is worth browsing through to see how something as simple as swapping data templates can provide a better user experience.

UNDERSTANDING THE BACK BUTTON

All Windows Phone 7 devices have three hardware buttons: Back, Start, and Search. You can change the behavior of only the Back button. In this section, you'll look at what the Back button does and how you can respond to a user pressing it.

Taking Advantage of the Back Button's Functionality

The Back button in a Windows Phone 7 device fulfills the same function as a Back button in a browser. Essentially, the device maintains a page history, and as you press the Back button, the device moves backward through this history. From the main page of an application, this means going back to whatever application was previously active, or, if none was active, returning to the device's home page.

NOTE *Using the Back button is one of the only ways to exit an application. There is no code that you can write to terminate an application; that is, there is no* App.Terminate() *method or anything similar. Instead, you rely on the user choosing to exit and can only respond to the user's action.*

Although this behavior is by design, some people in the developer community seem quite offended by the prospect of not being able to terminate their applications. However, it's unlikely that this situation will change.

The user can also press the Back button on other pages in your application, with similar results: When the user presses this button, he is returned to the main page or to the page that was active before the previous navigation.

You can mimic the behavior of the Back button from pages in your application by calling the NavigationService.GoBack() method. This does not, however, result in exactly the same behavior as the Back button, as you'll see in the next section.

Responding to the Back Button

When the Back button is pressed, the PhoneApplicationPage.BackKeyPress event is raised. You can add a handler to this event if there is any cleanup to do or if you want to optionally cancel the operation. This is possible because the event handler is passed an argument of type CancelEventArgs. If you set the Cancel property of this argument to true, the back operation will be canceled, as in the following code:

```
private void MainPage_BackKeyPress(
    object sender, System.ComponentModel.CancelEventArgs e)
{
    e.Cancel = true;
}
```

However, you should be *extremely* sure that this is what you want to do. The Back button is part of the standard Windows Phone 7 interface, and in general, it should do what the user expects it to do. User interfaces that defy expectations are usually not good user interfaces.

NOTE *If you want to get your application certified (see Chapter 15) then the Back button must function as intended. The Windows Phone 7 Application Certification Requirements document includes the following specification that must be adhered to:*

5.2.4 Use of Back Button

To maintain a consistent user experience, the Back button must only be used for backwards navigation in the application.

➤ *Pressing the Back button from the first screen of an application must exit the application.*

➤ *Pressing the Back button must return the application to the previous page.*

➤ *If the current page displays a context menu or a dialog, the pressing of the Back button must close the menu or dialog and cancel the backward navigation to the previous page.*

➤ *For games, when the Back button is pressed during gameplay, the game can choose to present a pause context menu or dialog or navigate the user to the prior menu screen. Pressing the Back button again while in a paused context menu or dialog closes the menu or dialog.*

For more information, see the document at `http://windowsteamblog` `.com/windows_phone/b/wpdev/archive/2010/10/29/updated-version-of-` `windows-phone-7-application-certification-requirements.aspx.`

If you use `NavigationService.GoBack()` instead of the Back button to navigate backward, no `BackKeyPress` event is raised. Instead, if you want to intercept back functionality wherever it comes from, you need to handle the `NavigationService.Navigating` event, as in this example that shows a handler called `NavigationService_Navigating()`:

```
private void NavigationService_Navigating(
    object sender, System.Windows.Navigation.NavigatingCancelEventArgs e)
{
    if (e.NavigationMode == System.Windows.Navigation.NavigationMode.Back)
    {
        e.Cancel = true;
    }
}
```

As this event is raised for all sorts of navigation, you should check that the `NavigationMode` property of the event handler argument is `NavigationMode.Back` before canceling.

In the following steps, you'll see an example of handling the Back button without breaking the "user interface contract" of Back button functionality.

1. Create a new application using the Windows Phone Application template called `BackButton`.

2. Modify the code in `MainPage.xaml.cs` so that it looks like Listing 6-3.

LISTING 6-3: Modifying the code in MainPage.xaml.cs

```
public partial class MainPage : PhoneApplicationPage
{
    int backAttempts = 0;

    public MainPage()
    {
        InitializeComponent();

        BackKeyPress += new EventHandler<System.ComponentModel.CancelEventArgs>(
            MainPage_BackKeyPress);
    }

    private void MainPage_BackKeyPress(
        object sender, System.ComponentModel.CancelEventArgs e)
    {
        switch (backAttempts++)
        {
            case 0:
                message1.Opacity = 0.5;
                message2.Visibility = Visibility.Visible;
                e.Cancel = true;
                break;
            case 1:
                message2.Opacity = 0.5;
                message3.Visibility = Visibility.Visible;
                e.Cancel = true;
                break;
        }
    }

    private void StayButton_Click(object sender, RoutedEventArgs e)
    {
        NavigationService.Navigate(new Uri("/SecondPage.xaml", UriKind.Relative));
    }
}
```

Code Snippet BackButton\MainPage.xaml.cs

3. Modify the code in `MainPage.xaml` so that it looks like Listing 6-4.

LISTING 6-4: Modifying the code in MainPage.xaml

```xaml
<phoneNavigation:PhoneApplicationPage ... >

  <Grid x:Name="LayoutRoot" Background="Transparent">
    <Grid.RowDefinitions>
      <RowDefinition />
      <RowDefinition />
      <RowDefinition />
      <RowDefinition />
    </Grid.RowDefinitions>
    <TextBlock Grid.Row="0" TextAlignment="Center" VerticalAlignment="Center"
      Text="It's nice here, you should stay a while."
      Style="{StaticResource PhoneTextExtraLargeStyle}" TextWrapping="Wrap"
      Name="message1" />
    <TextBlock Grid.Row="1" TextAlignment="Center" VerticalAlignment="Center"
      Text="Please don't go back!"
      Style="{StaticResource PhoneTextExtraLargeStyle}"
      Visibility="Collapsed" Name="message2" />
    <TextBlock Grid.Row="2" TextAlignment="Center" VerticalAlignment="Center"
      Text="Last chance..." Style="{StaticResource PhoneTextExtraLargeStyle}"
      Visibility="Collapsed" Name="message3" />
    <Button Grid.Row="3" Content="Stay" Click="StayButton_Click" />
  </Grid>

</phoneNavigation:PhoneApplicationPage>
```

Code Snippet BackButton\MainPage.xaml

4. Add a new Windows Phone portrait page to the application called `SecondPage` and modify the code in `SecondPage.xaml` so that it looks like Listing 6-5.

LISTING 6-5: Modifying the code in SecondPage.xaml

```xaml
<phoneNavigation:PhoneApplicationPage ... >

  <Grid x:Name="LayoutRoot" Background="Transparent">
    <TextBlock TextAlignment="Center" VerticalAlignment="Center"
      Text="Hooray! Thanks for sticking around :)"
      Style="{StaticResource PhoneTextExtraLargeStyle}"
      TextWrapping="Wrap" />
  </Grid>

</phoneNavigation:PhoneApplicationPage>
```

Code Snippet BackButton\SecondPage.xaml

5. Run the application, and when it is displayed, tap the Stay button.

6. From the `SecondPage.xaml` page, tap the Back button to return to the main page.

7. From the main page, tap the Back button twice and note how the application responds (see Figure 6-4).

8. Tap the Back button one more time to terminate the application and return to the home page.

FIGURE 6-4: Application response.

How It Works

In this example, you saw the Back button functionality and how to respond to the Back button by adding a handler to the `BackKeyPress` event. The application contains three text elements, and the event handler you wrote changes the visibility of these elements prior to enabling the Back button functionality.

The event handler uses a private field called `backAttempts` to keep track of the number of times the Back button is pressed. The first time it is pressed, the opacity of the first text element, `message1`, is set to 50 percent. Next, the second text element, `message2`, is made visible, and finally the event is canceled:

```
switch (backAttempts++)
{
   case 0:
      message1.Opacity = 0.5;
      message2.Visibility = Visibility.Visible;
      e.Cancel = true;
      break;
```

The second time the Back button is pressed, the event handler performs similar manipulations on `message2` and `message3`:

```
   case 1:
      message2.Opacity = 0.5;
      message3.Visibility = Visibility.Visible;
      e.Cancel = true;
      break;
}
```

Finally, the third time the Back button is pressed, the event handler does nothing, and the Back button functionality is not canceled.

This application's "confirm exit" functionality can be quite useful in many applications, especially where you want to prevent data loss. Alternatively, you might want to save data to isolated storage when the Back button is pressed, before the application terminates.

VIBRATION

Vibration has been a feature of mobile phones almost since they first appeared on the market. Manufacturers were quick to see the benefit of a "silent" ring, such as in business meetings. Practically every mobile device now has vibration functionality, so it makes sense that you should be able to access it from application code.

 NOTE *You may have noticed earlier in this section, in the information on the Windows Phone 7 hardware specification, that vibration was not listed as a required feature of Windows Phone 7 devices. Instead, vibration is included as an optional feature for these devices. Therefore, you shouldn't rely on this functionality for your applications, and you should be sure to alert users in other ways, where required.*

You can use vibration functionality in mobile devices for several purposes, including these:

➤ As an alternative or supplementary signal for incoming calls or messages

➤ As a means of alerting users at important points in an application

➤ To enhance the gaming experience

➤ To provide haptic feedback to users as they interact with an application

Haptic technology simply means technology that users interact with through the sense of touch. Many mobile devices today don't include a hardware keypad or keyboard, and haptic technology allows you to provide feedback when user interface elements are triggered. This, along with visual changes, makes it clearer what has happened and provides a better user experience.

The Windows Phone 7 SDK provides a very simple implementation of vibration functionality. Essentially, all you can do is start and stop vibration; you can't control its strength or character. To use vibration functionality, you need an instance of the `Microsoft.Devices.VibrateController` class. This is defined in the `Microsoft.Devices.dll` assembly (which isn't added to applications by default), and you can obtain a reference to the controller through the `VibrateController.Default` static property. Once you have this reference, you can call the `Start()` and `Stop()` methods to start and stop vibration.

When you call `Start()`, you must pass a `TimeSpan` parameter that specifies how long the vibration will last; in addition, you can interrupt the vibration by calling `Stop()`. The maximum length you can specify for `TimeSpan` is five seconds, although in practice you are unlikely to require such a long period of vibration. For one thing, such a long vibration would be very annoying; also, you would risk draining the device's battery extremely quickly.

The following code illustrates how to trigger a one-second vibration when a button is pressed:

```
private void Button_Click(object sender, RoutedEventArgs e)
{
    Microsoft.Devices.VibrateController.Default.Start(new TimeSpan(0, 0, 1));
}
```

Unfortunately, as with a lot of other hardware functionality, the emulator doesn't provide any indication that vibration is working, so it is difficult to test (or indeed illustrate) vibration functionality without a real device.

TUNING IN TO THE FM RADIO

FM radio functionality is now included on many mobile devices as standard, presumably in an effort to reduce the number of gadgets you need to carry around with you. While there is likely to be an application built into the Windows Phone 7 operating system to control the radio (if present), there is also a very simple API that you can use to do so from within your applications.

 NOTE *You should treat FM radio functionality, like vibration functionality, as optional in your code because it is not included in the Windows Phone 7 hardware specification.*

To control the radio, you simply need to manipulate an instance of the FMRadio class, which is located in the Microsoft.Devices.Radio namespace. You can get an instance through the FMRadio.Instance property. You can then turn the radio on or off by using the FMRadio.PowerMode property (which you set to RadioPowerMode.On or RadioPowerMode.Off) and change the frequency by using the Frequency property. Setting the frequency will automatically power on the radio if it is off.

You can also control the frequency band in use though the FMRadio.CurrentRegion property, which can be RadioRegion.UnitedStates, RadioRegion.Japan, or RadioRegion.Europe. By doing this, you can ensure that an attempt to tune the frequency to a non-available value will raise an ArgumentException error. It is therefore worth checking for this exception when setting the frequency.

Finally, you can check the signal strength with the FMRadio.SignalStrength property, a double value that may be between 0 and 1.

Like vibration, the FM radio doesn't do much in the emulator, but the code is simple enough for you to quickly try it out for yourself if you want to.

ACCELERATING WITH THE ACCELEROMETER

Every Windows Phone 7 device contains an *accelerometer*, which is basically a motion-detecting sensor. It measures acceleration in three dimensions and makes this information available to applications. This acceleration includes gravity, so the phone knows which way is up (used under the hood for orientation detection) as well as other sources, such as those imparted by a user.

There are a number of uses for accelerometer data, from user interface streamlining to gaming. Games developers in particular have been quick on the uptake, and already there are, for example, driving games that let you steer by tilting a device, and innumerable marble maze–type games.

In this section, you'll see how to access accelerometer data and see some examples of using that data in applications. You'll also look at how to simulate sensor data, which is essential when working in the emulator.

The AccelerometerSensor Sensor

The Windows Phone 7 SDK includes sensor types in the `Microsoft.Devices.Sensors` namespace, for which you need the `Microsoft.Devices.Sensors.dll` assembly referenced by your project. At the time of writing, there are four types in this namespace, as shown in Table 6-2.

TABLE 6-2: Sensor Namespace Types

TYPE	CLASSIFICATION	DESCRIPTION
Accelerometer	Class	This class provides access to the accelerometer sensor. You can use the `Start()` and `Stop()` methods to start and stop the sensor, and you can keep track of the sensor state in the `State` property. When running, the sensor indicates reading changes through its `ReadingChanged` event.
Accelerometer FailedException	Class	This exception can be thrown during a call to `Start()` or `Stop()` for an `Accelerometer` instance. The failure is indicated through the `Message` property and a property called `ErrorId`, which is set by the underlying device driver.
Accelerometer ReadingEventArgs	Class	This class wraps accelerometer sensor data in an event argument type. The reading is exposed through `X`, `Y`, and `Z` properties (double values between -1 and 1) that indicate acceleration along three orthogonal axes. In addition, the `Timestamp` property indicates when the reading was taken.
SensorState	Enumeration	This enumeration shows the current state of a sensor. This is used as the type of the `State` property of `Accelerometer`.

The `SensorState` enumeration defines a standard set of values for states appropriate to sensors. Table 6-3 shows these values.

TABLE 6-3: SensorState Enumeration Values

VALUE	DESCRIPTION
Ready	The sensor is available in the current device and is happily generating readings.
Disabled	The sensor is available in the current device, but it is disabled and not generating readings.
Initializing	The sensor is available in the current device, but it is currently initializing and not yet generating readings.
NoData	The sensor is available in the current device, but for some reason it is unable to generate readings.
NoPermissions	The sensor is available in the current device, but the calling context doesn't have permissions to access it.
NotSupported	The sensor doesn't exist in the current device.

Although only the `Accelerometer` sensor class exists at the time of writing, it's reasonable to expect that additional sensor types will work in a similar way. They are likely to have `Start()` and `Stop()` methods and expose their state by using a value from the `SensorState` enumeration.

 NOTE *Sensors must be calibrated in order to be effective. Unfortunately, at the time of writing, the API doesn't yet implement calibration, so the code in this section assumes that this has happened through some other procedure.*

As indicated in the table, using the accelerometer involves the following:

1. Create an instance of the `Accelerometer` class.

2. Attach a handler to the `ReadingChanged` event.

3. When you want to start responding to events, call the `Start()` method of the accelerometer sensor.

4. When you no longer want to respond to events, call the `Stop()` method.

As a best practice, you should also check for `AccelerometerFailedException` exceptions. Note also that currently no details are available about how often the `ReadingChanged` event may be raised, but it is safe to assume that it will be quite frequent if this sensor is to be usable in, for example, gaming applications.

A little later, you'll see how to simulate readings in your applications. In the emulator, the accelerometer sensor raises events that all have the following readings:

x: 0

y: 0

z: -1

These settings simulate holding the device upright; the -1 value for z indicates the acceleration due to gravity.

TRY IT OUT Using the Accelerometer

In the following steps, you'll create an application that uses the accelerometer as input for a pedometer application that records the number of steps you take while walking with the device.

1. Create a new application using the Windows Phone Application template called `AccelerometerPedometer`.

2. Add a reference to the `Microsoft.Devices.Sensors.dll` assembly to the project.

3. Add a new class to the project called `PedometerStatistics` and modify the code in `PedometerStatistics.cs` so that it looks like Listing 6-6.

Available for download on Wrox.com

LISTING 6-6: Modifying the code in PedometerStatistics.cs

```
using System;
using System.ComponentModel;

namespace AccelerometerPedometer
{
    public class PedometerStatistics : INotifyPropertyChanged
    {
        private const double DistancePerStep = 0.4;
        private const double DoughnutsPerStep = 7.4E-5;

        private int stepsTaken;
        private TimeSpan activeDuration;
        public event PropertyChangedEventHandler PropertyChanged;

        public int StepsTaken
        {
            get
            {
                return stepsTaken;
            }
```

continues

LISTING 6-6 *(continued)*

```csharp
      private set
      {
         stepsTaken = value;
         OnPropertyChanged("StepsTaken");
         OnPropertyChanged("DistanceTravelled");
         OnPropertyChanged("Doughnuts");
         OnPropertyChanged("SecondsPerStep");
         OnPropertyChanged("ActiveDuration");
      }
   }

   public string DistanceTravelled
   {
      get
      {
         return string.Format("{0} m", StepsTaken * DistancePerStep);
      }
   }

   public string Doughnuts
   {
      get
      {
         return string.Format("{0} doughnuts", StepsTaken * DoughnutsPerStep);
      }
   }

   public string SecondsPerStep
   {
      get
      {
         return StepsTaken == 0 ? "N/A" : string.Format("{0} s / step",
            Math.Round((double)activeDuration.TotalSeconds
                    / (double)StepsTaken, 2));
      }
   }

   public string ActiveDuration
   {
      get
      {
         return string.Format("{0} h, {1} m, {2} s", activeDuration.Hours,
            activeDuration.Minutes, activeDuration.Seconds);
      }
   }

   public void TakeStep(TimeSpan timeSinceLastStep)
   {
      activeDuration += timeSinceLastStep;
      StepsTaken++;
   }
```

```
        private void OnPropertyChanged(string propertyName)
        {
            if (PropertyChanged != null)
            {
                PropertyChanged(this, new PropertyChangedEventArgs(propertyName));
            }
        }
    }
}
```

Code Snippet AccelerometerPedometer\PedometerStatistics.cs

4. Modify the code in `MainPage.xaml.cs` so that it looks like Listing 6-7.

LISTING 6-7: Modifying the code in MainPage.xaml

```
using System;
using System.Windows;
using Microsoft.Phone.Controls;
using Microsoft.Devices.Sensors;

namespace AccelerometerPedometer
{
    public partial class MainPage : PhoneApplicationPage
    {
        private bool isRunning;
        private Accelerometer accelerometer;
        private DateTime lastEventTime;
        private const double SignificantMagnitudeThreshold = 0.5;
        private AccelerometerReadingEventArgs previousReading;

        public MainPage()
        {
            InitializeComponent();

            Stats = new PedometerStatistics();
            accelerometer = new Accelerometer();
            accelerometer.ReadingChanged +=
                new EventHandler<AccelerometerReadingEventArgs>(
                    accelerometer_ReadingChanged);
        }

        public PedometerStatistics Stats { get; private set; }

        private void StartStopButton_Click(object sender, RoutedEventArgs e)
        {
            if (isRunning)
            {
                try
                {
                    accelerometer.Stop();
                    StartStopButton.Content = "Start";
```

continues

LISTING 6-7 *(continued)*

```
                PageTitle.Text = "Paused";
                isRunning = false;
            }
            catch (AccelerometerFailedException ex)
            {
                MessageBox.Show(ex.Message);
            }
        }
        else
        {
            try
            {
                accelerometer.Start();
                StartStopButton.Content = "Stop";
                PageTitle.Text = "Running";
                lastEventTime = DateTime.Now;
                isRunning = true;
            }
            catch (AccelerometerFailedException ex)
            {
                MessageBox.Show(ex.Message);
            }
        }
    }

    private void accelerometer_ReadingChanged(object sender,
        AccelerometerReadingEventArgs e)
    {
        if (previousReading == null)
        {
            previousReading = e;
            return;
        }

        if (GetChangeMagnitude(previousReading, e)
            > SignificantMagnitudeThreshold)
        {
            // Ensure that reading is processed on UI thread.
            Dispatcher.BeginInvoke(
                () =>
                {
                    Stats.TakeStep(DateTime.Now - lastEventTime);
                    lastEventTime = DateTime.Now;
                });
        }

        previousReading = e;
    }
```

```
          private double GetChangeMagnitude(
              AccelerometerReadingEventArgs previousReading,
              AccelerometerReadingEventArgs reading)
          {
              double changeX = reading.X - previousReading.X;
              double changeY = reading.Y - previousReading.Y;
              double changeZ = reading.Z - previousReading.Z;

              return Math.Sqrt(
                  changeX * changeX + changeY * changeY + changeZ * changeZ);
          }
      }
  }
```

Code Snippet AccelerometerPedometer\MainPage.xaml.cs

5. Modify the code in `MainPage.xaml` so that it looks like Listing 6-8.

Available for
download on
Wrox.com

LISTING 6-8: Modifying the code in MainPage.xaml

```
<phoneNavigation:PhoneApplicationPage ... Name="Root">
  <Grid x:Name="LayoutRoot" Background="Transparent">
    ...

    <StackPanel x:Name="TitlePanel" Grid.Row="0" Margin="12,17,0,28">
      <TextBlock x:Name="ApplicationTitle" Text="PEDOMETER"
        Style="{StaticResource PhoneTextNormalStyle}"/>
      <TextBlock x:Name="PageTitle" Text="Paused" Margin="9,-7,0,0"
        Style="{StaticResource PhoneTextTitle1Style}"/>
    </StackPanel>

    <Grid x:Name="ContentPanel" Grid.Row="1">
      <Grid.RowDefinitions>
        <RowDefinition Height="2*" />
        <RowDefinition />
      </Grid.RowDefinitions>

      <StackPanel Orientation="Vertical" Margin="10"
        DataContext="{Binding ElementName=Root, Path=Stats}">
        <TextBlock Text="Active Duration"
          Style="{StaticResource PhoneTextGroupHeaderStyle}" />
        <TextBlock Name="DurationText" Text="{Binding ActiveDuration}"
          Style="{StaticResource PhoneTextAccentStyle}" />
        <TextBlock Text="Steps Taken"
          Style="{StaticResource PhoneTextGroupHeaderStyle}" />
        <TextBlock Name="StepsTakenText" Text="{Binding StepsTaken}"
          Style="{StaticResource PhoneTextAccentStyle}" />
        <TextBlock Text="Average Time / Step"
          Style="{StaticResource PhoneTextGroupHeaderStyle}" />
        <TextBlock Name="AverageTimeText" Text="{Binding SecondsPerStep}"
          Style="{StaticResource PhoneTextAccentStyle}" />
        <TextBlock Text="Approximate Distance Travelled"
          Style="{StaticResource PhoneTextGroupHeaderStyle}" />
```

continues

LISTING 6-8 *(continued)*

```xml
        <TextBlock Name="DistanceText" Text="{Binding DistanceTravelled}"
          Style="{StaticResource PhoneTextAccentStyle}" />
        <TextBlock Text="Equivalent no. of Doughnuts"
          Style="{StaticResource PhoneTextGroupHeaderStyle}" />
        <TextBlock Name="DoughnutText" Text="{Binding Doughnuts}"
          Style="{StaticResource PhoneTextAccentStyle}" />
      </StackPanel>

      <Button Grid.Row="1" Name="StartStopButton" Content="Start"
          Click="StartStopButton_Click" />
    </Grid>
  </Grid>
</phoneNavigation:PhoneApplicationPage>
```

Code Snippet AccelerometerPedometer\MainPage.xaml

6. Run the application. Figure 6-5 shows the startup display.

7. Tap Start. If you're using a real device, the accelerometer starts, and you can have fun with it! If, however, you're using the emulator, the readings are constant, and no steps are detected or displayed.

How It Works

In this example, you've used the accelerometer data to create a pedometer application. Unfortunately, unless you have a real device to test this on, you won't be able to get any accelerometer data; instead, you'll just get a fixed reading that simulates gravity, as described earlier. Obviously, this is a fairly major hindrance to application development using this sensor, and it will remain so unless the emulator is upgraded to allow you to simulate this kind of sensor data. In the meantime, you have to simulate this data programmatically, which is the subject of the next section, "Simulating Accelerometer Data." Before moving on to simulation, though, it's time to look through the code for this example to see what result you should expect.

FIGURE 6-5: The startup display.

The first thing you did in this example was to add a class called `PedometerStatistics`. This class encapsulates the state of the pedometer and exposes strings for data binding to the XAML user interface. This class implements `INotifyPropertyChanged`, so it can notify the user interface when property changes occur, and the user interface can update its display accordingly.

 NOTE *The* `PedometerStatistics` *class is an example of a data model. This is an important concept in relation to Model-View-ViewModel (MVVM) application development, which you'll learn more about later in this book.*

The key piece of information that `PedometerStatistics` records is, of course, the number of steps taken. It uses this information, along with timing, to determine roughly how far you've traveled and how many doughnuts you've burned off. (Sadly, my estimates suggest that you have to walk an *extremely* long way to burn off even a single doughnut.)

These metrics are exposed through simple properties. The main functionality of this class is available through the `TakeStep()` method.

```
public void TakeStep(TimeSpan timeSinceLastStep)
{
    activeDuration += timeSinceLastStep;
    StepsTaken++;
}
```

Code Snippet AccelerometerPedometer\PedometerStatistics.cs

This method must be called with a parameter that indicates how much time has passed since the previous step. This could be recorded internally, but this class would then have to maintain state, indicating various values such as when the application was paused. Therefore, for simplicity, this information is maintained in the main application code. The time since the preceding step is added to the current total, and the step count is incremented. When this count is incremented, property notifications are raised for all properties that depend on it:

```
public int StepsTaken
{
    get
    {
        return stepsTaken;
    }
    private set
    {
        stepsTaken = value;
        OnPropertyChanged("StepsTaken");
        OnPropertyChanged("DistanceTravelled");
        OnPropertyChanged("Doughnuts");
        OnPropertyChanged("SecondsPerStep");
        OnPropertyChanged("ActiveDuration");
    }
}
```

For example, the `SecondsPerStep` property gets a value that involves the number of steps taken and the time taken.

In the main page code, this state is exposed through the `Stats` property, and this is bound directly to the user interface so that its subproperties can be accessed. For example, the `DurationText` property is accessed in the XAML as shown in the following code.

```
<StackPanel Orientation="Vertical" Margin="10"
  DataContext="{Binding ElementName=Root, Path=Stats}">
  <TextBlock Text="Active Duration"
    Style="{StaticResource PhoneTextGroupHeaderStyle}" />
```

```
<TextBlock Name="DurationText" Text="{Binding ActiveDuration}"
   Style="{StaticResource PhoneTextAccentStyle}" />
...
</StackPanel>
```

Code Snippet AccelerometerPedometer\MainPage.xaml

When the application starts, the main page code creates an instance of the `PedometerStatistics` class that's ready for binding. It also instantiates the `Accelerometer` sensor and attaches an event handler to its `ReadingChanged` event, as shown in the following code.

```
public MainPage()
{
    ...

    Stats = new PedometerStatistics();
    accelerometer = new Accelerometer();
    accelerometer.ReadingChanged +=
        new EventHandler<AccelerometerReadingEventArgs>(
            accelerometer_ReadingChanged);
}
```

Code Snippet AccelerometerPedometer\MainPage.xaml.cs

The main page code also includes a handler for the `StartStopButton` button in the user interface, which either starts or stops the accelerometer, as appropriate. It tracks whether the accelerometer is currently running through the `isRunning` field. It also changes the text on the button to Stop after starting the sensor or Start after stopping it so that having a single button doesn't become confusing. Finally, this code catches any exception that may be raised when manipulating the sensor, such as `AccelerometerFailedException` when starting the sensor. The code for this is simple:

```
try
{
    accelerometer.Start();
    StartStopButton.Content = "Stop";
    PageTitle.Text = "Running";
    lastEventTime = DateTime.Now;
    isRunning = true;
}
catch (AccelerometerFailedException ex)
{
    MessageBox.Show(ex.Message);
}
```

If the accelerometer starts, the `accelerometer_ReadingChanged()` event handler is called. You're interested in abrupt accelerations (signifying steps, which will jolt the device) rather than smooth movements. To detect these abrupt accelerations, you obtain the magnitude of the change between the current and previous readings through a simple manipulation of the reading values:

```
private double GetChangeMagnitude(
        AccelerometerReadingEventArgs previousReading,
    AccelerometerReadingEventArgs reading)
{
    double changeX = reading.X - previousReading.X;
    double changeY = reading.Y - previousReading.Y;
    double changeZ = reading.Z - previousReading.Z;

    return Math.Sqrt(
        changeX * changeX + changeY * changeY + changeZ * changeZ);
}
```

For efficiency, you could change this code so that you don't call Math.Sqrt(), but the code is included here to demonstrate how to obtain the magnitude of what is, in effect, a three-dimensional vector.

In accelerometer_ReadingChanged(), the previous value is stored when the first reading is obtained in a private field called previousReading. The first reading is therefore ignored. For subsequent readings, the magnitude of the change is compared with a threshold:

```
private void accelerometer_ReadingChanged(object sender,
    AccelerometerReadingEventArgs e)
{
    if (previousReading == null)
    {
        previousReading = e;
        return;
    }

    if (GetChangeMagnitude(previousReading, e)
            > SignificantMagnitudeThreshold)
    {
```

If the magnitude is large enough (in this code, the threshold is deemed to be 0.5), the PedometerStatistics.TakeStep() method is called with the time since the preceding step:

```
        // Ensure that reading is processed on UI thread.
        Dispatcher.BeginInvoke(
            () =>
            {
                Stats.TakeStep(DateTime.Now - lastEventTime);
                lastEventTime = DateTime.Now;
            });
    }
}
```

This call must be made on the user interface thread, so the local dispatcher is used to marshal the call.

Note that the state, and therefore the active duration, is updated only when an event occurs. Therefore, the active duration is accurate only when an event occurs and will not be updated otherwise. It would be simple enough to display the elapsed active time with a timer, but this hasn't been done here in order to keep the code simple.

So, now you've seen how to consume accelerometer data. However, in order to test your applications properly, you really need to simulate data to see code in action.

Simulating Accelerometer Data

When you develop using an emulator, you're at the mercy of the capabilities of that emulator, which may not exactly match those of actual devices. This is certainly the case for the emulator at the time of writing, which has no way to simulate anything other than trivial, constant accelerometer data.

If you don't have a test device, there are a number of ways you can approach this problem. If you're technically minded, you might want to look into hardware solutions. Various people have published information on the Internet detailing how you might do this, such as by using input from a Wii controller.

The rest of us are left with a software solution, which might mean playing back a predetermined sequence of simulated events or using a random stream. Regardless of the method used, though, you must to some extent abstract the code in your application that handles sensor data events from the actual source of these events. During testing, you can attach your event handler to whatever simulated data source you like.

Again, you can take simple or complicated approaches to achieve this end. One new and exciting way to do this is to use Reactive Extensions for .NET (also known as the Rx Framework), a technology new to .NET 4. However, quite a lot of explanation is required to use this, and the code, while elegant, can be quite difficult to understand.

TRY IT OUT   Simulating Accelerometer Data

In the following steps, you'll see a simple solution to the simulation problem. In it, you'll use a wrapper class to generate accelerometer events. This wrapped class, as you'll see, can be put into either simulation or "real" mode, as circumstances dictate.

1. Create a new application using the Windows Phone Application template called `AccelerometerPedometerSimulator`.

2. Add a reference to the `Microsoft.Devices.Sensors.dll` assembly to the project.

3. Remove the existing `MainPage.xaml` and `MainPage.xaml.cs` files from the project.

4. Add the `AccelerometerPedometer.cs`, `MainPage.xaml`, and `MainPage.xaml.cs` files from the previous Try It Out section.

5. Change all occurrences of the string `AccelerometerPedometer` in the files you have added to `AccelerometerPedometerSimulator` (including the namespace names and the `x:Class` attribute of the `<phone:PhoneApplicationPage>` element in the XAML file).

6. Add a new class to the project called `AccelerometerReading` and modify the code so that it looks like Listing 6-9.

LISTING 6-9: Modifying the code in the AccelerometerReading class

Available for
download on
Wrox.com

```
using System;
using Microsoft.Devices.Sensors;

namespace AccelerometerPedometerSimulator
```

```
{
   public class AccelerometerReading
   {
      public AccelerometerReading(AccelerometerReadingEventArgs reading)
      {
         X = reading.X;
         Y = reading.Y;
         Z = reading.Z;
      }

      public AccelerometerReading(double x, double y, double z)
      {
         X = x;
         Y = y;
         Z = z;
      }

      public double X { get; private set; }
      public double Y { get; private set; }
      public double Z { get; private set; }

      public double GetChangeMagnitude(AccelerometerReading previousReading)
      {
         double changeX = X - previousReading.X;
         double changeY = Y - previousReading.Y;
         double changeZ = Z - previousReading.Z;

         return Math.Sqrt(
            changeX * changeX + changeY * changeY + changeZ * changeZ);
      }
   }
}
```

Code Snippet AccelerometerPedometerSimulator\AccelerometerReading.cs

7. Add a new class to the project called `AccelerometerReadingWrapperEventArgs` and modify the code so that it looks like Listing 6-10.

LISTING 6-10: Modifying the code in the AccelerometerReadingWrapperEventArgs class

```
using System;

namespace AccelerometerPedometerSimulator
{
   public class AccelerometerReadingWrapperEventArgs : EventArgs
   {
      public AccelerometerReadingWrapperEventArgs(AccelerometerReading reading)
      {
         Reading = reading;
```

continues

LISTING 6-10 *(continued)*

```
        }

        public AccelerometerReading Reading { get; private set; }
    }
}
```

Code Snippet AccelerometerPedometerSimulator\AccelerometerReadingWrapperEventArgs.cs

8. Add a new class to the project called `AccelerometerSensorWrapper` and modify the code so that it looks like Listing 6-11.

LISTING 6-11: Modifying the code in the AccelerometerSensorWrapper class

```
using System;
using System.ComponentModel;
using System.Threading;
using Microsoft.Devices.Sensors;

namespace AccelerometerPedometerSimulator
{
    public class AccelerometerSensorWrapper
    {
        private BackgroundWorker generateReadingsWorker;
        private Accelerometer accelerometer;
        private bool isSimulation;
        public event EventHandler<AccelerometerReadingWrapperEventArgs>
            ReadingChanged;

        public AccelerometerSensorWrapper(bool isSimulation)
        {
            this.isSimulation = isSimulation;

            if (!isSimulation)
            {
                accelerometer = new Accelerometer();
                accelerometer.ReadingChanged +=
                    new EventHandler<AccelerometerReadingEventArgs>(
                        accelerometer_ReadingChanged);
            }
        }

        public void Start()
        {
            if (isSimulation)
            {
                if (generateReadingsWorker == null)
                {
                    generateReadingsWorker = new BackgroundWorker();
```

```csharp
            generateReadingsWorker.DoWork += new DoWorkEventHandler(
                generateReadingsWorker_DoWork);
            generateReadingsWorker.WorkerSupportsCancellation = true;
            generateReadingsWorker.RunWorkerAsync();
        }
    }
    else
    {
        accelerometer.Start();
    }
}

public void Stop()
{
    if (isSimulation)
    {
        if (generateReadingsWorker != null)
        {
            generateReadingsWorker.CancelAsync();
            generateReadingsWorker = null;
        }
    }
    else
    {
        accelerometer.Stop();
    }
}

private void accelerometer_ReadingChanged(object sender,
    AccelerometerReadingEventArgs e)
{
    OnReadingChanged(new AccelerometerReading(e));
}

private void OnReadingChanged(AccelerometerReading reading)
{
    if (ReadingChanged != null)
    {
        ReadingChanged(this,
            new AccelerometerReadingWrapperEventArgs(reading));
    }
}

public void generateReadingsWorker_DoWork(
    object sender, DoWorkEventArgs e)
{
    BackgroundWorker worker = sender as BackgroundWorker;
    Random random = new Random();
    while (!worker.CancellationPending)
    {
        // Get and raise event for reading.
        AccelerometerReading reading = new AccelerometerReading(
            random.NextDouble() * 2.0 - 1,
            random.NextDouble() * 2.0 - 1,
            random.NextDouble() * 2.0 - 1);
```

continues

LISTING 6-11 *(continued)*

```
        OnReadingChanged(reading);

        // Pause before next reading.
        Thread.Sleep(random.Next(1000) + 500);
      }
    }
  }
}
```

Code Snippet AccelerometerPedometerSimulator\AccelerometerSensorWrapper.cs

9. Modify the code in `MainPage.xaml.cs` so that it looks Listing 6-12.

LISTING 6-12: Modifying the code in MainPage.xaml.cs

```csharp
public partial class MainPage : PhoneApplicationPage
{
    private const bool SimulateAccelerometer = true;

    private bool isRunning;
    private AccelerometerSensorWrapper accelerometerWrapper;
    private DateTime lastEventTime;
    private const double SignificantMagnitudeThreshold = 0.5;
    private AccelerometerReading previousReading;

    public MainPage()
    {
        InitializeComponent();

        Stats = new PedometerStatistics();
        accelerometerWrapper =
            new AccelerometerSensorWrapper(SimulateAccelerometer);
        accelerometerWrapper.ReadingChanged +=
            new EventHandler<AccelerometerReadingWrapperEventArgs>(
                accelerometerWrapper_ReadingChanged);
    }

    ...

    private void StartStopButton_Click(object sender, RoutedEventArgs e)
    {
        if (isRunning)
        {
            try
            {
                accelerometerWrapper.Stop();
                ...
            }
            ...
        }
```

```
            else
            {
                try
                {
                    accelerometerWrapper.Start();
                    ...
                }
                ...
            }
        }

        private void accelerometerWrapper_ReadingChanged(object sender,
            AccelerometerReadingWrapperEventArgs e)
        {
            if (previousReading == null)
            {
                previousReading = e.Reading;
                return;
            }

            if (e.Reading.GetChangeMagnitude(previousReading)
                > SignificantMagnitudeThreshold)
            {
                ...
            }

            previousReading = e.Reading;
        }
    }
}
```

Code Snippet AccelerometerPedometerSimulator\MainPage.xaml.cs

10. Run the application and then tap Start. Data starts to be displayed.
After a while, the display looks similar to Figure 6-6.

How It Works

In this example, you've added a simulated data stream to the previous
example, and you've used it to demonstrate how that example responds to
accelerometer data. In order to make this simulation easier, you create a
wrapper class that can act as either a real or simulated data stream. Once
configured, you can use this class from your main code transparently, so
you can concentrate on using the data rather than on obtaining it. The
wrapper class is then reusable, so any other application you make that
requires the same sensor data could use it just as easily.

The first thing you do in this example is to create a class to represent
accelerometer readings, `AccelerometerReading`. This class stores readings,
regardless of whether they are real or simulated. It also avoids a tricky
problem: the fact that the event arguments class that the accelerometer
uses to store reading data, `AccelerometerReadingEventArgs`,
doesn't have a public constructor. It is therefore more difficult to
reuse the `AccelerometerReadingEventArgs` class in your code.

FIGURE 6-6: The
pedometer display with
simulated data.

`AccelerometerReading` has two constructors so that it can be initialized in one of two ways. First, it can be initialized with an instance of `AccelerometerReadingEventArgs` returned from the real sensor:

```
public AccelerometerReadingWrapper(
        AccelerometerReadingEventArgs reading)
{
    X = reading.X;
    Y = reading.Y;
    Z = reading.Z;
}
```

Or it can be initialized by using simulated measurements:

```
public AccelerometerReadingWrapper(double x, double y, double z)
{
    X = x;
    Y = y;
    Z = z;
}
```

You also provide a utility method to extract the magnitude of a change between one instance of this class and another:

```
public double GetChangeMagnitude(
        AccelerometerReading previousReading)
{
    double changeX = X - previousReading.X;
    double changeY = Y - previousReading.Y;
    double changeZ = Z - previousReading.Z;

    return Math.Sqrt(
        changeX * changeX + changeY * changeY + changeZ * changeZ);
}
```

Next, you create a new event argument type to use the new reading type, `AccelerometerReadingWrapperEventArgs`. After preparing the "plumbing," you create the actual sensor wrapper, `AccelerometerSensorWrapper`. This code includes a little multithreading code in order to allow the simulated data to be created in the background, but it's not too complicated. To keep things simple, you use the `BackgroundWorker` class.

 NOTE *Multithreading is important if you want to create responsive user interfaces. However, we don't discuss multithreading in great depth in this book.*

The code for this class starts by declaring the fields that are required and an event that will be raised when a real or simulated reading arrives:

```
public class AccelerometerSensorWrapper
{
    private BackgroundWorker generateReadingsWorker;
```

```
private Accelerometer accelerometer;
private bool isSimulation;
public event EventHandler<AccelerometerReadingWrapperEventArgs>
    ReadingChanged;
```

In the constructor, you configure the real accelerometer sensor if the class is running in nonsimulated mode:

```
public AccelerometerSensorWrapper(bool isSimulation)
{
    this.isSimulation = isSimulation;

    if (!isSimulation)
    {
        accelerometer = new Accelerometer();
        accelerometer.ReadingChanged +=
            new EventHandler<AccelerometerReadingEventArgs>(
                accelerometer_ReadingChanged);
    }
}
```

This code in the constructor is, as you might expect, much like the code in the previous Try It Out section, since you're doing the same thing.

NOTE *Configuration is not required for simulated mode because this is done on-the-fly, as you'll see in a moment.*

Next, the code includes Start() and Stop() methods, which either delegate to the matching methods of the real sensor or start and stop the simulation:

```
public void Start()
{
    if (isSimulation)
    {
        if (generateReadingsWorker == null)
        {
            generateReadingsWorker = new BackgroundWorker();
            generateReadingsWorker.DoWork += new DoWorkEventHandler(
                generateReadingsWorker_DoWork);
            generateReadingsWorker.WorkerSupportsCancellation = true;
            generateReadingsWorker.RunWorkerAsync();
        }
    }
    else
    {
        accelerometer.Start();
    }
}
```

```
public void Stop()
{
    if (isSimulation)
    {
        if (generateReadingsWorker != null)
        {
            generateReadingsWorker.CancelAsync();
            generateReadingsWorker = null;
        }
    }
    else
    {
        accelerometer.Stop();
    }
}
```

To start the simulation, you create an instance of the BackgroundWorker class and provide it with a method that contains the code you want it to run in the background — in this case, generateReadingsWorker_DoWork(). Then you start running it by calling RunWorkerAsync(). To stop it, you call CancelAsync(), which sets a flag called CancellationPending that can be detected in generateReadingsWorker_DoWork().

The next code in the wrapper sensor class raises the ReadingChanged event when a sensor reading is generated by the real sensor:

```
private void accelerometer_ReadingChanged(object sender,
    AccelerometerReadingEventArgs e)
{
    OnReadingChanged(new AccelerometerReading(e));
}
```

This code calls the OnReadingChanged() method, which is the code that actually raises the event (so you can reuse it for simulated readings):

```
private void OnReadingChanged(AccelerometerReading reading)
{
    if (ReadingChanged != null)
    {
        ReadingChanged(this,
                new AccelerometerReadingWrapperEventArgs(reading));
    }
}
```

Finally, the generateReadingsWorker_DoWork() method uses a random number generator to create random X, Y, and Z readings once every 0.5 to 1.5 seconds:

```
public void generateReadingsWorker_DoWork(
        object sender, DoWorkEventArgs e)
{
    BackgroundWorker worker = sender as BackgroundWorker;
```

```
        Random random = new Random();
        while (!worker.CancellationPending)
        {
            // Get and raise event for reading.
            AccelerometerReading reading = new AccelerometerReading(
                random.NextDouble() * 2.0 - 1,
                random.NextDouble() * 2.0 - 1,
                random.NextDouble() * 2.0 - 1);
            OnReadingChanged(reading);

            // Pause before next reading.
            Thread.Sleep(random.Next(1000) + 500);
        }
    }
}
```

After creating the wrapper, you make the required modifications to the main code, mainly to remove unused sections. You also change the event hander to use the new event argument type and the step detection algorithm to use the new `GetChangeMagnitude()` helper method. In essence, though, the code for the application remains more or less the same.

SUMMARY

In this chapter, you looked at various ways to interact with Windows Phone 7 devices. This included a discussion of the ways in which development for mobile devices differs from more traditional software development, and a look at the features you can expect in Windows Phone 7 devices.

You looked at how to consider device orientation in your applications, how to use the Back button, how to trigger vibration, and how to use the FM radio. Next, you took a look at the accelerometer sensor. Sadly, the accelerometer sensor is currently the only sensor that you can write code for with the release available at the time of writing this book. However, the generic techniques you learned in this chapter are likely to apply to all sensors as they become available (hopefully by the time you read this). In particular, the techniques you learned for simulating sensor data will be invaluable.

In the next chapter, you'll look at more platform-specific Windows Phone 7 features and how to create applications that fit into the framework you have available. There is some overlap with the subject of this chapter — for example, you could argue that multitouch is a hardware feature — and you'll look more at how to interact with the software features that the Windows Phone 7 environment provides.

EXERCISES

1. A Windows Phone 7 device supports some of the following hardware features. Which of them can you guarantee that a device will support?

a) Accelerometer

b) Thermometer

c) Compass

d) Vibration

e) Altimeter

2. If you want a page of your application to be viewable only in portrait orientation, how would you prevent the page from changing to landscape orientation?

3. How would you disable the Back button for a page? Why wouldn't you want to do this?

4. How would you detect whether the accelerometer sensor is disabled in a device?

5. Modify the `AccelerometerPedometerSimulator` application to play back the following readings, which should be stored in a resource file called `Readings.xml` (shown in Listing 6-13).

LISTING 6-13: Readings.xml

```xml
<?xml version="1.0" encoding="utf-8" ?>
<Readings>
  <Reading t="600" x="0.1" y="-0.5" z="1" />
  <Reading t="1400" x="-0.7" y="0" z="0.6" />
  <Reading t="950" x="0.3" y="-0.2" z="0.2" />
  <Reading t="1000" x="0" y="-0.4" z="0" />
  <Reading t="1200" x="0.4" y="0.9" z="-0.3" />
  <Reading t="800" x="0" y="1" z="-0.9" />
</Readings>
```

Code Snippet AccelerometerPedometerSimulator\Readings.xml

For each reading, the x, y, and z attributes show you the parameters, and the t attribute shows how long to pause before the next reading. If your code works, four steps should be taken when you run the application. What is the average time per step with this input?

> **HINT**
>
> If you change the properties of the XML file in the solution so that the build action is `Resource`, you can obtain an XML reader by using the following code:
>
> ```
> System.Xml.XmlReader readingsToUse =
>     System.Xml.XmlReader.Create(
>     System.Windows.Application.GetResourceStream(new Uri(
>     "AccelerometerPedometerSimulator;component/Readings.xml",
>     UriKind.Relative)).Stream);
> ```
>
> Remember to close the reader when you no longer need it.

Answers to the Exercises can be found in the Appendix.

▶ WHAT YOU LEARNED IN THIS CHAPTER

TOPIC	KEY CONCEPTS
Mobile versus traditional development	Mobile devices have different capabilities from desktop PCs. You're restricted by less processing power and a smaller display, but the trade-off is that you can use hardware features unique to mobile devices (for example, location awareness and assorted environmental sensors). In short, you should not view mobile device hardware as a limitation.
Device orientation	Users can hold mobile devices in several orientations, and Windows Phone 7 devices expose this orientation to your applications. You can respond to orientation changes and write your applications in such a way that they function in the best possible way in any given orientation. In addition, you can specify that a given page can be viewed only in a given orientation and will not change its appearance if the orientation changes.
The Back button	All Windows Phone 7 devices have a Back button. You can write code that is executed when a user presses this button, such as to confirm that the user wants to navigate away from a page. However, you should exercise caution when doing this and avoid making your application behave in a way that the user wouldn't predict. Windows Phone 7 devices also have a Search button and a Start button, but you can't write code that responds to them.
Vibration	You can cause a Windows Phone 7 device to vibrate by using the vibration controller from your code. This can be a great way to provide feedback, although you shouldn't overuse it. The maximum duration permitted for a single vibration is five seconds.
FM radio	If a Windows Phone 7 device has an FM radio, you can control it using very simple code. However, you should be sure to check for exceptions when you set the radio frequency.
Accelerometer sensor	Every Windows Phone 7 device includes an accelerometer sensor that detects forces applied to the device. The sensor raises events as these forces are detected, and you can take advantage of this functionality in your code. You can use this information to enhance the user experience of your applications, as it is an alternative source of input data.
Sensor simulation	Due to the limitations of the Windows Phone 7 emulator, you must simulate accelerometer readings if you don't have an actual device for testing. You might also want to simulate readings to test your applications, such as with a predetermined stream of data rather than random input. You can do this in a number of ways, including wrapping the sensor and its data in classes that can be used to expose real or simulated data.

7

Launchers, Choosers, and Advanced User Input

WHAT YOU WILL LEARN IN THIS CHAPTER:

➤ Using the application bar

➤ Understanding launchers and choosers

➤ Using launchers and choosers to perform common tasks, including manipulating contacts, making calls, and sending messages

➤ Controlling the software input panel (SIP)

➤ Responding to multitouch input

In the previous chapter, you looked at how mobile device hardware differs from standard PC hardware and how you can use the additional functionality. In this chapter, you'll learn about features provided by the Windows Phone 7 operating system and how to interact with them. There is some overlap between these subjects because the Windows Phone 7 operating system is shaped by the hardware on which it resides. For example, multitouch, which is the ability to interact with software by using two or more fingers on a touchscreen, is obviously hardware-related. In this case, the operating system provides an additional layer of abstraction for you, which enables you to work directly with gestures instead of raw data from the hardware. In addition, you can follow a number of best practices to make your applications feel more in tune with the Windows Phone 7 operating system.

Many of the features you'll look at in this chapter relate to a direct interaction with the Windows Phone 7 operating system. For example, you'll examine functionality that you control through launchers and choosers, which allow you to communicate with built-in functionality such as making phone calls.

You'll start by looking at the application bar, which is a standard user interface control that you're encouraged to use in your applications. Proper use of this control will ensure that your applications work in the same intuitive way as the applications provided as part of Windows Phone 7. Next, you'll look at launchers and choosers, which enable your applications to trigger phone calls, take pictures with the built-in camera, add and remove contacts, and more.

Finally, you'll look at more advanced user input. For example, you'll learn about controlling the SIP to change the type of input that a user can make, such as numbers instead of letters. You'll also look at responding to multitouch input and gestures, and at how to simulate this kind of input in the emulator.

USING THE APPLICATION BAR

Many applications use a standard user input element, such as a menu, to provide quick access to frequently used functionality. In Windows applications, for example, you're probably used to seeing the standard text-based menu, with entries such as File and Edit, as well as toolbar icons and the newer Ribbon icons. You could implement similar menus in Windows Phone 7 applications, but the preferred way of achieving this is to use the built-in application bar. All Microsoft-supplied Windows Phone 7 applications provide the application bar, and if you use it as well, you'll provide users with a consistent user experience.

The application bar can be opaque or semi-transparent and can contain up to four icons in a panel at the bottom of the device screen. It can also give users access to a list of additional text menu commands via a pop-up selection panel.

The Windows Phone 7 toolkit allows you to add buttons and text items that look and respond just like the built-in ones. Microsoft has even provided a downloadable pack of icons for you to use (included in the download of Expression Blend for Windows Phone, available at `www.microsoft` `.com/expression/windowsphone/`), as shown in Figure 7-1.

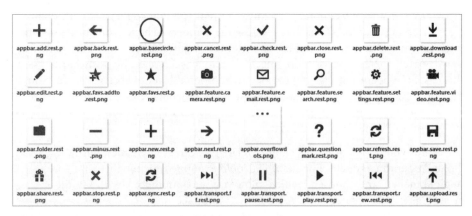

FIGURE 7-1: Application bar icons for Windows Phone 7.

NOTE *The downloadable application bar icons come in white-on-black and black-on-white versions. You can choose which set to use based on the color scheme in use on the device, and there are also vector versions in* .ai *files. On a phone with the default color scheme, you'll use the white-on-black versions, but because they have a transparent background, they're a little difficult to see in Explorer thumbnails. This is why Figure 7-1 shows the inverted versions.*

Figure 7-2 shows an example of the application bar, both in its default size and in pop-up mode with the text menu items. This pop-up appears when you tap the ellipsis (. . .) button. Note that descriptive text for the icons is visible only when the pop-up is visible.

FIGURE 7-2: The application bar in default mode (left) and pop-up mode (right).

Adding an Application Bar

To add an application bar to a page, you provide a value for the `PhoneApplicationPage` `.ApplicationBar` property. This property is of type `Microsoft.Phone.Shell.IApplicationBar`, and you can use an instance of type `Microsoft.Phone.Shell.ApplicationBar`, which supports the required interface.

You can do all this in code if you like, but it's usually better to provide all the information you need in XAML. For example, you can use the following XAML to add an empty application bar:

```
<phone:PhoneApplicationPage ... >
  <phone:PhoneApplicationPage.ApplicationBar>
    <shell:ApplicationBar IsVisible="True" />
  </phone:PhoneApplicationPage.ApplicationBar>
  ...
</phone:PhoneApplicationPage>
```

The `shell` namespace is included by default in a new page, and it maps to the .NET namespace `Microsoft.Phone.Shell`.

One thing to consider when you add an application bar is whether you want it to be semi-transparent and float over the page content or whether you want to make it opaque. You can set the `Opacity` property of the `ApplicationBar` control to achieve this, to 1 for opaque or 0.5 for semi-transparent. (You can use other values, but the recommended best practice is to use one of these two.) This property affects the space made available to your page content. An opaque application bar will reduce the page area, whereas a semi-transparent application bar makes the whole page available. This effect actually modifies the dimensions of the page, so you must ensure that your application responds correctly if you're using proportional scale factors, such as in grids with * sizing.

Adding Application Bar Icons

As mentioned in the previous section, application bar icons are contained in the `Buttons` property of the application bar. This property is a collection to which you can add instances of the `ApplicationBarIconButton` class. This class has the members shown in Table 7-1.

TABLE 7.1: ApplicationBarIconButton Members

MEMBER	DESCRIPTION
IconUri	You use this property to specify the URI of an icon image.
Text	You should set this property to a short descriptive term for the icon.
IsEnabled	If this property is `false`, the button will be disabled and will appear grayed out.
Click	This event is fired when the button is pressed; handle it in your code to respond to this.

To add an icon, you must include both `IconUri` and `Text`.

NOTE *The* `ApplicationBarIconButton` *class doesn't inherit from* `DependencyObject`, *and its properties aren't dependency properties. This means that you can't bind to its properties, which can be a little frustrating. Instead, you must rely on code-behind to change property values — for example, to set whether a button is enabled depending on what a user currently has selected in a page.*

You can use the following XAML to create an application bar with two icons added:

```
<phone:PhoneApplicationPage.ApplicationBar>
  <shell:ApplicationBar IsVisible="True">
    <shell:ApplicationBar.Buttons>
      <shell:ApplicationBarIconButton IconUri="/images/monkey.png" Text="monkey"
        Click="Monkey_Click" />
      <shell:ApplicationBarIconButton IconUri="/images/badger.png" Text="badger"
        Click="Badger_Click" />
    </shell:ApplicationBar.Buttons>
  </shell:ApplicationBar>
</phone:PhoneApplicationPage.ApplicationBar>
```

If you create your own icon, you must make it a 48 x 48-pixel image with your icon on a transparent background. The circle surrounding the icon is overlaid over your image automatically, so you don't have to include it. To make the icon appear completely within this circle, you should use only the center 26 x 26 area of the image.

You should add icon images to a project with the Build Action setting Content and the Copy to Output Directory setting Copy Always. You'll see this in practice shortly, in a Try It Out section, but first you'll look at adding text menu items.

Adding Application Bar Text Menu Items

To add a text menu item, you add an instance of the `ApplicationBarMenuItem` class to the `ApplicationBar.MenuItems` property. The `ApplicationBarMenuItem` class is similar to the `ApplicationBarIconButton` class; in fact, the only difference is that it doesn't have the `IconUri` property. Instead, the text you place in `Text` is used for display purposes. Any text you add here will automatically be converted to lowercase letters, to encourage a standardized look and feel to Windows Phone 7 applications.

The following XAML shows an application bar with menu items added:

```
<phone:PhoneApplicationPage.ApplicationBar>
  <shell:ApplicationBar IsVisible="True">
    <shell:ApplicationBar.MenuItems>
      <shell:ApplicationBarMenuItem Text="pirate" Click="Pirate_Click" />
      <shell:ApplicationBarMenuItem Text="ninja" Click="Ninja_Click" />
    </shell:ApplicationBar.MenuItems>
  </shell:ApplicationBar>
</phone:PhoneApplicationPage.ApplicationBar>
```

TRY IT OUT   Using the Application Bar

In the following steps, you'll build a simple application that includes an application bar with icons and menu items. Later in the chapter, you'll add functionality to this application; in particular, you'll add functionality to the event handlers for some of the buttons and menu items. A fair amount of the code in the Try It Out section is devoted to styling this application, but rest assured that although it's a lot to type in now, you'll be reusing it later.

1.   Using the Windows Phone application template, create a new application called **AdventureHolidays**.

2.   Add a new class called `AdventureHoliday` to the application and modify the code in `AdventureHoliday.cs` so that it looks like Listing 7-1.

LISTING 7-1: Adding the AdventureHoliday class and modifying the code in AdventureHoliday.cs

```csharp
using System.ComponentModel;

namespace AdventureHolidays
{
    public class AdventureHoliday : INotifyPropertyChanged
    {
        private string name;
        private string description;
        private string contactNumber;
        private bool isFavorite;
        public event PropertyChangedEventHandler PropertyChanged;

        public string Name
        {
            get
            {
                return name;
            }
            set
            {
                if (name != value)
                {
                    name = value;
                    OnPropertyChanged("Name");
                }
            }
        }

        public string Description
        {
            get
            {
                return description;
            }
```

```
        set
        {
           if (description != value)
           {
              description = value;
              OnPropertyChanged("Description");
           }
        }
     }

     public string ContactNumber
     {
        get
        {
           return contactNumber;
        }
        set
        {
           if (contactNumber != value)
           {
              contactNumber = value;
              OnPropertyChanged("ContactNumber");
           }
        }
     }

     public bool IsFavorite
     {
        get
        {
           return isFavorite;
        }
        set
        {
           if (isFavorite != value)
           {
              isFavorite = value;
              OnPropertyChanged("IsFavorite");
           }
        }
     }

     private void OnPropertyChanged(string propertyName)
     {
        if (PropertyChanged != null)
        {
           PropertyChanged(this, new PropertyChangedEventArgs(propertyName));
        }
     }
  }
}
```

Code Snippet AdventureHolidays\AdventureHoliday.cs

3. Add a new class called BoolToOpacityConverter to the application and modify the code in BoolToOpacityConverter.cs so that it looks like Listing 7-2.

LISTING 7-2: Adding the BoolToOpacityConverter class and modifying BoolToOpacityConverter.cs

```csharp
using System;
using System.Globalization;
using System.Windows;
using System.Windows.Data;

namespace AdventureHolidays
{
    public class BoolToOpacityConverter : IValueConverter
    {
        public object Convert(object value, Type targetType, object parameter,
            CultureInfo culture)
        {
            if ((bool)value)
            {
                return 1.0D;
            }
            else
            {
                return 0.2D;
            }
        }

        public object ConvertBack(object value, Type targetType, object parameter,
            CultureInfo culture)
        {
            return DependencyProperty.UnsetValue;
        }
    }
}
```

Code Snippet AdventureHolidays\BoolToOpacityConverter.cs

4. Modify the code in MainPage.xaml so that it looks like Listing 7-3.

LISTING 7-3: Modifying the code in MainPage.xaml

```xml
<phone:PhoneApplicationPage ...
    xmlns:local="clr-namespace:AdventureHolidays"
    xmlns:vsm="clr-namespace:System.Windows;assembly=System.Windows"
    Name="Root">

    <phone:PhoneApplicationPage.Resources>

        <local:BoolToOpacityConverter x:Key="boolToOpacityConverter" />
```

```xml
<DataTemplate x:Key="adventureHolidayTemplate">
  <Grid Margin="8,0,8,0">
    <Grid.ColumnDefinitions>
      <ColumnDefinition Width="48" />
      <ColumnDefinition />
    </Grid.ColumnDefinitions>
    <Grid.RowDefinitions>
      <RowDefinition Height="Auto" />
      <RowDefinition />
    </Grid.RowDefinitions>
    <Image Source="/images/appbar.favs.rest.png"
      Opacity="{Binding IsFavorite,
        Converter={StaticResource boolToOpacityConverter}}" />
    <TextBlock Grid.Column="1" Text="{Binding Name}"
      Style="{StaticResource PhoneTextLargeStyle}" TextWrapping="Wrap" />
    <TextBlock Grid.Column="1" Grid.Row="1" Margin="16,0,0,0"
      Text="{Binding ContactNumber}" />
  </Grid>
</DataTemplate>

<Style x:Key="listBoxItemStyle" TargetType="ListBoxItem">
  <Setter Property="Template">
    <Setter.Value>
      <ControlTemplate TargetType="ListBoxItem">
        <Border CornerRadius="8" x:Name="itemBorder"
          Background="{TemplateBinding Background}"
          BorderThickness="2" BorderBrush="Transparent">
          <vsm:VisualStateManager.VisualStateGroups>
            <vsm:VisualStateGroup x:Name="CommonStates">
              <vsm:VisualState x:Name="Normal" />
            </vsm:VisualStateGroup>
            <vsm:VisualStateGroup x:Name="SelectionStates">
              <vsm:VisualState x:Name="Unselected">
                <Storyboard>
                  <ColorAnimation Storyboard.TargetName="itemBorder"
                    Storyboard.TargetProperty=
                      "(BorderBrush).(SolidBrush.Color)"
                    To="Transparent" Duration="00:00:00.2" />
                </Storyboard>
              </vsm:VisualState>
              <vsm:VisualState x:Name="Selected">
                <Storyboard>
                  <ColorAnimation Storyboard.TargetName="itemBorder"
                    Storyboard.TargetProperty=
                      "(BorderBrush).(SolidBrush.Color)"
                    To="Yellow" Duration="00:00:00.5" />
                </Storyboard>
              </vsm:VisualState>
            </vsm:VisualStateGroup>
          </vsm:VisualStateManager.VisualStateGroups>
          <ContentPresenter Content="{TemplateBinding Content}"
            HorizontalAlignment="Left"
            Margin="{TemplateBinding Padding}" Visibility="Visible" />
        </Border>
```

continues

LISTING 7-3 *(continued)*

```
                </ControlTemplate>
              </Setter.Value>
            </Setter>
        </Style>

    </phone:PhoneApplicationPage.Resources>

    <phone:PhoneApplicationPage.ApplicationBar>
      <shell:ApplicationBar IsVisible="True">
        <shell:ApplicationBar.Buttons>
          <shell:ApplicationBarIconButton
            IconUri="/images/appbar.questionmark.rest.png"
            Text="description" Click="Description_Click" />
          <shell:ApplicationBarIconButton IconUri="/images/appbar.favs.rest.png"
            Text="toggle fav" Click="ToggleFavorite_Click" />
          <shell:ApplicationBarIconButton IconUri="/images/appbar.delete.rest.png"
            Text="delete" Click="Delete_Click" />
          <shell:ApplicationBarIconButton
            IconUri="/images/appbar.feature.email.rest.png"
            Text="email" Click="Email_Click" />
        </shell:ApplicationBar.Buttons>
        <shell:ApplicationBar.MenuItems>
          <shell:ApplicationBarMenuItem Text="call" Click="Call_Click" />
          <shell:ApplicationBarMenuItem Text="reset list" Click="ResetList_Click" />
        </shell:ApplicationBar.MenuItems>
      </shell:ApplicationBar>
    </phone:PhoneApplicationPage.ApplicationBar>

    <Grid x:Name="LayoutRoot" Background="Transparent">
      <Grid.RowDefinitions>
        <RowDefinition Height="Auto"/>
        <RowDefinition Height="*"/>
      </Grid.RowDefinitions>

      <StackPanel x:Name="TitlePanel" Grid.Row="0" Margin="12,17,0,28">
        <TextBlock x:Name="ApplicationTitle" Text="ADVENTURE HOLIDAYS"
          Style="{StaticResource PhoneTextNormalStyle}"/>
        <TextBlock x:Name="PageTitle" Text="holiday list" Margin="9,-7,0,0"
          Style="{StaticResource PhoneTextTitle1Style}"/>
      </StackPanel>

      <Grid x:Name="ContentPanel" Grid.Row="1" Margin="12,0,12,0">
        <ListBox x:Name="AdventureHolidayList"
              ItemsSource="{Binding ElementName=Root, Path=AdventureHolidays}"
              ItemTemplate="{StaticResource adventureHolidayTemplate}"
              ItemContainerStyle="{StaticResource listBoxItemStyle}" />
      </Grid>
    </Grid>
</phone:PhoneApplicationPage>
```

Code Snippet AdventureHolidays\MainPage.xaml

5. Modify the code in `MainPage.xaml.cs` so that it looks like Listing 7-4.

Available for
download on
Wrox.com

LISTING 7-4: Modifying the code in MainPage.xaml.cs

```
using System;
using System.Collections.ObjectModel;
using System.Windows;
using Microsoft.Phone.Controls;

namespace AdventureHolidays
{
    public partial class MainPage : PhoneApplicationPage
    {
        private ObservableCollection<AdventureHoliday> adventureHolidays;

        public MainPage()
        {
            InitializeComponent();
        }

        public ObservableCollection<AdventureHoliday> AdventureHolidays
        {
            get
            {
                if (adventureHolidays == null)
                {
                    adventureHolidays = new ObservableCollection<AdventureHoliday>();
                    LoadAdventureHolidays();
                }

                return adventureHolidays;
            }
        }

        public AdventureHoliday SelectedItem
        {
            get
            {
                return AdventureHolidayList.SelectedItem as AdventureHoliday;
            }
        }

        private void LoadAdventureHolidays()
        {
            adventureHolidays.Clear();
            adventureHolidays.Add(new AdventureHoliday
            {
                Name = "Egyptian Excavation",
                Description = "Hunt for lost treasure and hidden hieroglyphs in"
                    + " the desert sands of Giza.",
                ContactNumber = "1-800-555-0101"
            });
```

continues

LISTING 7-4 *(continued)*

```
        adventureHolidays.Add(new AdventureHoliday
        {
            Name = "Galapagos Galore",
            Description = "Explore all of the Galapagos Islands during this"
                + " two-week cruise. If you're lucky, you might see a volcano"
                + " erupt!",
            ContactNumber = "1-800-555-0102"
        });
        adventureHolidays.Add(new AdventureHoliday
        {
            Name = "Amazing Astronaut Adventure",
            Description = "A once-in-a-lifetime trip to the International"
                + " Space Station. Participate in science experiments and peer"
                + " at the Earth from above.",
            ContactNumber = "1-800-555-0103",
            IsFavorite = true
        });
        adventureHolidays.Add(new AdventureHoliday
        {
            Name = "Bumps and Balloons",
            Description = "Soar over the Alps in a hot air balloon.",
            ContactNumber = "1-800-555-0104"
        });
        adventureHolidays.Add(new AdventureHoliday
        {
            Name = "Elevated Eating in Edinburgh",
            Description = "Eat gourmet local produce on a platform 100 feet"
                + " above Edinburgh.",
            ContactNumber = "1-800-555-0105"
        });
        adventureHolidays.Add(new AdventureHoliday
        {
            Name = "Canoeing in the Canyon",
            Description = "See the Grand Canyon from a canoe on the Colorado"
                + " River.",
            ContactNumber = "1-800-555-0106"
        });
        adventureHolidays.Add(new AdventureHoliday
        {
            Name = "Riding Route 66",
            Description = "Pick your perfect pony and ride as much or as little"
                + " of Route 66 as you want. Disclaimer: ponies will need to be"
                + " changed at regular intervals.",
            ContactNumber = "1-800-555-0107"
        });
    }

    private void Description_Click(object sender, EventArgs e)
    {
        if (SelectedItem != null)
        {
```

```
            MessageBox.Show(SelectedItem.Description, SelectedItem.Name,
               MessageBoxButton.OK);
        }
    }

    private void ToggleFavorite_Click(object sender, EventArgs e)
    {
        if (SelectedItem != null)
        {
            SelectedItem.IsFavorite = !SelectedItem.IsFavorite;
        }
    }

    private void Delete_Click(object sender, EventArgs e)
    {
        if (SelectedItem != null)
        {
            adventureHolidays.Remove(SelectedItem);
        }
    }

    private void Email_Click(object sender, EventArgs e)
    {
        // Email selected adventure holiday to a contact.
    }

    private void Call_Click(object sender, EventArgs e)
    {
        // Call contact number for selected adventure holiday.
    }

    private void ResetList_Click(object sender, EventArgs e)
    {
        LoadAdventureHolidays();
    }
    }
}
```

Code Snippet AdventureHolidays\MainPage.xaml.cs

6. Add a directory called Images to the solution. Also add the following images from those included with Expression Blend for Windows Phone (discussed earlier in this chapter):

```
appbar.delete.rest.png
appbar.favs.rest.png
appbar.feature.email.rest.png
appbar.questionmark.rest.png
```

You'll find these images in the C:\Program Files (x86)\Microsoft SDKs\Windows Phone\ v7.0\Icons\dark directory after installing Blend. (They're also available in the downloadable code for this chapter.)

7. In the Solution Explorer window, select each of the images you've added. Then set Build Action to Content and set Copy to Output Directory to Copy always, as shown in Figure 7-3.

8. Run the application. You should see a list of adventure holidays. You can select items from the list and use the application bar icons to toggle whether they are marked as favorites, to delete them, and to view descriptive information. You can also use the pop-up menu to reset the list. (Note that this application isn't yet complete; you'll add more functionality later in the chapter.) Figure 7-4 shows two screenshots of the running application.

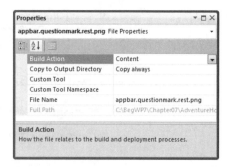

FIGURE 7-3: Setting image file properties.

FIGURE 7-4: The list of holidays in the `AdventureHolidays` application (left) and details of a specific holiday (right).

How It Works

In this example, you created a simple list application that demonstrates how you can use the application bar. To support the list, you made a simple data model class called `AdventureHoliday`. Next, you added a value converter, `BoolToOpacityConverter`, to convert `bool` values to `Opacity` values. This converter is used in the XAML for the main page to display "favorite" items with a star that has an `Opacity` setting of 1.0 and others with an `Opacity` setting of 0.2.

Next, you added the XAML for the main page. This started with a definition of three resources:

➤ An instance of BoolToOpacityConverter

➤ A data template for use with AdventureHoliday items

➤ A ListBoxItem style that defines a new control template

There's nothing too unusual about any of these, although it is worth looking closely at the use of VisualStateManager to control the styling of list box items. You can simplify the process of styling the item list by supplying a storyboard for changes to the Selected and Unselected states.

At this point, the most interesting section of the XAML is the part that defines the application bar:

```
<phone:PhoneApplicationPage.ApplicationBar>
  <shell:ApplicationBar IsVisible="True">
    <shell:ApplicationBar.Buttons>
      <shell:ApplicationBarIconButton
        IconUri="/images/appbar.questionmark.rest.png"
        Text="description" Click="Description_Click" />
      <shell:ApplicationBarIconButton IconUri="/images/appbar.favs.rest.png"
        Text="toggle fav" Click="ToggleFavorite_Click" />
      <shell:ApplicationBarIconButton IconUri="/images/appbar.delete.rest.png"
        Text="delete" Click="Delete_Click" />
      <shell:ApplicationBarIconButton
        IconUri="/images/appbar.feature.email.rest.png"
        Text="email" Click="Email_Click" />
    </shell:ApplicationBar.Buttons>
    <shell:ApplicationBar.MenuItems>
      <shell:ApplicationBarMenuItem Text="call" Click="Call_Click" />
      <shell:ApplicationBarMenuItem Text="reset list" Click="ResetList_Click" />
    </shell:ApplicationBar.MenuItems>
  </shell:ApplicationBar>
</phone:PhoneApplicationPage.ApplicationBar>
```

This defines four buttons and two menu items:

➤ **Description** — This button displays a description for the current selection.

➤ **Toggle-favorite** — This button changes the value of the IsFavorite property for the selection and changes the associated display.

➤ **Delete** — This button removes the selection from the list.

➤ **Email** — This button sends the current item to a contact as an email. (You'll implement this functionality later in this chapter.)

➤ **call** — This menu item calls the number in the ContactNumber property of the selected item. (Again, you'll implement this functionality later in the chapter.)

➤ **reset list** — This menu item returns the list to its original state.

Each of these buttons and menu items has a corresponding event handler in the code-behind. The code-behind starts with the code necessary to create and bind the list. First, there is an underlying storage field called `adventureHolidays`:

```
private ObservableCollection<AdventureHoliday> adventureHolidays;
```

This is an instance of `ObservableCollection<AdventureHoliday>` so that any changes to the list are reflected automatically in the user interface. This list is exposed through the `AdventureHolidays` property:

```
public ObservableCollection<AdventureHoliday> AdventureHolidays
{
    get
    {
        if (adventureHolidays == null)
        {
            adventureHolidays = new ObservableCollection<AdventureHoliday>();
            LoadAdventureHolidays();
        }

        return adventureHolidays;
    }
}
```

When this property is first accessed, it initializes the collection through a method called `LoadAdventureHolidays()`. In a more advanced implementation, this method might obtain information from some other source, such as a web service, but for simplicity, it currently sets some hardcoded values. (There's no need to repeat the code for that here as it's quite lengthy but extremely simple.)

For convenience, the current item is also made available through a property:

```
public AdventureHoliday SelectedItem
{
    get
    {
        return AdventureHolidayList.SelectedItem as AdventureHoliday;
    }
}
```

The application bar functionality is encapsulated in a number of event handlers, starting with `Description_Click()` for the description icon, which simply shows a message box with the `Description` property of the current item if an item is selected:

```
private void Description_Click(object sender, EventArgs e)
{
    if (SelectedItem != null)
    {
        MessageBox.Show(SelectedItem.Description, SelectedItem.Name,
            MessageBoxButton.OK);
    }
}
```

Next is the event handler for toggling favorites, `ToggleFavorite_Click()`:

```
private void ToggleFavorite_Click(object sender, EventArgs e)
{
    if (SelectedItem != null)
    {
        SelectedItem.IsFavorite = !SelectedItem.IsFavorite;
    }
}
```

As you might expect, this simply inverts the value of the item's `IsFavorite` property. The data model supports `INotifyPropertyChanged`, so this change in value is immediately reflected in the user interface. Next up is `Delete_Click()`, which removes the current item from the list:

```
private void Delete_Click(object sender, EventArgs e)
{
    if (SelectedItem != null)
    {
        adventureHolidays.Remove(SelectedItem);
    }
}
```

The next two event handlers, `Email_Click()` and `Call_Click()`, are not yet implemented, but the final one, `ResetList_Click()`, is:

```
private void ResetList_Click(object sender, EventArgs e)
{
    LoadAdventureHolidays();
}
```

This simply calls the same `LoadAdventureHolidays()` initialization method used when the application starts.

Application Bar Best Practices

Now that you've seen how simple it is to add an application bar to an application, there are a few things you need to be aware of. If you want to maximize usability, you must be careful in your implementation. In theory, you can use any icon you like, with any color scheme, but under those circumstances, it would be quite easy to make something that doesn't fit into the theme used in the rest of Windows Phone 7. In general, you want to make your interface as intuitive as possible, and this means either reusing the supplied icons (as in the previous example) or designing your icons so that they have a similar look and feel. Remember that because the Windows Phone 7 operating system adds circles for you, as noted earlier, sticking to a 26 x 26-pixel image in the center of a 48 x 48-pixel square is generally the best policy.

You should also divide your functionality into frequent and infrequent use, with icons being used for the most frequently used functionality and menu items for other functionality. And you might consider avoiding using menu items unless absolutely necessary because they require more interaction than icons.

Finally, one thing you didn't do in this Try It Out section is control the `IsEnabled` property of application bar icons and menu items. As mentioned earlier, you can't do this by binding; instead, you must manually change these values in code-behind. A disabled icon or menu item appears grayed out and can't be tapped. Keeping icons visible in this way provides excellent user experience feedback based on context, as it alerts users to functionality even when it is currently unavailable.

USING LAUNCHERS AND CHOOSERS

You can use launchers and choosers to make your application interact with other applications that are built into Windows Phone 7. For example, you can enable your application to access phone contacts as well as built-in hardware such as the camera.

Launchers and choosers work in essentially the same way. However, whereas a launcher implies "fire-and-forget" functionality, a chooser may (but does not always) return data to your application. When you trigger either a launcher or a chooser, your application is temporarily suspended until either the launcher or chooser completes or the user interrupts the operation. This suspension is known as *tombstoning*, and it has debugging implications, as you'll see shortly.

One of the reasons launchers and choosers are so useful is that they can provide additional information when your application triggers them. For example, when sending an email, you can provide content for the email body, or when launching a web search, you can set the text to search for. This interactivity between applications is part of what makes the Windows Phone 7 user experience great: it allows you to build into and extend an integrated user experience.

All launchers and choosers are contained in the `Microsoft.Phone.Task` namespace. This namespace also contains some other types, such as event arguments, that support the available launchers and choosers.

A number of launchers and choosers are currently available to Windows Phone 7 developers, and more are being added all the time. Before you take a look at them, though, you'll learn some general information about launchers and choosers.

An Overview of Launchers

Launchers trigger Windows Phone 7 functionality that doesn't return a specific result. You can use launchers to trigger the following functionality:

➤ Compose an email or SMS (text) message.

➤ Interact with the Windows Phone Marketplace.

➤ Make a phone call.

➤ Trigger a search.

➤ Open a web browser.

Each launcher consists of a single class that you can configure and then trigger by using its `Show()` method. Depending on the specific launcher, the functionality may occur immediately, or it may require an additional step from the user; for example, the phone call task initially displays a phone number, and the user can decide whether he or she wants to call the number.

 NOTE *The launcher* Show() *method is defined for each launcher because there is no common base class. It is possible that some future launchers will use a different method.*

While a launcher is active, the application that triggered it becomes inactive. The application is reactivated when the launcher finishes. However, the user may decide to quit the launcher by pressing the Home button, thereby bypassing the application reactivation. Therefore, you can make no assumptions in your application about what was achieved (or not achieved) by a launcher.

An Overview of Choosers

Choosers trigger Windows Phone 7 functionality that can either return a result to your application or simply notify you that an operation was successful. You can use choosers to trigger the following functionality:

➤   Take a new photo or select an existing photo.

➤   Get an email address or a phone number from a contact.

➤   Save an email address or a phone number to a new or existing contact.

All choosers inherit from the same base class in the `Microsoft.Phone.Tasks` namespace: `ChooserBase<TTaskEventArgs>`. The generic type argument is the event argument type that is used for completion notification, and it must inherit from `TaskEventArgs`. The base class defines a method called `Show()` that is used to trigger the chooser and an event called `Completed` that is raised when the chooser returns.

As with launchers, your application becomes inactive while a chooser executes, and it may or may not be reactivated again, depending on what the user does. A chooser also may or may not return data, as the user may cancel the operation.

When you use a chooser, you must initialize it and attach an event handler to `Completed` in the constructor of your page. This is required because of the life cycle of Windows Phone 7 applications and how the reactivation process works.

When a chooser completes, you can look at the event arguments returned to see what happened. The `TaskEventArgs` class defines an `Error` property that will contain exception information if an error occurred during the chooser operation. It also defines a `TaskResult` property that lets you know what happened through the `TaskResult` enumeration, which has the members shown in Table 7-2.

TABLE 7-2: TaskResult Enumeration Members

MEMBER	DESCRIPTION
None	No status is returned by the chooser.
OK	The chooser completed successfully.
Cancelled	The user canceled the chooser operation.

Some choosers use an event argument that derives from TaskEventArgs rather than simply using TaskEventArgs. This enables them to pass additional information, such as an email address.

Tombstoning

As mentioned earlier in this chapter, while a launcher or chooser is executing, your application is inactivated in a process known as tombstoning. Luckily for developers, Microsoft has made the debugger aware of this, and it doesn't detach. (Earlier versions of the Windows Phone 7 toolkit weren't so smart.) When the launcher or chooser completes and returns control to your application, the debugger carries on where it left off.

Something to be aware of is that your application might not be relaunched directly after a launcher or chooser executes; the user might decide to do something else, such as return to the home screen or do some browsing. The next time your application is started, however, it will be as if the launcher or chooser has just returned. For choosers, this means that the Completed event fires, so be prepared.

 WARNING *Tombstoning doesn't save your application state for you. If there is anything you need to save, you have to save it manually, in response to activation and deactivation events.*

Working with Contacts

Contact information is perhaps the most fundamental aspect of Windows Phone 7 devices. After all, whatever else a phone might be, it's still a phone, and you still use it to make calls. With recent smartphones, mobile email has also become the norm. The core functionality of managing contacts, making calls, and sending emails involves the built-in applications, but there are times when you'll also want your applications to make use of this functionality. For example, you might want to add contact details from an "about" page in your application, or maybe you need to send an email with predetermined content to a contact.

There are four choosers that you can use to manipulate contacts: two for getting and saving email addresses and two for getting and saving phone numbers. In the next two sections, you'll look at each of these. Note that these choosers don't deal with contacts directly. Rather, they deal with items that are part of contact information.

Adding Contact Information

If you are using the Windows Phone 7 emulator, you may have noticed that you start out with no contacts defined. Depending on the emulator version you're using, you also may not have direct access to the contacts application. However, you can still add contacts by using the following two choosers in code:

➤ SaveEmailAddressTask — Used to save an email address to a new or existing contact

➤ SavePhoneNumberTask — Used to save a phone number to a new or existing contact

Before you trigger these tasks, you must define them at the page level and then create them and add event handlers in the constructor for your page. (As noted earlier, event handlers are essential for all choosers.) The following is an example of doing this for SavePhoneNumberTask:

```
private SavePhoneNumberTask savePhoneNumberTask;

public MainPage()
{
    InitializeComponent();

    savePhoneNumberTask = new SavePhoneNumberTask();
    savePhoneNumberTask.Completed += (o, e) =>
        {
            if (e.TaskResult == TaskResult.OK)
                MessageBox.Show("Phone number saved.");
            else
                MessageBox.Show("Phone number not saved.");
        };
}
```

This code uses lambda syntax to define a delegate event handler for the SavePhoneNumberTask .Completed event. It's a handy technique if you want to use a simple handler without making a new method. The code displays a message that indicates whether the phone number was saved.

Once you have created a chooser, you can trigger it by calling its Show() method, but first you need to set the data you want to save. You do this by setting the Email property of SaveEmailAddressTask or the PhoneNumber property of SavePhoneNumberTask. For example, for the savePhoneNumberTask chooser from the preceding code snippet, you might write code such as the following:

```
savePhoneNumberTask.PhoneNumber = "1-800-555-10111";
savePhoneNumberTask.Show();
```

For both of these choosers, the next step is to create a new contact or choose a contact to which you want to save the email or phone number. You can also choose the type of phone number (cell, home, and so on) or email (personal, work, and so on) to save to the contact.

Reading Contact Information

To read contact information, use another two chooser tasks:

➤   `EmailAddressChooserTask` — Used to get an email address from a contact

➤   `PhoneNumberChooserTask` — Used to get a phone number from a contact

These work just like `SaveEmailAddressTask` and `SavePhoneNumberTask` except that you don't have to set the `Email` or `PhoneNumber` properties before calling `Show()`. Instead, you use either the `EmailResult.Email` property or the `PhoneNumberResult.PhoneNumber` property to read the chosen email address or phone number. These values are passed through the event arguments for the `Completed` event for the associated chooser.

For example, the following code shows how to configure an instance of `PhoneNumberChooserTask`:

```
private PhoneNumberChooserTask phoneNumberChooserTask;

public MainPage()
{
    InitializeComponent();

    phoneNumberChooserTask = new PhoneNumberChooserTask();
    phoneNumberChooserTask.Completed += (o, e) =>
        {
            if (e.TaskResult == TaskResult.OK)
                MessageBox.Show(e.PhoneNumber);
            else
                MessageBox.Show("No phone number selected.");
        };
}
```

This code simply displays the selected phone number, or a message if none is selected in the chooser for some reason.

After this is configured, triggering the chooser requires the following simple code:

```
phoneNumberChooserTask.Show();
```

The launcher displays the contacts in the phone. When the user selects one of these contacts, either a result is returned immediately or, if more than one result is available for the contact (for example, if the contact has multiple email addresses), the user can select the required item.

In the following Try It Out, you'll see the four contact-related choosers in action.

TRY IT OUT   **Manipulating Contacts**

1.   Using the Windows Phone application template, create a new application called **ContactManipulator**.

2.   Modify the code in `MainPage.xaml` so that it looks like Listing 7-5.

LISTING 7-5: Modifying the code in MainPage.xaml

```xml
<phone:PhoneApplicationPage ... >
  <Grid x:Name="LayoutRoot" Background="Transparent">

    ...

    <StackPanel x:Name="TitlePanel" Grid.Row="0" Margin="12,17,0,28">
      <TextBlock x:Name="ApplicationTitle" Text="CONTACT MANIPULATOR"
        Style="{StaticResource PhoneTextNormalStyle}"/>
      <TextBlock x:Name="PageTitle" Text="contact details" Margin="9,-7,0,0"
        Style="{StaticResource PhoneTextTitle1Style}"/>
    </StackPanel>

    <Grid x:Name="ContentPanel" Grid.Row="1" Margin="12,0,12,0">
      <Grid.RowDefinitions>
        <RowDefinition Height="Auto" />
        <RowDefinition Height="Auto" />
        <RowDefinition Height="*" />
        <RowDefinition Height="Auto" />
        <RowDefinition Height="Auto" />
        <RowDefinition Height="*" />
      </Grid.RowDefinitions>
      <Grid.ColumnDefinitions>
        <ColumnDefinition />
        <ColumnDefinition />
      </Grid.ColumnDefinitions>
      <TextBlock Grid.Row="0" Grid.ColumnSpan="2" Text="Phone Number"
        Style="{StaticResource PhoneTextTitle2Style}" />
      <TextBox Grid.Row="1" Grid.ColumnSpan="2" x:Name="PhoneNumberBox"
        Text="1-800-555-0101" />
      <Button Grid.Row="2" Grid.Column="0" x:Name="SavePhoneNumberButton"
        Content="Save Number" Click="SavePhoneNumberButton_Click" />
      <Button Grid.Row="2" Grid.Column="1" x:Name="GetPhoneNumberButton"
        Content="Get Number" Click="GetPhoneNumberButton_Click" />
      <TextBlock Grid.Row="3" Grid.ColumnSpan="2" Text="Email"
        Style="{StaticResource PhoneTextTitle2Style}" />
      <TextBox Grid.Row="4" Grid.ColumnSpan="2" x:Name="EmailBox"
        Text="someone@somewhere.com" />
      <Button Grid.Row="5" Grid.Column="0" x:Name="SaveEmailButton"
        Content="Save Email" Click="SaveEmailButton_Click" />
      <Button Grid.Row="5" Grid.Column="1" x:Name="GetEmailButton"
        Content="Get Email" Click="GetEmailButton_Click" />
    </Grid>
  </Grid>

</phone:PhoneApplicationPage>
```

Code Snippet ContactManipulator\MainPage.xaml

3. Modify the code in `MainPage.xaml.cs` so that it looks like Listing 7-6.

LISTING 7-6: Modifying the code in MainPage.xaml.cs

```csharp
using System.Windows;
using Microsoft.Phone.Controls;
using Microsoft.Phone.Tasks;

namespace ContactManipulator
{
    public partial class MainPage : PhoneApplicationPage
    {
        private SavePhoneNumberTask savePhoneNumberTask;
        private SaveEmailAddressTask saveEmailAddressTask;
        private PhoneNumberChooserTask phoneNumberChooserTask;
        private EmailAddressChooserTask emailAddressChooserTask;

        public MainPage()
        {
            InitializeComponent();

            // Create choosers.
            savePhoneNumberTask = new SavePhoneNumberTask();
            saveEmailAddressTask = new SaveEmailAddressTask();
            phoneNumberChooserTask = new PhoneNumberChooserTask();
            emailAddressChooserTask = new EmailAddressChooserTask();

            // Attach event handlers.
            savePhoneNumberTask.Completed += (o, e) =>
              DisplayResult("SavePhoneNumberTask", e);
            saveEmailAddressTask.Completed += (o, e) =>
              DisplayResult("SaveEmailAddressTask", e);
            phoneNumberChooserTask.Completed += (o, e) =>
            {
                DisplayResult("PhoneNumberChooserTask", e);
                PhoneNumberBox.Text = e.PhoneNumber ?? PhoneNumberBox.Text;
            };
            emailAddressChooserTask.Completed += (o, e) =>
            {
                DisplayResult("EmailAddressChooserTask", e);
                EmailBox.Text = e.Email ?? EmailBox.Text;
            };
        }

        private void DisplayResult(string taskName, TaskEventArgs e)
        {
            string message = string.Format(
                "Error: {0}\nResult: {1}",
                e.Error == null ? "None" : e.Error.Message,
                e.TaskResult);
            MessageBox.Show(message, taskName, MessageBoxButton.OK);
        }
```

```
private void SavePhoneNumberButton_Click(object sender, RoutedEventArgs e)
{
    savePhoneNumberTask.PhoneNumber = PhoneNumberBox.Text;
    savePhoneNumberTask.Show();
}

private void GetPhoneNumberButton_Click(object sender, RoutedEventArgs e)
{
    phoneNumberChooserTask.Show();
}

private void SaveEmailButton_Click(object sender, RoutedEventArgs e)
{
    saveEmailAddressTask.Email = EmailBox.Text;
    saveEmailAddressTask.Show();
}

private void GetEmailButton_Click(object sender, RoutedEventArgs e)
{
    emailAddressChooserTask.Show();
}
    }
}
```

Code Snippet ContactManipulator\MainPage.xaml.cs

4. Run the application. Figure 7-5 shows the display you should now see.

5. Press the Save Number button, create a new contact to save the number to, and then save the number as a home number. If all goes well, you should see the success message shown in Figure 7-6.

FIGURE 7-5: The contact details display.

FIGURE 7-6: The success message, which indicates that a phone number has been saved.

6. Enter a different number in the text box, and then repeat the process but add the new number (as a mobile number) to the contact you added in step 5.

7. Tap the Get Number button and then select the contact you added and the mobile number for that contact (see Figure 7-7). When you return to the application, the text box should be updated to show the number you have selected.

8. Use the Save Email and Get Email buttons to repeat the process for email addresses.

FIGURE 7-7: Updated contact details.

How It Works

This simple example shows how to use the four contact-related choosers in an application that lets you save and load phone and email data to and from contacts. The simple user interface consists of two text boxes for entering data (some dummy data is supplied) and buttons for saving and loading that data.

The code-behind initializes the four choosers as discussed earlier. The following example shows `EmailAddressChooserTask`:

```
public partial class MainPage : PhoneApplicationPage
{

    ...

    private EmailAddressChooserTask emailAddressChooserTask;

    public MainPage()
    {

        ...

        emailAddressChooserTask = new EmailAddressChooserTask();

        ...

        emailAddressChooserTask.Completed += (o, e) =>
        {
            DisplayResult("EmailAddressChooserTask", e);
            EmailBox.Text = e.Email ?? EmailBox.Text;
        };
    }
```

The event handler delegate calls a helper method called `DisplayResult()` and sets the `EmailBox` text in the user interface to the returned email address if it isn't null (using the null-coalescing operator (`??`) for simplicity). The `DisplayResult()` method simply calls `MessageBox.Show()` with appropriate text:

```
private void DisplayResult(string taskName, TaskEventArgs e)
{
    string message = string.Format(
        "Error: {0}\nResult: {1}",
        e.Error == null ? "None" : e.Error.Message,
        e.TaskResult);
    MessageBox.Show(message, taskName, MessageBoxButton.OK);
}
```

The remainder of the code consists of the four button click event handlers, which configure (if required) and show the choosers:

```
private void SavePhoneNumberButton_Click(object sender, RoutedEventArgs e)
{
    savePhoneNumberTask.PhoneNumber = PhoneNumberBox.Text;
    savePhoneNumberTask.Show();
}

private void GetPhoneNumberButton_Click(object sender, RoutedEventArgs e)
{
    phoneNumberChooserTask.Show();
}

private void SaveEmailButton_Click(object sender, RoutedEventArgs e)
{
    saveEmailAddressTask.Email = EmailBox.Text;
    saveEmailAddressTask.Show();
}

private void GetEmailButton_Click(object sender, RoutedEventArgs e)
{
    emailAddressChooserTask.Show();
}
}
```

You might have noticed that every time a chooser returns, the data in the text boxes is reset (except in the case of those you're populating with the Get Number and Get Email buttons). As noted earlier, tombstoning doesn't result in an automatic save of your application data; you must save manually if you want that behavior. Please don't try to use the numbers shown in this example to call Neil Armstrong; they aren't his real ones.

Making Voice Calls

To make a voice call, use the `PhoneCallTask` launcher. After you create an instance of this launcher, you can set the number to call via the `PhoneNumber` property and then call the `Show()` method, as in the following example:

```
PhoneCallTask phoneCallTask = new PhoneCallTask();
phoneCallTask.PhoneNumber = "1-800-555-0101";
phoneCallTask.Show();
```

A confirmation message displays, as shown in Figure 7-8.

If the number is associated with a contact in the phone, the contact name will be displayed when the call is made. Alternatively, you can set the `DisplayName` property of the launcher to specify a name to be displayed.

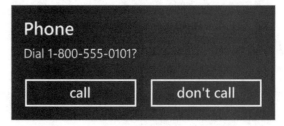

FIGURE 7-8: Voice call confirmation message.

Using Email and SMS Messaging

You can send email and SMS messages by using the `EmailComposeTask` and `SmsComposeTask` launchers. You must configure these launchers according to the messaging system you're using. For emails, you can set the `To`, `Cc`, `Subject`, and `Body` properties, as shown in this example:

```
EmailComposeTask emailComposeTask = new EmailComposeTask();
emailComposeTask.To = "someone@somewhere.come";
emailComposeTask.Cc = "someoneelse@somewhere.come";
emailComposeTask.Subject = "New cheese";
emailComposeTask.Body =
    "I just tried some Isle of Butte cheddar, you have to get some!";
emailComposeTask.Show();
```

For SMS, you can set the `To` and `Body` properties:

```
SmsComposeTask smsComposeTask = new SmsComposeTask();
smsComposeTask.To = "1-800-555-0101";
smsComposeTask.Body = "Tried the cheese. I prefer gorgonzola.";
smsComposeTask.Show();
```

In both cases, the Windows Phone 7 device gives users the option to edit all aspects of the message before sending, which makes sense because they might want to personalize messages or add additional recipients. For SMS messages, the user will see the screen shown in Figure 7-9, which allows a user to customize a message.

Interacting with the Camera

The Windows Phone 7 architecture allows for some fairly advanced ways of interacting with the camera, including making "photos extras applications" that can manipulate photos and interact with the camera seamlessly. However, here you'll look at the simpler technique of launching the camera and reading a result. You'll also look at how to get access to previous results.

Launching the Camera

To launch the camera, you need to use the `CameraCaptureTask` chooser. This has no initialization parameters, and it returns a result in its event

FIGURE 7-9: The SMS message screen.

arguments, which are of type `PhotoResult`. As with other choosers, you must have a page-level private field for the chooser, and you must create and initialize the chooser in the page constructor, as in the following example:

```
private CameraCaptureTask cameraCaptureTask;

public MainPage()
{
    InitializeComponent();

    cameraCaptureTask = new CameraCaptureTask();
    cameraCaptureTask.Completed += new EventHandler<PhotoResult>(
        cameraCaptureTask_Completed);
}
```

The result comes back as a stream reference, and you must read data from this stream to get the picture that was taken.

Reading Photo Results

The camera result event argument type, `PhotoResult`, returns the image as a stream in its `ChosenPhoto` property. You can read this directly into a `BitmapImage` object (a type you'll find in the `System.Windows.Media.Imaging` namespace) by using the `BitmapImage.SetSource()` method, as in this example:

```
private BitmapImage imageResult;

private void cameraCaptureTask_Completed(object sender, PhotoResult e)
{
    if (e.TaskResult == TaskResult.OK)
    {
        imageResult = new BitmapImage();
        imageResult.SetSource(e.ChosenPhoto);
    }
}
```

After you have the `BitmapImage` instance, you can do what you like with it. For example, you can set it as the `Source` property for an `Image` control on a page.

The `PhotoResult` event arguments include the image itself and the filename of the image in a property called `OriginalFileName`. For freshly taken pictures, this won't be a very user-friendly string, but, as you'll see in the next section, this property can still be useful.

If you're using the emulator, you can use the basic camera simulator, which returns an image of a black square on a white background. The square moves around while the camera application waits for you to take pictures, so if you take several pictures, they will be different, which is handy for testing. (At the time of writing, this emulator appears to be in the 64-bit version of the emulator only.) Alternatively, some sources on the Internet claim to have worked some magic to make the emulator work with a webcam, and you might want to investigate this if you're feeling brave.

Getting a Saved Image

You can use the `PhotoChooserTask` chooser to access other images stored in the Windows Phone 7 device's memory. This returns the same event argument type, `PhotoResult`, as `CameraCaptureTask`, which makes the `OriginalFileName` property more useful: It shows a filename that the user may have set.

The `PhotoChooserTask` chooser allows you to specify some additional information that can be useful, depending on how you want to use the resultant image. For example, if you want to get an image that is 100 pixels square, you can set the `PixelHeight` and `PixelWidth` properties to 100. The user is then presented with a cropping tool in the photo application so that the image that is returned has the specified dimensions. These properties are set to 0 by default, meaning "no restrictions." You can also set the `ShowCamera` property to `true` if you want to allow the user to take a new photo instead of selecting an existing one; this property is `false` by default.

The emulator comes with some sample images for you to look at, which makes it easier to test photo chooser functionality.

Using Other Launchers

A few more launchers are included in the Windows Phone 7 SDK, and more are being created all the time. The following sections whiz you through the ones you haven't seen yet.

Media Players

The `MediaPlayerLauncher` launcher is unique in that it is the only current launcher to include the word *Launcher* in its class name. You can use this launcher to enable users to view media such as video and audio files. However, using this launcher isn't the only way to do this; you can also embed media in your pages by using the `<MediaElement>` control. The difference between these two approaches is that, like other launchers, `MediaPlayerLauncher` spawns a new process, using the built-in media player application. This provides a familiar user interface that, like other launchers, helps to tie your application into the Windows Phone 7 experience.

The `MediaPlayerLauncher` launcher can display media in three different locations:

➤ Saved media on the device, in isolated storage

➤ Media contained in the application

➤ Remote media elsewhere on the Internet

You can specify the location from which to get media by using a combination of the `Location` and `Media` properties of the launcher, which are of types `MediaLocationType` and `Uri`. For remote media, you just need to set `Media` to an absolute URI, as in this example:

```
MediaPlayerLauncher mediaPlayerLauncher = new MediaPlayerLauncher();
mediaPlayerLauncher.Media = new Uri("http://somewhere.com/sometune.mp3",
    UriKind.Absolute);
mediaPlayerLauncher.Show();
```

For local media, you can set `Location` to `MediaLocationType.Data` for saved data or to `MediaLocationType.Install` for media bundled in your application. Then you can set the `Media` property to a relative URI, as in this example:

```
MediaPlayerLauncher mediaPlayerLauncher = new MediaPlayerLauncher();
mediaPlayerLauncher.Location = MediaLocationType.Install;
mediaPlayerLauncher.Media = new Uri("MyGreatVideo.wmv", UriKind.Relative);
mediaPlayerLauncher.Show();
```

The default for the `Location` property is `MediaLocationType.None`, which results in `FileNotFound` exceptions if you try to launch local media.

As well as specifying the file to view, you can also customize the media player slightly by choosing what controls to display. You do this by setting the `Controls` property to a `MediaPlaybackControls` value. The default is `All`, but you can also specify `None` or any combination of `Pause`, `Stop`, `FastForward`, `Rewind`, and `Skip`. For example, to show just the pause and stop controls, you would use this:

```
MediaPlayerLauncher mediaPlayerLauncher = new MediaPlayerLauncher();
mediaPlayerLauncher.Controls =
    MediaPlaybackControls.Pause | MediaPlaybackControls.Stop;
```

As you can see here, the | operator allows you to combine values.

Marketplace

There are several launchers for interacting with the Windows Phone Marketplace. You can use `MarketplaceHubTask` to launch the Marketplace client application, `MarketplaceSearchTask` to search it, and `MarketplaceDetailTask` and `MarketplaceReviewTask` to look at the details or review pages for a product. These last two are probably worth including in any about page for your applications, as they encourage feedback.

In Chapter 15, you'll see `MarketplaceDetailTask` in action.

Web Browser and Search

The last two launchers available to you are `SearchTask`, which enables you to search the web, and `WebBrowserTask`, which enables you to navigate to a web page in the built-in web browser. Both of these launchers are extremely simple to use. To search, you set the `SearchQuery` property of `SearchTask` to your desired search term or terms:

```
SearchTask searchTask = new SearchTask();
searchTask.SearchQuery = "wrox";
searchTask.Show();
```

To browse, you set the `URL` property of `WebBrowserTask` to your desired location:

```
WebBrowserTask webBrowserTask = new WebBrowserTask();
webBrowserTask.URL = "www.wrox.com";
webBrowserTask.Show(); WebBrowserTask
```

In the following Try It Out, you'll add launchers and choosers to the application you created earlier.

Adding Launchers and Choosers to the Adventure Holiday List Application

1. Open the `AdventureHolidays` solution you created earlier in the chapter and modify the code in `MainPage.xaml.cs` so that it looks like Listing 7-7.

LISTING 7-7: Modifying the code in MainPage.xaml.cs

```csharp
using System;
using System.Collections.ObjectModel;
using System.Windows;
using Microsoft.Phone.Controls;
using Microsoft.Phone.Shell;
using Microsoft.Phone.Tasks;

namespace AdventureHolidays
{
    public partial class MainPage : PhoneApplicationPage
    {
        private ObservableCollection<AdventureHoliday> adventureHolidays;

        private EmailAddressChooserTask emailAddressChooserTask;

        public MainPage()
        {
            InitializeComponent();

            emailAddressChooserTask = new EmailAddressChooserTask();
            emailAddressChooserTask.Completed +=
                new EventHandler<EmailResult>(emailAddressChooserTask_Completed);

            PhoneApplicationService.Current.Deactivated +=
                new EventHandler<DeactivatedEventArgs>(Current_Deactivated);
        }

        ...

        private void Email_Click(object sender, EventArgs e)
        {
            if (SelectedItem != null)
            {
                emailAddressChooserTask.Show();
            }
        }

        private void Call_Click(object sender, EventArgs e)
        {
            if (SelectedItem != null)
            {
                PhoneCallTask phoneCallTask = new PhoneCallTask();
```

```
            phoneCallTask.PhoneNumber = SelectedItem.ContactNumber;
            phoneCallTask.DisplayName = SelectedItem.Name;
            phoneCallTask.Show();
        }
    }

    ...

    private void emailAddressChooserTask_Completed(object sender, EmailResult e)
    {
        AdventureHoliday adventureHoliday =
            PhoneApplicationService.Current.State["SelectedItem"]
                as AdventureHoliday;

        if (adventureHoliday != null && e.TaskResult == TaskResult.OK)
        {
            EmailComposeTask emailComposeTask = new EmailComposeTask();
            emailComposeTask.To = e.Email;
            emailComposeTask.Subject = adventureHoliday.Name;
            emailComposeTask.Body = string.Format(
                "I thought you might be interested in this:\n\n{0}",
                adventureHoliday.Description);
            emailComposeTask.Show();
        }
    }

    private void Current_Deactivated(object sender, DeactivatedEventArgs e)
    {
        if (PhoneApplicationService.Current.State.ContainsKey("SelectedItem"))
        {
            PhoneApplicationService.Current.State.Remove("SelectedItem");
        }

        if (SelectedItem != null)
        {
            PhoneApplicationService.Current.State.Add(
                "SelectedItem", SelectedItem);
        }
    }
}
}
```

Code Snippet AdventureHolidays\MainPage.xaml.cs

2. Run the application, select an item, and tap the Call menu item from the pop-up menu. A call window appears, as shown in Figure 7-10.

3. Cancel the call and then tap the email application bar icon. If you have any contacts with email addresses stored in the device, you can select one, and an email will be created, ready for sending.

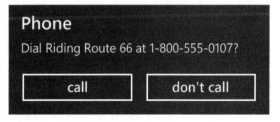

FIGURE 7-10: A call window.

How It Works

In this example, you added code to the handlers for the call and email functionality in order to call the number associated with an item or send an item to a contact. The call functionality was simple, as it merely required a launcher, which you configured with data from the selected item:

```
private void Call_Click(object sender, EventArgs e)
{
    if (SelectedItem != null)
    {
        PhoneCallTask phoneCallTask = new PhoneCallTask();
        phoneCallTask.PhoneNumber = SelectedItem.ContactNumber;
        phoneCallTask.DisplayName = SelectedItem.Name;
        phoneCallTask.Show();
    }
}
```

Emailing a contact was more difficult; it required both a chooser to select an email address and a launcher to send the email. You also had to store the selected item in application state while the application was suspended.

First, you created a chooser for the email functionality and attached a handler to its `Completed` event in the page constructor:

```
private EmailAddressChooserTask emailAddressChooserTask;

public MainPage()
{
    InitializeComponent();

    emailAddressChooserTask = new EmailAddressChooserTask();
    emailAddressChooserTask.Completed +=
        new EventHandler<EmailResult>(emailAddressChooserTask_Completed);
```

Also in the constructor, you added a hander to the `Deactivated` event of the current `PhoneApplicationService` instance:

```
    PhoneApplicationService.Current.Deactivated +=
        new EventHandler<DeactivatedEventArgs>(Current_Deactivated);
}
```

This handler is responsible for storing the current selected item, after first ensuring that any previously stored item is discarded:

```
private void Current_Deactivated(object sender, DeactivatedEventArgs e)
{
    if (PhoneApplicationService.Current.State.ContainsKey("SelectedItem"))
    {
        PhoneApplicationService.Current.State.Remove("SelectedItem");
    }
```

```
        if (SelectedItem != null)
        {
            PhoneApplicationService.Current.State.Add(
                "SelectedItem", SelectedItem);
        }
    }
```

Next, the code for the email functionality starts with the code to launch an email chooser:

```
    private void Email_Click(object sender, EventArgs e)
    {
        if (SelectedItem != null)
        {
            emailAddressChooserTask.Show();
        }
    }
```

When this chooser returns, the code checks the persisted state for a selected item and the `TaskResult` that was returned. If a persisted item exists and the user selected an item, the user can send an email:

```
    private void emailAddressChooserTask_Completed(object sender, EmailResult e)
    {
        AdventureHoliday adventureHoliday =
            PhoneApplicationService.Current.State["SelectedItem"]
                as AdventureHoliday;
        if (adventureHoliday != null && e.TaskResult == TaskResult.OK)
        {
```

To enable email sending, you simply needed to configure properties of an `EmailComposeTask` launcher and then call its `Show()` method:

```
            EmailComposeTask emailComposeTask = new EmailComposeTask();
            emailComposeTask.To = e.Email;
            emailComposeTask.Subject = adventureHoliday.Name;
            emailComposeTask.Body = string.Format(
                "I thought you might be interested in this:\n\n{0}",
                adventureHoliday.Description);
            emailComposeTask.Show();
        }
    }
```

Alternatively, you could simplify things by just using this launcher and letting users enter their own `To` data, as required.

THE SOFTWARE INPUT PANEL (SIP)

In this section, you'll take a closer look at how users enter text into text boxes in Windows Phone 7 applications. You've seen the keyboard entry several times already (for example, see Figure 7-9, earlier in this chapter). This keyboard entry display is known as the SIP.

Several methods of input are available in most mobile devices, including, in some cases, voice recognition. However, alphanumeric input is perhaps the most prevalent. Depending on what a text box is intended to contain, though, you might want to have a little more control over a user's input. For example, if the user is entering a phone number, letters are not required. In this case, you might want to display only a numeric keypad.

There is no way of completely customizing the SIP with your own selection of letters, numbers, and symbols. Thankfully, though, you can have the SIP display in various modes that restrict or enhance user input capabilities in a more generic (but no less useful) way.

Controlling the SIP

The SIP is controlled by the `InputScope` property of a text box. In XAML, you can set this property with a string value that is the name of a member of the `InputScopeNameValue` enumeration. This is quite a large enumeration; it has 62 members. However, not every member has a unique associated SIP display.

If you don't set the `InputScope` property, the value is assumed to be `Default`, which gives a basic alphanumeric keypad. For example, setting it to `TelephoneNumber` gives the SIP display shown in Figure 7-11.

The Windows Phone 7 documentation details eight separate modes for the SIP, as shown in Table 7-3.

FIGURE 7-11: The SIP display for an `InputScope` property value of `TelephoneNumber`.

TABLE 7-3: SIP Modes

MODE	DESCRIPTION
Default	Standard alphanumeric input
Text	Alphanumeric input with shortcuts to text emoticons
Email Address	Alphanumeric input with a shortcut key for .com and an @ key
Phone Number	12-key numeric input, as shown in Figure 7-11
Web Address	As `Email Address`, but with a different look for the Enter key
Maps	As `Default`, but with a different look for the Enter key
Search	Semi-transparent SIP with a different look for the Enter key and a .com button
SMS Address	As `Default`, but with easy access to numeric input

In practice, the implementation of the SIP is slightly different from what Table 7-3 shows. For example, the Search SIP is identical to the Web Address SIP, and the SMS Address SIP does not appear to be implemented at the time of writing.

The downloadable code for this chapter includes a simple test application, called SoftwareInputPanel, that enables you to see how InputScope affects the SIP. This application displays a text box and all members of the InputScopeNameValue enumeration in a list. If you select an item from the list and then tap the text box, you see the associated SIP display appear.

Figure 7-12 shows a screenshot from this test application, with InputScopeNameValue.Chat selected. Note that some SIP modes, including this one, show a text auto-completion bar like the one that's visible in Figure 7-12.

It is worth experimenting to find the most appropriate SIP modes for your applications, and it will also be worth experimenting again when new releases of Windows Phone 7 come out. More modes and changes to modes are appearing incrementally. Table 7-4 shows the current InputScope values required to get the different SIP modes.

FIGURE 7-12: The SIP with InputScopeNameValue .Chat selected.

TABLE 7-4: InputScope Values for SIP Modes

MODE	INPUTSCOPE VALUE
Default	Default
Text	Text
Email Address	EmailSmtpAddress
Phone Number	TelephoneNumber
Web Address	Url
Maps	Maps
Search	Search
SMS Address	Not defined

Some of the other InputScope options give you other, non-documented or slightly tweaked displays. For example, the CurrencyAmount value appears to display the same SIP mode as Default, but it starts on the numeric and symbol page rather than the alphabetic one. Again, experimentation seems to be the best strategy.

USING MULTITOUCH

Touchscreen technology has been available for many years now, but until recently, it was quite uncommon to find it used on a computer, especially a mobile one. Instead, you were more likely to find it in places such as airports and museums, providing a way to interact with exhibits or browse associated information. Those touchscreens were quite primitive and generally responded only to a single touch location at one time. As technology has improved, we now see far more advanced touchscreens everywhere, and using them is becoming the normal way to work with the latest smartphones. Newer screens also have a major advantage over the old ones: They can respond to multiple points of interaction simultaneously. This is known as *multitouch*.

Multitouch enables complex interaction, as combinations of touchpoints can do more interesting things than multiple single touchpoints. With multitouch, you can combine two or more points of interaction into complex gestures, such as pinching or rotating, that are impossible with a single touchpoint. Some gestures can be simpler, such as swiping a finger across the screen, so they don't always require multitouch, but multitouch extends the possibilities dramatically. Some applications, such as playing with a virtual piano keyboard, don't require multitouch interaction. Others, such as web browsing and photo manipulation, rely on it.

In this section, you'll look at what is possible and how you can respond to multitouch events and gestures in your Windows Phone 7 applications. You'll also see how to simulate multitouch when developing with the emulator.

Simulating Multitouch

The Windows Phone 7 emulator supports multitouch input, but unless you are developing on a PC with a multitouch screen, achieving this can be tricky. If you do have a multitouch monitor, lucky you: You can skip this section and head straight to the code! For the rest of us, there are a few options available. The simplest is to find a friend with a multitouch device and get that person to help out, but that may not be possible. The most complex option is to simulate the events through code, much as you did with the accelerometer in Chapter 6. Multitouch simulation is rather more complicated, though, as it involves more events and can be difficult to drive from fake data. (There would have to be a lot of fake data, and using random input wouldn't be very useful.)

Thankfully, there's a middle ground that is possible with minimal effort. Instead of using a touchscreen, you can "trick" your operating system into thinking that you have multitouch capabilities by using a third-party driver, and you can combine this with alternative hardware input, such as a webcam or more than one mouse. This sounds a bit odd, and it is indeed a little tricky to set up, but once you've done it, it makes testing multitouch applications a lot easier.

The best way to find suitable multitouch simulation options is to search for them online. One of the best that's available at the moment is Multi-Touch Vista, which you can find at `http://multitouchvista.codeplex.com`. This site takes the multiple-mouse device route and is a very effective way to get going with multitouch. It's a little fiddly to set up, and you'll need two USB mouse devices. However, step-by-step instructions are available, and once you have it set up, it's simple to use.

NOTE *All the multitouch examples in this chapter are developed using the "multiple mice" method of simulation.*

Manipulation Events

Windows Phone 7 is designed to make multitouch simple. While it is possible to get at the low-level data for touch input, such as the coordinates and sizes of each touchpoint, in practical applications, you probably won't need to. Instead, you'll find it easier to work with manipulations. A *manipulation* contains data that includes the following helpful information:

➤ **The object being manipulated** — This enables you to have several objects onscreen that can be individually moved or scaled.

➤ **The translation and scale transformation applied to the object** — You can use this information to move and size objects.

➤ **The input velocities** — This becomes important when a manipulation ends, as you might want the object being manipulated to continue moving (that is, to have inertia). You use this functionality, for example, in lists so that you can "flick" through items.

➤ **The input origin** — For multitouch manipulations such as scaling, this allows you to define a center point.

During a multitouch operation, three events are used. First, a `ManipulationStarted` event is raised. Next, while the manipulation is under way, a series of `ManipulationDelta` events are raised. Finally, when the manipulation finishes, a `ManipulationCompleted` event is raised. Each of these events has its own event argument type that inherits from `RoutedEventArgs`.

 NOTE *Silverlight defines another event,* `ManipulationInertiaStarting`, *which happens directly after a manipulation and before an additional series of "inertial"* `ManipulationDelta` *events and a final* `ManipulationCompleted` *event. This event is not supported in Windows Phone 7, and so no inertial* `ManipulationDelta` *events will occur. If you want to use inertia, you have to code for it manually, using the final manipulation velocities.*

This section looks at each of these events in turn and then at how to access low-level input. Finally, it ties things together with a code example.

The ManipulationStarted Event

The `ManipulationStarted` event has an event argument of type `ManipulationStartedEventArgs`. This type has two useful properties:

➤ `ManipulationContainer` — This property, of type `UIElement`, tells you what object is being manipulated — that is, which UI element is touched by the first manipulation point. This is important both for applying later transformations to that object and for using transformation coordinates relative to that object.

➤ `ManipulationOrigin` — This property tells you the starting point of the manipulation, which will be a `Point` instance contained by the object being manipulated.

Sometimes you aren't interested in the `ManipulationContainer` property. This is the case, for example, if you're viewing a single object and don't want to require users to touch that object. Instead, you could route any manipulations from anywhere on the page to that object — which is useful if the object can get small!

The ManipulationDelta Event

The `ManipulationDelta` event is the bread and butter of multitouch. You get a series of these events and can respond to them as they arrive to provide live feedback. This event has an argument of type `ManipulationDeltaEventArgs`. It includes `ManipulationContainer` and `ManipulationOrigin` properties, which are identical to those for `ManipulationStartedEventArgs`, as well as the following:

➤ `DeltaManipulation` — This tells you the change in manipulation since the previous `ManipulationDelta` event. This property is of type `ManipulationDelta`, which you'll look at in a moment.

➤ `CumulativeManipulation` — This tells you the total manipulation since it started, also in the form of a `ManipulationDelta` object.

➤ `Velocities` — This tells you the current velocities of manipulation — that is, how fast and in what directions the manipulation is changing. This property is of type `ManipulationVelocities`.

➤ `IsInertial` — This is currently not used in Windows Phone 7, but it would identify `ManipulationDelta` events that are inertial. It is a Boolean value that, at the time of writing, is always `false`.

Both the `ManipulationDelta` and `ManipulationVelocities` types inherit from `DependencyObject` and define two dependency properties and associated property accessors. The two properties on each object relate to scale and translation, respectively, and are all of type `Point`. The `ManipulationDelta` type has properties called `Scale` and `Translation`, and `ManipulationVelocities` has `ExpansionVelocity` and `LinearVelocity`.

A typical use of this event is to move an object as it is dragged by a user's finger. To do this, you might look at `DeltaManipulation.Translation`, which would tell you how much the touchpoint has moved since the previous event. You could apply this directly to a user interface element, which would then respond to the finger-dragging operation.

Scaling works in the same way but requires two touchpoints. You could work out for yourself how multiple touchpoints move relative to each other, but this event makes it easy for you to simply interrogate the `DeltaManipulation.Scale` property to determine the magnitude of the manipulation. And, again, you could apply this manipulation directly to a user interface element. If the manipulation doesn't include scaling (for example, if there's only a single touchpoint), the `Scale` property will be a `Point` with 0 values for `X` and `Y`.

You'll see both scaling and translation in action shortly, in the code example. This chapter doesn't look at velocity in any more detail, but as you've seen from the property definitions, it's easy to work out.

The ManipulationCompleted Event

A manipulation finishes with a single `ManipulationCompleted` event, with an argument of type `ManipulationCompletedEventArgs`. This also includes `ManipulationContainer` and `ManipulationOrigin` properties, as well as the following:

➤ `TotalManipulation` — This tells you the total manipulation over the lifetime of the manipulation, as a `ManipulationDelta` object.

➤ `FinalVelocities` — This tells you the final velocities of manipulation and is of type `ManipulationVelocities`.

➤ `IsInertial` — This is always `false`.

You can use the `TotalManipulation` and `FinalVelocities` properties just like the properties of the same types for `ManipulationDeltaEventArgs`. The only difference here is when the event occurs. Depending on what you want to achieve, you might use this event, rather than the individual delta events, to apply the manipulation in one go at the end rather than as it progresses.

Accessing Low-Level Input Data

As you've seen with the three manipulation events, it's easy to respond to multitouch manipulations in Windows Phone 7. However, in making things easy for you, manipulations also hide some information that you might have been interested in, such as the individual touchpoints that comprise a manipulation.

Admittedly, you might not need to get at this information, although you would need it if you wanted to use gestures, as discussed later in this chapter. If you want this information, it's simple enough to get — regardless of how complicated your code for making use of it might be.

To get low-level multitouch data, you can use the `System.Windows.Input.Touch` class. This exposes a single static event called `FrameReported`, which is raised every time touch input is reported. The event arguments that are returned by this event are of type `TouchFrameEventArgs`. The class enables you to get information on touchpoints in the form of `TouchPoint` objects. You do this by using one of two methods, `GetPrimaryTouchPoint()` or `GetTouchPoints()`, as follows:

```
private void Touch_FrameReported(object sender, TouchFrameEventArgs e)
{
    TouchPoint primaryTouchPoint = e.GetPrimaryTouchPoint(this);
    TouchPointCollection touchPoints = e.GetTouchPoints(this);

    // Do something with touchpoint information...
}
```

Both of these methods take a single UIElement parameter that determines the coordinates used for the TouchPoint instance returned. The coordinates are relative to the object passed, so passing this in a page class, as in the preceding code, means that they will be relative to the page position. Alternatively, you can pass an instance of the UIElement parameter that you're interested in, according to the functionality you require.

Once you have a TouchPoint instance or a collection of TouchPoint instances, you can look at the following dependency properties:

> ➤ Position — This Point value gives the position of the center point of the touchpoint, relative to the requested UIElement.

> ➤ Size — This gives you a Size instance that specifies the size of the touchpoint (so you can tell the size of the finger being used).

> ➤ Action — This is a TouchAction enumeration value, which might be Down, Move, or Up. This tells you whether the touchpoint is new (Down), moving, or being removed.

> ➤ TouchDevice — This somewhat confusingly named property lets you find out information about the particular touchpoint in use. It has a subproperty called Id that enables you to keep track of individual touchpoints if there are several. It also has a DirectlyOver sub-property that tells you the UIElement that the touchpoint is over.

With all this information at your disposal, you can perform advanced multitouch analysis, such as analyzing gestures. Or, more simply, you could use this information to write a piano-playing application, as noted earlier.

TRY IT OUT   **Responding to Multitouch Events**

In the following Try It Out, you'll create a simple image-manipulation application that will respond to and report on multitouch input.

1. Create a new Windows Phone 7 application called **ImageViewer**.

2. Add a directory called Images to the solution and add the following images (included with Expression Blend for Windows Phone):

```
appbar.feature.camera.rest.png
appbar.refresh.rest.png
```

You'll find these images in the C:\Program Files (x86)\Microsoft SDKs\Windows Phone\ v7.0\Icons\dark directory. They're also available in the downloadable code for this chapter.

3. Select each of the images you've added in the Solution Explorer window and change the properties to set Build Action to Content and Copy to Output Directory to Copy always.

4. Modify the code in MainPage.xaml so that it looks like Listing 7-8.

LISTING 7-8: Modifying the code in MainPage.xaml

```xaml
<phone:PhoneApplicationPage ...
  ManipulationDelta="PhoneApplicationPage_ManipulationDelta"
  x:Name="Root">

  <phone:PhoneApplicationPage.ApplicationBar>
    <shell:ApplicationBar IsVisible="True">
      <shell:ApplicationBar.Buttons>
        <shell:ApplicationBarIconButton
          IconUri="/images/appbar.feature.camera.rest.png"
          Text="load image" Click="LoadImage_Click" />
        <shell:ApplicationBarIconButton IconUri="/images/appbar.refresh.rest.png"
          Text="reset" Click="Reset_Click" />
      </shell:ApplicationBar.Buttons>
    </shell:ApplicationBar>
  </phone:PhoneApplicationPage.ApplicationBar>

  <Grid x:Name="LayoutRoot" Background="Transparent">
    <Grid.RowDefinitions>
      <RowDefinition Height="Auto"/>
      <RowDefinition Height="*"/>
      <RowDefinition Height="Auto"/>
    </Grid.RowDefinitions>

    <StackPanel x:Name="TitlePanel" Grid.Row="0" Margin="12,17,0,28">
      <TextBlock x:Name="ApplicationTitle" Text="MULTITOUCH"
        Style="{StaticResource PhoneTextNormalStyle}"/>
      <TextBlock x:Name="PageTitle" Text="image viewer" Margin="9,-7,0,0"
        Style="{StaticResource PhoneTextTitle1Style}"/>
    </StackPanel>

    <Canvas x:Name="ContentPanel" Grid.Row="1" Margin="12,0,12,0">
      <Image x:Name="DisplayImage" Height="534" Width="456">
        <Image.RenderTransform>
          <TransformGroup>
            <ScaleTransform x:Name="scaleTransform" ScaleX="1" ScaleY="1" />
            <TranslateTransform x:Name="translateTransform" />
          </TransformGroup>
        </Image.RenderTransform>
      </Image>
      <ItemsControl Height="534" Width="456"
        ItemsSource="{Binding ElementName=Root, Path=TouchPoints}" />
    </Canvas>
  </Grid>

</phone:PhoneApplicationPage>
```

Code Snippet ImageViewer\MainPage.xaml

5. Modify the code in `MainPage.xaml.cs` so that it looks like Listing 7-9.

LISTING 7-9: Modifying the code in MainPage.xaml.cs

```csharp
using System;
using System.Collections.ObjectModel;
using System.Windows;
using System.Windows.Input;
using System.Windows.Media.Imaging;
using Microsoft.Phone.Controls;
using Microsoft.Phone.Tasks;

namespace ImageViewer
{
    public partial class MainPage : PhoneApplicationPage
    {
        private PhotoChooserTask photoChooserTask;

        public MainPage()
        {
            InitializeComponent();

            // Configure the photo chooser.
            photoChooserTask = new PhotoChooserTask();
            photoChooserTask.Completed +=
                new EventHandler<PhotoResult>(photoChooserTask_Completed);

            // Configure touchpoint monitor.
            TouchPoints = new ObservableCollection<Point>();
            Touch.FrameReported += new TouchFrameEventHandler(Touch_FrameReported);
        }

        public ObservableCollection<Point> TouchPoints { get; private set; }

        private void Touch_FrameReported(object sender, TouchFrameEventArgs e)
        {
            // Update monitored points.
            TouchPointCollection touchPoints = e.GetTouchPoints(this);
            TouchPoints.Clear();
            foreach (TouchPoint touchPoint in touchPoints)
            {
                TouchPoints.Add(touchPoint.Position);
            }
        }
```

```csharp
private void photoChooserTask_Completed(object sender, PhotoResult e)
{
    // Load the new image and then reset the transformation.
    if (e.TaskResult == TaskResult.OK)
    {
        BitmapImage bmp = new BitmapImage();
        bmp.SetSource(e.ChosenPhoto);
        DisplayImage.Source = bmp;
    }
    Reset();
}

private void PhoneApplicationPage_ManipulationDelta(
    object sender, ManipulationDeltaEventArgs e)
{
    // Scale the image.
    if (e.DeltaManipulation.Scale.X != 0D
        && e.DeltaManipulation.Scale.Y != 0D)
    {
        scaleTransform.ScaleX *= e.DeltaManipulation.Scale.X;
        scaleTransform.ScaleY *= e.DeltaManipulation.Scale.Y;
    }

    // Move the image.
    translateTransform.X += e.DeltaManipulation.Translation.X;
    translateTransform.Y += e.DeltaManipulation.Translation.Y;
}

private void LoadImage_Click(object sender, EventArgs e)
{
    photoChooserTask.Show();
}

private void Reset_Click(object sender, EventArgs e)
{
    Reset();
}

private void Reset()
{
    // Reset the transformation.
    scaleTransform.ScaleX = 1D;
    scaleTransform.ScaleY = 1D;
    translateTransform.X = 0D;
    translateTransform.Y = 0D;
}
    }
}
```

Code Snippet ImageViewer\MainPage.xaml.cs

6. Run the application, and then tap the camera-shaped load image application bar icon.

7. Select one of the sample pictures from the photo chooser.

8. When the application resumes, drag the image around with a single touchpoint or scale it with two touchpoints (if you have a suitable touchscreen device or multiple mouse devices). The image moves or scales as shown in Figure 7-13. (The dots near the bottom of the image correspond to two touchpoints from two mouse devices, using the simulating utility driver mentioned at the beginning of this section.)

9. If you lose track of the image position or size, tap the reset button to reset the size and scale.

How It Works

In this example, you created a simple application that's capable of moving and resizing images from your device. Admittedly, it provides much less functionality than the built-in viewer, but it does help to illustrate some multitouch principles. Much of the application uses code that you've already seen in this chapter, such as the application bar and photo chooser, so you can concentrate on the multitouch-specific parts here.

FIGURE 7-13: Scaling an image with two touchpoints.

The first thing to note is the XAML added to subscribe to the `ManipulationDelta` event, which is on the root page element:

```
<phone:PhoneApplicationPage ...
  ManipulationDelta="PhoneApplicationPage_ManipulationDelta"
  x:Name="Root">
```

This picks up all manipulations in the page so that users don't have to interact directly with the image. This is useful if the image becomes too small to interact with easily.

Next comes the XAML to display the image:

```
<Image x:Name="DisplayImage" Height="534" Width="456">
  <Image.RenderTransform>
    <TransformGroup>
      <ScaleTransform x:Name="scaleTransform" ScaleX="1" ScaleY="1" />
      <TranslateTransform x:Name="translateTransform" />
    </TransformGroup>
  </Image.RenderTransform>
</Image>
```

The image dimensions are chosen to fit into the available space. The image also includes a `RenderTransform` definition, which here is set to essentially an empty definition. This transformation scales the image to 100% width, 100% height, and no translation (that is, no change to its position). More importantly, it defines `Name` properties for `ScaleTransform` and `TranslateTransform` so you can access these properties from code-behind.

The user interface also includes a coordinate overlay so that you can see where the touchpoints are. This is simply an `ItemsControl` element:

```
<ItemsControl Height="534" Width="456"
  ItemsSource="{Binding ElementName=Root, Path=TouchPoints}" />
```

This will bind to a collection of `Point` objects, for which the default `ToString()` item template is sufficient for your purposes. It will display `Point` values in `X, Y` format.

The code-behind starts by defining and configuring a `PhotoChooserTask`, using code you've already seen in this chapter, and then configures a monitor for touchpoints by subscribing to the `Touch .FrameReported` event:

```
TouchPoints = new ObservableCollection<Point>();
Touch.FrameReported += new TouchFrameEventHandler(Touch_FrameReported);
```

The event handler obtains `TouchPoint` instances relative to the page, extracts the `Point` position of these instances, and populates an `ObservableCollection<Point>` property accordingly:

```
public ObservableCollection<Point> TouchPoints { get; private set; }

private void Touch_FrameReported(object sender, TouchFrameEventArgs e)
{
    // Update monitored points.
    TouchPointCollection touchPoints = e.GetTouchPoints(this);
    TouchPoints.Clear();
    foreach (TouchPoint touchPoint in touchPoints)
    {
        TouchPoints.Add(touchPoint.Position);
    }
}
```

Next, you have the event handler that is raised when the `PhotoChooserTask` completes. This handler sets the source of the image in the user interface and also resets the image position and scale, using a method called `Reset()`:

```
private void photoChooserTask_Completed(object sender, PhotoResult e)
{
    // Load the new image and then reset the transformation.
    if (e.TaskResult == TaskResult.OK)
    {
        BitmapImage bmp = new BitmapImage();
        bmp.SetSource(e.ChosenPhoto);
        DisplayImage.Source = bmp;
    }
    Reset();
}

private void Reset()
{
    // Reset the transformation.
    scaleTransform.ScaleX = 1D;
    scaleTransform.ScaleY = 1D;
    translateTransform.X = 0D;
    translateTransform.Y = 0D;
}
```

Next is the code to handle the page-level `ManipulationDelta` event:

```
private void PhoneApplicationPage_ManipulationDelta(
    object sender, ManipulationDeltaEventArgs e)
{
    // Scale the image.
    if (e.DeltaManipulation.Scale.X != 0D && e.DeltaManipulation.Scale.Y != 0D)
    {
        scaleTransform.ScaleX *= e.DeltaManipulation.Scale.X;
        scaleTransform.ScaleY *= e.DeltaManipulation.Scale.Y;
    }

    // Move the image.
    translateTransform.X += e.DeltaManipulation.Translation.X;
    translateTransform.Y += e.DeltaManipulation.Translation.Y;
}
```

This code looks at the `DeltaManipulation` data from the event arguments and applies it directly to the two transformation elements defined in the XAML. You can modify the position simply by summing with the existing position data. Similarly, you can modify the scale by multiplying with the current scale data (initially `1.0D`).

Finally, the code includes the simple event handlers for the application bar icons. The first of these shows the photo chooser, and the second resets the image scale and position using the `Reset()` method discussed earlier:

```
private void LoadImage_Click(object sender, EventArgs e)
{
    photoChooserTask.Show();
}

private void Reset_Click(object sender, EventArgs e)
{
    Reset();
}
    }
}
```

This example has shown you how to apply simple manipulations to user interface elements. In order to do anything more complicated, however, you need more than manipulations. In this case, you'll probably want to investigate gestures, which are described next.

Using Gestures

Using gestures is a way to look at touch input at a higher level. Manipulations, as you have seen, go some way toward providing access to simple gestures. They let you see scaling from multiple touchpoints without having to know anything about the touchpoints themselves, for example. Scaling using a pinch gesture is just one of several possible gestures.

The XNA framework (an alternative tool for writing Windows Phone 7 applications, which you'll look at in Chapter 11) includes several more built-in gestures. Among others, these include gestures such as "flick," indicating a quick flick of a finger across the screen; "hold," indicating a finger left for a short period on a UI element; and "double-tap," for a double finger tap. You can probably think of many more gestures that you might want to use in your applications. How about tracing the outline of a circle to select a region, or drawing a question mark to request contextual help, for example? Sadly, none of these are built into the tools you have available to write Silverlight applications for Windows Phone 7 devices.

So you have a choice. You can, if you want to, define your own gestures, using the `Touch.FrameReported` event and/or simple mouse events, such as `MouseLeftButtonUp`. To detect a double tap, for example, you could look for two `MouseLeftButtonUp` events that occur within a specified short period of time. For rotation events, you would have to analyze the motion of two touchpoints to work out the center and angle of rotation. For more complicated gestures, such as the aforementioned question mark, you'd have to perform more complex analysis. You'd also have to add code to differentiate between different gestures, and you'd have to do all this while keeping your application responsive. That may all sound like fun, but not everyone would have the time or inclination to do such things.

Fortunately, there are plenty of people out there on the web who love puzzles like this. Here's one system you might like to try out: `http://blogs.claritycon.com/blogs/windows_phone_7/archive/2010/07/19/wp7-gesture-recognizer-and-behavior-triggers.aspx`. This one gives you gesture behaviors that you can apply to UI elements and also gives you a degree of confidence in the accuracy of more complex gestures such as circles. There are probably plenty more similar systems out there that you'll be able to find if you look hard enough.

SUMMARY

This chapter examined some of the unique features that enable you to interact with Windows Phone 7 applications and that Windows Phone 7 applications can use to access built-in features. You saw how to add an application bar containing icons and short text commands to your applications. This is a great way to expose common functionality, especially if you design your icons to fit in with the Windows Phone 7 style. This will make your user interfaces as intuitive as possible.

Next, you moved on to launchers and choosers, and you saw how to take advantage of Windows Phone 7 functionality. Again, by delegating responsibility to other applications in the Windows Phone 7 operating system, you can increase usability in your applications. You also don't have to worry too much about things like contact databases; all that is built in, so why replicate it?

Finally, you looked at customizing user text input with the SIP and multitouch input. Multitouch, in particular, is something that you can make fantastic use of if you want to. This is still a relatively new technology, and exciting new ways of using it are emerging all the time.

In the next chapter, you'll look at how to interact with remote services, including location information and more.

EXERCISES

1. A designer supplies you with a set of application bar icons that are multicolored 48 x 48 pixel images. Is it a good idea to use them in your application?

2. Which of the following functionality can you implement with launchers and choosers? Which launchers and choosers would you use to do so?

    a)   Send an email.

    b)   Take a photo.

    c)   Play a video.

    d)   Vibrate the device.

    e)   Set user input to numeric.

3. What is tombstoning and how does it influence your application design?

4. What event would you use to scale a user interface element at the end of a user manipulation? What properties of the event argument would be of interest?

5. Try writing some code that would respond to a tap-and-hold gesture. Write an application that displays a colored circle that toggles between two colors after it has a tap-and-hold gesture applied to it for one second.

> **TIP**
>
> You can use a `MouseLeftButtonDown` event to check for the beginning of a tap-and-hold operation, but you need to remember to check for `MouseLeftButtonUp` and `MouseMove` events of more than a few pixels to cancel a gesture in progress.)

Answers to the Exercises can be found in the Appendix.

▶ **WHAT YOU LEARNED IN THIS CHAPTER**

TOPIC	KEY CONCEPTS
Using the application bar	Windows Phone 7 includes a control that you can use to define an application bar for your applications. This is the preferred way to get application bar functionality because it fits into the Windows Phone 7 look and feel, especially if you adhere to the style guidelines. You can add up to four icons and a selection of text commands to the pop-up application bar.
Working with launchers and choosers	You can use launchers and choosers to access built-in Windows Phone 7 device functionality, such as email and camera applications. Choosers may return information; launchers never do. During the operation of a launcher or chooser, an application enters a suspended state through a process known as tombstoning. You should persist any application state when this happens and load it again later, when your application resumes.
Exploring the modes of the SIP	Text input on a Windows Phone 7 device takes place through a virtual keyboard known as the SIP. Depending on what text you want users to enter, you can change the mode of the SIP (for example, to numeric-only input). Several modes exist, including modes specific to operations, such as chat and URL entry mode.
Including multitouch functionality	Windows Phone 7 devices can respond to complex multitouch input. You can use raw input data to get access to individual touchpoint coordinates and characteristics, or you can use manipulations to get a higher-level view of user actions. Manipulations give you scale and translation information directly so that you don't have to work that out for yourself. However, this can be limiting for more advanced applications.
Implementing gesture detection	Using gestures is a way of getting a higher-level view of multitouch operations, including scaling via a pinch gesture, than manipulations provide. Windows Phone 7 Silverlight applications are quite limited in gesture support, so to achieve more complex gesture detection, you have to write your own code that analyzes touchpoint input or use a third-party library.

Windows Phone 7 Services and Cloud Services

WHAT YOU'LL LEARN IN THIS CHAPTER:

➤ Understanding what web services are

➤ Using location services

➤ Understanding cloud computing and cloud services

➤ Using the range of Microsoft cloud services that are available

➤ Using the Bing Maps cloud service

One of the most useful and exciting features of Windows Phone 7 devices are that they are (mostly) connected to the Internet. The *mostly* modifier is included here because, unlike with desktop PCs, the connection on a Windows Phone 7 device may be intermittent (for example, if you're on a train going through a tunnel). Sadly there's not much you can do about that with current technological limitations; even in cities, you find "dead spots" with little or no Internet access. However, even with limited Internet access you can still write mobile applications that communicate with the Internet to send and receive data. You've probably seen plenty of them already, from built-in email to Twitter clients.

In this chapter and the following two chapters, you'll look at how to access remote applications from your applications. This chapter concentrates on using existing services, but don't worry: You'll see how to make your own soon enough. Specifically, in this chapter, you'll look at web services and, later on, cloud services. Web services, as you'll see, are components that exist somewhere on the Internet that your applications can use to add functionality. Cloud services are essentially the same thing but are more tightly coupled with other applications through cloud computing. Again, you'll learn all about what this means later.

To illustrate service interaction, this chapter examines location services, which enable your applications to determine where a user's device is located. This opens up a huge number of possibilities for creating "location-aware" applications.

Finally, you'll look at some of the possibilities that cloud computing has to offer, including accessing various Microsoft cloud-based services. In particular, you'll look at the Bing Maps services.

WHAT ARE SERVICES?

Over the past few years, people have become increasingly accustomed to the "always on" Internet, and we expect our devices to be connected all (or at least most) of the time. You should be able to pop open a browser any time you like and have access to information anywhere in the world. You also need email applications to fetch new mail for you whenever it is available, without you having to manually log on somewhere to get it. Other applications, such as RSS feed readers, instant messaging clients, and so on also get information from the Internet in the same way. These are examples of using *web services* to communicate with other applications that exist somewhere on the Internet.

Figure 8-1 shows the sort of connections you can expect from a Windows Phone 7 application. The application connects to a web service, which can connect to a number of other web services and data sources. The application "consumes" this service and all the functionality it provides, and users of the application might not be aware that this process is occurring.

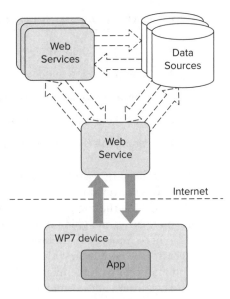

Web services allow you to send and receive information. For example, you might access a web service for high scores that enables games that you write to send a user's best score to an online database that's available to other users.

It's important to bear in mind that a device's Internet connection may not always be available, and you need to take this into account in your applications. You don't, for example, want a user's hard-fought high score to be discarded and your application to crash due to a temporary service outage.

FIGURE 8-1: A high-level view of Windows Phone 7 and web service interaction.

To get a better feel for web services, it's best to dive in and look at a great example of using web services in a Windows Phone 7 device: location services.

FINDING YOURSELF WITH LOCATION SERVICES

Since devices have "gone mobile," there's been a huge demand for location-aware applications. As soon as people started to think about the possibilities, it was clear that a fantastic new wave of applications would appear. In fact, this has occurred, in the manner of direction-finding applications, restaurant-finding applications, and social media applications such as Foursquare. There's also a new class of augmented-reality applications that combine location information, orientation, and device cameras to overlay location-based information on a view of the world around you.

As location information is becoming so prevalent, the Windows Phone 7 system is designed to make it easy for you to access that information. A Windows Phone 7 device can obtain information through a number of sources, including Global Positioning System (GPS), Wi-Fi, and nearby cellular towers. The device uses this information in combination with a location web service to expose information to your applications, as shown in Figure 8-2.

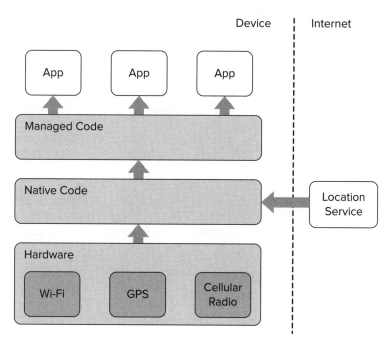

FIGURE 8-2: How apps receive location information through hardware and web services.

In this section, you'll look first at the differences between these sources of location information and then move on to see how you can use the information you receive. You'll also see how, as an application developer, you can simulate location information during development.

Location Data Sources Overview and Comparison

As mentioned in the previous section, Windows Phone 7 devices can use multiple sources of location information to determine a location. In this section, you'll look at and compare GPS, Wi-Fi, and cellular location sources.

GPS Location Services

GPS is probably the first thing that springs to mind when you think of location services. You can find it in use by a multitude of satellite navigation devices in cars, and, more recently, mobile phone devices. Windows Phone 7 includes GPS as one of its required device features.

GPS works by examining signals received from a number of satellites in orbit around the earth. At any one time, several of these will be "visible," and a device that contains GPS hardware can use these signals to calculate its position. The accuracy of this calculation can vary, and only the military has access to the most precise location information, which can reportedly obtain positions to the accuracy of inches. Civilian applications can only get a position to within a few yards — but this is easily accurate enough for most applications.

The advantages of GPS are that it is available pretty much anywhere on the planet with a clear view of the sky and that it is very accurate. The disadvantage of using GPS is that both receiving and processing signals can be quite power-intensive. Therefore, using GPS is required only when a high degree of accuracy is necessary. GPS signals are also easily blocked by tall buildings or when you're inside or underground. Another problem with GPS is that locating visible satellites can take a little while. However, you can locate satellites more quickly when you're using a fast Internet connection, such as Wi-Fi; this is called Assisted GPS (A-GPS).

Wi-Fi Location Services

Wi-Fi location tracking uses known locations of local Wi-Fi hotspots to track your position. This is possible only when there are nearby Wi-Fi networks, so it isn't much use when you're in rural areas. The actual mechanism of location detection is similar to that of GPS, as the device can combine multiple nearby Wi-Fi signals to calculate a position. It can also work with a single Wi-Fi source, although the accuracy in this case isn't that great.

Wi-Fi location detection is best for indoor use and in densely populated areas where multiple known Wi-Fi networks exist. If these sources are mapped accurately, Wi-Fi can be fairly accurate, but it's not as accurate as GPS. Wi-Fi is also less power-intensive than GPS, but it's more power-intensive than the final option used in Windows Phone 7: cellular data.

Cellular Location Services

Mobile communication devices have an existing connection to the world through cellular networks. There are different types of these networks, such as 3G and EDGE networks, but essentially they all work the same way. Regions known as *cells* are serviced by antennae that communicate with your device. These cells can be quite small in densely populated urban areas to cope with the load generated by lots of people, and they can be quite large in rural areas. And, of course, there are still plenty of places in the world where you struggle to get a cellular connection at all.

Where you do get a connection, you're likely to be in range of several transmitters at once. Devices can use signals from these transmitters to triangulate a position. This isn't as accurate as either Wi-Fi or GPS, but it can provide a rough estimate of position fairly quickly and with fairly low processing requirements. Again, this doesn't work where you don't have a signal, but it can often be quite useful. If you have an application that needs to know only what city a device is in, for example, cellular data is definitely good enough.

Obtaining Location Information

Windows Phone 7 exposes location information to you via a very simple interface. In fact, you hardly need to know about the underlying technologies discussed in the previous section, although knowing about them does make it easier to understand the results and best-practice usage. Rather than choose between GPS, Wi-Fi, or cellular data, you simply say how accurate you want results to be, and the code and underlying hardware will sort things out for you.

In this section, you'll look at the interface that Windows Phone 7 provides and how to use it to obtain location information. You'll also see how to configure the service, how user permission works for the service, and how to make sense of its output.

The GeoCoordinateWatcher Class

To get location data, you use the `System.Device.Location.GeoCoordinateWatcher` class, which is located in the `System.Device.dll` assembly. This assembly isn't included in Windows Phone 7 applications by default, so you must add a reference to it in order to use it. When you create an instance of this class, you can (optionally) pass in an accuracy level to use through a `GeoPositionAccuracy` enum value. You have only two options: `Default` and `High`. If you use `High`, the accuracy will be higher, but so will the battery usage. Under the hood, the location-detecting hardware is likely to concentrate on the more accurate information, such as GPS. The following code shows how to use the `GeoCoordinateWatcher` class:

```
GeoCoordinateWatcher geoCoordinateWatcher =
    new GeoCoordinateWatcher(GeoPositionAccuracy.High);
```

Once you have a `GeoCoordinateWatcher` instance, you can listen for two events that will be raised. The first, `StatusChanged`, lets you know whether the watcher is enabled, disabled, or not producing data. The second, `PositionChanged`, lets you know when a new position has been detected. You can further configure the `PositionChanged` event by setting the `GeoCoordinateWatcher` `.MovementThreshold` property to a minimum change in position (expressed in meters) that is required to generate an event.

Putting this together, you might initialize the location service as shown in the following code:

```
GeoCoordinateWatcher geoCoordinateWatcher =
    new GeoCoordinateWatcher(GeoPositionAccuracy.High);
geoCoordinateWatcher.MovementThreshold = 10.0D;
geoCoordinateWatcher.PositionChanged +=
    new EventHandler<GeoPositionChangedEventArgs<GeoCoordinate>>(
        geoCoordinateWatcher_PositionChanged);
geoCoordinateWatcher.StatusChanged +=
    new EventHandler<GeoPositionStatusChangedEventArgs>
        (geoCoordinateWatcher_StatusChanged);
```

This code initializes a `GeoCoordinateWatcher` instance with a movement threshold of 10 meters and adds event handlers for the `PositionChanged` and `StatusChanged` events. You'll look at these handlers in the next two sections.

After you have this instance, you can start and stop listening to position changes with the `Start()` and `Stop()` methods:

```
geoCoordinateWatcher.Start();
// Location service is active until...
geoCoordinateWatcher.Stop();
```

Location Service Status

When you start the location service, a `StatusChanged` event is raised. This event uses event arguments of type `GeoPositionStatusChangedEventArgs`, which has a single property called `Status` of type `GeoPositionStatus`. Looking at this property tells you the status of the service, which can be one of the following:

➤ `GeoPositionStatus.Disabled` — This can mean one of two things: Either the device has no location service available for some reason (maybe it got dropped on the floor), or the user has disabled it. You'll look at user permission for location in the "Getting Permission from the User" section, shortly.

➤ `GeoPositionStatus.NoData` — This means the service is available but is not currently generating data. This might be due to a loss of signal, or perhaps because you haven't yet called `Start()`.

➤ `GeoPositionStatus.Initializing` — This means the service is starting up. This can take up to a few minutes if the signal is low, but it is usually just a few seconds.

➤ `GeoPositionStatus.Ready` — This means the location service is up-and-running and generating data.

The first status change event should let you know that the service is initializing. Shortly afterward, there should be a second event to let you know that the service is ready. However, if there's a startup problem or you're using the emulator, the second status event will contain the `NoData` status. You can also look at the `GeoCoordinateWatcher.Status` property at any time to see the current status.

As soon as the service is ready, it starts to generate `PositionChanged` events and changes the value of its `Position` property.

Geographic Coordinates

As the location of a Windows Phone 7 device changes, `PositionChanged` events are raised. These events use the argument type `GeoPositionChangedEventArgs<GeoCoordinate>`. This has a `Position` property of type `GeoPosition<GeoCoordinate>`, which in turn has a `Location` property of type `GeoCoordinate` that actually contains the location information. The `GeoPosition<T>` class simply wraps the coordinate and adds a `TimeStamp` property of type `DateTimeOffset` that tells you when the coordinate was generated.

The `GeoCoordinate` instance has all the properties you need to identify a location, as shown in Table 8-1.

TABLE 8-1: GeoCoordinate Properties

PROPERTY	DESCRIPTION
IsUnknown	Tells you whether the position is unknown. This is a Boolean value that will be `true` when the status of the service is `NoData`, `Initializing`, or `Disabled` because the service will not know where the device is at this point. You can also get an instance of the `GeoCoordinate` class with this property set to `true` through the static `GeoCoordinate.Unknown` property.
Latitude	Contains the latitude, expressed as the number of degrees away from the equator. Positive values are degrees north, and negative values are degrees south. Values are therefore between −90 and 90.
Longitude	Contains the longitude expressed in a number of degrees away from the Greenwich Meridian. Positive values are degrees east, and negative values are degrees west. Values are between −180 and 180.
Altitude	Gives you the height of the location, in meters.
HorizontalAccuracy	Gives you the accuracy of the location on the ground, in terms of a radius of meters.
VerticalAccuracy	Gives you the accuracy of the `Altitude` property, in meters.
Speed	For a moving position, lets you know the speed in meters per second.
Course	For a moving position, lets you know where you're heading, in degrees, with north being 0.

There are also some helpful methods on `GeoCoordinate`, such as `GetDistanceTo()`, which can get the distance between two coordinates, in meters. You can use this to determine the distance traveled (as the crow flies) from a starting point by using code such as the following:

```
private GeoCoordinate startPosition;

private void geoCoordinateWatcher_StatusChanged(
    object sender, GeoPositionStatusChangedEventArgs e)
{
    if (e.Status == GeoPositionStatus.Ready)
    {
        startPosition = geoCoordinateWatcher.Position.Location;
    }
}
```

```
private void geoCoordinateWatcher_PositionChanged(
    object sender, GeoPositionChangedEventArgs<GeoCoordinate> e)
{
    double distanceFromStart = startPosition.GetDistanceTo(e.Position.Location);
    // Code here would use the distance value determined above.
}
```

Civic Addresses

Having a geographic location in terms of latitude and longitude is great, but often you want to find out more details about where a Windows Phone 7 device is located. It might, for example, be useful to obtain a street address in some instances. To do this, you can use the CivicAddressResolver class to get a CivicAddress instance, as follows:

```
private CivicAddress GetAddressFromGeoCoordinate(GeoCoordinate coordinate)
{
    CivicAddressResolver resolver = new CivicAddressResolver();
    return resolver.ResolveAddress.(coordinate);
}
```

Alternatively, you can use the ResolveAddressAsync() method and wait for the CivicAddressResolver.ResolveAddressCompleted event to be raised. In both cases, you'll end up with a CivicAddress value that contains address information in properties including AddressLine1, AddressLine2, and City, among others.

Unfortunately, at the time of writing, although the CivicAddressResolver class exists in the framework, it's not implemented. If you need to get more detailed information from a geographic location, you'll have to resort to other means. There are, for example, web services available that you can use to obtain this information.

Getting Permission from the User

Users of Windows Phone 7 devices have the option to disable location services from the options menu. It is even possible to grant or deny permissions to individual applications. If this has happened, you can't use the GeoCoordinateWatcher class to get locations.

The GeoCoordinateWatcher.Permission property tells you whether this has happened by giving you a member of the GeoPositionPermission enum, which can be Unknown, Granted, or Denied. You can use this property, for example, to display a dialog to users, informing them that they must enable location services to get the full functionality of your application. Even if permission is granted, a call to the GeoCoordinateWatcher.Start() method may result in a dialog asking the user whether to grant location services permissions.

Simulating Location Data

As with other Windows Phone 7 device-specific functionality, location service data is not available in the emulator. Instead, you must simulate it. You can do this in a number of ways, but the simplest is to wrap the service in a class, in the same way you wrapped the accelerometer sensor in Chapter 6.

The only difference here is that there are two event handlers to add to the service to simulate, and it's worth raising events for both of them in your wrapper class. When it comes to the actual simulation, you can use whatever system you want — random numbers, stored data, and so on.

Using the Location Service

In the following steps, you'll see the location service in action. The code wraps the service in a class that allows simulation so that you can see an example of how to do this. Of course, if you have an actual device, you can switch it to real data easily enough.

1. Create a new Windows Phone Application called **WhereAmI**.

2. Add to the project a reference to the System.Device.dll assembly.

3. Add a class called GeoCoordinateWatcherWrapper and modify the code in GeoCoordinateWatcherWrapper.cs so that it looks like Listing 8-1.

LISTING 8-1: Modifying the code in GeoCoordinateWatcherWrapper.cs

```
using System;
using System.ComponentModel;
using System.Device.Location;
using System.Threading;

namespace WhereAmI
{
    public class GeoCoordinateWatcherWrapper
    {
        private BackgroundWorker generateReadingsWorker;
        private GeoCoordinateWatcher geoCoordinateWatcher;
        private DateTime startTime;
        private bool isSimulation;
        private GeoPositionAccuracy accuracy;
        private double movementThreshold;
        public event EventHandler<GeoPositionChangedEventArgs<GeoCoordinate>>
            PositionChanged;
        public event EventHandler<GeoPositionStatusChangedEventArgs> StatusChanged;
        private GeoPosition<GeoCoordinate> lastPosition;
        private GeoPosition<GeoCoordinate> simulationRootPosition;

        public GeoCoordinateWatcherWrapper(
            GeoPositionAccuracy accuracy = GeoPositionAccuracy.Default,
            double movementThreshold = 10.0,
            bool isSimulation = false)
        {
            this.isSimulation = isSimulation;
            this.accuracy = accuracy;
            this.movementThreshold = movementThreshold;

            if (!isSimulation)
            {
                geoCoordinateWatcher = new GeoCoordinateWatcher(accuracy);
                geoCoordinateWatcher.MovementThreshold = movementThreshold;
                geoCoordinateWatcher.PositionChanged +=
                    new EventHandler<GeoPositionChangedEventArgs<GeoCoordinate>>(
                        geoCoordinateWatcher_PositionChanged);
```

continues

LISTING 8-1 *(continued)*

```
            geoCoordinateWatcher.StatusChanged +=
                new EventHandler<GeoPositionStatusChangedEventArgs>(
                    geoCoordinateWatcher_StatusChanged);
        }
        else
        {
            this.lastPosition = new GeoPosition<GeoCoordinate>(
                DateTimeOffset.Now, GeoCoordinate.Unknown);
            this.simulationRootPosition = new GeoPosition<GeoCoordinate>(
                DateTimeOffset.Now,
                new GeoCoordinate(
                    29.976274,
                    31.131392,
                    10,
                    100,
                    5,
                    0,
                    0));
        }
    }

    public GeoPosition<GeoCoordinate> Position
    {
        get
        {
            if (!isSimulation)
            {
                return geoCoordinateWatcher.Position;
            }
            else
            {
                return lastPosition;
            }
        }
    }

    public void Start()
    {
        if (isSimulation)
        {
            if (generateReadingsWorker == null)
            {
                lastPosition = simulationRootPosition;
                OnStatusChanged(GeoPositionStatus.Initializing);
                generateReadingsWorker = new BackgroundWorker();
                generateReadingsWorker.DoWork += new DoWorkEventHandler(
                    generateReadingsWorker_DoWork);
                generateReadingsWorker.WorkerSupportsCancellation = true;
                generateReadingsWorker.RunWorkerAsync();
                OnStatusChanged(GeoPositionStatus.Ready);
            }
        }
```

```
        else
        {
            geoCoordinateWatcher.Start();
        }

        startTime = DateTime.Now;
    }

    public void Stop()
    {
        if (isSimulation)
        {
            if (generateReadingsWorker != null)
            {
                generateReadingsWorker.CancelAsync();
                generateReadingsWorker = null;
                OnStatusChanged(GeoPositionStatus.NoData);
            }
        }
        else
        {
            geoCoordinateWatcher.Stop();
        }
    }

    private void geoCoordinateWatcher_PositionChanged(
        object sender, GeoPositionChangedEventArgs<GeoCoordinate> e)
    {
        this.OnPositionChanged(e.Position);
    }

    private void geoCoordinateWatcher_StatusChanged(
        object sender, GeoPositionStatusChangedEventArgs e)
    {
        this.OnStatusChanged(e.Status);
    }

    private void OnPositionChanged(GeoPosition<GeoCoordinate> position)
    {
        if (PositionChanged != null)
        {
            PositionChanged(this,
                new GeoPositionChangedEventArgs<GeoCoordinate>(position));
        }
        lastPosition = position;
    }

    private void OnStatusChanged(GeoPositionStatus status)
    {
        if (StatusChanged != null)
        {
            StatusChanged(this, new GeoPositionStatusChangedEventArgs(status));
        }
    }
```

continues

LISTING 8-1 *(continued)*

```
private void generateReadingsWorker_DoWork(object sender, DoWorkEventArgs e)
{
    BackgroundWorker worker = sender as BackgroundWorker;
    Random random = new Random();
    while (!worker.CancellationPending)
    {
        // Get and raise event for reading.
        GeoCoordinate location = new GeoCoordinate(
            29.976274 + (random.NextDouble() - 0.5) / 1000,
            31.131392 + (random.NextDouble() - 0.5) / 1000,
            10,
            100,
            5,
            0,
            0);
        OnPositionChanged(
            new GeoPosition<GeoCoordinate>(
                new DateTimeOffset(DateTime.Now), location));

        // Pause before next reading.
        Thread.Sleep(random.Next(1000) + 500);
    }
}
```

Code Snippet WhereAmI\GeoCoordinateWatcherWrapper.cs

4. Modify the code in `MainPage.xaml` so that it looks like Listing 8-2.

LISTING 8-2: Modifying the code in MainPage.xaml

```
<phone:PhoneApplicationPage ... x:Name="Root">

    <Grid x:Name="LayoutRoot" Background="Transparent">
        <Grid.RowDefinitions>
            <RowDefinition Height="Auto"/>
            <RowDefinition Height="*"/>
            <RowDefinition Height="Auto"/>
            <RowDefinition Height="Auto"/>
        </Grid.RowDefinitions>

        <StackPanel x:Name="TitlePanel" Grid.Row="0" Margin="12,17,0,28">
            <TextBlock x:Name="ApplicationTitle" Text="LOCATION"
                Style="{StaticResource PhoneTextNormalStyle}"/>
            <TextBlock x:Name="PageTitle" Text="where am i?" Margin="9,-7,0,0"
                Style="{StaticResource PhoneTextTitle1Style}"/>
        </StackPanel>
```

```
<Grid x:Name="ContentPanel" Grid.Row="1" Margin="12,0,12,0">
  <ScrollViewer x:Name="logView">
    <ItemsControl ItemsSource="{Binding ElementName=Root, Path=MessageLog}">
      <ItemsControl.ItemTemplate>
        <DataTemplate>
          <TextBlock Text="{Binding}"
              Style="{StaticResource PhoneTextNormalStyle}"
              TextWrapping="Wrap" />
        </DataTemplate>
      </ItemsControl.ItemTemplate>
    </ItemsControl>
  </ScrollViewer>
</Grid>

<Grid Grid.Row="2">
  <Grid.ColumnDefinitions>
    <ColumnDefinition />
    <ColumnDefinition />
    <ColumnDefinition />
  </Grid.ColumnDefinitions>

  <Button x:Name="startButton" Grid.Column="0" Height="100" Content="Start"
    Click="startButton_Click" />
  <Button x:Name="stopButton" Grid.Column="1" Height="100" Content="Stop"
    Click="stopButton_Click" />
  <Button x:Name="mapButton" Grid.Column="2" Height="100" Content="Map"
    Click="mapButton_Click" />

</Grid>
</Grid>

</phone:PhoneApplicationPage>
```

Code Snippet WhereAmI\MainPage.xaml

5. Modify the code in `MainPage.xaml.cs` so that it looks like Listing 8-3.

LISTING 8-3: Modifying the code in MainPage.xaml.cs

```
using System;
using System.Collections.ObjectModel;
using System.Device.Location;
using System.Windows;
using Microsoft.Phone.Controls;

namespace WhereAmI
{
    public partial class MainPage : PhoneApplicationPage
    {
        private GeoCoordinateWatcherWrapper geoCoordinateWatcherWrapper;
```

continues

LISTING 8-3 *(continued)*

```csharp
public MainPage()
{
    InitializeComponent();

    MessageLog = new ObservableCollection<string>();
    MessageLog.Add("I don't know where you are... yet!");

    geoCoordinateWatcherWrapper =
        new GeoCoordinateWatcherWrapper(isSimulation: true);

    geoCoordinateWatcherWrapper.PositionChanged +=
        new EventHandler<GeoPositionChangedEventArgs<GeoCoordinate>>(
            geoCoordinateWatcherWrapper_PositionChanged);
    geoCoordinateWatcherWrapper.StatusChanged +=
        new EventHandler<GeoPositionStatusChangedEventArgs>(
            geoCoordinateWatcherWrapper_StatusChanged);
}

public ObservableCollection<string> MessageLog { get; private set; }

private void geoCoordinateWatcherWrapper_StatusChanged(
    object sender, GeoPositionStatusChangedEventArgs e)
{
    // Ensure reading is processed on UI thread.
    Dispatcher.BeginInvoke(
        () =>
        {
            MessageLog.Insert(0, string.Format(
                "Status changed to: {0}", e.Status));
        });
}

private void geoCoordinateWatcherWrapper_PositionChanged(
    object sender, GeoPositionChangedEventArgs<GeoCoordinate> e)
{
    // Ensure reading is processed on UI thread.
    Dispatcher.BeginInvoke(
        () =>
        {
            MessageLog.Insert(0, string.Format(
                "Position changed to: {0}{1}, {2}{3}",
                Math.Abs(e.Position.Location.Latitude),
                e.Position.Location.Latitude > 0 ? "N" : "S",
                Math.Abs(e.Position.Location.Longitude),
                e.Position.Location.Longitude > 0 ? "E" : "W"));
        });
}

private void startButton_Click(object sender, RoutedEventArgs e)
{
    geoCoordinateWatcherWrapper.Start();
}
```

```
private void stopButton_Click(object sender, RoutedEventArgs e)
{
    geoCoordinateWatcherWrapper.Stop();
}

private void mapButton_Click(object sender, RoutedEventArgs e)
{
    // Not yet implemented.
}
    }
}
```

Code Snippet WhereAmI\MainPage.xaml.cs

6.   Run the application and tap Start. The log starts, as shown in Figure 8-3.

How It Works

In this example, you've created a simple location-detection and reporting application that uses location services. You've also created a wrapper for location services to make it easier to simulate location data during development. This wrapper currently generates a stream of coordinate readings that are near a fixed point. It's a fairly well-known geographic location, in fact. Later, when you look at Bing Maps, you'll find out where it is. At the moment, the Map button in the application doesn't do anything, but you'll wire it up in an example later in this chapter.

You started by creating the `GeoCoordinateWatcherWrapper` wrapper class. This wrapper is designed to mirror the interface provided by `GeoCoordinateWatcher`, and so it defines `PositionChanged` and `StatusChanged` events and `Start()` and `Stop()` methods. These members have the same types and signatures as the matching members of `GeoCoordinateWatcher`. This enables client code to use the wrapper in the same way as using a `GeoCoordinateWatcher` instance.

FIGURE 8-3: The WhereAmI application in action.

In the code, after defining a host of private fields for holding various data and the exposed events, you added the constructor with parameters that client code can use to set basic parameters and whether to use simulated data:

```
public GeoCoordinateWatcherWrapper(
    GeoPositionAccuracy accuracy = GeoPositionAccuracy.Default,
    double movementThreshold = 10.0,
    bool isSimulation = false)
{
    ...
}
```

This constructor either creates a `GeoCoordinateWatcher` instance with the requested parameters and adds `PositionChanged` and `StatusChanged` event handlers or sets up some initial simulation data — the first `lastPosition` value and `simulationRootPosition`. The `lastPosition` value is exposed through the Position property for simulations. The Position property will return the live position from the GeoCoordinateWatcher instance for non-simulated data.

The Start() method either calls the GeoCoordinateWatcher.Start() method or starts the BackgroundWorker instance that will generate simulated data. For simulations, two StatusChanged events are also raised; they contain GeoPositionStatus.Initializing and GeoPositionStatus .Ready values. Similarly, the Stop() method either stops the live service with GeoCoordinateWatcher .Stop() or signals the BackgroundWorker to stop.

There's not much else to say about the GeoCoordinateWatcherWrapper class that you haven't already seen in the accelerometer simulation sample in Chapter 6. Also, the XAML for this example is very simple, so there's no need to look at that in any more detail.

The code in MainPage.xaml.cs starts by defining a field to hold the wrapper, geoCoordinateWatcherWrapper:

```
public partial class MainPage : PhoneApplicationPage
{
    private GeoCoordinateWatcherWrapper geoCoordinateWatcherWrapper;
```

Next, in the constructor, a property called MessageLog is initialized, and an initial message is added:

```
public MainPage()
{
    InitializeComponent();

    MessageLog = new ObservableCollection<string>();
    MessageLog.Add("I don't know where you are... yet!");
```

The MessageLog property is a list of strings that are displayed in the simple user interface for the application. This collection is observable, so any changes to it will instantly be reflected in the user interface.

Next, the constructor creates the wrapper in simulation mode (using the default values for the other parameters of the GeoCoordinateWatcherWrapper constructor) and attached event handlers:

```
geoCoordinateWatcherWrapper = new GeoCoordinateWatcherWrapper(
    isSimulation:true);
geoCoordinateWatcherWrapper.PositionChanged +=
    new EventHandler<GeoPositionChangedEventArgs<GeoCoordinate>>(
        geoCoordinateWatcherWrapper_PositionChanged);
geoCoordinateWatcherWrapper.StatusChanged +=
    new EventHandler<GeoPositionStatusChangedEventArgs>(
        geoCoordinateWatcherWrapper_StatusChanged);
}
```

Both of these event handlers simply add a message to MessageLog. geoCoordinateWatcherWrapper _StatusChanged() adds a message containing the new status, and geoCoordinateWatcherWrapper _PositionChanged() adds a message containing the new position:

```
private void geoCoordinateWatcherWrapper_StatusChanged(
    object sender, GeoPositionStatusChangedEventArgs e)
{
    // Ensure reading is processed on UI thread.
    Dispatcher.BeginInvoke(
        () =>
        {
            MessageLog.Insert(0, string.Format("Status changed to: {0}", e.Status));
        });
}

private void geoCoordinateWatcherWrapper_PositionChanged(
    object sender, GeoPositionChangedEventArgs<GeoCoordinate> e)
{
    // Ensure reading is processed on UI thread.
    Dispatcher.BeginInvoke(
        () =>
        {
            MessageLog.Insert(0, string.Format("Position changed to: {0}{1}, {2}{3}",
                Math.Abs(e.Position.Location.Latitude),
                e.Position.Location.Latitude > 0 ? "N" : "S",
                Math.Abs(e.Position.Location.Longitude),
                e.Position.Location.Longitude > 0 ? "E" : "W"));
        });
}
```

In both cases, the `Dispatcher.Invoke()` method is used to ensure thread-safe access to `MessageLog`.

The remaining code in this application simply allows the Start and Stop buttons in the user interface to trigger the `Start()` and `Stop()` methods in the wrapper. There's also a handler for the Map button, which, as mentioned at the beginning of this section, you'll implement later.

Location Service Best Practices

There are a few points to bear in mind when using location services. First, as discussed earlier, using these services can result in a significant drain on the device battery. For this reason, you should use location services only for as long as you need to. Often, you'll only require a single initial reading, in which case you can start the watcher, get a position, and then stop the watcher again.

Another way to minimize usage is to use the higher-accuracy setting only if you really need to. If you only need a rough position, such as the city where the user is located, there's no need to use high accuracy.

You should also be aware that, in general usage, the accuracy of readings will not be fantastic. Signal noise due to location, atmospheric conditions, and so forth may mean that consecutive readings may be a significant distance apart. This can result in many similar readings even if the device isn't moving. You can reduce the amount of readings you receive by setting the movement threshold to a suitably large amount, perhaps 10 to 20 meters or so. Alternatively, if you don't care about noise and want a lot of updates, you can set the threshold to 0 for continuous readings, which will come in at around 1 per second.

Finally, remember that it can take a while before readings start to come in as the hardware can take a while to initialize. In the worst-case scenario, it might be around 2 minutes before data starts to come in (although in most cases it should take a lot less time). Obviously, you'll want to design your applications accordingly. You certainly wouldn't want them to freeze before there is data because users will wonder what's happening and may just give up waiting and do something else.

USING CLOUD SERVICES

Recently, the idea of web services has been extended with the concept of *software as a service* (SaaS, also known as Software plus Services, or S+S), which involves accessing applications directly on the Internet. Rather than use a large application installed on a PC, with SaaS you use a smaller application, or *thin client*, and subscribe to functionality on the Internet, usually for a subscription fee rather than a one-time charge. There are a number of advantages to this, not the least of which is that functionality can be kept up-to-date without users ever having to install patches or updates. Of course, this also requires an Internet connection, so the model is not perfect yet, as connections can still be intermittent — especially for mobile devices.

With *cloud computing*, the applications you use, along with the data consumed by those applications and any functionality that links those applications to other applications, is all accessed remotely. You can even save your data to remote file stores rather than to local storage hardware. The advantage here is that there is a reduced dependency on the device being used. In some cases, such as when using a web browser as a client, there might be very little dependency on device hardware.

In practice, cloud computing is still a work in progress, although it's developing fast with systems such as Microsoft Azure arriving to assemble cloud applications. However, one of the most well-defined parts of cloud computing is cloud services, and this is where Windows Phone 7 fits in. *Cloud services* are web services that are specifically designed to provide cloud computing functionality; that is, they supply building blocks that you can build on.

In this section, you'll look at the cloud services that Microsoft provides now and will provide in the future. You can also expect other companies to provide cloud services at some point, but at the moment, with the field being so new, there's not a lot to look at.

Using Microsoft Cloud Data

Microsoft sees cloud computing very much as "the next big thing." As such, it is investing heavily in cloud services, and many of its next-generation applications are already using these services. Many of these applications are available to Windows Phone 7 applications, including Windows Live Messenger Connect, Bing, Xbox LIVE, Zune, and Azure.

At the time of writing, much of this cloud functionality is still in its early stages. Some, such as the Bing Maps part of Bing, is mature enough to start using, but most is not very mature yet. In this section, you'll learn about what's available and what will hopefully be available in the future.

Windows Live Messenger Connect

Windows Live is Microsoft's main web and application portal. It includes a vast range of functionality, including email, calendars, instant messaging, online file storage, office application connectivity, and more. Windows Live Messenger Connect is a collection of web services and APIs intended to expose Windows Live functionality to third-party applications. It also gives devices such as Windows Phone 7 devices access to all this.

Currently, Windows Live Messenger Connect is at a private beta stage. You can see what's on offer in more detail at http://msdn.microsoft.com/en-us/windowslive/default.aspx. At this site you can request an invitation to join the beta and experiment with an "interactive SDK" to see how you might use the services on offer.

Bing

Bing is primarily known as Microsoft's search engine. In actual fact, there's a bit more to it than that, including Bing Maps and more. There is an API available for remote client usage, which is part of a Microsoft initiative currently known as Project Silk Road. The Bing API, currently in version 2.0, enables you to perform search operations with web services.

 NOTE *You can get access to the Bing API at* www.bing.com/developers.

At the moment, Windows Phone 7 developers are very interested in the separate Bing Maps API. You can get access to this at www.bingmapsportal.com, and once you've signed up and obtained a key, you can start to embed maps and use the API for other services from your applications. You'll see an example of how to do this shortly.

XBox LIVE

XBox LIVE is Microsoft's gaming community platform. Any XBox or indeed Windows Phone 7 games that you play can hook into XBox LIVE services in order to exchange information and interact with the larger gaming community. These services include accessing a user's account info, gaming statistics, and other community services. Much of this is built into the main XBox LIVE application that ships with Windows Phone 7. However, through the API, you should also be able to access it outside this application, in your own applications. Unfortunately, at the time of writing, very little information is available about how you might go about doing this. Hopefully, this will change soon, as it has potential for creating some very interesting applications.

Zune

Zune is Microsoft's media-playing platform and marketplace. Through the web service API, you should be able to get marketplace information and even perform purchases. Again, at the time of writing, the only way to access the Zune cloud services is through the Zune application on a Windows Phone 7 device.

Azure

The Windows Azure platform is the culmination of Microsoft's cloud computing development. It brings together a service architecture and a common set of tools that you can use to create cloud computing applications. It also provides a number of services, such as online storage, that you can use in applications. It is still very much "in development," but it is already looking very interesting. You can find out much more at `www.microsoft.com/cloud/` and `www.microsoft.com /windowsazure/`.

 NOTE *Unfortunately, Azure does come at a price: You must sign up for services, hosting, and so on in order to enable your applications to use it. It is worth investigating, but really an entire book or more can be devoted to this subject.*

Using Bing Maps in a WP7 Application

It is worth digging into the Bing Maps services in more detail because they are the most mature of Microsoft's cloud services. The latest version of the Windows Phone 7 SDK even includes a Bing Maps control that you can use in your applications. In this section, you'll see how to get connected and how to use that control.

 NOTE *The Bing Maps API is extensive, and here you'll see only a small subset of what is possible. For more information, please refer to the MSDN documentation at* `http://msdn.microsoft.com/en-us/library/ee681884.aspx`.

Signing Up for Bing Maps

In order to use Bing Maps in your applications, you must sign up for an account. You can do that, as noted in the previous section, at `www.bingmapsportal.com`. You need a Windows Live ID to do this, so you have to sign up for one of those as well if you don't already have one.

Once you have a Bing Maps account, you can create keys that you can then use in your applications. To do so, you must provide a name for your application and a URL for it. For Windows Phone 7 applications, the URL is obviously not very important, as you'll be using the key in a smart client. You might like to provide a product information or company page for this value instead. Several types of keys are available, depending on expected usage; you can find details in the Bing Maps terms and conditions. If you want to try out the code in this section, you should get a developer key.

 NOTE *You can create up to five keys with a Bing Maps account, and you can track usage information for those keys through your account.*

Using the Bing Maps Silverlight Control

When you have a key, using a Bing Maps control in an application is extremely simple. All you need to do is to put a `Map` control on the page and put your key in its `CredentialsProvider` property. To use this control, you must first reference the `Microsoft.Phone.Controls.Maps.dll` assembly and reference the `Microsoft.Phone.Controls.Maps` namespace in your XAML. For example, you can use the following XAML page (where <*My Key*> is your API key):

```
<phone:PhoneApplicationPage
    ...
    xmlns:m="clr-namespace:Microsoft.Phone.Controls.Maps;
assembly=Microsoft.Phone.
Controls.Maps">

    <Grid x:Name="LayoutRoot" Background="Transparent">
        <m:Map x:Name="myMap" CredentialsProvider="<My Key>" />
    </Grid>

</phone:PhoneApplicationPage>
```

This would fill the page with a map that users can interact with in a basic way, such as dragging to move the position around and zooming in with a double tap gesture.

From code-behind you can programmatically control the map. For example, you can set the location to view using the `Map.SetView()` method. This has a number of overloads that you can use, including several that use `GeoCoordinate` values. You also need to set the zoom level when you set the location. The zoom level is a `double` value greater than or equal to 1, where 1 is fully zoomed out. The maximum zoom varies, depending on the imagery for the place in the world you're looking at, but it goes up to around 19.

For example, the following code would set the location to a `GeoCoordinate` value and a zoom level of 15 (which corresponds to a fairly deep zoom, perhaps showing you a few football fields):

```
myMap.SetView(myGeoCoordinate, 15D);
```

Adding Control Elements

To make your map more useful, you can add controls — for example, to enable zooming in and out with buttons. You simply need to add buttons whose event handlers call the relevant methods or manipulate the relevant properties of the map. In the case of zooming, you just need to set the `ZoomLevel` property of the map, like this:

```
myMap.ZoomLevel += 1;
```

This code adds 1 to `ZoomLevel`, so it results in zooming in. Similarly, you can zoom out by subtracting 1 from `ZoomLevel`.

Using Overlays and Child Controls

One of the most useful features when working with Bing Maps is the ability to add overlays and child controls. These might be complex objects showing information about a location, or they might be simple controls such as pushpins. The overlays and child controls you add will be stored in the map and made visible or hidden according to the visible location. You can do this in XAML simply by adding overlay controls to the `Children` property of the map control, as in this example:

```
<m:Map x:Name="myMap" CredentialsProvider="<My Key>">
  <m:Map.Children>
    <m:Pushpin x:Name="myPin" />
  </m:Map.Children>
</m:Map>
```

This code adds a `Pushpin` control to the map. Its location is controlled with the `Location` property, which is of type `GeoCoordinate`. This familiar data type makes it easy to position wherever you wish.

There are other similar controls that you can use, and you can also create your own. In the following example, which builds on the earlier example in this chapter, you'll see how this works in practice as you add mapping functionality to a location-aware application.

TRY IT OUT Using Bing Maps

1. Make a copy of the `WhereAmI` application from earlier in the chapter and rename it **WhereAmIOnAMap.**

2. Open the solution and add to the project a reference to the `Microsoft.Phone.Controls.Maps.dll` assembly.

3. Modify the code in `MainPage.xaml` so that it looks like Listing 8-4, using your Bing Maps API key in place of `<My Key>`:

LISTING 8-4: Modifying the code in MainPage.xaml

```
<phone:PhoneApplicationPage
  ...
  xmlns:m="clr-namespace:Microsoft.Phone.Controls.Maps;
    assembly=Microsoft.Phone.Controls.Maps"
  xmlns:o="clr-namespace:Microsoft.Phone.Controls.Maps.Overlays;
    assembly=Microsoft.Phone.Controls.Maps"
  ...>

  <Grid x:Name="LayoutRoot" Background="Transparent">
    ...
    <Grid x:Name="ContentPanel" Grid.Row="1" Margin="12,0,12,0">
      <ScrollViewer x:Name="logView">
        ...
      </ScrollViewer>
      <m:Map Visibility="Collapsed" x:Name="LocationMap"
        CredentialsProvider="<My Key>" Mode="Aerial">
        <m:Map.Children>
          <o:Scale />
          <m:Pushpin x:Name="locationPin">
            <m:Pushpin.Template>
              <ControlTemplate>
                <Grid Height="30" Width="30">
                  <Ellipse Fill="Red" Stroke="Black" StrokeThickness="2"
                    Margin="3" Opacity="0.4" />
```

```
                          <Rectangle Fill="White" Height="2" />
                          <Rectangle Fill="White" Width="2" />
                      </Grid>
                  </ControlTemplate>
              </m:Pushpin.Template>
          </m:Pushpin>
        </m:Map.Children>
      </m:Map>
    </Grid>


    ...
  </Grid>

</phone:PhoneApplicationPage>
```

Code Snippet WhereAmIOnAMap\MainPage.xaml

4. Modify the code in `MainPage.xaml.cs` so that it looks like Listing 8-5.

LISTING 8-5: Modifying the code in MainPage.xaml

```csharp
using System;
using System.Collections.ObjectModel;
using System.Device.Location;
using System.Windows;
using Microsoft.Phone.Controls;
using Microsoft.Phone.Controls.Maps.Core;
using Microsoft.Phone.Controls.Maps;

namespace WhereAmI
{
    public partial class MainPage : PhoneApplicationPage
    {
        ...

        private void mapButton_Click(object sender, RoutedEventArgs e)
        {
            // Toggle control visibility.
            LocationMap.Visibility = LocationMap.Visibility == Visibility.Collapsed
                ? Visibility.Visible : Visibility.Collapsed;

            locationPin.Location = geoCoordinateWatcherWrapper.Position.Location;
            LocationMap.SetView(geoCoordinateWatcherWrapper.Position.Location, 15D);
        }
    }
}
```

Code Snippet WhereAmIOnAMap\MainPage.xaml.cs

5. Run the application, tap the Start button, and when results come in, tap the Map button. The location is displayed with a custom pushpin, as shown in Figure 8-4.

How It Works

In this example, you've added Bing Maps functionality to the location service example from earlier in this chapter. This was actually a remarkably simple task because the Bing Maps API is so easy to use.

You started by adding the Bing Maps assembly to your project because this assembly contains the Bing Maps Silverlight control. Next, you added the map to your XAML as follows:

FIGURE 8.4: Your location on a map.

```
<m:Map Visibility="Collapsed" x:Name="LocationMap"
   CredentialsProvider="<My Key>"
   Mode="Aerial">
   <m:Map.Children>
     <o:Scale />
     <m:Pushpin x:Name="locationPin">
       <m:Pushpin.Template>
         <ControlTemplate>
           <Grid Height="30" Width="30">
             <Ellipse Fill="Red" Stroke="Black" StrokeThickness="2" Margin="3"
               Opacity="0.4" />
             <Rectangle Fill="White" Height="2" />
             <Rectangle Fill="White" Width="2" />
           </Grid>
         </ControlTemplate>
       </m:Pushpin.Template>
     </m:Pushpin>
   </m:Map.Children>
</m:Map>
```

There are several things to note in this code. First, the Map control was initially invisible. To simplify the code, you simply added the control on top of the existing display, and toggling its visibility switches the display. Next, you set the Mode property of the control to Aerial. In XAML, you can set this property to Aerial or Road (the default). This property is actually of type MapMode, and in code-behind, you'd set it to an instance of AerialMode or RoadMode; you can create your own mode if you are feeling advanced, but setting it to AerialMode or RoadMode is fine for most purposes. You can build up modes with a number of customizations to define exactly how you want the map to look.

You also included two overlay children: Scale (taken from the Microsoft.Phone.Controls.Maps .Overlays namespace, hence the different tag name prefix) and Pushpin. The Scale control simply displays a scale so you can see the zoom level. Pushpin, as you saw earlier, puts a pin on the map. In this code, though, you provided an alternative control template for the pushpin, which illustrates the control you have over the look and feel of your Bing Maps applications. The pushpin you used looks like a semi-transparent red circle with a white cross through it — appropriate for showing a location on a map.

In the code-behind, you simply had to toggle the map visibility:

```
private void mapButton_Click(object sender, RoutedEventArgs e)
{
    // Toggle control visibility.
    LocationMap.Visibility = LocationMap.Visibility == Visibility.Collapsed
        ? Visibility.Visible : Visibility.Collapsed;
```

And then you set the location both of the pushpin and the map to the location stored in the `GeoCoordinateWatcherWrapper` instance:

```
    locationPin.Location = geoCoordinateWatcherWrapper.Position.Location;
    LocationMap.SetView(geoCoordinateWatcherWrapper.Position.Location, 15D);
}
```

You used a zoom level of 15 here to give a good view of the location, which I'm sure you recognize as being some pointy Egyptian thingies.

Additional Bing Maps API Functionality

The Bing Maps API includes more than just mapping functionality. You can also get access to some additional useful services:

➤ **Geocode Service** — This service enables you to translate between `GeoCoordinate` and `Address` values. You can either supply an address and get back a location coordinate or vice versa. It supplies the functionality of the currently non-functional `CivicAddressResolver` civic address-resolving class, so it's quite useful.

➤ **Imagery Service** — This service gives you access to the image data that is used to build maps.

➤ **Route Service** — This service lets you calculate routes from one location to another. It includes options such as routes to take or avoid, and it can take traffic conditions into account.

➤ **Search Service** — This service allows you to perform location-aware searches, such as getting nearby restaurants or other places of interest.

In order to use these services, though, you need to understand a bit more about the internal structure of web services and how to call them in a more low-level way. You'll learn about this in the next chapter, where you'll learn more about web service protocols and how to create your own services.

SUMMARY

In this chapter, you've looked at how to use Windows Phone 7 to access various web and cloud services. In particular, you've focused on location services and how to make sense of the data you get from such services. You saw how the technology works and how the different systems of location detection differ from one another. You also looked at best practices for using location data.

Next, you concentrated on cloud services. Cloud services are exciting and are just now becoming realistic for use. You looked at the various services that Microsoft is developing, although sadly most of them are in relatively early stages of development.

You focused in this chapter on one cloud service that is both usable and well supported for Windows Phone 7 devices: Bing Maps. You saw how easy it is to use the Bing Maps Silverlight control and how easy it is to customize the output.

All the services you've looked at in this chapter have one thing in common: All the service communication is more-or-less hidden from you. Not all web services work like this, particularly any that you create yourself. For those, you need to dig a little deeper into how to make and receive calls to and from services on the Internet and what protocols you must use to do so. This is the subject of the next chapter, where you'll learn a lot more about how to use web and cloud services.

EXERCISES

1. Web services are:

   a) Delivery companies from which you can obtain silk.

   b) Modules of functionality that you can access over the Internet.

   c) A way of accessing data in databases around the world.

   d) Exciting but not very useful for Windows Phone 7 devices.

   e) A way to get coffee.

2. You have written an application that can obtain the locations of fondue restaurants. How would you use location services in your application, and how would you ensure that you didn't drain the device battery too fast?

3. What class would you use for obtaining location information?

4. How would you determine the distance between two `GeoCoordinate` instances?

5. What do you need to do before using the Bing Maps Silverlight control?

6. What class would you use to place a scale indicator on a Bing Maps Silverlight control, and how would you add it to a Bing Maps control in XAML?

Answers to the Exercises can be found in the Appendix.

▶ WHAT YOU LEARNED IN THIS CHAPTER

TOPIC	KEY CONCEPTS
Using web services	Web services encapsulate units of functionality that you can access over the Internet. Many existing web services, including the ones that you looked at in this chapter, can be accessed through managed classes. Others, which you'll look at in more detail in Chapter 9, require more low-level code.
Adding location services	The Windows Phone 7 location service makes use of GPS, Wi-Fi, and cellular hardware to detect the location of a device. These three options range from high to low accuracy and power consumption. When the location service is running, it reports location in terms of latitude, longitude, and altitude. It also reports a degree of accuracy and, for moving devices, an estimated direction and speed. Windows Phone 7 also includes a civic address-resolving service, but it is currently not enabled. You should use the location service sparingly to avoid excessive power consumption.
Using cloud services	Cloud services extend the web service metaphor by providing application building blocks and SaaS functionality. This is part of a move toward subscription cloud computing with remote access rather than device-bound applications. This includes distributed functionality and data storage. While cloud computing is very much in its infancy, it is an exciting area with huge potential, particularly in relation to mobile devices such as Windows Phone 7 devices.
Getting to know Microsoft cloud services	Microsoft's strategy includes a major push toward cloud computing, and a raft of services will become increasingly important in the future. This includes mobile office functionality, instant messaging, XBox LIVE, and more. For now, much of this is very much at the prototype stage, although the Bing service API is mature enough for use today.
Using Bing Maps	Bing Maps services provide a great example of how cloud services will develop in the future. The Bing Maps Silverlight control provides a simple way to integrate maps into your applications. You can manipulate this control programmatically and customize almost every aspect of it, from the look and feel to complex overlays. You can also connect to additional Bing Maps services, including search, location resolution, and route-finding functionality, although this requires more low-level service access.

Creating and Consuming Web Services

➤ Understanding the types of web services and the differences between them

➤ Making web requests and receiving responses from code

➤ Consuming RESTful services

➤ Creating and consuming WCF services

➤ Creating RESTful services with WCF

In Chapter 8, you learned about web and cloud services and how to access some of them from a Windows Phone 7 device. All the services you used in that chapter were abstracted through other code, so you didn't have to worry about managing the underlying communication. Although this makes things easy for you, it's a little limiting. There are plenty more services available on the Internet that aren't abstracted in this way, and of course you can make your own, too. If you make your own, you need a way to access them, and you won't be able to add code to the Windows Phone 7 libraries, so you need lower-level access.

In this chapter, you'll look at how to achieve this. You'll see what kinds of protocols are available to you for web service communication and how to use them. You'll also see how to use Representational State Transfer (REST) services and how to create and use your own Windows Communication Foundation (WCF) and WCF REST services.

SERVICE ARCHITECTURE PRIMER

All services that exist on the Internet must, logically, be accessed over Internet channels. The underlying structure of the Internet requires you to communicate over Hypertext Transfer Protocol (HTTP) to do this. This means that HTTP communications exist behind all services.

HTTP uses a request/response methodology. Your application makes a request to a web service, and in return, it can receive a response. For example, you might send a request to a web service for product names that start with the letters *sta* and receive a response containing a list of results. However, responses are optional; sometimes you don't need them. And responses without requests (known as *push notifications*) require a different way of thinking about things and different programming techniques, as you'll see in Chapter 10.

Various service architectures are built on top of HTTP and make use of the way in which it works. Some, like REST, are simple in nature and provide, by intention, a thin wrapper on top of HTTP. Others, like WCF, are more complex and supply you with a host of powerful features that would otherwise require a lot of code to implement independently.

In this section, you'll learn about HTTP, REST, and WCF services in a little more detail so that you have a little background before you dive into writing code. This section isn't intended to provide exhaustive descriptions of these services. Instead, the information here should help to clarify things as you start to use web services.

HTTP

HTTP is a technology that you're probably intimately familiar with, even if you don't know it. Every time you use a web browser, you're using HTTP to obtain web pages. You submit an HTTP request in the form of a uniform resource locator (URL), such as `www.wrox.com`, and you receive a response in the form of a web page. Figure 9-1 shows the general architecture of this, which applies to all client/server interactions.

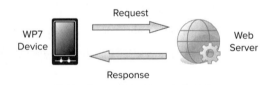

FIGURE 9-1: HTTP request/response architecture.

Sometimes you send other requests, such as when you enter information in a form and submit it. A URL is one form of uniform resource identifier (URI). HTTP also supports the notion of uniform resource names (URNs) to identify specific resources. You can think of these as being like the ISBN that identifies this book, whereas a URL is more like the address of the shop where you bought it (literally, if you bought it online).

HTTP defines several types of requests that you can use, each of which has an accompanying method, often known as the *verb*. When you're making a request from a browser, you're typically using the GET method. To send form data, you use the POST method. Two other methods are important in some web service schemes: PUT to upload data and DELETE to delete it.

In addition to the verb you use, an HTTP request can also include information in the form of a set of headers and a message body. Headers are normally used to provide metadata about the response you require, such as the language you want it in. They can also be used for other purposes, such as exchanging security tokens for authorization. The message body can be anything you like (for example, the form data mentioned above when used in a POST request).

So you can probably see how HTTP, without any additional technology or protocol, would enable you to transmit data over the Internet in a client/server situation. Assuming that you have access to a web server that can process HTTP requests, you can easily send data to it from a Windows Phone 7 device and return data, as requested. You can even define your own vocabulary to indicate a request for data, a request to save data to a database, and so on. However, it's usually better to use a more established service protocol on top of HTTP, as this can save you a lot of work.

REST

REST defines certain processes that you can use to manipulate remote resources. This manipulation uses representations of resources rather than the resources themselves — hence the name. The form of the representation is left to the user, but it typically uses a well-known encoding scheme such as JavaScript Object Notation (JSON) or some form of Extensible Markup Language (XML). A resource representation can be translated by a REST service into whatever form is required, such as a database row. Similarly, the Windows Phone 7 client can use its own representations, such as C# objects.

Web services that use REST are sometimes referred to as *RESTful* web services. A RESTful web service usually exposes one or more base URIs that refer to collections of resources. Individual resources can then be referred to using some kind of identifier underneath the base URI — perhaps a product name, but usually some kind of unique identifier such as a product ID. A base RESTful service collection URI looks something like this:

```
http://www.mygreatshopofgreatness.com/products
```

An individual resource would have a URI like this:

```
http://www.mygreatshopofgreatness.com/products/14159
```

When you have a URI, you can perform actions (that is, transitions between states) by using an HTTP method. The GET method gets you a list of items from a collection URI or a resource representation from a resource URI, for example.

Specific REST implementations may define additional operations, such as searching data. You'll see more of this later in the chapter, when you access a well-known RESTful service.

WCF

WCF is the Microsoft standard for web services. In fact, it's a lot more than that because it's not limited to HTTP. It can work on top of other communication protocols such as Transmission Control Protocol / Internet Protocol (TCP/IP) for local network communication and more. Essentially, WCF enables you to define URI endpoints for communication, wherever those might be, and bind them to protocols that include security and other information. A particular service may have several endpoints and protocol bindings to make it accessible in various ways. This address and binding information is supplied through *contracts*. Services also define the payloads required for communications through another type of contract. WCF services can expose these contracts to clients in order to become self-describing. If you have all the contracts associated with a WCF service, you have all the information required to use it, regardless of the technology you use to do so. WCF is built with the .NET Framework like Windows Phone 7, so the examples you'll see in this chapter are .NET based, but other platforms can use WCF just as easily.

The data payload used for request and response messages for WCF takes the form of a Simple Object Access Protocol (SOAP) message. SOAP messages include header and payload information and are written using XML, which is another bonus for cross-platform compatibility. Over HTTP, the SOAP message is the payload of the HTTP request or response. Over other protocols, the SOAP message may be encoded in different ways.

Usually when you use WCF, though, you don't need to worry a lot about the implementation details described above. The .NET Framework is able to abstract most of the functionality for you so that you end up with quite simple code in both the client and service. You might define a service that adds two numbers together, for example. After the .NET Framework and development tools have worked their magic, accessing this service from a client is practically identical to calling a method on a class in the client. To achieve this, you use the contracts exposed by the service to create a *proxy* class using a tool, and then you simply call methods on that proxy class. Under the hood, web requests will be created, sent, configured, returned, and so on as required by the service and the communication contracts.

WEB REQUESTS AND RESPONSES

Silverlight supplies several classes that you can use to make and receive requests over HTTP. Depending on the level of access you require, you can use either the WebClient class for simplicity or the WebRequest and WebResponse classes for flexibility. The latter classes are a little more difficult to use as they require slightly more complicated asynchronous code. However, they give you more control over how things work. Web access through all these classes must be performed asynchronously. This enables you to keep the client responsive, so it isn't a bad thing.

Using WebClient

To use the WebClient class, you create an instance, attach an event handler to one of several events it exposes, and then make a request using one of several methods. Each method has a corresponding event. For example, the DownloadStringAsync() method raises the DownloadStringCompleted event when it completes. This method performs an HTTP GET operation on a URI. To perform a POST operation, you use the UploadStringAsync() method. There are also methods that you can use to work with streams of data rather than string data.

For example, to perform an HTTP GET on some data at a particular URI, you might write the following:

```
WebClient webClient = new WebClient();
webClient.DownloadStringCompleted += new DownloadStringCompletedEventHandler(
webClient_DownloadStringCompleted);
```

```
webClient.DownloadStringAsync(
    new Uri("http://www.mygreatshopofgreatness.com/products/14159"));
```

In the event handler, you can look at the `Result` property of the `DownloadStringCompletedEventArgs` argument to get the result as a string.

You can also set HTTP request headers through the `Headers` property, and after a result is returned, you can see the HTTP response headers in the `ResponseHeaders` property.

Using WebRequest and WebResponse

There are two main differences regarding how you access data over HTTP with `WebRequest` and `WebResponse` compared to using `WebClient`:

> You must use streams rather than strings to send and receive data.

> You must use the .NET async pattern to make calls rather than use event-based asynchronous code.

Using streams is simple enough, as you can use the `StreamReader` and `StreamWriter` classes to read data from or write data to streams, respectively. The .NET asynchronous pattern is a little more difficult at first. However, once you're used to it, it's easy to use, as you'll see in the following section.

Making Asynchronous Calls

Asynchronous programming is an enormous topic and not one this book can cover in depth. However, you don't need to know a lot in order to use `WebRequest` and `WebResponse`. Essentially, you can perform asynchronous calls as follows:

1. Call the asynchronous `BeginXXX()` method, passing a callback delegate and, optionally, some state that will be passed to the callback method.

2. While the call is in progress, control is handed back to your application, so the user interface remains responsive, and you can get on with other tasks while you wait for the callback to occur; this is similar to waiting for an event to be raised by `WebClient`.

3. When the callback method is called, call the `EndXXX()` method corresponding to the `BeginXXX()` method you used previously to get the result. You must pass the `IAsyncResult` value that is passed to the callback method as a parameter to the `EndXXX()` method.

This is a somewhat simplified view of asynchronous calls as there are many more options available, but it's all you need to know for now.

 WARNING *You must beware of the fact that the callback method from an asynchronous call can be called from a background thread, so you must use the Dispatcher to modify the user interface from a callback if you need to.*

Performing an HTTP GET Request

The first step in making an HTTP request using `WebRequest` is to create a request object. There is no public constructor for this class. Instead, you can use the static `GetHttpWebRequest()` method and pass a URI string parameter. The method returns an `HttpWebRequest` instance (which derives from `WebRequest`) that you can use to send requests. You can then use the `BeginGetResponse()` asynchronous method to make a GET request:

```
HttpWebRequest request = WebRequest.CreateHttp(
    "http://www.somewherethatinterestsyou.com/");
request.BeginGetResponse(GetResponseCallback, request);
```

In this code, the callback that is called is the `GetResponseCallback()` method. Note also that the `request` object is passed as the second parameter to `BeginGetResponse()`. This object is then passed to the callback so that you can call the `EndGetResponse()` method as follows:

```
private void GetResponseCallback(IAsyncResult result)
{
    HttpWebResponse response =
        (result.AsyncState as HttpWebRequest).EndGetResponse(result)
        as HttpWebResponse;
    ... // Read response result.
}
```

The `result.AsyncState` property contains the `request` object passed to `BeginGetResponse()`. You call the `EndGetResponse()` method of this object, passing the `IAsyncResult` callback parameter, and obtain a `WebResponse` object, which you can cast to `HttpWebResponse`. Once you have the `HttpWebResponse` value, you can get the response stream by using `response` `.GetResponseStream()` and read out the result.

Performing an HTTP POST Request

Performing an HTTP POST request is just the same as performing an HTTP GET request, but with two additional steps:

1.   You must set the `Method` property of the request to POST.

2.   You must write any data to be posted to a request stream before getting a response.

The first step is easy. The second step requires another asynchronous method call, to `WebRequest` `.BeginGetRequestStream()`. Once you have written data to the stream return value that you get from `WebRequest.EndGetRequestStream()`, you can call `BeginGetResponse()` asynchronously as before:

```
HttpWebRequest request = WebRequest.CreateHttp(
    "http://www.somewherethatinterestsyou.com/post");
request.Method = "POST";
request.BeginGetRequestStream(GetRequestStreamCallback, request);

...
```

```
private void GetRequestStreamCallback(IAsyncResult result)
{
    Stream requestStream =
        (result.AsyncState as HttpWebRequest).EndGetRequestStream(
            result) as Stream;
    ... // Write to request stream.
    request.BeginGetResponse(GetResponseCallback, request);
}

private void GetResponseCallback(IAsyncResult result)
{
    HttpWebResponse response =
        (result.AsyncState as HttpWebRequest).EndGetResponse(result)
        as HttpWebResponse;
    ... // Read response result.
}
```

TRY IT OUT Web Requests and Responses

In the following steps, you'll see an example of using both the WebClient and WebRequest and WebResponse methods to access data over HTTP. You'll also see how to read a response from a stream with a StreamReader object.

1. Create a new Windows Phone Application called **HttpResponseGetter**.

2. Modify the code in MainPage.xaml so that it looks like Listing 9-1.

LISTING 9-1: Modifying the code in MainPage.xaml

Available for download on Wrox.com

```xml
<phone:PhoneApplicationPage ... >

  <Grid x:Name="LayoutRoot" Background="Transparent">
    ...

    <StackPanel x:Name="TitlePanel" Grid.Row="0" Margin="12,17,0,28">
      <TextBlock x:Name="ApplicationTitle" Text="HTTP RESPONSE GETTER"
        Style="{StaticResource PhoneTextNormalStyle}"/>
    </StackPanel>

    <Grid x:Name="ContentPanel" Grid.Row="1" Margin="12,0,12,0">
      <Grid.RowDefinitions>
        <RowDefinition Height="Auto"/>
        <RowDefinition Height="Auto"/>
        <RowDefinition Height="*"/>
      </Grid.RowDefinitions>
      <Grid.ColumnDefinitions>
        <ColumnDefinition />
        <ColumnDefinition />
      </Grid.ColumnDefinitions>
      <TextBox Grid.Row="0" Grid.ColumnSpan="2" Name="UrlTextBox"
        Text="http://www.wrox.com/" />
      <Button Grid.Row="1" Grid.Column="0" Content="Use WebClient"
        Name="GetResponseWebClientButton"
        Click="GetResponseWebClientButton_Click" />
```

continues

LISTING 9-1 *(continued)*

```xml
      <Button Grid.Row="1" Grid.Column="1" Content="Use Raw"
        Name="GetResponseRawButton"
        Click="GetResponseRawButton_Click" />
      <ScrollViewer Grid.Row="2" Grid.ColumnSpan="2">
        <TextBlock HorizontalAlignment="Left" Name="ResponseText"
          VerticalAlignment="Top" TextWrapping="Wrap" />
      </ScrollViewer>
    </Grid>
  </Grid>

</phone:PhoneApplicationPage>
```

Code Snippet HttpResponseGetter\MainPage.xaml

3. Modify the code in `MainPage.xaml.cs` so that it looks like Listing 9-2.

LISTING 9-2: Modifying the code in MainPage.xaml.cs

```csharp
using System;
using System.IO;
using System.Net;
using System.Windows;
using Microsoft.Phone.Controls;

namespace HttpResponseGetter
{
    public partial class MainPage : PhoneApplicationPage
    {
        private WebClient webClient;

        public MainPage()
        {
            InitializeComponent();

            webClient = new WebClient();
            webClient.DownloadStringCompleted +=
                new DownloadStringCompletedEventHandler(
                    webClient_DownloadStringCompleted);
        }

        private void GetResponseWebClientButton_Click(
            object sender, RoutedEventArgs e)
        {
            webClient.DownloadStringAsync(new Uri(UrlTextBox.Text));
        }

        private void webClient_DownloadStringCompleted(
            object sender, DownloadStringCompletedEventArgs e)
        {
            SetText(e.Result);
        }
```

```
private void GetResponseRawButton_Click(
   object sender, RoutedEventArgs e)
{
   HttpWebRequest request = WebRequest.CreateHttp(
      UrlTextBox.Text);
   request.BeginGetResponse(
      GetResponseRawButtonCallback, request);
}

private void GetResponseRawButtonCallback(IAsyncResult result)
{
   HttpWebResponse response =
      (result.AsyncState as HttpWebRequest).EndGetResponse(
         result) as HttpWebResponse;
   string returnValue = null;
   using (StreamReader sr = new StreamReader(
      response.GetResponseStream()))
   {
      returnValue = sr.ReadToEnd();
      SetText(returnValue);
   }
}

private void SetText(string text)
{
   Dispatcher.BeginInvoke(
      new Action(() => ResponseText.Text = text));
}
   }
}
```

Code Snippet HttpResponseGetter\MainPage.xaml.cs

4. Run the application and tap either button. (You can also change the URL from which to get data, if you wish.) After a short pause, the HTTP response is shown, as in Figure 9-2.

How It Works

In this example, you created a simple application that can get a response from an HTTP GET request to a URI. The response shown in the example, from www.wrox.com, is an HTML page. Other URIs provide other data, such as REST representations, WCF SOAP packages, images, media files, and so on. The user interface for the application contains a text box for entering a URI, two buttons to use the two methods of performing an HTTP GET operation, as discussed earlier in this section, and a text block in a scroll viewer for viewing the result.

For the first technique, using WebClient, you must first create a WebClient instance and store it for future use. You do this in the page constructor:

FIGURE 9-2: The HTTP response getter in action.

```
public MainPage()
{
    InitializeComponent();

    webClient = new WebClient();
```

You also add an event hander to the `DownloadStringCompleted` event to use when requests complete:

```
    webClient.DownloadStringCompleted +=
        new DownloadStringCompletedEventHandler(
                webClient_DownloadStringCompleted);
}
```

Sending the HTTP GET request simply means calling the `DownloadStringAsync()` method of the `WebClient` instance, using the URI from the text box:

```
private void GetResponseWebClientButton_Click(
        object sender, RoutedEventArgs e)
{
    webClient.DownloadStringAsync(new Uri(UrlTextBox.Text));
}
```

The event handler calls in to a helper method for setting the result text through the page `Dispatcher` property:

```
private void webClient_DownloadStringCompleted(
        object sender, DownloadStringCompletedEventArgs e)
{
    SetText(e.Result);
}

private void SetText(string text)
{
    Dispatcher.BeginInvoke(new Action(() => ResponseText.Text = text));
}
```

To use the `WebRequest` technique, you create an `HttpWebRequest` instance and then call `BeginGetResponse()`, again using the URI from the user interface:

```
private void GetResponseRawButton_Click(object sender, RoutedEventArgs e)
{
    HttpWebRequest request = WebRequest.CreateHttp(UrlTextBox.Text);
    request.BeginGetResponse(GetResponseRawButtonCallback, request);
}
```

The callback gets the `HttpWebResponse` result and then uses a `StreamReader` object to read the data returned through the `GetResponseStream()` method. For simplicity, the `ReadToEnd()` method of the `StreamReader` instance is used to get all the data. In practice, you might want to read the data a bit at a time if there's lots of it:

```
private void GetResponseRawButtonCallback(IAsyncResult result)
{
    HttpWebResponse response =
        (result.AsyncState as HttpWebRequest).EndGetResponse(result)
        as HttpWebResponse;
    string returnValue = null;
    using (StreamReader sr = new StreamReader(response.GetResponseStream()))
    {
        returnValue = sr.ReadToEnd();
        SetText(returnValue);
    }
}
```

 COMMON MISTAKES *Note that this example doesn't include all the exception handling that you would use in a real-world example. Many of the calls made can fail for various reasons, such as a "404 not found" response for an invalid URI or an authentication failure for a secure location.*

To expand on this last point, both of the techniques you have looked at in this section allow you to authenticate to web services in a variety of ways, but that is beyond the scope of this chapter.

Cached Responses

There is one more important point to note when using low-level HTTP requests and responses. HTTP responses will be cached by the Windows Phone 7 device. This is done in order to achieve greater efficiency, but it can cause problems when it comes to web service access. For example, if the data you get back from a particular URI represents the state of an object (which is a common case with REST services, as you'll see shortly), subsequent requests will return the same data because it will be cached. This may be true even if the data has changed, which isn't necessarily what you want to happen.

This caching behavior is determined by the response from a URI. It is possible to send back HTTP headers with a response that instruct the client not to cache data. Alternatively, you can ensure that you don't use the same URI more than once; for example, you can include a dummy parameter in the request URI, such as the current time. In general, though, it's best if this is handled on the server. Later in the chapter, when you create your own WCF REST service, you'll see how to do this.

REST-BASED SERVICES

Now that you've seen how to perform HTTP requests and receive HTTP responses, you're most of the way to using RESTful services. You can use exactly the same code from the previous section to do this, with one change: You need to process the data you send and receive so that the service understands it.

Consuming a RESTful Service

To show how easy it is to use a RESTful service, the best thing to do is to try one out. The exact syntax of these services varies between implementations, but it's usually easy to find out what to do.

In this section and in the following Try It Out, you'll see how to use the Flickr REST service application programming interface (API). You can find full details of the available services and ways to call them at www.flickr.com/services/api/. This page includes links to various language implementations, including .NET, but you can also use the simple REST interface.

> **NOTE** *You need an API key in order to use the Flickr services. You need to register with the site at* www.flickr.com *if you haven't already done so, and then you can get a key at* www.flickr.com/services/apps/create/. *Basic membership of Flickr is completely free, and you don't need to provide any payment details.*

Many of the Flickr API calls require user authentication. Basically, you must direct users to an authentication page provided by Flickr, where they can enter a username and password. In return, the page provides you with a token that you can use for authentication. This token, known as a mini-token, must first be exchanged for a full token. After this process (which effectively and sensibly prevents your application from obtaining a user's authentication details), you can make calls on the user's behalf. This includes modifying photo details and so on. Various levels of authorization apply to subsequent calls. For example, users can modify photos that they own but not other people's photos.

Many API calls don't require authentication, so there's plenty you can do without requiring user login. All calls, regardless of whether they require authentication, share a common format. The URI of a call includes a specific base address for the API and some parameters such as a function name. For POST calls, there may also be a required message body, such as the text of a comment to add to a photo.

Parameters take the form of query string parameters. This is a convention whereby a URI can include extra information in the form of a number of name/value pairs, as follows:

```
http://<base address>?param1=value1&param2=value2
```

In this URI, the ? symbol precedes a number of *param=value* pairs, each separated from the next with an ampersand (&) symbol. In order to use this syntax, you must "escape" some characters. This means you must encode them in such a way as to be understandable without breaking the URI. For example, if your parameter value includes an & symbol, you must instead use the string %26. You can use existing .NET methods to do this automatically and to decode a previously encoded string, as in the following examples:

```
HttpUtility.UrlEncode(stringToEncode);
HttpUtility.UrlDecode(stringToDecode);
```

TRY IT OUT RESTful Services

In the following steps, you'll use the `flickr.people.findByUsername` and
`flickr.people.getPublicPhotos` API calls to get details about a user's photo stream:

1. If you don't already have one, obtain an API key from Flickr. (Remember that to do so, you must register at Flickr.)

2. Create a new Windows Phone Application called `FlickrStatViewer` and add a reference to `System.Xml.Linq.dll`.

3. Add a new class called `FlickrUriHelper` to the application and modify the code in `FlickrUriHelper.cs` so that it looks like Listing 9-3.

LISTING 9-3: Modifying the code in FlickrUriHelper.cs

```
using System.Collections.Generic;
using System.Text;

namespace FlickrStatViewer
{
    public class FlickrUriHelper
    {
        private const string UriBaseFormatString =
            "http://api.flickr.com/services/rest/?method={0}";
        private const string ParameterFormatString = "&{0}={1}";
        private const string ApiKeyParameter = "api_key";

        public string ApiKey { get; set; }

        public string GetUri(
            string method, Dictionary<string, string> parameters)
        {
            StringBuilder sb = new StringBuilder();
            sb.AppendFormat(UriBaseFormatString, method);
            sb.AppendFormat(ParameterFormatString, ApiKeyParameter,
                ApiKey);
            foreach (var parameter in parameters)
            {
                sb.AppendFormat(ParameterFormatString, parameter.Key,
                    parameter.Value);
            }

            return sb.ToString();
        }
    }

    public class PhotoInfo
    {
        public string Title { get; set; }
        public string DateTaken { get; set; }
```

continues

LISTING 9-3 *(continued)*

```
    public string Views { get; set; }
  }
}
```

Code Snippet FlickrStatViewer\FlickrUriHelper.cs

4. Modify the code in `MainPage.xaml` so that it looks like Listing 9-4.

LISTING 9-4: Modifying the code in MainPage.xaml

```
<phone:PhoneApplicationPage ... >

  <Grid x:Name="LayoutRoot" Background="Transparent">
    <Grid.RowDefinitions>
      <RowDefinition Height="Auto"/>
      <RowDefinition Height="*"/>
    </Grid.RowDefinitions>

    <StackPanel x:Name="TitlePanel" Grid.Row="0" Margin="12,17,0,28">
      <TextBlock x:Name="ApplicationTitle" Text="FLICKR STAT VIEWER"
        Style="{StaticResource PhoneTextNormalStyle}"/>
    </StackPanel>

    <Grid x:Name="ContentPanel" Grid.Row="1" Margin="12,0,12,0">
      <Grid.RowDefinitions>
        <RowDefinition Height="Auto" />
        <RowDefinition Height="Auto" />
        <RowDefinition Height="Auto" />
        <RowDefinition Height="*" />
      </Grid.RowDefinitions>
      <Grid Grid.Row="0">
        <Grid.ColumnDefinitions>
          <ColumnDefinition Width="Auto" />
          <ColumnDefinition Width="*" />
        </Grid.ColumnDefinitions>
        <TextBlock VerticalAlignment="Center" Text="Username:"
          Style="{StaticResource PhoneTextAccentStyle}" />
        <TextBox Grid.Column="1" Name="UsernameBox"
          Text="Karlequin" />
      </Grid>
      <Button Grid.Row="2" Name="GetPhotoStatsButton"
        Content="Get Photo Stats" Click="GetPhotoStatsButton_Click" />
      <ScrollViewer Grid.Row="3">
        <ItemsControl Name="PhotoStats">
          <ItemsControl.ItemTemplate>
            <DataTemplate>
              <Border Margin="2" Background="Indigo"
                BorderBrush="YellowGreen" BorderThickness="4"
                Padding="2,0,0,0" CornerRadius="8">
```

```
    <Grid>
      <Grid.RowDefinitions>
        <RowDefinition Height="Auto" />
        <RowDefinition Height="28" />
      </Grid.RowDefinitions>
      <Grid.ColumnDefinitions>
        <ColumnDefinition Width="Auto" />
        <ColumnDefinition Width="*" />
        <ColumnDefinition Width="Auto" />
        <ColumnDefinition Width="80" />
      </Grid.ColumnDefinitions>
      <TextBlock Grid.ColumnSpan="4"
        Text="{Binding Title}"
        Style="{StaticResource PhoneTextTitle3Style}" />
      <TextBlock Grid.Column="0" Grid.Row="1" Text="Date:"
        Style="{StaticResource PhoneTextAccentStyle}" />
      <TextBlock Grid.Column="1" Grid.Row="1"
        Text="{Binding DateTaken}" />
      <TextBlock Grid.Column="2" Grid.Row="1"
        Text="Views:"
        Style="{StaticResource PhoneTextAccentStyle}" />
      <TextBlock Grid.Column="3" Grid.Row="1"
        Text="{Binding Views}" Margin="0,0,4,0" />
    </Grid>
    </Border>
    </DataTemplate>
    </ItemsControl.ItemTemplate>
    </ItemsControl>
    </ScrollViewer>
    </Grid>
  </Grid>
</phone:PhoneApplicationPage>
```

Code Snippet FlickrStatViewer\MainPage.xaml

5. Modify the code in `MainPage.xaml.cs` so that it looks like Listing 9-5 (including your API key, as noted in the code).

LISTING 9-5: Modifying the code in MainPage.xaml.cs

```
using System;
using System.Collections.Generic;
using System.Linq;
using System.Net;
using System.Windows;
using System.Xml.Linq;
using Microsoft.Phone.Controls;

namespace FlickrStatViewer
{
    public partial class MainPage : PhoneApplicationPage
    {
```

continues

LISTING 9-5 *(continued)*

```csharp
private FlickrUriHelper flickrUriHelper;

public MainPage()
{
   InitializeComponent();

   flickrUriHelper =
      new FlickrUriHelper { ApiKey = "<YOUR KEY HERE>" };
}

private void GetPhotoStatsButton_Click(
   object sender, RoutedEventArgs e)
{
   HttpWebRequest getUserRequest = WebRequest.CreateHttp(
      flickrUriHelper.GetUri(
         "flickr.people.findByUsername",
         new Dictionary<string,string>
         {
            { "username",
              HttpUtility.UrlEncode(UsernameBox.Text) }
         }));
   getUserRequest.BeginGetResponse(GetUserRequestCallback,
      getUserRequest);
}

private void GetUserRequestCallback(IAsyncResult result)
{
   HttpWebResponse response =
      (result.AsyncState as HttpWebRequest).EndGetResponse(result)
      as HttpWebResponse;
   XDocument resultXml = XDocument.Load(
      response.GetResponseStream());
   string userNsid = (from user in resultXml.Descendants("user")
      select user.Attribute("nsid").Value).FirstOrDefault();

   HttpWebRequest getPhotosRequest = WebRequest.CreateHttp(
      flickrUriHelper.GetUri(
         "flickr.people.getPublicPhotos",
         new Dictionary<string, string>
         {
            { "user_id", userNsid },
            { "extras", "date_taken,views" }
         }));
   getPhotosRequest.BeginGetResponse(GetPhotosRequestCallback,
      getPhotosRequest);
}

private void GetPhotosRequestCallback(IAsyncResult result)
{
   HttpWebResponse response =
      (result.AsyncState as HttpWebRequest).EndGetResponse(result)
      as HttpWebResponse;
```

```
XDocument resultXml = XDocument.Load(
    response.GetResponseStream());
Dispatcher.BeginInvoke(new Action(
    () =>
        PhotoStats.ItemsSource =
        from photo in resultXml.Descendants("photo")
        select new PhotoInfo
        {
            Title = photo.Attribute("title").Value,
            DateTaken = photo.Attribute("datetaken").Value,
            Views = photo.Attribute("views").Value
        }));
        }
    }
}
```

Code Snippet FlickrStatViewer\FlickrUriHelper.cs

6. Run the application. Enter the name of a Flickr user (or simply use this author's account: Karlequin) and tap Get Photo Stats. You see a list of photos and associated data, as shown in Figure 9-3.

FIGURE 9-3: Flickr stats for Karlequin.

How It Works

In this example, you created an application that uses the Flickr REST API to obtain stats from a user's photo stream. You started by creating a helper class to format URIs for use with the Flickr REST API. These URIs all use the same base address and require two parameters each, to specify the name of the method to call and the API key, as follows:

```
http://api.flickr.com/services/rest/?method=<method name>&api_key=<key>
```

Most API methods also require additional methods. The code in the `FlickrUriHelper` class includes some constant format strings and values to enable you to create these API URIs with ease:

```
public class FlickrUriHelper
{
    private const string UriBaseFormatString =
        "http://api.flickr.com/services/rest/?method={0}";
    private const string ParameterFormatString = "&{0}={1}";
    private const string ApiKeyParameter = "api_key";
```

The class also has an `ApiKey` property so that you have to set it only once:

```
public string ApiKey { get; set; }
```

The rest of the code in the class defines a method called `GetUri()` that's used to create a method call with an arbitrary list of name/value parameters:

```
public string GetUri(
        string method, Dictionary<string, string> parameters)
{
    StringBuilder sb = new StringBuilder();
    sb.AppendFormat(UriBaseFormatString, method);
    sb.AppendFormat(ParameterFormatString, ApiKeyParameter,
        ApiKey);
    foreach (var parameter in parameters)
    {
        sb.AppendFormat(ParameterFormatString, parameter.Key,
            parameter.Value);
    }

    return sb.ToString();
}
}
```

This method assumes that the strings passed to it are already escaped, which is fine in this example, as you can control this.

The code in this file also includes a simple data class that's used later to store photo information, `PhotoInfo`.

Next, you created the XAML for the main page. This simply contains a text box, a button to tap, and a scrollable result view.

The code in `MainPage.xaml.cs` starts with a reference to an instance of the helper class created earlier, which is initialized in the constructor with the API key. Next is the event handler for the button on the page, `GetPhotoStatsButton_Click()`. This code uses the value from the text box for the `username` parameter for the `flickr.people.findByUsername` API method. The parameter value is escaped for safety, and the method is invoked asynchronously, using code like that you saw earlier.

```
private void GetPhotoStatsButton_Click(
        object sender, RoutedEventArgs e)
{
```

```
        HttpWebRequest getUserRequest = WebRequest.CreateHttp(
            flickrUriHelper.GetUri(
                "flickr.people.findByUsername",
                new Dictionary<string,string>
                {
                    { "username",
                            HttpUtility.UrlEncode(UsernameBox.Text) }
                }));
        getUserRequest.BeginGetResponse(GetUserRequestCallback,
                getUserRequest);
    }
```

The callback for this API method call, `GetUserRequestCallback()`, extracts the result as an XML document. You can see the expected document format on the Flickr API documentation page:

```
<user nsid="12037949632@N01">
  <username>Stewart</username>
</user>
```

Elsewhere in the API documentation, you can find the general response format for API calls. Where no error occurs, the preceding XML is wrapped in a document as follows:

```
<?xml version="1.0" encoding="utf-8" ?>
<rsp stat="ok">
  [xml-payload-here]
</rsp>
```

Alternatively, if an error occurs, the error details are sent back in a document as follows:

```
<?xml version="1.0" encoding="utf-8" ?>
<rsp stat="fail">
  <err code="[error-code]" msg="[error-message]" />
</rsp>
```

For simplicity, the code in this example doesn't check for error messages. Instead, it simply extracts the important information in the response for the `flickr.people.findByUsername` API method, which is the `nsid` attribute of the `<user>` element. This is a unique identifier that you can use to identify a user in subsequent calls. In the code, this value is extracted using simple LINQ-to-XML syntax:

```
private void GetUserRequestCallback(IAsyncResult result)
{
    HttpWebResponse response =
            (result.AsyncState as HttpWebRequest).EndGetResponse(result)
        as HttpWebResponse;
    XDocument resultXml = XDocument.Load(
            response.GetResponseStream());
    string userNsid = (from user in resultXml.Descendants("user")
        select user.Attribute("nsid").Value).FirstOrDefault();
```

Once the `nsid` value is obtained, it's used in a call to the `flickr.people.getPublicPhotos` API method, in a parameter called `user_id`. Another parameter, `extras`, is used to instruct the API method to return additional information — in this case, the date the photo was taken and the number of times it's been viewed:

```
HttpWebRequest getPhotosRequest = WebRequest.CreateHttp(
    flickrUriHelper.GetUri(
        "flickr.people.getPublicPhotos",
        new Dictionary<string, string>
        {
            { "user_id", userNsid },
            { "extras", "date_taken,views" }
        }));
getPhotosRequest.BeginGetResponse(GetPhotosRequestCallback,
        getPhotosRequest);
}
```

The last method in the code, `GetPhotosRequestCallback()`, handles the final result. The API lists the expected (non-error) response to the API method as follows:

```
<photos page="2" pages="89" perpage="10" total="881">
  <photo id="2636" owner="47058503995@N01"
    secret="a123456" server="2" title="test_04"
    ispublic="1" isfriend="0" isfamily="0" />
  <photo id="2635" owner="47058503995@N01"
    secret="b123456" server="2" title="test_03"
    ispublic="0" isfriend="1" isfamily="1" />
  <photo id="2633" owner="47058503995@N01"
    secret="c123456" server="2" title="test_01"
    ispublic="1" isfriend="0" isfamily="0" />
  <photo id="2610" owner="12037949754@N01"
    secret="d123456" server="2" title="00_tall"
    ispublic="1" isfriend="0" isfamily="0" />
</photos>
```

The parent `<photos>` element contains useful pagination information that you can use to locate the result returned as part of a larger set. You can request a specific page of photos with the call if you like, using the `page` and `per_page` parameters.

Each `<photo>` child element contains some basic information, such as the page title and enough information to generate a URI for the photo. (See www.flickr.com/services/api/misc .urls.html for details about Flickr URIs.) As the code includes a request for some more information, `datetaken` and `views` attributes are also included. Again, you use LINQ-to-XML syntax to get data from the response. This time, you use it to create a collection of `PhotoInfo` objects, which is assigned to the `ItemsSource` property of the `ItemsControl` in the XAML. This must be done on the user interface thread, so you use `Dispatcher`:

```
private void GetPhotosRequestCallback(IAsyncResult result)
{
    HttpWebResponse response =
        (result.AsyncState as HttpWebRequest).EndGetResponse(result)
        as HttpWebResponse;
    XDocument resultXml = XDocument.Load(
        response.GetResponseStream());
```

```
        Dispatcher.BeginInvoke(new Action(
            () =>
                PhotoStats.ItemsSource =
                from photo in resultXml.Descendants("photo")
                select new PhotoInfo
                {
                    Title = photo.Attribute("title").Value,
                    DateTaken = photo.Attribute("datetaken").Value,
                    Views = photo.Attribute("views").Value
                }));
        }
    }
}
```

This example hopefully shows you enough to get started using the Flickr API, and indeed it shows enough to use other REST APIs. As long as you can find some documentation for the API you want to use, doing this is generally not too difficult.

Creating RESTful Services

There are a number of ways to create your own REST services. You can, if you wish, write code that listens to requests at a particular base URI and processes parameters sent. (One way to do this would be to implement an .ashx handler.) Parsing parameters and requests, building responses, and so on can involve a lot of work, though.

An alternative to writing the code yourself is to use a framework to help you. There are many of these available, or you can simply use WCF to do the heavy lifting for you. For more complex scenarios, you can also use the WCF REST Starter Kit, which builds on WCF to add additional capabilities. You can find out more about this at http://msdn.microsoft.com/en-us/netframework/cc950529.aspx.

Later in this chapter, you will see how to create a REST service with WCF. Before that, though, you need to learn a lot more about WCF, which you'll do in the next section.

WCF SERVICES

As you learned earlier in the chapter, WCF is the Microsoft standard for web services. WCF services are extremely flexible, and you can use them in all manner of situations, from the most basic request and response to the most complicated secure services. In this section, you'll use WCF services at their simplest, with most of the configuration using the default settings.

Entire books are devoted to WCF services and their usage, and this isn't the place to go into details. In this section, you'll get a glimpse of how powerful even the simplest WCF services can be and how easily they can be put together. You'll also see how to implement REST services with WCF.

Tools for Creating WCF Services

You can't create WCF services in Microsoft Visual Studio Express 2010 for Windows Phone (VSE for WP). Instead, you must have either the full version of Visual Studio or Microsoft Visual Web Developer 2010 Express (VWD). The advantage of the latter is that, like VSE for WP, it is completely free. You can download it from www.microsoft.com/express/ if you don't already have it or the full version of Visual Studio.

Hosting WCF Services

WCF services must be hosted somewhere, such as on a web server. Don't panic, though. This doesn't mean you need to upload them anywhere when you're developing your applications (although obviously you do need to upload them if you release your code). For testing, you can use either a local web server installation or simply the built-in ASP.NET Development Server that is included in the integrated development environment (IDE). This latter option is the easiest and is perfect for simple services, so that's what you'll use in the examples in this chapter.

Creating WCF Services

The development process for consuming a homemade WCF service from a Windows Phone 7 application is roughly as follows:

1. Create a new WCF service project in VWD.

2. Define the service contract and any required data contracts. A service contract defines what operations are available to clients, and a data contract specifies how custom types are serialized. Often, for simple types, as in the examples in this chapter, no data contracts are required.

3. Implement the service contract.

4. Compile and run the project so that the service is running in the ASP.NET Development Server. You may at this point decide to (temporarily) fix the URI for the service for testing; otherwise, the port that the server is exposed through may change.

5. Optionally, test the service by using the WCF Test Client, which is built into the IDE.

6. Create a new Windows Phone Application in VSE for WP.

7. Add a service reference to the WCF service, using the URI of the service in the ASP.NET Development Server.

8. Consume the service through the supplied proxy class. You can do this without having to write any low-level HTTP access code.

9. Test with a satisfied smile.

Now, you could spend a lot of time learning about these steps in more detail. However, it's a lot more fun to dive in, get your hands dirty, and learn how all this works by working through an example or two.

WCF Services Example Application

In this section, you'll create an application that will enable you to view and edit a collection of notes that are stored on a remote server and accessed through a service. In theory, you can use a system like this to maintain a centralized note store that you can access from multiple clients. You can even share notes with friends. However, to keep things simple, this implementation has a single list of notes and no user registration or authentication.

The service, which you'll create in the first of two Try It Out sections, will support four operations:

- ➤ Get a list of note titles.
- ➤ Load a note body by its title.
- ➤ Save a note with title and body.
- ➤ Delete a note by its title.

In a real-world implementation, you'd probably store note data in a database, accessed through the service. However, for the sake of simplicity, this example uses a simple XML file stored on your local disk.

TRY IT OUT Creating a WCF Service

The client, which you'll create in this exercise, uses all the service operations to provide full note-editing capability.

1. In VWD, create a new C# WCF Service Application called **NotesService**. It's the first time you've used this IDE in this book. Figure 9-4 shows how the New Project dialog looks.

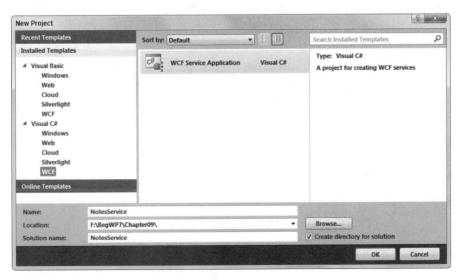

FIGURE 9-4: Creating a WCF service application.

2. Remove the auto-generated `IService1.cs`, `Service1.svc`, and `Service1.svc.cs` files from the project. (`Service1.svc.cs` will be deleted automatically when you remove `Service1.svc`.)

3. In Solution Explorer, right-click the `NotesService` project and select Add ➪ New Item...

4. Using the Add New Item dialog, add a WCF service called `NotesService`, as shown in Figure 9-5.

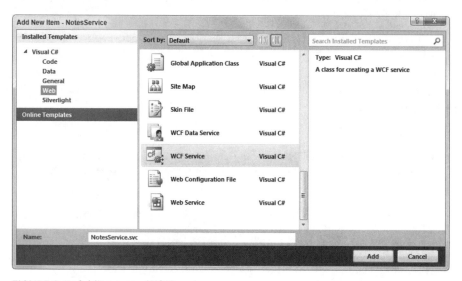

FIGURE 9-5: Adding a new WCF service.

5. Modify the code in `INotesService.cs` so that it looks like Listing 9-6.

LISTING 9-6: Modifying the code in INotesService.cs

```csharp
using System.Collections.Generic;
using System.ServiceModel;

namespace NotesService
{
    [ServiceContract]
    public interface INotesService
    {
        [OperationContract]
        IEnumerable<string> GetNoteTitles();

        [OperationContract]
        string LoadNote(string title);

        [OperationContract]
        void SaveNote(string title, string body);

        [OperationContract]
```

```
            void DeleteNote(string title);
        }
    }
```

Code Snippet NotesService\INotesService.cs

6. Modify the code in NotesService.svc.cs so that it looks like Listing 9-7.

LISTING 9-7: Modifying the code in INotesService.svc.cs

```csharp
using System.Collections.Generic;
using System.IO;
using System.Linq;
using System.Xml.Linq;

namespace NotesService
{
    public class NotesService : INotesService
    {
        private const string NotesFile = @"c:\Temp\notes.xml";

        private XDocument ReadNotesFile()
        {
            XDocument document;
            if (File.Exists(NotesFile))
            {
                document = XDocument.Load(NotesFile, LoadOptions.None);
            }
            else
            {
                document = new XDocument();
                document.Add(new XElement("Notes"));
                WriteNotesFile(document);
            }

            return document;
        }

        private void WriteNotesFile(XDocument notes)
        {
            notes.Save(NotesFile, SaveOptions.None);
        }

        public IEnumerable<string> GetNoteTitles()
        {
            XDocument notes = ReadNotesFile();
            return from n in notes.Descendants("Note")
                select n.Attribute("title").Value;
        }
```

continues

LISTING 9-7 *(continued)*

```csharp
public string LoadNote(string title)
{
   XDocument notes = ReadNotesFile();
   return (from n in notes.Descendants("Note")
      where n.Attribute("title").Value == title
      select n.Value)
      .FirstOrDefault();
}

public void SaveNote(string title, string body)
{
   XDocument notes = ReadNotesFile();
   var existingNote = (from n in notes.Descendants("Note")
      where n.Attribute("title").Value == title
      select n)
      .FirstOrDefault();
   if (existingNote != null)
   {
      existingNote.Value = body;
   }
   else
   {
      notes.Element("Notes").Add(new XElement(
         "Note", new XAttribute("title", title), body));
   }

   WriteNotesFile(notes);
}

public void DeleteNote(string title)
{
   XDocument notes = ReadNotesFile();
   var existingNote = (from n in notes.Descendants("Note")
      where n.Attribute("title").Value == title
      select n)
      .FirstOrDefault();
   if (existingNote != null)
   {
      existingNote.Remove();
   }

   WriteNotesFile(notes);
}
   }
}
```

Code Snippet NotesService\NotesService.svc.cs

7. Ensure that your C: drive has a directory called Temp in the root directory or change the value of the NotesFile constant to an alternative directory.

8. In Solution Explorer, right-click NotesService.svc and select Set As Start Page.

9. Run the application.

10. When the WCF Test Client dialog appears, expand the nodes in the left pane so that you can see the service operations and then double-click `SaveNote()`.

11. In the SaveNote tab on the right, enter values for the title and body parameters and then click Invoke. If there are no errors, the dialog should show a null response, as shown in Figure 9-6.

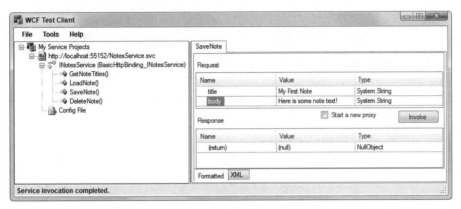

FIGURE 9-6: The WCF Test Client dialog.

12. Click the XML tab to see the SOAP request and response XML.

13. Add more notes if you wish and test the other operations in the same way.

14. In the system tray on the Start bar, right-click the ASP.NET Development Server icon and select Show Details. The dialog displayed should be similar to Figure 9-7.

15. Close the dialog and stop debugging. Notice that the ASP.NET Development Server continues to run.

FIGURE 9-7: ASP.NET Development Server details.

How It Works

In this example, you created a fully working, albeit simple, WCF service that can store, edit, and retrieve notes. You started by defining a service contract, which takes the form of an interface with the `[ServiceContract]` attribute:

```
[ServiceContract]
public interface INotesService
{
    ...
}
```

You then added operation contracts to the service contract. These are method signatures with the [OperationContract] attribute applied, for example:

```
[OperationContract]
IEnumerable<string> GetNoteTitles();
```

Next, you implemented the code for the service. This code starts with a hard-coded data store location and two methods used to quickly read and write data to and from this file, using the handy XML XDocument class:

```
public class NotesService : INotesService
{
    private const string NotesFile = @"c:\Temp\notes.xml";

    private XDocument ReadNotesFile()
    {
        XDocument document;
        if (File.Exists(NotesFile))
        {
            document = XDocument.Load(NotesFile, LoadOptions.None);
        }
        else
        {
            document = new XDocument();
            document.Add(new XElement("Notes"));
            WriteNotesFile(document);
        }

        return document;
    }

    private void WriteNotesFile(XDocument notes)
    {
        notes.Save(NotesFile, SaveOptions.None);
    }
```

The ReadNotesFile() method creates a file with a root <Notes> element if one doesn't already exist, and then it returns either the new or existing file contents. WriteNotesFile() simply saves the document that is passed to it. Obviously, this method is quite trusting, as it could be passed any document, so your code is clearly not production ready. However, it is simple and serves as a good illustration.

If you open up the saved document in the text editor of your choice and look at the data inside, you'll see something like this:

```
<?xml version="1.0" encoding="utf-8"?>
<Notes>
  <Note title="My First Note">Here is some note text!</Note>
  <Note title="Shopping">Must remember to buy cheese.</Note>
  <Note title="Cheese">Must remember to go shopping.</Note>
  <Note title="Note">C#</Note>
</Notes>
```

Back in the service implementation, the code continues with the first service operation, GetNoteTitles():

```
public IEnumerable<string> GetNoteTitles()
{
    XDocument notes = ReadNotesFile();
    return from n in notes.Descendants("Note")
        select n.Attribute("title").Value;
}
```

This method calls the ReadNotesFile() method you've seen already and extracts the title elements of all notes, using simple LINQ-to-XML syntax. It then returns the resultant collection of strings.

The remaining methods are equally simple and use similar LINQ-to-XML syntax to achieve their purpose. The SaveNote() method is the most interesting of these, as it checks for an existing note with a given title before saving the note body. You can therefore never have two notes with the same title. Of course, having more than one note with the same title might be behavior you want, and in that case, you wouldn't do this. However, the rest of the code would get more complicated, and you'd probably still need a way to uniquely identify individual notes. In a database, you'd use a primary key for this.

That's all the code in the example. The service requires no data contract, so you didn't add one. You may not be surprised to know after looking at this code, though, that data contracts use an attribute called [DataContract] (as well as some others). You also didn't define any fault contracts (which describe how errors are transmitted to the client) or message contracts (which define the messaging structure), and you left the endpoint and binding settings at their defaults. You can define these in the Web.config file for the project, which you can look at if you like, but at the moment, you don't really need an in-depth understanding of what is there.

When you started the service running and accessed it through the WCF Test Client, the endpoint address was generated from the name of the service and a server location:

```
http://localhost:55152/NotesService.svc
```

The localhost part of this address refers to your local web server, and the numeric part is the TCP port on which the server is listening. (It is 55152 in this case, but it will probably be a different number on your computer because it is auto-generated.)

Make a note of your endpoint address, as you'll need it in the next Try It Out.

TRY IT OUT   Consuming a WCF Service

In this example, you'll create a Windows Phone 7 application that uses the WCF service you just made in the preceding Try It Out.

1.   In VSE for WP, create a new Windows Phone Application called **NotesClient**.

2.   In Solution Explorer, right-click the NotesClient project and select Add Service Reference...

3. In the Add Service Reference dialog, enter the endpoint address you noted earlier and click Go. (The ASP.NET Development Server must be running for this to work. If it isn't, run the WCF project again.)

4. In the Services pane, change the Namespace value to NotesService, as shown in Figure 9-8, and then click OK. You can expand the service reference to see the supported operations if you wish.

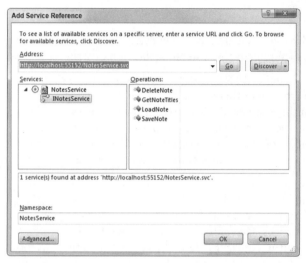

FIGURE 9-8: The Add Service Reference dialog.

5. Modify the code in MainPage.xaml so that it looks like Listing 9-8.

Available for download on Wrox.com

LISTING 9-8: Modifying the code in MainPage.xaml

```xml
<phone:PhoneApplicationPage ...
  Loaded="PhoneApplicationPage_Loaded">

  <Grid x:Name="LayoutRoot" Background="Transparent">
    <Grid x:Name="ContentPanel" Grid.Row="1" Margin="12,0,12,0">
      <Grid.RowDefinitions>
        <RowDefinition Height="Auto" />
        <RowDefinition Height="*" />
        <RowDefinition Height="Auto" />
      </Grid.RowDefinitions>
      <TextBlock Text="My Notes"
        Style="{StaticResource PhoneTextExtraLargeStyle}"
        VerticalAlignment="Center" />
      <Button Name="AddButton" Content="Add New"
        VerticalAlignment="Center" HorizontalAlignment="Right"
        Click="AddButton_Click" />
```

```xml
    <ScrollViewer Grid.Row="1">
      <ListBox Name="Notes" SelectionChanged="Notes_SelectionChanged">
        <ItemsControl.ItemTemplate>
          <DataTemplate>
            <Grid>
              <Grid.ColumnDefinitions>
                <ColumnDefinition Width="*" />
                <ColumnDefinition Width="Auto" />
              </Grid.ColumnDefinitions>
              <TextBlock Text="{Binding}"
                  VerticalAlignment="Center" />
            </Grid>
          </DataTemplate>
        </ItemsControl.ItemTemplate>
      </ListBox>
    </ScrollViewer>
    <Grid Grid.Row="2" Name="NoteEditor" Height="400"
      Visibility="Collapsed">
      <Grid.RowDefinitions>
        <RowDefinition Height="Auto" />
        <RowDefinition Height="*" />
        <RowDefinition Height="Auto" />
      </Grid.RowDefinitions>
      <Grid.ColumnDefinitions>
        <ColumnDefinition Width="100" />
        <ColumnDefinition Width="*" />
      </Grid.ColumnDefinitions>
      <TextBlock Text="Title:" Margin="8,20,0,0"
        Style="{StaticResource PhoneTextAccentStyle}"/>
      <TextBox Grid.Column="1"  Name="TitleBox" />
      <TextBlock Grid.Row="1" Text="Body:" Margin="8,20,0,0"
        VerticalAlignment="Top"
        Style="{StaticResource PhoneTextAccentStyle}" />
      <TextBox Grid.Row="1" Grid.Column="1" AcceptsReturn="True"
        VerticalScrollBarVisibility="Visible" Name="BodyBox"
        TextWrapping="Wrap" />
      <Grid Grid.Row="2" Grid.ColumnSpan="2">
        <Grid.ColumnDefinitions>
          <ColumnDefinition Width="*" />
          <ColumnDefinition Width="*" />
          <ColumnDefinition Width="*" />
        </Grid.ColumnDefinitions>
        <Button Name="DeleteButton" Content="Delete"
          Click="DeleteButton_Click" />
        <Button Name="SaveButton" Grid.Column="1" Content="Save"
          Click="SaveButton_Click" />
        <Button Name="CancelButton"  Grid.Column="2" Content="Cancel"
          Click="CancelButton_Click" />
      </Grid>
    </Grid>
  </Grid>
  </Grid>
</phone:PhoneApplicationPage>
```

Code Snippet NotesClient\MainPage.xaml

6. Modify the code in `MainPage.xaml.cs` so that it looks like Listing 9-9.

LISTING 9-9: Modifying the code in MainPage.xaml.cs

```csharp
using System;
using System.ComponentModel;
using System.Windows;
using System.Windows.Controls;
using Microsoft.Phone.Controls;
using NotesClient.NotesService;

namespace NotesClient
{
    public partial class MainPage : PhoneApplicationPage
    {
        private NotesServiceClient notesService;
        private string selectedNoteTitle;

        public MainPage()
        {
            InitializeComponent();

            notesService = new NotesServiceClient();
            notesService.GetNoteTitlesCompleted +=
                new EventHandler<GetNoteTitlesCompletedEventArgs>(
                    notesService_GetNoteTitlesCompleted);
            notesService.LoadNoteCompleted +=
                new EventHandler<LoadNoteCompletedEventArgs>(
                    notesService_LoadNoteCompleted);
            notesService.SaveNoteCompleted +=
                new EventHandler<AsyncCompletedEventArgs>(
                    notesService_SaveNoteCompleted);
            notesService.DeleteNoteCompleted +=
                new EventHandler<AsyncCompletedEventArgs>(
                    notesService_DeleteNoteCompleted);
        }

        private void PhoneApplicationPage_Loaded(
            object sender, RoutedEventArgs e)
        {
            notesService.GetNoteTitlesAsync();
        }

        private void notesService_GetNoteTitlesCompleted(
            object sender, GetNoteTitlesCompletedEventArgs e)
        {
            Dispatcher.BeginInvoke(
                new Action(() => Notes.ItemsSource = e.Result));
        }

        private void AddButton_Click(object sender, RoutedEventArgs e)
        {
            Notes.SelectedItem = null;
            TitleBox.Text = "New note";
            BodyBox.Text = string.Empty;
```

```csharp
      NoteEditor.Visibility = Visibility.Visible;
}

private void CancelButton_Click(object sender, RoutedEventArgs e)
{
   NoteEditor.Visibility = Visibility.Collapsed;
   Notes.SelectedItem = null;
}

private void Notes_SelectionChanged(
   object sender, SelectionChangedEventArgs e)
{
   if (e.AddedItems != null && e.AddedItems.Count == 1)
   {
      selectedNoteTitle = e.AddedItems[0] as string;
      TitleBox.Text = selectedNoteTitle;
      notesService.LoadNoteAsync(selectedNoteTitle);
   }
   else
   {
      selectedNoteTitle = null;
      NoteEditor.Visibility = Visibility.Collapsed;
   }
}

private void notesService_LoadNoteCompleted(
   object sender, LoadNoteCompletedEventArgs e)
{
   BodyBox.Text = e.Result;
   NoteEditor.Visibility = Visibility.Visible;
}

private void SaveButton_Click(object sender, RoutedEventArgs e)
{
   NoteEditor.Visibility = Visibility.Collapsed;
   if (!string.IsNullOrEmpty(selectedNoteTitle)
      && selectedNoteTitle != TitleBox.Text)
   {
      notesService.DeleteNoteAsync(selectedNoteTitle);
   }

   notesService.SaveNoteAsync(TitleBox.Text, BodyBox.Text);
}

private void notesService_SaveNoteCompleted(
   object sender, AsyncCompletedEventArgs e)
{
   notesService.GetNoteTitlesAsync();
}

private void DeleteButton_Click(object sender, RoutedEventArgs e)
{
   NoteEditor.Visibility = Visibility.Collapsed;
   notesService.DeleteNoteAsync(TitleBox.Text);
}
```

continues

LISTING 9-9 *(continued)*

```
        private void notesService_DeleteNoteCompleted(
            object sender, AsyncCompletedEventArgs e)
        {
            NoteEditor.Visibility = Visibility.Collapsed;
            notesService.GetNoteTitlesAsync();
        }
    }
}
```

Code Snippet NotesClient\MainPage.xaml.cs

7. Run the application. You should see a list containing any notes you added with the WCF Test Client earlier. You can tap to edit a note, add new notes, delete the selected note, and so on. Figure 9-9 shows the application in action.

How It Works

In this example, you created a simple Windows Phone 7 client application that consumes the service you made earlier. Much of the presentation and C# code in this example should be familiar to you, so in this section you focused on the WCF-specific tasks and code that you've performed and written.

The first thing you did was add a service reference. You did this by entering the address of the endpoint for your WCF service. When you do this, Visual Studio sends a request for information to the endpoint, using a metadata service that your service exposes. Not all services expose such data, and you can easily configure it to be disabled, if you wish to do so. Having metadata exposed in this way, though, gives all the information that clients require to use the service, so in general it's a good thing to do.

FIGURE 9-9: The NotesClient application in action.

Visual Studio uses this metadata to construct several classes and associated configuration, including a proxy class through which you can access the service without writing any HTTP access code. The primary source of configuration for the service you added is stored in `ServiceReferences.ClientConfig`, which contains the following:

```
<configuration>
  <system.serviceModel>
    <bindings>
      <basicHttpBinding>
        <binding name="BasicHttpBinding_INotesService"
            maxBufferSize="2147483647"
            maxReceivedMessageSize="2147483647">
          <security mode="None" />
        </binding>
      </basicHttpBinding>
```

```
        </bindings>
        <client>
          <endpoint address="http://localhost:55152/NotesService.svc"
            binding="basicHttpBinding"
            bindingConfiguration="BasicHttpBinding_INotesService"
            contract="NotesService.INotesService"
            name="BasicHttpBinding_INotesService" />
        </client>
      </system.serviceModel>
    </configuration>
```

Some binding information here tells you how the service is configured, along with the endpoint configuration. You can see the endpoint address that you added in this section. If you were to move the service elsewhere, such as somewhere online, you could simply update this address, and the proxy code would continue to work.

You could do all manner of tweaking to this file and in the Web.config file that contains the WCF service configuration. However, as stated earlier, at this point you just need to know the basics.

In the XAML file, you created a fairly simple user interface with a list of note titles and a detail view for a selected note or a new note. The user interface for the detail view includes buttons to save and delete notes, as well as a cancel button to clear the selection and hide the detail view.

The C# for the page starts by storing a reference to the generated proxy class, NotesServiceClient (created in the constructor), as well as a string variable to store the title of the note being edited, if any.

Event handlers are added to some events that the proxy class exposes. As with HTTP calls, here you perform all service communication asynchronously. To simplify the code, the proxy class raises events when calls are completed. You just have to call the "begin" method on the proxy, and then it will make the call and raise an event for you. There are therefore four events to handle, one for each service operation:

```
        notesService.GetNoteTitlesCompleted +=
            new EventHandler<GetNoteTitlesCompletedEventArgs>(
                notesService_GetNoteTitlesCompleted);
        notesService.LoadNoteCompleted +=
            new EventHandler<LoadNoteCompletedEventArgs>(
                notesService_LoadNoteCompleted);
        notesService.SaveNoteCompleted +=
            new EventHandler<AsyncCompletedEventArgs>(
                notesService_SaveNoteCompleted);
        notesService.DeleteNoteCompleted +=
            new EventHandler<AsyncCompletedEventArgs>(
                notesService_DeleteNoteCompleted);
```

The first thing the application does when it is started is to call the GetNoteTitles() service operation. This happens in the PhoneApplicationPage_Loaded() handler. When the call completes, the notesService_GetNoteTitlesCompleted() event handler is called:

```
    private void notesService_GetNoteTitlesCompleted(
            object sender, GetNoteTitlesCompletedEventArgs e)
    {
```

```
Dispatcher.BeginInvoke(
    new Action(() => Notes.ItemsSource = e.Result));
}
```

This method simply sets the `ItemsSource` property of the list in the user interface to the collection of strings returned. As with other asynchronous callbacks that you've seen in this chapter, you must use the `Dispatcher` to do this to ensure that the user interface is updated on the correct thread.

The rest of the code in this application calls the remaining service operations in a similar way and also ensures that the user interface updates appropriately.

WCF REST Services

In the previous section, you saw how easy it is to create a simple WCF service. Much of the rest of the power of WCF comes through additional configuration. Through this configuration you can change the security model used, the communication protocols, and so on. Also, you can provide alternative endpoints for communication. This includes providing a REST endpoint for the service in addition to, or as a replacement for, the default endpoint that is provided for you.

Converting a WCF service to REST can in fact be quite a painless experience. Essentially, you have to do the following:

➤   Ensure that the endpoint for your service is configured to use REST.

➤   Add attributes to your service contract operations to specify the HTTP method and URI format that should be used to access them.

➤   Configure caching where necessary (to avoid caching problems when reading changed data, as described earlier in the chapter).

Configuring Endpoints

WCF endpoints, as you have learned earlier in this chapter, are what WCF services expose to allow clients to communicate with them. To recap, an endpoint consists of the following:

➤   An address that describes where the endpoint is located, for example, a URI

➤   A binding that describes how the endpoint should be accessed, for example, through HTTP

➤   A contract that describes what can be communicated, which may include service operations, data contracts, and so on

All of these can be configured down to the smallest detail, or you can cut some corners and use *behaviors*. A behavior modifies or extends the way in which an endpoint functions and can encapsulate several aspects of an endpoint's configuration in a simple, reusable way.

One such behavior, which is called `WebHttpBehavior`, enables WCF service endpoints to use REST. This behavior isn't added to WCF service endpoints by default, so you have to add it yourself. You can either do this programmatically if you are creating endpoints from code, through configuration if you are defining them through configuration files, or in the `.svc` service file. This latter technique is perhaps the simplest and involves specifying a service factory that will be used to create endpoints for you. OK, this may not sound all that simple, but trust me, in practice it is. All you need to do to achieve this is to add the following to the ServiceHost declaration in the .svc file:

```
<%@ ServiceHost Language="C#" Debug="true" Service="..." CodeBehind="..."
    Factory=System.ServiceModel.Activation.WebServiceHostFactory %>
```

Once you have done this, the next step is to configure the contract.

Configuring Service Operations

You have seen earlier in this chapter that you define WCF service contracts using interfaces, and that you use the [OperationContract] attribute to define an operation, for example:

```
[OperationContract]
IEnumerable<string> GetNoteTitles();
```

Configuration for REST simply involves using one of two other attributes in an operation definition: [WebGet] for HTTP GET operations or [WebInvoke] for other HTTP methods. In both cases, further customization is usually necessary in order to specify what URI is required for the operation, through a UriTemplate property. This is because the service endpoint is just one URI, but each operation requires a unique URI to differentiate itself from other operations. The operations will use REST syntax, so these URIs may also include parameter information. An operation URI will be combined with the service endpoint (also known as the base URI) to define the operation's access syntax.

For simple operations, the URI template you use may simply be a path relative to the base URI, for example:

```
[WebGet(UriTemplate = "/")]
```

Or:

```
[OperationContract]
[WebGet(UriTemplate = "/titles")]
IEnumerable<string> GetNoteTitles();
```

Where parameters are required for an operation, you must provide matching placeholders in the URI template, which consist of the name of the parameter enclosed in curly braces. For example:

```
[OperationContract]
[WebGet(UriTemplate = "/save?title={title}&body={body}")]
void SaveNote(string title, string body);
```

An important point to note here is that when parameters are passed in a URI, they *must* be encoded appropriately. Recall from earlier in this chapter the two methods that you can use to encode or decode strings for URIs:

```
HttpUtility.UrlEncode(stringToEncode);
HttpUtility.UrlDecode(stringToDecode);
```

You will see these methods used a lot in REST service implementations.

On a related note, you can also put parameter placeholders into the path itself, instead of adding them as query string parameters. For example:

```
[WebGet(UriTemplate = "/{category}/{id}"]
```

However, if you do this you must take care, as some characters, even when encoded, will not be permitted in certain situations. The ? character, for example, can be encoded to the string %3f. If you are hosting in Internet Information Services (IIS), including this character or its encoded representation in a URI path will cause the following error: *A potentially dangerous Request.Path value was detected from the client (?)*. The error will cause the request from the client to fail. There are ways around this, but they are quite advanced and come with their own problems, so it's generally best to avoid these.

Configuring Caching

Once you have configured your endpoints and operations, the final step is to ensure that results aren't cached if they shouldn't be. This means adding two headers to the HTTP response from your service, as shown in Table 9.1.

TABLE 9.1: HTTP Response Headers to Disable Client-Side Caching

HEADER	VALUE
Cache-Control	no-cache
Pragma	no-cache

This is something that you must do from code in the operation implementation. You can use the following code:

```
WebOperationContext.Current.OutgoingResponse.Headers.Add(
    "Cache-Control", "no-cache");
WebOperationContext.Current.OutgoingResponse.Headers.Add(
    "Pragma", "no-cache");
```

You must do this in every service operation that shouldn't be cached.

Modifying the Notes Example to Use REST

Some of the code snippets in this section have used the NotesService code from the earlier Try It Out sections to illustrate the modifications necessary to change that service to use REST. The downloadable code for this chapter includes REST versions of both NotesService and NotesClient, which show these modifications in more detail.

The .svc file for the service in NotesService is modified as follows:

```
<%@ ServiceHost Language="C#" Debug="true" Service="NotesService.NotesService"
    CodeBehind="NotesService.svc.cs"
    Factory=System.ServiceModel.Activation.WebServiceHostFactory %>
```

The service contract is modified as follows:

```
[ServiceContract]
public interface INotesService
{
    [OperationContract]
    [WebGet(UriTemplate="/titles")]
    IEnumerable<string> GetNoteTitles();

    [OperationContract]
    [WebGet(UriTemplate="/load?title={title}")]
    string LoadNote(string title);

    [OperationContract]
    [WebGet(UriTemplate = "/save?title={title}&body={body}")]
    void SaveNote(string title, string body);

    [OperationContract]
    [WebGet(UriTemplate = "/delete?title={title}")]
    void DeleteNote(string title);
}
```

Also, the implementations of the GetNoteTitles() and LoadNote() methods are modified to include non-caching headers, for example:

```
public IEnumerable<string> GetNoteTitles()
{
    WebOperationContext.Current.OutgoingResponse.Headers.Add(
        "Cache-Control", "no-cache");
    WebOperationContext.Current.OutgoingResponse.Headers.Add(
        "Pragma", "no-cache");

    XDocument notes = ReadNotesFile();
    return from n in notes.Descendants("Note")
            select n.Attribute("title").Value;
}
```

Finally, note that some methods use the HttpUtility.UrlDecode() method to decode values sent from the client in URIs.

The client code is modified to use REST by having the WCF service reference removed and instead using WebClient to make simple HTTP calls. This doesn't use any new code that you haven't already encountered when accessing the Flickr REST services, so you can look through that in your own time.

SUMMARY

This chapter took you on a whistle-stop tour through the basics of web services. You started by looking at how you can access content on the Internet, using low-level HTTP access classes. In theory, you could stop there and implement web services using nothing else. However, you saw from the code in this chapter that it would take a lot of work to implement even the simplest of web services.

Next, you looked at a simple web service standard, REST. REST simplifies the calls you need to make, or at least imposes some structure on them, but it can still be slightly tricky to use as you still have to use fairly low-level HTTP calls to make it work.

In the last part of this chapter, you looked at WCF services and worked through an example. You created a simple web service and connected it to a simple Windows Phone 7 Silverlight application. You saw just how simple it can be to get a system like this up-and-running and also how simple it can be to expose your services through REST.

Obviously, there's much more that can be said about web services, especially WCF, which is capable of so much more. You'll see some more techniques in action in the next chapter, which looks at how you can make web services push notifications to a Windows Phone 7 client. You'll also find a wealth of information about WCF on the web and in many books. You'll quickly find that there is plenty to learn, and some of it is quite advanced, but the rewards are very much worthwhile.

EXERCISES

1. Which of the following are valid HTTP methods (verbs)?

a) GET

b) ZAP

c) DELETE

d) POST

e) PUT

f) EXSANGUINATE

2. You want to make an HTTP POST request from an application without having to write any asynchronous code. Instead, you'd prefer to respond to a completed event. What class, method, and event would you use to do this?

3. The XAML for a page has a button called GetDataButton that triggers a GetDataButton_Click() handler, and you want to set the text of a TextBlock called ResultTextBox to the result of a GET request. What's wrong with using the following code to do this?

```
public partial class MainPage : PhoneApplicationPage
{
    public MainPage()
    {
        InitializeComponent();
    }

    private void GetDataButton_Click(
        object sender, RoutedEventArgs e)
    {
        HttpWebRequest request = WebRequest.CreateHttp(
            "www.somewherewithdata.com/getdata");
```

```
        request.Method = "GET";
        request.BeginGetResponse(GetDataButtonCallback, request);
    }

    private void GetDataButtonCallback(IAsyncResult result)
    {
        HttpWebResponse response =
            (result.AsyncState as HttpWebRequest).EndGetResponse(
            result) as HttpWebResponse;
        string returnValue = null;
        using (StreamReader sr = new StreamReader(
            response.GetResponseStream()))
        {
            ResultTextBox.Text = sr.ReadToEnd();
        }
    }
}
```

4. Modify the `FlickrStatViewer` example from earlier in this chapter so that if an error is returned from the `flickr.people.findByUsername` API call, the application displays a message box containing the error and doesn't call `flickr.people.getPublicPhotos`. The message box should include both the error code and message.

5. How would you connect a Windows Phone 7 Silverlight application to a WCF service at a known URI?

6. All the WCF service calls you made from the `NotesClient` example were practically instantaneous because the service was on the local computer. How would you improve the user interface to deal with slow calls over the Internet?

Answers to the Exercises can be found in the Appendix.

▶ **WHAT YOU LEARNED IN THIS CHAPTER**

TOPIC	KEY CONCEPTS
Web service architecture	There are many ways to create web services and many ways to communicate with them. However, if you access them over the Internet, you must use an Internet protocol, and the most ubiquitous of these is HTTP. HTTP is a request/response architecture that involves communication of messages between URI addresses and resources. Request messages can be of various types, such as GET and POST, and they may include additional information in headers and a message body. Response messages can also include header and body information. Web services add an additional layer of structure on top of HTTP, depending on the framework in which you write them. Two of these frameworks, both of which are examined in this chapter, are REST and WCF.
Web requests and responses	You can use the WebClient class to make and receive web requests in a simple way. Alternatively, you can use the WebRequest and WebResponse classes to get a finer degree of control over communication. Both techniques involve making calls asynchronously. This means that after you send a request but before the response is returned, you still have an active user interface to maintain. Also, when a response is received, it may be on a background thread, and you must ensure that you transfer control back to the user interface before doing anything that might affect the response.
REST services	REST is a simple framework for web services. You can communicate with RESTful services by using ordinary web requests and responses. The meaning of a REST service call may be inferred from context, such as the path from the base URI and the HTTP method used to access the endpoint. Alternatively, as in many implementations, additional information may be sent to a service through query string parameters, headers, or a message body. For example, the Flickr API is accessible through REST services and uses query string parameters. There are several implementations of REST that you can use to create .NET REST services, including WCF.
WCF services	WCF services are more complex than plain REST services in concept, but in practice WCF services can be extremely simple to create and use. This is partly due to the helpful tools that the IDE supplies for you to build, test, reference, and call operations. You can create a service by using Visual Web Developer Express and consume it in a Windows Phone 7 application with a bare minimum of code that takes a matter of minutes to write. With only a little more effort, you can use the WebHttpBehavior behavior and the [WebGet] and [WebInvoke] attributes to make your WCF services RESTful. WCF is extremely powerful and flexible, and there are ways to introduce security, alternative transports, and much more, often through configuration only.

10

Web Services Push Notifications

WHAT YOU WILL LEARN IN THIS CHAPTER:

➤ Understanding how push service architecture works

➤ Understanding participant requirements for push services

➤ Understanding the difference between toast, tile, and raw push notifications

➤ Configuring a push notification channel

➤ Sending and receiving push notification messages

In the previous two chapters, you learned how to access web services from Windows Phone 7 applications, both through helper classes and directly. You also learned about the protocols used to communicate with web services and how to create simple Windows Communication Foundation (WCF) services for yourself. Push notifications take web services to a new level. With a push notification, you don't have to write code to call a web service operation. Instead, a push notification involves a web service talking to your application without prompting. It can even work when your application isn't running.

You've probably come across many applications that support push notifications without really knowing it. Some examples are email, social media applications that tell you your friends' updates, and all kinds of other applications that provide notifications, from shopping to music. Not all applications want or require push notification functionality, of course, but many do. Having these notifications at your disposal provides a lot of power.

In this chapter, you'll learn how push notifications work in Windows Phone 7 devices, what types of notifications are available, and how to write applications that make use of this exciting technology.

PUSH NOTIFICATION ARCHITECTURE

In essence, push notifications involve a web service sending messages to an application. However, in actuality, the process is more complex. With push notifications, an application doesn't expose any kind of endpoint that your web service can communicate with directly. Even if the web service were to communicate directly, it wouldn't be able to talk to the application if it weren't running.

Rather than enabling direct communication in this way, the push notification architecture mediates communication between a web service and an application through a universal push cloud service that communicates with a push client on the Windows Phone 7 device on which the application exists. The device then communicates with the application and can start it up if necessary.

In this section, you'll look at how push notifications work in a little more detail, including the participating components, registration, notification channels, and the types of push notification that are available.

Push Notification Components

Four components participate in Windows Phone 7 push notifications:

➤ **Application** — This receives push notifications.

➤ **Push notification web service** — This sends notifications.

➤ **Central push notification service** — This receives notifications from the service and forwards them to a Windows Phone 7 device.

➤ **Push client on the Windows Phone 7 device** — This handles notifications and interacts with the client application.

In the following sections you'll learn how these components interact.

Registering a Push Notification Service

Before your application can use the central push notification service, the application must first register with it. Registration means that your application is saying, "Hi. I want to receive push notifications from a web service. Can you set that up please?" The central push service replies, "Sure, no problem. Here are some instructions that you can give your web service so that its messages get through to you." Once this registration is done, the central push notification service will be able to route messages to your application.

Figure 10-1 provides an overview of this process, which includes the following steps:

1. Your application registers with the central push notification service through the push client.

2. The push notification service stores the registration and hands back instructions, also through the push client.

3. Your application sends those instructions to your web service.

4. Your web service sends a message to the central push notification service, using the instructions it received.

5. The central push notification service forwards the message to the push client on the Windows Phone 7 device where the client application is hosted.

6. The push client takes appropriate action, such as forwarding the message to your client application if it is running or displaying some kind of notification if it isn't.

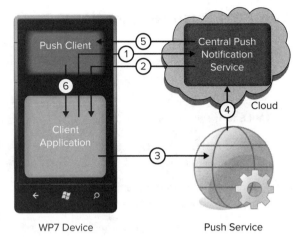

FIGURE 10-1: Push service architecture.

 NOTE *Windows Phone 7 devices allow only the built-in application plus 15 other applications to use push notifications at any one time. In order to register a 16th application, you must first unregister one of the others.*

Creating and Opening Notification Channels

When your application registers with the central push notification service, it actually creates what is known as a *notification channel*. You can create a notification by supplying a unique name and, optionally, a service name. (However, the service name isn't optional for secure services, and it must match the fully qualified domain name of the service.) After you create a new notification channel, you must open it, which causes the central push notification service to create and register it internally. Once created and opened, a notification channel exposes the following functionality:

➤ A uniform resource identifier (URI) that your services can use to send notifications, which is what was referred to in the previous section as the "instructions" that you pass on to your service. This may change over the lifetime of a notification channel.

➤ Configuration methods that you can use to indicate which types of push notification your application uses. (See the following section.)

➤ Events that are raised in case of errors, updates to the notification URI, and incoming notifications (if received when your application is running).

Your application needs to create a new notification channel only once, the first time it needs it. The next time you run the application, you must reuse the channel you have already created. If you attempt to create a new notification channel with the same name as an existing one, you'll receive an error.

Types of Push Notifications

There are three types of push notifications that you can send to your application through the push notification service. Table 10-1 lists them, the information they contain, and what happens when they're received.

TABLE 10-1: Push Notification Types

TYPE	CONTENT	EFFECT WITH APPLICATION RUNNING	EFFECT WITH APPLICATION NOT RUNNING
Toast	Two strings: a title and a message body	Event raised in application	Pop-up message displayed
Tile	A title, an image, and a numeric value	Tile updated	Tile updated
Raw	Up to 1KB of raw data, which can be anything you like	Event raised in application	None; message discarded

It's worth spending some time looking at what these notifications mean and why you'd use each of them.

Toast Notifications

Toast notifications are useful when you want to send a general alert that something important has happened, such as new content becoming available. When the application is running, it can respond to the notification instantly and format the title and body of the message any way you wish. When the application isn't running, it doesn't receive this information directly. Instead, the Windows Phone 7 shell displays a pop-up message with the title and body. At this point, the user can either dismiss the message with a swipe or tap it to open the application.

 COMMON MISTAKES *One important thing to be aware of with toast notifications is that they can be quite intrusive because they interrupt the user. This is fine for infrequent and important notifications, but if you overuse this type of notification, you're really just inviting people to uninstall your application.*

Tile Notifications

Tile notifications provide a less intrusive way to alert users that new content is available, as they enable you to modify your application tile. This unfortunately works only if your tile is pinned to the device start page, but it can still be useful. Tiles are updated for notifications regardless of whether your application is running, although you might not see the effect until you return to the start page.

Three parts of an application tile can be modified:

➤ The tile background image (either stored locally or obtainable via a URI)

➤ A number that appears in the top-right corner of the tile

➤ The tile title

You can use these three pieces of information to provide all sorts of feedback. The numeric value is often used to display things like the number of new messages or news stories available, but you'll probably think of other ways to use it. The title may be redundant if your image is clear enough about what your application is, and maybe you'll use the title to display other information. Alternatively, because you can't customize the layout of these three things, you may remove the title and numeric count and dynamically generate images for backgrounds, as required. Your only limitation here is that the image must be less than 80KB in size and take no longer than 15 seconds to download.

 NOTE *Tile notifications go directly to tiles, and your application (running or not) doesn't receive any kind of notification when they arrive.*

Raw Notifications

With raw notifications, you can send any information you want, but only running applications receive this information. However, raw notifications are still useful. There are several ways you might use them, from displaying a simple notification to triggering a poll-mode web service call from the application to get more details.

SENDING AND RESPONDING TO PUSH NOTIFICATIONS

Now that you know how the push notification architecture works and what's possible, it's time to look at some code. First, you'll look at how to register an application with the push notification framework by creating and configuring a notification channel. Next, you'll look at how to use the URI endpoint in the channel to register with a simple Representational State Transfer (REST) service that you'll create. Next, you'll look at how to use this service to send push notifications to your application and see what happens.

Creating and Configuring a Notification Channel

As you've learned, the first step in using the push notification framework is to create a notification channel in your application. This means using the `HttpNotificationChannel` class. To create a new channel using this class, you can call its constructor. You can either pass a single string parameter with the channel name like so:

```
HttpNotificationChannel notificationChannel =
    new HttpNotificationChannel("ChannelName");
```

Or you can pass two parameters, where the second is the domain of the web service that will send notifications, as follows:

```
HttpNotificationChannel notificationChannel =
    new HttpNotificationChannel("ChannelName", "www.somewhere.com");
```

It's good practice to use the version with two parameters even for unauthenticated web services, although for testing with local services, you can omit it. The channel name isn't really that important. You can call it whatever you want, and it won't clash with other applications or devices.

To get an existing notification channel, you can use the static `Find()` method, which just needs the channel name:

```
HttpNotificationChannel notificationChannel =
    HttpNotificationChannel.Find("ChannelName");
```

If no channel is found, this method returns `null`.

When you first create a channel, it's not active. To make it active, and to receive a URI that you can use with your push service, you must call the `Open()` method. Subsequently, when you find an existing channel, it's likely to have a URI already, and if it does, calling `Open()` generates an exception. However, the URI may not be the same as the last time you used the channel, so you should re-register with your services just in case.

When you call `Open()`, or if the URI changes and your application is running, the push client generates a `ChannelUriUpdated` event, so you should subscribe to that before you open the channel. Once this event is raised, you can find the URI for the channel in the event arguments and also in the `ChannelUri` property of the `HttpNotificationChannel` object.

When you have a channel with a channel URI, the next step is to configure it for the type of notification you want to receive. Raw notifications are always received if your application is running, but for toast and tile notifications, you must explicitly instruct the push client to listen. To do this, you call either or both of the `BindToShellToast()` or `BindToShellTile()` methods of the `HttpNotificationChannel` object. You can do this only if the push client is not already bound, so you should check the `IsShellToastBound` and `IsShellTileBound` properties first.

If you want to update the tile image using tile notifications, you need to do one more thing. You must pass a parameter to the `BindToShellTile()` method that specifies where the tile images are stored, in the form of a collection of domain URIs. Here's an example:

```
notificationChannel.BindToShellTile(
    new Collection<Uri>
    {
        new Uri("http://www.myshelltileimagedomain.com/"),
        new Uri("http://www.myothershelltileimagedomain.com/")
    });
```

If you try to pass a shell image URI to your application that isn't in the list, the image is not updated.

To receive events when your application is running, you must subscribe to the `ShellToast NotificationReceived` event for toast notifications and/or the `HttpNotificationReceived` event for raw notifications. You can also subscribe to the `ErrorOccurred` event if you want to respond to any errors that may occur during channel configuration or operation.

TRY IT OUT Creating a Push Notification Application

You know enough now to assemble a simple push notification–aware application. In the following steps, you'll create one, although it won't actually be fully functional until you create a service to go with it a little later in the chapter:

1. Create a new Windows Phone 7 application called **PushApplication**.

2. Modify the code in `MainPage.xaml` as shown in Listing 10-1.

LISTING 10-1: Modifying the code in MainPage.xaml

Available for download on Wrox.com

```xaml
<phone:PhoneApplicationPage ...>

  <Grid x:Name="LayoutRoot" Background="Transparent">
    <Grid.RowDefinitions>
      <RowDefinition Height="Auto"/>
      <RowDefinition Height="*"/>
    </Grid.RowDefinitions>

    <StackPanel x:Name="TitlePanel" Grid.Row="0" Margin="12,17,0,28">
      <TextBlock x:Name="ApplicationTitle" Text="PUSH DEMO"
        Style="{StaticResource PhoneTextNormalStyle}"/>
      <TextBlock x:Name="PageTitle" Text="wrox updates"
        Margin="9,-7,0,0"
        Style="{StaticResource PhoneTextTitle1Style}"/>
    </StackPanel>

    <StackPanel x:Name="ContentPanel" Grid.Row="1" Margin="12,0,12,0">
      <TextBlock Text="Status"
        Style="{StaticResource PhoneTextAccentStyle}" />
      <TextBlock x:Name="StatusText" TextWrapping="Wrap" Text="None."
        Style="{StaticResource PhoneTextNormalStyle}" />
      <TextBlock Text="Channel URI"
        Style="{StaticResource PhoneTextAccentStyle}" />
      <TextBlock x:Name="ChannelUriText" TextWrapping="Wrap"
        Text="None."
        Style="{StaticResource PhoneTextNormalStyle}" />
      <TextBlock Text="Message Received"
        Style="{StaticResource PhoneTextAccentStyle}" />
      <TextBlock x:Name="MessageText" TextWrapping="Wrap" Text="None."
        Style="{StaticResource PhoneTextNormalStyle}" />
    </StackPanel>
  </Grid>
</phone:PhoneApplicationPage>
```

Code Snippet PushApplication\MainPage.xaml

3. Modify the code in `MainPage.xaml.cs` as shown in Listing 10-2.

LISTING 10-2: Modifying the code in MainPage.xaml.cs

```csharp
using System;
using System.Collections.ObjectModel;
using System.IO;
using System.Text;
using Microsoft.Phone.Controls;
using Microsoft.Phone.Notification;

namespace PushApplication
{
    public partial class MainPage : PhoneApplicationPage
    {
        private const string tileImageDomain = "http://localhost/";
        private const string notificationChannelName =
            "WroxPushApplicationNotificationChannel";
        private HttpNotificationChannel notificationChannel;

        public MainPage()
        {
            InitializeComponent();

            GetOrCreateNotificationChannel();
        }

        private void GetOrCreateNotificationChannel()
        {
            StatusText.Text = "Getting or creating channel.";
            notificationChannel =
                HttpNotificationChannel.Find(notificationChannelName);
            if (notificationChannel == null)
            {
                // Channel doesn't exist, so create it.
                notificationChannel =
                    new HttpNotificationChannel(notificationChannelName);
            }

            notificationChannel.ErrorOccurred +=
                new EventHandler<NotificationChannelErrorEventArgs>(
                    notificationChannel_ErrorOccurred);
            notificationChannel.ChannelUriUpdated +=
                new EventHandler<NotificationChannelUriEventArgs>(
                    notificationChannel_ChannelUriUpdated);
            notificationChannel.HttpNotificationReceived +=
                new EventHandler<HttpNotificationEventArgs>(
                    notificationChannel_HttpNotificationReceived);
            notificationChannel.ShellToastNotificationReceived +=
                new EventHandler<NotificationEventArgs>(
                    notificationChannel_ShellToastNotificationReceived);
```

```csharp
    if (notificationChannel.ChannelUri == null)
    {
        notificationChannel.Open();
    }
    else
    {
        RegisterAndConfigureChannelUri();
    }
}

private void notificationChannel_ErrorOccurred(
    object sender, NotificationChannelErrorEventArgs e)
{
    Dispatcher.BeginInvoke(
        () => StatusText.Text = string.Format(
        "An error of type {0} occurred.", e.ErrorType));
}

private void notificationChannel_ChannelUriUpdated(
    object sender, NotificationChannelUriEventArgs e)
{
    RegisterAndConfigureChannelUri();
}

private void RegisterAndConfigureChannelUri()
{
    // Nothing to register with yet, for now display the URI.
    Dispatcher.BeginInvoke(
        () => ChannelUriText.Text =
            notificationChannel.ChannelUri.ToString());

    // Bind notifications.
    if (!notificationChannel.IsShellToastBound)
    {
        notificationChannel.BindToShellToast();
    }

    if (!notificationChannel.IsShellTileBound)
    {
        notificationChannel.BindToShellTile(new Collection<Uri>
            { new Uri(tileImageDomain) });
    }

    Dispatcher.BeginInvoke(
        () => StatusText.Text = "Channel active and configured.");
}

private void notificationChannel_ShellToastNotificationReceived(
    object sender, NotificationEventArgs e)
{
    StringBuilder sb = new StringBuilder();
    sb.AppendLine("Toast message:");
```

continues

LISTING 10-2 *(continued)*

```csharp
        foreach (string key in e.Collection.Keys)
        {
            sb.AppendFormat("{0}=\"{1}\"", key, e.Collection[key]);
            sb.AppendLine();
        }

        string message = sb.ToString();
        Dispatcher.BeginInvoke(
            () => StatusText.Text = "Toast notification received.");
        Dispatcher.BeginInvoke(() => MessageText.Text = message);
    }

    private void notificationChannel_HttpNotificationReceived(
        object sender, HttpNotificationEventArgs e)
    {
        StreamReader reader = new StreamReader(e.Notification.Body);
        StringBuilder sb = new StringBuilder();
        sb.AppendLine("Raw message:");
        sb.Append(reader.ReadToEnd());
        string message = sb.ToString();

        Dispatcher.BeginInvoke(
            () => StatusText.Text = "Raw notification received.");
        Dispatcher.BeginInvoke(() => MessageText.Text = message);
    }
  }
}
```

Code Snippet PushApplication\MainPage.xaml.cs

4.   Run the application. After a short pause, the channel URI is shown, as in Figure 10-2.

How It Works

In this example, you created a simple push-aware application. The XAML user interface you added contains a few placeholders for displaying information from notifications received while the app is running and also shows the channel URI once the channel is created and configured. The XAML code is extremely straightforward, and there's no need to repeat it here.

The C# code starts with the fields `tileImageDomain` (to store the permitted tile image domain for binding tile notifications), `notificationChannelName` (to store the channel name), and `notificationChannel` (to hold the channel itself). The page constructor initializes `notificationChannel` with a call to `GetOrCreateNotificationChannel()`. This method sets the status message and then finds or creates a notification channel using the name defined in `notificationChannelName`:

FIGURE 10-2: The push application, showing its channel URI.

```
private void GetOrCreateNotificationChannel()
{
    StatusText.Text = "Getting or creating channel.";
    notificationChannel =
        HttpNotificationChannel.Find(notificationChannelName);
    if (notificationChannel == null)
    {
        // Channel doesn't exist, so create it.
        notificationChannel =
            new HttpNotificationChannel(notificationChannelName);
    }
```

Next, event handlers are added to the four events that the notification channel can raise when an error occurs, when its URI is updated, and when toast or raw notifications are received:

```
notificationChannel.ErrorOccurred +=
    new EventHandler<NotificationChannelErrorEventArgs>(
        notificationChannel_ErrorOccurred);
notificationChannel.ChannelUriUpdated +=
    new EventHandler<NotificationChannelUriEventArgs>(
        notificationChannel_ChannelUriUpdated);
notificationChannel.HttpNotificationReceived +=
  new EventHandler<HttpNotificationEventArgs>(
        notificationChannel_HttpNotificationReceived);
notificationChannel.ShellToastNotificationReceived +=
    new EventHandler<NotificationEventArgs>(
        notificationChannel_ShellToastNotificationReceived);
```

Finally, the method checks the `ChannelUri` property to see if the channel is already open (the property will be null if the channel isn't open), and opens the channel if necessary.

```
    if (notificationChannel.ChannelUri == null)
    {
        notificationChannel.Open();
    }
    else
    {
        RegisterAndConfigureChannelUri();
    }
}
```

Notice that the preceding code contains a call to `RegisterAndConfigureChannelUri()` (which does exactly as its name suggests, as you'll see in a moment), even for an open channel. It's good practice to include this because the URI may have changed since the previous execution of this application.

If an error occurs while the channel is being opened, the `notificationChannel_ErrorOccurred()` event handler displays the error type. More details are available through the `NotificationChannelErrorEventArgs` argument, so you can drill in to find out exactly what the problem is. Perhaps there are already 15 applications configured for push notifications, or maybe the current power-saving settings prevent this channel registration activity.

Assuming that the channel is opened, the `ChannelUriUpdated` event fires, and the `notificationChannel_ChannelUriUpdated()` method is called. This method simply forwards a call to the `RegisterAndConfigureChannelUri()` method, which updates the status text and binds the toast and tile notification listeners in the shell:

```
private void RegisterAndConfigureChannelUri()
{
    // Nothing to register with yet, for now just display the URI.
    Dispatcher.BeginInvoke(
        () => ChannelUriText.Text = notificationChannel.ChannelUri.ToString());

    // Bind notifications.
    if (!notificationChannel.IsShellToastBound)
    {
        notificationChannel.BindToShellToast();
    }

    if (!notificationChannel.IsShellTileBound)
    {
        notificationChannel.BindToShellTile(new Collection<Uri>
            { new Uri(tileImageDomain) });
    }

    Dispatcher.BeginInvoke(
        () => StatusText.Text = "Channel active and configured.");
}
```

Next come two event handlers for toast and raw notifications that may be received when the application is running. These will be used later to display the notification content.

Sending Push Notification Service Messages

In the preceding Try It Out section, you created an application that's ready and waiting for push notifications. However, you currently don't have a service that can send these notifications. In the next section, you'll build a simple REST service that enables you to register a channel URI and send push notification messages. Before doing that, though, it's worth taking a look at exactly how you send a notification message.

Essentially, all you need to do is to send an HTTP POST request to the channel URI. The headers and body of the request you send specify the type and properties of notification that you want to send. You then get a response message that tells you whether the notification was successfully sent by the central push notification service. Behind the scenes, the central push notification and push client do all the heavy lifting for you.

Sending Toast Notifications

To send a toast notification, you must set the HTTP headers listed in Table 10-2.

TABLE 10-2: HTTP Headers for Sending Toast Notifications

HEADER	VALUE	MEANING
X-WindowsPhone-Target	toast	This header specifies that the message is a toast notification.
X-NotificationClass	2, 12, or 22	This header tells the service how urgent the notification is by saying how soon the message should be delivered. A value of 2 means you want the message to be delivered immediately, 12 means delivery should be within 450 seconds, and 22 means within 900 seconds.

You can send a toast notification by using the following code:

```
HttpWebRequest sendRequest =
    (HttpWebRequest)WebRequest.Create(subscriptionUri);
sendRequest.Headers.Add("X-WindowsPhone-Target", "toast");
sendRequest.Headers.Add("X-NotificationClass", "2");
```

The message body you need to send for a toast notification is Extensible Markup Language (XML), so you should also set the ContentType property of the request to text/xml:

```
sendRequest.ContentType = "text/xml";
```

The XML message you need to send must use the following template:

```
<?xml version="1.0" encoding="utf-8"?>
<wp:Notification xmlns:wp="WPNotification">
  <wp:Toast>
    <wp:Text1>Title</wp:Text1>
    <wp:Text2>Message</wp:Text2>
  </wp:Toast>
</wp:Notification>
```

The two highlighted sections of the preceding code snippet indicate where you would put the title and message for the toast notification.

Sending Tile Notifications

To send a tile notification, you must set the HTTP headers listed in Table 10-3.

TABLE 10-3: HTTP Headers for Sending Tile Notifications

HEADER	VALUE	MEANING
X-WindowsPhone-Target	tile	This header specifies that the message is a tile notification.
X-NotificationClass	1, 11, or 21	This header tells the service how urgent the notification is by saying how soon the message should be delivered. A value of 1 means you want the message to be delivered immediately, 11 means delivery should be within 450 seconds, and 21 means within 900 seconds.

As with toast notification, the message body you need to send for a tile notification is XML, so again you should also set the ContentType property of the request to text/xml.

The XML message you need to send must use the following template:

```
<?xml version="1.0" encoding="utf-8"?>
<wp:Notification xmlns:wp="WPNotification">
  <wp:Tile>
    <wp:BackgroundImage>ImageURI</wp:BackgroundImage>
    <wp:Count>Count</wp:Count>
    <wp:Title>Title</wp:Title>
  </wp:Tile>
</wp:Notification>>
```

Here, ImageURI is the URI to the tile background image, and Count and Title are the values to display on the tile.

 NOTE *As you saw earlier, any remote tile background image URI must use a domain specified in the* BindToShellTile() *method you called in your Windows Phone 7 application. Also, the image should be a 173 x 173-pixel image with a maximum size of 80KB and a maximum download time of 15 seconds.*

Sending Raw Notifications

To send a raw notification, you must set the HTTP header listed in Table 10-4.

TABLE 10-4: HTTP Header for Sending Raw Notifications

HEADER	VALUE	MEANING
X-NotificationClass	3, 13, or 23	This header tells the service how urgent the notification is by saying how soon the message should be delivered. A value of 3 means you want the message to be delivered immediately, 13 means delivery should be within 450 seconds, and 23 means within 900 seconds.

The message body for a raw notification is simply a stream of bytes, so there's no need to set the ContentType property of the request. You can send up to 1KB of data in this way.

Receiving Notification Response Messages

When you send a notification request using any of the three message types detailed in this section, you get a response that contains the three HTTP headers listed in Table 10-5.

TABLE 10-5: HTTP Headers Received in Notification Response Messages

HEADER	MEANING
X-NotificationStatus	This header tells you the notification was successful if it contains the message Received. The status can also be Dropped or QueueFull if the message failed to be received for some reason. If a particular notification type is not supported (or you've missed some request headers), the status will be Suppressed.
X-SubscriptionStatus	This header tells you the status of the notification channel, and it is Active for active channels and Expired for expired channels.
X-DeviceConnectionStatus	This header tells you if the device is currently connected. If it is, the value is Connected; if it isn't, the value might be Disconnected, TempDisconnected, or InActive.

For messages that are received and processed successfully, the values you expect to see are Received, Active, and Connected. For a full list of the various combinations that are possible and their meaning, refer to http://msdn.microsoft.com/en-us/library/ff941100(v=vs.92).aspx

Tracking Push Notifications

Sometimes, if your service is sending messages to many channel URIs, you might find it hard to keep track of requests and responses. In order to simplify matters, you can add an additional header to your requests, X-MessageID, which must contain a universally unique identifier (UUID), such as a Guid instance:

```
string messageId = Guid.NewGuid().ToString();
sendRequest.Headers.Add("X-MessageID", messageId);
```

If you use this header, the identifier will be returned in the response headers, which enables you to easily match responses with requests.

Creating a Push Notification Service

Now that you know how to format the messages you need to send to achieve push notifications, it's time to build a service that sends them.

TRY IT OUT   Creating a Push Notification Service

The following steps show you how to create a service that uses REST to enable a single application to register a channel URI. It also exposes REST operations that will make it simple for you to send all three types of messages simply by typing an address into a browser:

1. In Visual Web Developer Express, create a new WCF service application called **PushService**.

2. Remove the auto-generated Service1.svc and IService1.cs files and add a new WCF service called PushService to the project.

3. Modify the code in PushService.svc as shown in Listing 10-3.

LISTING 10-3: Modifying the code in PushService.svc

```
<%@ ServiceHost Language="C#" Debug="true"
    Service="PushService.PushService"
    CodeBehind="PushService.svc.cs"
    Factory="System.ServiceModel.Activation.WebServiceHostFactory" %>
```

Code Snippet PushService\PushService.svc

4. Modify the code in IPushService.cs as shown in Listing 10-4.

LISTING 10-4: Modifying the code in IPushService.cs

```
using System.ServiceModel;
using System.ServiceModel.Web;


namespace PushService
{
    [ServiceContract]
    public interface IPushService
```

```
    {
        [OperationContract]
        [WebGet(UriTemplate = "/Register?uri={uri}")]
        void Register(string uri);

        [OperationContract]
        [WebGet(UriTemplate = "/SendRaw?payload={payload}")]
        string SendRaw(string payload);

        [OperationContract]
        [WebGet(UriTemplate =
        "/SendToast?title={title}&message={message}")]
        string SendToast(string title, string message);

        [OperationContract]
        [WebGet(UriTemplate =
        "/SendTile?imagePath={imagePath}&count={count}&title={title}")]
        string SendTile(string imagePath, string count, string title);
    }
}
```

Code Snippet PushService\IPushService.cs

5. Modify the code in `PushService.svc.cs` as shown in Listing 10-5.

LISTING 10-5: Modifying the code in PushService.svc.cs

```
using System;
using System.IO;
using System.Net;
using System.Text;
using System.Web;
using System.Xml.Linq;

namespace PushService
{
    public class PushService : IPushService
    {
        private static string registeredUri;

        public void Register(string uri)
        {
            registeredUri = HttpUtility.UrlDecode(uri);
        }

        public string SendToast(string title, string message)
        {
            WebHeaderCollection headers = new WebHeaderCollection
            {
                { "X-WindowsPhone-Target", "toast" },
                { "X-NotificationClass", "2" }
            };

            XNamespace wp = "WPNotification";
```

continues

LISTING 10-5 *(continued)*

```
    XDocument doc = new XDocument(
       new XDeclaration("1.0", "utf-8", "no"),
       new XElement(wp + "Notification",
          new XElement(wp + "Toast",
             new XElement(wp + "Text1", title),
             new XElement(wp + "Text2", message))));

    return Send(doc.ToString(), true, headers);
}

public string SendTile(string imagePath, string count,
    string title)
{
    WebHeaderCollection headers = new WebHeaderCollection
    {
       { "X-WindowsPhone-Target", "token" },
       { "X-NotificationClass", "1" }
    };

    XNamespace wp = "WPNotification";
    XDocument doc = new XDocument(
       new XDeclaration("1.0", "utf-8", "no"),
       new XElement(wp + "Notification",
          new XElement(wp + "Tile",
             new XElement(wp + "BackgroundImage", imagePath),
             new XElement(wp + "Count", count),
             new XElement(wp + "Title", title))));

    return Send(doc.ToString(), true, headers);
}

public string SendRaw(string payload)
{
    WebHeaderCollection headers = new WebHeaderCollection
    {
       { "X-NotificationClass", "3" }
    };

    return Send(payload, false, headers);
}

private string Send(
    string messageToSend, bool sendAsXml,
    WebHeaderCollection headers)
{
    HttpWebRequest sendRequest =
       (HttpWebRequest)WebRequest.Create(new Uri(registeredUri));
    sendRequest.Method = "POST";
    foreach (string headerKey in headers.Keys)
    {
       sendRequest.Headers.Add(headerKey, headers[headerKey]);
    }
```

```csharp
            if (sendAsXml)
            {
                sendRequest.ContentType = "text/xml";
                sendRequest.ContentLength = messageToSend.Length;
                using (StreamWriter writer =
                    new StreamWriter(sendRequest.GetRequestStream()))
                {
                    writer.Write(messageToSend);
                }
            }
            else
            {
                byte[] messageBytes = Encoding.UTF8.GetBytes(
                    messageToSend);
                sendRequest.ContentLength = messageBytes.Length;
                using (Stream requestStream =
                    sendRequest.GetRequestStream())
                {
                    requestStream.Write(messageBytes, 0,
                        messageBytes.Length);
                }
            }

            HttpWebResponse response =
                (HttpWebResponse)sendRequest.GetResponse();
            string notificationStatus =
                response.Headers["X-NotificationStatus"];
            string subscriptionStatus =
                response.Headers["X-SubscriptionStatus"];
            string deviceConnectionStatus =
                response.Headers["X-DeviceConnectionStatus"];

            XDocument doc = new XDocument(
                new XDeclaration("1.0", "utf-8", "yes"),
                new XElement("Response",
                    new XElement("NotificationStatus", notificationStatus),
                    new XElement("SubscriptionStatus", subscriptionStatus),
                    new XElement("DeviceConnectionStatus",
                        deviceConnectionStatus)));

            return doc.ToString();
        }
    }
}
```

Code Snippet PushService\PushService.svc.cs

6. Add two `.png` images named `Cheese1.png` and `Cheese2.png` to the root of the project. (They can be any images you like; the downloadable code includes some samples.)

7. Run the web service application and make a note of the URI it uses, either from the browser window or via the Show Details option on the development server task icon (for example, `http://localhost:50533/`).

8. Make a copy of the `PushApplication` application you made earlier (or simply edit the existing one).

9. In Visual Studio 2010 Express for Windows Phone, modify the code in `MainPage.xaml.cs` as shown in Listing 10-6 (using the port for the service you just created).

LISTING 10-6: Modifying the code in MainPage.xaml.cs

```csharp
using System;
using System.Collections.ObjectModel;
using System.IO;
using System.Net;
using System.Text;
using Microsoft.Phone.Controls;
using Microsoft.Phone.Notification;

namespace PushApplication
{
    public partial class MainPage : PhoneApplicationPage
    {
        private const string tileImageDomain =
            "http://localhost:50533/";
        private const string registrationUri =
            "http://localhost:50533/pushservice.svc/register?uri={0}";

        ...

        private void RegisterAndConfigureChannelUri()
        {
            Dispatcher.BeginInvoke(
                () => ChannelUriText.Text =
                    notificationChannel.ChannelUri.ToString());

            // Register Channel URI.
            HttpWebRequest request = HttpWebRequest.Create(
                string.Format(registrationUri, HttpUtility.UrlEncode(
                    notificationChannel.ChannelUri.ToString())))
                as HttpWebRequest;

            request.BeginGetResponse(GetResponseCallback, request);
        }

        private void GetResponseCallback(IAsyncResult result)
        {
            // Bind notifications.
            if (!notificationChannel.IsShellToastBound)
            {
                notificationChannel.BindToShellToast();
            }
```

```
        if (!notificationChannel.IsShellTileBound)
        {
            notificationChannel.BindToShellTile(
                new Collection<Uri> { new Uri(tileImageDomain) });
        }

        Dispatcher.BeginInvoke(
            () => StatusText.Text = "Channel active and configured.");
    }


    ...
  }
}
```

Code Snippet PushService\MaingPage.xaml.cs

10. Run the application.

11. When the main screen is displayed, open a browser window and navigate to the following addresses in turn (using the port number for your service):

```
http://localhost:50533/PushService.svc/SendRaw
    ?payload=Cheese%20is%20your%20friend.
http://localhost:50533/PushService.svc/SendToast?title=New%20Cheese!
    &message=Have%20you%20tried%20gouda?
```

12. After each address, observe the changes in the application, as shown in Figure 10-3.

FIGURE 10-3: Raw and toast messages in a Windows Phone 7 application.

13. Close the application by tapping the Back button.

14. On the application screen, tap and hold the PushApplication icon until the dialog shown in Figure 10-4 displays, and then tap "pin to start."

15. When the start screen is displayed with your pinned application tile, open a browser window and navigate to the following addresses in turn (again using the port number for your service):

```
http://localhost:50533/PushService.svc/SendTile
  ?imagePath=http://localhost:50533/Cheese2.png&count=10
  &title=Daily%20Cheese
http://localhost:50533/PushService.svc/SendToast
  ?title=New%20Recipe
  &message=Cheese%20on%20toast!
```

16. After you have entered the addresses, observe the changes in the emulator, as shown in Figure 10-5.

How It Works

In this example, you created a RESTful push notification service, connected it to your Windows Phone 7 application, and used it to send push notification messages. To make things simple, you exposed the notification API in a simple way so that you could send notifications using a web browser.

You started by adding the `WebServiceHostFactory` factory to your service to gain REST functionality, as described in Chapter 9. Next, you defined four operations for the service:

➤ `Register` — This operation enables the Windows Phone 7 application to register a channel URI with the service. The endpoint URI is `/Register?uri={uri}`. When appended to the root URI of the service, that makes a full URI of `http://localhost:50533/PushService .svc/Register?uri={uri}`.

➤ `SendRaw` — This operation enables you to send raw notification messages by adding your payload (which must be 1KB or less) to the endpoint `/SendRaw?payload={payload}`.

➤ `SendToast` — This operation enables you to send toast notification messages by including a title and message in the endpoint `/SendToast?title={title}&message={message}`.

➤ `SendTile` — This operation enables you to send tile notification messages by including an image URI, title, and count in the endpoint `/SendTile?imagePath={imagePath}&count={count}&title={title}`.

Next, you implemented these operations in the service. The `Register()` method simply stores a single URI in a private static field called `registeredUri`.

FIGURE 10-4: Pinning the application.

FIGURE 10-5: Tile and toast notifications in action.

COMMON MISTAKES *It isn't generally a good idea to store a single channel URI as in this example. If you have multiple devices and/or applications that use your service then each channel URI received will wipe out the last. In a real-life application, you'd persist a collection of channel URIs in a file or database and keep track of which ones were active. Then, instead of sending single notifications, you might send the same notification to all your stored URIs. For a sample application, though, and for testing, this is fine. The only limitation imposed is that you must keep the service running after registration so that the channel URI isn't lost.*

Each of the push notification methods works in more or less the same way. For example, here is `SendToast()`:

```
public string SendToast(string title, string message)
{
    WebHeaderCollection headers = new WebHeaderCollection
    {
        { "X-WindowsPhone-Target", "toast" },
        { "X-NotificationClass", "2" }
    };

    XNamespace wp = "WPNotification";
    XDocument doc = new XDocument(new XDeclaration("1.0", "utf-8", "no"),
        new XElement(wp + "Notification",
            new XElement(wp + "Toast",
                new XElement(wp + "Text1", title),
                new XElement(wp + "Text2", message))));

    return Send(doc.ToString(), true, headers);
}
```

First, you set the headers that you want to include, in this case `X-WindowsPhone-Target` and `X-NotificationClass`. Next, you build the message payload. For tile and toast messages, this takes the form of an XML document that is built using `XDocument`, with special attention given to the required Windows Phone 7 notification namespace, `WPNotification`. This namespace must be applied to all elements. The `SendRaw()` method is simpler in that it just sends a string, taken from the query string parameter passed to the service endpoint.

All three methods call the generic `Send()` method, which actually does the sending. This method starts by creating an `HttpWebRequest` object by using the stored channel URI, setting its HTTP method to `POST`, and adding the headers passed as method parameters:

```
private string Send(
    string messageToSend, bool sendAsXml, WebHeaderCollection headers)
{
    HttpWebRequest sendRequest =
        (HttpWebRequest)WebRequest.Create(new Uri(registeredUri));
    sendRequest.Method = "POST";
    foreach (string headerKey in headers.Keys)
    {
        sendRequest.Headers.Add(headerKey, headers[headerKey]);
    }
```

If the message is XML (for toast and tile notifications), ContentType is then set to text/xml, and the data is written to the request stream:

```
if (sendAsXml)
{
    sendRequest.ContentType = "text/xml";
    sendRequest.ContentLength = messageToSend.Length;
    using (StreamWriter writer =
        new StreamWriter(sendRequest.GetRequestStream()))
    {
        writer.Write(messageToSend);
    }
}
```

For raw messages, the message is sent as a stream of Byte values:

```
else
{
    byte[] messageBytes = Encoding.UTF8.GetBytes(messageToSend);
    sendRequest.ContentLength = messageBytes.Length;
    using (Stream requestStream = sendRequest.GetRequestStream())
    {
        requestStream.Write(messageBytes, 0, messageBytes.Length);
    }
}
```

Next, the request is sent synchronously and the response is stored:

```
HttpWebResponse response = (HttpWebResponse)sendRequest.GetResponse();
```

Finally, the returned message headers are extracted and returned to the browser as an XML document:

```
string notificationStatus =
    response.Headers["X-NotificationStatus"];
string subscriptionStatus =
    response.Headers["X-SubscriptionStatus"];
string deviceConnectionStatus =
    response.Headers["X-DeviceConnectionStatus"];

XDocument doc = new XDocument(new XDeclaration("1.0", "utf-8", "yes"),
    new XElement("Response",
        new XElement("NotificationStatus", notificationStatus),
        new XElement("SubscriptionStatus", subscriptionStatus),
        new XElement("DeviceConnectionStatus", deviceConnectionStatus)));

return doc.ToString();
}
```

You probably noticed this document appearing in the browser as you sent push notifications, as in this example, which illustrates a successful message:

```
<Response>
  <NotificationStatus>Received</NotificationStatus>
  <SubscriptionStatus>Active</SubscriptionStatus>
  <DeviceConnectionStatus>Connected</DeviceConnectionStatus>
</Response>
```

Next, you added two images ready for sending tile notifications (hopefully some good ones, or, failing that, some pictures of cheese) and then updated the Windows Phone 7 application to use your push service.

First, you stored the URIs for the domain used for tile images and the service registration endpoint:

```
public partial class MainPage : PhoneApplicationPage
{
    private const string tileImageDomain = "http://localhost:50533/";
    private const string registrationUri =
        "http://localhost:50533/pushservice.svc/register?uri={0}";
```

Next, you added code to `RegisterAndConfigureChannelUri()` to send the channel URI you get from the central push notification service to your push service:

```
private void RegisterAndConfigureChannelUri()
{
    Dispatcher.BeginInvoke(
        () => ChannelUriText.Text = notificationChannel.ChannelUri.ToString());

    // Register Channel URI.
    HttpWebRequest request = HttpWebRequest.Create(
        string.Format(registrationUri, HttpUtility.UrlEncode(
            notificationChannel.ChannelUri.ToString())))
        as HttpWebRequest;

    request.BeginGetResponse(GetResponseCallback, request);
}
```

The call to your service must be made asynchronously, so you also moved the bind notifications into the callback for the service call.

When you finished the code, you set it all in motion and then sent toast and raw push notifications. First, with the application running, you consumed the toast and raw push notifications in the event handlers you added earlier, which simply wrote the message content to the screen. Next, you closed the application, pinned it to the start page, and sent tile and toast notifications. With very little effort, you made the tile image, count, and title update, and created a toast message. All you had to do to send this was to enter an address into a browser, so this is quite impressive. It's especially impressive when you consider that behind the scenes a whole host of messages are being sent back and forth between different subsystems.

SUMMARY

In this chapter, you've seen how to send and receive push notifications in Windows Phone 7 applications. To start, you learned how the push notification architecture works and what participants are required for it to hold together. Next, you looked at what's involved in preparing for push notifications by registering with the central notification service. You learned about notification channels, and you learned that you must create or find a channel and then register a channel URI with a service in order to send notifications.

Next, you learned about the three types of notifications — toast, tile, and raw. In particular, you learned that best-practice use for notifications is generally to use them sparingly, especially when it comes to intrusive toast notifications, which interrupt the user.

After learning about the architecture, you moved on to implement a push notification system. You built a Windows Phone 7 application consumer and a REST service to send push notifications. You saw how simple it can be to send notifications and how useful these notifications can be.

There is, of course, more that you can do. It's possible to include callbacks in secured push services so that you can detect when a device goes offline, for example. You've seen all the essentials, but when it comes to actually using push notifications, you're limited only by your imagination. You can expect to see innovative uses of push notifications in the years to come. This technology is still relatively new, and you have the power to create that "killer app" you've always dreamed of, or you can just have fun by making an application that describes a new type of cheese every day.

EXERCISES

1. Which of the following agents participate in push notifications? (Choose all that apply.)

   a) Your Windows Phone 7 application

   b) The push client on your device

   c) A WPF Windows application

   d) Your local post office

   e) The central push notification service, somewhere in the cloud

2. When is it appropriate to send raw notifications? Can you guarantee that they'll be received?

3. What is the purpose of binding to toast notifications?

4. The following code configures a Windows Phone 7 notification channel for tile notifications (myNotificationChannel is an instance of the HttpNotificationChannel class):

```
if (!myNotificationChannel.IsShellTileBound)
{
    myNotificationChannel.BindToShellTile();
}
```

How does this code limit the use of such notifications?

5. What would happen if you sent a notification message to a device that is switched off?

Answers to the Exercises can be found in the Appendix.

▶ WHAT YOU LEARNED IN THIS CHAPTER

TOPIC	KEY CONCEPTS
Push notification architecture	Push notifications must be sent through a notification channel instance that's supplied by the central push notification service. You must communicate the channel URI for a channel to a web service, which can then use it to send push notifications. The web service sends notifications to the central push notification service, which in turn sends it to the push client on a device. This push client then forwards the message to your application, if it is running, or takes appropriate action such as displaying the message or updating your application tile. There are three types of notifications: toast, tile, and raw.
Toast notifications	Toast notifications can be consumed directly in your applications or can be used to display onscreen alerts if your application isn't running. Users can tap this alert to open your application or dismiss it. Toast notifications should be used with discretion as they can be quite intrusive.
Tile notifications	Running applications ignore tile notifications. Instead, applications use them to update the tile associated with an application. You can set the tile background image, the tile title, and a numeric indicator. You can't, however, customize the layout of these elements.
Raw notifications	You can send any information you like in a raw notification, as long as the message size is less than or equal to 1KB. Raw notifications are received only by running applications, and they're probably the most versatile notification type. However, because the payload is small, you might want to use them to initiate a pull request from an application rather than send lots of data in small chunks.
Notification channels	When you create a notification channel, it persists beyond the lifetime of an application. You can therefore reuse existing channels after you've created them. You can configure channels by specifying what types of notifications should be bound to the push client. You must also check and, if necessary, re-register the channel URI as you need it, as it may change without warning.
Sending notifications	You send push notifications by sending an HTTP POST message to a channel URI. The message headers of such messages configure the type of notification, and the message body contains the properties of the notification, such as the title and body of a toast notification. The central push notification service will reply with a message that includes headers to inform you of the status of the notification, the channel, and the device due to receive the notification. You can also use an ID header to correlate requests and responses.

11

XNA for Windows Phone 7

WHAT IS XNA?

"XNA's not acronymed" is the official line on what XNA stands for. First released in 2007, XNA is a platform for developing games. Initially, it was just for Xbox and Windows (on the PC), but more recently, it has been used to build games for Zune and for Windows Phone 7.

There are techniques you can use to write a game for multiple platforms at once. And there's a special directive in C# — the #if preprocessor directive — that lets you include or exclude bits of code, depending on which platform you are building for. (Although XNA was designed with code reuse in mind, we don't recommend trying it on the first couple of games you write.)

XNA comes with some well-designed solutions to many of the problems that game developers typically face. This chapter walks though the construction of a simple Windows Phone 7 game and shows how you can leverage XNA to create your own games.

COMPARING XNA AND SILVERLIGHT

Most games are proactive: Unless they are paused, something is happening, and it's up to the user to react to the game or else lose. It's this time-based challenge that makes up part of the fun of the game.

Silverlight is a great framework for building reactive applications. What do we mean by reactive? Think about most of the software you use today. If you aren't interacting with it, telling it what you want it to do, it will be inert. It's only when the user triggers some event by typing on the keyboard or by clicking with the mouse that the application needs to react. Turn-based games such as chess or poker are also event-based, reactive applications (except, perhaps, when the turn timer is counting down or when a computer is playing its turn).

It is actually possible to create proactive games with Silverlight. Creating a `DispatcherTimer` object with a time interval will generate a `Tick` event every time that interval elapses until you stop the timer. You can control how fluid the game seems by setting `DispatcherTimer` to trigger more often.

Silverlight excels at displaying 2-D graphics. It makes it easy for programmers to design and animate fonts, colors, shapes, and paths. Although Windows Phone 7 does a great job of rendering simple animations, it can struggle with a heavily animated game. Often you don't see these problems when developing on a PC, because your computer is much more powerful than a phone.

By its very design, XNA is much better than Silverlight at handling complex animation. Because XNA is written from the ground up for real-time games, even on the limited hardware available on a phone, you can use XNA to achieve excellent performance.

Deciding whether to use Silverlight or XNA to build a game often comes down to a couple of key factors:

➤   How do you want to render the game? For 2-D games, Silverlight offers a much richer rendering model with shapes, paths, and animations. XNA can only draw images and text to the screen (no primitive shape support). For a 3-D game on Windows Phone 7, XNA gives you much more control and performance than Silverlight.

➤   How much performance do you need to get out of your hardware? A properly written Windows Phone 7 XNA game almost always outperforms a properly written Windows Phone 7 Silverlight game.

AN XNA GAME: TANK

In this chapter, you'll create a simple but functional game with XNA. This game is creatively named Tank, as it puts the player in charge of a vehicle that he or she can drive across the screen with his or her thumb. In the game, a missile can be launched at the tank from the corners of the screen. These missiles home in on the tank, but the player can shoot them down (see Figure 11-1).

FIGURE 11-1: The finished Tank game, running in the emulator.

If you follow all the steps in this chapter, you'll create the Tank game shown in Figure 11-1. The following Try It Out walks you through how to start this new XNA project.

Creating the Windows Phone Tank Game

Following are the first steps for creating the Tank Windows Phone game using XNA:

1. In Visual Studio, choose File ➪ New Project.

2. From the left side of the New Project dialog, select XNA Game Studio 4.0.

3. Select the Windows Phone Game template option and type the name of the project, **Tank**, in the Name field (see Figure 11-2).

FIGURE 11-2 The New Project dialog.

4. Click OK. Visual Studio creates a number of files for you, and you can see them in the Solution Explorer (see Figure 11-3).

How It Works

Visual Studio has a number of pre-installed templates for various types of projects. Because they contain all the boilerplate code you need to get started, they make it very easy to get something up-and-running. In this example, the Windows Phone Game template creates an empty game that does nothing but has all the required code in place. All you have to do is add your own code in the right places (which you'll do soon). You can find more complete sample projects on the Internet, but because this chapter shows you how to build a game from scratch, this hollow shell of an XNA game project is ideal.

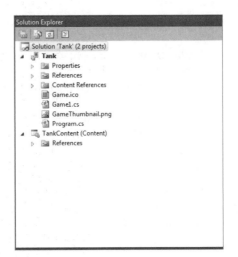

FIGURE 11-3 A fresh XNA solution.

What's in My Solution?

The key file of any XNA solution is the Game class, in this case Game1, which is covered in the next section, "The Game Class." The following files come with your brand-new solution:

➤ **The C# project Tank** — In Windows Explorer, this file is called Tank.csproj. It's used to track all of your C# code. Just like any C# project, it has a folder for references, but it also has Content References that contains all the content libraries the Tank project uses. At the moment, the project uses only TankContent.

➤ **Game.ico** — Games that are written for Windows require an icon, and this is the icon for the Tank game. If you're not building a multiplatform game (and you aren't in this chapter), you can safely ignore Game.ico.

➤ **Game1.cs** — Game1 is ultimately responsible for everything your game does.

➤ **GameThumbnail.png** — This .png image shows how our game will look in the game browser of a phone, before the game is even launched.

➤ **Program.cs** — Windows Phone 7 doesn't use this file, so you should see that its contents have been removed via the #if directive (unless you're running on Xbox or Windows).

➤ **The content project, TankContent** — Though TankContent is empty right now (if you ignore its references), this project is responsible for storing all your images, font definitions, sound files, and 3-D resources (such as meshes and textures).

➤ **The content project's references** — These references tell the content project how to process various resources (for example, sound files, images) into something that XNA can use. When these don't work for the kinds of source data files being used, game developers write their own content pipeline extensions, but you don't need to build any pipeline extensions for your game.

The Game Class

The Game class is the heart of any XNA system. To tie your code into the XNA framework, you inherit from `Microsoft.Xna.Framework.Game` and override the appropriate methods. When you create a new XNA project, Visual Studio writes these method stubs for you.

When Windows Phone 7 launches your game, it constructs a Game and hands over control by calling the `Run()` method. Figure 11-4 shows a simple workflow for this process.

The most important part of the workflow is the game loop. Almost all game programming systems have a game loop, which has two stages: update and draw. The game tries to call each of these methods up to 30 times per second. The other steps in the life cycle basically support these two game loop stages.

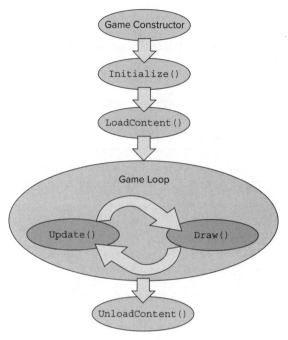

FIGURE 11-4: The XNA game life cycle.

Let's take a look at the contents of the `Game1.cs` file, and figure out what each of the steps in a Game's life cycle does.

The Game Constructor

Right at the top of the `Game1.cs` file are the constructor and a couple fields:

```
GraphicsDeviceManager graphics;
SpriteBatch spriteBatch;

public Game1()
{
    graphics = new GraphicsDeviceManager(this);
    Content.RootDirectory = "Content";

    // Frame rate is 30 fps by default for Windows Phone.
    TargetElapsedTime = TimeSpan.FromTicks(333333);

    // Pre-autoscale settings.
    graphics.PreferredBackBufferWidth = 480;
    graphics.PreferredBackBufferHeight = 800;
}
```

These two fields, `graphics` and `spriteBatch`, are used to store objects that are created once during the game's startup and are then available to the game loop's methods. As you add functionality to your games, you'll often add new fields to store either game state or useful resources. `graphics` is a `GraphicsDeviceManager` field that is used to configure the screen itself, and the `spritebatch` is a `SpriteBatch` field that is used to support 2-D drawing in XNA.

Inside the constructor, you see that the template has created the `graphics` field. The `GraphicsDeviceManager` class's constructor requires a `Game` instance, and this code is actually inside the `Game` methods, so you can provide the current `Game` class by using the keyword `this`. Having created the `GraphicsDeviceManager` class, you're now able to configure screen-related settings such as resolution.

The next thing the constructor does is set the folder where content files (that is, digital art assets) are to be found. It does this by accessing the game's preexisting `Content` property and setting `RootDirectory` to the string `"Content"`. This string is supposed to match the content project's `Content Root Directory` property. You should never have to change either of these, but if they get out of sync, you may see an error of type `ContentLoadException`. To fix these errors, you need to make sure each of these properties is set to a valid directory name, such as the default: `"Content"`.

Next, the template sets the `TargetElapsedTime` setting of the game to 333,333 "ticks." The helpful comment that comes with the template tells you that this is setting the game's frame rate to 30 frames per second. If you have your calculator handy, you'll be able to figure out that a tick is one ten-millionth of a second. This is the only supported setting for Windows Phone 7, so it's best to leave it as is.

Finally, the template changes the preferred width and height of the `GraphicsDeviceManager` class's `BackBuffer`. The back buffer is, in essence, where all the things you draw to the screen are prepared, just before it's shown to the user. You can think of it as a second screen, behind the visible one (hence *back*), that collects (that is, *buffers*) drawing commands until drawing is complete. When this new screen is ready to display, it replaces the visible one in an instant. If you were programming in a different framework, you might have to manage this double-buffering yourself; otherwise, there would be a visible flicker to your game (albeit at a very high rate) as each visual element appeared one by one.

You might have noted that the `SpriteBatch` class has still not been created, and that's okay at the moment because you're not trying to use it. (You'd get a `NullReferenceException` if you tried to use it now.) The `SpriteBatch` class is first used in the `Draw()` method, but the game is going to call `Initialize()`, `LoadContent()`, and `Update()` before then. The following sections discuss these three methods, and the `UnloadContent()` method that occurs when you exit the game.

The Initialize() Method

The template for the new project will have created an `Initialize()` method that looks like this:

```
/// <summary>
/// Allows the game to perform any initialization it needs to before starting to
/// run.
/// This is where it can query for any required services and load any non-graphic
/// related content.  Calling base.Initialize will enumerate through any components
/// and initialize them as well.
/// </summary>
protected override void Initialize()
{
    // TODO: Add your initialization logic here

    base.Initialize();
}
```

This method stub doesn't yet contain any custom logic. Overriding the method `Initialize()` and then calling `base.Initialize()` is the same as simply not overriding it. You could delete this whole declaration right now and not affect the way the program runs. However, the `// TODO:` comment indicates that you're meant to be doing something, perhaps adding some "initialization logic". We do this later in this chapter in the "Cross-Component Communication" section.

The LoadContent() Method

This is the default `LoadContent()` code:

```
/// <summary>
/// LoadContent will be called once per game and is the place to load
/// all of your content.
/// </summary>
protected override void LoadContent()
{
    // Create a new SpriteBatch, which can be used to draw textures.
    spriteBatch = new SpriteBatch(GraphicsDevice);

    // TODO: use this.Content to load your game content here
}
```

This creates the `SpriteBatch` object. Its constructor requires a `GraphicsDevice` object, and the current `Game` class has one available via the conveniently named `GraphicsDevice` property. If you'd tried to retrieve it inside the `Game`'s constructor, the `Game` wouldn't have had a chance to create one yet, so the `SpriteBatch` constructor would have thrown an `ArgumentNullException` error.

As you can see from the `TODO` comment, the `LoadContent()` method is also useful for loading game content (such as fonts and images, which XNA calls textures). You'll do this in just a few more pages.

 NOTE There's no call to `base.LoadContent()`. The base implementation does absolutely nothing and therefore can be left out.

The UnloadContent() Method

Here's what the `UnLoadContent()` method looks like:

```
/// <summary>
/// UnloadContent will be called once per game and is
/// the place to unload all content.
/// </summary>
protected override void UnloadContent()
{
    // TODO: Unload any non ContentManager content here
}
```

`UnloadContent()` is the first method that is declared in a different order than how the game actually runs. This method doesn't get called until the game is exiting. Therefore, you can move it to the end of the class — if you keep it at all. The template's comment in this case is a little inaccurate: Only content that's not loaded by `ContentManager` needs to be explicitly unloaded here. Because you're never going to do this for your Tank game, you can go ahead and delete it now. (However, if you don't delete it, nothing bad will happen; it will just be ornamental.)

The Update() Method

The Update() method is responsible for updating the state of the game's world, which could be in response to any of the following:

➤ Time passing

➤ User input (via the accelerometer or touchscreen)

➤ Collisions and other physics

➤ Artificial intelligence (such as the computer player reaching a decision)

➤ Network/Bluetooth communication (for multiplayer games)

For example, your completed Tank game might check whether the user is trying to steer the tank, move the tank accordingly, move all missiles and bullets on the screen, and then check whether any missiles have hit the tank or are hit by bullets — and so on.

Here's the default template's implementation of Update():

```
/// <summary>
/// Allows the game to run logic such as updating the world,
/// checking for collisions, gathering input, and playing audio.
/// </summary>
/// <param name="gameTime">
/// Provides a snapshot of timing values
/// </param>
protected override void Update(GameTime gameTime)
{
    // Allows the game to exit
    GamePadState gamePadState = GamePad.GetState(PlayerIndex.One);
    if (gamePadState.Buttons.Back == ButtonState.Pressed)
        this.Exit();

    // TODO: Add your update logic here

    base.Update(gameTime);
}
```

For now, the Update() method is simply checking whether the user is pressing the Back button on the phone in order to quit the application. Unlike with the LoadContent() method though, it's important to call base.Update(). You'll see why shortly.

The Draw() Method

Visual Studio creates a default draw implementation as follows:

```
/// <summary>
/// This is called when the game should draw itself.
/// </summary>
/// <param name="gameTime">
```

```
/// Provides a snapshot of timing values.
/// </param>
protected override void Draw(GameTime gameTime)
{
    GraphicsDevice.Clear(Color.CornflowerBlue);

    // TODO: Add your drawing code here

    base.Draw(gameTime);
}
```

Draw() is responsible for rendering the current state of the game to the screen. The image that's rendered on each Draw() method is called a *frame*. You'll often hear the term *frame rate* used when talking about game performance; a low frame rate looks jerky to the user and usually occurs when the Draw() method is too complex for the hardware available.

The first thing this default method implementation does is clear the GraphicsDevice property. Next, you can see another one of those useful but bossy TODO comments, indicating that this is where you put your drawing code (whether 2-D or 3-D). Then, the base.Draw() method is called, giving the Game superclass an opportunity to do any important drawing.

 NOTE *An interesting performance optimization in the XNA framework is that the Draw() method might be skipped up to three times if it's taking too much time to execute, giving priority to the Update() method. This approach helps to make the game play smoothly, even if the frame rate isn't as high as normal.*

Running the Tank Game

You can go ahead and run the Tank game at this point, to see what happens. To do so, you click the little green "play" triangle in Visual Studio's toolbar or press F5 on your keyboard. As when you run a Silverlight application, you see the Windows Phone 7 emulator launch, and after a short wait, the emulator fires up your game. You should see an empty blue screen. In the next section, you'll learn how to make this screen more interesting.

DRAWING 2-D GRAPHICS

The easiest way to build a game is with 2-D drawing, where you *paint* flat images and text onto the screen. When we talk about 2-D game programming versus 3-D game programming, we're really talking about the set of APIs used to program the drawing code. A 2-D API is typically much simpler than a 3-D API, which entails a scene graph, lighting sources, camera positions, textures, shaders, and more!

When you build a 2-D XNA game, rendering images (that is, AKA textures) to the screen is the primary way of giving visual feedback to the user. XNA gives you a lot of ways to manipulate these images, by giving you control over the following:

➤ The position on the screen

➤ The size of the image

➤ The angle of the image (to point it at something else)

➤ Color tinting, to allow for some variation on the same reusable image

➤ Drawing order, so that backgrounds can be behind game objects and so on, giving the impression that something's in front of something else

➤ Transparency of images that are on top of other images

You use two classes when doing 2-D drawing on XNA. You use `ContentManager` to load images into memory, and you use `SpriteBatch` class to paint these images to the screen.

 COMMON MISTAKES *With XNA, you have to provide all your images ahead of time; there's no easy way to compose images together at runtime. Silverlight lets you put things together using rectangles, paths, and other shapes, but with XNA, you need to draw your images in an image-editing program (such as Microsoft Paint or any of a number of other programs). The quality of these images will have a strong effect on the perceived quality of your game. The Internet is a potential source of pictures, but be sure to check copyrights and licenses on anything you find online. If you want to build a really polished-looking game to sell, you might consider investing in the services of a professional designer.*

The SpriteBatch Class

The `SpriteBatch` class has a number of methods that are able to draw images and text to the device's screen. There are many overloads of the `Draw()` and `DrawString()` methods. Some take many arguments and give you control over everything, and others take fewer arguments and provide intelligent defaults for the drawing parameters that you haven't provided.

When using the `SpriteBatch` class, you always have to wrap calls to it in `Begin()` and `End()` methods, as in the following example:

```
protected override void Draw(GameTime gameTime)
{
    GraphicsDevice.Clear(Color.Black);

    spriteBatch.Begin(); // line 5
    spriteBatch.Draw(tankTexture, new Vector2(50, 100), Color.White); // line 6
    spriteBatch.End(); // line 7

    base.Draw(gameTime);
}
```

You've already seen how a `Game` object can obtain a `SpriteBatch` class, in the section "The Game Class." By default, Visual Studio uses the recommended method, so you shouldn't have to change the code. `Game` also usefully provides an instance of the `ContentManager` class, discussed next.

The ContentManager Class

`ContentManager` is a useful XNA class that makes resources in the game's content project available to the game. It's made available as a property called `Content` on your game. You can use the `Load()` method (from your own game's `LoadContent()` method) to bring any file that was in your content project into memory.

The XNA `Content` project can natively load `.bmp`, `.dds`, `.dib`, `.hdr`, `.jpg`, `.pfm`, `.png`, `.ppm`, and `.tga` images. We recommend using `.png` files because of their superior support for partially transparent images and because most image-manipulation software is able to create files in the `.png` format.

You might use the `Content` project to store other items in addition to images:

➤ Sprite font definitions to make the required glyphs (characters) from a particular font available to the game

➤ Sound effects (short sound bites that enhance onscreen occurrences) and music (typically long-playing tracks that add ambience)

➤ 3-D meshes (A *mesh* is a collection of triangles in 3-D space that define the shape of a 3-D object.)

➤ Data/config files, such as the layout of a level in your game or a list of tweakable game constants (for example, how much damage each spell can do, how much money each weapon costs)

CUSTOMIZING THE CONTENT PIPELINE

Seasoned game developers often get excited about the content pipeline when they first learn about it. It's a customizable system that's capable of converting "source assets" (that is, files that represent creative output — the ones you add to the content project) into an appropriate format for an XNA game's consumption. Because most of the conversion occurs when you compile your program and not when you run it, your game starts up a lot faster — just as when you compile your C# files into DLL files.

The content pipeline is architected in such a way that developers can even customize the process, adding their own steps to any stage of the content pipeline. This means you can have your own, or third-party, formats in the content library, and the XNA game will be able to load the content as though Microsoft supported it out-of-the-box. For more information on this process, see `http://msdn` `.microsoft.com/en-us/library/bb447745.aspx`.

How to Draw Images

There are two simple steps involved in drawing an image on the screen:

1. Load the image into a field with `ContentManager`.

2. Render the image by using `SpriteBatch`.

The loading must be done during the game's `LoadContent()` method. Drawing should occur during the game's `Draw()` method. You don't often get this lucky with naming conventions!

Loading Images with ContentManager

Once an image is in the `Content` project, Visual Studio automatically deploys the image along with your code whenever you compile the project. The image is available to your game via the `Load(string assetName)` method of the `ContentManager` object, which is provided through a property of the game named `Content`. This method's return type is generic, which means that you have to specify the type of asset you want when you call it. You can use `ContentManager` for loading many different asset types, but images that are intended for rendering in 2-D are best represented by the `Texture2D` class. Because drawing is done in a different method than loading, you have to store this variable at the class level. (Class-level variables are often called *fields*.)

Rendering Images with the SpriteBatch Class

The `SpriteBatch` class that is provided with `Game` in a default XNA project is ideal for rendering 2-D images and text to a device's screen. A `SpriteBatch` class is good at doing a batch of things at once; you get better performance out of it when you build up your drawing commands within a `Begin() ... End()` region.

The `SpriteBatch.Draw()` method has many overloads. You can think of the simpler ones as having exactly the same behavior as the method with the most parameters — but with a lot of defaults provided. Table 11-1 lists all the arguments available to `Draw()`. If you examine this table, you can determine what the other methods do. You should be able to read the MSDN documentation to find out what defaults are provided.

TABLE 11-1: Arguments to the Draw() Method

ARGUMENT	DESCRIPTION
`Texture2D texture`	The image to draw.
`Vector2 position`	The location to draw the image.
`Rectangle? sourceRectangle`	The section of the original image to draw. You can use this to draw only a part of a single image. With an argument specifying a 50 x 30 rectangle starting at (0, 10), you'll see one side of the tank clipped off. You'll see a great use for this when you start animating your images. Because this is a nullable rectangle (`Rectangle?`), you could pass null here, in which case the whole image would be used (just like with your first call to `Draw()`).
`Color color`	The tint color. In this case, you're using a partly transparent green, to give the new tank a ghostly appearance.
`float rotation`	You can have an image rotated by specifying an angle, in radians. In your Tank game, you specify 1/4 Pi, which translates to 45 degrees (one-eighth of a full circle).

ARGUMENT	DESCRIPTION
Vector2 origin	The origin point is the position on the image where the rotation and scale will be "from" — the one point on the image that will still be in the same place after it's been stretched and turned. In your Tank game, you specify the top left corner, although often the center of the image is the best place, as you'll see later in this chapter.
Vector2 scale	You can scale the width and height of an image independently, with the X and the Y values of the vector that's passed in here. Note that this is the first time a vector has been used as something other than a location — but it won't be the last time! The argument (8, 3.5) means that you're stretching it 8 times the normal width and 3.5 times the normal height. You should use the term 3.5f instead of just 3.5 because the Vector2 class works only with floats.
SpriteEffects effects	This argument, which is a value from the enumeration SpriteEffects, can be None, FlipHorizontally, FlipVertically, or if you want to flip in both directions, the flag FlipHorizontally | FlipVertically.
float layerDepth	layerDepth can be used to determine the order in which images are drawn to the screen. This can be important when you want one image to cover another. If you have a background image, then you obviously don't want it to be on top of all the action. However, in order for layerDepth to have any effect, you need to use a different overload of the SpriteBatch.Begin() method. For now, you rely on the order of Draw() method calls, with subsequent Draw() calls going on top of previous ones.

TRY IT OUT   Drawing Images

You need to either create your own image to represent a tank (a .png file) or use the tank.png asset provided in Chapter11.zip. Once you have a suitable image on disk, you need to add it to your content project:

1. In Solution Explorer, locate your content project (called TankContent, if you named your solution Tank).

2. Right-click the project and select Add and then Existing Item.

3. Navigate to your tank image and click Add to confirm your selection. You should now be able to see that your image file is a part of your Content project. If you used your own image, make sure it's called tank.png.

4. Create a new field to hold an image in your Game class, as shown in the following:

```
public class Game1 : Microsoft.Xna.Framework.Game
{

    GraphicsDeviceManager graphics;
    SpriteBatch spriteBatch;
    Texture2D tankTexture;
```

Code Snippet Draw\Tank\Tank\Game1.cs

5. Add the following code to your LoadContent() method:

```
protected override void LoadContent()
{
    // Create a new SpriteBatch, which can be used to draw textures.
    spriteBatch = new SpriteBatch(GraphicsDevice);

    tankTexture = Content.Load<Texture2D>("Tank");
}
```

Code Snippet Draw\Tank\Tank\Game1.cs

6. Replace your Draw() method so that it looks as follows:

```
protected override void Draw(GameTime gameTime)
{
    GraphicsDevice.Clear(Color.Black);

    spriteBatch.Begin();

    spriteBatch.Draw(tankTexture, new Vector2(50, 100), Color.White);

    spriteBatch.Draw(tankTexture,
        new Vector2(100, 100),
        new Rectangle(0, 10, 50, 30),
        new Color(100, 255, 100, 150),
        MathHelper.PiOver4,
        new Vector2(0, 0),
        new Vector2(8, 3.5f),
        SpriteEffects.FlipHorizontally,
        0);

    spriteBatch.End();

    base.Draw(gameTime);
}
```

Code Snippet Draw\Tank\Tank\Game1.cs

7. Run the application. Figure 11-5 shows the expected result.

How It Works

In this example, you drew the same image to the device's screen twice, but with different parameters. To do this, you had to do the following:

1. Add the image to the content project.

2. Create a new field in the `Game` class for storing a `Texture2D` object.

3. Load the image into this new field in the `LoadContent()` method. The string `"Tank"` needs to match the name of the file in your content project.

4. Use `Begin()` on the `SpriteBatch` class.

5. Call the `Draw()` method of the `SpriteBatch` class from within your `Draw()` method. This is done twice, once with the simplest `Draw()` method available, and once with the most complex overload. The field storing the tank image is passed in so that the `SpriteBatch` class knows what image to draw.

6. `End()` the `SpriteBatch` class.

FIGURE 11-5: Drawing an image twice, with different parameters.

How to Draw Text

Often, you'll want to display something like the user's current score or the text of a menu item. The `SpriteBatch` class makes this very easy to do; in fact, you might have already spotted the `DrawString()` method. The only thing that's missing right now is a font. Fonts have to be packaged as part of a game, just like images.

Making Fonts Available through the Content Manager

A bitmap font (the type of font used in XNA) is a collection of images, where each image represents a character. (These character-specific images are called *glyphs*.)

As with images, the `Content` project is used to specify which fonts should be available to a game. Unlike with images, however, you don't add the existing font file itself. Instead, you need to add a new file that defines which font should be imported. This `spritefont` file looks as follows:

```xml
<?xml version="1.0" encoding="utf-8"?>
<XnaContent xmlns:Graphics="Microsoft.Xna.Framework.Content.Pipeline.Graphics">
  <Asset Type="Graphics:FontDescription">
    <FontName>Kootenay</FontName>
    <Size>14</Size>
    <Spacing>0</Spacing>
    <UseKerning>true</UseKerning>
    <Style>Regular</Style>
```

```
<CharacterRegions>
  <CharacterRegion>
    <Start>&#32;</Start>
    <End>&#126;</End>
  </CharacterRegion>
</CharacterRegions>
  </Asset>
</XnaContent>
```

Normally, Microsoft likes to build clever screens that let you edit this type of XML through a graphical user interface so that you never have to see the underlying code, but when it comes to `spritefont` files, you have to edit the file yourself.

The key things you might want to change are the font name and the size (displayed in bold in the example above). Because XNA games embed fonts, not all of the standard Windows fonts are actually legal to use in your games, so Microsoft has commissioned a set of fonts that are free for developers to use. Figure 11-6 displays these fonts.

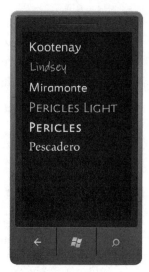

FIGURE 11-6: Fonts available in XNA.

SAVING MEMORY WITH CHARACTERREGIONS

Sometimes, you're interested in only a few characters, such as 0 to 9. In such a case, you can exclude all other glyphs included in your content project by editing the `CharacterRegions` section of the XML. This can make your game's final package slightly smaller and faster to start up. Conversely, if you need to use fancy non-Latin characters (such as the copyright symbol, Unicode character 169; or a snowman, Unicode character 9731), you can add another region to the file.

As with images, fonts are made available through the `Load` method of the content manager. This time, you need to request an object of type `SpriteFont`.

In order to render text to the screen, in your `Draw()` method, you need to call `SpriteFont`'s `DrawString` method.

TRY IT OUT Drawing Text

These steps take you through what you need to do in order to draw some text onto a screen. You add this code to the code from the Try It Out titled "Drawing Images":

1. Add a sprite font to your content project by selecting Add New Item and then Sprite Font. You can just use the default font definition XML for now.

2. Declare a new field to hold `SpriteFont`:

```
public class Game1 : Microsoft.Xna.Framework.Game
{

    GraphicsDeviceManager graphics;
    SpriteBatch spriteBatch;
    Texture2D tankTexture;
    SpriteFont font;
```

Code Snippet Draw\Tank\Tank\ Game1WithFont.cs

3. In your `LoadContent()` method, load the font from the content manager by adding the following:

```
protected override void LoadContent()
{
    // Create a new SpriteBatch, which can be used to draw textures.
    spriteBatch = new SpriteBatch(GraphicsDevice);

    tankTexture = Content.Load<Texture2D>("Tank");
    font = Content.Load<SpriteFont>("font");
}
```

Code Snippet Draw\Tank\Tank\ Game1WithFont.cs

You now have a `SpriteFont` object in your content project and loaded into your game, ready to use in your game's `Draw` method.

4. Add the following call to `spritebatch.DrawString()`:

```
protected override void Draw(GameTime gameTime)
{
    GraphicsDevice.Clear(Color.Black);

    spriteBatch.Begin();

    spriteBatch.Draw(tankTexture, new Vector2(50, 100), Color.White);

    spriteBatch.Draw(tankTexture,
        new Vector2(100, 100),
        new Rectangle(0, 10, 50, 30),
        new Color(100, 255, 100, 150),
        MathHelper.PiOver4,
        new Vector2(0, 0),
        new Vector2(8, 3.5f),
        SpriteEffects.FlipHorizontally,
        0);

    spriteBatch.DrawString(font,
        "stick em up!",
        new Vector2(50, 600),
        Color.Magenta);

    spriteBatch.End();
```

```
    base.Draw(gameTime);
}
```

5. Run the application. You should get a result like the one shown in Figure 11-7.

How It Works

In this exercise, you loaded a font from the content project. You then added code to your `Draw()` method. The first argument is the `SpriteFont` variable. Next, you passed in the string that you wanted to display. In a real game, you often need to calculate this dynamically. Then, you specify the location where you want the top-left corner of the text block to be. Finally, you specify the color for the text you're drawing.

This example used a simple overload of the `DrawString()` method. There are many more overloads to the `DrawString()` method. As with images, you can control scale, rotation, transparency, and color.

FIGURE 11-7: Drawing text to the screen.

Measuring the Size of a String

If you want to center an image on the screen, you subtract half the size of the image from the point where you want to place it. You might simply know an image's size beforehand, since you drew it yourself, or you could query the `Width` and `Height` properties of the image object.

Text is a little more complicated, however. Knowing the font size doesn't help a lot because different letters (such as w and i) are different widths — and the extent of the difference depends on the font's glyphs.

Fortunately, the `SpriteFont` object can measure a string for you. Here's the `Draw()` code you could use to center a piece of text on the screen:

```
string text = "stick em up!"; // line 1
Vector2 center = new Vector2(240, 600); // line 2
Vector2 textSize = font.MeasureString(text); // line 3

float x = center.X - (textSize.X / 2); // line 5
float y = center.Y - (textSize.Y / 2); // line 6

spriteBatch.DrawString(font, text, new Vector2(x, y), Color.Magenta);
```

First, you create a variable to hold the text (line 1). Because you use the text in two different places (measuring on line 3 and drawing on line 5), it's important to make sure you have to change the string in only one place. Line 2 represents the position where you want your text centered — in the vertical center of the screen, near the bottom. Line 3 is the important one: It is where you ask the font for a vector that represents the size of the string. Now that you have the size of the text, you can calculate the correct X and Y for positioning your text.

UPDATING GAME STATE

As discussed earlier, the `Update()` method of the Tank game is responsible for updating the state of the game's world in response to various types of inputs, especially the passing of time. But what do we mean by "the state of the world"? Software uses variables to hold state, and fields (that is, class-level variables) represent more persistent state. But none of the fields you've used so far represent the conceptual world that is the Tank game.

Here are some examples of conceptual things that a game could include, along with potential types that could hold the state for these variables in an XNA game:

CONCEPT	TYPE
Position	Vector2
Speed	Vector2
Acceleration	Vector2
Angle/direction	float
Alive/dead	bool
Score	int
Health points/lives	int
The last time something occurred	DateTime
How long something might take	TimeSpan

The Versatility of Vectors

As it turns out, that's the hard way to translate vectors. The `Vector2` class in XNA has all sorts of nifty methods. Mathematically, you use it to add one vector to another. As it turns out, `Vector2` *overloads* the plus operator. This means that even though an instance of `Vector2` isn't a number, you can simply add two `Vector2`s together. And you can use `x += y` as shorthand for `x = x+y`. Here's how you could refactor the code to make use of this versatility:

```
protected override void Update(GameTime gameTime)
{
    // Allows the game to exit
    GamePadState gamePadState = GamePad.GetState(PlayerIndex.One);
```

```
    if (gamePadState.Buttons.Back == ButtonState.Pressed)
        this.Exit();

    // TODO: Add your update logic here
    tankPosition += new Vector2(1.5f, 2.5f);

    base.Update(gameTime);
}
```

This new code is much easier to understand, and it takes less typing, too!

Let's take a step back to really look at what vectors are. In Latin, *vector* means "one who carries," and we can think of a vector as representing an object's movement. If something moves in a straight line, we can represent it with a direction and a distance. In two dimensions, we can represent a direction with a single angle, so a 2-D vector can be represented as an *angle* and *distance*. (Adjectives for distance include *length* and *magnitude*.) In XNA, it's best if the angle is measured from a line pointing east of the vector's origin because it simplifies conversions between coordinate systems. Figure 11-8 shows you a vector with its angle and length.

When we use angle and length to represent a vector, it's often called the *polar coordinate* system. This is a good way to represent a vector if it's the kind of game object that might slowly change direction, such as a vehicle that needs to be steered. However, it's not easy to add together polar vectors, like those shown in Figure 11-9.

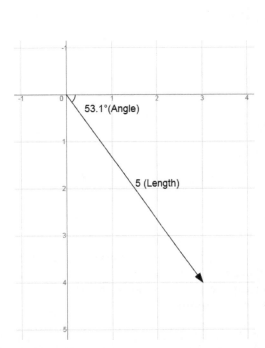

FIGURE 11-8: A single vector in polar coordinates.

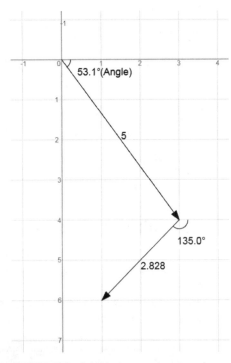

FIGURE 11-9: Adding two vectors in polar coordinates.

For the kinds of computation that you often do in XNA, it's often more efficient to use a Cartesian coordinate system, where you store the horizontal and vertical extent of the vector as an X and Y pair (see Figure 11-10).

By representing a 2-D vector as an X and Y pair, in order to add two vectors together, all you have to do is add the X and Y components individually, as shown in Figure 11-11.

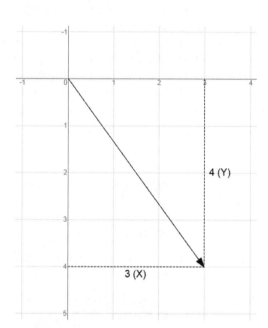

FIGURE 11-10: A single vector in Cartesian coordinates.

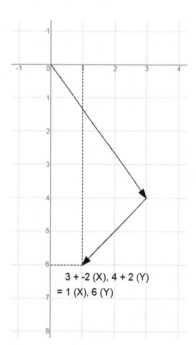

FIGURE 11-11: Adding two vectors in Cartesian coordinates.

Because a `Vector2` class in XNA is in fact a pair of X and Y values and most of XNA's libraries work with `Vector2` parameters, it's easy to see which is the preferred coordinate system to work with. However, if you ever find that you need to work with polar coordinates, you can use a simple formula to convert between the two.

The following formula converts polar to Cartesian coordinates:

$$X = Length = Cosine\,(Angle)$$

$$Y = Length = Sine\,(Angle)$$

The following formula converts Cartesian to polar coordinates:

$$Angle = arctan2(Y, X)$$

$$Length = \sqrt{X^2 + Y^2}$$

Each of these mathematical functions (cosine, sine, arctan2, and square root) is available on the `System.Math` class: They are `Math.Cos()`, `Math.Sin()`, `Math.Atan2()`, and `Math.Sqrt()`, respectively. Note that these methods expect angles to be in radians, so you can either natively work in radians yourself or convert as needed:

$$Angle\ in\ radians = Angle\ in\ degrees \times \frac{2\pi}{360}$$

In addition to using vectors to represent a movement, you can use vectors in XNA to represent positions. In fact, this is what's happening when you pass `Vector2` into one of the `SpriteBatch.Draw()` methods. If you have one vector representing a position (such as the `tankPosition` field in the update example) and another vector representing a translation or movement, you can simply add these together to get the next position. This is what you did in the update method itself. Conversely, if you have two positions, you can get the difference between them by simply subtracting them. Just like plus (+), the minus (-) operator is overloaded on the `Vector2` class.

Table 11-2 lists some useful Vector2 mathematical operations and methods.

TABLE 11-2: `Vector2` Operations

OPERATION	EXAMPLE	EXPLANATION
Addition	`newLocation = oldLocation + speed;`	Represents movement (on locations) or acceleration (on translations).
Subtraction	`delta = thisPosition - thatPosition;`	Finds the difference between two locations.

Multiplication	`speed = speed * new Vector2(5,5)`
	 or
	 `speed = speed * 5`
	 or
	 `speed *= 5`
		Increases the speed/amount of translation. When multiplying a vector by a single number, the direction/angle is unchanged.

Division	`speed = speed / new Vector2(5,5)`
	 or
	 `speed = speed / 5`
	 or
	 `speed /= 5`
		Decreases speed/amount of translation.

Length	`float distance = delta.Length();`	Calculates the length of a vector using Pythagoras' theorem. `LengthSquared()` is a faster operation.

Normalize	`speed = speed / speed.Length();`
	 or
	 `speed.Normalize()`
		Makes a vector have a length of 1. This is useful when you want to set a speed to an absolute value without altering direction. Be sure to normalize the vector before you multiply it.

OPERATION	EXAMPLE	EXPLANATION
Clamp	`pos = Vector2.Clamp(pos, topLeft, btmRight);`	Returns a vector that has been "clamped" to stay inside a rectangle. Three vectors are required: the vector to clamp, the top-left (minimum) point of the rectangle, and the bottom-right (maximum) point of the rectangle. This is useful when you want to ensure that game elements stay onscreen.

Keeping in Time

Whenever you move an object in an XNA game, you should move it by a magnitude that's proportional to the passing of time. Because a phone's limited processor has to be shared with the built-in programs that keep the phone running, you can't guarantee that you will get an update call at a steady rate. This is where the `Update()` method's `gameTime` parameter comes in.

You may have noticed that both `Update()` and `Draw()` — the two parts of the XNA game loop — both accept a parameter of type `GameTime`. The `GameTime` class has only three properties:

➤ `ElapsedGameTime` — This `TimeSpan` property tells you how much time has passed since the last time the XNA framework called your method; it's tracked separately for `Update()` and `Draw()`. This will come in handy very soon.

➤ `TotalGameTime` — This `TimeSpan` property tells you how much time has passed since the game was first launched.

➤ `IsRunningSlowly` — This `bool` is true if the game is having trouble calling your methods at the required rate. You could consider deferring complex update or draw logic if this is the case.

In the next code example, you'll see how to use these properties to ensure that the game's state updates happen smoothly.

The TouchPanel Class

The primary sensor for reading input from a user is the touchscreen. Silverlight is event based and provides various touch events for you to subscribe to. XNA is more procedural: You're supposed to poll the sensors for information during your game's update phase. This is why XNA provides the static `TouchPanel` class. (Microsoft's full documentation on this class is available at http://msdn .microsoft.com/en-us/library/microsoft.xna.framework.input.touch.touchpanel.aspx.) Two types of input can be read from the `TouchPanel` class:

➤ **Gestures** — Gestures are high-level inputs, such as tap, double tap, pinch, and drag. (For a full list of gestures, see http://msdn.microsoft.com/en-us/library/microsoft.xna

.framework.input.touch.gesturetype.aspx). If you need to respond to something like a double tap, this is a great API because Microsoft engineers have already done the hard work of interpreting whether two taps are close enough to count as a double tap or two separate taps. In order to work with gestures, you need to do the following:

1. Register which gestures your game is interested in by setting the EnabledGestures property at the start of the game.

2. Check whether the IsGestureAvailable property is true during the update phase.

3. Call the ReadGesture() method to get information (an instance of a GestureSample) about the gesture that just occurred or is occurring.

➤ Touches — These are lower-level inputs than gestures. If you call the GetState() method, you get back a list of all the touches (zero to many instances of the TouchLocation class) that are currently applied to the phone's screen. By working with touches directly, you can glean more information faster, but you also need to write more code.

Driving the Tank

It's time to build a proper control system for the Tank game. You need some way for players to give input to the game and control the tank's movement. On a PC, you could listen for keypresses or mouse input. On an Xbox, you could listen for game pad presses. On Windows Phone 7, you could listen for screen touches, but you need to consider the unique physical aspects of the phone. One factor is that a human finger can't be seen through, so a game that forces users to keep their fingers on top of the action can get annoying. It's okay to have the user occasionally reach out and tap the screen, but for a function such as steering, it's a good idea to build a control system that stays at the edge of the game.

To create a Windows Phone 7 control system, you can build a thumbpad that sits at the bottom left of the screen, as in Figure 11-12.

 WARNING *The remaining Try It Out sections in this chapter build on the previous ones, so if you don't do them in order, you'll need to download the source code for this chapter and find the completed code for the Try It Out that you missed.*

FIGURE 11-12: A thumbpad.

TRY IT OUT Controlling the Tank with a Thumbpad

In the following steps, you control the tank with a thumbpad.

1. Create a new XNA Game project by selecting File ⇨ New Project ⇨ XNA Game Studio ⇨ Windows Phone Game.

2. Open the Game class and replace the constructor with the following code:

Available for
download on
Wrox.com

```
public Game1()
{
    graphics = new GraphicsDeviceManager(this)
    {
        PreferredBackBufferWidth = 800,
        PreferredBackBufferHeight = 480,
        SupportedOrientations = DisplayOrientation.LandscapeLeft,
        IsFullScreen = true,
    };

    Content.RootDirectory = "Content";

    // Frame rate is 30 fps by default for Windows Phone.
    TargetElapsedTime = TimeSpan.FromTicks(333333);
}
```

Code Snippet ControlTankWithThumb\Tank\Tank\Game1.cs

3. Add the tank image back to your content project, just as you did in the Try It Out titled "Drawing Images."

4. Add the thumbpad to your content project. You can provide your own 200 x 200 .png image or use the file Thumbpad.png provided in the downloadable zip file Chapter11.zip. If you use your own image, make sure it's called Thumbpad.png.

5. Add the following fields to your class to store these images:

Available for
download on
Wrox.com

```
public class Game1 : Game
{
    GraphicsDeviceManager graphics;
    SpriteBatch spriteBatch;

    Texture2D tankTexture;
    Texture2D padTexture;
```

Code Snippet ControlTankWithThumb\Tank\Tank\Game1.cs

6. Load these images in your LoadContent() method:

Available for
download on
Wrox.com

```
protected override void LoadContent()
{
    // Create a new SpriteBatch, which can be used to draw textures.
    spriteBatch = new SpriteBatch(GraphicsDevice);

    tankTexture = Content.Load<Texture2D>("Tank");
```

```
        padTexture = Content.Load<Texture2D>("Pad");
    }
```

Code Snippet ControlTankWithThumb\Tank\Tank\Game1.cs

7. Add the following fields to your class to store the state of your game:

```
public class Game1 : Game
{

    GraphicsDeviceManager graphics;
    SpriteBatch spriteBatch;

    Texture2D tankTexture;
    Texture2D padTexture;

    Rectangle padArea = new Rectangle(0, 280, 200, 200);

    Vector2 tankPosition = new Vector2(50, 50);
    float padAngle;
```

Code Snippet ControlTankWithThumb\Tank\Tank\Game1.cs

8. Update the `Draw()` method to render the thumbpad and the tank:

```
protected override void Draw(GameTime gameTime)
{
    GraphicsDevice.Clear(Color.Black);

    Vector2 padCenter = new Vector2(padArea.Center.X, padArea.Center.Y);

    spriteBatch.Begin();
    spriteBatch.Draw(tankTexture,
        tankPosition,
        null,
        Color.White,
        padAngle,
        new Vector2(20, 25),
        1,
        SpriteEffects.None,
        0);

    spriteBatch.Draw(padTexture,
        padCenter,
        null,
        Color.White,
        padAngle,
        new Vector2(100, 100),
        1,
        SpriteEffects.None,
        0);

    spriteBatch.End();

    base.Draw(gameTime);
}
```

Code Snippet ControlTankWithThumb\Tank\Tank\Game1.cs

9. Add the following code to your `Update()` method to update the state of the game (where the template has the comment `// TODO: Add your update logic here`):

```
// Find any touches inside the thumbpad's bounds
var touches = from touch in TouchPanel.GetState()
            let position = touch.Position
            where padArea.Contains((int)position.X, (int)position.Y)
            select position;

if (!touches.Any())
{
    return;
}

Vector2 padCenter = new Vector2(padArea.Center.X, padArea.Center.Y);
Vector2 padDelta = (touches.First() - padCenter);

float padRadius = padArea.Width / 2;
float padMagnitude = padDelta.Length() / padRadius;
padMagnitude = MathHelper.Clamp(padMagnitude, 0, 1f);

double elapsedSeconds = gameTime.ElapsedGameTime.TotalSeconds;
double magnitude = 300 * elapsedSeconds * padMagnitude;

Vector2 direction = padDelta;
direction.Normalize();

tankPosition += direction * (float)magnitude;

tankPosition = Vector2.Clamp(tankPosition,
    new Vector2(0, 0),
    new Vector2(800, 480));

padAngle = (float)Math.Atan2(padDelta.Y, padDelta.X);
```

Code Snippet ControlTankWithThumb\Tank\Tank\Game1.cs

10. Run your game to see what this new code does. Touch or click on the thumbpad to see the tank drive around.

How It Works

In this exercise, you first ensured that the XNA game would be able to load the required images by adding them to your content project. Then, you made these images available by creating fields to store them and loading them in your `LoadContent()` method.

In step 6, you declared your first "state" fields, which (unlike the other fields) are updated constantly by the game's `Update()` method. The field `tankPosition` stores the location where the tank should be drawn, and the field `padAngle` records the direction in which both the tank and the thumbpad should point. The field `padArea` is not conceptually a state variable; it's just declared as a field because at least two methods need to make use of the same rectangle.

Next, you drew the loaded images at the correct locations. Notice how the `padAngle` state variable is passed into each of the `spriteBatch.Draw()` methods; this rotates each image to point in the direction the user is driving the tank (calculated in step 8).

You implemented all the update logic for the game, which is complex:

➤   The first statement is a LINQ query to find all the touches that occurred within the bounds of the thumbpad. You check to see if there are in fact any of these touches, and if there aren't, you return from the `Update()` method. From now on, you are assuming that the user has in fact touched the thumbpad.

➤   The next lines calculated the vector difference (that is, delta) between the center of the thumbpad and the first of the user's touches. (You ignore all but the first touch on the thumbpad.) This delta is a raw indication of which direction the user is trying to drive the tank, and its length (that is, distance from the center) tells you the speed that the user wants:

```
Vector2 padCenter = new Vector2(padArea.Center.X, padArea.Center.Y);
Vector2 padDelta = (touches.First() - padCenter);
```

➤   Then you calculated the length of the delta as a ratio of the radius of the thumbpad. However, because the LINQ query picks up touches in the corner of the thumbpad, you need to clamp this ratio so that it can't be longer than 1:

```
float padRadius = padArea.Width / 2;
float padMagnitude = padDelta.Length() / padRadius;
padMagnitude = MathHelper.Clamp(padMagnitude, 0, 1f);
```

➤   The next lines multiplied the top speed of the tank (in pixels per second; currently 300) by the number of actual seconds that have passed since the last update and then by the magnitude of the user's current input. This variable, `magnitude`, becomes the length of the tank's movement.

```
double elapsedSeconds = gameTime.ElapsedGameTime.TotalSeconds;
double magnitude = 300 * elapsedSeconds * padMagnitude
```

➤   Then you made a copy of the actual delta, normalized it (to make its length 1), and translated the tank itself (`tankPosition`) by this normalized vector multiplied by the magnitude. This complex way of moving the tank ensures that the tank moves by exactly the right amount for the elapsed game time:

```
Vector2 direction = padDelta;
direction.Normalize();

tankPosition += direction * (float)magnitude;
```

➤   Then you clamped the tank's location to ensure that it didn't drive off the screen:

```
tankPosition = Vector2.Clamp(tankPosition,
    new Vector2(0, 0),
    new Vector2(800, 480));
```

➤   Finally, you calculated the angle at which the tank and thumbpad should point:

```
padAngle = (float)Math.Atan2(padDelta.Y, padDelta.X);
```

SIMPLIFYING YOUR CODE WITH GAME COMPONENTS

So far, you've written all your code in one file, the Game subclass. You've not done anything too complicated, but you can see how your Update() and Draw() methods get longer every time you add a feature to your game. You're going to be writing a lot more code soon, and you wouldn't be following good object-oriented design principles if you just kept tacking code onto the same method.

One of the tenets of object-oriented programming is modularity. The concept of modularity involves separating concerns into distinct areas, as well as formalizing interfaces (that is, how one module is allowed to interact with another). Normally, when two classes interact with one another through just the public methods, fields, and properties, there is a high degree of modularity. This is achieved because each class is hiding relatively numerous and complex methods and fields with the private keyword, publishing (through the public keyword) only what other classes need to know about. However, when all the code is in one big class, all fields and methods are effectively public, and there's no easy way to tell what code fulfills what concern. (Okay, you can tell what code does drawing — it's in the Draw() method — but there's no way to tell tank code from thumbpad code.)

What you need to do is separate the responsibilities out into different classes. Conceptually (and object-oriented design is about modeling concepts, not necessarily modeling physical things), the Tank game contains two "things" right now: a tank and a thumbpad. Let's look at how you can use some helpful classes in XNA to encapsulate these responsibilities.

The GameComponent and DrawableGameComponent Classes

Conceptually, a GameComponent class is a modular part (or component) of a game. Technically, it's a subclass (that you write yourself) of Microsoft.Xna.Framework.GameComponent. A game has a collection of these (Components), and in your Game subclass, you'd add new instances of your GameComponent classes.

As with Game, methods that you should override on GameComponent include Initialize() and Update(). These are called by the parent Game method at the appropriate times. You can set the Enabled (a Boolean) and UpdateOrder (an integer) properties to control whether and when the Update() method is called.

Have you noticed what's missing? A GameComponent class is not actually designed to do any drawing; it's for things that merely process an update message. If you create a subclass of DrawableGameComponent instead, you'll also be able to override the LoadContent() and Draw() methods. For the purposes of the Tank game, these are all you need to create.

The DrawableGameComponent class declares very similar methods to Game. When you add these to your game's Components collection, the game becomes responsible for calling these methods at the appropriate times. However, the game can't update or draw its subcomponents if you've overridden the Update() or Draw() methods on your game and omitted the call to base.Update() or base.Draw().

 NOTE *The base class,* DrawableGameComponent, *requires the current* Game *method to be passed to its constructor. This is then made available through a property named* Game.

Sharing Services

One special consideration is that the main `Game` method will declare a `SpriteBatch` object, and it needs to share its `SpriteBatch` object with its components. If the `SpriteBatch` object is created after the game's components (which is usually the case), you can still make the `SpriteBatch` object available to the components by putting the `SpriteBatch` object into the game's `Services` collection. This is the recommended approach for sharing services between components with XNA.

Cross-Component Communication

If everything is in your `Game` class, then all fields are available to each feature of the game. Although this is convenient, it doesn't reflect good object-oriented programming practices. Specifically, it violates the principle of *encapsulation*. A well-encapsulated piece of code calls only public methods and properties of another class. This means that the implementation beneath the public interface of that other class is free to change, and you'll be less likely to break a large section of your system.

TRY IT OUT Introducing GameComponents

You can refactor your current game into a form that will make it much easier to add more features. You start by creating a reusable base class (that inherits from `DrawableGameComponent`). After that, you can move much of the code from the `Game` class `TankGameComponent` subclasses. Here are the steps:

1. Add a new class, called **TankGameComponent,** to your game project and implement it as shown in Listing 11-1. Notice how it inherits from `DrawableGameComponent`:

Available for download on Wrox.com

LISTING 11-1: The new TankGameComponent class

```
public class TankGameComponent : DrawableGameComponent
{
    protected SpriteBatch spriteBatch;

    public TankGameComponent(Game game)
        : base(game)
    {
    }

    public override void Initialize()
    {
        spriteBatch = (SpriteBatch)Game.Services.GetService(typeof(SpriteBatch));
        base.Initialize();
    }
}
```

Code Snippet GameComponents\Tank\Tank\GameComponents\TankGameComponent.cs

2. Add another class, called `Thumbpad`, to your game project. Add the code from Listing 11-2 to the `Thumbpad` class:

LISTING 11-2: The new Thumbpad base class

```csharp
public class Thumbpad : TankGameComponent
{
    Texture2D padTexture;
    Rectangle padArea = new Rectangle(0, 280, 200, 200);
    float angle;
    Vector2 movement;

    public Thumbpad(Game game)
        : base(game)
    {
        DrawOrder = int.MaxValue;
        UpdateOrder = int.MinValue;
    }

    public float Angle
    {
        get { return angle; }
    }

    public Vector2 Movement
    {
        get { return movement; }
    }

    protected override void LoadContent()
    {
        padTexture = Game.Content.Load<Texture2D>("Pad");
    }

    public override void Update(GameTime gameTime)
    {

        // Find any touches inside the thumbpad's bounds
        var touches = from touch in TouchPanel.GetState()
                    let p = touch.Position
                    where padArea.Contains((int)p.X, (int)p.Y)
                    select p;


        movement = Vector2.Zero;

        if (touches.Any())
        {
            Vector2 padCenter = new Vector2(padArea.Center.X, padArea.Center.Y);
            Vector2 padDelta = (touches.First() - padCenter);

            if(padDelta != Vector2.Zero)
            {
                float padRadius = padArea.Width / 2f;
                float padMagnitude = padDelta.Length() / padRadius;
```

continues

LISTING 11-2 *(continued)*

```
            padMagnitude = MathHelper.Clamp(padMagnitude, 0, 1f);

            Vector2 direction = padDelta;
            direction.Normalize();

            movement = direction * padMagnitude;
            angle = (float)Math.Atan2(padDelta.Y, padDelta.X);
        }
    }
}

public override void Draw(GameTime gameTime)
{
    Vector2 padCenter = new Vector2(padArea.Center.X, padArea.Center.Y);
    spriteBatch.Draw(padTexture,
                padCenter,
                null,
                Color.White,
                Angle,
                new Vector2(100, 100),
                1,
                SpriteEffects.None,
                0);
    }
}
```

Code Snippet GameComponents\Tank\Tank\GameComponents\Thumbpad.cs

3. Add another class, called PlayerTank, to your game. Implement with the code in Listing 11-3:

LISTING 11-3: The new PlayerTank class

```
public class PlayerTank : TankGameComponent
{
    Texture2D tankTexture;
    Vector2 tankPosition = new Vector2(50, 50);
    Thumbpad thumbpad;

    public PlayerTank(Game game, Thumbpad thumbpad)
        : base(game)
    {
        this.thumbpad = thumbpad;
    }

    protected override void LoadContent()
    {
        tankTexture = Game.Content.Load<Texture2D>("Tank");
    }

    public override void Update(GameTime gameTime)
    {
        double elapsedSeconds = gameTime.ElapsedGameTime.TotalSeconds;
```

```
        double speed = 300 * elapsedSeconds;

        Vector2 thumbpadMovement = thumbpad.Movement;

        tankPosition += thumbpadMovement*(float) speed;

        tankPosition = Vector2.Clamp(tankPosition,
                            new Vector2(0, 0),
                            new Vector2(800, 480));
    }

    public override void Draw(GameTime gameTime)
    {
        float thumbpadAngle = thumbpad.Angle;

        spriteBatch.Draw(tankTexture,
                    tankPosition,
                    null,
                    Color.White,
                    thumbpadAngle,
                    new Vector2(20, 25),
                    1,
                    SpriteEffects.None,
                    0);
    }
}
```

Code Snippet GameComponents\Tank\Tank\GameComponents\PlayerTank.cs

4. Now that these features exist outside the game, you can simplify the Game class to match Listing 11-4:

LISTING 11-4: The updated and simplified Game1 class

```
public class Game1 : Game
{
    GraphicsDeviceManager graphics;
    SpriteBatch spriteBatch;

    public Game1()
    {
        graphics = new GraphicsDeviceManager(this)
                    {
                        PreferredBackBufferWidth = 800,
                        PreferredBackBufferHeight = 480,
                        SupportedOrientations = DisplayOrientation.LandscapeLeft,
                        IsFullScreen = true,
                    };

        Content.RootDirectory = "Content";
```

continues

LISTING 11-4 *(continued)*

```
        TargetElapsedTime = TimeSpan.FromTicks(333333);

        // create and add GameComponents
        Thumbpad thumbpad = new Thumbpad(this);
        Components.Add(thumbpad);
        Components.Add(new PlayerTank(this, thumbpad));
    }

    protected override void Initialize()
    {
        spriteBatch = new SpriteBatch(GraphicsDevice);
        Services.AddService(typeof(SpriteBatch), spriteBatch);
        base.Initialize();
    }


    protected override void Update(GameTime gameTime)
    {
        // Allows the game to exit
        GamePadState gamePadState = GamePad.GetState(PlayerIndex.One);
        if (gamePadState.Buttons.Back == ButtonState.Pressed)
           this.Exit();

        base.Update(gameTime);
    }

    protected override void Draw(GameTime gameTime)
    {
        GraphicsDevice.Clear(Color.Black);

        spriteBatch.Begin();
        base.Draw(gameTime);
        spriteBatch.End();
    }
}
```

Code Snippet GameComponents\Tank\Tank\Game1.cs

5. Run your game. It should behave exactly the way it used to behave. You've simply introduced encapsulation into the program.

How It Works

In this exercise, you created a helpful base class for all your drawable game components to inherit from. Because you're building a 2-D game, all drawable game components need access to the game's SpriteBatch class. This class simply loads SpriteBatch from the game's services collection, ready for use before Draw() is ever called.

Next, you extracted all the thumbpad-related features out of the game into a new game component. This new class inherits from your new base class, so it's able to simply reference spriteBatch within its Draw() method. It has fields for the thumbpad's angle and the movement that the current thumbpad interaction represents. It now exposes these as public properties. This means that other components can read these properties from the class, even though they're private. The `Update()` method and the `Draw()` method are essentially cut straight out of the game class.

You also extracted all the Tank-related features of the game into another game component. As with the thumbpad, the trigger component inherits from your new base class because it needs access to the `SpriteBatch` class. Note that now that `PlayerTank` doesn't have direct access to the fields that represent the thumbpad's state anymore, it uses a reference to the thumbpad to read these values via the public properties. This is an example of the desirable object-oriented property of *encapsulation*. At first, encapsulation might seem like a lot of extra work, but as your game gets more and more complex, and you make changes to the way things work, encapsulation makes it much easier to change the way things work. You could have placed the thumbpad into the Game's `Services` collection, allowing `PlayerTank` to retrieve the thumbpad from there, but instead you've made this dependency as obvious to other programmers as possible by passing it through the constructor.

Figure 11-13 shows the inheritance hierarchy of the new game components.

In step 4, you updated the `Game` class to accommodate the new game components. The constructor now performs the very important job of creating instances of the new classes and adding them to the game's collection of game components:

```
// create and add GameComponents
Thumbpad thumbpad = new Thumbpad(this);
Components.Add(thumbpad);
Components.Add(new PlayerTank(this, thumbpad));
```

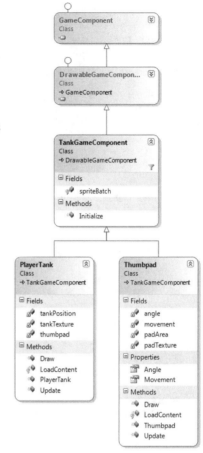

FIGURE 11-13: The game component hierarchy.

If you leave out this step, nothing will ever call the methods of your components, and your game will look like it's doing nothing.

The new `Initialize()` method now makes the `SpriteBatch` class available to the `TankGameComponent` objects, and the call to `base.Initialize()` ensures that all the `GameComponent` objects have their own `Initialize()` methods called. All the `Update()` method needs to do now is ensure that the game's components have their `Update()` methods called. However, the `Draw()` method has to begin the `SpriteBatch` class before the child components have their `Draw()` method called. The `Game` class is now much more maintainable because the only thing it is responsible for is creating and managing its components.

How to Create a Trigger Thumbpad

Now that you have a taste for inheritance, you can use it to add a new feature to the Tank game. Say that you want a second thumbpad on the right hand side of the screen. Unlike the first thumbpad, it's just a trigger that you press, so instead of having `Angle` and `Movement` properties, it will have a single `IsPressed` property. Now that there are two different kinds of thumbpad, you need to reconsider the names you're giving your classes. One thumbpad controls the tank like a joystick (so call it `Joystick`), and the other is a trigger button (that you can call `Trigger`). They will probably need to share some code, so you can call the common base class `Thumbpad`. Figure 11-14 demonstrates this new class hierarchy.

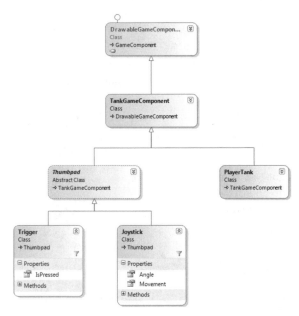

FIGURE 11-14: Joystick and trigger inheritance hierarchy.

These two classes have the following in common:

➤ They both have a display area.

➤ They both analyze touches that occur in the display area during the update phase.

➤ They both render a single texture to the game screen.

➤ They both need to be called at the beginning of the update phase and at the end of the draw phase.

TRY IT OUT Creating a Trigger Thumbpad

In the following steps, you create a trigger thumbpad.

1. Add a new image, named `target.png`, to your content project. You can use the one provided in `Chapter11.zip`, which looks as shown in Figure 11-15.

2. Update your `Thumbpad` class so that it matches Listing 11-5:

FIGURE 11-15
`target.png`.

LISTING 11-5: The updated Thumbpad base class

```
public abstract class Thumbpad : TankGameComponent
{
    readonly string textureName;
    readonly protected Rectangle padArea;
    protected Texture2D padTexture;

    protected Thumbpad(Game game, Rectangle padArea, string textureName)
        : base(game)
    {
        this.padArea = padArea;
        this.textureName = textureName;
        DrawOrder = int.MaxValue;
        UpdateOrder = int.MinValue;
    }

    protected override void LoadContent()
    {
        padTexture = Game.Content.Load<Texture2D>(textureName);
    }


    public override void Update(GameTime gameTime)
    {
        var touches = from touch in TouchPanel.GetState()
                    let position = touch.Position
                    where padArea.Contains((int)position.X, (int)position.Y)
                    select position;

        UpdateWithTouches(touches);
    }

    protected abstract void UpdateWithTouches(IEnumerable<Vector2> touches);
}
```

Code Snippet GameComponentsWithThumbpad\Tank\Tank\GameComponents\Thumbpad.cs

3. Create a new class called `Joystick` with the content from Listing 11-6:

LISTING 11-6: The new Joystick class

```
public class Joystick : Thumbpad
{
    float angle;
    Vector2 movement;

    public Joystick(Game game)
        : base(game, new Rectangle(0, 280, 200, 200), "Pad")
    {
```

continues

LISTING 11-6 *(continued)*

```
    }

    public float Angle
    {
        get { return angle; }
    }

    public Vector2 Movement
    {
        get { return movement; }
    }

    protected override void UpdateWithTouches(IEnumerable<Vector2> touches)
    {
        movement = Vector2.Zero;

        if (!touches.Any())
        {
            return;
        }

        Vector2 padCenter = new Vector2(padArea.Center.X, padArea.Center.Y);
        Vector2 padDelta = (touches.First() - padCenter);

        if (padDelta != Vector2.Zero)
        {
            float padRadius = padArea.Width / 2f;
            float padMagnitude = padDelta.Length() / padRadius;
            padMagnitude = MathHelper.Clamp(padMagnitude, 0, 1f);

            Vector2 direction = padDelta;
            direction.Normalize();

            movement = direction * padMagnitude;
            angle = (float)Math.Atan2(padDelta.Y, padDelta.X);
        }
    }

    public override void Draw(GameTime gameTime)
    {
        Vector2 location = new Vector2(padArea.Center.X, padArea.Center.Y);
        Vector2 spriteCenter = new Vector2(padArea.Width, padArea.Height) / 2f;
        spriteBatch.Draw(padTexture,
            location,
            null,
            Color.White,
            Angle,
            spriteCenter,
            1,
            SpriteEffects.None,
            0);
    }
}
```

4. Create a new class called `Trigger` with the code from Listing 11-7:

LISTING 11-7: The new Trigger class

```
public class Trigger : Thumbpad
{
    bool isPressed; //true if the trigger is being touched

    public Trigger(Game game)
        : base(game, new Rectangle(600, 280, 200, 200), "Target")
    {
    }

    public bool IsPressed
    {
        get { return isPressed; }
    }

    protected override void UpdateWithTouches(IEnumerable<Vector2> touches)
    {
        isPressed = touches.Any();
    }

    public override void Draw(GameTime gameTime)
    {
        Color tint = IsPressed ? Color.Orange : Color.White;
        spriteBatch.Draw(padTexture, padArea, tint);
    }
}
```

Code Snippet GameComponentsWithThumbpad\Tank\Tank\GameComponents\Trigger.cs

5. Change your game's constructor so that it looks like Listing 11-8:

LISTING 11-8: The updated Game1 class

```
public Game1()
{
    Rectangle area = new Rectangle(0, 0, 800, 480);
    graphics = new GraphicsDeviceManager(this)
    {
        PreferredBackBufferWidth = area.Width,
        PreferredBackBufferHeight = area.Height,
        SupportedOrientations = DisplayOrientation.LandscapeLeft,
        IsFullScreen = true, // gets rid of the status bar
    };


    Content.RootDirectory = "Content";
```

continues

LISTING 11-8 *(continued)*

```
    TargetElapsedTime = TimeSpan.FromTicks(333333);

    // setup components:
    Joystick joystick = new Joystick(this);
    Trigger trigger = new Trigger(this);
    PlayerTank tank = new PlayerTank(this, joystick, trigger, area);

    Components.Add(trigger);
    Components.Add(joystick);
    Components.Add(tank);
}
```

Code Snippet GameComponentsWithThumbpad\Tank\Tank\Game1.cs

6. Update your `PlayerTank` class so that it looks like Listing 11-9:

LISTING 11-9: The updated PlayerTank class

Available for
download on
Wrox.com

```
public class PlayerTank : TankGameComponent
{
    readonly Joystick joystick;
    readonly Trigger trigger;
    readonly Rectangle tankBounds;

    Texture2D tankTexture;
    Vector2 tankPosition = new Vector2(50, 50);


    public PlayerTank(Game game, Joystick joystick, Trigger trigger, Rectangle rect)
        : base(game)
    {
        this.joystick = joystick;
        this.trigger = trigger;
        this.tankBounds = rect;
    }

    protected override void LoadContent()
    {
        tankTexture = Game.Content.Load<Texture2D>("Tank");
    }

    public override void Update(GameTime gameTime)
    {
        double elapsedSeconds = gameTime.ElapsedGameTime.TotalSeconds;
        double speed = 300 * elapsedSeconds;

        Vector2 joystickMovement = joystick.Movement;

        tankPosition += joystickMovement*(float) speed;

        tankPosition = Vector2.Clamp(tankPosition,
                            new Vector2(0, 0),
```

```
                             new Vector2(800, 480));
    }

    public override void Draw(GameTime gameTime)
    {
        float joystickAngle = joystick.Angle;

        spriteBatch.Draw(tankTexture,
                    tankPosition,
                    null,
                    Color.White,
                    joystickAngle,
                    new Vector2(20, 25),
                    1,
                    SpriteEffects.None,
                    0);
    }
}
```

Code Snippet GameComponentsWithThumbpad\Tank\Tank\GameComponents\PlayerTank.cs

7. Run the game to see the effect of your changes. You should see both thumbpads on the screen, and the trigger should turn orange when pressed.

How It Works

First, you added an image to your content project to represent the trigger thumbpad.

Then, you altered the Thumbpad class to make it a reusable base class for Trigger and Joystick. This involved:

➤ Making the class abstract in order to support the abstract method UpdateWithTouches().

➤ Requiring a string called textureName to be passed into the constructor. This is used to load the texture for this thumbpad, padTexture.

➤ Requiring a Rectangle object that represents the area of this thumbpad. This is used by the Update() method, when filtering out the current touches, ready to pass to the abstract method UpdateWithTouches().

Next, you created the first Thumbpad subclass: Joystick. You passed the correct area rectangle and the correct texture name to the base class constructor. You provided an implementation of the UpdateWithTouches() method that replicates the behavior of the old thumbpad.

You then declared the new Trigger class. This class has a different area than the joystick. The Rectangle object (with the x, y, width and height arguments of 600, 280, 200, 200) represents the bottom-right side of the screen. This area, along with the texture name Target, is passed to the base class:

```
public Trigger(Game game)
    : base(game, new Rectangle(600, 280, 200, 200), "Target")
```

In this new class, you provided a very simple implementation of the `UpdateWithTouches()` method, which simply checks whether the user is touching anywhere inside the trigger. This property, `IsPressed`, is made available to other classes through a public property:

```
public bool IsPressed
{
    get { return isPressed; }
}
```

In the `Draw()` method, a tint of orange is applied to the drawing if the trigger is currently pressed.

Next, you updated the `Game` class to correctly instantiate and track its components, including the new `Trigger` class.

Finally, you updated the `PlayerTank` class to accept both of the thumbpads in its constructor. You added fields to track these, and you renamed the variables that used to refer to `thumbpad` to now refer to `joystick`, since this is now the class that handles driving the tank.

GameComponent Life Cycles

In the Tank game, you've added all the components to the game in the game's constructor. However, it's conceivable that some components might have their own lifetime within the context of a play session. For example, you might write a `GameComponent` object that represents the high score screen and have it added to the game only when a level is completed. To go back to playing, the user can then just remove the high score screen. However, it's not a good idea to add and remove game components many times a second because doing so involves performance overhead, and things like the draw and update order of the game's components become difficult to manage. The upcoming section "Handling Many Objects Efficiently" looks at a better way to handle short-lived game components.

MORE XNA TIPS AND TRICKS

You've learned the basic building blocks of XNA, which are required for practically every XNA game. This section presents a number of techniques that may come in handy as you build the rest of the game components required to complete the Tank game.

Handling Many Objects Efficiently

Now that you have a trigger on your screen, say that you want to make bullets come out of the tank when you hold down the trigger. This is the first time you've needed transient objects in the game — that is, things that are on the screen for only a limited period of time. Conceivably, you could add a `GameComponent` object called `Bullet` to the game every time the tank fires, and you could remove it when it hits enemies or a wall. However, it's not efficient to keep adding and removing `GameComponent` objects from the game, and the logical flow might become difficult to follow if a component is removing itself from the game during an update.

Rather than think of each component as an *entity* within the game, you can think about each component taking responsibility for a *concept* within the game. There's only one player tank, one joystick, and one trigger, so you can just create a GameComponent object to represent these. If you're going to need many game entities to appear and disappear during the game, then you should write a single GameComponent object to manage all these entities at once. Of course, you'll likely need a class to represent each entity, but you should make a single GameComponent object to manage a list of these instead. Listing 11-10 is how you'd write a class that represents all the tank's bullets on the screen:

LISTING 11-10: The new Particle class

Available for
download on
Wrox.com

```
public class Particle
{
    public Particle(Vector2 position, float angle, float velocity)
    {
        Position = position;
        Angle = angle;
        Velocity = velocity;
    }

    public Vector2 Position { get; set; }
    public float Angle { get; set; }
    public float Velocity { get; set; }

    public void Move(TimeSpan elapsedGameTime)
    {
        float length = (float)(Velocity * elapsedGameTime.TotalSeconds);
        Vector2 v = new Vector2((float)Math.Cos(Angle),
                                (float)Math.Sin(Angle));

        Position += v * length;
    }

    public bool IsInside(Rectangle rectangle)
    {
        return rectangle.Contains((int)Position.X, (int)Position.Y);
    }

    public bool IsNear(Vector2 other, int distance)
    {
        // compare the square of two distances since sqrt takes extra calculations
        return (Position - other).LengthSquared() < distance * distance;
    }
}
```

Code Snippet Tank\Tank\Tank\GameComponents\Particle.cs

This class is essentially just for storing information — a position, an angle, and a velocity. This information is all stored in public properties, which must be initialized by the constructor.

The preceding example makes use of a few methods:

➤ **Move()** — This method simply moves Particle by the right number of pixels (elapsed game time in seconds multiplied by velocity).

➤ **IsInside()** — This method can tell you if the Particle is inside any specified rectangle.

➤ **IsNear()** — This method compares the distance of this particle's Position to another Vector2 object. Because Length() is a much more expensive operation than LengthSquared(), this method opts to compare the distance between two points *squared* with the specified distance *squared*.

Now you can write a GameComponent object called BulletManager,- whose primary responsibility is to track the location of each bullet Particle, as shown in Listing 11-11.

LISTING 11-11: The new BulletManager class

```csharp
public class BulletManager : TankGameComponent
{
    readonly List<Particle> bullets = new List<Particle>();
    readonly PlayerTank tank;
    readonly Rectangle bulletBounds;

    Texture2D texture;

    public BulletManager(Game game, PlayerTank tank, Rectangle bulletBounds)
        : base(game)
    {
        this.tank = tank;
        this.bulletBounds = bulletBounds;

        tank.BulletFired += Tank_OnBulletFired;
    }

    public List<Particle> Bullets
    {
        get { return bullets; }
    }

    void Tank_OnBulletFired(object sender, EventArgs eventArgs)
    {
        bullets.Add(new Particle(tank.Position, tank.Angle, 700));
    }

    protected override void LoadContent()
    {
        texture = Game.Content.Load<Texture2D>("Bullet");
    }

    public override void Update(GameTime gameTime)
    {
        RemoveOutOfBoundsBullets();
        MoveBullets(gameTime);
```

```
    }

    void RemoveOutOfBoundsBullets()
    {
        for (int i = bullets.Count - 1; i >= 0; i--)
        {
            if (!bullets[i].IsInside(bulletBounds))
            {
                bullets.RemoveAt(i);
            }
        }
    }

    void MoveBullets(GameTime gameTime)
    {
        foreach (Particle bullet in bullets)
        {
            bullet.Move(gameTime.ElapsedGameTime);
        }
    }

    public override void Draw(GameTime gameTime)
    {
        foreach (Particle m in bullets)
        {
            spriteBatch.Draw(texture, m.Position - new Vector2(5), Color.White);
        }
    }
}
```

Code Snippet Tank\Tank\Tank\GameComponents\BulletManager.cs

This class keeps a list of `Particle` objects named `bullets`. The `BulletManager` constructor requires `Game` (like all `GameComponent` objects), `PlayerTank`, and `Rectangle` (which represents the bounds of the game; bullets that fly out of this area should be thrown away, or they will pointlessly eat up memory and processor cycles).

In the constructor you subscribe to the `BulletFired` event on `PlayerTank`. This event should be raised by `PlayerTank` whenever it wants to signal to other components that it's fired its cannon; you'll see the implementation of this soon. The `Tank_OnBulletFired()` method handles this event by adding a new `Particle` object to the `Bullets` collection. The `Update()` method has two responsibilities, which have been split into separate methods. In the `RemoveOutOfBoundsBullets()` method, you loop through the list of bullets, removing any that have left the bounds of the game:

```
    void RemoveOutOfBoundsBullets()
    {
        for (int i = bullets.Count - 1; i >= 0; i--)
        {
            if (!bullets[i].IsInside(bulletBounds))
            {
                bullets.RemoveAt(i);
            }
        }
    }
```

Note that this isn't an ordinary `for` loop (let alone `for each`); by looping backward, you can avoid getting into trouble as you remove items from the very collection you loop through. In the `MoveBullets()` method, you simply allow each bullet to move. Drawing is a simple matter of drawing the bullet `texture`, centered at each bullet's `Position`.

Listing 11-12 shows the new and improved `PlayerTank` class, modified to trigger an event whenever the `Trigger` component is being touched. The class keeps track of the last time a bullet was fired in order to limit the rate at which the player can fire bullets:

LISTING 11-12: The updated PlayerTank class

```
public class PlayerTank : TankGameComponent
{
    readonly Joystick joystick;
    readonly Trigger trigger;
    readonly Rectangle tankBounds;
    readonly TimeSpan fireRate = TimeSpan.FromMilliseconds(600);

    TimeSpan lastHurt = TimeSpan.FromSeconds(-60);
    Texture2D texture;
    TimeSpan lastShot;
    Vector2 origin;

    public event EventHandler BulletFired;

    public PlayerTank(Game game, Joystick joystick, Trigger trigger, Rectangle rect)
        : base(game)
    {
        this.joystick = joystick;
        this.trigger = trigger;
        this.tankBounds = rect;
        Position = new Vector2(300, 300);
    }

    public Vector2 Position { get; private set; }
    public int DamageTaken { get; set; }
    public int Kills { get; set; }
    public float Angle { get { return joystick.Angle; } }

    public void Damage(GameTime gameTime, int damage)
    {
        lastHurt = gameTime.TotalGameTime;
        DamageTaken += damage;
    }

    protected override void LoadContent()
    {
        texture = Game.Content.Load<Texture2D>("Tank");
    }

    public override void Update(GameTime gameTime)
    {
```

```
        double elapsedSeconds = gameTime.ElapsedGameTime.TotalSeconds;
        double speed = 300 * elapsedSeconds;

        Position += joystick.Movement * (float)speed;

        Position = Vector2.Clamp(Position,
                          new Vector2(tankBounds.Left, tankBounds.Top),
                          new Vector2(tankBounds.Right, tankBounds.Bottom));

        if (trigger.IsPressed)
        {
            if ((gameTime.TotalGameTime - lastShot) > fireRate)
            {
                if (BulletFired != null)
                {
                    BulletFired(this, EventArgs.Empty);
                }
                lastShot = gameTime.TotalGameTime;
            }
        }
    }

    public override void Draw(GameTime gameTime)
    {
        bool recentlyHurt = (gameTime.TotalGameTime - lastHurt).TotalSeconds < 0.5;
        Color color = recentlyHurt ? Color.Red : Color.White;
        origin = new Vector2(30, 20);
        const SpriteEffects None = SpriteEffects.None;
        spriteBatch.Draw(texture, Position, null, color, Angle, origin, 1, None, 0);
    }

}
```

Code Snippet Tank\Tank\Tank\GameComponents\PlayerTank.cs

In the `Update()` method you check the time since the last shot, and only if a `TimeSpan` value greater than `fireRate` has passed do you fire the cannon again. `lastShot` is then reset. There's another new method (and associated fields), called `Damage()`, which you'll make use of soon. If you'd like to go ahead and run the game now, you just need to change your `Game` class to match Listing 11-13:

LISTING 11-13: Updating the Game class

```
public class TankGame : Game
    {
        readonly GraphicsDeviceManager graphics;

        public TankGame()
        {
            Content.RootDirectory = "Content";

            Rectangle area = new Rectangle(0, 0, 800, 480);
            graphics = new GraphicsDeviceManager(this)
                {
```

continues

LISTING 11-13 *(continued)*

```
                        PreferredBackBufferWidth = area.Width,
                        PreferredBackBufferHeight = area.Height,
                        SupportedOrientations = DisplayOrientation.LandscapeLeft,
                        IsFullScreen = true, // gets rid of the status bar
                };


        // Frame rate is 30 fps by default for Windows Phone.
        TargetElapsedTime = TimeSpan.FromTicks(333333);

        // setup components:
        Joystick joystick = new Joystick(this);
        Trigger trigger = new Trigger(this);
        PlayerTank tank = new PlayerTank(this, joystick, trigger, area);
        BulletManager bulletManager = new BulletManager(this, tank, area);

        Components.Add(trigger);
        Components.Add(joystick);
        Components.Add(tank);
        Components.Add(bulletManager);
    }

    private SpriteBatch spriteBatch;

    protected override void Initialize()
    {
        spriteBatch = new SpriteBatch(GraphicsDevice);
        Services.AddService(typeof(SpriteBatch), spriteBatch);
        base.Initialize();
    }

    protected override void Update(GameTime gameTime)
    {
        // Allows the game to exit
        if (GamePad.GetState(PlayerIndex.One).Buttons.Back == ButtonState.Pressed)
            Exit();
        base.Update(gameTime);
    }

    protected override void Draw(GameTime gameTime)
    {
        GraphicsDevice.Clear(Color.Black);
        spriteBatch.Begin();
        base.Draw(gameTime);
        spriteBatch.End();
    }
}
```

Code Snippet Tank\Tank\Tank\TankGame.cs

You should now be able to control the tank and fire bullets.

Playing Sounds

You can play sound effects in XNA. There are actually two types of sounds in the XNA framework: SoundEffect objects are short-lived sounds that play in response to something happening in the game, and Song objects are meant for long-playing, ambient music. If you'd like to play music throughout the duration of a game, with the possibility of pulling music from the phone's own music collection, you should look into the Microsoft.Xna.Framework.Media.Song and Microsoft.Xna.Framework.Media.MediaPlayer classes. For the Tank game, assume that you just want to play a sound effect whenever the tank fires its cannon.

First, you need to add to your content project a sound file such as a WMA or MP3 file. We've provided one called Canon.mp3 in the downloadable Chapter11.zip. Next, you need to load the resource as a SoundEffect object:

Available for download on Wrox.com

```
protected override void LoadContent()
{
    texture = Game.Content.Load<Texture2D>("Bullet");
    cannon = Game.Content.Load<SoundEffect>("Cannon");
}
```

Code Snippet Tank\Tank\Tank\GameComponents\Bulletmanager.cs

Don't forget to declare a field to hold this SoundEffect:

Available for download on Wrox.com

```
public class BulletManager : TankGameComponent
{
    readonly List<Particle> bullets = new List<Particle>();
    readonly PlayerTank tank;
    readonly Rectangle bulletBounds;

    Texture2D texture;
    SoundEffect cannon;
```

Code Snippet Tank\Tank\Tank\GameComponents\Bulletmanager.cs

Finally, you need to call Play() on this SoundEffect object at the appropriate time:

Available for download on Wrox.com

```
void Tank_OnBulletFired(object sender, EventArgs eventArgs)
{
    bullets.Add(new Particle(tank.Position, tank.Angle, 700, TimeSpan.Zero));
    cannon.Play(1, 0, tank.Position.X / bulletBounds.Width - 0.5f);
}
```

Code Snippet Tank\Tank\Tank\GameComponents\Bulletmanager.cs

Advanced Geometry: Homing Missiles

As with BulletManager, you might like to create a GameComponent object that manages a collection of enemy missiles. These missiles could fly around the screen, homing in on the tank's location, and if they hit the tank, the tank could take some damage. If a tank's bullet hits a missile, the missile should be destroyed. For now, let's look at how to copy the `BulletManager` object and make the enemy missiles home in on the tank. You'll need the texture `Enemy.png` available in your content project.

Add the following code from Listing 11-14 to a new `MissileManager` class in your project.

LISTING 11-14: The new MissileManager class

```
public class MissileManager : TankGameComponent
{
    readonly List<Particle> missiles = new List<Particle>();
    readonly PlayerTank tank;
    readonly Rectangle missileBounds;

    Texture2D texture;

    public MissileManager(Game game, PlayerTank tank, Rectangle missileBounds)
        : base(game)
    {
        this.tank = tank;
        this.missileBounds = missileBounds;
    }

    public List<Particle> Missiles
    {
        get { return missiles; }
    }

    protected override void LoadContent()
    {
        texture = Game.Content.Load<Texture2D>("Enemy");
    }

    public override void Update(GameTime gameTime)
    {
        RemoveOutOfBoundsMissiles();
        MoveMissiles(gameTime);
    }

    void RemoveOutOfBoundsMissiles()
    {
        for (int i = missiles.Count - 1; i >= 0; i--)
        {
            if (!missiles[i].IsInside(missileBounds))
            {
                missiles.RemoveAt(i);
            }
        }
    }

    void MoveMissiles(GameTime gameTime)
    {
```

```
        foreach (var missile in missiles)
        {
            double rotation = gameTime.ElapsedGameTime.TotalSeconds * 0.7;
            missile.HomeOn(tank.Position, (float)rotation);
            missile.Move(gameTime.ElapsedGameTime);
        }
    }

    public override void Draw(GameTime gameTime)
    {
        foreach (var missile in missiles)
        {
            spriteBatch.Draw(texture,
                missile.Position,
                null,
                Color.White,
                missile.Angle,
                new Vector2(30, 30),
                1,
                SpriteEffects.None,
                0);
        }
    }

    public void SpawnMissile(Vector2 position, float angle)
    {
        missiles.Add(new Particle(position, angle, 130));
    }
}
```

Code Snippet Tank\Tank\Tank\GameComponents\MissileManager.cs

As you can see, `MissileManager` is very similar to `BulletManager`, except that it doesn't subscribe to the `BulletFired` event of the tank. Instead, the tank is used in the `MoveMissiles ()` method: `missile.HomeOn(tank.Position, (float)rotation);` We need to add the `HomeOn()` method to the `Particle`. Here's how you'd implement this method, which steers a `Particle` object toward a vector:

```
public void HomeOn(Vector2 target, float rotation)
{
    Vector2 targetDelta = target - Position;

    // headingTangent represents a 90 degree tangent from this particle's heading
    float f = Angle - MathHelper.PiOver2;
    Vector2 headingTangent = new Vector2((float)Math.Cos(f), (float)Math.Sin(f));

    float dotProduct = Vector2.Dot(headingTangent, Vector2.Normalize(targetDelta));

    if (Math.Abs(dotProduct) < 0.01)
    {
        //we're almost pointing directly at the target
        return;
```

```
        }

    if (dotProduct < 0)
    {
        // steer anticlockwise
        Angle += rotation;
    }
    else
    {
        //steer clockwise
        Angle -= rotation;
    }
}
```

Code Snippet Tank\Tank\Tank\GameComponents\Particle.cs

This method accepts a vector called `target` to tell the particle what to aim for, as well as a rotation amount to specify how much the particle should turn. It's easy for a human to look at two vectors and tell whether one is to the left or to the right, and it turns out that this is the most efficient way to get the computer to do the same thing. You use a mathematical concept called the dot product of two vectors, which is quite interesting, and you should look it up if you're interested. However, what you really need to know here is that (according to MSDN), given two vectors of length 1 (unit vectors), the dot product will be:

➤ Greater than zero if the angle between the two vectors is less than 90 degrees

➤ Less than zero if the angle between the two vectors is more than 90 degrees

➤ Closer to zero as the angle difference approaches 90 degrees

This means that, given a vector pointing from the particle's current location to its target, and given an angle that's 90 degrees from the particle's angle, you can easily tell which way the missile needs to turn. Note that you test to see if the missile needs to turn at all by checking how close to zero `dotProduct` is:

```
    if (Math.Abs(dotProduct) < 0.01)
    {
        //we're almost pointing directly at the target
        return;
    }
```

Nonvisual Components

Instead of being fired by the tank (via the user), missiles should be spawned onto the screen by the game. (Game designers often say "spawn" when they're talking about creating visible game entities.) This is what the `SpawnMissile()` method in `MissileManager` is for, and you can use it with a nonvisual `MissileSpawner` class. Unlike with other game components presented so far, you don't need to inherit from `DrawableGameComponent` because `MissileSpawner` only needs to override `GameComponent`'s `Update()` method. Create a new class to match Listing 11-15.

LISTING 11-15: The new MissileSpawner

```
public class MissileSpawner : GameComponent
{
    static readonly Dictionary<Vector2, float> SpawnPoints =
        new Dictionary<Vector2, float>
            {
                {new Vector2(1, 1), (float) (Math.PI*0.25)},
                {new Vector2(799, 1), (float) (Math.PI*0.75)},
                {new Vector2(1, 479), (float) (Math.PI*1.75)},
                {new Vector2(799, 479), (float) (Math.PI*1.25)},
            };

    readonly MissileManager missileManager;
    readonly Random random = new Random();

    TimeSpan spawnRate = TimeSpan.FromSeconds(3);
    TimeSpan lastSpawn;

    public MissileSpawner(Game game, MissileManager missileManager)
        : base(game)
    {
        this.missileManager = missileManager;
    }

    public override void Update(GameTime gameTime)
    {
        if ((gameTime.TotalGameTime - lastSpawn) > spawnRate)
        {
            int randomIndex = random.Next(SpawnPoints.Count);
            var spawnPoint = SpawnPoints.ElementAt(randomIndex);
            missileManager.SpawnMissile(spawnPoint.Key, spawnPoint.Value);

            lastSpawn = gameTime.TotalGameTime;

            //speed up the spawn rate so that the game gets more challenging
            if (spawnRate > TimeSpan.FromSeconds(0.5))
            {
                spawnRate -= TimeSpan.FromSeconds(0.05);
            }
        }
    }
}
```

Code Snippet Tank\Tank\Tank\GameComponents\MissileSpawner.cs

At the top of this class, you initialize a static dictionary that maps each corner of the game's screen to an ideal initial angle — pointing inward. These four points are where the missiles will be launched from in the Update() method. Update() first checks whether it's ready to launch another missile:

```
if ((gameTime.TotalGameTime - lastSpawn) > spawnRate)
```

Note that `spawnRate` is the `TimeSpan` representing the rate at which you'd like to launch your missiles. You pull a random `spawnPoint` object out of the dictionary and pass it to the `missileManager.SpawnMissile()` method. To make the game become more challenging as time goes on, you actually speed up the spawn rate, too.

Detecting Collisions

The Tank game is nearly complete! There are only two things left to do before the game is fully playable. The first of these tasks is to make the bullets destroy the missiles and make missiles hurt the tank. You can do this with the code in Listing 11-16.

LISTING 11-16: The CollisionManager class

```
class CollisionManager : GameComponent
{
    readonly PlayerTank tank;
    readonly BulletManager bulletManager;
    readonly MissileManager missileManager;

    public CollisionManager(Game game,
                            PlayerTank tank,
                            BulletManager bulletManager,
                            MissileManager missileManager)
        : base(game)
    {
        this.tank = tank;
        this.bulletManager = bulletManager;
        this.missileManager = missileManager;

        //this component should update last
        UpdateOrder = Int32.MaxValue;
    }

    public override void Update(GameTime gameTime)
    {
        BulletsDestroyMissiles();

        int hits = MissilesHitTank();
        if (hits > 0)
        {
            tank.Damage(gameTime, hits);
        }

    }

    void BulletsDestroyMissiles()
    {
        List<Particle> missiles = missileManager.Missiles;

        foreach (var bullet in bulletManager.Bullets)
        {
            for (int j = missiles.Count - 1; j >= 0; j--)
            {
```

```
                    Particle missile = missiles[j];

                    // have we hit the missile?
                    if (bullet.IsNear(missile.Position, 30))
                    {
                        missiles.RemoveAt(j);
                        tank.Kills++;
                    }
                }
            }
        }

        int MissilesHitTank()
        {
            int hits = 0;
            var missiles = missileManager.Missiles;
            for (int i = missiles.Count - 1; i >= 0; i--)
            {
                Particle missile = missiles[i];

                // has the missile hit the tank?
                if (missile.IsNear(tank.Position, 40))
                {
                    missiles.RemoveAt(i);
                    hits++;
                }
            }
            return hits;
        }
    }
```

Code Snippet Tank\Tank\Tank\GameComponents\CollisionManager.cs

CollisionManager defines the interaction between the tank, the bullets, and the missiles, so it needs to reference all three of these other components. During the Update() method, it first checks whether the tank's bullets have destroyed any missiles, and then it checks the missiles to see if any of them have hit the tank. No matter how many missiles hit the tank, you call Damage() only once. The implementation of the BulletsDestroyMissiles() method requires two loops: one to go through all bullets (which don't get destroyed unless they exit the game bounds) and a second to remove any missiles that are hit by a bullet. You use the Particle.IsNear() method, with 30 pixels as the maximum distance between a bullet and a missile to count as a hit. At the end of the method you increment the tank's kills for scoring purposes.

The MissilesHitTank() method is similar to BulletsDestroyMissiles(), except that it tracks the number of missiles that have hit the tank.

Rendering Smooth Text with a Drop Shadow

There's just one more feature to add to the Tank game: displaying the player's current score. Say that you want track kills (that is, missiles shot down with bullets) versus damage (that is, missiles that have hit the tank). You might have noticed when using SpriteBatch.DrawString() before that the text looks quite blocky and jagged. You can fix this by drawing a double-size font at half-scale. For this purpose, you might want to change the font size of your `spritefont` file to 36. Also, to make the text look a bit more appealing, you can render a drop shadow underneath it. Achieving this is a simple matter of calling `DrawString()` twice, as shown in Listing 11-17.

LISTING 11-17: The ScoreDisplay component

```
public class ScoreDisplay : TankGameComponent
{
    readonly PlayerTank tank;
    SpriteFont scoreFont;

    public ScoreDisplay(Game game, PlayerTank tank)
        : base(game)
    {
        this.tank = tank;

        // draw this on top of everything else
        DrawOrder = int.MaxValue;
    }

    protected override void LoadContent()
    {
        scoreFont = Game.Content.Load<SpriteFont>("ScoreFont");
    }

    public override void Draw(GameTime gameTime)
    {
        const string Format = "{0} Kills / {1} Lives lost";
        string message = string.Format(Format, tank.Kills, tank.DamageTaken);

        // the text shadow is drawn at 11,11
        spriteBatch.DrawString(
            scoreFont,
            message,
            new Vector2(11f, 11f),
            Color.Gray,
            0,
            Vector2.Zero,
            0.5f,
            SpriteEffects.None, 0);

        // the text itself is at 10,10
        spriteBatch.DrawString(
            scoreFont,
            message,
            new Vector2(10, 10),
            Color.LightGray,
            0,
            Vector2.Zero,
            0.5f,
            SpriteEffects.None, 0);
    }
}
```

Code Snippet Tank\Tank\Tank\GameComponents\ScoreDisplay.cs

The ScoreDisplay component only needs a reference to the PlayerTank itself; this is where the scores come from. The Draw() method first formats a string to display to the user, and then it passes the same string into two different spriteBatch.DrawString() calls, each with a slightly different color and position.

In order to run the game now, you should set up all the components with the code in listing 11-18 in your game's constructor:

LISTING 11-18: The updated Game class

```
public TankGame()
{
    Content.RootDirectory = "Content";

    Rectangle area = new Rectangle(0, 0, 800, 480);
    graphics = new GraphicsDeviceManager(this)
                {
                    PreferredBackBufferWidth = area.Width,
                    PreferredBackBufferHeight = area.Height,
                    SupportedOrientations = DisplayOrientation.LandscapeLeft,
                    IsFullScreen = true, // gets rid of the status bar
                };


    // Frame rate is 30 fps by default for Windows Phone.
    TargetElapsedTime = TimeSpan.FromTicks(333333);

    // setup components:
    Joystick joystick = new Joystick(this);
    Trigger trigger = new Trigger(this);
    PlayerTank tank = new PlayerTank(this, joystick, trigger, area);
    MissileManager missileManager = new MissileManager(this, tank, area);
    BulletManager bulletManager = new BulletManager(this, tank, area);
    MissileSpawner missileSpawner = new MissileSpawner(this, missileManager);
    CollisionManager collisionManager =
            new CollisionManager(this, tank, bulletManager, missileManager);

    ScoreDisplay scoreDisplay = new ScoreDisplay(this, tank);

    Components.Add(trigger);
    Components.Add(joystick);
    Components.Add(tank);
    Components.Add(missileManager);
    Components.Add(bulletManager);
    Components.Add(missileSpawner);
    Components.Add(collisionManager);
    Components.Add(scoreDisplay);
}
```

Code Snippet Tank\Tank\Tank\TankGame.cs

SUMMARY

In this chapter, you've seen how to build a simple 2-D game with XNA. The chapter started by covering the basic game loop of an XNA game and its performance implications. You now have an idea of what kinds of programs suit XNA versus Silverlight, the two platforms available to develop with Windows Phone 7.

You looked at how to draw images and text to a phone's screen within an XNA game loop, and then you learned how to update the game's state within the same life cycle by reading touch input from the user and understanding the vital `Vector2` class.

You moved on to how to make it easier to build big, complex games with the help of `GameComponent` objects, and you applied these techniques to the Tank game that you built in this chapter.

Finally, you read about some different techniques that may be useful when creating an XNA game, and you used each of these techniques to complete more features of the Tank game.

In the next chapter, you'll learn more about Silverlight and how to use Expression Blend to easily create complex visuals and animations.

EXERCISES

1. How would you animate the flame that's drawn at the back of the missile sprite to make it look more realistic?

2. How could you make "powerups" (for example, things that make the tank move faster or fire faster) appear randomly on the screen? How would you make it so that the tank could pick them up? How would you apply these powerups to the tank?

3. How would you create different screens for your game, so that it launched with a new game screen and finished with a high score screen?

Answers to the Exercises can be found in the Appendix.

► **WHAT YOU LEARNED IN THIS CHAPTER**

TOPIC	KEY CONCEPTS
The Game class and its life cycle	The game controls everything in XNA. You subclass Game and override its methods in order to provide your own behavior and visuals to the game. The XNA framework manages the game loop for you.
Drawing 2-D images and text	For a 2-D game, the SpriteBatch class is essential. You need to use it to draw images and text. Your content project manages images and fonts, which simplifies the efficient loading of resources within XNA.
Updating the game's state	Different classes can be used to represent different aspects of a game's state, and you learned which classes are appropriate when.
The Vector2 class	For a 2-D game, the Vector2 class is good at storing positions and movements, and it provides a lot of helpful methods for doing geometric calculations.
GameComponent objects	GameComponent objects are optional, but without them, you end up with a very large Game class, and it becomes very difficult to manage this when you want to add new features to your game. GameComponent objects alleviate this by separating conceptual concerns into different classes. This is an example of best-practice object-oriented programming.

12

Microsoft Expression Blend

WHAT YOU WILL LEARN IN THIS CHAPTER:

➤ Navigating the Blend user interface

➤ Creating and styling simple forms in Blend

➤ Managing and editing themes and resources

➤ Creating Silverlight animations with storyboards

➤ Setting up and previewing data bindings

Microsoft Expression Blend (or simply *Blend*) is a visual editor for Windows Presentation Foundation (WPF) and Silverlight user interfaces. Although Visual Studio 2010 comes with a serviceable visual editor for WPF and Silverlight, Blend has always been a couple of steps ahead for visual design.

Blend is part of Microsoft's Expression suite of media products, introduced in 2005. Expression currently has four product lines:

➤ Expression Blend, which this chapter is about

➤ Expression Media Encoder, for transcoding and publishing video

➤ Expression Web, for designing HTML

➤ Expression Design, for drawing and editing images and vector art

Some media companies might use all four of these products — for example, for hosting streaming video in a Silverlight video player in a web page with icons on the web page and in the Silverlight video player. However, all you need to build great-looking applications for Windows Phone 7 (WP7) is Blend.

By now you should be familiar with some basic Silverlight and XAML concepts from previous chapters. In this chapter, we concentrate on how Blend can speed up the XAML creation process.

THE BLEND INTERFACE

When you launch Blend for the first time, you are greeted with a startup screen, as shown in Figure 12-1. At this point, you can choose to create a new project, open an existing one, or simply close the welcome screen.

 NOTE *Once this screen is dismissed, it's easy to create or open a project again: You just look in the File menu.*

FIGURE 12-1: The Blend startup screen.

To create a new project, you need to select Windows Phone Application (see Figure 12-2). (The other options require a paid version of Blend.) You can call the project whatever you like and place it in any directory you like. All the examples in this book are in C#, so C# is the recommended Language setting.

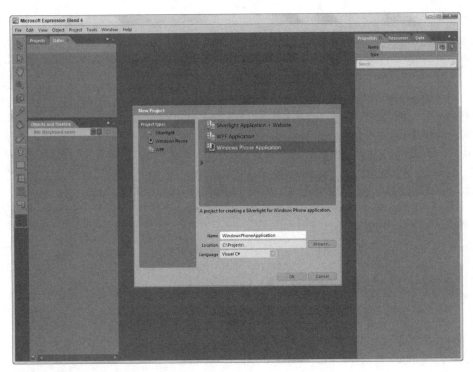

FIGURE 12-2: Creating a new project.

Using Blend's Tools and Panels

After you create a new WP7 project, you see the main Blend user interface. Similarly to Visual Studio, Blend surrounds a central tabbed document area (called the artboard) with various panels and tool boxes. However, Blend is a more focused user interface than Visual Studio:

➤ All Blend elements are gray by design, and the contents of the artboard are the only source of color on the screen.

➤ There are fewer items in the Blend toolbar than in the Visual Studio toolbar.

➤ The panels in Blend are simpler and do fewer things than those in Visual Studio.

➤ Almost everything that Blend can do is either on the screen or a single click away on a background tab panel.

CAN BLEND EDIT C# CODE?

Although Blend is technically capable of editing C# code, Visual Studio has a much more powerful editor. Blend and Visual Studio work with the same solution and project structure, so you can have the same solution open in both tools at the same time.

Blend has the following panels:

➤ **Tools** — This sidebar (shown in figure 12-3) lets you choose controls to add to the artboard. When a tool icon has a triangle in the bottom left (such as the gradient tool), it means you can click and hold to see more controls in the same category.

➤ **Project** — This panel shows the files in the currently open solution and projects. This panel is useful for opening new files.

➤ **Assets** — This panel enables you to search for items that are hard to find on (or not yet on) the toolbar.

➤ **Device** — This WP7-specific feature of Blend lets you emulate changing device settings, such as theme and orientation. It's also where you choose where your application will be tested when you build and run it from Blend.

➤ **Objects & Timeline** — This panel shows the logical structure of the objects in the user interface. When you're editing the storyboard, this panel also shows you the properties of the objects that are being animated.

➤ **Properties** — You use this panel to configure objects after adding them to the artboard.

➤ **Resources** — This panel makes it easy to access resources such as styles and templates.

➤ **Data** — You use this panel to configure design data in Blend.

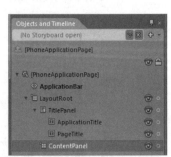

FIGURE 12-3: The Tools panel.

➤ **Results** — You can see any errors that occurred during compilation in this window. It will automatically bring itself into view when errors occur.

These panels are arranged around the sides of the artboard. If you don't see the panel you are looking for, you will be able to bring it into view via the Window menu.

The artboard shows you the actual user interface that you're working on. You can use it to view the designer, the XAML, or both. You can use the artboard to select, move, and add items to your user interface. The tabs above the artboard let you select which open document to work on. It's often quite educational to have both the designer and the XAML visible, so you can see what Blend is doing to your XAML code in real-time.

CREATING FORMS

This section looks at how Blend makes it easy to create a new Windows Phone 7 Form.

Adding Layout Panels

To put controls on a WP7 application page, the first thing you need is a layout panel. When you create a new page in Blend, the Page template already contains a number of components, as shown in Figure 12-4.

FIGURE 12-4: Default controls in a New Page template.

LayoutRoot is a `Grid` that's the root layout control of the whole `Page`. It contains two more layout panels: a `StackPanel` named *TitlePanel* and a `Grid` named *ContentPanel*.

If you're happy to have the page title and the application title at the top of the page, you should go ahead and add your own content to the `Grid` named *ContentPanel*. If you want a full-screen application, you can delete *TitlePanel* and *ContentPanel* and add your own content to *LayoutRoot*.

When you use a `StackPanel`, the order of its contents is the only thing that affects where the child items are placed. You can change the orientation of a `StackPanel`, but there are no properties that you need to set on the child items. If you need to rearrange items in a `StackPanel`, you can either reorder them by dragging them around in the Objects and Timelines panel or by selecting them and then selecting Object ➪ Order ➪ Bring Forward or Object ➪ Order ➪ Send Backward options.

Placing items in a `Canvas` is different from placing items in a `StackPanel`. A `Canvas` doesn't care what order you put the items in, and there are no properties on the `Canvas` that affect the layout of its children. Instead, once an item is inside a `Canvas`, Blend adds a couple of new properties to the Layout section of the Properties panel: `Left` and `Top`. You can position items within the canvas by setting these pixel values. The canvas will never try to rescale the child items either; each item will use its own `Width` and `Height`.

A `Grid` is the most common and also the most complex layout panel. To use a `Grid`, you need to configure the grid's rows and columns, as well as the child item's `Row`, `Column`, `RowSpan`, and `ColumnSpan`. To create rows and columns on a grid in Blend, you just need to select the `Grid` and click in the row or column header area, as shown in Figure 12-5. To select the row and column that a child item belongs to, you can either drag it around the grid or manually set the values in the Layout section of the Properties panel. (Row, column, row span, and column span appear only on items that are children of a grid.)

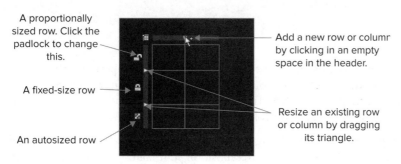

A proportionally sized row. Click the padlock to change this.

A fixed-size row

An autosized row

Add a new row or column by clicking in an empty space in the header.

Resize an existing row or column by dragging its triangle.

FIGURE 12-5: Configuring a grid in Blend.

Adding Controls

Once you have a layout panel, you can put controls in it. The easiest way to do this is to select a control in the tool box (by simply clicking it) and then dragging it to an area on the artboard where you want to see the item placed. Blend does a good job of figuring out what kinds of layout properties can place the control where you specify, but sometimes you need to double-check either the layout section of the Properties panel or the generated XAML.

If the control that you want to add isn't immediately visible in the tool box, you have two choices: You can either go to the Assets panel and use the search bar there or you can click on the assets icon (a double chevron) in the toolbar, which pops up a temporary dialog that behaves just like the Assets panel. Once you find the control you want, you just click on it to select it and then drag a box onto the artboard, as you would with any other control.

PENCILS AND PENS

Two exceptions to this "drag a box on the screen" technique are the pencil and pen tools. You use these to create Path objects, and instead of dragging a box, you drag lines onto the screen. The pencil is intended for freehand drawing (one big drag), while the pen can be used to create smoother lines (by adding together multiple points).

You can add images to a page in a number of ways:

➤ You can add an `Image` control and then select any image file in your project as an image source.

➤ You can drag an image file from the Projects panel onto the artboard.

➤ You can drag an image file from Windows Explorer. This has the same effect as the previous techniques but also copies the image into your project.

➤ You can paste an image from the Clipboard directly onto the artboard. This is not recommended because the image will usually be of poorer quality than the file that you copied from.

Editing Properties

Once a control is on the artboard, you usually want to configure it. Every property that's changed on a control will be reflected in your XAML, so you could always edit them in the XAML. However, Blend is all about making complex XAML changes easy for you, and now we'll look at the different ways you can use Blend to set a control's properties.

When a control is added to the artboard, Blend usually sets a few layout properties on the control to reflect the location you specified. If you continue to reposition your control by dragging it or its borders around on the artboard, Blend will continue to update these layout properties. You can see this for yourself by switching the artboard into split view, where you can see both XAML and the designer, and dragging your control around.

You can edit properties in Blend's Properties panel. This panel displays all the available properties of the currently selected control and offers smart editors for each type property.

PROPERTY PEGS

Have you noticed the little square at the right of each property? The ToolTip for this square is Advanced Options. Colloquially, this square is sometimes known as the *peg*. When you click it, you're presented with a number of advanced options that you can apply to the property. The color of the peg has specific meanings:

➤ Unfilled means the property hasn't been set for this control, and the default value will be applied.

➤ White means that the property has been given an ordinary value.

➤ Green means that the property has been given a value that refers to a resource.

➤ Orange means that the property is set with a binding.

You can also use the peg's menu to reset a property, which will delete the property setter attribute from the control's XAML.

The Property panel is divided into sections:

➤ **Brushes** — Any property of the control that is of type Brush appears in this section. Figure 12-6 shows this section, and at the top is a list of these properties. You use the five tabs at the bottom of this section for choosing the brush for the selected property:

➤ **No Brush** — Clears the value of the property.

➤ **Solid Color Brush** — Enables you to select a single color for the brush.

➤ **Gradient Brush** — Defines a linear or radial gradient.

➤ **Tile Brush** — Enables you to choose and configure an image brush, for when you want the background of a grid to be an image, for example.

➤ **Brush Resources** — Contains all the brushes that are already defined in an accessible resource dictionary.

➤ **Appearance** — Contains properties that affect the way a control looks, such as opacity, border thicknesses and rounding, and so on.

➤ **Layout** — Contains all the properties related to a control's position. If a control belongs to a canvas or a grid, you also see properties that let you configure the placement of the control in that layout panel, such as `Canvas.Left` or `Grid.Row`.

➤ **Common Properties** — Contains properties that don't belong in the preceding categories but are still commonly used, such as the `Text` property of a `TextBlock`.

➤ **Text** — Use this section to configure font, font size, italics, paragraph spacing, and so on when you've selected a control that displays text.

➤ **Transform** — Provides you with an intuitive but advanced user interface for editing the visual transformation of a Silverlight object. You can scale, skew, or rotate (2D and 3D) your control. These transforms occur after layout is calculated, so a control that's had its size doubled may unintentionally overlap with neighboring controls.

➤ **Miscellaneous** — Contains all the properties that don't appear anywhere else. In fact, this is the default location for properties, so the control's properties are listed in the Miscellaneous section.

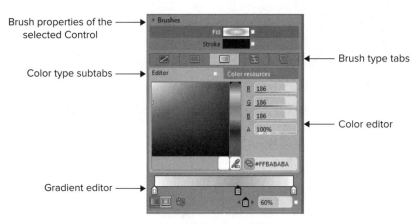

Brush properties of the selected Control

Color type subtabs

Brush type tabs

Color editor

Gradient editor

FIGURE 12-6: The Brushes section of the Properties panel.

TRY IT OUT Creating a Simple WP7 Page

In the following steps, you'll create a simple WP7 page in Blend. You'll start by creating a new project:

1. Create a new WP7 project in Blend. You can do this with the New Project button on the startup screen or by selecting File ➪ New Project. Select "Windows Phone 7 Application" and click OK. Blend opens the main XAML file for you: MainPage.xaml. If it doesn't, double-click MainPage .xaml in the Projects panel to open it. Notice that the page has already been set up with some default contents, including an application title and a page title.

2. Click *LayoutRoot*, which is the root layout control for the page, and press the Delete key on your keyboard. (Or, right-click *LayoutRoot* and select Delete.) This deletes the contents of the page.

3. Add a new root layout control to your application by clicking on the Grid icon in the Tools panel. With the Grid icon selected, drag a small rectangle onto the empty space on the artboard. The grid appears exactly where you dragged the rectangle.

4. Make the Grid fill the entire page by right-clicking it and selecting Auto Size ➪ Fill. This has the same effect as going to the grid's properties and resetting the grid's margin to zero.

5. Split the Grid into four rows by clicking in an empty space in the Grid's row-editing area — the light blue line just to the left of the grid (see Figure 12-5). When you're hovering your mouse over the correct area, the mouse cursor has a plus symbol added to it, and an orange gridline appears over the grid to give you a preview of where the grid will be split. Click in this area at three different places to create four rows (see Figure 12-7).

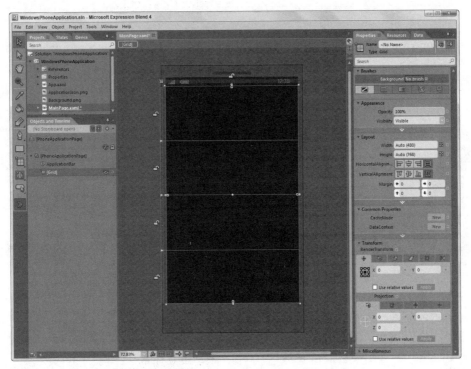

FIGURE 12-7: Adding rows to a grid.

6. Add a heading to the page by clicking on the `TextBlock` tool and dragging a large rectangle into the top row of the grid. When you release the mouse, you can type in some text and edit the text's properties. Type in a heading like Log In and play around with the font settings in the properties panel.

7. Add a new column to the grid by clicking in the blue bar above the grid roughly in the middle. Notice that Blend automatically adjusts the `ColumnSpan` setting of the header text block to keep it in position.

8. Add a button to the bottom two cells by choosing the button tool and then drawing a rectangle that covers both of the bottom cells. Change its text to Go. Make it nice and big by setting all four of its margin properties to 20. There are four empty cells remaining.

9. Add a `TextBlock` control to each of the left cells, one with the text User Name and the other with the text Password. Add a `TextBox` control to the top-right empty cell and add a `PasswordBox` control to the bottom-right empty cell. To access the `TextBox` and `PasswordBox` controls, you have to hold the mouse down on the `TextBlock` icon on the tools panel. Don't worry about placing these too neatly; you'll tidy them up soon. Test your app by pressing F5. You should see the same form running in the emulator.

> **NOTE** *A* `TextBlock` *control is for read-only* blocks *of text, while the* `TextBox` *and* `PasswordBox` *controls are for editable* boxes *of text.*

10. Select the four controls just added by choosing the Selection tool and dragging a box around all four. In the properties panel on the left side of the screen, look for the Layout section. Set the vertical alignment to be centered and set the margins to be 15 pixels left and right and 0 pixels top and bottom (see Figure 12-8).

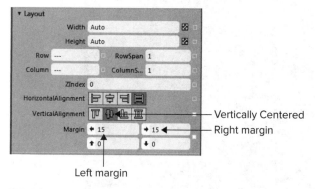

    — Vertically Centered
    — Right margin

    Left margin

FIGURE 12-8: Layout properties of four controls.

11. Now that each control has been configured to correctly sit within its grid cell(s), adjust the location of each grid splitter until the proportions seem right. Press F5 to test it again. Again, the emulator should show you the form just the way it looked in Blend.

How It Works

In this exercise, you used Blend's WYSIWYG editor to add a layout panel and some controls to a WP7 page. You edited the properties of these objects by interacting with various Blend components, such as the artboard (and especially the grid row and column editor), the properties panel, and context-sensitive menus. Everything you do through Blend you can also do (eventually) by hand-editing the XAML file. It's worth repeating this exercise with the XAML code visible in split view (which you open by pressing F11). One of the best ways to learn XAML is to make experimental changes in the Blend interface and observe the changes that Blend applies to your XAML in real-time.

Modifying Visual Design

Blend is especially useful for editing the visual look and feel of Silverlight. When you use it, you get immediate feedback on how your form is going to look, as you tweak colors, borders, shapes, sizes, and so on. This section explains all the different tools in Blend that help you to efficiently design the visual user experience of your page.

You can manipulate the visual aspects of a form by adding new items, such as images, shapes, and borders, or by adjusting the properties of existing controls, such as setting the background color of a grid or the size of a text block's font.

 COMMON MISTAKES *It's a lot of fun to tweak the way a Silverlight user interface looks, and Blend makes it easy to do so. However, Microsoft has put many hours of design into the standard look and feel of its phones, so it's often acceptable to leave the visual theme alone. In some situations, however, you may need to completely redesign the way everything looks, such as:*

➤ *When you're trying to match an existing corporate brand*

➤ *When you have real design experience or when you have help from some-one with proper design credentials*

➤ *When you're quite confident that you can do a good job with it*

If you end up customizing your look and feel in a way that Microsoft's testers don't find aesthetically pleasing, they might return your application with a suggestion to reset your styles to the default ones.

Adding Visual Elements

Images are a great way to give some depth to an application. You can place them in the background or in the foreground. The easiest way to add an Image control to the artboard in Blend is to drag an image file from Windows Explorer onto the artboard. PNG files work best. One disadvantage of using images is that they don't scale well, so you should try to obtain images that are already the desired size.

You can use shapes in the same way that you use images, but by their vector-based nature, they typically look better than images when resized. You can design your own shapes in a number of ways:

➤ Use the ellipse and rectangle tools to add these shapes to the artboard.

➤ Use the pen and pencil tools to design complex shapes.

➤ If you have Expression Design, draw vectors in Design and then export them to XAML.

➤ If you have Adobe Illustrator or Photoshop, import files built in those tools directly into Blend. You do this by selecting File ➪ Import Adobe Illustrator/Photoshop File. Sometimes, Blend can't import all aspects of these files, but it generally does a good job with paths, shapes, backgrounds, and colors.

➤ Create a Path control from almost any other object by selecting Object ➪ Path ➪ Convert to Path from the main menu. This works well on text, especially icon fonts like wingdings.

One easy way (at least traditionally) to group related items together in a form is by placing a border around the items. Microsoft's Metro design guidelines don't make a lot of use of borders for this purpose, preferring to instead use whitespace. However, you can use the Border control to choose a background, a border brush, thickness, and corner rounding. You can add a border to a page by simply selecting some controls, right-clicking, and choosing Group Into ➪ Border.

Modifying Properties

Each control has a number of properties that affect its visual appearance. You can experiment with the Brushes, Appearance, Text, and Transform sections of the property editor when you want to restyle existing controls.

For example, you might want to change the background of a button or the font of a `TextBlock`. You can make such changes through Blend's Properties panel. If you need to go another step further and completely change the visual behavior of an existing control, you can create a new template for that control. Blend provides a lot of help with this, and you'll learn how to do that in a later section of this chapter, "Themes and Resources."

TRY IT OUT Decorating a Page

Available for download on Wrox.com

This Try It Out builds on the previous Try It Out, where you added a few simple controls to a page. If you skipped that section, you can download the solution from the code snippet TIO-Create a simple wp7 page. To decorate that page, follow these steps:

1. To change the color of the `Username` TextBlock, select the TextBlock either in the artboard or the Objects and Timeline panel, set its `Foreground` property to a solid color brush, choose a hue, and choose a brightness and saturation (see Figure 12-9).

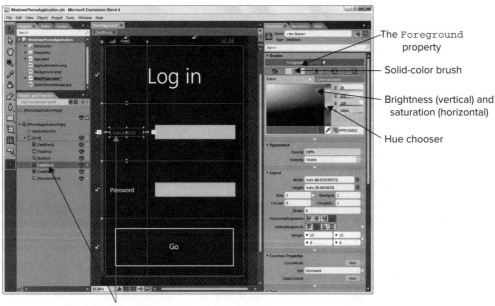

The two places you can click to select the `TextBlock` Control

FIGURE 12-9: Setting a solid-color brush.

2. Set the other TextBlock so that it has the theme accent color (that is, the theme color that the phone's user has chosen). To do so, select the `Password` TextBlock from either the artboard or the Objects and Timeline panel, select the `Foreground` property, select the Brush Resources brush type, and choose `PhoneAccentBrush` (see Figure 12-10). The color will now change in Blend, depending on the settings in the Device panel, and it will change on an actual phone depending on the theme settings.

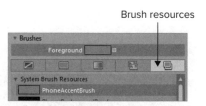

FIGURE 12-10: Brush Resources.

3. To set a gradient that utilizes the theme accent color, select the Login Button and then select the `Background` property. Select the Gradient brush type and select the first gradient color stop. Then select the Color Resources tab, choose `PhoneAccentColor`, set the other gradient color stop to `PhoneBackgroundColor`, and choose between a radial gradient and a linear one. See Figure 12-11.

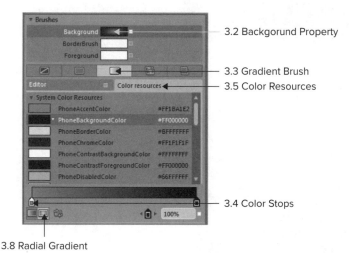

FIGURE 12-11: Setting a theme-aware gradient.

4. To wrap the whole screen in a border, right-click the main grid and choose Group Into ➪ Border. Then select the new border, change its `BorderBrush` property to the brush resource `PhoneBorderBrush`, change its `BorderThickness` setting to 1 for each edge, change its `CornerRadius` setting to 4, and change its `Margin` setting to 15 for each edge. See Figure 12-12.

5. Select the `Ellipse` tool, holding the mouse down on the rectangle tool until the shape submenu opens, if needed. Then drag an ellipse anywhere on the grid, set its `Stroke` property to the phone's accent brush, set its `Fill` property to an image brush, and choose an image for the brush. You can either use an image that's already part of your project, such as `ApplicationIcon.png`, or you can add your own (see Figure 12-13).

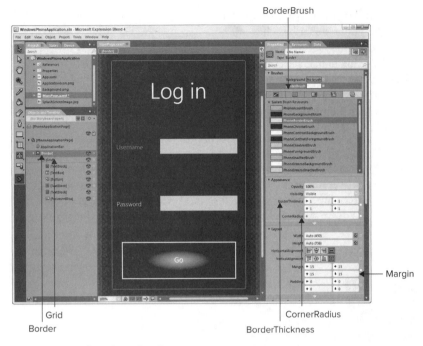

FIGURE 12-12: Creating a border.

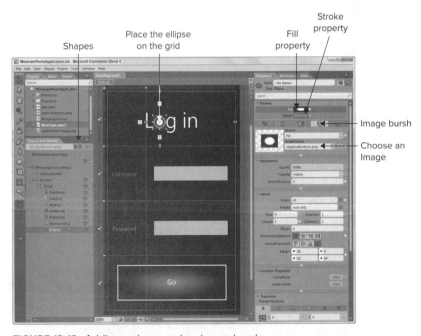

FIGURE 12-13: Adding a shape and an image brush.

6. Run the application by pressing F5. Note that the Username TextBlock doesn't change colors when you change the phone's theme settings.

How It Works

In step 1, you set the color of the Username TextBlock to a particular color, and in step 2 you set the color of the Password TextBlock to the theme color. It's recommended you use the theme accent color whenever you need a splash of color so that the user always sees the color that he or she liked enough to select as the theme color. Setting specific colors is useful when the color has meaning (for example, red means stop or warning) or when you need to tie an application's visuals to a brand, such as a company logo.

In step 3, you utilized a theme color in a gradient by selecting the color from the color picker tab instead of the brush resources tab. In step 4 you customized a border, and in step 5 you looked at a very simple placement of an ellipse.

You can use techniques like these to gain full control over how your application looks. Blend can help you to build unique visual themes for an application.

THEMES AND RESOURCES

You can easily restyle applications and controls in the Silverlight framework. (This process is also known as *skinning*, or *theming*.) Blend makes this restyling even easier, as explained in this section.

Managing Resources

In Silverlight, a Resource is simply an object that's declared in a ResourceDictionary in XAML. Because it's in the ResourceDictionary, it's made available to all the children of the item that owns that ResourceDictionary. This means that if you declare a resource in the ResourceDictionary of a Page, you can use that resource from anywhere in that page. In XAML, you access the value of a resource with the syntax {StaticResource keyName}, where keyName is the key name chosen for the resource (with the syntax x:Key="keyName").

Using resources is a perfect way to reuse objects and values in Silverlight. You can specify something once, reference it from multiple places, and when you update the original resource in Blend or Visual Studio all the references will reflect these changes.

Making Your Own Resources

Blend makes it easy to work with resources. Most property values can be extracted into a resource: In the property's Advanced Options menu (the peg, discussed earlier in this chapter, in the sidebar "Property Pegs"), there's an option called Convert to New Resource. Invoking this brings up a dialog from which you can pick a name for the resource and choose where to keep it. This dialog lets you keep the resource in a number of places:

> ➤ **Application** — Resources stored at the application level (inside App.xaml) are available to all controls in the entire application.

➤ **This Document** — Choose between storing the resource in the current document (as with a page or user control) or in the element that contains the property. The second option wouldn't be useful in a lot of cases, but you might want to store a new resource in the current document so that it's available to any controls in there but not in other controls.

➤ **Resource Dictionary** — These can simply be elements in the XAML of another object, but you can also create a file of type `ResourceDictionary`. In this case, Blend knows you're trying to create a reusable library of resources, so it always offers all resource dictionaries that are referenced by your application as places to store the new resource.

Having created a resource, you should be able to find it (and, if you like, edit it) in the location you specified, either by looking directly at the XAML or in Blend's Resources panel.

When a resource exists, you can select another control with a property of the same type (resources don't have to be for the same objects; they just have to be of the same type) and look in the Local Resource menu of the peg of that property. You should see the names of all available resources in that list. Brush and color resources get special treatment. Brush resources (which can be solid brushes, gradients, or images) can be found in the Brush Resource tab of the Brushes section of the Property panel (refer to Figure 12-6 to see where this is placed). Color resources (these look the same as solid color brushes but can be used as the contents of gradients and solid-color brushes) are available in the Color Resources subtab of the Solid Color and Gradient Brush tabs.

Using System Resources

As mentioned earlier in this chapter, WP7 uses the concept of themes. In the Settings application, you can switch between light and dark themes, and you can choose a single accent color. After you do this, the rest of the phone's user interface changes to match these color themes. In Blend, you can emulate these user choices within the Device panel. This theming is implemented with resources: You can use a number of predefined system resources to ensure that your application always fits in with the user's theme. You can't edit these resources, but you can choose them for your properties under the System Resources menu item of the property peg.

Reusing Code with Styles

In Silverlight, you can use a `Style` to set multiple properties on a control at once. In fact, a `Style` is little more than a collection of `Setter` objects, each of which has a `Property` property (which you can set with a string) and a `Value` property, which can be anything. All controls that inherit from `FrameworkElement` have a `Style` property, and setting this property applies all the setters in that new property value to the control.

You can create, for example, a `Style` that gives a `Border` a `BorderThickness` of 1, a `BorderBrush` of White, and a `CornerRadius` of 5. This sounds like a strange thing to do, when you can just go ahead and set all these properties directly. But if you place a style in a resource dictionary, you can reuse it. Then you can apply the same style to multiple `Border` controls with ease! You can even alter the original style and have all the `Border` controls update to match in one swoop. Here's how the XAML would look for such a Style:

```
<phone:PhoneApplicationPage.Resources>
    <Style x:Key="AwesomeBorder" TargetType="Border">
        <Setter Property="BorderThickness" Value="1"/>
```

```
        <Setter Property="CornerRadius" Value="5"/>
        <Setter Property="BorderBrush" Value="White"/>
    </Style>
</phone:PhoneApplicationPage.Resources>
```

Because `Styles` are usually stored in a resource dictionary, they usually have keys associated with them. This means that you usually apply a `Style` by referencing the `ResourceDictionary`, as in the following example:

```
<Border Style="{StaticResource AwesomeBorder}" >
    <!-- Content of Border -->
    <Grid />
</Border>
```

In addition to having a collection of setters, a style is likely to have a `TargetType` property, which just means it is intended to target a specific type of control. This is useful because many of the properties that you may want to style are specific to the particular control you are styling, and it's important to be clear what you're trying to set. As well as providing a bit of type safety, setting the `TargetType` helps Blend show you an example of the control you are styling.

Every `FrameworkElement` control (including things like buttons and text boxes, but excluding layout controls such as grids) has a default system style that sets up a few default values. If you don't explicitly set a style on a control, it will look for an implicit style. You can actually override the built-in system style by adding a style to an accessible resource dictionary that doesn't have a key.

If you want to create a new style in Blend, you first need an instance of the control that you want to style on the screen. You select it and then select the menu item Object ➪ Edit Style ➪ Create Empty or Object ➪ Edit Style ➪ Edit a Copy. The option Edit a Copy copies the existing style of the control into a new style, giving you a lot more setters to start with. It's a good choice to use if you don't want to drastically change the look of something that's already styled. To create a style with no key, in the Create Style Resource dialog, you select the option Apply to All.

If you create a new style or start editing an existing one, Blend's artboard changes scope, drilling down into that style. You see a set of breadcrumbs at the top of the artboard, and the Objects and Timeline panel contains a single item: <> Style. While you can't add any more controls (you're not up to the templating bit yet!), you can use the property panel just as you normally would, except that Blend automatically puts your edits into the style as setters instead of changing an object directly. The pegs will be white only for properties that the current style is setting.

A number of system styles are built into WP7, and the most useful of them are the ones that target TextBlocks. If you select a TextBlock and then select Object ➪ Edit Style ➪ Apply Resource, you see a number of built-in text styles such as `PhoneTextHugeStyle` and `PhoneTextAccentStyle`. These are useful for when you want to maintain standards with the default WP7 look and feel.

Editing Control Templates

One important function of styles is to set up a control's `Template`. A *template* defines the subcomponents of a control. For example, a button in WP7 is actually made up of a `Border` control and a `ContentControl` control. While a style can change a few default properties, a template represents every single detail of how a control looks. Usually, as in the following example, a template is defined within a style, as just another setter:

```
<Style x:Key="AwesomeButton" TargetType="Button">
    <Setter Property="Background" Value="Transparent"/>
    <Setter Property="Padding" Value="10,3,10,5"/>
    <Setter Property="Template">
        <Setter.Value>
            <ControlTemplate TargetType="Button">
                <Grid>
                    <!-- Continued... -->
```

Blend makes it easy to edit a control's template. Just as with a style, you first select a control, or you add one to the page if none exist yet. Then you select Object ⇨ Edit Template ⇨ Edit a Copy. As when you're editing styles, the artboard drills down into the template, allowing you to edit the contents of the control but nothing else. Anything you change here doesn't actually affect the control directly; rather, it is added to the style's template setter value.

When you are editing a control's template in Blend, if you go into the States panel, you can see a list of the visual states of the control. By selecting them, you can see and edit how the control should look when it's in a particular visual state. Visual states are almost like styles, in that they represent a number of property setters. (Visual states are, in fact, storyboards, which are discussed in the following section, "Animation.") For example, in the disabled state, a button's border and content become gray: {StaticResource PhoneDisabledBrush}. You'll learn more details later in this chapter, in the section "Visual States."

TRY IT OUT   Changing the Style and Template of the Button Control

Let's take a look at how to change the visual style for a button in Blend. You can follow along with the following steps, which are also shown in Figure 12-14.

1. Create a new project by pressing Ctrl+Shift+N and then selecting Windows Phone Application.

2. Add a new Button control anywhere in the page and select it.

3. In Blend's main menu, go Object ⇨ Edit Style ⇨ Edit a Copy. Accept the default values in the Create Style Resource dialog box. Blend replaces the contents of the Objects and Timeline panel with a single item named Style.

4. Set the button's background to PhoneChromeBrush.

5. Set the button's BorderThickness property to 1 on the top and left and 5 on the bottom and the right.

6. Start editing the button's template by right-clicking the style in the Objects and Timeline panel and selecting Edit Template ⇨ Edit Current.

7. Now that there are a few items in the Objects and Timeline panel (the contents of a standard button), select the border named ButtonBackground.

8. Set the border's CornerRadius setting to 5 and its Margin setting to 0.

9. Exit Edit Template mode by clicking the [Button] breadcrumb at the top of the artboard.

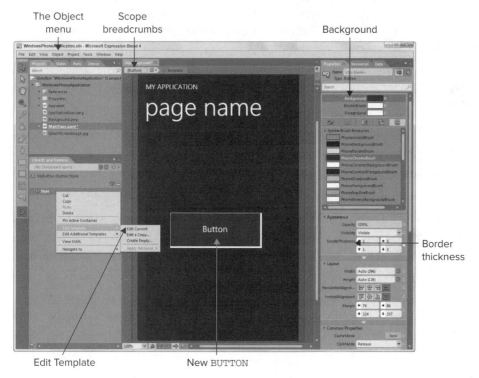

FIGURE 12-14: Editing a button's style.

How It Works

You needed to perform steps 1 to 3 to get Blend into its Edit Style mode. In step 3 you accept the name that Blend suggested; later, you can use this name to reuse the style. In steps 4 and 5, you changed some of the button's style properties. In step 6, you delved into the template of the style, which gave you even more control over the look of the control (steps 7 and 8). In step 9, you brought Blend back into its normal editing mode.

ANIMATION

Silverlight is very good at creating and displaying animations. All you have to do is specify that you want a property of a control (such as a color, an opacity, or a position) to animate to a new value and how long you'd like that animation to take, and Silverlight takes care of interpolating all the values in between. To make animations appear more natural, you can even use easing functions.

Managing Animations with Storyboards

You can use a storyboard to manage animations in Silverlight. You can create a new storyboard in Blend and then add any number of animations to it by choosing a time in the Timeline panel and setting a property at that point. Silverlight will automatically animate that property to the chosen value in a smooth manner when the storyboard is begun.

Whereas a style represents a set of property setters for a single control, a storyboard is composed of a set of property setters for a number of controls, with timing information included. A storyboard defines the following:

➤ Which controls are to be affected

➤ Which properties of these controls are to be affected

➤ What values these properties should have

➤ When these property values should take effect

When you open a storyboard for editing, the Objects and Timeline panel transforms to show a timeline like the one shown in Figure 12-15. It also adds any storyboarded properties to each object as sub-items in the tree. Each of these properties has one or more keyframes in the Objects and Timeline panel. This gives you a great visual indication of when different values are going to affect different properties. You can drag a keyframe horizontally in Blend's timeline to change the time when it takes effect. When you select a keyframe, you can change the Value property (the new target value to which the storyboard will animate the property), and Blend lets you choose from various easing options. Easing is what makes an animation look smooth and natural; real life objects don't change speed instantly, they "ease" into their acceleration and deceleration.

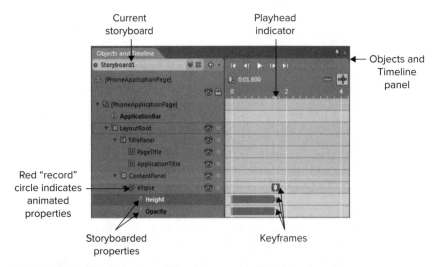

FIGURE 12-15: The Objects and Timeline panel in Storyboard mode.

TRY IT OUT   Animating Objects with a Storyboard

Let's take a look at how to create a simple animation with a storyboard in Blend. Refer to Figure 12-16 as you complete these steps:

1. Create a new project by pressing Ctrl+Shift+N and then selecting Windows Phone Application.

2. Add a new ellipse to the page, at the top left of the grid named `ContentPanel`.

3. Create a new storyboard by clicking the New Storyboard button in the Objects and Timeline panel. Accept the default name.

4. Drag the playhead indicator to the two second mark.

5. Drag the ellipse to the bottom-right corner of the page.

6. Expand the ellipse's properties in the Objects and Timeline panel and select the `TranslateY` property. Blend selects the first keyframe for that property, but you can click on individual keyframes, too. Currently, you have only one keyframe per property.

7. Change the easing function for the `TranslateY` keyframe to Bounce Out.

8. Test your animation by clicking the Play Storyboard button.

9. Close your animation by clicking the Close Storyboard button.

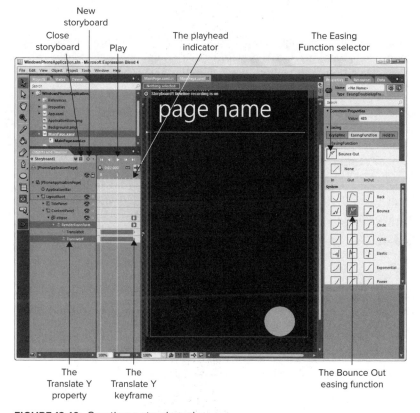

FIGURE 12-16: Creating a storyboard.

How It Works

When you open or create a storyboard in Blend, Blend changes modes. It displays the timeline in the Objects and Timeline panel, and many of the changes you make to an object's properties are actually stored in the storyboard rather than the object, so the properties you select apply only at the time that's current in the storyboard. You have to be careful about whether you are in Timeline Recording mode, but by keeping an eye on the XAML that Blend is creating, you can tell exactly when your property changes are being applied directly to your object or whether they are being subsumed into your animation.

If you want to view the results of a storyboard outside Blend, you need to trigger the storyboard by calling `Storyboard1.Begin()` in code somewhere, such as the `Loaded` event of your page or the `Click` event of a button.

Visual States

Visual states are a powerful feature of Silverlight. Consider, for example, a check box. Visually, it can be held down, disabled, or neither. At the same time, it can be checked, unchecked, or indeterminate. (*Indeterminate* is the rarely used third state of check boxes, which usually looks like a filled-in box.) Visual states let you specify how a control should look in each of these states and also allow you to specify what kinds of transitions occur between these states.

Each visual state is effectively a storyboard, setting a number of properties on a number of controls. `VisualStateManager` is responsible for making sure that within each group, only one storyboard can be active. This means that a check box can't be both pressed and disabled, but it can be disabled and checked.

Visual states can apply to existing control templates or to your own controls and pages. For existing controls such as buttons and check boxes, the visual states are triggered by the control's behavior. If you're creating your own visual states for your own controls, you'll often have to trigger them manually from code with a call to `VisualStateManager.GoToState()`.

If you go to Blend's States panel when you're editing the template of a control, you see all the states available to that control already listed. Often a control's template already has a few different states set up. From this panel, shown in Figure 12-17, you can do the following:

➤   Add and remove state groups.

➤   Add and remove states.

➤   Configure the default time and easing for a transition within a state group.

➤   Add a specific transition to say exactly how to move from one particular state to another particular state.

➤   Select a state so that you can choose some new property values to represent this state.

➤   Pin a state to show how the control looks when it's in that state.

NOTE *Because you can pin one state from every state group, pinning is an invaluable tool to show you how your control's different states will interact.*

Preview
transitions

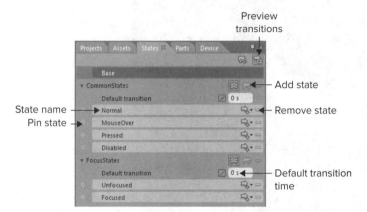

State name — Normal
Pin state —

Add state

Remove state

Default transition
time

FIGURE 12-17: The States panel when you're editing a button template.

TRY IT OUT   Using the Visual State Editor

Available for
download on
Wrox.com

The following steps build on the previous Try It Out, "Changing the Style and Template of the Button Control." If you skipped that section, you can download the code snippet TIO-Re-template the Button. In this Try It Out, you'll add animations to a button template to give it smoother interactions. Refer to Figure 12-18 as you go:

1. Right-click the button and select Edit Template ⇨ Edit Current.

2. Open the States panel. Inspect how the button looks in each state by selecting a state. For example, MouseOver and FocusStates don't apply in a mouseless environment.

3. Change the default transition length for common states to 0.1 seconds.

4. Select the state Pressed to preview the pressed state.

5. Select the border ButtonBackground and change its Y projection rotation to −45.

6. Move out of state editing mode by clicking on Base in the States panel.

7. Change the X center of rotation to 0.

8. Run the application by pressing F5 and watch what happens when you click the button.

The States panel

Default transition length for CommonStates

The Pressed state

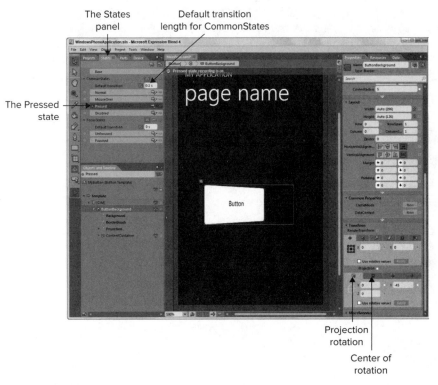

Projection rotation

Center of rotation

FIGURE 12-18: Editing visual states.

How It Works

In step 3, you stopped the transitions from being instant and forced them to interpolate over a 0.1-second space. In steps 4 and 5, you made the button rotate when pressed, but this looked silly until you anchored the rotation at the left side of the button in step 7.

DATA BINDING IN BLEND

Data binding is a wonderful feature of Silverlight. At the most basic level, data binding is about tying together the values of two properties of different objects. It's especially useful when it's used to bind a property of a control to a value in your class model.

Binding to Datacontext

Imagine that a class represents a customer's order, and it has a property of type `string` named `Address`. You can just bind a text box's text property to the `Address` property, and Silverlight will make sure these values stay in sync. To do this in XAML (assuming that the current `DataContext` is an instance of `Order`), you'd just need the following code:

```
<TextBox Text="{Binding Address, Mode=TwoWay}"/>
```

`Mode=TwoWay` ensures that the `Address` property is not only read from the order but is also written back into it when the user types some text.

To set up the same data binding in Blend, you need to use the property peg (see the section "Editing Properties," earlier in this chapter, for more details on pegs). If the current property is capable of being bound, then the menu item Data Binding is available. Clicking it launches the Create Data Binding dialog, shown in Figure 12-19. To create the same XAML as previously, you need to do the following:

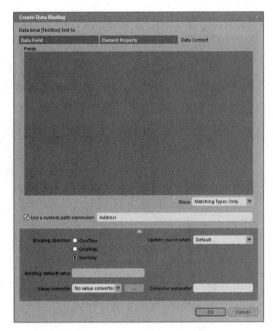

FIGURE 12-19: The Create Data Binding dialog.

1. Select the Data Context tab.

2. Select the Use a Custom Path Expression check box. Type the name of the property you're binding to (`Address`) in the adjacent text box.

3. Choose the Binding Direction setting TwoWay.

4. Press OK to dismiss the dialog. You should now see an orange border around the property, and the peg will be colored orange, too.

You might wonder why there's a big empty box labeled Fields in the Create Data Binding dialog box, and you might also wonder why Blend seems to be making things harder in this case. The problem is that Blend doesn't know that you're expecting the current `DataContext` object to be an instance of `Order`, so it can't find out what fields might exist. This is why you have to manually type a binding path, which opens you up to spelling mistakes that the compiler can't catch! Fortunately, there are a few ways you can help Blend as you'll see in the upcoming section "Putting Sample Data into the Blend Artboard."

Binding to Elements

In addition to the use just discussed, another use for data binding is to tie together the values of two controls' properties. For example, you can bind a `TextBlock` control's `IsReadOnly` property to a `CheckBox` control's `IsChecked` property. The XAML for this would look as follows:

```
<CheckBox x:Name="checkBox" />
<TextBox IsReadOnly="{Binding IsChecked, ElementName=checkBox}" Width="400"/>
```

In order to generate this XAML from Blend, you need to select the property peg of the text box's `Text` property. Instead of clicking the Data Binding item, though, you select the Element Property Binding menu item. At this point, the mouse cursor changes into a target icon, and you can click the check box to "target" it. A simple dialog appears, letting you select which property to bind to. As an alternative to this, the Element Property tab of the Create Data Binding dialog (Figure 12-19) also lets you choose a control and a property.

Putting Sample Data into the Blend Artboard

So far, we've covered how to use Blend to set up data bindings on properties. Typing the equivalent code into your XAML wouldn't be incredibly difficult though, would it? But we've left the most useful data binding feature of Blend untouched: sample data.

By letting Blend know what kinds of objects you're planning to give it at runtime (a *sample* of your *data*), you enable Blend to do the following:

➤ Suggest correct property paths in the Create Data Binding dialog (see Figure 12-19).

➤ Display the page in the Blend artboard itself exactly as it would look at runtime, with the sample data filling out the provided data bindings.

There are three different options in the Sample Data menu (the second icon from the right in the Data panel):

➤ **New Sample Data** — This option creates a sample data item that lets you pick and choose what kinds of properties (types, names, and sample values) should be available (as a data context) to the controls in your artboard at design time.

➤ **Import Sample Data from XML** — This option is similar to the first, except that it tries to infer the values and properties that are stored in an existing XML file for you.

➤ **Create Sample Data from Class** — This option is useful throughout a project. It enables you to populate an existing object model with some sample data and then have Blend render those sample values.

NOTE *The first two options are great if you want to start by prototyping an application's visuals before you make a start on any coding, because you can quickly whip together some sample data that you would eventually replace with real data.*

What's great about this design-time data is that it disappears when you actually run your application. So you get the best of both worlds: some simple, quick data for your page to bind to in Blend and the ability to replace that sample data with real data of exactly the same class at runtime.

TRY IT OUT Data Binding, Collections, and Design Data

In the following steps, you'll see how quick and easy it is to put together a data-driven form in Blend, with a proper preview of how the data will look at runtime, even with collections of data. Follow these steps to create and utilize some design-time data:

1. Create a new project by pressing Ctrl+Shift+N and then selecting Windows Phone Application.

2. Select File ➪ New Item. Choose Class and name it **Order**. Add the following code under the class's constructor:

```
public double Total {get;set;}
public string Address {get;set;}
public System.Collections.ObjectModel.ObservableCollection<Product> Products {get;set;}
```

3. Select File ➪ New Item. Choose Class and name it `Product`. Add the following code under the class's constructor:

```
public string Name {get;set;}
public string Description {get;set;}
public bool IsSelected {get;set;}
public double Price {get;set;}
```

4. Make sure your project compiles by pressing Ctrl+Shift+B. Building your project also helps Blend find your classes in its class chooser dialogs.

5. Go back to your `MainPage.xaml` file. Then go to the Data panel, open the Create Sample Data menu, and choose Create Sample Data from Class (see Figure 12-20).

6. Choose your `Order` class in the resultant class chooser dialog (Figure 12-21), and then click OK.

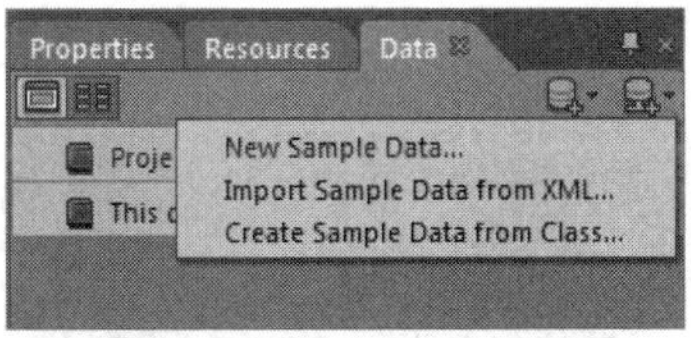

FIGURE 12-20: Creating sample data from a class.

FIGURE 12-21: The class chooser dialog.

7. In the Data panel, expand the tree of your `OrderSampleData` data source until you see the `Name` property. Click the ABC icon to edit the type of sample data provided here. Set the maximum word count to 1 (see Figure 12-22). Select the Address format for the `Address`.

8. Create three rows in the `ContentPanel` grid.

9. From the Data panel, drag `Address`, `Products`, and `Total` from the `ContentPanel` grid onto the artboard one by one. Arrange them into rows so that all three controls are visible (see Figure 12-23).

FIGURE 12-22: Editing sample data generator properties.

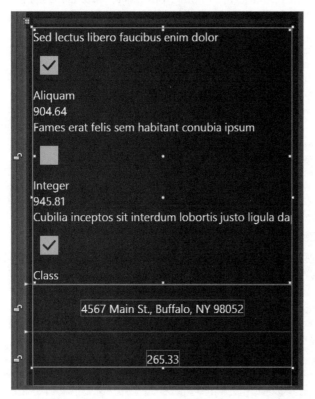

FIGURE 12-23: Placing data items on a grid.

10. Right-click the `ListBox` control that was added when you added the products. Choose Edit Additional Templates ⇨ Edit Generated Items (ItemTemplate) ⇨ Edit Current.

11. Right-click the template's root layout control, a stack panel, and select Change Layout Type ⇨ Grid. Divide the grid into four quarters. Move each of the four controls into one of the cells, as in Figure 12-24.

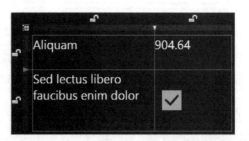

FIGURE 12-24: Laying out the item template.

12. Group the grid into a new border. Set the following properties on the border:

➤ Set `Background` to a gradient from the color resource `PhoneBackgroundColor` to the color resource `PhoneChromeColor`.

➤ Set `BorderBrush` to the color resource `PhoneBorderBrush`.

➤ Set each `BorderThickness` value to 1.

➤ Set `Width` to 330.

➤ Set `Padding` to 12.

How It Works

In steps 2 and 3, you created some simple data classes that your user interface is going to bind to. In step 5, 6, and 7, you set up some sample data in Blend. This actually created an XML file under a new folder, named `SampleData`, in your project.

In step 9, you pulled elements from your sample data onto your page. Blend automatically creates controls for you when you do this, and it sets the correct binding on them. An alternative would be to place whichever control you preferred onto the page and then drag the data onto the control to create a binding.

In steps 10, 11, and 12, you restyled the data template for the `ListBox` control.

SUMMARY

In this chapter, you've looked at how to use Blend to create the Silverlight XAML for which you'd normally use Visual Studio. This chapter concentrates on the areas in which Blend is a much better tool for the job.

First, you looked at creating a simple form with text boxes and buttons. Then you looked at how to change the visual aspects of them with colors, borders, gradients, and images.

Next, you looked at how to reuse system resources such as colors and how doing so can help your application fit the current theme of the user's phone. You also re-templated a `Button` control and learned that re-templating gives you power over how a control looks.

You looked at how to create a storyboard, which is an animation that can be used in any arbitrary context. Many of the built-in controls in WP7 utilize some kind of animation, and you looked at how to leverage visual states to control transitions between different states of a control (for example, when a button is clicked).

Finally, you looked at the data binding capabilities of Blend. You learned that Blend can provide a true WYSIWYG experience when you leverage its sample data features.

1. If all of Blend's panels were hidden, and you wanted to change the theme color of the phone in the artboard, how would you do it?

2. Name three different controls and three different properties that can be used to change the way an existing form looks.

3. Why should you try to use system resources such as Styles and Colors instead of making your own?

4. Why should you always try to apply easing to your animations?

5. If you don't want to go to the trouble of writing a new class or typing out your own XML, what type of sample data is most appropriate to get you some design-time sample data in the artboard?

    a) New Sample Data

    b) Import Sample Data from XML

    c) Create Sample Data from Class

Answers to the Exercises can be found in the Appendix.

▶ **WHAT YOU LEARNED IN THIS CHAPTER**

TOPIC	KEY CONCEPTS
Blend's user interface	Blend's user interface is made up of the artboard, where you see what the user interface you're building looks like as you work on it. Surrounding this are various panels that let you configure different parts of your interface. For example, the States panel lets you work on visual states, and the Properties panel lets you configure different properties about the control that you currently have selected on the artboard. In addition, the tool box lets you drag new controls onto the artboard.
Creating and styling forms	Blend's artboard is an excellent WYSIWYG editor for Silverlight user interfaces. It provides a lot of support for layout, particularly with respect to grids. It also makes it easy to quickly change the way your existing controls look.
Themes and resources	Blend's Resources panel helps you manage all your different resources. It also lets you delve into a template or style and edit it directly.
Animations	Blend is the only tool with good support for creating Silverlight animations. You learned how to create storyboards to animate a control's properties as well as how to create visual states to transition between the states of a control's templates.
Data binding	Blend's support for data binding can be very useful if it's used the right way. You learned how to invoke the data binding editor to bind a control property and how sample data can make this feature even better.

13

Using the Silverlight for Windows Phone Toolkit and Creating Panoramic User Interfaces

WHAT YOU WILL LEARN IN THIS CHAPTER:

➤ Acquiring the Silverlight for Windows Phone Toolkit

➤ Using the powerful new toolkit controls

➤ Using the transitions available in the toolkit

➤ Detecting gestures with `GestureService` and `GestureListener`

➤ Using the `Panoramic` control for large user interfaces

In the first few chapters of this book, you learned about the vast number of Silverlight controls that are available in Windows Phone 7 applications. You also learned about the various hardware features. In addition to the standard hardware features and Silverlight controls, Microsoft has provided a separate toolkit download that contains great controls and features that have not yet been added to the standard API platform. The Silverlight for Windows Phone Toolkit comes complete with several new controls that you can use, including `AutoCompleteBox`, `ListPicker`, `LongListSelector`, `DatePicker`, `TimePicker`, `ToggleSwitch`, and `WrapPanel`.

The Silverlight for Windows Phone Toolkit provides several page transitions that you can apply for a nonstandard transition effect between page changes in your application. It also gives you an easy way to create a context menu like the ones you have seen built into the standard Windows Phone 7 menu features. Finally, the toolkit also provides a `GestureService` and `GestureListener` object to help facilitate the easy detection of various gestures that the user can perform on the device. In this chapter, you'll see how to use of all these new controls and features in your own application to provide an even richer user experience than can be made available using only the standard Silverlight controls.

Later in this chapter, you'll also see how to use one final control that is part of the standard Windows Phone 7 developer kit. The `Panoramic` control enables you to easily create large user interfaces that can cover multiple horizontal screens. You've already seen this control in action as it is used in several of the hubs available on the phone, including the music and video hub. In this chapter, you'll see how to quickly make a panoramic user interface and use this control to display it.

OVERVIEW OF THE SILVERLIGHT FOR WINDOWS PHONE TOOLKIT

The Silverlight for Windows Phone Toolkit is a set of controls and classes that you can use in addition to the standard controls that come in the Windows Phone 7 developer kit. These additional controls provide you with features for autocomplete, time and date picking, gesture recognition, and more. Not only does the toolkit provide additional rich controls for your applications, it is also an open source project, which means you can download the controls in binary form as well as the entire source code for the controls. This means if you need to make any customizations or modifications to the controls, you can do so. You can also examine the code to get a better understanding of how some of the Windows Phone 7 controls are created.

To get your hands on the toolkit, you need to go to `www.silverlight.codeplex.com`. There you'll see download choices for the web version of the toolkit as well as the phone version. You should download the phone version and run the installer after the download has completed. When the installation program has finished, you can add the binary DLL files to your project and use all the controls included in the toolkit.

SILVERLIGHT FOR WINDOWS PHONE TOOLKIT CONTROLS

When you've finished installing the toolkit, you'll need the binary DLL files on your hard drive. To use any of these controls in your own project, however, you need to add a reference. When the installer is complete, a new .NET library is added to the list of available references. If a project is open, you can right-click the References folder and select Add Reference. The references dialog shown in Figure 13-1 appears. You need to select the `Microsoft.Phone.Controls.Toolkit` reference. This assembly includes the new toolkit.

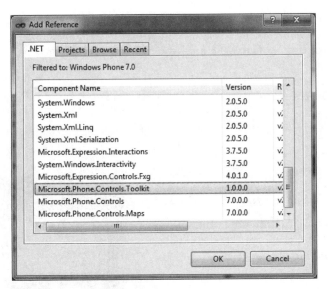

FIGURE 13-1: The Add Reference dialog.

After you add the reference, you can add the new controls to your XAML code by adding a new namespace declaration at the top of any XAML page. Typically, you add the following code and then access the toolkit controls by using the `toolkit:` syntax:

```
xmlsn:toolkit="clr-namespace:Microsoft.Phone.Controls;
assembly=Microsoft.Phone.Controls.Toolkit"
```

Now that you know how to add the required toolkit references and libraries to a Windows Phone 7 project, you can begin to use some of these new controls.

The AutoCompleteBox Control

If you have been to Google in the past few years, you no doubt have noticed its auto-suggest feature. As you type a search term, Google displays a drop-down list of search results that match what you have started typing. Google attempts to figure out what your final search term will be, and it displays possibilities as you type to give you a faster way to search. You may also have noticed that this auto-suggest feature is popping up on many other sites that require data entry or search capabilities. The Silverlight Toolkit for the web provides the `AutoCompleteBox` control to help facilitate adding auto-suggest features to your Silverlight applications. Now with the toolkit for the phone, you can also add auto-suggest functionality to your Windows Phone 7 applications.

Assuming that you've added the required reference and namespace, using the `AutoCompleteBox` control is not very difficult. There is only one real prerequisite to using the control: You must have a collection of data.

There are two main ways of using the `AutoCompleteBox` control. The first and easiest is to just use the default behavior of the control and set the `ItemsSource` property to a collection of objects. Assuming that you have a collection of string values, you simply add the following XAML code:

```
<toolkit:AutoCompleteBox x:Name="AutoComplete" VerticalAlignment="Top" />
```

Then, in the code-behind, you set `ItemsSource` to the collection of strings:

```
AutoComplete.ItemsSource = searchTerms;
```

If you were to run the application now, you would be presented with a typical drop-down list of choices, like the one shown in Figure 13-2.

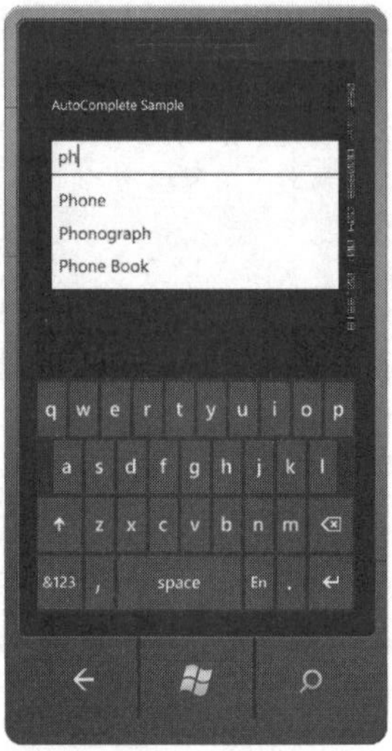

As you can see, after a couple of letters have been entered using the onscreen keyboard, a list of possible selections appear. You can easily determine which item is selected by handling the `SelectionChanged` event in your code-behind page.

In addition to the standard behavior, you also have the option of customizing the list of items that appear in the drop-down control. Instead of just a line with the string being displayed, you can customize the drop-down items to be just about any valid Silverlight control combination. For example, let's say you want to display a `WebSite` object that contains both an `SiteID` field and a `SiteName` field. You can override the `ItemTemplate` property of the `AutoCompleteBox` control to display a `StackPanel` control that shows both of these fields, using the following code:

FIGURE 13-2: The `AutoCompleteBox` control drop-down.

```
<toolkit:AutoCompleteBox x:Name="AutoComplete"
        ValueMemberPath="SiteName" VerticalAlignment="Top">
    <toolkit:AutoCompleteBox.ItemTemplate>
        <DataTemplate>
            <StackPanel Orientation="Horizontal">
                <TextBlock Text="{Binding SiteID}" />
                <TextBlock Text="{Binding SiteName}" Margin="10,0,0,0" />
            </StackPanel>
        </DataTemplate>
    </toolkit:AutoCompleteBox.ItemTemplate>
</toolkit:AutoCompleteBox>
```

Notice how the `ValueMemberPath` property is used here. The `AutoCompleteBox` control uses this property to determine which of the `WebSite` object's properties should be compared against the text being entered in the control. You need to set this anytime a non-string collection is used as the `ItemsSource` of the control.

TRY IT OUT Using the AutoCompleteBox Control

In this example, you'll add an `AutoCompleteBox` control to an application in order to allow users to search for foods. While a user is searching for the food to select, you want to show the user the calorie count for the food. This requires the use of a custom `ItemTemplate` control. Follow these steps:

1. Create a new Windows Phone 7 application, using the default project template. Call this application **AutoCompleteSample**.

2. Open the `MainPage.xaml` file and replace its contents with the code shown in Listing 13-1.

LISTING 13-1: Modifying the Code in MainPage.xaml

```xml
<phone:PhoneApplicationPage
    x:Class="AutoCompleteSample.MainPage"
    xmlns="http://schemas.microsoft.com/winfx/2006/xaml/presentation"
    xmlns:x="http://schemas.microsoft.com/winfx/2006/xaml"
    xmlns:phone="clr-    namespace:Microsoft.Phone.Controls;
assembly=Microsoft.Phone"
    xmlns:shell="clr-namespace:Microsoft.Phone.Shell;assembly=Microsoft.Phone"
    xmlns:d="http://schemas.microsoft.com/expression/blend/2008"
    xmlns:mc="http://schemas.openxmlformats.org/markup-compatibility/2006"
    xmlns:toolkit="clr-namespace:Microsoft.Phone.Controls;
assembly=Microsoft.Phone.Controls.Toolkit"
    mc:Ignorable="d" d:DesignWidth="480" d:DesignHeight="768"
    FontFamily="{StaticResource PhoneFontFamilyNormal}"
    FontSize="{StaticResource PhoneFontSizeNormal}"
    Foreground="{StaticResource PhoneForegroundBrush}"
    SupportedOrientations="Portrait" Orientation="Portrait"
    shell:SystemTray.IsVisible="True">

    <!--LayoutRoot is the root grid where all page content is placed-->
    <Grid x:Name="LayoutRoot" Background="Transparent">
        <Grid.RowDefinitions>
            <RowDefinition Height="Auto"/>
            <RowDefinition Height="*"/>
        </Grid.RowDefinitions>

        <!--TitlePanel contains the name of the application and page title-->
        <StackPanel x:Name="TitlePanel" Grid.Row="0" Margin="12,17,0,28">
            <TextBlock x:Name="ApplicationTitle" Text="AutoComplete Sample"
Style="{StaticResource PhoneTextNormalStyle}"/>
        </StackPanel>

        <!--ContentPanel - place additional content here-->
        <Grid x:Name="ContentPanel" Grid.Row="1" Margin="12,0,12,0">
            <toolkit:AutoCompleteBox x:Name="AutoComplete"
ValueMemberPath="FoodID" VerticalAlignment="Top">
                <toolkit:AutoCompleteBox.ItemTemplate>
                    <DataTemplate>
                        <StackPanel Orientation="Horizontal">
```

continues

LISTING 13-1 *(continued)*

```
                                    <TextBlock Text="{Binding FoodName}" />
                                    <TextBlock Text="{Binding CalorieCount}"
        Margin="10,0,0,0" />
                        </StackPanel>
                    </DataTemplate>
                </toolkit:AutoCompleteBox.ItemTemplate>
            </toolkit:AutoCompleteBox>
        </Grid>
    </Grid>
</phone:PhoneApplicationPage>
```

Code Snippet AutoCompleteSample\MainPage.xaml

3. Add to the project a new class file called `Food.cs` that contains a collection of foods, along with their respective calorie counts. To do so, add the code shown in Listing 13-2.

LISTING 13-2: Modifying the Code in Food.cs

```
namespace AutoCompleteSample
{
    public class Food
    {
        public int FoodID { get; set; }
        public string FoodName { get; set; }
        public int Calories { get; set; }
    }
}
```

Code Snippet AutoCompleteSample\Food.cs

4. Provide the `ItemsSource` of the `AutoCompleteBox` control with a collection of `Food` objects and let the user know which food was selected. To do this, open the `MainPage.xaml.cs` code-behind file and replace it with the code shown in Listing 13-3.

LISTING 13-3: Modifying the Code in MainPage.xaml.cs

```
using System;
using System.Collections.Generic;
using System.Windows;
using System.Windows.Controls;
using Microsoft.Phone.Controls;

namespace AutoCompleteSample
{
    public partial class MainPage : PhoneApplicationPage
```

```
        {
            // Constructor
            public MainPage()
            {
                InitializeComponent();

                this.Loaded += new RoutedEventHandler(MainPage_Loaded);
                AutoComplete.SelectionChanged += new
SelectionChangedEventHandler(AutoComplete_SelectionChanged);
            }

            private void AutoComplete_SelectionChanged(object sender,
SelectionChangedEventArgs e)
            {
                MessageBox.Show(String.Format("You selected {0}",
(AutoComplete.SelectedItem as Food).FoodName));
            }

            private void MainPage_Loaded(object sender, RoutedEventArgs e)
            {
                List<Food> foods = new List<Food>();

                foods.Add(new Food { FoodID = 1,
FoodName = "Chicken", Calories = 200 });
                foods.Add(new Food { FoodID = 2,
FoodName = "Cheese", Calories = 70 });
                foods.Add(new Food { FoodID = 3,
FoodName = "Pizza", Calories = 500 });
                foods.Add(new Food { FoodID = 4,
FoodName = "Popcorn", Calories = 100 });
                foods.Add(new Food { FoodID = 5,
FoodName = "Apple", Calories = 30 });
                foods.Add(new Food { FoodID = 6,
FoodName = "Apricot", Calories = 60 });
                foods.Add(new Food { FoodID = 7,
FoodName = "Beef", Calories = 140 });
                foods.Add(new Food { FoodID = 8,
FoodName = "Bacon", Calories = 80 });
                foods.Add(new Food { FoodID = 9,
FoodName = "Fries", Calories = 350 });
                foods.Add(new Food { FoodID = 10,
FoodName = "Potato", Calories = 150 });

                AutoComplete.ItemsSource = foods;
            }
        }
    }
}
```

Code Snippet AutoCompleteSample\MainPage.xaml.cs

5. Build and run the application. After the emulator displays the main screen, try to enter the letters **ch**. You now see the Chicken and Cheese options, as shown in Figure 13-3.

6. Select the Cheese option, and you will see the `FoodID` property of the selected item displayed using the `MessageBox` control.

How It Works

In this example, you added an `AutoCompleteBox` control to the application to help users search for foods. Because the goal was to show both foods and their calorie counts, you needed to override the `ItemTemplate` property. You also needed to set the `ValueMemberPath` property because you were setting `ItemsSource` to a collection of `Food` objects. You needed to tell the `AutoCompleteBox` control which of the `Food` properties should be used when comparing the text being entered by the user. In this case, you needed to search the `FoodName` property. Finally, because in most applications you would be interested in the actual `FoodID` property for coding purposes, you added a handler for the `SelectionChanged` event, and in that handler you had access to the `SelectedItem` property of the `AutoCompleteBox` control. Once you had access to that object, you simply cast it to a `Food` type and displayed the `FoodID` property in the `MessageBox` control.

FIGURE 13-3: The `AutoCompleteBox` list showing food choices.

The DatePicker Control

Another useful control in the toolkit is `DatePicker`. You can use the `DatePicker` control to set the initial date on the phone. This control isn't part of the standard SDK. Luckily, it's available as part of the Silverlight for Windows Phone Toolkit, and using it is just about the easiest way to enable users to perform date selection.

To get started with the `DatePicker` control, you just add the following XAML code to a page:

```
<toolkit:DatePicker x:Name="Picker" ValueChanged="Picker_ValueChanged" />
```

The `ValueChanged` event gives you a way to detect when the user has finished selecting the date. As you can see, there isn't much code required to get this working. When you add this control to the page, you see what appears to be a `TextBox` control with the current date being displayed, as shown in Figure 13-4.

When the user touches any area of the `TextBox` control, the date selection screen appears. The user can finish the selection by clicking one of the buttons displayed at the bottom of the screen. Figure 13-5 shows the date selection screen of the control.

FIGURE 13-4: The
DatePicker control.

FIGURE 13-5: The
DatePicker date
selection screen.

When the user completes the date selection, you can easily access the result in the code-behind
page by adding an event handler for the ValueChanged event. The previous XAML declares a
ValueChanged handler called Picker_ValueChanged. The code-behind for this handler might look
something like the following:

```
private void Picker_ValueChanged(object sender, DateTimeValueChangedEventArgs e)
{
    string previousDate = e.OldDateTime.Value.Date.ToShortDateString();
    string selectedDate = e.NewDateTime.Value.Date.ToShortDateString();
}
```

Notice that the DateTimeValueChangedEventArgs object gives you easy access to both the original
date displayed and the newly selected date. Overall, this control is easy to work with and similar to
the TimePicker control.

The TimePicker Control

The TimePicker control gives you an excellent way to provide users with the capability to choose
a time value in your application. As with the DatePicker control, you can add an instance of
TimePicker with just one line of XAML code:

```
<toolkit:TimePicker x:Name="TimePicker" ValueChanged="TimePicker_ValueChanged" />
```

Once you have added this XAML to your page, your user is once again presented with a `TextBox` control, but this control displays the current time. When the user touches in the area of the control, a time selection screen appears (see Figure 13-6).

As you can see, this is similar to what the `DatePicker` control provides. And as with the `DatePicker` control, you can add an event handler for the `ValueChanged` event to access the selected time. The following code shows an example of a handler for this:

```
private void TimePicker_ValueChanged(object sender,
DateTimeValueChangedEventArgs e)
{
    TimeSpan previousTime = e.OldDateTime.Value.TimeOfDay;
    TimeSpan selectedTime = e.NewDateTime.Value.TimeOfDay;
}
```

You can easily make use of the same `DateTimeValueChangedEventArgs` object as before to retrieve both the previous time and the newly selected time values.

FIGURE 13-6: The `TimePicker` time selection screen.

The ContextMenu Control

Another great addition to the Silverlight for Windows Phone Toolkit is the `ContextMenu` control. You may have seen context menus being displayed on the phone when you touch and hold your finger down in some standard Windows Phone 7 applications. The default SDK doesn't give you an easy way to provide this functionality. Luckily, the toolkit does.

As with a traditional context menu, you need to plan on having several menu options. You also need to determine what controls the user should press and hold to enable the display of the `ContextMenu` control. Creating a new `ContextMenu` control involves first adding a container to host the controls responsible for displaying the menu. Say that you want a `StackPanel` control containing `Button` controls. You want the `ContextMenu` control to be displayed when the user touches and holds any of the `Button` controls in the `StackPanel`. So far, you need the following XAML code:

```
<StackPanel>
    <StackPanel>
        <Button Content="Press and hold here" />
        <Button Content="Or Press and hold here" />
    </StackPanel>
    <StackPanel>
        <Button Content="No Context menu here" />
        <Button Content="No Context menu here either" />
    </StackPanel>
</StackPanel>
```

Now you add a declaration of the `ContextMenuService.ContextMenu` control. You should place this control just under the container you want to use to display the `ContextMenu` control. Because you want only the first two Button controls to enable the menu, you modify the code to look like the following:

```
<StackPanel>
    <StackPanel>
        <toolkit:ContextMenuService.ContextMenu>
            <toolkit:ContextMenu>

            </toolkit:ContextMenu>
        </toolkit:ContextMenuService.ContextMenu>
        <Button Content="Press and hold here" />
        <Button Content="Or Press and hold here" />
    </StackPanel>
    <StackPanel>
        <Button Content="No Context menu here" />
        <Button Content="No Context menu here either" />
    </StackPanel>
</StackPanel>
```

As you can see, an instance of the ContextMenu control has been added to the first StackPanel control containing Button controls. This means that after you add menu items, touching and holding either of the two Button controls results in the menu being displayed. Say that you want to add three menu options. To do this, you add three MenuItem declarations, with the Header and Tag properties set:

```
<StackPanel>
    <StackPanel>
        <toolkit:ContextMenuService.ContextMenu>
            <toolkit:ContextMenu>
                <toolkit:MenuItem Header="Menu Item 1" Tag="1"
Click="MenuItem_Click" />
                <toolkit:MenuItem Header="Menu Item 2" Tag="2"
Click="MenuItem_Click" />
                <toolkit:MenuItem Header="Menu Item 3" Tag="3"
Click="MenuItem_Click" />
            </toolkit:ContextMenu>
        </toolkit:ContextMenuService.ContextMenu>
        <Button Content="Press and hold here" />
        <Button Content="Or Press and hold here" />
    </StackPanel>
    <StackPanel>
        <Button Content="No Context menu here" />
        <Button Content="No Context menu here either" />
    </StackPanel>
</StackPanel>
```

The Tag property is used to hold the number of the MenuItem control so that in the code-behind you can easily determine which MenuItem object is selected. Notice that a Click event handler is declared for all the MenuItem controls All these MenuItem controls can share the same event handler because the Tag property is used to distinguish among the three choices. If you were to build and run this example, you could click and hold the left mouse button in the emulator to get the new `ContextMenu` control to display. The screen shown in Figure 13-7 displays.

Now you just need to add code to the `MenuItem_Click` event handler to find out which selection was made. You could use the following code to access this information:

```
private void MenuItem_Click(object sender, RoutedEventArgs e)
{
    string selected = ((MenuItem)sender).Tag.ToString();
}
```

FIGURE 13-7: A ContextMenu control being displayed.

SILVERLIGHT FOR WINDOWS PHONE TOOLKIT PAGE TRANSITIONS

In addition to providing new controls, the Silverlight for Windows Phone Toolkit includes several easy-to-use `Page Transition` classes. By simply wrapping your application pages in these transition classes, you can create dynamic user interface effects for moving between pages in a multi-page application.

To get started with transitions, you need to understand a little about how they work. Basically, each page has both an IN transition and an OUT transition defined. For both the IN and OUT transitions, you can specify a transition effect to apply for when the user moves forward and backward through the page. Let's break this down with some code. Say that your application has multiple pages. The first thing you need to do is add a declaration for `TransitionService` at the page level, like this:

```
<phone:PhoneApplicationPage
    x:Class="PhoneToolkitSample.Samples.NavigationTransitionSample1"
    xmlns="http://schemas.microsoft.com/winfx/2006/xaml/presentation"
    xmlns:x="http://schemas.microsoft.com/winfx/2006/xaml"
    xmlns:phone="clr-namespace:Microsoft.Phone.Controls;assembly=Microsoft.Phone"
    xmlns:shell="clr-namespace:Microsoft.Phone.Shell;assembly=Microsoft.Phone"
    xmlns:d="http://schemas.microsoft.com/expression/blend/2008"
    xmlns:mc="http://schemas.openxmlformats.org/markup-compatibility/2006"
    xmlns:toolkit="clr-
namespace:Microsoft.Phone.Controls;assembly=Microsoft.Phone.Controls.Toolkit"
    FontFamily="{StaticResource PhoneFontFamilyNormal}"
    FontSize="{StaticResource PhoneFontSizeNormal}"
    Foreground="{StaticResource PhoneForegroundBrush}"
    SupportedOrientations="Portrait" Orientation="Portrait"
    mc:Ignorable="d" d:DesignHeight="768" d:DesignWidth="480"
    shell:SystemTray.IsVisible="False">
    <toolkit:TransitionService.NavigationInTransition>
```

As you can see, you've started to create the IN transition definition. Now you need to decide on effects to be applied for when the user navigates into this page using a normal forward motion as well as when the user clicks the Back button on the phone device to get to this page. One effect you can use is `TurnstileTransition`. The emulator uses this transition effect automatically when the application starts running. The following code applies this transition when the page is reached both through a forward navigation motion and when the user presses the Back button on the phone device:

```
<toolkit:TransitionService.NavigationInTransition>
    <toolkit:NavigationInTransition>
        <toolkit:NavigationInTransition.Backward>
            <toolkit:TurnstileTransition Mode="BackwardIn"/>
        </toolkit:NavigationInTransition.Backward>
        <toolkit:NavigationInTransition.Forward>
            <toolkit:TurnstileTransition Mode="ForwardIn"/>
        </toolkit:NavigationInTransition.Forward>
    </toolkit:NavigationInTransition>
</toolkit:TransitionService.NavigationInTransition>
```

Note that in instances of the `TurnstileTransition` effect, the `Mode` property is set according to how the user is navigating to the page. In addition to this, you also need to set up the effects you want to apply when the user navigates away from this page. The following code sets up a `TurnstileTransition` effect for leaving the page:

```
<toolkit:TransitionService.NavigationOutTransition>
    <toolkit:NavigationOutTransition>
        <toolkit:NavigationOutTransition.Backward>
            <toolkit:TurnstileTransition Mode="BackwardOut"/>
        </toolkit:NavigationOutTransition.Backward>
        <toolkit:NavigationOutTransition.Forward>
            <toolkit:TurnstileTransition Mode="ForwardOut"/>
        </toolkit:NavigationOutTransition.Forward>
    </toolkit:NavigationOutTransition>
</toolkit:TransitionService.NavigationOutTransition>
```

This code is similar to the IN transition code, but the `Mode` property takes care of making everything look good. Of course, a screenshot of this in action is tough to create for a book, so you need to just try some of these transitions in the emulator to see for yourself. Before doing so, however, you need to take one more very important step. In the `App.xaml.cs` file, by default the main `Frame` object of the application is declared as `PhoneApplicationFrame`. This type of frame does not support the transition effects. Instead of using the `PhoneApplicationFrame` object, you should change the following `InitializePhoneApplication` method to use a `TransitionFrame` instead:

 WARNING *If you fail to change the following* `InitializePhoneApplication` *method to use a* `TransitionFrame` *instead, you won't see any of the declared transition effects take place.*

```
// Use TransitionFrame instead of PhoneApplicationFrame
// TransitionFrame has built-in support for transition effects

RootFrame = new TransitionFrame();
```

The toolkit supports many types of transition effects in addition to `TurnstileTransition`. Table 13-1 shows all the effects the toolkit offers.

TABLE 13-1: Silverlight for Windows Phone Toolkit Transition Effects

EFFECT	SUPPORTED MODE VALUES
TurnstileTransition	BackwardIn
	BackwardOut
	ForwardIn
	ForwardOut
RollTransition	
RotateTransition	In180Clockwise
	In180CounterClockwise
	In90Clockwise
	In90CounterClockwise
	Out180Clockwise
	Out180CounterClockwise
	Out90Clockwise
	Out90CounterClockwise
SlideTransition	SlideDownFadeIn
	SlideDownFadeOut
	SlideUpFadeIn
	SlideUpFadeOut
	SlideLeftFadeIn
	SlideLeftFadeOut
	SlideRightFadeIn
	SlideRightFadeOut
SwivelTransition	BackwardIn
	BackwardOut
	ForwardIn
	ForwardOut
	FullScreenIn
	FullScreenOut

SILVERLIGHT FOR WINDOWS PHONE TOOLKIT GESTURES

In addition to providing page transitions, the Silverlight for Windows Phone Toolkit also offers the ability to easily detect gestures. With just a few lines of XAML code, you can detect user gestures such as tap, flick, pinch, and drag movements. The gesture recognition works similarly to the ContextMenu control in that you add to your XAML a container on which you wish to listen for gestures. Then you set up a GestureListener control to determine which gesture events you want to handle in your code-behind file. You can easily detect multitouch pinch gestures and perhaps scale an image accordingly, or you could allow users to drag items in a container by listening and handling the drag events.

To get started with gesture detection, you first need a container to host both the service and the controls on which you want to detect gestures. In this example, you'll create a Border control that hosts a simple rectangle shape:

```
<Border>
    <Rectangle Fill="Blue" Width="200" Height="200" />
</Border>
```

Say that you want to detect both Flick and DoubleTap gesture events. To do this, you simply add the GestureService.GestureListener object to the Border control, using code like the following:

```
<Border>

    <Rectangle Fill="Blue" Width="200" Height="200" />
    <toolkit:GestureService.GestureListener>
        <toolkit:GestureListener Flick="HandleFlick"
DoubleTap="HandleDoubleTap"
/>
    </toolkit:GestureService.GestureListener>
</Border>
```

Notice that you simply add event handler declarations for both the Flick and DoubleTap gesture events, and this is all the code you need. Now in the code-behind, you have access to additional data about the Flick and DoubleTap events. In the following code, the Flick and DoubleTap event handlers display both the Angle of the Flick and update a TextBlock control to let the user know when a DoubleTap gesture has occurred:

```
private void HandleFlick(object sender, FlickGestureEventArgs e)
{
    GestureResult.Text = String.Format("Flick Detected - Angle: {0}",e.Angle);
}

private void HandleDoubleTap(object sender, GestureEventArgs e)
{
    GestureResult.Text = "Double Tap Detected";
}
```

If you were to build and run this code in the emulator, you could easily mimic the `Flick` gesture by quickly moving the mouse left or right while the left mouse button is down. The screen updates to show the `Angle` of the `Flick` shown in Figure 13-8.

Of course, mimicking the `DoubleTap` gesture is as simple as double-clicking the mouse on the screen. This results in the `HandleDoubleTap` method being called.

As stated earlier, you can catch several other gestures by using `GestureListener`, and they all provide the information necessary to handle the gesture event as well as manipulate objects on the screen or run custom code, based on the type of gesture detected. Table 13-2 shows all the gestures that can be detected.

FIGURE 13-8: A `Flick` gesture detected.

TABLE 13-2: Available Gestures in the Silverlight for Windows Phone Toolkit

GESTURE	SUPPORTED EVENTS
Flick	Flick
DoubleTap	DoubleTap
Pinch	PinchStarted
	PinchCompleted
	PinchDelta
Drag	DragStarted
	DragCompleted
	DragDelta
Hold	Hold

`Flick`, `Hold`, and `DoubleTap` are straightforward, and detecting these gestures just requires handling the events. `Pinch` and `Drag`, however, each have three separate events that you can listen for. The `Started` event is triggered as soon as the user begins a `Pinch` or `Drag` movement on the screen. The `Completed` event is thrown when the user releases his or her finger from the screen or, in the case of the emulator, releases the mouse button. Finally, the `Delta` event is fired as the motion is taking place, allowing you to update any user interface object accordingly during the actual gesture operation as opposed to forcing you to wait until the motion has completed.

THE PANORAMA CONTROL

In addition to the new controls and features in the Silverlight for Windows Phone Toolkit, another important control is available in the standard Windows Phone 7 SDK: `Panorama`. The `Panorama` control enables you to create a wide scrolling user interface that's similar to what you would find in the music and video hub on the phone. The `Panorama` control gives you a unique way to have what looks to the user like a multi-page application but in fact is just one continuous page. Figure 13-9 shows one of the standard `Panorama` controls in use on a Windows Phone 7 device.

FIGURE 13-9: A `Panorama` control on a Windows Phone device.

To get started using the `Panorama` control in your own application, you need to add a reference to the `Microsoft.Phone.Controls` assembly. Next, you need to figure out how to best lay out your application screen. Because the `Panorama` control works best with groups or categories, you should try to determine what categories are necessary for your app. Once you've determined how best to lay out the categories, you can add a new `Panorama` control to your XAML page. Don't forget to add a reference to the required namespace at the top of your file. For the `Panorama` control, you add the following namespace declaration:

```
xmlsn:controls="clr-namespace:Microsoft.Phone.Controls;
assembly=Microsoft.Phone.Controls"
```

Next, you simply add a `Panorama` control along with a `PanoramaItem` control for each of your categories. The following code shows a sample outline of a `Panorama` control being used:

```
<controls:Panorama Title="Panorama View">
<controls:PanoramaItem Header="Category 1">

</controls:PanoramaItem>
```

```
<controls:PanoramaItem Header="Category 2">

</controls:PanoramaItem>
<controls:PanoramaItem Header="Category 3">

</controls:PanoramaItem>
</controls:Panorama>
```

To add content to the `Panorama` control, you just add XAML code in between the opening and closing tags of the `PanoramaItem` control. You can use the `Title` property of the `Panorama` control to display a long-running application or page title. This text spreads out across all three categories, and as the user scrolls through the `PanoramaItem` controls, the `Title` control text flows across the screen. You can also add header text for each of the `PanoramaItem` controls.

<u>**TRY IT OUT**</u>   **Using the Panorama Control**

In the following steps, you'll create your own `Panorama` control–enhanced application that will show the user three categories of books. Each `Panorama` control view will display books from the categories Windows Phone 7, Silverlight, and ASP.NET. Follow these steps:

1.   Create a new Windows Phone 7 project using the standard project template and call this project **PanoramaSample**.

2.   When the project finishes loading, add a reference to the `Panorama` control. To do so, right-click the References folder in the Solution Explorer and add the `Microsoft.Phone.Controls` assembly, as shown in Figure 13-10.

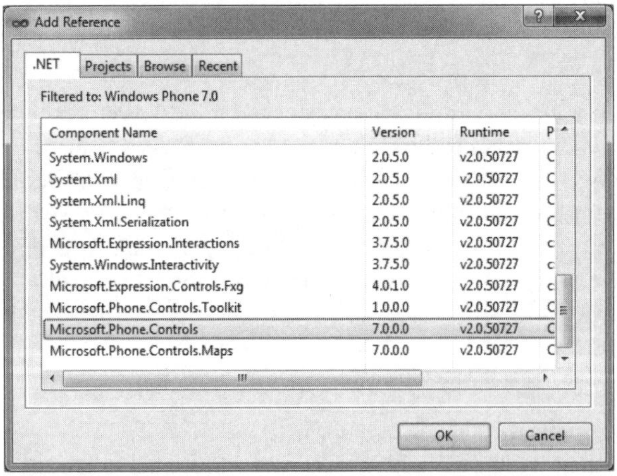

FIGURE 13-10: Adding a `Panorama` control reference.

3.   Add a new class file called `Book` to the project. This file represents each of the books that will be displayed in the `Panorama` control. Replace the contents of this new file with the code in Listing 13-4.

LISTING 13-4: Modifying the Code in Book.cs

```csharp
using System.Windows.Media.Imaging;

namespace Panorama_Sample
{
    public class Book
    {
        public string Title { get; set; }
        public BitmapImage Cover { get; set; }
    }
}
```

Code Snippet Panorama Sample\Book.cs

4. Define the `Panorama` control by opening the `MainPage.xaml` file and replacing its contents with the code shown in Listing 13-5.

LISTING 13-5: Modifying the Code in MainPage.xaml

```xml
<phone:PhoneApplicationPage
    x:Class="Panorama_Sample.MainPage"
    xmlns="http://schemas.microsoft.com/winfx/2006/xaml/presentation"
    xmlns:x="http://schemas.microsoft.com/winfx/2006/xaml"
    xmlns:phone="clr-
namespace:Microsoft.Phone.Controls;assembly=Microsoft.Phone"
    xmlns:shell="clr-namespace:Microsoft.Phone.Shell;assembly=Microsoft.Phone"
    xmlns:d="http://schemas.microsoft.com/expression/blend/2008"
    xmlns:controls="clr-
namespace:Microsoft.Phone.Controls;assembly=Microsoft.Phone.Controls"
    xmlns:mc="http://schemas.openxmlformats.org/markup-compatibility/2006"
    mc:Ignorable="d" d:DesignWidth="480" d:DesignHeight="768"
    FontFamily="{StaticResource PhoneFontFamilyNormal}"
    FontSize="{StaticResource PhoneFontSizeNormal}"
    Foreground="{StaticResource PhoneForegroundBrush}"
    SupportedOrientations="Portrait" Orientation="Portrait"
    shell:SystemTray.IsVisible="True">

    <phone:PhoneApplicationPage.Resources>
        <DataTemplate x:Key="ItemStyle">
            <StackPanel Orientation="Horizontal" Margin="10">
                <Image Source="{Binding Cover}" />
                <TextBlock Text="{Binding Title}" Margin="10,0,0,0" />
            </StackPanel>
        </DataTemplate>
    </phone:PhoneApplicationPage.Resources>

    <!--LayoutRoot is the root grid where all page content is placed-->
    <Grid x:Name="LayoutRoot" Background="Transparent">
        <Grid.RowDefinitions>
            <RowDefinition Height="Auto"/>
```

continues

LISTING 13-5 *(continued)*

```
                <RowDefinition Height="*"/>
            </Grid.RowDefinitions>

            <!--ContentPanel - place additional content here-->
            <controls:Panorama x:Name="MainPanorama"
    Title="Panoramic Book View">
                <controls:PanoramaItem Header="Win Phone 7">
                    <ListBox x:Name="WinPhoneList"
    ItemTemplate="{StaticResource ItemStyle}" />
                </controls:PanoramaItem>
                <controls:PanoramaItem Header="Silverlight">
                    <ListBox x:Name="SilverlightList"
    ItemTemplate="{StaticResource ItemStyle}" />
                </controls:PanoramaItem>
                <controls:PanoramaItem Header="ASP.NET">
                    <ListBox x:Name="AspNetList"
    ItemTemplate="{StaticResource ItemStyle}" />
                </controls:PanoramaItem>
            </controls:Panorama>
        </Grid>
    </phone:PhoneApplicationPage>
```

Code Snippet Panorama Sample\MainPage.xaml

5. Add some items to each of the ListBox controls that will hold the book information. Notice how each ListBox control uses data binding in the ItemTemplate to reduce the amount of code required. Open the MainPage.xaml.cs file and replace its contents with the code shown in Listing 13-6.

LISTING 13-6: Modifying the Code in MainPage.xaml.cs

```
using System;
using System.Collections.Generic;
using System.Windows;
using Microsoft.Phone.Controls;
using System.Windows.Media.Imaging;

namespace Panorama_Sample
{
    public partial class MainPage : PhoneApplicationPage
    {
        // Constructor
        public MainPage()
        {
            InitializeComponent();
            this.Loaded += new RoutedEventHandler(MainPage_Loaded);
        }

        private void MainPage_Loaded(object sender, RoutedEventArgs e)
```

```
            {
                List<Book> silverlight = new List<Book>();
                List<Book> aspnet = new List<Book>();
                List<Book> winphone = new List<Book>();

                silverlight.Add(new Book {
Title = "Professional Silverlight 4",
Cover = new BitmapImage(new Uri("Images/silver_1.png", UriKind.Relative)) });
                silverlight.Add(new Book {
Title = "Silverlight 4 PDS",
Cover = new BitmapImage(new Uri("Images/silver_2.png", UriKind.Relative)) });
                silverlight.Add(new Book {
Title = "Professional Silverlight 3",
Cover = new BitmapImage(new Uri("Images/silver_3.png", UriKind.Relative)) });
                silverlight.Add(new Book {
Title = "Professional Silverlight 2",
Cover = new BitmapImage(new Uri("Images/silver_4.png", UriKind.Relative)) });

                SilverlightList.ItemsSource = silverlight;

                aspnet.Add(new Book {
Title = "ASP.NET Design Patterns",
Cover = new BitmapImage(new Uri("Images/asp_1.png", UriKind.Relative)) });
                aspnet.Add(new Book {
Title = "Professional ASP.NET MVC 2",
Cover = new BitmapImage(new Uri("Images/asp_2.png", UriKind.Relative)) });
                aspnet.Add(new Book {
Title = "Beginning ASP.NET Security",
Cover = new BitmapImage(new Uri("Images/asp_3.png", UriKind.Relative)) });
                aspnet.Add(new Book {
Title = "ASP.NET 3.5 PDS",
Cover = new BitmapImage(new Uri("Images/asp_4.png", UriKind.Relative)) });

                AspNetList.ItemsSource = aspnet;

                winphone.Add(new Book {
Title = "Professional Windows Phone 7 Apps & Games",
Cover = new BitmapImage(new Uri("Images/winphone_1.png", UriKind.Relative)) });
                winphone.Add(new Book {
Title = "Professional Windows Phone 7 Game Dev",
Cover = new BitmapImage(new Uri("Images/winphone_2.png", UriKind.Relative)) });
                winphone.Add(new Book {
Title = "Windows Phone 7 24 Hour Trainer",
Cover = new BitmapImage(new Uri("Images/winphone_3.png", UriKind.Relative)) });

                WinPhoneList.ItemsSource = winphone;
            }
        }
}
```

Code Snippet Panorama Sample\MainPage.xaml.cs

6. Build and run the application. You should see a screen similar to the one shown in Figure 13-11.

7. You can now easily swipe the mouse on the emulator screen in order to display each of the three book categories.

How It Works

In this example, you created a `Panorama` control–enhanced user interface. You added three `PanoramaItem` controls, one for each category of books being displayed. To minimize the amount of code, you used a custom `ItemTemplate` control for the `ListBoxItem` objects and shared that template among all three `ListBox` controls by using a `StaticResource` declaration. As you can see, most of the code required involves just setting up collections of `Book` objects for populating the `ListBox` controls. The `Panorama` control does all the hard user interface work behind the scenes, giving you nice fluid transitions between category pages.

FIGURE 13-11: The `Panorama` control sample screen.

SUMMARY

In this chapter, you were introduced to the Silverlight for Windows Phone Toolkit as well as the `Panorama` control from the Windows Phone SDK. The toolkit provides several powerful controls in addition to the standard SDK controls. You saw how easy it is to add Google-type autocomplete functionality to your application by using the `AutoCompleteBox` control. You also saw how to enable users to easily choose dates and times by using the `DatePicker` and `TimePicker` controls. Next, you learned how to add fluid page transition effects to your multi-page applications by using `TransitionService` and transition effects.

You also learned about the `GestureService` and learned to easily detect various gestures, such as `Flick`, `DoubleTap`, `Drag`, `Pinch`, and `Hold`, by just listening for various events in the code-behind file.

Finally, you used the `Panorama` control to display a long horizontal user interface consisting of multiple category displays. The `Panorama` control took care of making sure each category page transitioned smoothly with a simple `Flick` gesture.

1. True or False: `PhoneApplicationFrame` provides full support for page transitions.

2. Which of the following are valid gestures that `GestureService` supports? (Choose all that apply.)

a)   `Flick`

b)   `Press`

c)   `Drag`

d)   `Close`

3. Which event can you listen for in the code-behind file to determine what item being displayed by the `AutoCompleteBox` control was selected by the user?

4.   What transition types does the Silverlight for Windows Phone Toolkit support?

5.   Which of the following `DatePicker` events can be used to determine what date the user selected?

a)   `Click`

b)   `Loaded`

c)   `ValueChanged`

d)   `ValueChanging`

Answers to the Exercises can be found in the Appendix.

▶ **WHAT YOU LEARNED IN THIS CHAPTER**

TOPIC	KEY CONCEPTS
Silverlight for Windows Phone Toolkit	The toolkit provides several new controls and features not included with the standard Windows Phone 7 SDK, including the following:
	AutoCompleteBox
	ToggleButton
	DatePicker
	TimePicker
	Gestures
	Page transitions
Panorama **control**	This control enables you to create multi-page applications using a scrollable user interface. You can add category pages by using PanoramaItem controls. The Panorama control provides smooth scrolling and auto-detection of Flick gestures.

14

Patterns, Frameworks, and Tests

WHAT YOU WILL LEARN IN THIS CHAPTER:

➤ Understanding patterns

➤ Using the MVVM pattern in Windows Phone 7 applications

➤ Using third-party frameworks

➤ Performing unit tests

➤ Writing unit tests for Windows Phone 7 applications

Throughout this book, you have learned many techniques that enable you to create Windows Phone 7 applications. However, having basic, low-level tools to do this will only take you so far. For larger-scale applications, particularly enterprise applications that may need to be developed by a team of programmers, more advanced, high-level techniques are essential for success.

In this chapter, you'll look at some of these techniques, in particular the implementation of patterns, frameworks, and tests. Each of these individually will make your applications more robust and more maintainable. As you will see, they also support each other in elegant ways, and the combination is far more than the sum of the parts. If you want to be the best programmer you can be and if you want to work on the best teams in the industry, the techniques in this chapter are must-haves.

Patterns, frameworks, and tests apply to a much wider range of development than Windows Phone 7 applications. In this chapter, you'll not only learn the basics but also see how to apply these techniques to Silverlight applications on Windows Phone 7 devices. You'll also focus on techniques that work well with this type of application rather than look at all the options and compare them.

USING PATTERNS

Application development involves regularly solving problems in order to achieve some goal, such as accessing a remote web service or displaying items in a list. You'll encounter the same problems time and again. Perhaps you will refer to solutions that others have posted on websites or written down in books to help you overcome a common problem. You might identify common types of applications and build your applications using code from them as starting points.

One thing that can help you when it comes to approaching problems in this way is the use of patterns. *Patterns* are agreed-on solutions to common problems. They might be relatively small and simple (such as a way to access a remote service through a proxy class) or larger scale (such as ways to structure your applications to realize some benefit). The .NET Framework has common patterns that you use daily, such as collection classes and events.

Entire books are devoted to the use of patterns, and although many of them are great, they can be extremely technical. When it comes to Windows Phone 7 Silverlight application development, the most useful patterns are the larger-scale, architectural ones that influence how you structure entire applications. In this section, you'll look at the patterns available in this area and see how they can benefit you.

Using Architectural Patterns

The Silverlight applications you've created so far in this book have, for the most part, followed a fairly simple scheme. Each page or user control has consisted of some XAML and some associated C# code (as shown schematically in Figure 14-1). This technique, while simple, has some disadvantages. The biggest of them is that the code and XAML are tightly coupled. Often, you'll refer to code elements such as event handlers by name in XAML code, and from C# code you'll manipulate named XAML elements and controls directly. For example, if you want to change the visibility of a control, you must give the control a name and then change the value of its `Visibility` property from your C# code.

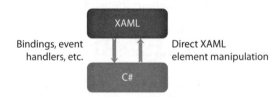

FIGURE 14-1: Standard Silverlight application architecture.

The advantages of this technique are its simplicity and the speed with which you can create new pages. However, the tight coupling of XAML and C# means that you lose a lot in maintainability. If you want to change the look and feel of a page, you generally have to change both the XAML and C# parts. It can also be easy to break the links between XAML and C#, because often the functionality of the code relies on structural aspects of the XAML code, such as exactly how deeply nested one control is in the page hierarchy.

By using a more advanced architectural pattern, you can remove many of the dependencies between XAML and C# code. Doing this has advantages as the two parts become more independent of each other, which means different people can work on them simultaneously (a user experience [UX], designer, and a programmer, for example). The logical separation also encourages cleaner and more maintainable code because the communication between the layers becomes more strictly defined within the scope of the pattern. This also makes your code more testable, as you'll see later in this chapter.

Architectural patterns have existed for many years and have evolved to suit different platforms and languages. The pattern that is currently accepted to be the best for Silverlight development on Windows Phone 7 devices is called Model–View–View-Model (MVVM).

Developing with MVVM

MVVM defines three parts (also known as layers, or tiers) that make up the architecture of an application. Each part references one of the others and does not need direct knowledge or references other than this. The parts are defined as follows:

➤ **Model** — This part contains the data and anything else the application requires, such as units of business logic.

➤ **View** — This part provides the user interface for the application.

➤ **ViewModel** — This part provides the interface between the view and the model, including all the interaction that is possible.

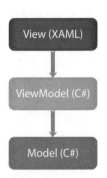

In a Silverlight implementation, you create views in XAML (with an associated, though often empty, C# class definition) and models and view models in C#. Figure 14-2 shows the relationship between these three parts. The arrows in the diagram show which part references which other part. For example, the view has a reference to the view model.

To understand this better, say that you want to make a car showroom application that enables users to browse through a collection of cars and send email messages to friends about cars that they like. In this case, you define models that represent cars, perhaps using a C# class called `CarModel`. You then create a XAML page or user control, called `CarView`, that displays the details of an individual car. Finally, you create a view model called `CarViewModel` to provide the linkage between the view and the model.

FIGURE 14-2: MVVM architecture.

TIP *Using suffixes in class names is a great way to keep track of what is what in an MVVM application.*

The `CarModel` class exposes car details through properties, such as `Make` and `Color`. The `CarViewModel` class might then have a property that contains a `CarModel` instance. It also exposes functionality to enable operations to be performed on or using this instance, such as the "email a friend" functionality. The `CarView` view uses Silverlight data binding techniques to access the data and functionality exposed by the view model. This last point is perhaps the most important: The power of Silverlight data binding is one of the main reasons MVVM is so popular.

NOTE *In addition to MVVM, other architectures that are in common use today include Model–View–Controller (MVC) and Model–View–Presenter (MVP). In MVC, the view renders the model directly but interacts with it through a controller. In MVP, the presenter maintains a reference to the view and controls it directly. Neither of these architectures takes full advantage of Silverlight data binding capabilities or provides the same level of logical separation between layers that MVVM does, so this chapter does not explore them.*

Associating Views with View Models

In MVVM, views are associated with view models. Without MVVM, this is obviously not an issue: When you create a page or user control, it's tightly coupled with its code implementation. With MVVM, you have two separate classes — the view and the view model — which must be associated with each other to be usable.

There are several ways of doing this, but the result you want to end up with is a XAML view with `DataContext` set to your view model. If you achieve this, binding to view model properties is simple. In essence, associating views with view models can take either a view-first or view model–first approach. With a view-first approach, you instantiate a view that then creates a view model it proceeds to use as its `DataContext`. If you implement your view as a user control, you can then simply drop it onto a page (or add it programmatically), and everything will work. Alternatively, you could use a locator-based approach, where views use a separate component to find a view model instance to use.

A view model–first approach works in the other direction. With this type of approach, you add a view model to a page and have a view wrapped around it, often using a data template. This works much like templating you've seen elsewhere in this book, as in displaying a list of items and providing item templates.

With the view model–first approach, you still have the problem of how and when to create your view model. The simplest solution here is to do it in XAML, for example, as a page resource:

```
<phone:PhoneApplicationPage.Resources>
  <local:MyViewModel x:Key="MyViewModelInstance" />
</phone:PhoneApplicationPage.Resources>
```

In the preceding code, you create a view model of type `MyViewModel` (which may include additional initialization attributes or XAML, not shown here), and you can then reference it from a view as follows:

```
<local:MyView DataContext="{StaticResource MyViewModelInstance}" />
```

This code can be part of a data template.

There is much discussion on various forums about the best way to achieve view/view model association, and many of the frameworks that exist for implementing MVVM supply helper classes (such as locators) to do the work for you. The best implementations tend to be those that make use of dependency injection to resolve instances of views and/or view models as required, but these techniques are beyond the scope of this book.

Change Notification Requirements

MVVM views bind to view model properties, often in a simple way, as in this example:

```
<TextBox Text="{Binding MyTextProperty}" />
```

The `DataContext` of the view containing this `TextBox` control is set to the view model, so this works with minimal effort. However, if you want changes to properties to be reflected in the view, you must raise change notifications back to the view. For this reason, practically every view model implements `INotifyPropertyChanged`.

In addition, if you expose collections of objects, you should use a collection that implements `INotifyCollectionChanged`, such as the generic `ObservableCollection<TItem>` class.

Raising Property Change Notifications

Implementing property change notifications is simple. The `INotifyPropertyChanged` interface has a single member; an event called `PropertyChanged`:

```
using System.ComponentModel;

public class MyViewModel : INotifyPropertyChanged
{
    public event PropertyChangedEventHandler PropertyChanged;
}
```

Typically, you raise this event by using a method as follows:

```
public class MyViewModel : INotifyPropertyChanged
{
    ...

    protected virtual void OnPropertyChanged(string propertyName)
    {
      var handler = this.PropertyChanged;
      if (handler != null)
      {
          handler(this, new PropertyChangedEventArgs(propertyName));
      }
    }
}
```

To raise notifications, you simply check property values as they change and call the `OnPropertyChanged()` method as required, as in this example:

```
public class MyViewModel : INotifyPropertyChanged
{
    ...

    private int myValue;
```

```
public int MyValue
{
   get
   {
      return this.myValue;
   }

   set
   {
      if (value != this.myValue)
      {
         this.myValue = value;
         this.OnPropertyChanged("MyValue");
      }
   }
}
}
```

Raising Collection Change Notifications

To ensure that collection change notifications are raised correctly, you simply use properties of type ObservableCollection<TItem> and ensure that, once created, the collection instance does not change; if it does, any code listening for a change event won't receive it. Here's an example:

```
public class MyViewModel : INotifyPropertyChanged
{
   public MyViewModel()
   {
      this.MyValues = new ObservableCollection<int>();
   }

   public ObservableCollection<int> MyValues { get; private set; }
}
```

The set accessor is private, so only the containing class can change the collection instance, although external code can still change the contents.

Should Notifications Come from Models or View Models?

You might wonder about the best place to raise notifications. Certainly, all view models that require changes should raise them, and it's quite rare to see a view model that doesn't implement the INotifyPropertyChanged interface. But what about models?

In fact, it can be a good idea to implement this change notification in model classes. However, whether you should do this depends on how the model classes are used elsewhere. If back-end systems also require change notification, then by all means you should implement change notification. If they don't, or if you want to reuse existing classes, implementing change notification isn't always appropriate. In such cases, it's better to wrap the properties of the model in properties exposed by the view model and raise notifications as you change underlying model values.

One thing to be aware of, though, is that if the model doesn't implement change notification, you won't detect changes to its properties that don't come through your view model. Depending on the rest of your application, this may or may not be an issue.

NOTE *More often than not in large scale applications, the model implementation may not be under your control. You might be forced to use models supplied by middle tier developers, in which case you might have no option other than to implement change notification in view models that wrap these models.*

TRY IT OUT Creating a Simple MVVM Application

In the following steps you'll create a simple MVVM application that includes the features you've learned about in previous sections. This example also illustrates how to deal with models that don't implement property change notifications by wrapping them in view model code:

1. Create a new Windows Phone Application called **CarList**.

2. Add a new class called `CarModel` and modify the code in `CarModel.cs` so that it looks like Listing 14-1.

Available for
download on
Wrox.com

LISTING 14-1: Modifying the code in CarModel.cs

```
using System.Windows.Media;

namespace CarList
{
    public class CarModel
    {
        public string Description { get; set; }
        public Color Color { get; set; }
    }
}
```

Code Snippet CarList\CarModel.cs

3. Add a new class called `CarViewModel` and modify the code in `CarViewModel.cs` so that it looks like Listing 14-2.

Available for
download on
Wrox.com

LISTING 14-2: Modifying the code in CarViewModel.cs

```
using System.ComponentModel;
using System.Windows.Media;

namespace CarList
{
```

continues

LISTING 14-2 *(continued)*

```
public class CarViewModel : INotifyPropertyChanged
{
    private CarModel carModel;

    public event PropertyChangedEventHandler PropertyChanged;

    public CarModel CarModel
    {
        get
        {
            return this.carModel;
        }
        set
        {
            this.carModel = value;
            this.OnPropertyChanged("Description");
            this.OnPropertyChanged("Color");
        }
    }

    public string Description
    {
        get
        {
            return this.carModel.Description;
        }
        set
        {
            if (value != this.carModel.Description)
            {
                this.carModel.Description = value;
                this.OnPropertyChanged("Description");
            }
        }
    }

    public Color Color
    {
        get
        {
            return this.carModel.Color;
        }
        set
        {
            if (value != this.carModel.Color)
            {
                this.carModel.Color = value;
                this.OnPropertyChanged("Color");
            }
        }
    }
```

```
        protected virtual void OnPropertyChanged(string propertyName)
        {
            var handler = this.PropertyChanged;
            if (handler != null)
            {
                handler(this, new PropertyChangedEventArgs(propertyName));
            }
        }
    }
}
```

Code Snippet CarList\CarViewModel.cs

4. Add a new class called ColorBrushConverter and modify the code in ColorBrushConverter.cs so that it looks like Listing 14-3.

LISTING 14-3: Modifying the code in ColorBrushConverter.cs

```
using System;
using System.Windows.Data;
using System.Windows.Media;

namespace CarList
{
    public class ColorBrushConverter : IValueConverter
    {
        public object Convert(object value, Type targetType,
            object parameter, System.Globalization.CultureInfo culture)
        {
            if (value is Color)
            {
                return new SolidColorBrush((Color)value);
            }

            return new SolidColorBrush(Colors.Transparent);
        }

        public object ConvertBack(object value, Type targetType,
            object parameter, System.Globalization.CultureInfo culture)
        {
            throw new NotImplementedException();
        }
    }
}
```

Code Snippet CarList\ColorBrushConverter.cs

5. Add a new Windows Phone 7 user control called `CarView` and modify the code in `CarView.xaml` so that it looks like Listing 14-4.

LISTING 14-4: Modifying the code in CarView.xaml

```xml
<UserControl x:Class="CarList.CarView" ...
    xmlns:local="clr-namespace:CarList">
  <UserControl.Resources>
    <local:ColorBrushConverter x:Key="ColorBrushConverter" />
  </UserControl.Resources>
  <StackPanel Background="{Binding Color,
    Converter={StaticResource ColorBrushConverter}}">
    <TextBlock Style="{StaticResource PhoneTextAccentStyle}" Text="Description" />
    <TextBox Text="{Binding Description, Mode=TwoWay}" />
  </StackPanel>
</UserControl>
```

Code Snippet CarList\CarView.xaml

6. Add a new class called `MainPageViewModel` and modify the code in `MainPageViewModel.cs` so that it looks like Listing 14-5.

LISTING 14-5: Modifying the code in MainPageViewModel.cs

```csharp
using System;
using System.Collections.Generic;
using System.Collections.ObjectModel;
using System.ComponentModel;
using System.Windows.Media;

namespace CarList
{
    public class MainPageViewModel : INotifyPropertyChanged
    {
        private CarViewModel selectedCar;
        private Random random;
        private List<string> carNames;
        private List<Color> carColors;

        public MainPageViewModel()
        {
            this.random = new Random();
            this.carNames = new List<string>
            {
                "Ferrari Enzo", "Ford Focus", "Audi S4", "Volkswagen Scirocco",
                "Porsche 911", "Lamborghini Gallardo", "Aston Martin DB9",
                "Lotus Elise", "Jaguar XF", "Bugatti Veyron", "Koenigsegg CCX",
```

```
            "Rolls-Royce Phantom"
        };

        this.carColors = new List<Color>
        {
            Colors.Black, Colors.White, Colors.Red, Colors.Orange,
            Colors.Yellow, Colors.Green, Colors.Blue, Colors.Purple,
            Colors.Brown
        };

        this.Cars = new ObservableCollection<CarViewModel>();
        for (int i = 0; i < 10; i++)
        {
            AddCar();
        }
    }

    public event PropertyChangedEventHandler PropertyChanged;

    public ObservableCollection<CarViewModel> Cars { get; private set; }

    public CarViewModel SelectedCar
    {
        get
        {
            return this.selectedCar;
        }
        set
        {
            if (value != this.selectedCar)
            {
                this.selectedCar = value;
                this.OnPropertyChanged("SelectedCar");
            }
        }
    }

    protected virtual void OnPropertyChanged(string propertyName)
    {
        var handler = this.PropertyChanged;
        if (handler != null)
        {
            handler(this, new PropertyChangedEventArgs(propertyName));
        }
    }

    private void AddCar()
    {
        this.Cars.Add(new CarViewModel
        {
```

continues

LISTING 14-5 *(continued)*

```
            CarModel = new CarModel
            {
                Description = this.carNames[this.random.Next(this.carNames.Count)],
                Color = this.carColors[this.random.Next(this.carColors.Count)]
            }
        });
    }
  }
}
```

Code Snippet CarList\MainPageViewModel.cs

7. Modify the code in `MainPage.xaml` so that it looks like Listing 14-6.

LISTING 14-6: Modifying the code in MainPage.xaml

```xml
<phone:PhoneApplicationPage ...
    xmlns:local="clr-namespace:CarList">
  <phone:PhoneApplicationPage.Resources>
    <local:MainPageViewModel x:Key="MainPageViewModel" />
  </phone:PhoneApplicationPage.Resources>

  <Grid x:Name="LayoutRoot" Background="Transparent"
    DataContext="{StaticResource MainPageViewModel}">
    <Grid.RowDefinitions>
      <RowDefinition Height="Auto"/>
      <RowDefinition Height="*"/>
    </Grid.RowDefinitions>

    <StackPanel x:Name="TitlePanel" Grid.Row="0" Margin="12,17,0,28">
      <TextBlock x:Name="ApplicationTitle" Text="MVVM DEMO"
        Style="{StaticResource PhoneTextNormalStyle}"/>
      <TextBlock x:Name="PageTitle" Text="car list" Margin="9,-7,0,0"
        Style="{StaticResource PhoneTextTitle1Style}"/>
    </StackPanel>

    <Grid x:Name="ContentPanel" Grid.Row="1" Margin="12,0,12,0">
      <Grid.RowDefinitions>
        <RowDefinition Height="*" />
        <RowDefinition Height="Auto" />
        <RowDefinition Height="Auto" />
        <RowDefinition Height="Auto" />
      </Grid.RowDefinitions>
      <ListBox x:Name="CarSelector"
        ScrollViewer.VerticalScrollBarVisibility="Visible"
        DisplayMemberPath="Description" ItemsSource="{Binding Cars}"
        SelectedItem="{Binding SelectedCar, Mode=TwoWay}" />
      <Button Grid.Row="1" Content="Add Car" />
      <local:CarView Grid.Row="2" DataContext="{Binding SelectedCar}" />
```

```
      <Button Grid.Row="3" Content="Send Email" />
    </Grid>
  </Grid>

</phone:PhoneApplicationPage>
```

Code Snippet CarList\MainPage.xaml

8. Run the application and select a car. The buttons don't work yet, but if you edit the car description, you see it updated in the list, as shown in Figure 14-3.

How It Works

In this example, you created a simple MVVM application that displays a list of cars and allows you to edit their names. It also stores a color for each car, and this color is used to format the background of the editing area.

You started by creating a model, a view model, and a view for a car. The model `CarModel` is simple; in fact, it is a Plain Old CLR Object (POCO) with two properties, `Description` and `Color`. You made this simple class to see how you wrap an object in a view model to get property change notifications, which is essential for the application to work properly. The view model implements `INotifyPropertyChanged` and raises the `PropertyChanged` event whenever either of its wrapper properties (also called `Description` and `Color`) change. For example, the implementation of `Description` is as follows:

FIGURE 14-3: The CarList application.

```
private CarModel carModel;

public string Description
{
   get
   {
      return this.carModel.Description;
   }
   set
   {
      if (value != this.carModel.Description)
      {
         this.carModel.Description = value;
         this.OnPropertyChanged("Description");
      }
   }
}
```

This wraps the `Description` property stored in an internal field called `carModel`. Notice that the `PropertyChanged` event is raised only if the property value changes.

The `carModel` field is also exposed through a `CarModel` property. Note that when this property is set, the values of `Color` and `Description` also change, so change notifications are raised.

The view for a car simply exposes the `Description` property through a `TextBox` control and uses a value converter (`ColorBrushConverter`) to get a background color from the car. Note that the use of value converters is extremely common in MVVM. The reason for this is that the view model effectively doesn't know anything about the view. Therefore, it shouldn't make assumptions about what the view will do to render the view model state. Instead, the view model exposes pertinent information, and the view is free to do as it chooses with it; in this case, the view chooses a background color, but it might just as easily write the color in text. Value converters provide the link here, and you can treat them as being part of the view.

Next, you created a view model for the main page rather than using code in `MainPage.xaml.cs`, as you have done in previous chapters. To use this view model in the view, you created an instance of it in the `MainPage.xaml` code and used it as the `DataContext` for the root element, as follows:

```
<phone:PhoneApplicationPage ...
    xmlns:local="clr-namespace:CarList">
  <phone:PhoneApplicationPage.Resources>
    <local:MainPageViewModel x:Key="MainPageViewModel" />
  </phone:PhoneApplicationPage.Resources>

  <Grid x:Name="LayoutRoot" Background="Transparent"
    DataContext="{StaticResource MainPageViewModel}">
    ...
  </Grid>

</phone:PhoneApplicationPage>
```

The `MainPageViewModel` class creates and exposes a list of cars with randomized descriptions and colors in a property called `Cars`, as follows:

```
public ObservableCollection<CarViewModel> Cars { get; private set; }
```

This is defined using an `ObservableCollection<CarViewModel>` collection so that if it changes, the view will be updated. At the moment, it changes only during the creation of the view model, so it's not so important right now, but it will be in the next example.

The `ObservableCollection<CarViewModel>` collection is bound to the `ItemsSource` of a `ListBox` control in the view, which also binds its `SelectedItem` property as follows:

```
<ListBox x:Name="CarSelector"
  ScrollViewer.VerticalScrollBarVisibility="Visible"
  DisplayMemberPath="Description" ItemsSource="{Binding Cars}"
  SelectedItem="{Binding SelectedCar, Mode=TwoWay}" />
```

This property is important because it allows the view to update the view model so that it is aware of the currently selected item through its `SelectedCar` property:

```
public CarViewModel SelectedCar
{
   get
   {
      return this.selectedCar;
   }
```

```
        set
        {
            if (value != this.selectedCar)
            {
                this.selectedCar = value;
                this.OnPropertyChanged("SelectedCar");
            }
        }
    }
}
```

As the selection changes, so does this property, and in turn, it raises a property change notification that the `CarView` view instance detects in the main page view:

```
<local:CarView Grid.Row="2" DataContext="{Binding SelectedCar}" />
```

In this way, the selected car is used as the `DataContext` for the view, which provides the association between the view and the view model for this control.

The rest of the code is fairly straightforward and not worth repeating here. There are, however, two buttons in the main page view that are left unfinished. The reason for this is that binding events raised in a view to commands in a view model is not straightforward. You'll return to this example and complete it after you've found out why.

Using Events and Commands in MVVM

Throughout this book, you've provided a lot of interactivity by implementing handlers for events. In an MVVM application, you can't do this because you can't add an event handler to an event that will call into a view model. Instead, you create commands in your view model and bind them to actions in the view.

In other flavors of XAML, such as Silverlight 4 and Windows Presentation Foundation (WPF), binding commands to the view is often very simple. `Button` controls, for example, have a `Command` property that you can bind to a view model. In the version of Silverlight used for Windows Phone 7 applications, though, the `Button` control has no such property. Other controls also lack appropriate properties; for example, it's not easy to receive a notification for a selected item changed event.

Happily, it is relatively simple to translate an event into a command by using helper classes. For example, you can use an attached property that, when added to a control, injects code to achieve a variety of needs. In this case, the helper attaches to the button click event and routes it to a specified command. You'll see an implementation of this in the next Try It Out.

Implementing commands requires a little bit of thought. The key is to provide an implementation of the `ICommand` interface. This interface exposes (among other things) an `Execute()` method that is called when a command is executed. So, if you define an `ICommand` property in a view model, you can bind it to wherever a command is required, using the aforementioned helper, if necessary.

Adding Command Bindings to CarList

In the following steps, you'll see how to bind commands. Follow these steps to extend the MVVM application you created earlier:

1. Open the **CarList** application you made earlier. Make a copy if you wish; the downloadable code has this version of the example in a directory called CarList (Part 2).

2. Add a new class called DelegateCommand and modify the code in DelegateCommand.cs so that it looks like Listing 14-7.

LISTING 14-7: Modifying the code in DelegateCommand.cs

```csharp
using System;
using System.Windows.Input;

namespace CarList
{
    public class DelegateCommand : ICommand
    {
        private readonly Predicate<object> canExecute;
        private readonly Action<object> execute;

        public event EventHandler CanExecuteChanged;

        public DelegateCommand(Action<object> execute)
            : this(execute, null)
        {
        }

        public DelegateCommand(Action<object> execute, Predicate<object> canExecute)
        {
            this.execute = execute;
            this.canExecute = canExecute;
        }

        public bool CanExecute(object parameter)
        {
            if (this.canExecute == null)
            {
                return true;
            }

            return this.canExecute(parameter);
        }

        public void Execute(object parameter)
        {
            this.execute(parameter);
        }
```

```
      public void RaiseCanExecuteChanged()
      {
         if (CanExecuteChanged != null)
         {
            CanExecuteChanged(this, EventArgs.Empty);
         }
      }
   }
}
```

Code Snippet CarList\DelegateCommand.cs

3. Modify the code in `MainPageViewModel.cs` so that it looks like Listing 14-8.

LISTING 14-8: Modifying the code in MainPageViewModel.cs

```
using System.Windows;
using System.Windows.Input;

namespace CarList
{
   public class MainPageViewModel : INotifyPropertyChanged
   {
      ...

      public MainPageViewModel()
      {
         ...

         this.SendEmailCommand = new DelegateCommand(
            this.SendEmailCommandExecute, this.SendEmailCommandCanExecute);
         this.AddCarCommand = new DelegateCommand(
            this.AddCarCommandExecute);
      }

      public ICommand SendEmailCommand { get; private set; }

      public ICommand AddCarCommand { get; private set; }

      ...

      private void AddCarCommandExecute(object commandParameter)
      {
         AddCar();
      }
```

continues

LISTING 14-8 *(continued)*

```
    private void SendEmailCommandExecute(object commandParameter)
    {
        MessageBox.Show(string.Format(
            "Email sent: I want a {0} {1}!",
            this.selectedCar.Color,
            this.selectedCar.Description));
    }

    private bool SendEmailCommandCanExecute(object commandParameter)
    {
        return this.selectedCar != null;
    }
    }
}
```

Code Snippet CarList\MainPageViewModel.cs

4. Add a new class called `ButtonCommandHelper` and modify the code in `ButtonCommandHelper.cs` so that it looks like Listing 14-9.

LISTING 14-9: Modifying the code in ButtonCommandHelper.cs

```
using System.Windows;
using System.Windows.Controls.Primitives;
using System.Windows.Input;

namespace CarList
{
    public static class ButtonCommandHelper
    {
        public static readonly DependencyProperty CommandProperty =
            DependencyProperty.RegisterAttached(
                "Command",
                typeof(ICommand),
                typeof(ButtonCommandHelper),
                new PropertyMetadata(null, OnCommandChanged));

        public static ICommand GetCommand(ButtonBase button)
        {
            return (ICommand)button.GetValue(CommandProperty);
        }

        public static void SetCommand(ButtonBase button, ICommand command)
        {
            button.SetValue(CommandProperty, command);
        }
```

```
        private static void OnCommandChanged(
            DependencyObject d, DependencyPropertyChangedEventArgs e)
        {
            var button = d as ButtonBase;
            if (button == null)
            {
                return;
            }

            var oldCommand = e.OldValue as ICommand;
            if (oldCommand != null)
            {
                button.Click -= OnButtonBaseClick;
            }

            var newCommand = e.NewValue as ICommand;
            if (newCommand != null)
            {
                button.Click += OnButtonBaseClick;
            }
        }

        private static void OnButtonBaseClick(object sender, RoutedEventArgs args)
        {
            var button = sender as ButtonBase;
            var command = GetCommand(button);
            if (command != null && command.CanExecute(null))
            {
                command.Execute(null);
            }
        }
    }
}
```

Code Snippet CarList\ButtonCommandHelper.cs

5. Modify the code in `MainPage.xaml` so that it looks like Listing 14-10.

LISTING 14-10: Modifying the code in MainPage.xaml

```
<Grid x:Name="ContentPanel" Grid.Row="1" Margin="12,0,12,0">
    ...
  <Button Grid.Row="1" Content="Add Car"
    local:ButtonCommandHelper.Command="{Binding AddCarCommand}" />
  <local:CarView Grid.Row="2" DataContext="{Binding SelectedCar}" />
  <Button Grid.Row="3" Content="Send Email"
    local:ButtonCommandHelper.Command="{Binding SendEmailCommand}" />
</Grid>
```

Code Snippet CarList\MainPage.xaml

6. Run the application. Now you can add more random cars by tapping the Add Car button, and you can pop up a message box by tapping the Send Email button, as shown in Figure 14-4. (The color formatting should keep your web developer friends happy.)

How It Works

In this example, you added command bindings to the CarList application. In order to do so, you made two main additions:

➤ An implementation of ICommand

➤ A helper to bind a button Click event to ICommand

FIGURE 14-4: The Send Email message box.

First, you added the DelegateCommand class, which is a helper class that makes it easy to create commands using delegates. You created an instance of this class by using an Action<object> delegate (that is, a delegate for a method that takes a single object type parameter and returns void) and a Predicate<object> delegate (that is, a delegate for a method that takes a single object type parameter and returns bool). You then called these delegates for the Execute() and CanExecute() methods, respectively.

You use the DelegateCommand class in the constructor of MainPageViewModel to set two new properties of type ICommand: SendEmailCommandExecute and AddCarCommand:

```
this.SendEmailCommand = new DelegateCommand(
    this.SendEmailCommandExecute, this.SendEmailCommandCanExecute);
this.AddCarCommand = new DelegateCommand(
    this.AddCarCommandExecute);
```

As a result, three new methods are wired up to the two commands you've created. The simplest of these, AddCarCommandExecute(), is used with AddCarCommand (which has no CanExecute() handler delegate because it's always executable):

```
private void AddCarCommandExecute(object commandParameter)
{
    AddCar();
}
```

This method simply calls the existing AddCar() method. Note that you could omit this method altogether by using a lambda expression in the delegate command constructor, as follows:

```
this.AddCarCommand = new DelegateCommand(_ => AddCar());
```

However, if you're not familiar with lambda expressions, this syntax might look a little odd, so the example uses simpler syntax.

After you create the commands and handlers in the view model, the next step is to use a helper to connect the view to the view model, as described in the section before this example. The class you added, ButtonCommandHelper, does this in a simple way. First, it defines a Command attached property with associated get and set accessor methods, GetCommand() and SetCommand(). A property change handler, OnCommandChanged(), is invoked when the attached property is set on a target control that derives from `ButtonBase`. This handler attaches or detaches the `OnButtonBaseClick()` handler to or from the `Click` event of the target button. The `OnButtonBaseClick` handler simply calls `CanExecute()` and `Execute()` on the `ICommand` instance stored in the `Command` attached property (if one exists) as follows:

```
private static void OnButtonBaseClick(object sender, RoutedEventArgs args)
{
    var button = sender as ButtonBase;
    var command = GetCommand(button);
    if (command != null && command.CanExecute(null))
    {
        command.Execute(null);
    }
}
```

This very simple implementation doesn't allow you to set command parameters; it passes a value of `null`. For this example, it's fine, but in general, it's better to use more robust and versatile implementations of this sort of helper, such as the behavior definitions found in many of the frameworks available for building Windows Phone 7 applications. Some of these are also usable with other types of controls and events. In fact, now that you know the basics of MVVM, it's time to look at some of the frameworks that are available.

USING MVVM FRAMEWORKS

One of the benefits of using an MVVM architecture is that a lot of your code is more reusable, enabling you to build more features faster. Sometimes, you end up reusing the same framework code (for example, the `ButtonCommandHelper` and `DelegateCommand` classes you saw earlier in this chapter) across completely different projects. Other developers have noticed this, too, and some have gone as far as extracting the reusable bits of code into a formal framework.

It's a good idea to use an existing third-party MVVM framework for any big projects because the implementations have been thoroughly tested and cover more ground than the samples you've seen in this chapter. For example, a fully featured implementation of `ButtonCommandHelper` would also disable the associated button whenever the command was not executable, and it would allow you to pass parameters from data bindings into the command. There's nothing stopping you from adding this functionality to your own classes; it's simply easier to use other people's work.

NOTE *All the current MVVM frameworks are open source, donated to the world by their original developers, so you should be able to just download the latest assemblies from the Internet and use them directly. Although you shouldn't ever have to pay for these open source frameworks, it's always worth remembering to read the license in case the terms do not suit you. For example, some licenses require attribution, and others may prevent you from modifying the framework code unless you agree to supply your changes back to the project.*

MVVM Framework Features

A number of MVVM frameworks are already available for Windows Phone 7, and even more are available for the desktop editions of Silverlight and WPF. These MVVM frameworks are constantly appearing and evolving, but there are a number of useful functions you can expect to find in a framework. The following list first addresses the features you're most likely to depend on in any MVVM application, and then it describes some more exotic features:

➤ **An implementation of `ICommand`** — You'll need a simple implementation of `ICommand` in order to run code when a user taps a button.

➤ **An attached property helper or behavior to bind an `ICommand` to a `Button` control** — Silverlight 4 introduced the `Command` property to the `Button` control, which enables you to directly bind the button to a view model's command. Silverlight for Windows Phone 7 has yet to catch up completely with Silverlight 4, so you need a helper class such as `ButtonCommandHelper`, described earlier in this chapter, in the section "Using Events and Commands in MVVM." This is the same technique that desktop Silverlight developers had to use in version 3. As Silverlight for Windows Phone 7 advances, you may find that this is no longer needed.

➤ **A base class for your view models that implements `INotifyPropertyChanged`** — Each of your view model classes can share a base implementation of `INotifyPropertyChanged`. You still need to call the method that raises this event from each of your property setters.

➤ **A message bus/event hub** — Some projects have a call for an application-wide, loosely coupled event hub. Think of it as a registry where any important actions are posted (such as the Internet connection being lost or the user logging out of your web service), and any view models that have registered themselves for such events will be notified. The emphasis here is on the loose coupling. In a finished application, there can be any number of view models that need to respond to the user going offline, whereas with an event such as a button being tapped, only one screen needs to handle that event. In the latter case, it's best to stick with standard, strongly typed .NET events. In simple cases, view models can subscribe to custom events on other view models, which can be easier to understand and debug than using an event hub. Not all projects require an event hub, but it's a good thing to have built into a framework for when you do need it.

➤ **Screen management** — Some MVVM frameworks provide you with more advanced view model base classes that do things such as track whether the view model is currently visible or sync up with the stack of screens that the user has navigated through so far (that is, the screens they see as they press the Back button).

Finding the Right Framework

To find out what frameworks are currently available, you can search on the Internet for "Windows Phone 7 MVVM framework." You'll find some blog posts that talk about such frameworks (often worth a read), as well as links to home pages for frameworks. Read through the feature lists, download samples, and try the frameworks out in your own applications. Depending on the size of your project, building a few prototypes could reap great dividends. Frameworks are there to make your life easier, so pick one that you like — and then work to get past the initial tricky learning curve.

At the time of writing, MVVM frameworks include Prism, Caliburn, MVVM Light, and Opus. All four of them provide a good starting point, although they vary in exactly what they provide. Links to the framework home pages are as follows:

➤ Prism: `http://compositewpf.codeplex.com/`

➤ Caliburn: `http://caliburn.codeplex.com/`

➤ MVVM Light: `http://mvvmlight.codeplex.com/`

➤ Opus: `http://opus.codeplex.com/`

ADDING UNIT TESTS

When you're writing code, you obviously want to know whether it works as you intend. Typically, this involves running the code (with or without a debugger attached) either on the emulator or on a real device. If you want to test an aspect of the user interface, such as whether tapping a button really takes you to a particular new page, this is easy — you just run the app, tap the button, and watch what happens.

Things get harder when you want to test whether a small unit of code, such as a calculation or piece of business logic, does what you expect — especially if that unit of code is buried deep within your application. For example, say that you want to check that a customer is at least 18 years old. Assuming that your application validates birthdays only after users have done their shopping and created an account, this test might be quite convoluted. In order to test your code, you'd need to tap your way through many screens before you can get to it. And if you know you need to check a number of different cases, you'll have to create a new account for each set of test inputs. After all this effort, you might find a bug in your code, and once you've fixed that bug, you'll need to re-run all your different test cases, by hand, again.

This can get tedious. However, there's an easy way to simplify this procedure. All you actually want to do is to call your code multiple times with multiple inputs and check that your expected result is returned each time. You don't necessarily depend on a customer being created with a valid order before you can do this; it's just something that your user interface enforces.

> ### THE BENEFITS OF UNIT TESTING
>
> Untested code often has more bugs in it than you think it does. For small, simple applications, it can be quite easy to run through the application by hand and make sure everything's fine. As applications get bigger, it becomes more necessary to automate your testing so that the tests are easy and quick to run, repeatable, and recorded in a reliable place (your source code).
>
> Unit tests can also help prevent regression errors (where some code did work fine but then broke when a change was made). If you're about to start changing some code that was written by another person (or by you some time ago), having unit tests covering the fragile parts of that code is incredibly useful.

Manual Unit Testing

The simplest way to run a few unit tests is to create a new page that is not for end users to see. Such a page is often referred to as a *test harness*. This test harness needs only a few buttons on it; each of these buttons will run some tests. It's up to you whether you make one button run 10 tests or make 10 buttons with one test each. When it's time to run your test harness, you can temporarily make that page the default page.

Creating Some Basic Unit Tests

The following steps show an example of creating manual unit tests:

1. Create a new Windows Phone Application called **AgeCalculator**.

2. Add a new class called `Calculator` and add a `CalculateAge()` method so that it looks like Listing 14-11.

LISTING 14-11: Modifying the code in Calculator.cs

```
public class Calculator
{
    public static int CalculateAge(DateTime birthday, DateTime currentDate)
    {
        return (int)((currentDate - birthday).TotalDays / 365);
    }
}
```

Code Snippet AgeCalculator\Calculator.cs

3. Add a new page (by selecting Windows Phone Portrait Page in the New Item dialog) named `UnitTests` and add a button to the XAML. Add a click event handler to the button (`Click="button1_Click"`) and add the code to the code behind the XAML (`UnitTests.xaml.cs`) so that it looks like Listing 14-12.

LISTING 14-12: Modifying the code in UnitTests.xaml.cs

```
private void button1_Click(object sender, RoutedEventArgs e)
{
    // Test case where birthday hasn't occurred this year.
    Test(12, new DateTime(1998, 6, 1), new DateTime(2011, 1, 1));

    // Test case where birthday has occurred this year.
    Test(35, new DateTime(1975, 1, 2), new DateTime(2011, 1, 1));

    // Test case where birthday is on a leap day.
    Test(11, new DateTime(2000, 2, 29), new DateTime(2011, 2, 28));
}
```

```
private void Test(int expectedAge, DateTime birthday, DateTime currentDate)
{
    int age = Calculator.CalculateAge(birthday, currentDate);
    if(expectedAge != age)
    {
        string s = "Expected {0} but was {1} for {2:dd MMM yyyy}"
            + " and {3:dd MMM yyyy}";
        MessageBox.Show(string.Format(s, expectedAge, age,
            birthday, currentDate));
    }
}
```

Code Snippet AgeCalculator\UnitTests.xaml.cs

4. Open the WMAppManifest.xml file, found in your project's Properties folder. Look for the DefaultTask element and change it to start up UnitTests.xaml instead of MainPage.xaml, as shown in Listing 14-13.

Available for download on Wrox.com

LISTING 14-13: Modifying the code in WMAppManifest.xml

```
<DefaultTask Name ="_default" NavigationPage="UnitTests.xaml"/>
```

Code Snippet AgeCalculator\Properties\WMAppManifest.xml

5. Launch your application and tap the button. A message box appears, as shown in Figure 14-5.

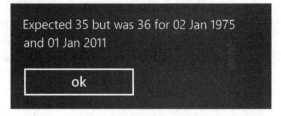

How It Works

In this example, you created three tests for a particularly tricky calculation. These tests are much easier to run than if you had tested the application through a finished user interface.

FIGURE 14-5: A message showing a failed test.

First, you added the CalculateAge() method to the new Calculator class. This was the system under test (SUT). Then you created a test harness in a new page and added your tests to the click handler of a new Button control on that test harness. Finally, you changed the WMAppManifest.xml file so that your test harness was the first page that you see when you launch the application. You can change this back to MainPage.xaml whenever you want to run the real application rather than the tests.

The result you saw was that a message box appeared, indicating that a test failed. The text shown tells you the expected result and the actual result. This is important and useful information when it comes to fixing your code. (As an exercise, you can provide a better algorithm for determining ages from two dates.)

This ad hoc test harness approach to writing unit tests has served programmers well for decades. However, there are a few disadvantages to this way of doing things:

➤ You have to remember to run the tests, and it's annoying to have to keep switching the start page.

➤ A finished application might have hundreds of tests — which means a lot of buttons!

➤ The test code is mixed in with the production code, bloating the size of your download and potentially confusing developers.

➤ It can be difficult to wade through each of the failures.

The following sections look at how some more modern approaches to unit testing can alleviate this.

Unit Testing Frameworks

Ever since a fateful airplane trip when Kent Beck and Erich Gamma wrote the first version of JUnit (for Java), developers have had a better way to organize and write unit tests. Using JUnit involves writing a special test method, marking it as such, and letting the unit testing framework find that test and run it for you. The framework automatically catches any exceptions that occur and marks that test as failed. If no exception is thrown, the method counts as passed. Often, the framework comes with some helper classes that can throw these exceptions for you. You'll now learn about one such framework for Windows Phone 7.

Microsoft's Silverlight team has an open source project where they regularly post new Silverlight frameworks and code (much more often than the official releases of Silverlight). Known as the Silverlight Toolkit, it can be found at `http://silverlight.codeplex.com`. The Silverlight Toolkit contains both a unit testing framework for desktop Silverlight and a set of controls for Windows Phone 7. Unfortunately, at the time of writing, it doesn't contain a unit testing framework for Windows Phone 7. However, one of the key contributors on the toolkit has created a Windows Phone 7 version of the unit testing tools, available at `www.jeff.wilcox.name/2010/05/sl3-utf-bits/`. The assemblies required for this framework (`Microsoft.Silverlight.Testing.dll` and `Microsoft.VisualStudio.QualityTools.UnitTesting.Silverlight.dll`) are also included in the downloadable code for this chapter, as part of the following Try It Out. Hopefully this will also be included in future versions of the toolkit.

TRY IT OUT   Creating Unit Tests in a Unit Testing Framework

Windows Phone 7 is a newer platform, and it is likely that some standard, semi-official unit testing frameworks will start to emerge. Chances are great that they will take on a form very similar to what you're about to see in this Try It Out:

1. Create a new Windows Phone Application called **FrameworkedAgeCalculator**.

2. Add a new class called `Calculator` and add a `Calculate()` method so that `Calculator.cs` looks like Listing 14-14 (identical to the class used in the previous Try It Out section):

LISTING 14-14: Modifying the code in Calculator.cs

```
public class Calculator
{
    public static int CalculateAge(DateTime birthday, DateTime currentDate)
    {
        return (int)((currentDate - birthday).TotalDays / 365);
    }
}
```

Code Snippet FrameworkedAgeCalculator\Calculator.cs

3. Add to your solution a second Windows Phone Application project named **FacUnitTests**.

4. Add a reference from `FacUnitTests` to the project `FrameworkedAgeCalculator`.

5. Download the `Microsoft.Silverlight.Testing.dll` and `Microsoft.VisualStudio .QualityTools.UnitTesting.Silverlight.dll` assemblies from `www.jeff.wilcox .name/2010/05/sl3-utf-bits/` and place them in a project folder called `lib` in the `FacUnitTests` project directory.

6. Add references to `FacUnitTests` for the two assemblies you have just saved. (Ignore the warnings that appear.)

7. In the `FacUnitTests` project, open the `MainPage.xaml` file and turn off the system tray by setting `shell:SystemTray.IsVisible` to `"False"` in the `Page` element.

8. In the same file, add a `Loaded` event handler, by adding `Loaded="MainPage_OnLoaded"` to the `Page` element.

9. Go to the code behind this XAML file, `MainPage.xaml.cs`, by pressing F7. Modify the code so that it looks like Listing 14-15.

LISTING 14-15: Modifying the code in MainPage.xaml.cs

```
using System.Windows;
using Microsoft.Phone.Controls;
using Microsoft.Silverlight.Testing;

namespace FacUnitTests
{
    public partial class MainPage : PhoneApplicationPage
    {
        public MainPage()
        {
            InitializeComponent();
        }

        private void MainPage_OnLoaded(object sender, RoutedEventArgs e)
        {
            var testPage = UnitTestSystem.CreateTestPage();
```

continues

LISTING 14-15 *(continued)*

```
        BackKeyPress += (o, a) =>
            a.Cancel = ((IMobileTestPage)testPage).NavigateBack();
        ((PhoneApplicationFrame)Application.Current.RootVisual).Content =
            testPage;
        }
    }
}
```

Code Snippet FrameworkedAgeCalculator\MainPage.xaml.cs

10. Create a new class in the `FacUnitTests` project named **Tests** and modify the code in `Tests.cs` so that it looks like Listing 14-16.

LISTING 14-16: Modifying the code in Tests.cs

```
using System;
using FrameworkedAgeCalculator;
using Microsoft.VisualStudio.TestTools.UnitTesting;

namespace FacUnitTests
{
    [TestClass]
    public class Tests
    {
        [TestMethod]
        public void TwelveAndAHalf()
        {
            Assert.AreEqual(12, Calculator.CalculateAge(
                new DateTime(1998, 6, 1),
                new DateTime(2011, 1, 1)));
        }

        [TestMethod]
        public void BornOnALeapDay()
        {
            Assert.AreEqual(11, Calculator.CalculateAge(
                new DateTime(2000, 2, 29),
                new DateTime(2011, 2, 28)));
        }

        [TestMethod]
        public void Turns35Tomorrow()
        {
            Assert.AreEqual(35, Calculator.CalculateAge(
                new DateTime(1975, 1, 2),
                new DateTime(2011, 1, 1)));
        }
    }
}
```

Code Snippet FrameworkedAgeCalculator\Tests.cs

11. Run your unit tests by right-clicking the `FacUnitTests` project and then either choose Debug ➪ Start New Instance or click Set as Startup Project and then press the F5 key.

12. If you receive warnings about loading assembly files that have been downloaded from the web, locate the files in Windows Explorer and then right-click each of them in turn and click Properties ➪ Unblock.

13. Wait for the first screen that is displayed to time out. (This screen allows you to select subsets of tests; in this case, you want to run all of them.)

14. Tap Tests and then Turns35Tomorrow to drill into a failed test. Figure 14-6 shows the result.

How It Works

In this example, you created the same three tests as in the previous Try It Out section, "Creating Some Basic Unit Tests." However, this time you used a unit testing framework.

FIGURE 14-6: Failed test details.

Using this framework, you defined a class as containing tests with the `TestClass` attribute and individual test methods with the `TestMethod` attribute, as in this example:

```
[TestClass]
public class Tests
{
    [TestMethod]
    public void TwelveAndAHalf()
    {
        . . .
    }

    . . .
}
```

Notice that this example defines three tests. It's a good idea to keep your tests simple and to have lots of them. Adding a test is as straightforward as adding a new method, so the low friction will hopefully encourage you to write more tests than if you were manually building a test harness with lots of buttons.

Within each test, you use the `Assert.AreEqual()` method to check an expected result (the first method parameter) against an actual result (the second method parameter). Here's an example:

```
[TestMethod]
public void TwelveAndAHalf()
{
    Assert.AreEqual(12, Calculator.CalculateAge(
        new DateTime(1998, 6, 1),
        new DateTime(2011, 1, 1)));
}
```

In this test, someone born June 1, 1998, is expected to be 12 on January 1, 2011.

There are numerous other static methods on the `Assert` class that you can use to check other conditions, such as whether an expression evaluates to `true` or `false` or whether an object is `null`. In all cases, an exception is thrown if the assertion fails, and the testing framework uses this to mark the test as failed.

When you ran your test project, you saw a user interface telling you which tests (methods, grouped by class) failed. By tapping an item, you can drill down into details. You saw details of the failed test, `Turns35Tomorrow()`, in the example. As you can see, this is a nice user interface for viewing test results, especially as your test count grows.

WHAT MAKES A GOOD UNIT TEST?

Here are some qualities that you should always strive to achieve with your unit tests:

➤ **Fast** — Unit tests should execute quickly. You might have hundreds of them, and you want to be able to run them as often as you like. Otherwise, bugs might slip in under your nose!

➤ **Isolated** — It shouldn't matter what order your unit tests run in; each should represent an isolated unit of work. Wanting to run a number of tests in sequence tells you that you're trying to test a full user interaction story rather than simple units of functionality. There are different frameworks for this.

➤ **Repeatable** — If a test passes once, and the code doesn't change, the test should continue to pass, with no exceptions (pun intended). One common cause for a test being unrepeatable is when your code calls `DateTime.Now` to get the current date and then does some calculation that fails, for example, whenever the number of seconds is a multiple of 10.

➤ **A good indicator of the problem** — It should be easy to go from a failing test to seeing where the code is broken. Tests that try to test too many things at once score poorly here, as do tests that are badly named. The test's name should explain the case that's being considered; for example, `BornOnALeapDay` is much better than `DatesAreCorrect`.

Mocking Dependencies

So far, we've dealt only with unit tests that test from one "side" of your code. The tests call your code, wait for a result, and then check the result. This is fine for calculations. But what do you do when you need to test some code that depends on some external system, such as the phone's GPS or a web service on the Internet? These external systems have their own state, so a unit test that relies on such a system won't be repeatable. Calling web services on the Internet is bound to be quite slow, too. Even if your application seems fast, running 200 unit tests that all call the same web server will take an appreciable amount of time. Fortunately, you can "mock" (or "stub") these external systems in order to isolate the unit of code that you'd like to test. Another reason to create a mock is that sometimes you want to write a unit test for some code that depends on other code that hasn't yet been written.

 NOTE *A test that uses external systems is usually called an "integration test." Developers know that integration tests run slowly and sometimes fail for spurious reasons. However, sometimes integration tests catch bugs that unit tests do not catch, so they are an important tool to have in your belt.*

Let's say you're writing an application that records a phone's location every time a user taps a button, and the app sends that location to a web service (perhaps for sharing with friends). If you're writing unit tests for the application, you shouldn't be concerned with the internal workings of the web service. Alternatively, if you're testing the web service, you don't need to know how the client application functions. In both cases, you only need to know about the "contract" shared between the application and the web service. The best way to implement such a contract is through an interface definition, which describes, at a low level, what operations are supported. Your client application can call methods defined by this interface (for example, UpdateMyLocation()) and not worry about what happens next.

So, to make the client "testable" without actually calling the web service, you simply have to provide an alternative implementation of the interface that the web service functionality uses. This alternative implementation is called a mock, or stub, implementation, and typically you pass it into the constructor of one of your classes. A typical unit test might then be "When method X is called, I expect my code to call the UpdateMyLocation() method on the interface." In real-life operation, this code calls the web service. For testing, though, you have a verifiable call to a mock object.

To make a mock object for testing, then, all you need to do is to implement an interface for a type used by the code being tested. To make things simpler, a number of frameworks can create these objects for you, such as Moq and Rhino Mocks. You can find these frameworks on the Internet easily. With frameworks such as these, you can create mocks simply by saying "give me a mock that implements interface X" and then using that in testing. You can also provide expected behavior, such as return values, and monitor when methods and properties are accessed. All this means that your unit tests will actually be unit tests — that is, only the code you want to test is actually tested.

Unit Testing MVVM Applications

In this section, you have seen how to write unit tests so that you don't have to manually tap your way through an application to individually test parts of it as you go. Unit tests are fantastic for maintainability. Every time you make a change to an application, you simply need to run all the existing tests to ensure that your change hasn't broken anything. If a bug is reported, you can hopefully reproduce it by adding a test, fixing the bug, and running the new set of tests so you know that you haven't introduced any new problems (at least none that you are currently testing for).

The reason unit testing works so well in MVVM applications is that your view models are decoupled from your views. You can write unit tests for view models that are completely independent of the user interface. Instead of testing the user interface, you test *functionality*. Testing the user interface then becomes part of a different problem and can be left to designers and QA teams to worry about. This frees you up to concentrate on the more important aspects of writing code.

Test-Driven Development

When you're comfortable with unit tests, you might like to dig a little deeper and look into test-driven development (TDD). This programming methodology can at first seem a little backward, but in practice it can be very powerful. The idea is that you write tests first, before you write any other code. Then you write code that makes all your tests pass. At this point, you have production-ready code and a set of associated tests to work with.

For example, say that you're writing an application that includes business logic to convert Roman numerals into integers, to be implemented in a method with the signature `int ConvertToInt(string numerals)`. Before doing anything else, you can provide some tests, starting with this:

```
Assert.AreEqual(1, ConvertToInt("I"));
```

If you had only this test, your method could be simple and just return the value 1, so you really need to continue and add more, like this:

```
Assert.AreEqual(2, ConvertToInt("II"));
Assert.AreEqual(3, ConvertToInt("III"));
```

So far, so good. You could just return the number of characters, but what about something like this:

```
Assert.AreEqual(4, ConvertToInt("IV"));
Assert.AreEqual(2011, ConvertToInt("MMXI"));
```

Eventually, you can come up with a series of tests that covers all possible meaningful inputs. And you might also include some extras, such as testing for "what happens if I pass a `null` value to my method?"

If it passes all the tests you have written, the method you come up with is pretty much guaranteed to work in all situations (or at least as many as you can think of tests for). Such a method is likely to be much better and more robust than one you write first and test later.

SUMMARY

In this chapter, you looked at some techniques you can use to ensure that the code you write is as robust and maintainable as possible.

You started by looking at the MVVM architectural pattern and saw how it can give your applications a great separation of form and function. This enables you to work on user interfaces independently of other code, which is great for teams of developers and designers. There are a few challenges to overcome when writing in MVVM, such as mapping events to commands, but none of them are terribly difficult. This is where third-party frameworks come in, as they generally include a lot of boilerplate code so that you don't have to write it yourself.

In this chapter, you also looked at unit tests and saw how you can write code that can test the functionality of other code without requiring you to manually work through your application's user interface. This can save you a lot of time and effort, especially in cases where later changes can break existing code logic.

Combining patterns such as MVVM with third-party frameworks and unit testing takes a little bit more effort than simply hammering out code, but the end result is worth it. Rather than having flimsy code that hangs together as much by luck as technique and that is impossible for other developers to understand, you end up with proper, production-ready code that you can be proud of.

EXERCISES

1. Why would you use MVVM in your applications?

2. Extend the `ButtonCommandHelper` class used in the Try It Out "Adding Command Bindings to `CarList`" to support command parameters. Hint: Use a second attached property called `CommandParameter`.

3. How do most unit tests indicate test failure?

Answers to the Exercises can be found in the Appendix.

▶ **WHAT YOU LEARNED IN THIS CHAPTER**

TOPIC	KEY CONCEPTS
Patterns	Patterns are agreed-on solutions to common problems. Often when you write code, you can save yourself time by using patterns instead of working things out from first principles. In addition, common use of patterns enhances both reusability and maintainability, especially when new developers join a project, because using patterns makes it easier to see how things work.
MVVM	MVVM is an architectural-level pattern that specifies how different parts of your application work together. By separating out the user interface part of your application into views that are bound to view models, you decouple form from function and can work on these two facets independently. There are some coding challenges when using MVVM, such as button click handlers, but the extra effort is worthwhile.
MVVM frameworks	Frameworks, such as Prism, Caliburn, and MVVM Light, make it easier to code using MVVM. They do this by providing a common library of code to solve problems such as "how are views associated with view models?" and "how do I wire up a button click event to my view model?" Each framework has strong points and peculiarities, and it's worth experimenting with as many as possible before deciding which to use.
Unit tests	Using unit tests is a way to ensure that your code works the way it should without requiring you to manually run your application and work through the user interface. Instead, you provide code that tests your methods with different varieties of input and checks what happens. Unit tests should test code at its lowest level, taking into account only essential dependencies. Other dependencies can be mocked so that they don't take part in tests. You can also write tests before other code if you want to use TDD.
Unit test frameworks	Frameworks make it easier to write unit tests and to provide a user interface for viewing test results. One example is built into the Silverlight Toolkit, although some third-party code is required to make it work with Windows Phone 7.

15

Publishing Your Application

WHAT YOU WILL LEARN IN THIS CHAPTER:

➤ Joining the App Hub

➤ Submitting an application to the Windows Phone 7 Marketplace

➤ Avoiding common mistakes when submitting your application

➤ Marketing your application: pricing, advertising, target markets and Trial mode

So you've finished building an application, and now you'd like to put it out there for the world to see. Maybe you'd even like to try to make some money from it. Or perhaps you'd like to know what's involved in selling a Windows Phone 7 application before you get started. This chapter walks you through the process of publishing and creating a presence for your application in the Marketplace.

THE MARKETPLACE AND APP HUB

For the first time, Microsoft has implemented a "walled garden" (also known as a "curated" approach) for applications on a Windows Phone. Following in Apple's footsteps, Microsoft now prevents the installation of any application that Microsoft itself hasn't inspected, tested, and appraised. Although power users and developers may find this frustrating, in the end, the consumers win because the only applications that make it onto the phone are those that are almost guaranteed not to crash or rapidly wear out the battery.

Every Windows Phone 7 phone comes with an application called Marketplace (see Figure 15-1), which enables users to download, try, and buy new apps. You should familiarize yourself with Marketplace, because understanding the way it works is crucial to your success as an app developer.

FIGURE 15-1: The Windows Phone 7 Marketplace App.

If you want to install your own applications on a real phone, which you'll certainly want to do before you submit an application for testing, you need to "unlock" it. You can install any application on an unlocked phone, including the ones that you write and want to test.

To unlock a phone, you need to become a member of the online developer portal, App Hub. Once you're a verified member of this program, you can run the Windows Phone Developer Registration tool to unlock up to three phones per year (or one phone per year, if you are a student and enrolled with a student account). Joining App Hub costs $99 for an individual (at time of this book's publication). You also have to join this program to submit applications to the Windows Phone 7 Marketplace.

JOINING THE APP HUB

From the App Hub home page at `http://create.msdn.com`, click the Join button to go into the membership section of the site. Membership is linked to a Windows Live ID, so you will be prompted to either log in with an existing ID or sign up for a new one when you proceed with the registration. If you choose the latter, you will need to return to the App Hub registration page after verifying your Windows Live ID e-mail address.

After you have signed in with your Windows Live ID, the first step of the registration is selecting the country in which you want to do business, and the type of membership. The country is usually where you live, but if you are registering a company that's based in another country, you can choose that. This is the country where Microsoft will send revenue for app purchases, and you'll be responsible for paying any taxes in that country.

MEMBERSHIP TYPES

Company membership is for companies that are registered with their local government, and are planning on publishing apps on behalf of the company entity. At the time of writing, only one App Hub account can be created for a company.

Student membership is available to only students verified by Microsoft's DreamSpark (`www.dreamspark.com`) program for students. No registration fee is charged for this account.

Individual membership is for independent developers, who will have income from application sales contributing to their personal income.

Different membership types have different requirements. For example, getting a validated DreamSpark account requires confirmation from an academic institution. Other account types require a credit card to purchase your subscription. More information is available at the App Hub at `http://create.msdn.com/en-US/home/about/developer_registration_walkthrough`

On the second page, you provide personal contact information, such as your name and address. It's important to enter this information accurately; Microsoft needs to confirm the accuracy of the details before you can unlock your phone or release applications. Microsoft and its identity verification partner, GeoTrust, do this by emailing various requests to the email address that you provide, so make sure that the mailbox for the address you provide doesn't delete emails from Microsoft, App Hub, and GeoTrust as spam.

Your publisher name is what's shown to Marketplace users. You can use your own name or your company name, or you can make up a new "doing business as" name. (If you make up a name and start to successfully sell your applications, it would make sense to register this name as soon as possible.) The website that you provide here will theoretically be displayed to end users who come across your publisher name on the Marketplace, although currently this website isn't used in the phone's Marketplace app. If you don't have a website yet, you could even sign up for a free blog (just put "blog host" into your favorite search engine) to be your website.

On the next page, you enter your App Hub profile information. Information entered here is displayed only to other developers when you make posts on the App Hub forum. You'll also need an Xbox LIVE Gamertag; signing up to App Hub also buys you an Xbox LIVE subscription.

On the fourth page, you enter your credit card details to pay for your account. You must use a credit card that's from the same country you selected on the first page. (If you're signing up with DreamSpark, you skip this page.)

Next, you confirm that all the details you've just entered are correct, read some more information about the identity verification process, and click Finish to create your account. Before you can unlock your phone, you'll still need to complete the identity verification process, which is discussed in the next section.

Completing the Identity Verification Process

After you create an account with App Hub, you'll receive an email from GeoTrust within a few working days. The email asks you to print and sign a form and to submit this along with your government-issued ID. If your passport is from a different country than where you're living, it's a good idea to provide a copy of your visa, too, to prevent delay if GeoTrust later asks for it.

Setting Up Payee Information

If you're planning to charge for an application you create, you need to set up your payee details on App Hub, too. For free or ad-supported applications, you don't need to set up payee information. You can access the necessary form by clicking your own name to view your profile and then selecting Payee Details from the My Account menu.

On the Payee Details screen, you enter details such as your bank account name and number, payee address, and tax codes. The details on this form vary by country. You need to supply your U.S. taxpayer identification number. U.S. citizens should use their Social Security number. Citizens of other countries can apply for an Individual Tax Identification Number (ITIN) by filling out an IRS Form W-7; you can find instructions on how to do so on this web page. With a valid U.S. taxpayer identification number, you need to send a physical copy of a W-8 form to Microsoft. Again, the web page provides an explanation about how to do this and links to the appropriate forms.

 WARNING *You may be asked for a country-specific tax code, too, if you're based outside the United States. Providing this code may be optional, but providing it can give you tax benefits. If you expect to earn a lot of money from your application, it might be wise to consult an accountant.*

SUBMITTING AN APPLICATION FOR PUBLICATION

So you've finished your application and it's time to release it to the unsuspecting world? Whether you're charging for the application or want it to be free to download, you follow the same process. When you're logged into App Hub with a verified account, you have access to the Submit for Windows Phone button, which takes you to the Submit New App wizard.

 COMMON MISTAKES *At the time of publication, the Submit New App wizard (a Silverlight 4 application) exhibits a few bugs unless you use Microsoft's Internet Explorer browser. If you use a different browser and notice any inconsistencies or error messages, try switching to Internet Explorer.*

Uploading the XAP File

The first step of the wizard is the Upload page, where you can upload your application package. This is a file with a `.xap` (pronounced "zap") extension, which is generated when your Silverlight or XNA project is built. It's a good idea to build this file in release mode. To do so, follow these steps:

1. Open the Visual Studio solution for your application.

2. Look for the drop-down menu in the toolbar that says Debug. Change this to Release.

3. Rebuild your solution. The XAP file should now be in the `bin\Release` folder.

In addition to uploading your XAP file, you also need to enter the following information for your app to be published on the Marketplace:

➤ Your application's name

➤ The platform you're targeting (that is, Windows Phone 7)

➤ The primary language of your application (that is, the language you used in your user interface)

➤ A version number (start with 1.0)

In addition to this Marketplace data, you need to fill in a few fields, and your answers here remain private to you and Microsoft:

➤ **Developer Notes** — This is simply for your own reference, and you can leave it blank.

➤ **Tester Notes** — This is what testers at Microsoft will see when they start testing your application. You can provide a simple "how to use" description, but if your application requires users to have an account, it's a good idea to create an account for Microsoft's testers beforehand and provide the username and password here.

➤ **Requires Technical Exception** — This is what you use to request exemption from Microsoft's requirements or policy for submitting apps to the Marketplace. You need a convincing argument for this to be accepted, and it is better to wait for Microsoft's testing team to ask you to submit a request than to assume that one is required before you submit.

Describing the Application

The Description page is where you specify the details you'd like potential customers to see when they browse your app on the Marketplace. This screen has the following fields:

➤ **Application Title** — The title, as indicated on the previous screen.

➤ **Supported Languages** — You actually have to fill out this screen once for each of the languages your app supports. This field tells you which language you're currently describing.

➤ **Category and Subcategory** — By selecting the correct category for your application, you can help potential customers find your application faster. Not all categories have subcategories. You should choose the most specific category that represents your application so that users who are looking for an application like yours are more likely to find it. For example, if you've written a chess game, filing it under "Games/Board&Classic" will mean that it is easier for your target audience to find it than if you filed it under "Entertainment."

➤ **Detailed Description** — Here you can provide up to 2,000 characters of text describing your application. If your potential customers have gotten as far as reading this, then they are considering buying your application, so you should sell your application here. See the section "Creating Impressions That Count," later in this chapter, for more details on writing a good description.

➤ **Update Description** — Here you describe what's new in your latest release. You don't need to sell your application here — just list the new features and bug fixes.

➤ **Featured App Description** — If you're ever lucky enough to be featured on the Marketplace, then the 25 characters you enter here will be displayed to people browsing the Marketplace. Although you can barely fit a sentence into 25 characters, you should try very hard to explain what your app does in this space. Although this field is optional, it's a good idea to fill it out because you're unlikely to be considered for featuring if it's empty.

➤ **Keywords** — When a user does a search on the Marketplace, the search is based on the app's title, the developer, and the keywords entered here. Therefore, your choice of keywords is important. Try to think of five different words that users would potentially enter when searching for an application like yours.

➤ **ESRB, PEGI, and USK Ratings** — These are all ratings that big game developers have to get in order to sell their games at retail. Fortunately, the ratings are optional, so you should leave these fields blank.

➤ **Legal URL** — If you like, you can link to a web page that provides legal information regarding your application.

➤ **Support Email Address** — While providing a support email address is optional, doing so benefits you in two ways: You get valuable feedback about your application, and disgruntled users get a chance to vent. A well-thought-out response to a support request can mean the difference between a one-star review and a five-star review. It's a good idea to create a new email address to use here, though, as you'll be publishing this address to the world, and you don't want support messages to flood your personal inbox.

➤ **Required Device Capabilities** — This is calculated automatically by Microsoft by analyzing the XAP file you uploaded. You don't need to wait for this to complete before moving on to the next screen.

➤ **Push Notification Certificates** — This optional field displays only if you're using push notifications. After you've configured an SSL certificate in the My Account section of App Hub, you can pick which certificate to use.

Adding Artwork

On the Artwork page of the wizard, you upload a few images that will be used to identify your application on the Marketplace. These are different from the two images that are compiled into your XAP file from your original project; those two images are used on the phone itself once the application's installed.

APPLICATION IMAGES VERSUS SUBMISSION ARTWORK

The images you included in your Visual Studio solution are compiled into your XAP file, and will be used on the phone itself after the application is installed. The images uploaded as part of the submission process are used to represent your application in the Marketplace.

The first three images are meant to be representations of your application's icon, similar to the application icon you're using on the phone. However, these images must not contain any transparency, and they have to conform to the exact dimensions that the form requires. A user would see the large mobile app tile (173 x 173 pixels) and the small mobile app tile (99 x 99 pixels) when browsing the Marketplace on a Windows Phone device. The large PC app tile (200 x 200 pixels) is visible when browsing the Marketplace on a PC, such as with the Zune software.

You can optionally provide a background art image. Microsoft uses this 1000 x 800-pixel image as the background in the Marketplace if you're lucky enough to be featured. Providing a good panorama-style image here isn't necessary, but it can improve your chances of being featured, so it's highly recommended. As part of the Windows Phone 7 Application Submission Walkthrough, Microsoft has published their Best Practices for Application Marketing guidelines, recommending that you do the following:

➤ Keep your image simple, so that it doesn't clutter up the foreground of the Marketplace app.

➤ Entice the user to scroll horizontally, with a design that spans several 320 x 800-pixel sections.

➤ Make each screen strong enough to stand by itself.

You can also upload up to eight screenshots of your app. The more screenshots you provide, the more information a potential customer will be able to glean from the Marketplace, so upload as many representative, visually appealing screenshots as you can.

 NOTE *At the time of publication, it is not possible to take a screenshot from the phone. Instead, take a screenshot of the emulator running on your PC, and crop the phone frame.*

Pricing Your Application

In the Pricing step, you can indicate what you'd like to charge for your application, as well as the markets that you'd like to sell in, and whether your app supports a trial mode. This page contains the following fields:

➤ **Trial Supported** — Enable this option only if you've developed your application to have a restricted set of features when in trial mode. (See the upcoming section "Providing a Trial Mode" for more details on this.) Otherwise, you'll effectively be giving your application away for free, since users will be able to request a trial but will then be able to use the full version of your application. Offering a trial version is a great way to let users try your application before they decide whether to buy it.

➤ **Worldwide Distribution** — If you enable this option, your application will be available for purchase everywhere there is a Windows Phone 7 marketplace. If you disable this option, you'll be presented with a list of countries to select from.

➤ **Primary Offer Currency** — This is the currency in which you want to set the price.

➤ **Application Price** — Here you enter the amount you'd like to charge for the application. When you make a selection here, the form automatically updates the individual country prices. If you want to set the price on a per-country basis, you can disable Worldwide Distribution and then set each country's price individually.

Submitting Your Application

The final step of the wizard is where you choose whether your application should be published as soon as it passes certification. Normally, you'll want your app to go on sale as soon as possible, but if you have a release party planned, or if you need to turn on certain features on a web server first, then it might make sense to take control of the publish date yourself.

 NOTE Generally, game purchases peak on Saturdays, and applications on Tuesdays, so it would pay to choose your publication date yourself.

You can now review all the details of your application. When everything looks the way you want it, you can press the Submit for Certification button to pass your application on to Microsoft for testing and certification!

TESTING YOUR APPLICATION

Once you've submitted your application, Microsoft will submit it to the testing and certification process, whereby Microsoft engineers run your XAP and try to find bugs. If your application requires users to create an account or log in, you need to provide Microsoft's testers with some usable credentials. If your application passes testing, you get an email saying that it's ready to be placed on the Marketplace, which takes a few days. If your application fails testing, you get an email explaining why, along with some suggestions about how to improve your application. Once you've applied these suggestions, you can simply resubmit the app to Microsoft. This process may seem overbearing, but it's a critical way to ensure that end users have a good experience with each Marketplace app.

You should thoroughly familiarize yourself with Microsoft's "Windows Phone 7 Application Certification Requirements" document, available at `http://go.microsoft.com/?linkid=9730558`. This document lists all the official reasons that an application may fail testing, although Microsoft's testers are allowed to use some discretion. The following are some common mistakes that can prevent an application from passing testing:

➤ **Crashing** — Microsoft isn't likely to pass your app if it finds unhandled exceptions or unexpected termination of your application.

➤ **Freezing** — This occurs when an application permanently hangs (for example, due to an infinite loop) or is temporarily unresponsive (for example, performing network requests on the user interface thread or failing to display an appropriate progress bar when waiting for a background computation).

➤ **Not being designed for mobile devices** — Text sizes must be large enough to be legible, and buttons must be large enough to press.

➤ **Respecting themes** — You should test your Silverlight applications with different themes to ensure that all text is readable in both light and dark themes. White text on a white background is invisible. You can avoid this by using the built-in resource brushes instead of directly using brushes like white and black. You should also respect the user's choice of accent color.

➤ **Back button behaving unexpectedly** — Although you have full control over what the physical Back button on the phone can do, users expect that it will always take them back somewhere that they were, such as a previous screen or to quit the application.

➤ **Covering buttons with the keyboard** — Imagine a form with a text box in the top half and a button in the bottom half. If you tap the text box, the software keyboard will slide up and cover the button. Most users will find it incredibly difficult to dismiss this keyboard and press the button. The easiest way to fix this is to move the button into the application bar, which is never covered by the keyboard.

 COMMON MISTAKES *If you use push notification, you have to make sure that the user has had a chance to accept or decline push for your application before you turn it on. In addition, you need to provide an obvious, easy way for users to turn push off, either temporarily or permanently.*

PROVIDING A TRIAL MODE

Including a trial mode for your app is a great way to give users a chance to try out your application before purchasing it. When you submit your application, you can tell Microsoft whether your application supports a trial mode. If you choose No, your application must be bought outright or not downloaded at all. If you choose Yes, customers can download your application for free, and you must selectively cripple your application such that users can see how good your application is, but without all the full-version features. You can provide the crippled trial version to entice customers to eventually purchase your application.

> **NOTE** *The simple method call* `bool isTrial = new LicenseInformation()` `.IsTrial();` *tells you whether an application is in trial mode. Note that Microsoft recommends that you cache the results of this method call, as it can take a long time to compute.*

Many people think that building a time-based trial application is a good way to go, but a user can simply uninstall and then reinstall the app to reset the timer and continue using the trial version. It's better to reduce the features in the trial version. For a game, you might not let users play all the levels or use all the available characters or weapons. (But remember that you want to show them what they're missing to get them hungrier for the full version.) For a productivity application, you might prevent users from saving or emailing their files. Providing a less capable version as the trial is a much better approach than annoying the user with a 10-second nag screen or deliberately corrupting their data. You want users to like your application (even when it's in trial mode); otherwise, they'll buy something else!

When the user hits the limits of the trial mode (for example, by finishing level 2 or pressing the Email Me This Todo List button), it's a good time to give them the opportunity to visit the Marketplace and purchase your application. If they're politely taken to a place where they can purchase your application for little effort, you have a higher chance of getting their money!

TRY IT OUT   **Building a Trial Version of an Application**

In this Try It Out, you'll build a simple Silverlight application that has different behavior in the trial version than in the full version. This trial version will offer to take users to the Marketplace when they want to use full-version features. Here's how you create the app:

1.   Create a new project in Visual Studio by pressing Ctrl+Shift+N and then selecting Windows Phone Application, under the Silverlight for Windows Phone group. Name it **TrialModeApplication**.

2.   Add the following code to the `ContentPanel` grid in `MainPage.xaml:` like in Listing 15-1.

LISTING 15-1: Modifying the code in MainPage.xaml

```xaml
<Grid.RowDefinitions>
  <RowDefinition/>
  <RowDefinition/>
  <RowDefinition/>
</Grid.RowDefinitions>
<TextBlock x:Name="label" TextWrapping="Wrap">
  If you want to use this awesome feature,
  you'll need to purchase this application
</TextBlock>
<Button x:Name="buy" Click="Buy_Click" Content="Buy" Grid.Row="1"/>
<Button x:Name="continue" Click="Continue_Click" Content="Continue" Grid.Row="2"/>
```

Code Snippet TrialModeApplication\TrialModeApplication\MainPage.xaml

3. Replace the contents of `Mainpage.xaml.cs` with the code in Listing 15-2.

LISTING 15-2: Modifying the code in MainPage.xaml.cs

```csharp
using System.Windows;
using Microsoft.Phone.Controls;
using Microsoft.Phone.Marketplace;
using Microsoft.Phone.Tasks;

namespace TrialModeApplication
{
    public partial class MainPage : PhoneApplicationPage
    {
        bool isTrial;

        public MainPage()
        {
            InitializeComponent();

            isTrial = new LicenseInformation().IsTrial();

            if (!isTrial)
            {
                buy.Visibility = Visibility.Collapsed;
                label.Visibility = Visibility.Collapsed;
            }
        }

        void Buy_Click(object sender, RoutedEventArgs e)
        {
            var task = new MarketplaceDetailTask();
            task.Show();
        }

        void Continue_Click(object sender, RoutedEventArgs e)
```

continues

LISTING 15-2 *(continued)*

```
    {
        if (isTrial)
        {
            MessageBox.Show("You haven't paid for awesome feature, here's an ok one");
        }
        else
        {
            MessageBox.Show("Continuing to the awesome feature");
        }
    }
}
```

Code Snippet TrialModeApplication\TrialModeApplication\MainPage.xaml.cs

4.   Run the application. You should see a button titled, Continue. Click it and see which message displays.

5.   Replace the constructor in `MainPage.xaml.cs` with the following code:

Available for
download on
Wrox.com

```
public MainPage()
{
    InitializeComponent();

    isTrial = true; // new LicenseInformation().IsTrial();

    if (!isTrial)
    {
        buy.Visibility = Visibility.Collapsed;
        label.Visibility = Visibility.Collapsed;
    }
}
```

Code Snippet TrialModeApplication\TrialModeApplication\MainPage.xaml.cs

6.   Run the application. Click each button to see what happens. If you're taken to the Marketplace but see an error, don't worry, as this is expected.

How It Works

First, you created three rows in the main grid. You added a `TextBlock` control to the first row and a button to each of the remaining rows. You then added some code to the code-behind file of `MainPage` `.xaml`. In the `MainPage` constructor, this code checks to see whether the application is running in trial mode, and it stores this Boolean value in the class field `isTrial`. The constructor also hides the top two controls if the application is not in trial mode.

Next, you tested this application and hopefully discovered that in debug mode, `isTrial` always returns `false`. This is why in step 5 you overrode the value of `isTrial`, so that in step 6 you could test the behavior in trial mode. If you click the Buy button, a new `MarketplaceDetailTask` method with no further arguments is shown. If your application actually exists on the Marketplace, then clicking Buy takes the user to the page of the Marketplace for the full version of the application, where it is possible to purchase the application.

INCREASING APP SALES

Marketing isn't just about advertising. It's also about building a product that lots of people want (or that some people want a lot). If you're a programmer who's serious about making money from your Windows Phone 7 applications, you might despair to learn that to do your development effort justice, you need to spend almost as much time on promotion and polish as you've spent coding. There are two things you need to do in order to get sales:

➤ Find the right people.

➤ Convince them to buy your application.

Do your market research (show your app to some friends) and try to get inside the head of your customer. Most smartphone app sales are driven by word-of-mouth and website reviews, so the best way you can sell more copies is to have a better product.

Microsoft's Target Windows Phone 7 Market

There's no point trying to sell an application on the Windows Phone 7 Marketplace if the kinds of people who would want your application don't use Windows Phone devices. Don't feel guilty about making sweeping generalizations; it pays to think about what kinds of people have Windows Phone 7 phones and target those people.

Microsoft has a clear idea of what kinds of people it wants to buy its phones. Microsoft calls these folks "life maximizers," and this target audience has the following characteristics:

➤ Busy with both job and personal life

➤ Living an active life

➤ Juggling many priorities at once

➤ Used to using technology to help achieve goals

➤ More likely to be in a settled relationship than seeking a relationship

These people value the following:

➤ Keeping in touch with friends, family, and work, possibly all at once

➤ Accessing information quickly

➤ Avoiding the feeling of being overwhelmed

➤ Balancing their different priorities

➤ Growing personally and professionally

➤ Living life to the fullest

This information might help provide some inspiration about what kinds of applications are popular in the Marketplace.

You can also use this information to help make an application that suits these people better. For example, you should streamline your application as much as possible, so that it takes minimal taps and time to get to the desired information. Tasks that the user does more often should be closer to the home screen. You can see this concept present in many of the applications that come with the phone, such as the Zune music player.

Applications that let users connect to friends — whether a multiplayer game, photo sharing, or a dinner organizer — are going to be popular. Hooking into a number of different social media networks gives you more coverage. Some people prefer Facebook over Twitter, while others just stick to email. The social media landscape is always changing, whereas a phone's purpose (connecting people) is constant.

Try not to overwhelm the user with functionality. If your application has a lot of features, make sure the user is gently eased into them rather than presenting all the features on launch. It's far better to do one thing very well than do ten things poorly.

Creating Impressions That Count

The first things that potential customers see on the Marketplace are your app's icon and title. Once they tap on that the icon, users will see your description, screenshots, and reviews. If they like those, they might buy your application. So let's look at how you can engineer the description, screenshots, and reviews to create as many sales as possible.

Designing an Effective Icon

A good icon can go a long way toward increasing your reach. You want an icon that makes people curious about what the application does and whether it can help them, and you want it to give a strong impression of quality and polish.

Your icon should represent the purpose of your application. Users should get a sense of what your app is for just by looking at it. Equally as important, the icon should be visually appealing.

 NOTE *Microsoft has published a UI Design and Interaction Guide for Windows Phone 7. It's full of tips and suggestions regarding user experience, and might help you to think about what kind of icon you want. You can download it from* `http://go.microsoft.com/fwlink/?LinkID=183218.`

You might want to look at existing applications that you're competing with in order to come up with an icon that explicitly differentiates you. Once your application is submitted, yours will be nestled among those other icons, so you want something that stands out. Figure 15-2 shows a number of Stopwatch applications. Which icons catch your eye? Which ones make you think, "This application is polished and of a high standard?" Which ones make you think, "This is designed for my Windows Phone 7?"

FIGURE 15-2: Stopwatch applications in the Marketplace.

Once you've piqued a customer's curiosity, he or she will click on your icon. The icon takes potential customers to the Marketplace detail page for your application. At this point, they'll see your description screenshots and any reviews that your application has been given. These three elements can help close sales.

 NOTE *Make sure your icon looks good at different resolutions. If you draw your icon as an 800-pixel square and then scale it down to 200, 173, and 99 pixels, you'll find that your smaller icons look sharper than if you'd just started at 200 and scaled down to 173 and 99. Don't ever start with a 99-pixel square and then scale up because whenever you rescale an image to be bigger, it always gets blurry.*

Writing an Effective Description

You have 2,000 characters to convince a user to buy your app. Actually, you'll be lucky if users read that far, so try to convince them in even fewer characters. You should describe what your application does, possibly by comparing it to other applications. (However, keep in mind that people may not have heard of those other applications.) Use clear, concise, interesting language. Write in active voice to keep your text interesting and clear.

If you've already received favorable reviews outside the Marketplace, such as on Windows Phone 7 blogs or websites, you can complete the description with a testimonial or two. Potential customers generally trust the words of other customers (and even celebrities). That's why when you see a movie poster, you'll always see the best reviews of the movie quoted on the poster. You can edit the description later, so don't hesitate to revisit it when you've received a new testimonial.

Using Screenshots to Attract Potential Customers

You're allowed up to eight screenshots in your application's Marketplace detail page. A picture really is worth a thousand words, and there's no better way to show potential customers how your app looks. On top of how it looks, though, you should also convey the following to your customers:

> ➤ The richness of features in your application (with screenshots of a number of things that can be done)

> ➤ How features are used (that is, the user experience)

> ➤ How polished your application is

Reviews

When people use and review your application, reviews will start to appear under your screenshots. The average star score (out of 5) will be displayed next to your application. Having a high review score is incredibly desirable because there's a direct correlation between review scores and sales.

You have no direct control over your app's reviews; all you can do is build a great app with no bugs and hope that people are kind enough to say nice things! Don't be disheartened by bad reviews; people with negative opinions are much more likely to voice them than are people who like your app.

Getting the Word Out

There's no point having an attractive icon if no one even knows to look for it. What can you do to help people find your application? Let's take a look at some of the ways you can reach people before they find you in the Marketplace.

Application Website

You'll find that almost all the popular applications (across all marketplaces, not just Windows Phone 7 apps) have their own websites. A website gives the developer full control over how to present an app; for example, you can choose which reviews to quote, and you can use as many characters as you like to describe the app. Also, the site is more likely to come up than the Marketplace if a potential customer does a search on the Internet. You don't need a complex website; it can be a simple extension of what's on the Marketplace. However, your site is a great place to put an FAQ, an instruction manual, or a troubleshooting guide.

If a picture is a worth a thousand words, a video is worth a million. If you have the resources, put a two-minute video on your website and on YouTube or Vimeo. There's no better way for people to see what your application is like without installing it than via a video.

Word-of-Mouth Advertising

It's fun to imagine: You publish your application, you show it to your friends, they love it and tell their friends all about it, and they tell their friends all about it, and before you know it you've sold a million copies.

The real reason that word-of-mouth is effective is because it's *authentic*. Having a trusted friend, colleague, or family member rave about an application is much more likely to make you buy an application than anything else, because you know this person, this person knows you, and he or she probably knows what kinds of things you like.

The best way to rely on word-of-mouth is to build an application that's so useful and polished that the people who find your application immediately want to show it to their friends, regardless of whether they know you personally.

Being Featured at the Marketplace

Every few days, Microsoft features a new application on the Marketplace. Everyone who launches the Marketplace app will see it because of its prominence. During the feature period, the panorama image that its developer uploaded for the app is used as the background of the Marketplace app. Being featured usually results in a huge increase in sales, so you should do everything you can to ensure that you're eligible for featuring.

When you upload your application, you have the opportunity to provide a featured app description and a panorama image. Make sure to provide both of these things, or you won't have a chance at being featured.

Microsoft currently doesn't warn that it's planning to feature an application on the Marketplace. If you're featured, you may notice the Marketplace app icon, or someone you know may notice and let you know. While you're being featured and your visibility is high is a great time to do additional marketing (such as letting a review website know about your app, as discussed in the next section).

Review Websites

A number of Windows Phone 7 application review websites and blogs are springing up. While not all "life maximizers" read such websites, some may be on the lookout for new technology and rely on such websites for information. The people behind these websites are always looking for new applications to review, and you can make the job easy for them. Here's how to approach the people behind a website to get your application reviewed:

➤ Look for a few review websites that write their own content (instead of simply cross-posting other sites' content).

➤ Find the email address specifically for submissions or the personal email address of one of the reviewers. If you have a productivity app and you notice that one particular person is reviewing all the productivity apps, find that person's address and contact him or her directly. People are much more likely to respond when you contact them by name.

➤ A week before your application is likely to be ready for release is a good time to let reviewers know about it. It gives them enough time to do a proper write-up of your application, without being far enough away that they'll put it on their "I'll do it later" pile.

➤ Don't just paste your app's description into your message to reviewers. Make it easy for a reviewer to write a review. Read other reviews and think about what kinds of things they say. For example, a review will often say something like "It's similar to the XYZ application, but it has feature ABC." Let the reviewer know about anything special or different in your application.

➤ Send reviewers more screenshots than what you've uploaded to the Marketplace. They'll appreciate being able to offer more original content on their website and will pick the shots they think their readers might like best. If you have a video, send reviewers a link to it.

➤ Microsoft is putting together a program that enables developers to give their applications to friends for testing, before it's officially published at the Marketplace. Once this is in place, you'll be able to offer free review copies to reviewers. Do this. A reviewer doesn't want to pay you for the privilege of giving you free advertising.

Paying for Advertising

Although you can purchase untargeted Internet ads to boost sales, you're not likely to get a lot of bang for your buck. When you consider the percentage of the ad's audience who own Windows Phone 7 devices, the chances that they'll click your add and then buy your app, the cost of advertising, and the income from a sale, you can see that it's difficult to make a profit off an ad. However, if you target your ads properly, you have a better chance of making money. If you're writing a Windows Phone 7 game, the best place to advertise is probably on a Windows Phone 7 gaming website because most of the visitors will actually have a Windows Phone 7 device and want to play games. If you've built a Facebook client, why not advertise on Facebook? You'll actually find that most advertising networks (especially Facebook) give you quite a lot of options regarding your target audience.

Niche Markets

If you've built an application that appeals to a small market niche, then you have even more opportunity to get creative with your marketing. Golfing, photography, graduate-level mathematics, public speaking, programming — these are all hobbies with specific websites and communities. Although the websites that support these communities probably don't handle their own advertising network, by contacting them you might manage to get a mention on the website itself.

The Right Price

It can be difficult to figure out how much to charge for an application. If you have competitors in the Marketplace, you can decide to either charge more because you have more features or to undercut them. Otherwise, you should charge an amount that's proportional to the effort that's gone into the application.

Charging less than competitors can sometimes mean more profit, since more people end up buying your application. You can try changing the price to see at what point you make the most income, but you need to be aware that by charging too little, you'll make all the sales you were ever going to make at once. By charging too much, your sales will go very slowly, but at least there will always be a large pool of people out there who haven't yet bought your app.

Be wary of changing your price too often, too. People who paid a lot of money for your app and now see that it's free are very likely to leave bad reviews because they feel cheated. If your price is always fluctuating, a number of people will want to see how low your price goes before they buy, whereas if it's stable, they'll just go ahead and buy it.

It's not a good idea to launch at the cheapest price possible (99 cents). Knowing that your app is a 99-cent app (when it's not on sale) alters peoples' perception of the quality of your app; they may believe that it's not as good as something that costs more. Also, you want to leave yourself some wiggle room so that can put your application "on promotion" and temporarily lower the price.

Taking Advantage of Momentum

Imagine that a user wants to buy a new game. That user will likely go to the Marketplace app, choose the category Games, pick the Top list or the New list, and start scrolling down. The New list is easy to get onto (but very hard to stay on), so we won't go into that. The Top list is very interesting because anything that's on the Top list is probably quite good — so the user is more likely to buy it. The person might reason that if other people like these applications, there must be a good reason for it.

The exact algorithm is subject to change, but in general, the way you get your app onto the Top list is by making a lot of sales. So, basically, the best way to make lots of sales is to make lots of sales. You need to capitalize on your own success whenever something good happens. If you're getting near the top 25 list, it's the perfect time to drop the price or start a new ad campaign.

The App Hub website lets you track how many sales you're making each day, and you can check on the Marketplace yourself to see what rank you are.

CHECKING YOUR MARKETPLACE RANK

In the Marketplace section of Microsoft's Zune software (for the PC, not the phone), there are lists of the top paid and free apps. These lists show the top one hundred applications initially, but load another hundred every time you scroll to the bottom. The Marketplace app on the phone can show you this too, but loads fewer apps at a time. Unless you're a chart-topper, it's easier to find yourself on the PC than the phone.

Obtaining Feedback

Getting high-quality feedback on an application is priceless. There's no better way to improve your app than to get ideas from other people. By showing your application to other people, you can get suggestions that you never would have thought of. It's a really good idea to seek some feedback before you submit your app to the Marketplace: Show your app to your friends, tell them to play with it, and send the source code to people you trust. It's a good idea to spend a minimum of two weeks in such beta testing.

Ideally, you won't receive any feedback from Microsoft after submitting your application but will just pass straight through the certification process. If you're rejected from testing, then at least you'll have some useful criticism of your application to apply.

Once your application is deployed, you'll be getting feedback from real users in the form of reviews and support emails. Once again, keep an open mind and take as much of this feedback on board as you can. If 1 user cares enough to email you about something, chances are there are 20 other people who think the same thing.

SUMMARY

In this chapter, you looked at the Windows Phone Marketplace. You learned how to create an account, submit an application, and avoid some common causes of rejection.

You built a simple application that checked whether it's in trial mode and offered to take the user to the Marketplace to pay for the full version, if so.

You then looked at the wooly world of marketing, including a few basic techniques that might help you to get more sales, such as presenting your app as best you can on the Marketplace and getting coverage outside the Marketplace.

EXERCISES

1. True or False: You need to pay Microsoft to join its Developer Program before you can install your own applications on your own phone.

2. What are the different sizes of application icons that you need to submit with your application to represent it on the Marketplace? Can you use transparency on these images?

3. Will your application fail Microsoft's testing if you use your own colors for Silverlight controls instead of using the system resource colors, which change to reflect the user's preferences?

4. What's a better way of implementing a trial mode in a game — letting the user play the entire game for only a week or letting the user play as far as only the fifth level, regardless of the time period?

5. Do potential customers see your description or your icon on the Windows Phone 7 Marketplace first?

6. Should you go out and get websites to review your application, or will they find your application themselves (if they're any good at their jobs)?

Answers to the Exercises can be found in the Appendix.

▶ **WHAT YOU LEARNED IN THIS CHAPTER**

TOPIC	KEY CONCEPTS
Signing up for the Windows Phone 7 Developer program	You need to purchase an annual subscription to the Windows Phone 7 Developer program if you want to deploy your application to your phone or if you want to publish your application on the Marketplace.
Submitting an application to the Windows Phone 7 Marketplace	Submitting an application to the Marketplace involves uploading the application package and artwork, setting the price and global availability of the application, and deciding on its date of publication on the Marketplace.
Common testing errors	You should familiarize yourself with the Windows Phone 7 certification requirements. An app can fail testing for many reasons, and failing testing means it'll take longer to release your app.
Trial mode	It's a good idea to create a trial mode for your app, with crippled functionality. You can easily check whether your application is in trial mode. You should make it easy for users to purchase the full version of your app from the trial version.
Target markets	Microsoft's target customers for Windows Phone 7 devices typically are busy people with active lives. They don't want to be overwhelmed but want to use technology to get things done.
Presenting your application on the Marketplace	It's important to present your application well on the Marketplace. The time you invest here pays off a lot more quickly than the time you put into developing your application.
Presenting your application outside the Marketplace	The Marketplace isn't your only channel of promotion. You can also use websites to spread the word about your application.
Pricing	You may want to choose a price that's similar to the prices of any competing products. You should never start with a price of 99 cents; save that price for promotions.
How popularity affects sales	As in the music industry, the closer you are to the top of the charts, the more sales you make. You should do everything you can to try to keep up your sales momentum.
Feedback	It's incredibly valuable to get constructive criticism about your application — from friends, Microsoft, and your customers.

Solutions to Exercises

This appendix provides the solutions for the end-of-chapter exercises located at the end of each chapter 1–15.

CHAPTER 1 EXERCISE SOLUTIONS

Exercise 1 Solution

The answer is False. Make no mistake, if you already have a the professional version of Visual Studio 2010, then you can also use it and simply download and install the new Windows Phone 7 developer tools; and the installation package will recognize the fact that Visual Studio is installed and act accordingly. In that particular case, a copy of Expression Blend 4 for Windows Phone 7, along with the required Silverlight, XNA, and Windows Phone 7 emulator software will simply be integrated into your existing Visual Studio 2010 environment.

If you do not have the professional version, you can use the free Express version of Visual Studio, which is the version we use in this book.

Exercise 2 Solution

The Windows Phone 7 architecture consists of a, b, d, and e. WCF RIA Services is a client-side technology used for web-based Silverlight solutions and is not currently supported by Windows Phone. WPF is the full thick client programming solution for creating PC-based applications.

The Windows Phone 7 architecture consists of Runtime, Cloud Services, Portal Services, and Developer Tools.

Exercise 3 Solution

The answer is False. Unlike in previous versions of Windows Mobile, you can no longer just build an executable and distribute it yourself. If you wish want to make an application that is publically available, you will need to register for the Windows Phone 7 developer program and send your application through the verification and certification teams. Once it has been signed off as safe for devices, your application can be posted in the Windows Phone Marketplace for other users to find and download to their phones.

Exercise 4 Solution

The `TextBlock` control is a Silverlight control that can be used anywhere on the user interface to display static text. In the Try-It-Out section you were able to change the value of this to "Hello Windows Phone" and see the changes right in the design view of Visual Studio.

Exercise 5 Solution

The `PhoneApplicationPage` control located in all Windows Phone 7 applications is used as the top most parent that holds any additional user interface elements. You can think of it as the "main window" for an application that holds all other controls and elements must happen inside of it.

CHAPTER 2 EXERCISE SOLUTIONS

Exercise 1 Solution

The correct answer is False. You can easily support both `portrait` and `landscape` orientations in your applications by modifying the `SupportedOrientation` and `Orientation` properties of the `PhoneApplicationPage` control. Valid values for `SupportedOrientation` are `Landscape`, `Portrait`, and `PortraitOrLandscape`. The `Orientation` property should be set to the screen orientation you want to be the default when the application starts up.

Exercise 2 Solution

The answer is c (`GroupName`). When using several `RadioButton` controls on a page, you should set the `GroupName` property to be the same for all the `RadioButton` controls that you want to be a part of the mutually exclusive group. Then, when a user clicks a given `RadioButton` control, the currently selected control will automatically become unselected.

Exercise 3 Solution

Although there are a couple of ways to accomplish vertical and horizontal layouts, the `StackPanel` control provides the easiest way to do so. You can accomplish a similar layout by using a `Grid` or `Canvas` control, but doing so requires much more code than does using a simple `StackPanel` declaration. With the `StackPanel` control, you just set the `Orientation` property and add controls. No other work is necessary. On the other hand, with a `Grid` control, you need to add `RowDefinition` or `ColumnDefinition` objects for each control you're trying to display.

Exercise 4 Solution

When you want to launch the internal web browser on the phone and navigate to an external site, you need to set the `TargetName` property to "_blank."

Exercise 5 Solution

There are multiple options for subscribing to Silverlight control events. The first and easiest way is to add the event handler declaration right in the XAML file for the event you want to capture. For example, to handle the `Click` event of a `Button` control, you simply add the following code:

```
<Button x:Name="ButtonControl" Content="Click This" Click="ButtonControl_Click" />
```

In addition, you can subscribe to the `Click` event in the code-behind with code similar to the following:

```
ButtonControl.Click += new RoutedEventHandler(ButtonControl_Click);
```

In both cases, you also need to add an event-handling method called `ButtonControl_Click` with a method signature like the following:

```
private void ButtonControl_Click(object sender, RoutedEventArgs e)
{
}
```

CHAPTER 3 EXERCISE SOLUTIONS

Exercise 1 Solution

False. By default, you can use HTML color codes only when declaring brushes in XAML. If you need to use HTML color codes in the code-behind file, you have to create a custom conversion method that parses the color code into red, green, and blue components and then pass those into the `Color.FromARGB` method.

Exercise 2 Solution

Choices a and b are not valid shape objects in Silverlight. Silverlight provides the `Rectangle`, `Polyline`, `Polygon`, `Path`, `Ellipse`, and `Line` objects for drawing various shapes on the screen.

Exercise 3 Solution

When you use the `TransformGroup` object, the order in which transform effects are added matters. The transforms will be applied to the target object in the order in which the effects are added to the group.

Exercise 4 Solution

When you need a way to repeat a task on a timed basis, you should always use the `DispatcherTimer` object. This ensures that the repeated task will not interfere at all with the main user interface, and it also gives you the ability to run custom code during every `Tick` event.

Exercise 5 Solution

Choices c, e, and f are not valid transform effects. Silverlight provides the `RotateTransform`, `SkewTransform`, `ScaleTransform`, and `TranslateTransform` effects.

CHAPTER 4 EXERCISE SOLUTIONS

Exercise 1 Solution

The answer here is d, `BasedOn` styling. `BasedOn` styling allows you to create a base style containing values that will be common to a particular set of controls. That set of controls must be the same type, however. In this case, you can build a base style to hold the value for `Margin`, `Padding`, and `Background` and then create the additional styles for the rest of the `Button` objects that will contain the properties that differ.

Exercise 2 Solution

Choices a and b are the only valid animation objects in the list. You can use the `ColorAnimation` object to animate from one color to another over a specified period of time. You can use the `DoubleAnimation` object to change any property with a `double` type, such as `Opacity`. This object will perform the animation smoothly over a set period of time.

Exercise 3 Solution

True. Controls can be in multiple states as long as the states have been assigned to different `VisualStateGroup` declarations.

Exercise 4 Solution

The answer is d, override `OnApplyTemplate`. When creating custom controls that contain several Silverlight controls in the default style template, you should override the `OnApplyTemplate` method in order to gain access to any controls in the template.

Exercise 5 Solution

True. When creating custom controls, it is best to add corresponding `DependencyProperty` objects along with any custom properties. Doing so ensures that those properties are supported properly by tools such as Visual Studio and Expression Blend. Creating these properties also helps ensure that developers can use the controls in conjunction with scenarios such as data binding in XAML code.

CHAPTER 5 EXERCISE SOLUTIONS

Exercise 1 Solution

The answer is a and c. When an application requires you to write custom data files to Isolated Storage, you should make use of the `IsolatedStorageFile` object. If your application only needs to quickly save objects in a name/value pair format, you can use the `IsolatedStorageSettings` object instead.

Exercise 2 Solution

False. When your application is first being run, it can run custom code in the `Application_Launching` event handler. When your application is in the running state, no separate event is fired. After the `Launched` event has been processed, your application is considered to be running, and you can add custom code to the `Loaded` event handlers of various pages in the application.

Exercise 3 Solution

Your application is free to use any available memory on the device. You can check to see how much memory is available by checking the `AvailableFreeSpace` property of the `IsolatedStorageSettings.ApplicationSettings` object. Of course, you shouldn't use all the available space on the device because there will most likely be additional applications that also have storage requirements. Using all the available free space is a good way to ensure that users uninstall your application.

Exercise 4 Solution

When a user navigates to a certain page in your application, you can override the `OnNavigatedTo` method to run custom code. Alternatively, when a user navigates away from that page, you can also run custom code by overriding the `OnNavigatedFrom` method.

Exercise 5 Solution

The answer is c. When an application is interrupted by a phone event and the system determines that your application should be suspended, a `Deactivated` event is fired, and you can run custom code in the `Application_Deactivated` event handler. There is no `Application_Suspened` event handler defined in `App.xaml.cs`.

CHAPTER 6 EXERCISE SOLUTIONS

Exercise 1 Solution

The Windows Phone 7 hardware specification says that the accelerometer and compass are mandatory. Vibration is optional, and at the time of writing, there are no plans to include thermometer or altimeter sensors. It would probably be possible to get both of these environmental values through online services that could provide this information based on location information.

Exercise 2 Solution

You can restrict a page to portrait orientation only by setting the `PhoneApplicationPage` `.SupportedOrientations` property as follows:

```
<phone:PhoneApplicationPage ... SupportedOrientations="Portrait" ... >
```

Exercise 3 Solution

You can disable the Back button by canceling every event received. For example, you can do this with the following code:

```
private void MainPage_BackKeyPress(
    object sender, System.ComponentModel.CancelEventArgs e)
{
    e.Cancel = true;
}
```

However, you should avoid doing this because it prevents users from exiting the page by using the Back button. Remember that you should ensure that the button still functions as users expect it to.

Exercise 4 Solution

You can tell whether the accelerometer sensor is disabled in a device by looking at its State property. The value `SensorState.Disabled` indicates that it is disabled. Other sensors may also expose a property of this type.

Exercise 5 Solution

You can modify the `generateReadingsWorker_DoWork()` method of the `AccelerometerSensorWrapper` class as follows:

```
public void generateReadingsWorker_DoWork(object sender, DoWorkEventArgs e)
{
    // Load data.
    using (System.Xml.XmlReader readingsToUse = System.Xml.XmlReader.Create(
        System.Windows.Application.GetResourceStream(
        new Uri("AccelerometerPedometerSimulator;component/Readings.xml",
            UriKind.Relative)).Stream))
    {
        BackgroundWorker worker = sender as BackgroundWorker;
        while (!worker.CancellationPending)
        {
            // Get next reading.
            if (!readingsToUse.ReadToFollowing("Reading"))
            {
                break;
            }

            // Get and raise event for reading.
```

```
            AccelerometerReading reading = new AccelerometerReading(
                double.Parse(readingsToUse["x"]),
                double.Parse(readingsToUse["y"]),
                double.Parse(readingsToUse["z"]));
            OnReadingChanged(reading);

            // Pause before next reading.
            Thread.Sleep(int.Parse(readingsToUse["t"]));
        }
    }
}
```

The average time per step taken is approximately 1.3 seconds per step.

CHAPTER 7 EXERCISE SOLUTIONS

Exercise 1 Solution

The short answer is that it depends. There is no rule that says you *must* make application bar icons that fit with the Windows Phone 7 scheme. However, if you want to make your applications as usable as possible, you should probably do so. You should also be aware that Windows Phone 7 will overlay circles over your icons automatically, so unless they fit into a 26 x 26 square in the middle of the bitmap, it's possible that they will be obscured. If you really want to customize the application bar completely, you might have to use your own custom control instead.

Exercise 2 Solution

a. You can use `EmailComposeTask` to send an email message, and you might also want `EmailAddressChooserTask` to get an email address to send to if you're sending to an existing contact.

b. You can use `CameraCaptureTask` to take a photo.

c. You can use `MediaPlayerLauncher` to play a video, or you can embed a video in your page.

d. Vibration doesn't require launchers or choosers.

e. SIP changes aren't achieved using launchers or choosers.

Exercise 3 Solution

Tombstoning is the process by which an application is suspended while a launcher or chooser operates. Users may choose not to complete the required operation, but when the application resumes, it will be as if the launcher or chooser has completed. You must be aware of this and never require user input. You must also persist any state that you require as state is not maintained after tombstoning.

Exercise 4 Solution

You use the `ManipulationCompleted` event and the `ManipulationCompletedEventArgs` `.TotalManipulation.Scale` property to get the scale factor to apply.

Exercise 5 Solution

You can start by defining an ellipse in XAML and event handlers as follows:

```xml
<phone:PhoneApplicationPage ...
   MouseLeftButtonUp="PhoneApplicationPage_MouseLeftButtonUp"
   MouseMove="PhoneApplicationPage_MouseMove">

   <Grid x:Name="LayoutRoot" Background="Transparent">
     <Ellipse x:Name="Target" Height="300" Width="300" Stroke="White"
        StrokeThickness="10" MouseLeftButtonDown="Target_MouseLeftButtonDown" />
   </Grid>

</phone:PhoneApplicationPage>
```

Note that the MouseLeftButtonDown handler is defined on the ellipse, but to detect movement elsewhere, the MouseLeftButtonUp and MouseMove handlers are defined on the page.

Next, you need to define a timer in the code-behind; the DispatcherTimer will work. You also need some brushes to toggle the Fill property of the ellipse, a movement threshold beyond which the gesture will be aborted, and somewhere to store the initial touchpoint:

```csharp
using System;
using System.Windows;
using System.Windows.Input;
using System.Windows.Media;
using System.Windows.Threading;
using Microsoft.Phone.Controls;

namespace Exercise5Solution
{
    public partial class MainPage : PhoneApplicationPage
    {
        private const double MovementThreshold = 10;

        private DispatcherTimer timer;
        private Point startPosition;
        private SolidColorBrush brush1 = new SolidColorBrush(Colors.Red);
        private SolidColorBrush brush2 = new SolidColorBrush(Colors.Green);
```

The constructor can set the initial color for the ellipse (called Target):

```csharp
public MainPage()
{
    InitializeComponent();

    Target.Fill = brush1;
}
```

When a `MouseLeftButtonDown` event occurs, you start the timer (if there isn't already one in progress) and record the mouse position:

```
private void Target_MouseLeftButtonDown(
    object sender, MouseButtonEventArgs e)
{
    if (timer == null)
    {
        timer = new DispatcherTimer();
        timer.Interval = TimeSpan.FromSeconds(1);
        timer.Tick += GestureCompleted;
        timer.Start();
    }
}
```

If a `MouseLeftButtonDown` event occurs, you can check whether a timer exists and, if so, kill it:

```
private void PhoneApplicationPage_MouseLeftButtonUp(
    object sender, MouseButtonEventArgs e)
{
    if (timer != null)
    {
        timer.Stop();
        timer = null;
    }
}
```

You can do the same for `MouseMove`, but here you need to see how far the mouse has moved by using some simple math:

```
private void PhoneApplicationPage_MouseMove(object sender, MouseEventArgs e)
{
    if (timer != null)
    {
        Point currentPosition = e.GetPosition(this);
        if (Math.Sqrt(Math.Pow(currentPosition.X - startPosition.X, 2)
            + Math.Pow(currentPosition.Y - startPosition.Y, 2))
            > MovementThreshold)
        {
            timer.Stop();
            timer = null;
        }
    }
}
```

If the timer hasn't been stopped, the `Tick` event will fire, and in this handler you toggle the ellipse color between the `Brush` instances you have defined:

```
private void GestureCompleted(object source, EventArgs e)
{
    timer.Stop();
```

```
            timer = null;
            if (Target.Fill == brush1)
            {
                Target.Fill = brush2;
            }
            else
            {
                Target.Fill = brush1;
            }
        }
    }
}
```

This code is included in the downloaded code in the Exercise5 Solution project.

CHAPTER 8 EXERCISE SOLUTIONS

Exercise 1 Solution

The most appropriate answer is b. Answer c is also correct, but it's far too narrow a definition because web services can do much more.

Exercise 2 Solution

To start with, you would use location services only if requested, perhaps with a "near me" link. You might provide other options, such as letting users choose from a list of locations. You would then perform a one-shot location detection to locate nearby restaurants, and then you'd shut off the location service again. Default accuracy would be enough for this. If you were to also provide route-finding functionality to help users find restaurants, you might use high accuracy and keep the location service running while the user gets to the location.

Exercise 3 Solution

You use the GeoCoordinateWatcher class for obtaining location information.

Exercise 4 Solution

You use the GeoCoordinate.GetDistanceTo() method, which gets the distance between two GeoCoordinate instances, in meters.

Exercise 5 Solution

Before using the Bing Maps Silverlight control, you must obtain a usage key.

Exercise 6 Solution

You use the Scale class, which you would include in XAML as follows:

```
<m:Map CredentialsProvider="<My Key>"
  <m:Map.Children>
    <o:Scale />
  </m:Map.Children>
</m:Map>
```

This code assumes the following namespaces:

```
xmlsn:m="clr-namespace:Microsoft.Phone.Controls.Maps;
  assembly=Microsoft.Phone.Controls.Maps"
xmlsn:o="clr-namespace:Microsoft.Phone.Controls.Maps.Overlays;
  assembly=Microsoft.Phone.Controls.Maps"
```

CHAPTER 9 EXERCISE SOLUTIONS

Exercise 1 Solution

The valid HTTP methods (verbs) in the list are GET, DELETE, POST, and PUT (a, c, d, and e). ZAP isn't allowed, and EXSANGUINATE is just plain silly.

Exercise 2 Solution

You use the UploadStringAsync() method of the WebClient class and respond to the UploadStringCompleted event.

Exercise 3 Solution

The following call will fail:

```
ResultTextBox.Text = sr.ReadToEnd();
```

If you access the user interface, you must use Dispatcher, as in this example:

```
string text = sr.ReadToEnd();
Dispatcher.BeginInvoke(new Action(() => ResultTextBox.Text = text));
```

Exercise 4 Solution

Recall that the Flickr API error message format is as follows:

```
<?xml version="1.0" encoding="utf-8" ?>
<rsp stat="fail">
  <err code="[error-code]" msg="[error-message]" />
</rsp>
```

One way to achieve the desired result and extract this information in case of error is to modify the `GetUserRequestCallback()` method as follows:

```
private void GetUserRequestCallback(IAsyncResult result)
{
    HttpWebResponse response = (result.AsyncState as HttpWebRequest)
        .EndGetResponse(result) as HttpWebResponse;
    XDocument resultXml = XDocument.Load(response.GetResponseStream());
    string status = resultXml.Root.Attribute("stat").Value;
    if (status == "ok")
    {
        string userNsid = (from user in resultXml.Descendants("user")
            select user.Attribute("nsid").Value)
            .FirstOrDefault();
        HttpWebRequest getPhotosRequest = WebRequest.CreateHttp(
            flickrUriHelper.GetUri(
                "flickr.people.getPublicPhotos",
                new Dictionary<string, string>
                {
                    { "user_id", userNsid },
                    { "extras", "date_taken,views" }
                }));
        getPhotosRequest.BeginGetResponse(
            GetPhotosRequestCallback, getPhotosRequest);
    }
    else
    {
        string errorCode = resultXml.Root.Element("err")
            .Attribute("code").Value;
        string errorMessage = resultXml.Root.Element("err")
            .Attribute("msg").Value;
        Dispatcher.BeginInvoke(new Action(
            () =>
                MessageBox.Show(string.Format("{0} (error code {1})",
                errorMessage, errorCode),
                "An error has occurred.", MessageBoxButton.OK)));
    }
}
```

The code for this solution is in the downloadable code, in the folder `Exercise4Solution`.

Exercise 5 Solution

You use the Add Service Reference tool to generate proxy code. All you need to do this (assuming that the service exposes metadata) is the URI of the service.

Exercise 6 Solution

This is a fairly common situation. You have to strike a balance between having a responsive application and not allowing the user to perform potentially illegal or problematic actions, such as deleting an item and then editing it before the response from the delete operation returns. In fact, if one call fails for some reason, you may not even get results back in the same order as you sent the associated requests.

In the `NotesClient` application, you might disable some or all of the UI user interface controls while a call is in progress to prevent this. In order to prevent the user interface from being completely unresponsive, which may confuse users, you might include some kind of feedback, such as a spinning "waiting" icon.

CHAPTER 10 EXERCISE SOLUTIONS

Exercise 1 Solution

Answers a, b, and e participate in push notifications. You can argue that answer c possibly would, if you wrote an application to maintain channel URIs and provide a user interface for sending notifications to devices. Answer d is much more unlikely, though, unless the only Windows Phone 7 device you have access to belongs to your local mail carrier.

Exercise 2 Solution

Raw notifications are received only by applications that are currently running. If an application isn't running, notification messages are discarded.

Exercise 3 Solution

Binding to toast notifications (and indeed to tile notifications) is necessary because it instructs the push client on your device to listen for notifications. If you don't bind these notifications, they won't be received.

Exercise 4 Solution

When you call `BindToShellTile()`, you have the option of passing a list of domains from which tile image URIs will be accepted. If you don't supply such a list, you'll only be able to set the tile image to a resource that's local to the application.

Exercise 5 Solution

If a device is switched off, you'll receive the HTTP response header `X-DeviceConnectionStatus` with a value of `TempDisconnected`. If you also receive an `X-NotificationStatus` header value or `Received`, then the message is queued and will be delivered later when the device is switched on. Otherwise, you can try to send the message later.

CHAPTER 11 EXERCISE SOLUTIONS

Exercise 1 Solution

You can achieve this kind of animation by drawing a different, but similar, image every few hundred seconds in the place of the missile. You can either have a different image to represent each frame of the missile, or you could have one big image containing many frames and use the `sourceRectangle` parameter of the `Draw()` method to cut out the appropriate frame. You might like to track each missile's age so that the missiles don't all animate in unison. Source code for this solution is available for download. The name of the file is `code sample: Tank Exercise 1`.

Exercise 2 Solution

This kind of feature is best represented as a new `GameComponent` object. In terms of implementation, powerups are similar to missiles: They spawn randomly, and they collide with the tank. They differ in the way that they affect the tank in that they don't move and should disappear after a short time. Source code for this solution is available for download. The name of the file is `code sample: Tank Exercise 2`.

Exercise 3 Solution

Having multiple screens in an XNA game is easy to achieve with `GameComponent` objects. You just add and remove the appropriate components from the game's current `Components` collection. There must be code somewhere (possibly in the `Game` class itself) to control which screen should be made current at a particular time. Source code for this solution is available for download. The name of the file is `code sample: Tank Exercise 3`.

CHAPTER 12 EXERCISE SOLUTIONS

Exercise 1 Solution

The Device panel is the one that allows you to change the current theme and color of the phone in the artboard. To bring the Device panel into view, you need to select it from the Windows menu.

Exercise 2 Solution

Three controls that can be added to a form to add visual feedback are:

➤ An `Image`

➤ A `Border`

➤ A `Shape` such as a `Path`, `Rectangle` or `Ellipse`.

Exercise 3 Solution

When you apply a built-in (system) style to a control, you're guaranteed that when the user changes their theme and accent color settings, your application will fit right in. System styles will closely match other applications on the phone, conforming to Microsoft's "Metro" design guidelines.

Exercise 4 Solution

Cartoonists have known about easing since the early days of Mickey Mouse. By applying an appropriate type (ease in, ease out or both) and strength of easing, you can make animations look much more natural. The best animations are the ones that users don't even notice.

Exercise 5 Solution

Option a is the answer. New Sample Data will let you design a simple data class that Blend will create some sample instances of. This is good for prototyping because it's the quickest way to get something visible on the screen, but doesn't work with real production objects.

CHAPTER 13 EXERCISE SOLUTIONS

Exercise 1 Solution

False. The `PhoneApplicationFrame` object doesn't support page transitions. When you want to make use of the page transitions feature of the toolkit, you need to ensure that your application is using the `TransitionFrame` object instead. You can find this object in the `App.xaml.cs` file, under the `InitializePhoneApplication` method.

Exercise 2 Solution

The answers are a and c. Flick and Drag are the only valid gestures listed.

Exercise 3 Solution

When you need to determine which item was selected from an `AutoCompleteBox` control, you need to listen for the `SelectionChanged` event. In that event handler, you can cast the passed-in object to whatever data type you might have used for the collection of search items.

Exercise 4 Solution

The Silverlight for Windows Phone Toolkit provides the following page transition effects:

- ➤ TurnstileTransition
- ➤ RollTransition
- ➤ SlideTransition
- ➤ RotateTransition
- ➤ SwivelTransition

Exercise 5 Solution

The answer is c. When you need to find out what date was selected from the DatePicker control, you can listen for the ValueChanged event in your code-behind page. You can also listen for the same event when using the TimePicker control to determine the selected time value.

CHAPTER 14 EXERCISE SOLUTIONS

Exercise 1 Solution

You can use MVVM to separate views (user interface elements) from view models (functionality and business logic). This gives your applications a much better and more maintainable structure, which is particularly useful in large applications, such as those that have large teams of developers and designers.

Exercise 2 Solution

Modify the code for ButtonCommandHelper.cs so that it looks like the following:

```
public static class ButtonCommandHelper
{
    ...

    public static readonly DependencyProperty
        CommandParameterProperty =
            DependencyProperty.RegisterAttached(
                "CommandParameter",
                typeof(object),
                typeof(ButtonCommandHelper),
                new PropertyMetadata(null));

    public static object GetCommandParameter(
        ButtonBase button)
    {
        return button.GetValue(CommandParameterProperty);
    }

    public static void SetCommandParameter(
        ButtonBase button, object commandParameter)
    {
        button.SetValue(CommandParameterProperty, commandParameter);
    }

    ...

    private static void OnButtonBaseClick(object sender, RoutedEventArgs args)
    {
        var button = sender as ButtonBase;
        var command = GetCommand(button);
```

```
        var commandParameter = GetCommandParameter(button);
        if (command != null && command.CanExecute(commandParameter))
        {
            command.Execute(commandParameter);
        }
    }
}
```

Exercise 3 Solution

Most unit test frameworks throw exceptions when tests fail, although in practice these exceptions are handled by the framework and converted into user-friendly output you can peruse.

CHAPTER 15 EXERCISE SOLUTIONS

Exercise 1 Solution

True. You'll be unable to unlock any Windows Phone 7 devices until you've paid to join the program and your identity has been verified.

Exercise 2 Solution

You need to submit three completely opaque .png images at 200 x 200, 173 x 173, and 99 x 99 pixels.

Exercise 3 Solution

If you don't test your application under a number of different theme configurations, you're likely to fail testing because you might, for example, end up with white text on a white background. However, if you design your application to always have its own theme (and be legible under all theme combinations), you can happily ignore the user's selected theme.

Exercise 4 Solution

Never use a time-based trial mode because the user can always uninstall and then reinstall your application to reset the timer.

Exercise 5 Solution

The app's icon and title are the first things potential customers see of your application on the Marketplace.

Exercise 6 Solution

You need to proactively seek reviews from website authors if you want to reach as many potential customers as possible.

INDEX